HUMAN RESOURCE MANAGEMENT

TRANSFORMING THEORY INTO INNOVATIVE PRACTICE

The Irish say there is a pot of gold at the end of every rainbow. Those of us who have chased rainbows have discovered that rainbows always stay out of reach at the horizon. The pot of gold is found in the journey and in disovering the true friends who stick with you through the trials and tribulations of the journey – it is to these dear and true friends that I dedicate this book. And to Günter, Jameson and Jasmin who unquestionably have done and always will do the same—*CEJH*

To my mum and dad, whose love and self-sacrifice have brought me to where I am today—*YF*

For my friends and family, who provided support and encouragement when I needed it the most. And for the inifinite love and wisdom from my parents—*VES*

My thanks to Jim and Matthew for their encouragement and support and for allowing me the space to complete this work—*KF*

HUMAN RESOURCE MANAGEMENT

Charmine E.J. Härtel

Yuka Fujimoto

Victoria E. Strybosch

Karen Fitzpatrick

Transforming Theory into Innovative Practice

PEARSON

Prentice Hall

Pearson Education Australia
Unit 4, Level 3
14 Aquatic Drive
Frenchs Forest NSW 2086

www.pearsoned.com.au

Senior Acquisitions Editor: Frances Eden
Editorial Team Leader: Carolyn Robson
Editorial Coordinator: Roisin Fitzgerald
Copy Editor: Jennifer Coombs
Proofreader: Janice Keynton
Senior Permissions Coordinator: Liz de Rome
Cover design by Nada Backovic
Typeset by Midland Typesetters, Australia

Printed in Malaysia (CTP-VVP)

1 2 3 4 5 11 10 09 08 07

National Library of Australia
Cataloguing-in-Publication Data

Human resource management: transforming theory into innovative practice.

   Includes index.
   ISBN 978 0 73397 659 9.

   ISBN 0 7339 7659 X (pbk).

   1. Personnel management – Australia. I. Härtel, Charmine E. J., 1959–.

658.00994

An imprint of Pearson Education Australia
(a division of Pearson Australia Group Pty Ltd)

Brief contents

Contents

PART **2**

Issues, challenges and theoretical developments in strategic human resource management 83

PART **3**

Implementation of strategic human resource management   261

ABOUT THE AUTHORS

Dr Charmine E.J. Härtel is Professor of Organisational Behaviour and Director of Research for the Department of Management at Monash University. She received her doctorate from the top 5 ranked Industrial and Organizational Psychology program at Colorado State University and subsequently was the recipient of their Distinguished Alumni Award. Professor Härtel has 27 years of experience in the public and private sectors and is recognised internationally as a leading expert in the areas of organisational and employee development as demonstrated by her five awards for innovation in organisational practice. She has authored five books and over 50 refereed journal articles, which have appeared in journals such as *Journal of Management, Academy of Management Review, Applied Psychology: An International Review, Leadership Quarterly* and *Journal of Applied Psychology.*

Dr Yuka Fujimoto is a lecturer in human resource management at Deakin University in Melbourne. She has taught advanced human resource management, human resource development and staffing and rewarding and has researched widely in the area of diversity openness for the past seven years. Her research advocates the importance of diversity openness that fosters organisations and societies that enable every individual to flourish in their talent. Her research has been recognised as best papers at prestigious international conferences such as the Academy of Management, the Asia Academy of Management and the International Conference on Emotions and Organizational Life. Her research has been published in *Cross Cultural Management Journal: International, Asia Pacific Human Resource Management Journal* and *Journal of the Australian and New Zealand Academy of Management.*

Victoria E. Strybosch has taught, researched and published in the fields of human resource management, organisational change and generalist management since graduating from Monash University in 2001. She is currently based in London working in HRM, with the aim of expanding her training and development consultancy experience in the UK market.

Karen Fitzpatrick is Group HR Manager at Repco. She has been an HRM practitioner and educator for over 20 years, working in both the public and private sectors. In recent years she has held senior HRM roles with the Victorian Employers' Chamber of Commerce and Industry (VECCI) and the ANZ Banking Group. She is a Director of the Victorian TAFE Development Centre.

PREFACE

Human Resource Management: Transforming Theory into Innovative Practice aims to facilitate the development of critical and innovative thinking which will allow the reader to make strategic human resource management (SHRM) decisions in light of the unique features of any given business and its operating environment. Rather than simply providing the reader with definitions, theories and formulas of SHRM, this book takes an innovative step and specifically addresses the process of effective SHRM with directions on how the HR practitioner turns theory into practice.

In contrast to many books and journal articles preceding this work, this book moves a step beyond the emphasis on description, to the *process* characteristics of effective human resource management in practice. In particular, this book presents a model that readers can apply to individual topics in the book, which takes them from the point of problem or opportunity identification, through planning, implementation and evaluation, in a way that leads to innovation that is situated within the unique business context of the target organisation. The model, referred to as the SHRM Application Tool, captures the decision-making process that effective HR practitioners follow and provides a useful framework for transforming theory and research into actionable and innovative HR practices and policies. As such, we believe that this book represents an important turning point in this important management field.

The text has been divided into three parts. Part 1, 'Strategic human resource management in context', introduces the process of SHRM as well as strategies to engage and motivate employees. Part 2, 'Issues, challenges and theoretical developments in SHRM', considers many of the issues the HR practitioner needs to deal with to implement SHRM effectively. In particular, we address issues of knowledge, innovation, a learning culture and technology-based SHRM, and ethical and legal requirements related to HRM and HRM issues associated with increased workforce diversity as well as those operating in a global context. Part 3, 'Implementing strategic human resource management', emphasises the practical application of the functions associated with HRM. These include the recruitment, selection, training and development of employees, as well as performance and reward management.

At the end of each chapter you will find three key sections, the 'Contemporary SHRM Application Tool', 'A view from the field' and 'A manager's challenge'. In 'A manager's challenge' we provide an example of how Australian organisations or industries are dealing with the chapter topic; for example, in Chapter 4 we consider how Coles Myer is dealing with e-recruitment. In 'A view from the field' we challenge the reader to consider how they would proceed in a given situation; for example, in Chapter 6 we consider the effects of the Australian industrial relations reforms on the workforce. In the 'Contemporary SHRM Application Tool' section we provide a practical example of how the SHRM Application Tool can be used to contribute to the strategic decision-making process in organisations.

Applying the SHRM Application Tool

The SHRM Application Tool (illustrated below) forms the foundation of this book and is designed to enable students and educators alike to transfer their theory into practice. The steps in the tool are discussed below and they capture the critical questions that must be addressed to move from the identification of problems and opportunities to an innovative and customised response.

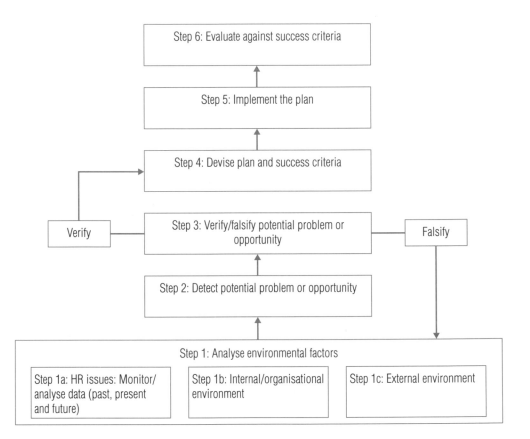

STEP 1: ANALYSE ENVIRONMENTAL FACTORS

An organisation must have mechanisms for monitoring its internal and external environment, including an analysis of past data (i.e. historical perspective), present data (i.e. current perspective) and future data (i.e. future trends perspective). The information it gathers and analyses enables it to make important decisions about the management of resources and strategic direction. The first step of the SHRM Application Tool, therefore, is an environmental analysis via the collection and analysis of timely and accurate information which enables the organisation to make timely and accurate decisions relevant to the alignment of its internal and external operating environment, strategic management and SHRM.

The activities involved in this step are numbered as Step 1 in the graphical representations of the SHRM Application Tool. The environment (internal and external) is presented separately from the history and present-day situation and trends to distinguish the general environmental issues from HR-related trends, which lead to potential HR-related problems and opportunities (Step 2).

STEP 2: DETECT POTENTIAL PROBLEM OR OPPORTUNITY

Once you have a picture of the organisation's present HR situation, you are in a position to conduct a gap analysis to list potential opportunities or problems. A common technique used for such purposes is the SWOT analysis; however, any gap analysis technique may be used to perform this step. The activities involved in this step are numbered as Step 2 in the graphical representations of the SHRM Application Tool. Beginning in Chapter 2, use of the SHRM Application Tool is illustrated for either an opportunity scenario or a problem scenario.

STEP 3: VERIFY/FALSIFY POTENTIAL PROBLEM OR OPPORTUNITY

Drawing on the information obtained from Step 1 and Step 2, you are now in a position to determine the most critical or dominant HR problems or opportunities (e.g. demotivated workers) that need to be managed at this point in time. This step involves gathering information to assist in the verification/falsification process, including the identification and evaluation of possible problem/opportunity alternatives. The activities involved in this step are numbered as Step 3 in the graphical representations of the SHRM Application Tool.

Although there are a variety of techniques you may wish to use to complete this step, it is important that your evaluation address two key questions:

1. Does the potential problem or opportunity identified fit with all the available evidence?
2. Is there a mismatch between the potential problem or opportunity identified and the evidence? Addressing this question ensures you have identified the root problem/opportunity rather than a symptom of it.

STEP 4: DEVISE PLAN AND SUCCESS CRITERIA

Once Step 3 is complete, you are ready to develop a plan to address the problem or opportunity identified (assuming you did not falsify the presence of the problem or opportunity). The activities involved in this step are numbered as Step 4 in the graphical representations of the SHRM Application Tool.

The aim of this step is to identify the functional activities which need to be implemented in order to address the problem or opportunity you identified in Step 3. The development of a plan should be guided by the criteria or indicators of a successful result (e.g. motivated workers, trust in management), and so it is important to identify how you will know if the plan has succeeded at this point in the process.

Two key questions that should be addressed in formulating the planned response are:

1. Does the plan address the problem/opportunity?
2. Are there any undesirable/unintended consequences of the preferred plan?

STEP 5: IMPLEMENT THE PLAN

Once the plan and success criteria are established, you should put the plan into action. At this stage you need to present a precise action plan. For example, employees are to respond to leadership questionnaire within two weeks and analysis is to be complete within the next two weeks. The activities involved in this step are numbered as Step 5 in the graphical representations of the SHRM Application Tool.

STEP 6: EVALUATE AGAINST SUCCESS CRITERIA

It is important to produce a report on whether the HR implementation (Step 5) brought about positive, negative or no change in the company. This evaluation allows other managers in the business to see the impact or value adding of HR activities as well as enabling continuous improvement to people management processes in the organisation. The activities involved in this step are numbered as Step 6 in the graphical representations of the SHRM Application Tool.

A book such as this which seeks to break the mould used in other books in its field cannot be developed without the insights, both critical and constructive, of those who have used, questioned or loved what has gone before. To that end, we give special thanks to our publisher, Pearson Education Australia, who ensured we received input from a range of educators and evaluators of HR textbooks; we also owe a debt of thanks to these anonymous reviewers. We also acknowledge the contributions of editorial assistants Shannon Lloyd, Deshani Ganegoda, Virginia Strybosch, Amanda Blyth, Dominique O'Keffe, Shobha Paranahewa and Debra Panipucci. Our gratitude also goes to Nell Kimberley for her insightful comments on the positioning of this book. Last, but not least, we thank Frances Eden and the staff and management of Pearson Education Australia for their diligence and hard work in bringing this innovative book to print.

Charmine E. J. Härtel, Yuka Fujimoto,
Victoria E. Strybosch and Karen Fitzpatrick

PART 1

Strategic human resource management in context

Chapter 1

The process of strategic human resource management

INTRODUCTION

This book was created to address what many practitioners, educators, students and other scholars have said is missing from the numerous publications on human resource management (HRM): a method for transforming theory and research into the practice of HRM within a specific organisation. The SHRM Application Tool is a unique feature of this text and provides readers with a clear illustration of the model used by many highly successful HR consultants and executives in their daily practice. The tool is used throughout the book to assist learning in two ways. First, a working example of the tool in use is provided in each chapter, modelling how a practitioner would use it to address an organisational matter relating to the chapter topic. Second, you are encouraged to practise using the tool to develop your own customised applications of theory and research to suit the unique circumstances of a specific organisation.

In Chapter 1 we introduce you to the essential elements of HRM. The first part of the chapter will help you to understand the history and development of HRM as well as its theory and practices. It also establishes the foundation for discussing strategic human resource management (SHRM). By understanding the basis of HRM and SHRM you will gain insight into the dynamic nature of the profession and the processes needed for effective SHRM.

The second part of this chapter introduces the SHRM Application Tool. This tool is based on a model formally known as the Process Model which was developed by Härtel for the purpose of educating students and consultants in the skills required to devise innovative HR strategies and practices. The Process Model was initially based on a systems model developed out of Härtel's decision-making and problem-solving research (Härtel & Härtel, 1996, 1997). This SHRM Application Tool will be the framework adopted for each chapter within the book. Therefore, each chapter will comprise a different version of the SHRM Application Tool depending on the specific topic and areas for discussion. These application tools will be used throughout the book as a framework for learning and understanding SHRM and learning how to develop and maintain effective SHRM within a contemporary organisational context.

Specifically, this chapter explores the nature of SHRM through a discussion of its historic roots, the more contemporary resource-based view (RBV) of SHRM and the stakeholder perspective, the relationship between the balanced scorecard for strategic management systems and the HR scorecard for high-performance HR work systems, and the process of SHRM.

Objectives

The primary objective of this chapter is to introduce you to the concept of SHRM and to advance your thinking about the process of effective SHRM. The chapter challenges the perspectives offered by most HR texts by emphasising the application of highly developed analytical thinking skills to transform theory and research into innovative practice. Researchers, students, educators and practitioners interested in updating their understanding of the latest thinking and practical techniques in the HR field will find the chapter equally useful.

After reading this chapter you should be able to:

- be familiar with key HRM terminology, concepts and definitions;
- describe why HRM is important to organisations;
- define the essential elements of the strategic approach to HRM;
- have an understanding of SHRM;
- understand how the RBV of the firm advanced the notion of SHRM;
- understand the importance of the relationship between the balanced scorecard for strategic management systems and the HR scorecard for high-performance work systems;
- identify issues that will face HR managers in the future;
- know the tool to analyse problems successfully;
- be familiar with the factors required to establish an effective HR environment;
- identify the old and new management paradigms;
- be familiar with an HR model to manage employees effectively.

Nature, origins and implications of strategic human resource management

management
A process involving planning, organising, leading and controlling the human, financial and material resources of the organisation.

The traditional **management** process involves planning, organising, leading and controlling the human, financial and material resources of the organisation. These resources can come either from within the organisation or from sources external to the organisation. For example, financial resources can be obtained from profits reinvested in the company (internal) or from increasing creditors or shareholders (external). Similarly, human resources can be internal to the organisation (i.e. an organisation's employees) or external (e.g. consultants).

As an organisation grows in size these management activities are divided and distributed in formal structures. For example, the management of financial resources becomes the responsibility of the Finance Department while the management of human resources becomes the responsibility of the Human Resource Management Department.

Human resource management, therefore, refers to the formal part of an organisation responsible for all aspects of the management of human resources. This includes strategy development and analysis; policy making, implementation and enforcement; systems, processes and procedures. In other words, it involves the activities needed to monitor, innovate, plan, and evaluate people including:

- *Job analysis, evaluation and classification:* to identify necessary skills.
- *Job design and work design:* to clarify work performance, scheduling and relations.
- *Recruitment:* to find the right people for the right job.
- *Selection:* to hire the right staff.
- *Induction, training and development:* to socialise staff and update their skills and careers.
- *Skills audit:* to know what skills and abilities your staff possess.
- *Performance management:* to develop, evaluate, motivate and discipline staff.
- *Managing compensation, rewards and benefits:* to ensure payment and benefits are adequate.
- *Research:* to monitor, evaluate and innovate staff continually.

Of course, HR departments vary considerably in terms of what they do, depending on the size of the organisation and the nature of the business. This means that in some organisations the HR department will do the set of tasks listed above and more, while in other organisations the HR department will do less. In all cases, the primary role of the HR department is to support the strategic direction of the organisation.

human resource management
The formal part of an organisation responsible for all aspects of the management of human resources.

THE HISTORY OF HRM

The idea of HRM has evolved from changes in the organisational environment, which demanded that organisations find better ways of looking after their employees (in addition to securing the value that people can bring to the organisation). In order to understand the role of SHRM properly it is important to understand the history of HRM.

ORGANISATIONAL BEHAVIOUR

In looking at the history of HRM, we begin by considering the study of the older, more established discipline of organisational behaviour from which HRM springs. **Organisational behaviour** is the study of each individual's and group's behaviours, attitudes and actions within an organisation. In particular, it looks at how people deal with being part of an organisation and why they work in a certain way. Understanding organisations and the behaviours of people is important to both managing the productivity of the organisation and ensuring the workplace is healthy for the individuals involved. Understanding organisational behaviour can also bring about a competitive advantage for the organisation. A **competitive advantage** refers to a process, system or source (i.e. social, cultural or human

organisational behaviour
The study of each individual's and group's behaviours, attitudes and actions within an organisation.

competitive advantage
A process, system or source (i.e. social, cultural or human capital) that one company does better than their competitors.

capital) that one company does better than their competitors. Hence, customers will remain loyal to the company, increasing market share and allowing for the overall achievement of strategic organisational goals. The field of HRM was founded on this idea, and involves three sources of capital:

social capital
The value that can be placed on the networks and relationships between people such as that gained from helping behaviours and sharing knowledge resources.

cultural capital
The value that can be placed on the core values and beliefs of the organisation and its people.

human capital
The value that can be placed on people's knowledge, skills, abilities and expertise.

1. **Social capital** refers to the value that can be placed on the networks and relationships between people such as that gained from helping behaviours and sharing of knowledge (Youndt & Snell, 2004). The social capital of an organisation includes not only the number and quality of relationships between employees within the organisation but also those between employees and individuals in other organisations and the community.

2. **Cultural capital** refers to the value that can be placed on the core values and beliefs of the organisation and its people. This means that certain values will be seen as worthy of being sought and possessed.

3. **Human capital** refers to the value that can be placed on people's knowledge, skills, abilities and expertise (Youndt & Snell, 2004). An organisation's human capital is well developed when its employees possess the capabilities it needs to maintain a competitive advantage.

Ever-increasing global competition coupled with the increasing popularity of knowledge management and continuous learning means that the capability of people to learn, interact and acquire knowledge underpins organisational success today. Consequently, a number of organisations are shifting their strategic focus from a task-focused approach to a people-focused approach, and a careful consideration of how the management of people can lead to competitive advantage. For example, Siemens, which historically has pursued an engineering-focused approach, has recently made a strategic decision to shift to a customer-focused approach. Next, we examine the chronology of different paradigms or assumptions about the best way to manage people at work.

THE SCIENTIFIC MANAGEMENT PARADIGM

scientific management
A method for managing people and work based on a concern for production and with an emphasis on efficiency.

The notion of managing people originated with the recognition that there could be 'one best way' for people to conduct their work tasks that would enable them to work quickly and effectively. This gave birth to the **scientific management** perspective, also known as Taylorism, where fact finding and specific time and method standards replaced the old rule of thumb method for managing people and work (see Taylor, 1911). This perspective placed an emphasis on production and on efficiency, but was soon considered to be impersonal and dehumanising for most organisational contexts. Taylorism is, however, not dead, as evidenced by the way many call centres are managed and evaluated (e.g. measurement of time spent per call).

THE HUMAN RELATIONS MOVEMENT

human relations movement
A joint focus on people and production based on a concern for people and with an emphasis on communication and the need to treat employees with dignity and respect.

From the evolution of the scientific management paradigm sprang the **human relations movement**, which placed a joint focus on people and production. The human relations perspective changed the focus of management from production to a concern for people, with emphasis being placed on communication and the need to treat employees with dignity and respect. Under this paradigm, management was required to focus on individual differences, interpersonal relations, group behaviour, employee attitudes, leadership and communication. Employees began to be seen as a source of competitive advantage.

A BEHAVIOURAL SCIENCE APPROACH

Changes in the workforce in the 1950s and 1960s saw a shift towards a more interdisciplinary approach: a **behavioural science approach** to HRM. It was felt that people would be motivated to perform better if they were more satisfied in their jobs. In order for this to occur work tasks had to be redesigned to be more interesting and challenging. This perspective focused management attention on dynamic systems, total organisational culture and climate, employee participation and an emphasis on both economic and humanistic concerns. The modern focus of HRM is on applying these principles of behavioural science in order to capitalise on the organisation's human talent.

> **behavioural science approach**
> Focused management attention on dynamic systems, total organisational culture and climate, employee participation and an emphasis on both economic and humanistic concerns.

Please read

Härtel, C. E. J. (1999), 'Global vision: Recognizing our organizational paradigms: Lessons from a historical review of the contribution of work psychology from three continents to occupational health and safety management', accessed from <http://siop.org/tip/backissues/TipOcto99/12Hartel.htm>.

In order to be effective in HRM it is necessary to have a balance of skills relating to both task- and people-related aspects as well as knowledge of the organisation as a whole. Thus HR personnel need to be familiar with the organisation's external environment, operating environment, culture and structure. These are vital to ensuring they are able to have an input into the design and implementation of goals and strategies. HR personnel need to be able to understand what the organisation does on a day to day basis as well as how to move organisational members through processes of change, negotiations and influences. Furthermore, the HR role is not a static position; as the circumstances and expectations around tasks and people change as a result of external and internal influences, so too do the skills and knowledge needed by HR professionals.

Managers can either emphasise task performance or people issues and have a choice over how they treat their employees. HRM styles can be differentiated in terms of being control or resource based. In the control-based style the organisation employs people to work and therefore it needs to organise tasks and processes to ensure employees can work to their full capacity. The resource-based philosophy, on the other hand, views people as assets rather than as a cost to the organisation. With opportunities to learn and grow, employees can provide the organisation with capabilities and capital through the development of knowledge, skills and social relationships. Below we identify four integrative philosophies which combine both control and resource-based styles (Bamberger & Meshoulam, 2000). According to the philosophies, organisations can either invest in their workers or acquire the human capital they need through the labour market. The choices they make are likely to be influenced by the changing characteristics of the workforce such as generational differences (Generation X and Y) and cultural diversity. Organisations also have a choice as to whether they closely monitor and control employees or focus on developing relationships.

traditional (or transactional) philosophy
Work tasks are tightly scripted and little accountability is given to individual workers.

paternalistic philosophy
When managers look after employees while maintaining high levels of control and hierarchy.

commitment philosophy
The development of an employee–employer relationship which maximises employee contribution and the application of skills and knowledge for the benefit of the organisation.

collaborative philosophy
Managers acknowledge the legitimacy of stakeholder views and are open to partnerships and involvement.

Theory X
The management assumption that employees prefer not to do work and need close supervision and control.

Theory Y
The management assumption that employees can be given greater responsibility as they are highly motivated and will be creative if given a chance.

- **Traditional (or transactional) philosophy.** Under this approach work tasks are tightly scripted and there is little accountability given to individual workers. With a view to minimising cost, managers attempt to exercise control and achieve maximum efficiency. Short-term temporary and contractual employees may be preferred.
- **Paternalistic philosophy.** Managers are seen as looking after employees while maintaining high levels of control and hierarchy. Employee discretion is limited by rules and regulations and promotion is based on compliance with those rules.
- **Commitment philosophy.** Managers following this philosophy focus on developing an employee–employer relationship that maximises employee contribution and the application of skills and knowledge for the benefit of the organisation. The employee is viewed as a resource and, consequently, individual attention is paid to each employee's ability to contribute to the organisation.
- **Collaborative philosophy.** Under this philosophy, managers acknowledge the legitimacy of stakeholder views and are open to partnerships and involvement. Information is shared and broad discussions are held in order to obtain decisions which are satisfactory to all parties involved.

There is no doubt that organisations are faced with conflicting pressures to minimise costs and maximise efficiency, thus there is a need for control while at the same time ensuring there are satisfactory relationships with all employees and other stakeholders. McGregor (1960) identified two opposing management assumptions, which he labelled Theory X and Theory Y. According to **Theory X**, employees prefer not to do work and need close supervision and control. In contrast, **Theory Y** refers to the view that employees can be given greater responsibility as they are highly motivated and will be creative if given a chance. Particular circumstances (e.g. nature of the business, nature of workforce) and strategies may require more control and a focus on cost minimisation, while others may require greater commitment and participation (Walton, 1985). Further, the philosophy employed may depend on what sector of the organisation you are looking at. For instance, unskilled labour may require more control and supervision whereas knowledge workers may require greater flexibility and independence. Subsequently, strategy makers are confronted with a choice on how to shape their environment (Child, 1997). What is important is that consistency in strategic direction exists across the organisation. This is discussed next.

TOWARDS A STRATEGIC APPROACH TO PEOPLE MANAGEMENT

Operating a business effectively requires a host of activities, including those associated with HRM, finance, accounting, marketing, public affairs, technology management, legal compliance and research and development. HRM exists as part of a larger system and to be effective it must be familiar with and congruent to the other parts in the system. To achieve business excellence HRM needs to be incorporated into the total strategic management process of an organisation. For this reason, it is important to understand how HRM fits into the larger picture of organisational life.

Since the 1970s, HR issues have increased in significance within the field of strategic management (Wright & Snell, 1991). To address the challenges and opportunities they face, organisations engage in a process of strategic management. **Strategic management** is the process of managing with a long-term (or strategic) focus, and is largely composed of organisational strategy, including strategy formulation and strategy implementation.

Organisational strategy refers to the action plan for becoming what an organisation's leadership envisions for it. Organisational strategy therefore is the result of organisational decisions about the goals, purpose, objectives and directions of the company and the way to realise these. The design of a strategy allows the management team to determine, to a large degree, the plans and policies required to achieve goals and the type of company it wants to be.

Organisational strategy consists of three levels. The *corporate* level refers to the decisions relating to which industry the organisation wishes to be in and how resources will be allocated. The *business* level refers to decisions surrounding how the organisation will operate within a given industry. The *functional* level refers to the decisions relating to operational functions within the business such as the financial strategy or marketing strategy.

Strategy formulation includes setting a mission, vision, strategy, goals and values, coupled with a consideration of the external environment (i.e. opportunities and threats) and the internal environment (i.e. strengths and weaknesses) of the organisation, using a SWOT or force field analysis.

The strategic direction of the organisation is communicated to its stakeholders via the wording of the organisational mission, vision and value statements.

- The organisational *mission* refers to the reason why the organisation exists in the first place, what it is here to do and what it stands for. It is the organisation's purpose.
- The organisational *vision* is a short and inspiring statement of what the organisation wants to be in the future.
- The *value* statement is the set of principles and beliefs that the organisation states to guide its members' behaviours in the pursuit of its vision. These are designed to shape how members of the organisation think and act on a day to day basis.

strategic management
The process of managing with a long-term focus, and which is largely composed of strategy formulation and strategy implementation.

organisational strategy
Design of organisational decision making which determines the goals, purpose, objectives and directions of the company.

strategy formulation
Includes setting a mission, vision, strategy, goals and values, coupled with a consideration of the external and internal environments.

Please read

Microsoft's (Indonesia) website to see their vision, mission and values: <http://www.microsoft.com/indonesia/backgrounder>.

INTEGRATING STRATEGY, STRUCTURE AND CULTURE

HRM and organisational strategy, structure and culture are intertwined, and changes in one are likely to have repercussions for one or more of the others. Organisational strategy should inform organisational structure and culture, especially at the beginning of an organisation's existence. As time goes on, an organisation's strategy is shaped in part by its culture and structure. This strategy–structure–culture dynamic is depicted in Figure 1.1.

FIGURE   **1.1**
The strategy–structure–
culture interaction

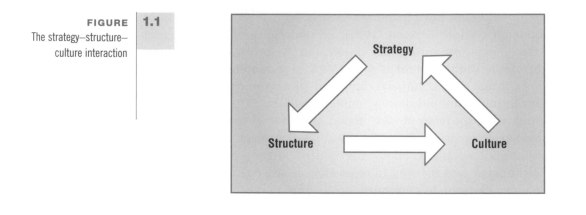

**organisational
structure**
The formal arrangement of
roles, processes and
relationships within the
organisation.

Organisational structure refers to the formal arrangement of roles, processes and relationships within the organisation. Generally, organisational structure is based around such things as functions or departments, products or geography. The characteristics of these organisational structures can vary with regard to the number of hierarchical levels, degree of centralisation and formalisation and the level of task specificity (Inzerilli & Laurent, 1983). For instance, in a highly centralised structure there are many levels of authority and control and decision making resides solely with top management. In contrast, decentralised structures consist of few management levels and greater employee involvement as decision making is delegated to the lower-level employees who are affected by the decision.

In the centralised structure, for instance, top management's decisions for the future dominate strategy formulation. In decentralised structure, however, lower level employees would have greater input into the strategy formulation. Thus, organisational structure is reflected in organisational culture (bureaucratic culture versus pluralistic culture). Simultaneously, organisational structure is affected by organisational strategy. For example, the CEO decides to restructure or lay off staff in order to pursue cost reduction strategies. This is sadly a typical example of strategy leading structure or/and culture.

organisational culture
A system of shared beliefs,
values and assumptions which
guide individual behaviour
within the organisation.

Organisational culture refers to a system of shared beliefs, values and assumptions which guides individual behaviour within the organisation. An organisation's culture is generally thought to reflect the ways people within an organisation have learned to cope with the internal and external environment, and the acceptance of what works and doesn't work is subsequently passed along to new employees as 'the way things are done around here'. Consequently, an organisation's culture is unique, reflecting the characteristics of the people, the organisation and the environment, in past and present. Therefore, even if two organisations are structured exactly the same, the meaning of the culture to organisational members may be different.

The strategy–structure–culture interaction suggests that changes in strategy may require changes in structure, and changes in structure may require changes in culture, which in turn will impact on strategy. For instance, as organisations grow larger, centralised decision making becomes less effective due to the increasing complexity of each decision. Thus, organisations that pursue a strategy of growth will be more likely to change to a more decentralised, flattened structure with decisions being broken into smaller elements and devolved to lower levels. Subsequently, organisational culture will need to be aligned with both strategy and structure to facilitate the greater responsibility and authority at the lower levels of the organisation. HRM is responsible for the activities which enable alignment between culture, strategy and structure, including hiring the right people, developing required skills through training and rewarding desired behaviours. The process of proactively integrating organisational culture, strategy and structure with HRM is referred to as strategic human resource management (SHRM).

WHAT IS THE DIFFERENCE BETWEEN HRM AND SHRM?

HRM implements the activities required to support organisational decisions. To be effective, these HRM activities must be aligned with the strategic direction of the organisation. SHRM, on the other hand, integrates HRM into the strategic decision-making process of the organisation so that human resources can have an active role in helping to define as well as implement strategic decisions. Thus, the main focus of SHRM is strategy, while the main focus of HRM is practice.

Since HRM is focused on the activities needed to implement decisions, it reacts to environmental aberrations. In contrast, SHRM is focused on vision and strategising to reach a desired state in the future and is thus proactive. Effective SHRM informs the organisation when it needs to change its overall strategy; it does not simply follow from the organisation's strategy. For example, consider an organisation that develops a strategy to enter a new foreign market. Effective SHRM would involve assessing the people management issues involved in implementing the strategy. If the assessment leads to the conclusion that the people management issues are such that the organisation is likely to fail in the new venture, the organisation's management team would be advised to abandon the strategy. If, however, the assessment indicates that the organisation is likely to succeed in pursuing the strategy, SHRM would then involve designing a people management strategy to support the new organisational strategy.

STRATEGIC HUMAN RESOURCE MANAGEMENT

Not all organisations execute HRM effectively. An effective HRM policy involves congruency, compatibility, clarity, stability, flexibility, understanding of the business and cultural appropriateness. Therefore, effective HRM entails intelligent decision-making processes, which involve environmental scanning, problem and opportunity identification, verification, implementation and evaluation in relation to its core activities. These elements are designed to enhance strategic ability and form the SHRM Application Tool described later in the chapter.

Strategic human resource management (SHRM) is the process of human resource management which is driven by planning, foresight and analytical decision making. It involves linking human resources with strategic objectives in order to improve performance. Therefore, SHRM involves setting employment standards and policies and developing a corporate culture that fits the organisation's operating environment and objectives, as well as identifying and implementing the activities and policies necessary to enact the chosen strategy for managing the employee–employer relationship. From this it is clear that SHRM

strategic human resource management
The process of human resource management which is driven by planning, foresight and analytical decision making.

integrates two ideas. The first is the notion that an organisation's human resources are important factors in both strategy formulation and implementation. The second is that the organisation's human resource practices are important in developing its pool of human resources for future strategy formulation processes.

Once an HR strategy is identified, it needs to be implemented. There are a number of activities that flow out of the HR strategy, such as structuring the organisation, designing jobs, staffing, training, reward systems and performance management, which are reflected in HRM polices and practices.

The activities involved in SHRM include such things as:

- determining the quantity and quality of employees required to meet organisational objectives;
- identifying effective ways to recruit desired staff;
- determining how to deploy people skills in the organisation through job characteristics and organisational structure;
- motivating employees to attain productivity targets;
- developing systems of accountability;
- pay and recognition; and
- ensuring legal requirements are met.

Linking SHRM with organisational performance

In this chapter, we have discussed why SHRM is important to an organisation's survival and sustainability. Throughout our discussion we have assumed that SHRM will lead to improved organisational performance. But how exactly is SHRM linked to organisational performance? We address this question next.

RESOURCE-BASED VIEW OF THE FIRM AND HRM

organisational resources
Tangible (e.g. finances, equipment, land, buildings, raw materials) or intangible commodities (e.g. knowledge, social networks, community relationships, trade secrets).

An organisation consists of resource inputs. These **organisational resources** are either tangible, such as finances, human and raw materials, or intangible, such as patents, copyrights, contracts or trade secrets (Hall, 1993). If these resources are unique they can enable the organisation to gain a competitive advantage.

Human resources have been argued to provide a particularly strong source of competitive advantage. Most companies have access to the same financial and material resources, yet what they do not have access to or are unable to copy are the people within the firm, their skills and how they work together. This view of the organisation and HRM is called the **resource-based view** (RBV) of the firm and it states that internal resources, which are rare, valuable, inimitable and non-substitutable, can provide sources of sustainable competitive advantage (Boxall, 1996). Therefore, an organisation can obtain an advantage over competitors if they can develop a core competency or capability in such resources as control systems, routines or learning mechanisms; human resource skills, knowledge and behaviours; or cultural resources or relationships that are built over time.

resource-based view
Internal resources, which are rare, valuable, inimitable and non-substitutable, can provide sources of sustainable competitive advantage (Boxall, 1996).

The ability of SHRM to provide enhanced business performance and competitive advantage arises both from matching HR practices and policies with overall strategic goals and from developing and focusing human resource skills and behaviours on organisational goals (cf. Colbert, 2004).

Wright, Dunford and Snell (2001) suggest that a competitive advantage can only be attained when HRM policies and practices motivate people through their thoughts and feelings to engage in behaviour that helps the organisation achieve its overall strategic goals. This means finding ways to shape the behaviours, norms, values, attitudes and perspectives of employees in a way which benefits both the employee and the organisation. For example, performance management can be used to set clear targets for an employee, identify training needs and clarify personal career interests and goals.

The business strategy of an organisation requires a unique set of behaviours and attitudes from employees and an appropriate HRM system that can generate these. Therefore, **effective SHRM** involves understanding both the internal and external operational requirements of the business and the social and behavioural requirements of the business. For example, a mining company operating in a small rural area which includes an Aboriginal community would need to consider government and state regulations relating to mining and Aboriginal land rights, understand the tasks and work context associated with the mining industry (e.g. safety issues), be aware of the economic importance it plays in the region, and understand diversity management issues relating to the demographics of the local community.

effective SHRM
Involves understanding both the internal and external operational requirements of the business and the social and behavioural requirements of the business.

Managing people is critical for an organisation to achieve its objectives, deliver results and be successful. There is substantial research evidence showing that there is a connection between how people are managed and the economic results achieved (Pfeffer & Veiga, 1999). Effective HR practices can deliver:

- increased productivity and less waste;
- greater collaborative problem solving;
- increased staff loyalty;
- fewer industrial problems and counterproductive behaviours;
- better skills in handling equipment;
- improved customer satisfaction and patronage;
- fewer accidents and an improved safety climate;
- lower turnover and absenteeism; and
- increased administrative, process and product innovation.

The RBV of the firm provides a valuable source of explanation about how SHRM leads to organisational performance. However, this framework is not without its limitations.

The RBV tends to be overly rationalistic. It assumes that organisations always choose the optimal decision for enhancing its performance. In doing this it does not take into account the ability of the environment to constrain and influence the organisation's decisions. For instance, the economy may increase the salary rates of talented and experienced applicants beyond what the organisation can afford.

The RBV tends to assume organisational discretion in HR practices. It has been proven that many organisational practices tend to be the same or similar among competitors over time (DiMaggio & Powell, 1983). This occurs due to legal requirements (such as equal employment opportunity legislation), societal expectations (such as negative views on child labour), labour market restrictions (such as the expectations of employees and potential employees as to their work environment and salary) and so forth.

The RBV is based on unitarist principles. It assumes that all employees are united in their efforts to achieve organisational goals and that they will exert the desired behaviours and use their skills to the benefits of goal attainment. In reality, though, the organisation does not have complete control over people. They exhibit discretion in what behaviours they exhibit and how much effort they exert. Further, it does not acknowledge the pluralist goals of its stakeholders.

The RBV reduces people to assets. It assumes that people are valuable to the organisation when they hold something that organisations cannot copy or substitute, such as skills or knowledge. This view, then, does not take into account the value that the organisation can obtain from subcontractors, temporary workers and consultants that their competitors can also acquire.

The RBV assumes that the resources which provide value are only those to which competitors cannot gain access. It is clear that there would be great value in having Dr Edward Deming (the statistician and management expert who created the notion of Total Quality Management, now adopted all over the world) on your payroll. However, there are also resources that are essential for organisational survival which are not distinctive (Deephouse, 1999). Thus, the organisation and competitors hold them alike. For example, banks must act like all other banks. They must attract funds from people in order to give funds to other people. To do this they need specific information technology and the typical range of services (i.e. cheque accounts and personal, business or housing loans).

Despite its limitations, the RBV of the firm has been instrumental in gaining legitimacy for the link between SHRM and organisational performance (Wright, Dunford & Snell, 2001). Most importantly, it has shifted the focus away from strategy based on external factors such as industry position to internal competencies and human resources. It has led to the increasing popularity of concepts such as knowledge management, learning organisations, flexible workforce and teamwork, each of which will be elaborated upon later in this book.

Please read
Wright, P. M., Dunford, B. B. & Snell, S. A. (2001), 'Human resources and the resource based view of the firm', *Journal of Management*, vol. 27, pp. 701–6.

THE MULTIPLE CONSTITUENCY MODEL
The RBV model shows how SHRM is linked to performance. Organisations, however, will still want to evaluate the value of their HR investment. Tsui's (1990) multiple constituency model shows that this is a difficult task. For example, consider the evaluation of a training program. Commonly, evaluation is conducted by asking participants in the training program to complete an evaluation form immediately after the conclusion of training. There are two obvious problems with this approach. First, trainees are likely to report how they felt about being part of the training, which may reflect the quality of the experience more than it does the actual skill development gained. Second, it relies on the self-ratings of the trainees, which may

not reflect how their manager would rate their performance on the skills which the training was intended to develop. How, when and by whom an HR activity is evaluated then affects the answer one obtains.

The basis of **Tsui's multiple constituency model** (1990) is that assessment of intangible organisational performance variables, such as SHRM, is difficult because of the multiple objectives of an organisation's constituencies. The model focuses on two components, how things currently work (*descriptive*) and how things ought to work (*normative*), and involves the analysis of three questions:

Tsui's multiple constituency model
A model that states an organisation has multiple constituencies whose objectives may conflict or differ.

1. What constituencies exist for the organisation? The context within which the organisation operates (i.e. its internal and external environments) such as industry, technology, workforce and structure suggests the relevant constituencies for the organisation.
2. What assessment does each constituency make as to the effectiveness of the organisation? It is clear from the above example that an organisation is unable to satisfy multiple constituencies at the same time. Therefore, it must seek out which is the most important constituent in terms of which has the most influence on organisational survival.
3. What factors influence the constituencies' evaluations? First, the environment may pose a direct influence on the organisational effectiveness assessment of a constituent. Second, the constituent may influence the organisation's environment by presenting particular opportunities and threats to the organisation. Third, the organisation itself can manage the opportunities and constraints posed by the environment by managing its interactions with constituencies and its responses to constituency expectations.

The systems approach, discussed earlier in this chapter, indicates that an organisation has a number of constituents or stakeholders and that the evaluation of one constituency will impact indirectly on the evaluations of others because an organisation which satisfies one constituent will not be satisfying other constituents. In other words, the perception of success is contingent on who you are asking and an organisation has a number of individuals from which these evaluative perceptions flow (Connolly, Conlon & Deutsch, 1980). For instance, management may view a strategy to improve innovation as being extremely successful in increasing the number of new products to market, whereas the organisation's shareholders may view it as being partially or even not successful if it does not bring about the financial return they are expecting. Lower-level employees too may view it as a failure as it did little to change their work tasks or give them more challenging roles.

Evaluating SHRM and organisational performance

So how do we know which organisational investments are effective and valuable? Traditionally this has been answered with financial analyses: assessing costs and calculating profits. However, financial assessments do not present a balanced view of investments. In addition to economic value, the organisation also obtains non-financial value from skills developed, location, knowledge, efficient processes, relationships between stakeholders and networks and the commitment between its stakeholders. Furthermore, financial measures are based on the past and they do not acknowledge why something happened the way it did, only that it did happen.

With success and competitive advantage contingent on HR skills, capabilities and knowledge, how do we measure the intangible value of investments in these areas? How do we place a value on such things as being able to retain talented employees? The balanced scorecard approach was developed by Kaplan and Norton (1996a) for just this purpose. It provides one way of assessing organisational performance taking into account intangible and intellectual assets.

CONSIDERING STAKEHOLDERS' VIEWS: MEASURING HRM PERFORMANCE BY USING THE BALANCED SCORECARD

An important aspect of the strategic management process is reviewing and evaluating the consequences of the strategic formulation and implementation process. In the current dynamic and internationally competitive environment, it is becoming important for organisations to measure their success in a simple, yet complete way (Kaplan & Norton, 1996b). The balanced score card created by Kaplan and Norton has been identified as one means of meeting this organisational need.

Based on the notion of goal conformity as a means to improve performance, the **balanced scorecard** translates an organisation's vision, mission, values and strategy into a comprehensive set of performance measures, which serve as the framework for a strategic management system (Kaplan & Norton, 1996b). Specifically, the balanced scorecard assesses past performance through financial measures (e.g. return on investment) mainly for shareholders and future performance gathered from the expectations and perspectives of certain stakeholders (see Figure 1.2). The four perspectives utilised to assess performance are:

balanced scorecard
Translates an organisation's vision, mission, values and strategy into a comprehensive set of performance measures, which serve as the framework for a strategic management system (Kaplan & Norton, 1996b).

1. The customers' perspective, or how customers see the organisation. The customers' perspective is undeniably a key component to future financial performance, because if the customer is not happy then sales will decrease.
2. The innovation and learning perspective, or how people can continue to improve. In the turbulent environment facing organisations today it is important that they learn and adapt to survive. If they do not monitor the environment and change accordingly they will be left behind by their competitors and sales will eventually decrease.
3. The internal perspective, or what people at work excel at. This perspective follows from the RBV of the firm, where if the organisation can gain core competencies in their resources then it will gain a competitive advantage and future sales will increase. Further, if the processes within the organisation are running efficiently and effectively then future output is guaranteed at minimum cost.
4. The financial perspective, or how the organisation appears to shareholders (Kaplan & Norton, 2000). This perspective highlights the financial results of past actions to give an indication of what future results may be.

The key to assessing performance, then, is the development of measures to assess goal attainment in each of these four areas. For instance, to assess financial success the organisation could measure return on equity; to assess customer satisfaction the organisation could measure their market share or number of complaints; to assess whether internal processes are successful the organisation

Translating vision and strategy: four perspectives

1.2 FIGURE
The balanced scorecard

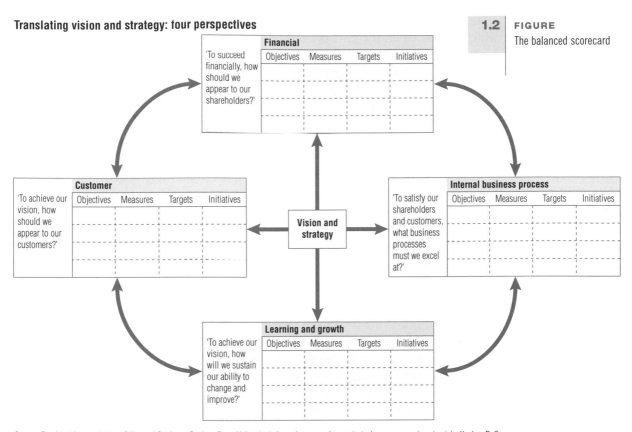

could measure cycle times or defect rates; to assess innovation and learning the organisation could measure rates of employee training and retention.

In addition to providing a more balanced way of assessing performance, Kaplan and Norton (1996b) suggest that the balanced scorecard can also align the organisation's strategy with the performance measures; it can provide the link between long-term strategies and short-term actions. The balanced scorecard has the capability of enhancing management's understanding of the organisation and the causal relationships between non-financial and financial measures. Subsequently, more effective HRM activities will be adopted, designed to contribute directly to one of the four perspectives, and these will be linked to the organisation's vision, mission, values, goals and strategy. When this is achieved (i.e. the balanced scorecard notion is applied specifically to HR), we refer to it as the HR scorecard. Management will also be able to evaluate better the extent to which the HRM system is assisting the organisation to meet its strategic goals and vision though the use of the HR scorecard. We will return to the concept of the HR scorecard in Chapter 10, where it will be discussed in relation to HR evaluation.

The balanced scorecard is not without its limitations. First, it is overly ambitious to attempt to suggest a complete list of cause and effect relationships that will drive a firm's future success. Second, if the organisation's environment is constantly changing, how important then are measures of customer satisfaction or share price, which are based on the past performance of the organisation? Third, the balanced scorecard approach fails to acknowledge the actions and perspectives of other stakeholders such as the government or competitors. If the government decides to ban the production of cigarettes, for instance, then cigarette companies will not have any future performance at all. Fourth, like the RBV of the firm, the balanced scorecard approach takes a rationalist view of organisations. It assumes that management will make the most optimal choice that will maximise value for customers, improve financial figures, build learning or improve internal processes. In reality, though, decisions are more complex than that and options may be constrained by the environment within which the organisation operates.

Please read

Kaplan, R. S. & Norton, D. P. (1996), *The Balanced Scorecard: Translating Strategy into Action*, Harvard Business School Press, Boston.

Thus far, we have discussed a number of criteria for HRM to be effective. These include taking a strategic (proactive) approach to people management, aligning policies and practices with the organisational strategy, considering the impact on stakeholders and other aspects of the business, intelligent decision-making processes, innovation based on an understanding of the business and cultural appropriateness, and balancing the needs of both the employee and the organisation so that each benefits. Next, we consider different models of SHRM and the value they bring to learning and practice.

<u>Models</u> of strategic human resource management

Organisations cannot rely on finding the types of people required to implement the decisions suggested by a given strategy at the time the strategy is finally identified. Planning is needed to get the right number of the right people in the right jobs at the right time. Therefore, for strategic decisions to be effective, an essential element is the anticipation of future HR needs. Lead time is needed to train and educate people as to the upcoming organisational changes as well as to hire or develop employees, evaluate compensation and reward systems, design new jobs or alter existing ones and research new options in HR such as new technology. For this to occur in a timely and organised manner, an analytical framework is needed.

There is an abundance of SHRM models in the literature. We will introduce you to only the most commonly used and accepted frameworks in SHRM research and practice. Following that, we will analyse what is missing in these models and present you with the SHRM Application Tool, which will help you to think about both the issues and practices of SHRM in a more practical and holistic way.

The most widely known model of HRM is that by Jackson and Schuler (1995). This model (see Figure 1.3) suggests that a variety of macro-level environmental characteristics influence the adoption of particular organisational HRM practices, policies and philosophies and, subsequently, organisational performance. This model shows that HR practitioners need to consider the laws and regulations,

1.3 FIGURE
Integrative framework for understanding HRM in context

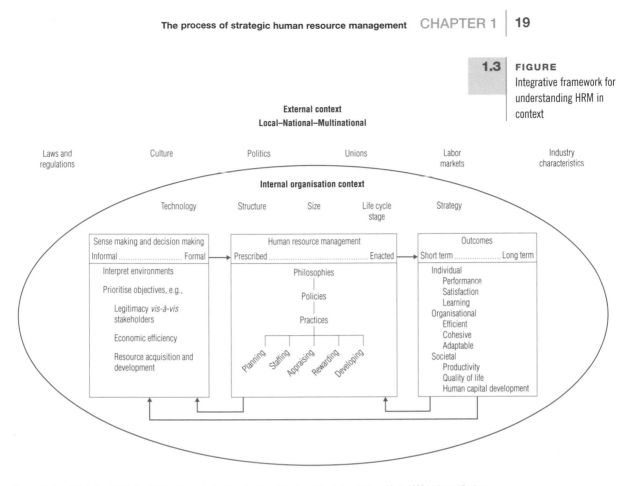

External context
Local–National–Multinational

| Laws and regulations | Culture | Politics | Unions | Labor markets | Industry characteristics |

Internal organisation context

Technology   Structure   Size   Life cycle stage   Strategy

| Sense making and decision making |
| Informal .... Formal |
| Interpret environments |
| Prioritise objectives, e.g., |
| Legitimacy *vis-à-vis* stakeholders |
| Economic efficiency |
| Resource acquisition and development |

| Human resource management |
| Prescribed .... Enacted |
| Philosophies |
| Policies |
| Practices |
| Planning   Staffing   Appraising   Rewarding   Developing |

| Outcomes |
| Short term .... Long term |
| Individual |
| Performance |
| Satisfaction |
| Learning |
| Organisational |
| Efficient |
| Cohesive |
| Adaptable |
| Societal |
| Productivity |
| Quality of life |
| Human capital development |

Source: Jackson & Schuler (1995). Reprinted, with permission, from the *Annual Review of Psychology*, Volume 46. © 1995 by Annual Reviews: www.annualreviews.org.

culture, politics and labour and industry partners (e.g. unions, markets, industry dynamics) relevant to the organisation. Further, the model shows that what information is interpreted, how information is interpreted, how decisions are made, and how people are communicated to and managed (and for what short-term and long-term goals) depends on the organisation's technology, structure, size, life cycle stage and strategy.

Similar to Jackson and Schuler's (1995) model, Kochan and Barocci (1985) provided an analytical framework for identifying the causal links between environmental changes, HRM policies and practices and the needs and goals of stakeholders (see Figure 1.4). They emphasise that analysis must recognise that HRM policies and practices need to adopt and respond to changes inside and outside the organisation. Any such analysis, they say, must be grounded in an accurate and comprehensive understanding of the history of the organisation, including 'shifts in the economic, legal, socio-political, demographic and technological contexts affecting the employment relationship' in the organisation of interest (Kochan & Barocci, 1985, p. 5).

The model by Klatt, Murdick and Schuster (1978) emphasises the importance of taking a systems approach with a focus on doing so at the planning and development stages (see Figure 1.5). Thus, in deciding on business objectives, an

FIGURE   1.4

Framework for analysing
HRM and industrial
relations at the level
of the firm

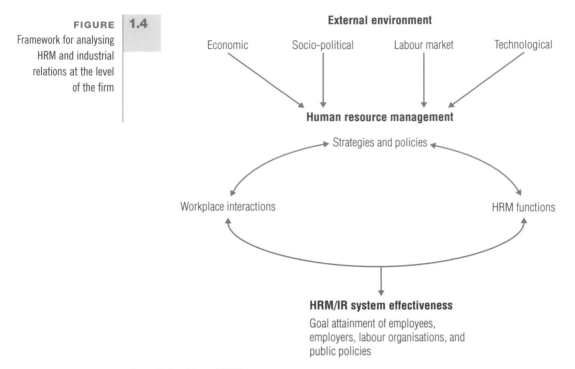

Source: Kochan & Barocci (1985).

organisation would also think through the HR implications, such as what type of employees and employee behaviours are required to achieve these objectives, how the organisation should be structured to achieve these objectives and what systems are required to ensure that individuals know what behaviours are required and are kept accountable for such.

The final model we discuss in this chapter is the SHRM framework by Lundy and Cowling (1996). Following Butler, Ferris and Napier (1991), these authors take a different perspective on HRM. They recognise that the SHRM process is a decision-making process and present it through the widely accepted decision-making technique of analysis, plan, implementation and evaluation (see Figure 1.6). In this book, we share and build on their perspective on SHRM as a decision-making process.

Lundy and Cowling underscore the vast amount of evidence showing that HRM often fails to add value within an organisation because it fails to take a strategic perspective, does not engage in planning behaviour and frequently fails to consider its interventions in relation to other features of the organisation. The tool presented in this book extends their notion of SHRM as a decision-making process.

As you can see, past frameworks tend to be a linear process. Yet in reality the relationship between analysis, choice and implementation is not so straightforward and past research has argued that it is dangerous to consider strategic decision making in a linear fashion, with orderly steps (Johnson & Scholes, 1989). The environment within which the organisation operates is constantly changing and on a number of levels, which means that to enable the organisation to be responsive to current needs, the analytical framework adopted

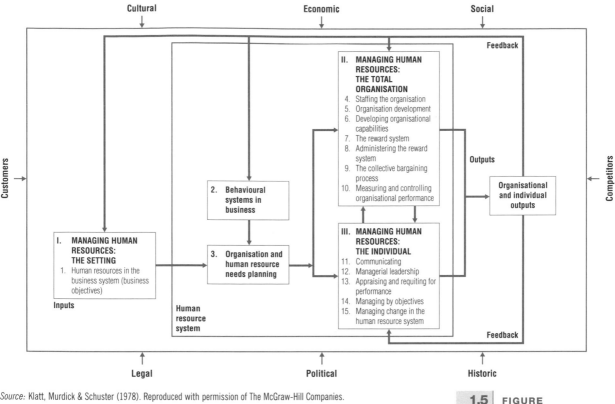

Source: Klatt, Murdick & Schuster (1978). Reproduced with permission of The McGraw-Hill Companies.

1.5 FIGURE

The human resource system in the business environment

by decision makers must involve a continuous process. What was successful in the past may not be successful now. We do acknowledge, however, that decisions can be made ad hoc without a process of steps, based on little information and implemented with little thought or preparation. It is clear though that such decision making is a gamble. Sometimes you may win but more often you may lose. Effective decision making has been proven to arise from a process of seeking information, identifying and evaluating alternatives and then selecting the 'best' alternative based on the current situation. This process forms the underlying framework of our SHRM Application Tool.

Also, past models of SHRM fail to acknowledge the evaluation component of SHRM. The outcomes of each action must be evaluated and fed back into future decisions including what was successful and aided organisational growth as well as what hindered growth and impeded employee satisfaction. It is important that both positive and negative outcomes are identified and analysed so that learning may occur. In addition, evaluation should occur at each level of the SHRM decision-making process; environmental influences should be evaluated as to their impact potential – what is most important and what is more trouble than it is worth. Plus, potential actions to address the issues revealed in the environmental analysis must be evaluated. It is extremely important to know whether the outcome of an action could be expected to have dire consequences for the organisation, and result in the termination of employment for the decision maker.

FIGURE 1.6
Strategic human resource
management

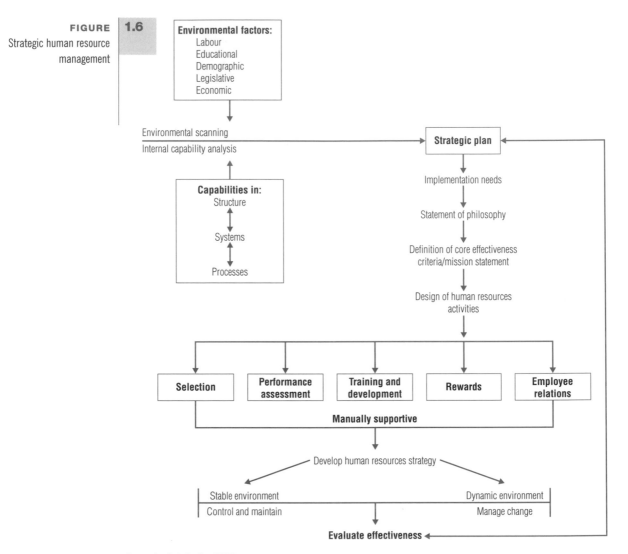

Source: Lundy & Cowling (1996).

It is evident in this chapter that the models described do not provide a clear process for identifying and addressing HRM issues. Instead, they describe what is involved in SHRM and the links between the environment and HRM practices. However, they do not provide specific steps for performing SHRM effectively, nor do they enable people to assess the appropriateness or effectiveness of potential HR actions and activities. Therefore, we combine the frameworks for analysing the process of SHRM with those based on the decision-making technique, to build on HR theory and take it to the next level. We present an SHRM Application Tool to show you how to put into practice in any given organisation effective SHRM. The SHRM Application Tool describes a process that will help you make optimal and timely HR decisions for your organisation.

The SHRM Application Tool is designed specifically to address these issues. It is a practice tool and will provide you with a base for making effective decisions based on the information you have. It will show you how environmental influences are interconnected, as too are the HRM activities that can be used to address SHRM issues. Finally, the tool will show you not only the bigger picture but also the steps to make decisions that are congruent with that framework.

The SHRM Application Tool

Managers are challenged by the role of constantly dealing with a never ending list of issues and they must do this within a dynamic organisational context with the aim of improving performance and stakeholder wellbeing. It is no wonder then that management practitioners are bombarded with a long list of possible ways of resolving the issues and it is confusing as to how they all fit together. The following SHRM Application Tool provides the answer. It will teach you a way to think about and analyse the organisation, its environment and issues as a whole. This model provides a continuous loop of constantly analysing and evaluating issues, actions and outcomes. Without acknowledgement of the process of SHRM, the HR professional is merely a personnel manager, undertaking only those tasks which enable the coordination of functions.

Earlier in this chapter it was said that effective SHRM is characterised by particular processes and management activities. The management activities or elements of SHRM, such as job analysis and design, staffing, training and performance management, are the tools used by organisations to manage people. In contrast, the decision-making process associated with SHRM guides the nature and use of these tools within the organisation. At this point, it is necessary to discuss the critical decision of how to arrange these tools or activities or how to relate them to each other in order to connect them into a whole. An effective decision-making system or process will enable the integration of components and ensure that each component supports organisational objectives, while an ineffective process will lead to ineffective people management. Thus, the system or process characterising effective SHRM is what enables an organisation to innovate, adapt, integrate and coordinate.

The SHRM Application Tool integrates the two components of strategic management, namely strategy formulation and strategy implementation. It also depicts the linking of organisational culture, strategies and structure with HR policies. It should be noted that, for effective SHRM, this process needs to be continuous, with ongoing monitoring of the environment, constant responses to opportunities and threats and regular evaluation with the aim of continuous improvement. This process enables decision makers to be better informed – not to make perfect decisions. Engaging in a continuous process such as the one described below is the best way of having up to date information on the organisation's current situation.

The SHRM Application Tool describes:
- the people and organisational practices and policies involved in the organisation;
- the context or environment in which the organisation operates and which it has little control over;

✓

**Checklist 1.1
SHRM
Application Tool**

❑ What is having or will have an impact on the organisation?

❑ What part of the organisation is affected by this and how is it affected?

❑ What do we need to know about this issue? e.g. What have other organisations done?

❑ What are our options?

❑ What are the potential outcomes of each option (both the positive and negative effects)?

❑ What is our best option based on the above and how will we act it out?

❑ Implement action plan.

❑ How did our action plan work? Did it address the original issue? What were its effects?

❑ Now that we have addressed the issue, what is having or will have an impact on the organisation?

- the profile of opportunities and threats including how the business can grow and who or what will stand in its way, both internally and externally to the organisation;
- the results of an assessment of the risk and rewards associated with pursuing the plan. This is one of the most important parts of the plan as it involves an 'assessment of everything that can go wrong and right, and a discussion of how the [HRM] team can respond' (Sahlman, 1997, p. 99).

The following process describes the SHRM Application Tool. Quite often the problems and opportunities faced by organisations are acted on without appropriate analysis. Do all potential opportunities and problems need to be analysed? If they do, can past assessments using the tool be used?

The answer to the first question is: Yes. Fully understanding the causes and effects of potential problems and opportunities will minimise surprises and enable proactive planning. The answer to the second question is an empathetic no. What has been successful in the past may not lead to success in the future due to constant changes in the internal and external environments of the organisation. It is important to analyse the current situation surrounding every opportunity and threat.

The SHRM Application Tool describes effective SHRM as the consistent application across all people management activities of a strategic decision-making process. The SHRM Application Tool presents techniques and frameworks for conducting a particular step. It is not suggested that you engage in all of these techniques, simply that you work out what technique or tool works best for you in your strategic analysis. The steps in this process are discussed in detail next.

STEP 1: ANALYSE ENVIRONMENTAL FACTORS

Through ongoing monitoring mechanisms, identify potential threats or opportunities. This refers to analysis of the relevant organisation, department and team objectives and operating environment (internal and external) for any existing or potential gaps in performance.

Environmental analysis, which is critical throughout the SHRM process, involves examining features of both the internal and external operating environment. Examples of things to consider in an environmental analysis are presented in Table 1.1.

An environmental analysis involves analysing:
- historical environmental effects; how the organisation arrived at its current situation. This may involve things such as the history of the relationship with unions;
- present factors and their effects on the organisation;
- expected future factors and their expected impact on the organisation.

INTERNAL ENVIRONMENT

In order to be effective in SHRM, the organisation must make an assessment of its present situation and compare it with a vision of the future. They then create an action plan to reach their vision. Finally, they must evaluate whether they achieved the vision by reassessing their present situation again. This assessment

---

TABLE **1.1**   **Environmental analysis**

Internal environments

- Ownership of the organisation (e.g. public or private sector, private or public companies and mergers or acquisitions)
- Size of the organisation (e.g. as simple or complex structures)
- Organisational strategy
- Organisational structure (e.g. bureaucratic, adhocratic, professional, centralised, divisionalised and 'flat' v. 'tall')
- Organisational culture
- Organisational history
- Resources

External environments

- Physical factors
- Technology
- Economic factors
- The labour market
- Industrial relations
- Political factors
- Social factors (e.g. social and community attitudes)
- Demographics (e.g. age, gender, minority groups, and education)
- Industry trends (e.g. service industries, telecommuting and privatisation)
- Cultural factors (e.g. employee rights and work and leisure)
- International factors (e.g. turbulent international environment, economic cycles, competitive and entrepreneurial cultures, international competitiveness v. international efficiency)

---

of their present situation involves an analysis of the organisation's strategy, structure and culture, and how these impact on each other. The results of this analysis are then assessed in relation to the organisation's HR policy.

Organisational ownership An individual, a group of individuals, the government or shareholders may own the organisation. The values of the organisation's owners impact on the direction of the company as well as the organisational climate. For instance, government-owned organisations operate in the public interest, whereas shareholder-owned organisations operate for the profitability of the organisation (through share price and dividend income).

Organisational size In a review of the literature, Verheul (2003) determined that firm size plays a role in shaping HRM practices. Small organisations have less need for developed and formalising practices as there tends to be direct communication between employees and owner–manager. Small businesses also rely more on developing commitment rather than control. Larger organisations, on the other hand, tend to face greater pressure for obtaining economies of scale (where average cost per item is reduced by sharing the costs over a greater number of items). These organisations are more visible in society, and their actions have wider implications for the environment than small family-owned businesses. As such, these organisations are more likely to have well-developed and formalised HRM and often conduct HRM functions (e.g. training) in-house. Furthermore, as discussed earlier, Kramar, McGraw and Schuler (1997) argued that centralised decision making is less effective in larger organisations due to the increasing complexity of each decision. Thus, organisational size impacts on the structure, direction and HR activities of the company.

Organisational strategy   Organisational strategy involves a course (or courses) of action necessary to meet the basic long-term goals and objectives of an organisation. It is important to identify the current organisational strategic direction with careful assessment of its prevailing goals and how the firm is positioned relative to its competitors. This will also involve an assessment of the organisation's ability to sustain its existing strategy taking into account the current environment in which it operates. Strategic decision making has important implications for HRM practices and policies. For instance, a cost-minimisation strategy may require a reduction in management levels to decentralise decision making to lower levels, a restructure of job roles or an increase in automation and technology, each resulting in people being made redundant.

Organisational structure   Organisational structure is concerned with the management levels, sectional arrangements and responsibilities necessary to execute organisational strategy. Specifically, there are three components to organisational structure: the designation of formal reporting relationships; the organisation of individuals into groups, groups into departments and departments into the firm; and the designation of systems for communicating, coordinating and integrating.

The type of structure utilised by the organisation depends on both internal and external forces such as technological advancements, pressure to grow internationally or a need for greater employee participation. As can be expected, then, the organisational structure has significant implications for the SHRM activities, in terms of the mix of recruitment, performance management, compensation and training and development. For example, an organisation in a highly competitive environment, characterised by a high level of technological change, may choose to pursue a strategy of flexibility and innovation through devolving responsibility for decisions to self-managed teams. Thus, it needs to recruit people whose working styles match this level of responsibility and autonomy, it needs to compensate people for their level of duties, and there needs to be constant training and development to keep abreast of the latest trends and technologies.

Molineux and Härtel (2004) suggest four levels of HR architecture: design, infrastructure, operational and assurance. They argue that it is important to consider the level in the organisation at which each factor is located. For instance, HR design should remain as a 'core corporate function' handled only by the upper levels of the organisation so that it can be integrated with organisational strategy and culture; HR infrastructure should be a centralised service; the operational HR functions should be decentralised to the lower levels in the organisation; and assurance of the HR system should also remain as a core corporate function.

Organisational culture   Organisational culture refers to the shared perspectives and beliefs within an organisation. It is a crucial but often overlooked management tool. Specifically, it includes the artefacts and patterns of employee behaviour, the beliefs and values of employees and the underlying assumptions evident in the organisation. The artefacts and behaviours within the organisation make up the visible level of culture as these can be seen. The invisible level of culture includes the beliefs and values and basic assumptions within the organisation. A system is needed to connect the HRM components into a holistic picture in order to understand and adapt the invisible side of culture.

- *Artefacts* are the material and non-material objects and patterns that intentionally or unintentionally communicate information about the organisation's technology, beliefs, values, assumptions and culture.
- *Patterns of behaviour* refer to the repeated rites and rituals within the organisation, which communicate information about the organisation's technology, beliefs, values, assumptions and culture.
- *Beliefs and values* refer to what people in the organisation believe in their mind to be true or not true, that is, realities and non-realities (beliefs) as well as what people really care about or have invested emotions in (values). Ethical and moral codes are composite systems of beliefs, values and judgements.
- *Underlying assumptions* refer to the beliefs and values that people in the organisation hold at the subconscious level of thought, unlike beliefs and values, which are expressed at a conscious level.

Organisational culture will impact on the HRM practices that will be considered in the organisation as well as those that are accepted. For instance, HRM practices of empowerment and self-managed work teams will conflict with a culture that is paternalistic and employees may face great difficulties in accepting the changes.

Organisational history Organisational history refers to the way in which the organisation has operated in the past, including past decisions, relationships and strategies. These are important to the organisation as past relationships with stakeholders such as unions, the environment and regulatory bodies can constrain or facilitate the organisational behaviours. Also under organisational history are the qualities and values of the founder of the organisation and their philosophies. Understanding where the organisation has come from and where it is currently at are important factors in developing a profile of the organisation and identifying its strengths and weaknesses.

Organisational resources Organisational resources are the inputs an organisation requires in order to produce its goods and services. They include such factors as financial, human and raw materials as well as skills, knowledge and social capital.

EXTERNAL ENVIRONMENT

Organisations operate in environments that are constantly changing. They are continuously faced with technological change, new governments and legislation, more sophisticated customers, globalisation of markets and different attitudes and customer tastes. Most organisations will find that what worked in the past will not work in the future. Subsequently, their decisions need to be made with up to date information about the environment.

Analysis of the environment may reveal changes which present the organisation with new opportunities or result in problems with their existing structures and practices.

The analysis involved in the SHRM Application Tool enables you to build alternative scenarios of the future. Bear in mind, though, that there are dangers to environmental analysis. If performed in a balance sheet fashion, where all environmental influences and their corresponding opportunities and threats are simply listed and addressed one at a time, then actions implemented tend to be piecemeal and the most important influences are overlooked.

Physical factors   Physical factors refer to the actual environment in which the organisation is located or where its goods and services are produced. This factor includes weather patterns (such as drought, hurricanes and tornadoes and floods) and characteristics of the environment (such as desert, swamp and earthquake faultlines).

Technological factors   Technological factors refer to the level of infrastructure and automation in the economy. They include such things as roads, airports, availability of electricity, healthcare and communication as well as the rate of technological change and level of development of products and processes (refer to Chapter 4 for a detailed discussion on technology and SHRM).

Economic factors   Economic factors refer to the general state of the economy in which the organisation operates. They include the current state of the business cycle (whether it is expanding, contracting or entering maturity), the level of unemployment, availability of credit, interest rates and inflation rates. These factors impact on the strategic direction of the organisation, influencing such decisions as whether it will pursue expansion or diversification of its business. It also impacts on HRM through the availability and quality of new recruits as well as expected wages (as discussed earlier, different economies have different wage expectations. For instance, the minimum hourly wage in China is 23 cents, whereas in the USA it is $5) (see Chapter 6 for a discussion on ethics and labour).

Labour market   The labour market refers to the availability of qualified personnel in the marketplace. Labour market conditions include unemployment levels, demographic diversity and market structure (Jackson & Schuler, 1995). Unemployment levels represent an imbalance in the supply of labour relative to the demand for labour. The unemployment level presents a significant challenge to the SHRM activities of an organisation. For instance, when the supply of qualified people is low, organisations may need to increase the attractiveness of the vacancy through higher compensation. Alternatively, the organisation can attempt to train existing employees to fill the position (see Chapter 8 for a discussion on the labour markets and recruitment and selection).

Industrial relations   Industrial relations refer to the relationship between management and its employees, with particular reference to negotiation of workplace conditions and contracts. Generally, the employee in the relationship is represented by a labour union (a group of workers usually external to the organisation appointed to represent the best interests of all employees within the particular industry). Organisational considerations under this factor include requirements surrounding negotiation of wages, working hours and training (see Chapter 6 for a detailed discussion on industrial relations and employment law).

Political and legal factors   Political and legal factors refer to the government activity, laws and regulations with which an organisation must comply. Different countries have different legal requirements and they differ in the extent to which legislation governs organisational actions. For instance, Europe has more extensive legal requirements than Australia. In European countries, organisations are required to set aside specific funds for training and development (Jackson & Schuler, 1995). In particular, these factors include political stability, political risk, export restrictions, taxes and corruption as well as laws governing wages, environmental protection, copyright and worker safety (refer to Chapter 6 for a discussion on workplace safety and the law).

Social factors   Social factors refer to the social and community attitudes which impact on the organisation's strategy. For instance, public demand for a clean environment constrains an organisation's options for waste removal as well as product outcomes such as the amount of energy used by appliances. Federal, state and local laws developed in response to community pressure also pose constraints on and provide opportunities for the organisation in relation to such factors as employee rights and minimum hours and wages (see Chapter 6 for a discussion on the employment relationship and labour law).

Demographic factors   Demographic factors refer to the characteristics of the population in which the organisation operates. They include age, population size and distribution, degree of migration and education, income levels and ethnic affiliation. This factor impacts on the characteristics and values of stakeholders within the organisation (employees and managers) as well as those external to the organisation (customers, shareholders, political groups and government). Demographic shifts hold important implications for HR practices such as allocation of holidays, recruiting new staff and training programs.

Diversity   Today, the workforce is composed of people of different race, gender, age, values, personalities, work behaviours, attitudes, needs and desires. Diversity is therefore one of the most important issues affecting SHRM. The organisation may need to alter the way it manages its people, including training and development, compensation, job design and performance management, to accommodate the personal needs and familial responsibilities of its employees (refer to Chapter 5 for a discussion on diversity).

Industry trends   Industry trends refer to the developments within the industry which present opportunities and threats to the organisation. They include the decisions of government such as privatisation of government services, the development of new modes of work such as telecommuting, where employees perform work off-site as opposed to in the organisation's building, as well as the emergence of new industries such as the service industry. For example, in less developed economies there are two main industries: a primary industry including mining and fishing, and a secondary industry including agriculture and manufacturing. In contrast, developed economies include a third industry, the service industry, which includes transport, tourism and entertainment.

Cultural factors   Cultural factors refer to the behaviours and customs particular to the culture of the country. Differences in human behaviour exist due to a need to adapt to the physical environment as well as social attitudes. These factors may include the centrality of religion, respect for elders, which behaviours constitute romantic interest, as well as rules for greeting others, eye contact and interpersonal contact/space (refer to Chapter 5 for a discussion on individual, national and international cultural differences).

International factors   International factors refer to the characteristics of the environment that are particular to cross-border operations, such as the degree of turbulence in the international economy, economic cycles, competitive and entrepreneurial cultures and international competitiveness in contrast to international efficiency (see Figure 1.7).

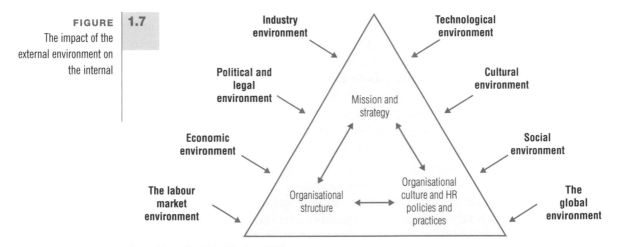

FIGURE 1.7
The impact of the external environment on the internal

Source: Adapted from Tichy & Fombrun (1982).

STEP 2: DETECT POTENTIAL PROBLEMS OR OPPORTUNITIES

Once you have a picture of the organisation's present situation you are able to assess where there are opportunities to grow and build strengths and where the organisation will face potential problems, for instance where stakeholders' interests are not being met; where the organisation is performing at below best practices; and whether changes are needed within the organisation in order for it to survive. Techniques include scenario planning and the widely adopted technique of gap analysis.

A **gap analysis** involves looking at what the organisation is currently doing and what it needs to be doing (i.e. best practices). The gap analysis will reveal the organisation's current and future human capital requirements (Molineux & Härtel, 2004). From the gap that emerges it is possible to identify areas which the organisation needs to build or improve on (see Figure 1.8).

gap analysis
Involves looking at what the organisation is currently doing and what it needs to be doing.

1.8 **FIGURE**
Gap analysis of a bank teller with poor quality service

It is important to determine whether your identified concern relates to an individual, group or the whole organisation and then identify the relevant purpose, vision and goals. A common way to determine the extent of a gap is to compare individual performance with the performance of other individuals, compare group performance with the performance of other groups and compare the organisation's performance with that of other organisations in the industry. For example, from the above gap analysis it is clear that the poor-service issue is occurring at the individual employee level. Therefore, attempts to minimise the gap must be directed at each individual, such as training, performance assessments and changes in job design. Other levels should not be discounted though, for the poor service may be occurring in only one geographic location or department, thus group-level initiatives must be put in place. Alternatively, poor service may be a feature across the entire organisation and is only translated to visible outcomes through the tellers. Thus, organisation-level initiatives need to be enacted to improve quality across the organisation.

Drawing from Hussey's (1995) HR audit we can evaluate the environmental influences on the organisation in terms of:
- potential changes;
- the potential impact of the potential changes;
- the probability of the changes and their impact; and
- the importance of the changes and impact relative to their probability.

In summary this step involves an analysis of the potential issues (both opportunities and threats) facing the organisation, based on the information gathered on the organisation's environment in Step 1. The level at which the issues are occurring must be identified (i.e. individual, group or organisational) and these must be assessed relative to the potential impact they will cause if they occur and the probability that they will occur. The final result, then, will be a list of potential opportunities and threats ranked in importance, enabling the organisation to focus on those that are most important or will have the greatest impact.

The issues identified may include such things as a need for a change in strategic direction. If this is the case, there are a number of tools available to identify which strategy would best suit the current or future environment. Two tools which require no previous skill are Porter's five forces and SWOT analysis.

Porter's five forces
A tool to model the influences in an organisation's environment and identify preferred strategic direction.

Porter's five forces (1979) is a tool to model the influences in an organisation's environment and identify preferred strategic direction (such as cost minimisation, product differentiation or market focus strategies). The purpose of this tool is to match organisational strategy to the opportunities and threats presented by five forces in its external environment. These five forces are:

1. *Intensity of rivalry.* Competition is increased when there are factors such as barriers to exiting the industry, low levels of industry growth and few differences between products.

2. *Barriers to entry.* Organisations are likely to be faced with new competitors when inputs and suppliers are easy to access and economies of scale are not necessary, thus any small organisation can compete with the well-established firms.

3. *Buyer power.* The power of consumers is maximised when there are substitutes available, when consumers have information and freedom to choose between products and when there are few buyers in the market.

4. *Supplier power.* The bargaining power of suppliers is increased when there is a threat that they will make their own products, when the volume of purchase means little to the supplier and when there are few suppliers in the industry.

5. *Threat of substitutes* (including technology change). Competition is increased if there are alternatives to the goods and services produced within the industry and there is little cost to the consumer in switching between them, for example watching videos or DVDs, or going to the cinema.

The Porter's five forces tool is not without its limitations. First, it assumes that an organisation strives purely for profitability and survival, with little regard for stakeholder satisfaction. Second, it completely ignores factors in the organisation's internal environment which may provide a competitive advantage (see the RBV of the organisation). Finally, the model assumes that organisations desire to achieve competitive advantages over all other players in the industry, overlooking alternatives such as strategic alliances and networks.

SWOT analysis
Involves a scan of the organisation's internal and external environments in order to match the organisation's internal strengths (S) and weaknesses (W) with its perceived opportunities (O) and threats (T).

A **SWOT analysis** involves a scan of the organisation's internal and external environments in order to match the organisation's internal strengths (S) and weaknesses (W) with its perceived opportunities (O) and threats (T) (Learned *et al.*, 1969). From this analysis the organisation will be able to see where a new strategy will be most advantageous (via the strength–opportunity match); where a new strategy will improve competitiveness (the weakness–opportunity match); where a new strategy will be need to continue competing (strength–threat match); and where a new strategy will protect the organisation (weakness–threat match).

As you can see, additional analysis is required on top of the tools mentioned in order to get a complete view of the issue.

STEP 3: VERIFY/FALSIFY POTENTIAL PROBLEM OR OPPORTUNITY

Once the important issues have been identified you need to put them into context by identifying all the environmental factors that may have caused or will be affected by the particular issue at hand. What are the expected outcomes of the issue (both the positive and negative outcomes that may occur if this issue is addressed and if it is not)? See Table 1.2 for an example.

For instance, if the problem or opportunity is a need to innovate, develop mechanisms for identifying relevant internal and external environmental issues which will enable the organisation to gain relevant core competencies.

This step sets the stage for considering the specific approaches available to address the issue, including what it is you actually want to achieve by solving this issue. If the issue is verified and it is decided to address it, the next step is planning. The planning stage involves identifying all the different ways the issue can be solved, evaluating the alternatives, selecting the alternative to pursue and developing a plan.

TABLE **1.2** **Verification of issue**

Issue: Need to increase innovation levels

	Causes of the issue	Positive things that will result	Negative things that will result
We *address* the issue	1. Industry is more competitive 2. Customers are demanding new products 3. Employees are asking for more challenging roles 4. Organisational mission and vision is becoming outdated	1. Become more competitive 2. Employee satisfaction and commitment likely to increase from more challenging tasks	1. Higher costs from continual training programs and higher wages of talented employees 2. Need entire organisation to be committed to constant change
We *do not address* the issue		1. Can focus costs on improving what we already do so that we can be the best at it 2. Reduce costs	1. Become less competitive 2. Talented employees likely to leave for more innovative roles at other companies

STEP 4: DEVISE PLAN AND SUCCESS CRITERIA
IDENTIFY ALTERNATIVES

There may be many possible courses of action in relation to a particular problem or opportunity identified in Step 2. This step involves the identification of all conceivable courses of action to address the problem or opportunity based on the information gathered in Step 3. Potential danger lies in not considering anything other than the most obvious action. However, it is important to keep a realistic view of the organisation at this step. There is no point in considering options that the organisation's structure, culture, processes and human capital will not be able to deliver (Molineux & Härtel, 2004).

There are a number of techniques available for creative problem solving that can be applied in any organisation. Two techniques that require no previous skills are brainstorming and mind mapping.

brainstorming
The process of idea generation via face to face groups.

Developed by Osborn (1957) in an attempt to improve employee creativity, **brainstorming** refers to the process of idea generation via face to face groups. However, it is not restricted to group activity; brainstorming has also been conducted by individuals with the output of each aggregated to a group level, called nominal groups (Sutton & Hargadon, 1996). To conduct a brainstorming session, the facilitator invites participants with relevant and complementary skills. In order to generate the large quantity of ideas that brainstorming is renowned for, it is important in each session to avoid criticising others, to note all ideas that come to mind regardless of feasibility or rationality and to combine and improve suggested ideas (Osborn, 1957, cited in Sutton & Hargadon, 1996).

Mind Mapping
A process of visually recording ideas with words, colours, codes and symbols.

Developed by Buzan (1970), **Mind Mapping** refers to a process of visually recording ideas with words, colours, codes and symbols. It enables you to use both the left and right parts of the brain to record large amounts of information and ideas and reveal the relationships between each. To produce a Mind Map® you start with a word or principal idea in the centre of the page. Then you record 5–10 words or principal ideas that are associated with this central word. Then you record 5–10 words associated with each of these secondary words and ideas (Buzan, 1989).

EVALUATE ALTERNATIVES

For each identified alternative, verify whether it addresses all the relevant issues. Assess what other effects (both positive and negative), in addition to the expected outcome, the action could have. Consideration of financial, logistical and human outcomes as well as the effects of taking no action should be given.

Evaluation consists of three components: suitability, feasibility and acceptability.

1. *Suitability*. To what extent does the alternative fit the situation? Does it capitalise on the organisation's strengths and address the organisation's weaknesses? Does it directly address the issue at hand? When choosing an alternative it is important to consider whether the options will fit the current organisational structure, strategy and culture or whether it demands large-scale change.

2. *Feasibility*. Is the alternative realistic to employ in terms of funding available and the existing capabilities of the organisation? Can the required resources be obtained? Is there time? Will the organisation be able to cope with any negative outcomes? When choosing an alternative you must consider the resources that will be required as well as the need for change in existing resources, structures and processes.

3. *Acceptability*. Do the benefits outweigh the costs? Will the plan fit the organisation's existing systems or will it require fundamental changes? Will the outcome contradict stakeholder expectations? When choosing an

alternative you must consider information from a wide range of sources in order to predict how acceptable the decision will be to each stakeholder group.

It is unlikely that there will be a clear-cut right or wrong choice of action to be pursued. The completion of this step will come down to a choice of action based on the decision makers' judgement based on the available information.

ESTABLISH SUCCESS CRITERIA

This step involves the identification of the functional activities needed to implement the alternative successfully, such as recruitment of new staff, training of existing staff and the purchase of new technology. To complete this step you must identify the preferred action plan, including criteria for evaluating its effectiveness in addressing the concern.

Rausch (2003) identified a number of factors that are important for effective managerial decisions. These are:

*   To communicate the plan clearly to all stakeholders, taking into account the information that they would like to have relative to the information that they need to have. Therefore, the plan needs to incorporate methods and timing of communication to stakeholders.
*   To gain acceptance of the final decision and plan by all the stakeholders participating in the plan. Participation is a critical factor in any plan, for if you do not win over the people needed to implement the plan, the plan is guaranteed to fail. It is important to identify the following: Who is required? How are they required (what is their role)? When are they required (what is the timeframe)? Where are they required (will they be moved to a new position or a new location)? Key questions also surround how to ensure participation by those needed to participate and how to ensure that participants are competent and able to implement the plan. Each of these questions needs to be addressed in the plan.
*   To achieve coordination of participants and satisfaction with the decision, it is important to assess how norms will be affected, including organisational culture and group norms as well as societal norms. It is also critical to determine where reviews and evaluations are needed to assess the outcome of each stage of the plan.

Part of planning involves considering where and when adjustments need to be made. There are two key aspects of this activity: (1) determining the primary changes required; and (2) determining the secondary changes needed to ensure the primary changes are properly aligned and do not conflict with existing practices (Molineux & Härtel, 2004). Practically, this is achieved using the process model to consider each element with respect to both primary and secondary changes.

Determining the location of various HR activities is also important, particularly in terms of whether the activities will be centralised or decentralised. For example, the negotiation of workplace conditions and agreements should be centralised and remain under the control and direction of top management, whereas activities such as performance management and training programs can be decentralised to the lower levels of the organisation (Molineux & Härtel, 2004). In addition, assessment of the value and importance to the organisation is essential, for if the activity is of high value to the organisation's core competency then it should be developed in-house and involve a full-time position as opposed to other employment alternatives such as outsourcing and part-time or casual work (cf. Molineux & Härtel, 2004).

STEP 5: IMPLEMENT THE PLAN

This step involves the translation of the decision into action; the implementation of the action plan decided in Step 4. Be aware that each action which is complex or likely to encounter high employee resistance will require its own 'application tool thinking' in order to devise an appropriate implementation plan for that specific action. For example, a plan which involves a change to top management may encounter resistance from those members who see a threat to their positions. To address this issue an assessment of all the external and internal factors that may contribute to the resistance is needed (such as the group norms of top management or views in the industry which may dictate that top management positions are immune from personnel cuts). Following this, a detailed assessment is needed on the positive and negative outcomes that may result from pursuing the action that threatens top management and the effects of potential resistance. Then alternative actions can be envisioned to combat the resistance before it arises and to turn the effort involved in resisting to effort directed at achieving the goals of the overall plan. Following this a plan is devised, implemented and evaluated.

If there is low risk, then the plan can be implemented with very little fuss; little thought is needed as to how each stakeholder group will react and adapt to the changes. An example of this is an organisation where employees are used to constant upgrades of computer programs. Thus, introducing an upgrade to the existing database program will encounter very little resistance or fear.

However, cases of high risk and greater uncertainty about whether the plan will work means that there may be problems with implementation, such as acceptance of the decision. In such a case more time is needed on process model thinking. More consideration is also needed for situations where previous routines and procedures are no longer effective and need to be changed. These situations may be uncomfortable for employees and require in-depth thinking for a sensitive change process. For example, in an organisation that encounters very little technological change employees will easily not accept upgrading the database program.

STEP 6: EVALUATE AGAINST SUCCESS CRITERIA

A vital component to any plan is an evaluation or review of whether it achieved what it set out to achieve; in particular, whether the predicted results emerged or whether unexpected results were obtained. Specifically, this step requires the decision maker to evaluate the effectiveness of the action against the criteria developed in Step 4. A gap analysis (described in Step 2) can be conducted to see where the plan achieved its aims and where it had shortcomings.

It is important to remember to look at both the positive effects of the actions implemented and the negative. Failures are just as important, if not more important, to organisations as successes for understanding why something did not work. They can tell us a lot about the organisation, its environment and its people. A critical factor here is to view the negative outcome in terms of when it occurred: when didn't the plan work and what were the defining circumstances? There is a tendency for organisations and academics to study 'best practice' and what has been successful for others, with a desire to replicate that success. As such, managers try out new policies, practices and ideas and discard them when they fail to yield the desired results. The problem with this, though, is that the need for change and the thought processes involved in attempting change have begun and when the plan is discarded the thought processes are unable to evolve to the next stage (Christensen & Raynor, 2003). There is no analysis of why it did not work in an attempt to move forward to a plan that will work. Christensen and Raynor (2003) argue that we cannot expect one cure to solve all business ailments, just as we cannot expect one medicine to cure all illnesses. It takes a process of finding what works for your business with its particular culture, processes, relationships and environment.

Evaluating the outcomes of the plan against the goals of the process is the final stage in our SHRM Application Tool. Yet the process should not conclude here. Achieving one's objective 'is not a cause for celebration; it is cause for new thinking' (Drucker, 1994, p. 103). The environment within which the organisation operates does not stop changing. Therefore, the decision makers should never stop analysing and planning for the future survival of the organisation.

Contemporary SHRM Application Tool

In practice the contribution of HRM tends to reside only in the implementation stage of plans, with such questions as: Do we need more staff or fewer staff for the change to be successful? Do we need to train existing staff to be able to handle the change? Will we need to change our compensation practices to be in line with the higher skilled staff? Will existing jobs need to be redesigned?

As we have shown, HRM should contribute throughout the decision-making process. HRM is in the best position to be able to identify and assess what are truly feasible alternatives and how the organisation can effectively implement the desired change. Integrating the RBV of the firm with the application tool described above reveals the SHRM Application Tool designed to provide a complete analysis of SHRM decision making (see Figure 1.9). This tool is used as a framework for learning throughout this book. An example of the SHRM Application Tool in action is provided at the end of each chapter to demonstrate how the tool can be applied to a particular area. The tool depicts the significance of SHRM as an integrative part of strategic formulation and implementation in dealing with dynamic environmental change (e.g. technology, demography, competition). Based on the RBV, SHRM components include human capital, employees' discretionary behaviours and the HRM system (i.e. policies and practices). It is evident that effective SHRM should demonstrate proactive critical analysis of its role in the strategic management process. It should identify any gaps or problems in the alignment of an organisation's internal and external operating environment, strategic management and SHRM; devise a plan and criteria to address the problem identified; and implement and evaluate the plan's effectiveness in the strategic management process. This learning cycle of SHRM can help to develop a better strategic management process to deal with the dynamic changing environment today's organisations face.

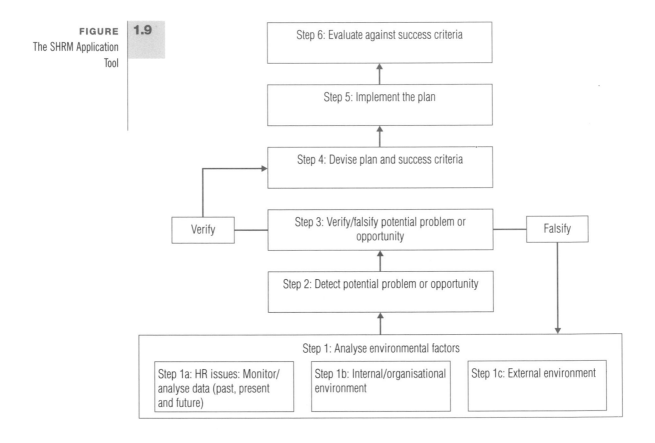

Today's global market is fast moving and increasingly competitive. Shareholders demand constant or improved return on their investments, governments push for value and competitive pricing in their purchases, and you and I demand lower bank fees and more functionality from our technology at a lower price. Given the enormity of these demands, it is no surprise that organisations are constantly reviewing their operations and searching for ways to improve productivity, flexibility, quality and innovation. Technology and digital communication developments have broadened the range of possible responses to these constant challenges.

Many organisations are responding to these challenges and opportunities by radically reviewing operating models to deliver increased reliability, faster time to market and lower operating costs. A component of emerging operating models is the increased utilisation of offshore suppliers, services or production facilities. Manufacturing organisations have utilised offshore production facilities for many years; however, increasing competitive pressures have led to the emergence of global sourcing strategies where service organisations (e.g. financial services) seek to access global markets for the delivery of 'back office' processes. These processes include the use of offshore centres. For example, financial services companies (such as Citibank) use offshore centres (primarily in India) for software development, accounts payable processing, insurance claims processing and payments processing and research facilities, and have established offshore call centres for product support, customer inquiries, and telesales.

This growing trend to the structuring of business operations is known as global sourcing, business process outsourcing (BPO) or offshoring. A.T. Kearney, the renowned international management consultancy firm, defines offshoring as 'the search for a lower cost location for business processing. It could include migrating existing processes or augmenting a current global footprint. When a company looks at an offshore location for its business processes, it can outsource to a third party, establish its own operating unit, called a captive, or create a joint venture with a local low cost operator'.

Some business commentators see continuous growth in offshoring as a natural progression in the development of the global economy. The significant labour cost savings, access to a skilled labour force and, in some cases, tax concessions make offshoring a compelling proposition. India, China, the Philippines, Malaysia, Singapore, Canada, Ireland, Eastern Europe, Latin America, Mauritius, the Baltic States and New Zealand all offer either scale or niche potential to those organisations exploring offshoring opportunities. Some of the world's most well known and successful brands including ABN AMRO, GE, Citibank, Microsoft, IBM, Accenture, HSBC, Deutsche Bank, Standard Chartered, Target Corporation, JP Morgan Chase, AXA, Zurich and American Express have engaged in significant offshoring exercises and continue to explore options for further development of their offshore presence.

The potential savings are considerable. The international management consultancy firm McKinsey and Company estimate that for every dollar American companies move offshore US$0.85 is saved. That's an 85 per cent cost saving! McKinsey claim that the quality of services they buy is often higher and the wages are lower, so companies can hire better qualified staff and invest more on supervision and training, which adds strategic value to their business.

One of the drivers of this trend is that the global economy is setting global benchmarks for organisational performance. Many organisations now compete in internationally deregulated markets where price is a significant component of the competitive advantage. The airline industry is one such example.

In January 2005 the Chief Executive Officer of Qantas, Geoff Dixon, made it clear that 'Qantas needed to compete effectively and that moving to more overseas based services was a consideration'. Qantas has already relocated 400 flight attendants to London in a bid to reduce costs and has plans to increase this number to 900.

Mr Dixon stated: 'We are, however, operating in a global market and there is no room for complacency simply because we are currently profitable and successful. There are major reasons for this: our close and constant attention to efficiencies, our decision to invest billions of dollars in new products and equipment, and the support of our staff for continued workplace change.' He went on to confirm 'That the airline was looking at a range of possibilities including joint ventures which would, if they came to fruition, involve new jobs being created in both Australia and other countries'.

The response to this announcement from the Australian community was mixed. Investors and shareholders viewed the evaluation of these options as a necessary and worthwhile investment, while staff members and unions feared possible restructuring and redundancies.

Other drivers of the offshoring trend include the pressures created by investors for short-term delivery of business results. Many companies now report quarterly and half yearly results to the market, and organisations failing to meet the expectations of share market analysts (or at least match the performance of their peers) can expect a reduction in their market capitalisation as investors move to stocks with perceived stronger performance. This can lead to demands within organisations to increase the speed, scale and scope of offshoring activities designed to improve profitability.

At St George Bank, Group Executive IT John Loebensteinin made a compelling point about offshoring: 'If any company is to stay competitive, it has to jump on the boat to keep development and operating costs in check and pass the savings on to customers. If it can't, it'll go under'.

Set against this seemingly inevitable trend is ongoing debate about the social, community and ethical issues raised by offshoring. There are community concerns about the people who will lose their jobs or find themselves in lower wage employment, and social concerns about the impact of this growing trend on future employment opportunities and the ability of affected nations to create sustainable industries in a fast-changing world. There is also a range of ethical concerns about moving jobs offshore to developing nations with significantly lower standards of living than those in the developed world.

Despite these concerns, one thing is certain: offshoring as an approach to business structure is here to stay. This trend presents new and complex issues and opportunities, particularly in the area of human resource management. Among these are the employee relations issues associated with offshoring jobs, downsizing, and redundancy and the new challenge of establishing and running an offshore workforce.

Discussion questions

1. Identify the SHRM challenges organisations face in responding to the compelling arguments for offshoring.
2. You are the General Manager of HR at Qantas. The Chief Executive Officer has asked for a brief report regarding the HR implications of offshoring. Which issues would you highlight?
3. Qantas is a major institution in Australian society. Evaluate the implications of its decision to move jobs offshore. In your answer, consider the role of business in society and the impact of offshoring on Australian business and society.

Source: Adapted from A.T. Kearney Executive Agenda (2004), vol. VII, no. 3, Third Quarter 2004, p. 50, <www.atkearney.com>, accessed 29 October 2005; P. Gray (2005), 'Destination India', *The Age*, 1 October, p. 44; McKinsey and Company (2004), 'Exploding the myths of offshoring', *The McKinsey Quarterly Web Exclusive*, July, <www.mckinseyquarterly.com>, accessed 27 October 2005; Qantas Statement on Overseas Jobs, 2005, *About Qantas Newsroom*, 18 January, <www.qantas.com>, accessed 24 October 2005.

New challenges for the HR manager   **A manager's challenge**

Present-day statistics of the booming Australian economy show its lowest unemployment rate and highest job market statistics since the 1970s. However, the business challenges such a lucrative economy poses for today's practitioners are far from similar to those faced 30 years ago. The ageing population of Australia has created a situation where 17 to 25 year olds entering the workforce are now 40% of that in the 1970s. Moreover, with the retirement of the baby boomers, people who leave the workforce considerably outnumber the people who are entering the workforce, consequentially creating a skill shortage detrimental to thriving Australian companies.

In light of this, the need to reinvent organisational HRM strategies has become more pronounced than ever before. As human resources and recruitment expert Sheryl Moon, Director of Manpower Services Australia (a global human resources solution provider), points out, in a global quest to seek out the best of skills and expertise Australia cannot consider itself an 'an island of isolation'. Australia already loses around 50 000 of its labour force permanently and a further 170 000 for longer than 12 months to foreign employers. In a global context Australian companies are challenged not only to preserve the local talent but also to attract global skills and knowledge. To meet this challenge, Ms Moon argues, Australian business requires changes to its recruitment strategies.

Such changes can include provision of referral bonuses to staff for recommendations they provide in bringing in new talent and strategies to attract underutilised labour groups such as mature workers, returning mothers and physically challenged people into the labour force. Companies can also encapsulate variety and fun into job roles by designing work that is flexible and requires employees' own decisional input. Further, managing an intergenerational workforce could ensure the continuity of organisational 'know-how', and integrate the wisdom of the company seniors with the creativity and diversity of the technology-savvy younger people.

From a global perspective, Michael Zanko (an Associate Professor in the School of Management, Marketing and Employment Relations at the University of Wollongong), stated that human resource development (HRD) was the most widely identified HRM issue (by 19 out of 21 economies) analysed in a study exploring HRM issues and trends in the Asia–Pacific region. The rationale for placing such emphasis on HRD, however, differed across countries; for example, HRD was considered useful in overcoming skills shortage for the knowledge-based economy in Singapore, while in Japan HRD was utilised for enhancing personal responsibility for career development. The USA, on the other hand, found HRD to be crucial in 'dealing with technology and globalisation through planned learning, increased education and sensitivity'.

Considering the multitude of issues influencing the current HRM field, professionals in the area are expected to ensure the development and sustainability of human resource capital, while balancing the needs of the organisation, aspirations of the workforce and values and expectations of the society.

Source: Adapted from Anonymous (2005), 'Creative solutions to HR headaches', *The Canberra Times*, 24 June, p. 13; M. Zanko (2003), 'Change and diversity: HRM issues and trends in the Asia Pacific region, *Asia Pacific Journal of Human Resources*, vol. 41, no. 1, pp. 75–87.

Using this book

The general model guiding the organisation of this book is presented in Figure 1.9. Based on this model, the book is divided into three main areas.
- The next chapter will complete your introduction to SHRM.
- Part 2 presents you with the business context. It will help you to understand how changes in the environment impact on organisations, and the issues that arise from these.

- This is followed by Part 3, where you will learn about the tools (or activities) of HRM that can address the issues analysed in Part 2. These tools are recruitment, training and development, performance management and compensation. This section concludes with a chapter on the defining features of an effective HR practitioner.

The text is ordered in this manner to help you to keep the business context in mind when learning about the components.

Summary

In this chapter we introduced you to the concept of strategic human resource management (SHRM). SHRM has evolved from a number of different perspectives. It is based on a holistic, or open-systems, approach where HRM must match the prevailing organisational culture, including at the level of assumptions. Strategy and structure were shown to interact with organisational culture and the characteristics of effective HRM policies were determined to make up the bottom line. Specifically, the topic uncovered how the resource-based view (RBV) of the firm advanced the role of SHRM in achieving a sustainable competitive advantage for an organisation. The balanced scorecard was identified as an essential means to assess organisational past and future performance with particular emphasis on the delivery of HR as a means of developing, implementing and evaluating an organisation's vision, mission, values, goals and strategy.

Key terms

balanced scorecard	management	strategic human resource
behavioural science approach	Mind Mapping	management
brainstorming	organisational behaviour	strategic management
collaborative philosophy	organisational culture	strategy formulation
commitment philosophy	organisational resources	SWOT analysis
competitive advantage	organisational strategy	Theory X
cultural capital	organisational structure	Theory Y
effective SHRM	paternalistic philosophy	traditional (or transactional)
GAP analysis	Porter's five forces	philosophy
human capital	resource-based view	Tsui's multiple constituency
human relations movement	scientific management	model
human resource management	social capital	

Review questions

1.1 How could HRM contribute to successful strategic management of the firm?

1.2 What is the resource-based view (RBV) of the firm and how has it advanced the notion of SHRM?

1.3 You are the HR manager for a mining company. You have been asked to highlight a plan of action for increasing computer training for the low-level employees who work in the mines. Outline the key issues explaining why this training is necessary and how the organisation may adopt the initiative.

1.4 What does the term organisational culture mean? How does it relate to SHRM?

1.5 How do HRM and SHRM differ? Use examples to illustrate the differences.

Exercises

1.1 Select an organisation that is important to you. List the characteristics of the external and internal environment that have the most impact on your chosen organisation.

Compare the tools that can be used in each stage of the SHRM Application Tool.

1.2 If a company is trying to increase year-to-date profit figures through reducing staff levels, what considerations must be taken into account?

1.3 Internet-based companies depend heavily on continuous improvement. 'Google' (www.google.com) is one of the world's leading search engines. Perform a SWOT analysis of Google and provide a plan to present to the managing director of the company.

1.4 Kate has just found out that her current job in tutoring International Cross-cultural Management will not exist next year due to the merging of the subject with International Management. Her university has offered her an administrative role but the pay is considerably lower and she is trying to pay off a home loan. She has searched for another tutoring job elsewhere but has been unable to find anything that suits her expertise. Should she accept the university's offer? What factors in the university's external and internal environment have put her in this dilemma? What are the positives and negatives of taking up the university's offer? What plan of action would you suggest?

1.5 Alex wants to open a trendy café on Darling Harbour, an extremely busy shopping area, 24 hours a day. What are the main factors she must take into consideration before she pursues her dream? What are the potential benefits or risks associated with this opportunity? What would be the first steps she must take?

References

Bamberger, P. & Meshoulam, I. (2000), *Human Resources Strategy: Formulation, Implementation, and Impact,* Sage, Thousand Oaks.

Boxall, P. (1996), 'The strategic HRM debate and the resource-based view of the firm', *Human Resource Management Journal,* vol. 6, no. 3, pp. 59–75.

Butler, J. E., Ferris, G. R. & Napier, N. K. (1991), *Strategy and Human Resources Management,* South-Western Pub. Co., Cincinnati, OH.

Buzan, T. (1970), *Make the Most of your Mind,* Colt Books, Cambridge.

Buzan, T. (1989), *Use Both Sides of Your Brain,* Plenum, New York.

Child, J. (1997), 'Strategic choice in the analysis of action, structure, organizations and environment: Retrospect and prospect', *Organizational Studies*, vol. 18, no. 1, pp. 43–76.

Christensen, C. & Raynor, M. (2003), 'Why hard-nosed executives should care about management theory', *Harvard Business Review*, vol. 81, no. 9, pp. 67–84.

Colbert, B. (2004), 'The complex resource-based view: Implications for theory and practice in strategic human resource management', *Academy of Management Review*, vol. 29, no. 3, pp. 341–58.

Connolly, T., Conlon, E. J. & Deutsch, S. J. (1980), 'Organizational effectiveness: A multiple-constituency approach', *Academy of Management Review*, vol. 5, no. 2, pp. 211–17.

Deephouse, D. L. (1999), 'To be different, or to be the same? It's a question (and theory) of strategic balance', *Strategic Management Journal*, vol. 20, no. 2, pp. 147–66.

DiMaggio, P. & Powell, W. (1983), 'The iron cage revisited: Institutional isomorphism and collective rationality in organizational fields', *American Sociological Review*, vol. 48, pp. 147–60.

Drucker, P. (1994), 'The theory of business', *Harvard Business Review*, September–October, pp. 95–104.

Hall, R. (1993), 'A framework linking intangible resources and capabilities to sustainable competitive advantage', *Strategic Management Journal*, vol. 14, no. 8, pp. 607–18.

Härtel, C. E. J. (1999), 'Global vision: Recognizing our organizational paradigms: Lessons from a historical review of the contribution of work psychology from three continents to occupational health and safety management', <http://siop.org/tip/backissues/TipOcto99/12Hartel.htm>, accessed 1 June 2005.

Härtel, C. E. J. & Härtel, G. F. (1996), 'Making decision making training work', *Training Research Journal: The Science and Practice of Training*, vol. 2, pp. 69–84.

Härtel, C. E. J. & Härtel, G. F. (1997), 'SHAPE-assisted intuitive decision making and problem solving: Information-processing-based training for conditions of cognitive busyness', *Group Dynamics: Theory, Research, and Practice*, vol. 1, no. 3, pp. 187–99.

Hussey, D. E. (1995), 'Human resources: A strategic audit', *International Review of Strategic Management*, vol. 6, pp. 157–95.

Inzerilli, G. & Laurent, A. (1983), 'Managerial views of organization structure in France and the USA', *International Studies of Management and Organization,* vol. 13, no. 1/2, pp. 97–118.

Jackson, S. & Schuler, R. (1995), 'Understanding human resource management in the context of organizations and their environments', *Annual Review of Psychology*, vol. 46, pp. 237–64.

Johnson, G. & Scholes, K. (1989), *Exploring Corporate Strategy: Text and Cases*, Prentice Hall, Hemel Hempstead.

Kaplan, R. S. & Norton, D. P. (1996a), *The Balanced Scorecard: Translating Strategy into Action*, Harvard Business School Press, Boston.

Kaplan, R. S. & Norton, D. P. (1996b), 'Using the balanced scoreboard as a strategic management system', *Harvard Business Review*, January–February, pp. 75–85.

Kaplan R. S. & Norton D. P. (2000), 'Having trouble with your strategy? Then map it', *Harvard Business Review*, September–October, pp. 167–76.

Klatt, L. A., Murdick, R. G. & Schuster, F. E. (1978), *Human Resources Management: A Behavioural Systems Approach*, R. D. Irwin, Homewood, Il.

Kochan, T. A. & Barocci, T. A. (1985), *Industrial Relations and Human Resource Management*, Little, Brown Inc., New York.

Kramar, R., McGraw, P. & Schuler, R. S. (1997), *Human Resource Management* in *Australia*, 3rd edn, Addison-Wesley, Melbourne.

Learned, E. P., Christiansen, C. R., Andrews, K. & Guth, W. D. (1969), *Business Policy, Text and Cases*, R. D. Irwin, Homewood, Il.

Lundy, O. & Cowling, A. (1996), *Strategic Human Resource Management*, Routledge, London.

McGregor, D. (1960), *The Human Side of Enterprise*, McGraw-Hill, New York.

Microsoft Indonesia. Mission and Vision, <http://www.microsoft.com/indonesia/back grounder>, accessed 26 September 2005.

Molineux, J. & Härtel, C. E. J. (2004), 'A model for the implementation of strategic human resource management', refereed paper presented at Australian and New Zealand Academy of Management Conference, Dunedin, New Zealand, December.

Osborn, A. (1957), *Applied Imagination*, Scribner, New York.

Pfeffer, J. & Veiga, F. (1999), 'Putting people first for organizational success', *Academy of Management Executive*, vol. 13, no. 2, pp. 37–48.

Porter, M. (1979), 'How competitive forces shape strategy', *Harvard Business Review*, March–April, pp. 137–45.

Rausch, E. (2003), 'Guidelines for management and leadership decision', *Management Decision*, vol. 41, no. 10, pp. 979–88.

Sahlman, W. (1997), 'How to write a great business plan', *Harvard Business Review*, vol. 75, no. 5, pp. 98–108.

Sutton, R. I. & Hargadon, A. (1996),

'Brainstorming groups in context: Effectiveness in a product design firm', *Administrative Science Quarterly*, vol. 41, pp. 685–718.

Taylor, F. W. (1911), *The Principles of Scientific Management*, Harper, New York.

Tichy, N. M. & Fombrun, C. J. (1982), 'Strategic human resource management', *Sloan Management Review*, vol. 23, no. 2, pp. 47–61.

Tsui, A. S. (1990), 'A multiple-constituency model of effectiveness: An empirical examination at the human resource subunit level', *Administrative Science Quarterly*, vol. 35, pp. 458–83.

Verheul, I. (2003), 'Commitment or control? Human resource management practices in female and male-led businesses', *EIM Business Policy and Research*, Scales Working Paper Series (N200306).

Walton, R. E. (1985), 'From control to commitment in the workplace', *Harvard Business Review*, vol. 63, pp. 77–84.

Wright, P. M. & Snell, S. A. (1991), 'Toward an integrative view of strategic human resource management', *Human Resource Management Review*, vol. 1, no. 3, pp. 203–25.

Wright, P. M., Dunford, B. B. & Snell, S. A. (2001), 'Human resources and the resource based view of the firm', *Journal of Management*, vol. 27, pp. 701–6.

Youndt, M. A. & Snell, S. A. (2004), 'Human resource configurations, intellectual capital, and organizational performance', *Journal of Managerial Issues*, vol. 16, no. 3, pp. 337–61.

2 Chapter

Strategies to engage and motivate employees

INTRODUCTION

In Chapter 1 the important fact that an organisation's greatest asset is its human resources was highlighted in detail. This was referred to as the resource-based view (RBV) of a firm, and the significant competitive advantages that employees provide an organisation were discussed. Chapter 2 focuses on the contemporary 'people' issues within the workplace and their implications for SHRM, such as motivating employees. This is achieved by learning about managing change and workplace relations, and how these relate to an employee's emotional and cognitive understanding within the workplace.

This chapter begins by introducing the different styles of strategic human resource management (SHRM), and assists in a clarification of the difference between 'hard' and 'soft' SHRM criteria. It also establishes the importance of management competencies required for successful managers in the twenty-first century (e.g. emotional intelligence, diversity management and the changing role of a manager to a mentor/coach), and how both the social and emotional environments impact on the way people think about, and act on, emotions in the workplace. Specifically, the changing role of a manager is important in the current business environment, which experiences many volatile changes, such as restructuring, mergers, acquisitions and bankruptcies. Therefore, managing during times of change is important because HR managers should know and understand the impact organisational change may have on a company and its human resources, and the way in which this can be managed effectively. By understanding the foundation of SHRM practices, it is possible to gain insight into the complex assessment of human needs required for effective SHRM.

Objectives

The primary objective of this chapter is to introduce the concept of employee behaviours and how these can be strategically aligned to the organisation's goals.

After reading this chapter you should be able to:

- identify how employees' focal and discretionary behaviours play a vital part in SHRM;
- know the key theories required to motivate people effectively;
- discuss the relevance of the psychological contract in today's workforce;
- explain SHRM in relation to business ethics;
- distinguish between the two different styles of strategic management;
- understand the importance of the combined use of soft and hard SHRM;
- identify how employees and employment have changed since the twentieth century;
- understand the role of resistance in change management;
- identify the value of emotional intelligence to SHRM.

Managing people

Undeniably, the most important and difficult job faced by managers is to manage people. Unlike other resources, which can be predicted quite reliably through forecasting, people are very difficult to predict. This is because every person has a unique set of values, attitudes, beliefs, experiences, expectations and ideas, therefore there is no 'one best way' to manage people. Indeed, most managers will attest that managing people is difficult because you never know how an employee will react to any given situation; what is humorous to one may be offensive to another. Managers must organise, lead and control people to achieve maximum productivity and employee wellbeing and they must do this knowing that no two people are alike. It is the role of management to direct employee behaviour towards organisational goals, and an understanding of why people work is essential to this task.

WORK VALUES: WHY DO PEOPLE WORK AT ALL?

What would you do if you had to fill in 24 hours a day, every day? Where would the money come from? What if no one worked? How would simple necessities such as furniture and electricity be produced? Surely work provides us with more than just money and something to do to fill in our time?

Work can be seen as a burden or as a central part of one's life, providing dignity and value to the self. The older (and wiser!) we get, the more we tend to value working and work opportunities; for many people, their job is a very important part of their life. In contrast, the younger generation tend to view work as simply a means to an end, and they may not take their job very seriously especially if they know it is not the job that they want for life. There is nothing wrong with either view, and it is imperative to remember that all human resources are important, no matter what their motivation for working is. Knowing what drives an individual to work, however, is essential for managers to know they are effective in motivating their staff.

protestant work ethic
'The degree to which
individuals place work at or
near the center of their lives'
(Mudrack, 1997, p. 217).

When work is viewed as central to an employee's life, it can form part of their personality. This has resulted in the development of the **protestant work ethic** (PWE) (see Table 2.1), which is a personality variable. The PWE represents 'the degree to which individuals place work at or near the center of their lives' (Mudrack, 1997, p. 217). In a review of literature, some scholars suggest that the work ethic personality characteristic developed from the idea that people have to work to gain a sense of purpose in life and that people can express their inner self through work (Marx, 1867/1977 and Weber, 1904/1905, cited in ter Bogt, Raaijmakers & van Wel, 2005). Thus, people with a strong work ethic view work as inherently good and a moral duty. Put simply, they believe that people *should* work.

TABLE 2.1 Protestant work ethic

1. Most people spend too much time in unprofitable amusements.
2. Our society would have fewer problems if people had less leisure time.
3. Money acquired easily (such as through gambling or speculation) is usually spent unwisely.
4. There are few satisfactions equal to the realization that one has done his or her best at a job.
5. The most difficult college courses usually turn out to be the most rewarding.
6. Most people who don't succeed in life are just plain lazy.
7. The self-made individual is likely more ethical than the person born to wealth.
8. I often feel that I would be more successful if I sacrificed certain pleasures.
9. People should not have more leisure time to spend in relaxation.
10. Anyone willing to work hard has a good chance of succeeding.
11. People who fail at a job have usually not tried hard enough.
12. Life would have very little meaning if we never had to suffer.
13. Hard work offers a greater likelihood of success.
14. The credit card is a ticket to careless spending.
15. Life would not be more meaningful if we had more leisure time.
16. The person who can approach an unpleasant task with enthusiasm is the person who gets ahead.
17. If people work hard enough, they are likely to make a good life for themselves.
18. I feel uneasy when there is little work for me to do.
19. A distaste for hard work usually reflects a weakness of character.

Source: Adapted from Mirels & Garrett (1971). © 1971 by the American Psychological Association. Adapted with permission.

Of course, not everybody feels this way. We have all had jobs we found boring or cumbersome; in essence, they were a burden. But, as previously mentioned, different people think, act and behave differently in organisations due to a variety of factors, and HR managers must be aware of and make allowances for this. Therefore, it is important to understand people's motivation for working.

So, why do people work?

The motivation for an individual to work may be derived from economic necessity, a sense of moral obligation or a need for identity construction. This motivation is acted out through behaviours labelled as focal or discretionary.

- **Focal behaviours** refer to those behaviours that the employee is bound to perform according to their job description and psychological contract.
- **Discretionary behaviours** refer to the behaviours that fall outside of the formal job requirements and are not recognised within the reward system, which can be performed at the discretion of the employee.

It is the role of management to understand the factors motivating its employees in order to ensure that the discretionary behaviours align with strategic organisational goals.

focal behaviours
Those behaviours that the employee is bound to perform according to their job description and psychological contract.

discretionary behaviours
The behaviours that fall outside of the formal job requirements and are not recognised within the reward system, which can be performed at the discretion of the employee.

Please read

Mudrack, P. E. (1997), 'Protestant work-ethic dimensions and work orientations', *Personality and Individual Differences*, vol. 23, no. 2, pp. 217–25.

Motivating employees

Motivating employees is an important task of management. But it is not as easy as it might seem. Managers can motivate to a certain extent, but employees must also motivate and take responsibility for themselves. The motivation of employees is seen as an integral part of work by both managers, who desire to encourage performance, and organisational researchers, who desire to develop predictive theories of management. Therefore, **work motivation** is defined as the stimulation of effort required to achieve, and maintain, organisational goals.

work motivation
The stimulation of effort required to achieve, and maintain, organisational goals.

Just as people can differ in their reasons to work, so they can also differ in their motivation to work. There are two reasons why people are motivated to work, and these tend to change over time as our personal and professional lives change. The first reason, intrinsic factors, refers to 'soft' factors such as a friendly and enjoyable work environment, challenging tasks and a genuine desire to help others (i.e. charity work). In contrast, extrinsic factors refer to 'hard' factors such as money, status, a big office and other more materialistic items. Generally, when we are younger and view work as an important social environment, we place more importance on intrinsic factors. At this stage of our lives, we tend not to be considering how this job might align with our professional development or career. However, as we mature our personal and professional lives change. For instance, we might purchase a car or home and get a mortgage. In this case, although it might still be important to consider intrinsic factors, financial needs force us to place priority on extrinsic factors, if nothing else than to survive. After all, although it would be nice to think that people work for other factors, the fact remains that most people work to earn money because they need money to survive. Many people, however, desire to maintain a balance between intrinsic and extrinsic factors and in their search for employment would prefer a job that can satisfy both.

Interestingly, the reasons why people work have changed over the years. Wiley (1997) conducted research in the USA on the most common motivator in organisations. In 1946, it was 'appreciation for task completion'. Approximately

40 years later, this had shifted to the second most important motivator, with an 'interesting job' the number one motivator in both the 1980 and 1986 surveys. In 1992, the most common motivator was 'good wages'. Hence, it is clear that as the external environment changes, and the business world becomes more turbulent and insecure, people shift their reason and motivation for working from intrinsic to extrinsic factors, which is congruent with the above discussion.

Please read

Ellemers, N., De Gilder, D. & Haslam, S. A. (2004), 'Motivating individuals and groups at work: A social identity perspective on leadership and group performance', *Academy of Management Review*, vol. 29, no. 3, pp. 459–78.

THEORIES OF MOTIVATION

Traditional views of motivation were based on scientific management principles and focused on financial reward for good work, and punishment or termination of employment for anything less. In direct contrast, the human relations movement arose, which emphasised that happy workers are more productive. These two views were captured in McGregor's (1960) Theory X and Theory Y, where employees are depicted as either holding a dislike of work and responsibility and need to be supervised closely (Theory X), or seeking responsibility and satisfaction in their work tasks (Theory Y). Flowing from these opposing paradigms has been a myriad of theories on work motivation. These can be classified as either content or process theories.

CONTENT THEORIES

content theories
Suggest that human beings have certain wants and needs that direct their behaviour.

Content theories suggest that human beings have certain wants and needs that direct their behaviour and these, in turn, are influenced by the environment. The prevalent content theories are discussed below.

Maslow's (1954) hierarchy of needs theory Abraham Maslow's theory is undoubtedly one of the most popular theories among laypersons of motivation within the social sciences field (Berl, Williamson & Powell, 1984). He proposed that human beings have five levels of needs and the desire to satisfy these needs drives behaviour (see Figure 2.1). The most basic of these needs is *physiological* (i.e. air, water, food and sleep). Once this need is satisfied, people strive to achieve higher-order needs in order of hierarchy: *safety and security* (i.e. security, stability and protection), *love and belongingness* (i.e. friendship, acceptance and affection) and *self-esteem* (i.e. achievement, competence, confidence, status, recognition and appreciation). Once these needs are achieved, people reach a desire for *self-actualisation* (i.e. purpose, personal growth and attainment of one's full potential).

In essence, Maslow's theory is based on three assumptions. First, that people must satisfy lower-order needs before moving on to the next need in the hierarchy. Second, that behaviour (or motivation) is only stimulated by unsatisfied needs. Third, that humans' needs range from the very basic to the more complex (i.e. physiological to self-actualisation) (Berl, Williamson & Powell, 1984).

2.1   FIGURE
Maslow's hierarchy of
needs theory and HRM

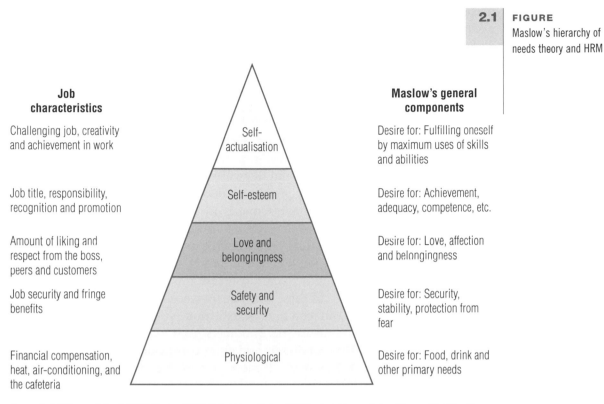

Job characteristics		Maslow's general components
Challenging job, creativity and achievement in work	**Self-actualisation**	Desire for: Fulfilling oneself by maximum uses of skills and abilities
Job title, responsibility, recognition and promotion	**Self-esteem**	Desire for: Achievement, adequacy, competence, etc.
Amount of liking and respect from the boss, peers and customers	**Love and belongingness**	Desire for: Love, affection and belongingness
Job security and fringe benefits	**Safety and security**	Desire for: Security, stability, protection from fear
Financial compensation, heat, air-conditioning, and the cafeteria	**Physiological**	Desire for: Food, drink and other primary needs

Source: Berl, Williamson & Powell (1984); Maslow (1954). Material from Maslow © 1954, adapted by permission of Pearson Education, Inc., Upper Saddle River, NJ.

The hierarchy of needs means that HR managers must understand that a satisfied need does not motivate an individual. So, this theory would suggest that the saying 'a happy worker is a productive worker' is incorrect, at least in terms of happiness meaning all needs are met. Maslow's theory also indicates that needs at higher levels are not activated until lower-level needs are met. Therefore, providing employees with opportunities for personal growth will not motivate if the employees seek recognition and status. Further, providing opportunities to acquire status will do little to motivate an employee who has fulfilled their need for status.

Alderfer's (1969) existence, relatedness, growth (ERG) theory This theory extends and refines Maslow's hierarchy of needs theory by collapsing the hierarchy into three basic needs. Alderfer argued that there are three elements underlying human needs. These are existence (or physiological and security), relatedness (or esteem and love) and growth (or self-actualisation). The main difference between Alderfer's ERG and Maslow's hierarchy of needs is that Alderfer's ERG allows for multiple needs to exist at any one time, whereas Maslow's theory argues that the lower-level need must be met before a higher-level need can be evoked.

In relation to HRM, and in addition to Maslow's theory, practitioners can use Alderfer's theory to recognise and understand that employees may have several needs at the one time (e.g. security because their job is in jeopardy and esteem because they might not believe they have the skills required to secure another job). Therefore, they must learn how to satisfy and manage those needs. More importantly, an effective and efficient HR manager will guide the employee to recognise this themselves so that they are aware of their own needs and can contribute towards meeting them.

Herzberg's (1968) two factor theory   Frederick Herzberg proposed that work factors can be grouped into two categories: hygiene and motivation. His theory suggests that in the work environment there are **hygiene factors**, which minimise discomfort and insecurity, thereby preventing dissatisfaction, such as an adequate salary and a pleasant work environment. In addition to these factors are 'motivators' or characteristics of the work environment that promote employee growth and development, such as responsibility and the work itself (Hertzberg, 1968). Herzberg argued that while hygiene factors do not motivate employees, their absence increases dissatisfaction. In contrast, **motivation factors** encourage effort; however, an absence of these will not increase dissatisfaction as will the hygiene factors, rather, it will lead to no satisfaction.

hygiene factors
Characteristics of the work environment which minimise discomfort and insecurity.

motivation factors
Characteristics of the work environment which promote employee growth and development.

According to Herzberg's theory, HR managers need to develop hygiene factors such as pay, status, working conditions and other contextual factors to attempt to eliminate dissatisfaction. However, HR managers are not motivating employees when they eliminate dissatisfaction. For HR managers to motivate employees they need to develop tasks that are meaningful, interesting and challenging, depending on the needs, wants and interests of the employee(s).

McClelland's (1955) acquired needs theory   David McClelland identified three needs in the workplace: achievement, affiliation and power. His theory suggests that the environment influences the strength of each of these needs. For instance, employees who strive for achievement will prefer work characterised by responsibility, challenging goals and feedback on performance. People who desire power, on the other hand, prefer work with high levels of control and with opportunities for recognition and attention. Finally, individuals who seek affiliation or relationships with other people will prefer work which provides opportunities for companionship and social approval.

According to McClelland's theory, HR managers must understand that the motivation of employees depends on the strength of each these needs. Therefore, the degree of responsibility and teamwork a person has in their job should be based on the individual employee's needs. For instance, teamwork will be a motivating factor for individuals seeking affiliation, whereas the ability to complete a task independently may motivate individuals seeking achievement.

process theories
Highlight thought patterns that underlie the decision of whether or not to engage in certain behaviours.

PROCESS THEORIES
While content theories depict human wants and needs, **process theories** highlight the thought patterns that underlie the decision of whether or not to engage in certain behaviours. The prevalent process theories are as follows.

Vroom's (1964) expectancy theory   Victor Vroom depicted work motivation as a function of desire and the expectation that it is achievable. This theory suggests that employees will be motivated to exert effort when they believe that it will result in a desired level of performance (*expectancy*) and this performance is linked to rewards (*instrumentality*) not punishment. Finally, the initial effort is, of course, dependent on the employee valuing the expected rewards (*valence*). This leaves us with a formula of motivation:

$$\text{Motivation} = \text{Expectancy} \times \text{Instrumentality} \times \text{Valence}$$

To maximise the attainment of performance levels, HR managers need to select workers who are competent and able to perform the tasks allocated to them. It is also important that performance goals and the psychological contract are clearly defined to ensure expected rewards follow achieved performance levels. Furthermore, according to expectancy theory, an important element of HRM is to identify individual needs to determine rewards that are of value to the employee. If rewards are seen as desirable then motivation levels will be high, and vice versa.

Adams' (1963) equity theory   J. Stacy Adam theorised that people are motivated by a desire to reduce the tension associated with the perception of inequity in the workplace. He argued that employees compare themselves to similar others to gauge how much effort to exert and what compensation to expect. Perceived inequity between one's own and similar other's situations will evoke emotional responses in the employee and may motivate them to reduce the tension experienced. For example, employees who feel underpaid may experience anger, whereas employees who feel overpaid may experience guilt, and each will modify work inputs to rectify the feelings.

Since perceptions of effort and rewards determine motivational outcomes, the HR manager must attempt to eliminate perceptions of inequity. They can do this by demonstrating that everyone in the organisation is treated equally. For example, as diversity management becomes an issue for managers in the twenty-first century, the HR manager can develop diversity awareness (through posters, policies and leading by example). This will decrease perceptions of inequity due to discrimination, thus increasing motivation. Increased motivation leads to increased productivity as employees perceive the exchange for their effort at work is fair, therefore more care is taken with work (i.e. fewer mistakes, less wastage, fewer accidents), which benefits all stakeholders.

Locke's (1968) goal setting theory   In contrast to Vroom's expectancy theory, Edwin Locke suggested that it is not the rewards or outcomes of performance that motivate, rather, motivation stems from the goal itself. The idea behind this theory is that setting goals enables the employee's attention and commitment to be focused on the particular task (Locke & Latham, 2002). In order to motivate employees, goals need to be specific not general; people need to reduce ambiguity about when the goal is achieved. Goals also need to be difficult but not impossible; people will not be motivated to exert effort for tasks that are exceptionally easy or impossible to achieve. Finally, convincing people that goal attainment is important evokes commitment to the goal and, hence, motivates behaviour (Locke & Latham, 2002).

According to this theory, the most important method for motivating employees is for HRM to provide clear and desirable performance targets. Thus, the provision of specific goals will motivate employees by providing direction to people in their work as well as clarifying performance expectations. Goal setting is particularly important for flexible work arrangements and participatory practices that require behavioural self-management.

Reinforcement theory Often referred to as organisational behaviour modification, B. F. Skinner (1953) developed reinforcement theory with his operant conditioning concept. The concept of conditioning suggests that over time people learn the relationship between their actions and their consequences and attempt to increase those behaviours with positive outcomes and minimise those behaviours with negative outcomes. **Conditioning**, then, refers to a permanent change in behaviour. Extending Pavlov's (1927) theory of classical conditioning, Skinner theorised that reinforcement of desired behaviour is an essential part of the motivation to change behaviour. According to operant conditioning, behaviour that is followed by a reinforcing consequence is more likely to be engaged in at a later date than behaviour followed by a punishing consequence. There are four basic processes in reinforcement theory:

conditioning
A permanent change in behaviour.

1. *Positive reinforcement:* behaviour resulting in pleasant consequences will evoke the motivation to repeat the behaviour.
2. *Negative reinforcement:* behaviour resulting in the withdrawal of an unpleasant consequence will evoke motivation to repeat the behaviour.
3. *Punishment:* behaviour resulting in an unpleasant consequence will evoke the motivation to avoid that behaviour.
4. *Extinction:* behaviour resulting in the withdrawal of a pleasant consequence will evoke the motivation to avoid that behaviour.

Although Skinner (1961) suggests that reinforcement is not necessary every time the behaviour occurs for it to be repeated, he also suggests that conditioned behaviours are not necessarily permanent. If reinforcement of a particular behaviour stops, it is possible that the behaviour will also cease (refer to Chapter 9 for a further discussion on operant conditioning).

Based on reinforcement theory, it is important for HR managers to clarify desired work behaviours and link these with valued rewards. Likewise, when HR managers identify undesirable work behaviours it is important to inform the employee what is being done wrong and what is required to do it right and punishment should also match the behaviour.

CRITIQUE

It is important to remember that some of these theories have been subjected to scrutiny in recent years. For example, despite Maslow's theory being known as 'the most popular' and 'general theory of motivation' (Berl, Williamson & Powell, 1984, p. 33), it has also been critiqued on three levels. First, and perhaps most importantly, Berl, Williamson & Powell (1984) questioned whether people really need to satisfy each lower-order need before they move on to the next. In their study conducted within the sales industry, the results elicited were in direct contrast to Maslow's theory. These scholars also suggest that little or no empirical support for Maslow's theory has been found and therefore they question the relevance of using Maslow's hierarchy of needs as a tool for motivating salespeople. However, they also acknowledge that salespeople are unique in that it has always been difficult to motivate salespeople because of the nature of their work, and that a unique approach is necessary to determine individual motivational levels.

A second and rather substantial critique is proposed by Trigg (2004). He identified several problems with Maslow's theory and developed an alternative theory to address these downfalls. His main critique of the theory is that 'individual needs are so innate, so that questions of social interaction and culture are seriously downgraded' (Trigg, 2004, p. 393). The problems he identified were:

1. Maslow's theory fails to take into account the link between the individual self, culture and learning;
2. Within economic applications, a needs-based approach (i.e. physiological needs) is replaced by social needs at the top of the hierarchy (i.e. self-esteem) (see Trigg, 2004 for a further discussion).
3. Scholars have critiqued Maslow's theory regarding its relevance across cultures. In a study conducted comparing Australia and Papua New Guinea (PNG), Onedo Ojuka's (1991) analysis indicated that 'cultural differences and differing stages of economic development affect the degree of importance attached to the five needs categories' proposed by Maslow (Onedo Ojuka, 1991, p. 121).

The applicability of Hertzberg's theory has also been questioned. Steers (1983, cited in Ramlall, 2004) stated that the most obvious implication of this theory is that motivation can only be increased through motivation factors (such as job enrichment) and not through hygiene factors (which maintain neutrality). Therefore, HR managers need to focus on the former factors by redesigning tasks which increase challenge, responsibility, personal growth and recognition.

Further, Adams' equity theory poses a further challenge for HRM. Everybody's perception of 'fair' differs because, as humans, people are unique and have different expectations and experiences. Yet, it is usually the HR department that determines the reward. If it doesn't align with what employees expect, the challenge is then for HRM to 'develop new reward systems that are perceived to be fair and equitable and distributing the reward in accordance with employee beliefs about their own value to the organization' (Ramlall, 2004, p. 55). Table 2.2 presents a summary of motivational theories and their relation to HRM practices, specifically employee retention.

In contrast, there has been support for Alderfer's ERG theory. Various scholars have cited it as 'the most current, valid, and researchable of the motivation content theories' (Ivancevich, Szilagyi & Wallace, 1977, cited in Berl, Williamson & Powell, 1984, p. 38), with another empirical study fully supporting the applicability and justification of this theory (Buhler, 1988) and yet another stating that

TABLE **2.2**   **Motivational theories, desired outcomes and relevant HR activities**

Desired outcome	Relevant motivational theories	Relevant HR activities
Increase worker effort	• Adams' Equity Theory • Alderfer's Existence, Relatedness, Growth (ERG) Theory • Herzberg's Two Factor Theory • Job Characteristics Theory • Locke's Goal Setting Theory • Maslow's Hierarchy of Needs Theory • McClelland's Acquired Needs Theory	• Career advancement and planning • Compensation and rewards • Selection • Performance management
Improve task performance	• Adams' Equity Theory • Herzberg's Two Factor Theory • Job Characteristics Theory • Locke's Goal Setting Theory • McLelland's Acquired Needs Theory • Reinforcement Theory • Vroom's Expectancy Theory	• Training and development of worker and supervisor • Compensation, benefits • Rewards • Selection • Performance management
Raise job satisfaction	• Adams' Equity Theory • Alderfer's Existence, Relatedness, Growth (ERG) Theory • Herzberg's Two Factor Theory • Job Characteristics Theory • Maslow's Hierarchy of Needs Theory • Vroom's Expectancy Theory	• Develop diversity-open and just culture • Provide each employee opportunity to develop and contribute • Make clear to all employees their contribution to the organisation and society
Increase organisational commitment	• Adams' Equity Theory • McClelland's Acquired Needs Theory • Reinforcement Theory • Vroom's Expectancy Theory	• Socialisation/induction • Career planning and opportunity • Training and development • Diversity openness • Creating organisational vision that includes adding value to society, and linking with each person's role
Increase organisational citizenship behaviours	• Alderfer's Existence, Relatedness, Growth (ERG) Theory • Maslow's Hierarchy of Needs Theory • McClelland's Acquired Needs Theory	• Diversity openness • Recognition • Development of high trust and collaborative culture • Recruitment and selection based on character not just skills
Reduce counterproductive work behaviours	• Adams' Equity Theory • Reinforcement Theory • Vroom's Expectancy Theory	• Training and development of workers and supervisors with focus on character and skills • Selection based on character not just skills • Performance management based on character not just skills • Rewards and punishment • Development of ethical culture
Reduce absenteeism	• Adams' Equity Theory • Alderfer's Existence, Relatedness, Growth (ERG) Theory • Herzberg's Two Factor Theory • Job Characteristics Theory • Maslow's Hierarchy of Needs Theory • Reinforcement Theory • Vroom's Expectancy Theory	• Exit interviews • Selection • Rewards and punishment • Development of collaborative and respectful culture

Desired outcome	Relevant motivational theories	Relevant HR activities
Reduce stress and burnout	• Adams' Equity Theory • Alderfer's Existence, Relatedness, Growth (ERG) Theory • Herzberg's Two Factor Theory • Job Characteristics Theory • Maslow's Hierarchy of Needs Theory • McClelland's Acquired Needs Theory • Vroom's Expectancy Theory	• Employee assistance programs • Job design • Training • Diversity openness • Flexible work arrangements • Selection • Consideration of whole person and work–life balance in HR policies and practices
Reduce turnover	• Adams' Equity Theory • Alderfer's Existence, Relatedness, Growth (ERG) Theory • Herzberg's Two Factor Theory • Job Characteristics Theory • Maslow's Hierarchy of Needs Theory • McClelland's Acquired Needs Theory	• Monetary and non-monetary rewards and compensation • Recruitment and selection • Exit interviews • Consider people's needs in HR policies and practices
Increase meaning at work	• Adams' Equity Theory • Alderfer's Existence, Relatedness, Growth (ERG) Theory • Herzberg's Two Factor Theory • Job Characteristics Theory • Locke's Goal Setting Theory • Maslow's Hierarchy of Needs Theory • McClelland's Acquired Needs Theory • Vroom's Expectancy Theory	• Training and development • Diversity management • Selection • Career planning • Develop culture that promotes quality relationships, authentic honest communication, collaboration and mutual respect • Make clear the contribution to society of each person's work
Increase accountability	• Adams' Equity Theory • Herzberg's Two Factor Theory • Locke's Goal Setting Theory • Reinforcement Theory	• Performance management • Rewards and punishment • Develop ethical culture

it represents a new trend which supersedes the theories of Maslow, McGregor and Hertzberg (Guest, 1976).

LIMITATIONS

The many variations of motivation theories arise due to the limitations of each theory. For instance, the majority of motivation theories assume people are motivated by biological and emotional needs. They assume people will do what they can to satisfy their needs, to reduce tension and discomfort or to gain rewards and other pleasant consequences.

This perspective overlooks the crucial role of value and beliefs in the choices people make with respect to their behaviour. That is, people do override their feelings of threat or discomfort or tolerate physical deprivation when important beliefs and values are brought into play. The motivational theories also tend to assume mistakes are undesirable. Yet, the increased emphasis on human capital and knowledge management arising from environmental competition is placing less emphasis on the achievement of work tasks and more on continuous learning. Thus, mistakes are desirable if they lead to new knowledge and process improvements.

Further, identity plays a role in the work behaviour an individual engages in. Unless you are born into wealth, a large portion of your life is spent at work. It makes sense then that the work we do influences our identity. Status, power and financial security are derived from the work we do (Collinson, 2003). Yet, the work we do and the behaviours we adopt are also influenced by a desire to protect and secure our identity. Collinson (2003; see also Noon & Blyton, 2002) suggests that people engage in 'survival strategies' or discretionary behaviour such as fiddling, joking or choreographing their reactions to maintain a particular image, in an attempt to maintain a particular identity. For instance, when employees struggle to maintain their identity in the face of a career bottleneck or a violation of the psychological contract, they may distance themselves physically through absenteeism or psychologically through splitting the self into a 'work self' and the 'real me outside of work'. These survival strategies enable the individual to engage in discretionary behaviours to get back some control and to construct meaning for work (see Axtell & Parker, 2003). Bunce and West (1994) found that behaviours such as creating a form to organise time more effectively helped nurses manage the stress of their work better.

Survival strategies are particularly evident for workers who only partially identify with employer's objectives and who desire to preserve as much life, energy, income and time as they can (Noon & Blyton, 2002). Therefore, the HR manager needs to motivate individuals to direct the energy behind these discretionary behaviours towards the goals of the organisation.

PSYCHOLOGICAL CONTRACTS AND MOTIVATION

Today's dynamic changing environment has radically changed the nature of the employer and employee relationships, namely, the psychological contract. **Psychological contracts** are defined as intangible, informal contracts that the employee perceives about their employment relationship. They include factors such as workplace conditions, expectations and obligations of both the employee and employer. Such contracts are important for HR managers to be aware of because they help predict and understand (and correlate with) organisational citizenship behaviour. They are also very useful in determining the person–organisation fit, which relates to the HRM functions of recruitment and selection, and which is also important to organisational success (Silverthorne, 2004).

Psychological contracts are broadly classified into three contracts, namely, transactional, relational and ideological contracts.

1. The *transactional* contract refers to an 'effort bargain', or the reciprocal exchange of effort for reward (Maguire, 2002). This is the type of contract that most employees have; put simply, it is what people receive for working (such as the exchange of skills for salary). This contract predominantly represents cognitively driven contracts, which lean toward the 'hard' HRM tenet (see under 'HRM styles and motivation' later in this chapter for a definition of hard HRM).

psychological contracts
Intangible, informal contracts that the employee perceives about their employment relationship.

2. The *relational* contract refers to the exchange of socioemotional currency. For example, the employee's commitment, loyalty and trust are exchanged for a sense of security, career development and the opportunity to belong (Thompson & Bunderson, 2003). This contract predominantly represents affectively driven contracts, which lean toward the 'soft' HRM tenet (see under 'HRM styles and motivation' later in this chapter for a definition of soft HRM).

3. The *ideology infused* contract refers to the exchange of effort in the belief that such efforts will be invested in the pursuit of a valued cause or principle. For example, the employee's voluntary helping or advocacy outside of work hours are exchanged to support the organisation's work towards a particular cause or ideal (Thompson & Bunderson, 2003).

Today, the nature of the psychological contract has changed dramatically due to fast-paced technological change, increased competition for scarce resources and the need for organisations to be more flexible and adaptable to their environment. Table 2.3 highlights the difference between old and new psychological contracts in industrialised society. While dynamic changes reciprocally occur in the external environment (e.g. competition, technology) and internal environment (e.g. restructuring, downsizing, outsourcing, re-engineering), employees' psychological contracts tend to face constant unpredictability. The unpredictable nature of psychological contracts has resulted in employees' negative attitudes, emotions and behaviours at work such as stress, anxiety and counterproductive work behaviours (Jordan, Ashkanasy & Härtel, 2003). This emerging trend implies that organisations are placing less strategic value on the relational contract (Maguire, 2002).

In today's workforce, instead of employees pursuing 'employment security' through a long-lasting parent–child dependent relationship with their employers,

TABLE 2.3   **Distinction between 'old' and 'new' characteristics of psychological contracts**

Old contract	New contract
• Organisation is 'parent' and employee is 'child'.	• Organisation and employee enter into 'adult' contracts focused on mutually beneficial work.
• Employees' identity and worth are defined by the organisation.	• Employees' identity and worth are defined by the employee.
• Those who stay are good and loyal; others are bad and disloyal.	• The regular flow of people in and out is healthy and should be celebrated.
• Employees who do what they are told will work until retirement.	• Long-term employment is unlikely; prepare for multiple relationships.
• The primary route for growth is through promotion.	• The primary route for growth is a sense of personal accomplishment.

Source: Kissler (1994) as cited in Maguire (2002).

they are pursuing 'employability security' by having an adult–adult partnership with their employers. They are adopting more self-dependent work and a self-directed learning approach to developing their own career path. A further management dilemma arises in the relational contract because, while organisations commit less to help develop employees' careers, they need employees' maximum commitment and loyalty to ensure their survival and success. The paradoxical nature of the contemporary relational contract has led employees to perceive management as violating their psychological contracts which, in turn, negatively affects their discretionary behaviours at work (Thite, 2001).

For the HR manager, organisations ought to consider employees' discretionary behaviours in their strategic management process by taking a relational approach, not in the old paternalistic sense, but based on continuous learning, open communication and nurturing relationships that provide employees with the opportunities and resources to manage their own careers (Atkinson, 2002). In this regard, SHRM should proactively represent employees' affective (e.g. negative emotions) and cognitive voice (e.g. perceived violation of psychological contracts) in strategic formulation and implementation.

Please read

Maguire, H. (2002), 'Psychological contracts: Are they still relevant?', *Career Development International*, vol. 7, no. 3, pp. 67–180.

HRM ETHICS

Another aspect affecting psychological contracts, motivation and HRM is ethics. Today, inquiries are increasing in relation to the ethics of organisations coping with the dynamic changing environment, while simultaneously managing employees' organisational citizenship behaviours, increasing their competitive advantage and return on investment (ROI) in the marketplace. As business ethics are concerned, in part, with the people relationship and how people are treated in the workplace, HRM takes a vital role in ethical management and its link with psychological contracts (Ackers, 2001).

HRM ethics can be evaluated through the following three normative ethical management theories: deontological; utilitarian; and stakeholder theories.

1. *Deontological* theory advocates that business is ethical when treating people with respect is the goal rather than letting business consequences (ROI and customer satisfaction) shape activities.
2. *Utilitarian* theory advocates that business is ethical when people are the means to maximise positive business consequences for the majority of stakeholders (e.g. shareholders).
3. *Stakeholder* theory advocates that business is ethical when all stakeholders mutually benefit (e.g. employees, shareholders, customers, suppliers, unions and the local community).

Among these theories, the deontological ethical value is embedded in the soft HRM perspective while the utilitarian ethical value is embedded in the hard HRM approach. The stakeholder ethical value is embedded in the combined tenet of soft and hard HRM as it takes each stakeholder's view into account in the strategic management process.

From the deontological point of view, management is unethical when employees are used only for business benefits. From the utilitarian point of view, however, employees' psychological, physical and monetary sufferings can be justified in order to achieve business benefits (Legge, 1998). It would be expected, based on the previous discussion of motivation theories, that a deontological and stakeholder ethical perspective would lead to a more motivated workforce than would a utilitarian perspective.

With the increasing strategic management focus on coping with the competitive volatile contemporary business environment, organisations tend to justify actions that produce negative emotional experiences in workers as a means to ensure organisational survival, reasoning that such mistreatment is necessary to protect stakeholders' jobs (i.e. employees, suppliers and business partners) and satisfy their customers and shareholders. The increasing management mentality of organisational survival, however, raises ethical questions such as 'Is it ethical to make employees work around the clock?' and 'Is it ethical to make them redundant for organisational survival or customer satisfaction?'. Shouldn't the value of humanity or quality of work life outweigh the significance of business success? This is a question that all HR managers need to consider, not just for the impact that it might have on the organisation, but on the employee and society as a whole.

Please read

Legge, K. (1998), 'The morality of HR', in *Strategic Human Resource Management: A Reader*, eds C. Mabey, G. Salaman & J. Storey, Sage/Open University Press, London.

ORGANISATIONAL JUSTICE

Another aspect affecting the motivation of employees is known as organisational justice. This issue is especially relevant during periods of organisational change, but can also affect the organisation and employees at any time. The theoretical foundation of organisational justice is that people evaluate situations that have important consequences for them and respond positively if they perceive the situation to be fair and negatively if the situation is perceived as unfair (Greenberg, 1990). As Paterson and Härtel (2002) explain, the early work on organisational justice draws on Adams' equity theory (1963) to propose that people compare the ratio of their inputs and outcomes with those of relevant others to determine the fairness of their outcomes. Therefore, HR managers need to understand the link between organisational justice and motivation, particularly with respect to how employees perceive job expectations and working conditions (through the use of psychological contracts) and the congruence of this with remuneration. This is especially important during recruitment and selection (i.e. when contracts are negotiated) and again during performance appraisals. In fact, research suggests that if employees feel they have been treated fairly, they demonstrate an increased acceptance of performance appraisals (Taylor *et al.*,

1995), personnel selection decisions (Ployhart & Ryan, 1998), labour unions (Skarlicki & Folger, 1997), and self-managing work teams (Kirkman *et al.*, 1996). Therefore, psychological contracts, ethics and organisational justice theory are imperative for the HR manager of the future.

HRM STYLES AND MOTIVATION

As discussed in Chapter 1, an organisation has a variety of stakeholders. It makes sense, then, that these stakeholders have multiple objectives and that very few of these tend to align with the organisation's objectives. Since there is no automatic congruence between individual and organisational needs, the role of management is to motivate employees to align their behaviours with organisational objectives.

However, aligning goals to meet organisational and individual needs is not a simple task. Stakeholders have different needs and wants of the organisation, each believing that their issue is more pertinent than another's. For example, customers and competitors have different needs, and each want something different from the company for the good of their own group. As a result, conflict is inevitable. **Conflict** occurs when people with different goals and perspectives interact. The role of management, therefore, is either to attempt to control the different perspectives and behaviours in order to eliminate conflict, or to manage this conflict so that it has constructive rather than destructive consequences (Shelton & Darling, 2004). In general terms, there are two styles of strategic management:

1. The **industrial organisation approach** is based on an economic ideal and is focused on issues such as resource allocation and profit maximisation. This approach assumes employees are rational and self-interested.

2. The **sociological approach** is based on a human ideal and is focused on issues such as profit sub-optimality. This approach assumes employees' rationality is 'bounded' by the limitations of human thoughts, thus employees can also be irrational and emotional in decision making. It also assumes that employees may compromise profits for mutual benefits.

The approach to HRM varies, then, based on the desired outcome and the philosophical position adopted on human behaviour. For instance, if the HR manager desires control and views HRM as a means to gain productivity improvements and employee efficiency, then they are more likely to use the industrial organisation approach in their HRM practices. In contrast, an HR manager who desires a healthy and satisfied workforce with high levels of wellbeing is more likely to adopt the sociological approach in their HRM practices.

HARD AND SOFT MODEL OF HRM PARADOX

HRM, as defined in Chapter 1, refers to the management of people at work. However, there is not just one simple method for managing people. Take the issue of motivation, for example. This chapter has discussed several theories of motivation, some of which support and build on other theories, and others which are unique. HRM is no exception. There are multiple theories relating to this issue, and in this chapter two of the most dominant models are addressed: hard and soft HRM.

---

conflict
Occurs when people with different goals and perspectives interact.

industrial organisation approach
Based on an economic ideal and is focused on issues such as resource allocation and profit maximisation.

sociological approach
Based on a human ideal and is focused on issues such as satisfying behaviour, and profit sub-optimality.

The hard and soft variants of HRM reflect the opposing perspective of the 'nature of people' versus 'managerial control strategies'. Hard HRM focuses on achieving high performance through the rational strategic approach, which is based on the belief that workers need to be controlled to achieve the bottom line (e.g. Theory X; see McGregor, 1960). **Hard HRM**, therefore, views human resources as costs and emphasises quantitative, calculative control-based strategies for managing people (Kamoche, 1991). This type of HRM is generally depicted in the media, for example through redundancies and the closing down of branch offices.

hard HRM
The management of people via calculative, control-based activities.

Soft HRM, on the other hand, focuses on gaining employees' commitment through quality of work life, based on the belief that employees need to be cared for, motivated, and self-directed through flexibility and adaptability rather than being controlled by management (e.g. Theory Y; see McGregor, 1960) (refer to Figure 2.2). This tenet of HRM views human resources as 'people' and thus strategies to manage employees emphasise communication, motivation and leadership (Kamoche, 1991). See Table 2.4 for a comparison of hard and soft HRM.

soft HRM
The management of people via activities designed to gain commitment and motivation.

These two views of HRM are important for an HR manager to understand. In terms of managing employees, this chapter advocates that soft HRM strategies are preferred. This is because it is a more humane way of managing people; it considers how decisions might impact on employees and determines less calculative ways to manage the organisation more efficiently and effectively and it leads to long-term benefits such as positive employer–employee resilience. In general terms, hard HRM is adopted when organisations either need to increase efficiency (i.e. due to increased pressure from competition) or are seeking to save costs. In today's turbulent business environment, the latter reason is the most common. However, it is a short-term solution to a long-term problem. Therefore, companies who adopt hard HRM find themselves resorting to it time and time again.

So which view of HRM is best? And how do these styles impact on employee motivation? According to the resource-based view (RBV) of SHRM, an organisation

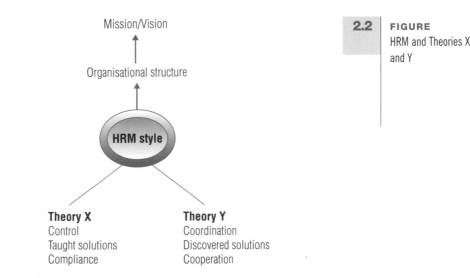

2.2 | **FIGURE**
HRM and Theories X and Y

Source: Adapted from Whiteley (1995).

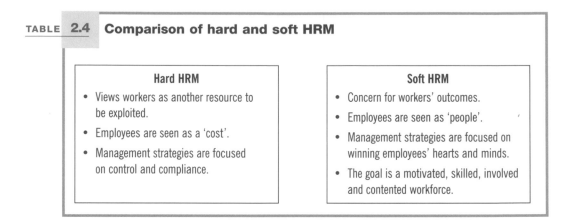

TABLE 2.4 Comparison of hard and soft HRM

Hard HRM	Soft HRM
• Views workers as another resource to be exploited.	• Concern for workers' outcomes.
• Employees are seen as a 'cost'.	• Employees are seen as 'people'.
• Management strategies are focused on control and compliance.	• Management strategies are focused on winning employees' hearts and minds.
	• The goal is a motivated, skilled, involved and contented workforce.

can gain a core competency in its people and improve its competitiveness in the marketplace. This view suggests the combined use of soft HRM (i.e. motivating employees' discretionary behaviours) and hard HRM (i.e. strategic control approach) (Guest, 1987) (see Figure 2.3). Further, empirical research indicates that no organisation adopts either a pure soft or hard HRM approach (Truss *et al.*, 1997). In fact, organisations tend to adopt a combination of the two. In a seminal article by Beer and Nohria (2000), these scholars indicate that during periods of organisational change hard HRM (referred to as Theory E) should be used initially to cut costs and increase efficiency, then soft HRM (referred to as Theory O) should be adopted to focus on the human side of the change. This

FIGURE 2.3
Integration of hard HRM and soft HRM into the strategic management process

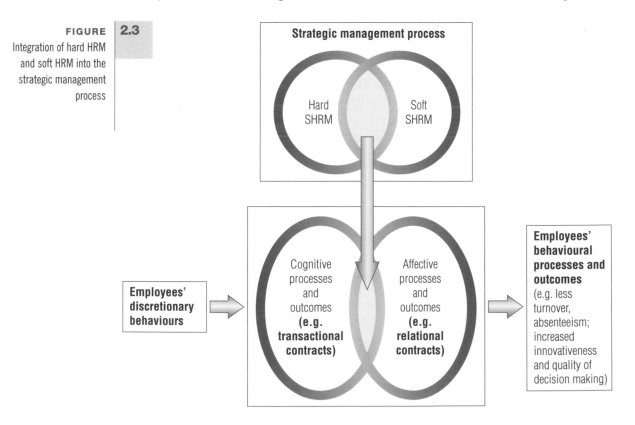

might include gaining employee trust after the restructuring, and motivating them to see the change as an opportunity rather than as a threat. Jack Welch from General Electric employed this combination during major change at the company and reported excellent results, not only regarding the financial position of the company but also the culture of the organisation (Beer & Nohria, 2000).

Further research indicates that, at the rhetorical level, many organisations embrace the soft HRM tenet of caring for workers' development and commitment; however, in practice, the hard HRM tenet of achieving the bottom line prevails. Kamoche (1991) suggests that organisations may adopt hard HRM for one particular group of employees and soft HRM for another, for example hard HRM for direct or periphery employees and soft HRM for core employees or managers (see also Legge, 1989). This paradox evokes ethical HRM issues in today's organisations. Is it possible for organisations to achieve an ethical standard for *all* stakeholders (particularly for employees)? Recent research warns organisations of the inhumane consequences of strategic downsizing (e.g. poor health, psychiatric morbidity) (Kusum, 2003). Although employees feel the brunt of this initially (through hard HRM), strategically it impacts on the organisation. After all, without its employees an organisation has nothing. This is why it is so important for HR managers to understand the *strategic* (or long-term) aspect of HRM.

Please read

Truss, C., Gratton, L., Hailey, V., McGovern, P. & Stiles, P. (1997), 'Soft and hard models of human resource management', *Journal of Management Studies*, vol. 34, no. 1, pp. 53–73.

INDIVIDUALISM VERSUS COLLECTIVISM

In addition to the hard and soft models of HRM, and their link with motivation, HR managers also need to consider the issue of cultural diversity when managing their workforce. This is especially pertinent for managers in the twenty-first century. **Workforce diversity** refers to any visible or invisible difference between organisational members, such as race, age, gender, sexuality, religion, educational level, work experience, disability, language, perceptions, attitudes, interests, lifestyle, expectations, values, needs and desires. Workplaces today are characterised by diversity in race, ethnicity, gender, lifestyle and values among an array of other things. Consequently, understanding how to manage diverse employees in the workplace is a critical need of modern management, especially given the rapid disappearance of cultural borders and the increasing popularity of teamwork (Richard, 2000).

Seminal work on diversity has been conducted in Australia by Härtel and Fujimoto (2004; see also Fujimoto, Härtel & Panipucci, 2005), who have researched group dynamics of individualists and collectivists, and the impact HRM has on the relationship between these two disparate cultural orientations. Although individualists differ from collectivists in their team orientation (i.e. **individualists** focus primarily on satisfying individual goals, whereas **collectivists** seek to benefit the group or community first), the HR manager

workforce diversity
Any visible or underlying difference between organisational members.

individualists
Focus primarily on satisfying individual goals.

collectivists
Seek to benefit the group or community first.

can motivate both by using a combination of individualist and collectivist HRM polices and practices.

In his study of cultural dimensions Hofstede (1980) found that, typically, individualism tended to align with Western cultures, such as Australia, the USA and New Zealand. However, collectivism tended to align with Eastern cultures, such as China, Japan and Thailand. For the HR manager, then, this has several implications and benefits. The most obvious implication that organisations need to be aware of is that, in today's workforce, managers manage people from a range of differing cultures, and their needs, wants and expectations will differ. This will also affect their reason for working, how they are motivated, how they view colleagues (hard versus soft HRM), their work ethic and their psychological contract. For example, if there is a promotion advertised in the HRM department, individualists will compete against others for this (i.e. through behaviours such as refusing to disclose information regarding the promotion or the interview to colleagues), whereas collectivists will help each other and openly share ideas and information. Of course, there is a significant benefit for HR mangers too; if both groups are managed appropriately, work performance for each group will improve as the manager openly sets an example of workplace diversity through encouraging the integration between people from different cultural orientations. Therefore, managing cultural diversity not only improves the emotional experience of employees' work life (which is reflected in such things as hope, confidence, satisfaction and reduced levels of stress, anxiety and tensions in the workplace), but it improves the operational aspect of the organisation also (Fujimoto, Härtel & Panipucci, 2005).

Motivating during times of change

It is possible to see from the theory presented so far in this chapter that motivating employees can be a complex and engaging task. Some employees are self-motivated and thus it is very easy to keep them motivated. Others require more guidance and control. Of course, as with all things in life, nothing is constant. Employees' motivation levels may change at any time. This is why it is very important that HR managers continually monitor the workplace to determine how employees are changing and align their motivational tools to ensure they develop a congruent fit with both the employee and the strategic focus of the organisation. It is only then that SHRM can truly be achieved.

Motivating employees can be challenging enough at the best of times, but what about at the worst? During periods of organisational change the organisation is often in disarray. Jobs may be lost, departments disseminated and people may panic about how the change will affect them. Therefore it is imperative to learn about how organisational change affects the ability to engage and motivate employees.

WHAT IS ORGANISATIONAL CHANGE?

Organisational change (or organisation development) is a term often heard today. But what does it mean? The literature is replete with discussions and definitions of organisational change, and although it appears on the surface to be a simple topic it can be a very complex issue affecting organisations today and well into the future. **Organisational change** refers to any alteration (whether planned or unplanned) which causes a shift in the status quo, and which affects the structure and resources of an organisation. For instance, many companies made the shift from using typewriters to computers in the 1980s. This is an example of planned organisational change as companies would have anticipated the need for this and then implemented goals to achieve this within certain timeframes. Other more contemporary examples are the restructuring, merging or acquisition of companies, or the implementation of a new software program.

organisational change
Any alteration (whether planned or unplanned) which causes a shift in the status quo, and which affects the structure and resources of an organisation.

TYPES OF ORGANISATIONAL CHANGE

There are several types of organisational change. First, the two most common types are planned and unplanned change. **Planned change** is any deliberate, structured execution of a shift in the status quo. Most large-scale changes these days are planned, simply because the HR manager (in conjunction with other senior managers) needs to determine the resources required to achieve the change, whether those resources are human, financial or technical. Furthermore, because 70 per cent of change efforts fail (Beer & Nohria, 2000), it is desirable that such changes be well thought out and planned in order to increase the likelihood of success. An example of a well-planned change would be the implementation of a new software program, where employees would recognise the need for the change (i.e. the old software is outdated) and welcome the new program. Once the new program is installed and training has been received, management would then ensure the new program is used from then on, and that employees do not revert back to the old system. This type of change is also discontinuous.

planned change
Any deliberate, structured execution of a shift in the status quo.

In contrast, unplanned change is as simple as its name suggests. It is where the organisation has not anticipated the change. For example, before the first terrorist attack this century (in the USA in 2001), most Western communities would not have anticipated that such attacks would occur and therefore may not have had adequate resources or procedures for dealing with such disasters. However, since then most organisations have implemented policies and procedures for dealing with this type of situation, thus turning it from an unplanned to a planned change. For example, in 2003, after an unanticipated emergency, Monash University developed a booklet containing emergency evacuation procedures and phone numbers, and made it compulsory for every office to contain this booklet. The impact of the policy and procedure changes on the role of the HRM department would be communicating the change to employees and overseeing its implementation.

The other types of organisational change are commonly referred to as incremental and radical change. **Incremental change** is a series of small changes. These tend to occur in organisations on a daily basis; sometimes people will not even realise they are occurring. For example, they might be minor changes in the organisation's culture (such as the shift from an informal to a formal dress code as the organisation expands and secures more clients). Or they might be as simple as a series of new recruitment forms to be used in the selection process.

incremental change
A series of small changes.

FIGURE
Incremental versus
radical change
2.4

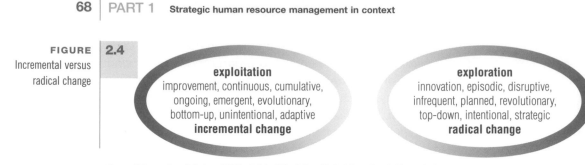

Source: Petersen, Boer & Gertsen (2004). © John Wiley & Sons Limited. Reproduced with permission.

radical change
Large-scale and drastic
change. It is usually
organisation-wide, innovative
and planned.

Radical change, in contrast, is large scale and drastic (see Figure 2.4). It is usually organisation-wide, innovative and planned. As with planned change, it requires that employees depart from the status quo and embrace the new change, which is why effective leadership is imperative in this situation. There are five stages of radical change (see Figure 2.5). *Planning* involves obtaining information, generating ideas and formulating how to achieve the goal; *enabling* entails explaining the plan and obtaining employee 'buy in' through involvement, empowerment and support; *launching* involves the implementation of phases to realise the change, and then achieving results and assessing success; *catalysing* is the phase of continual motivation through inspiring and energising to ensure employees do not revert to 'the old way'; and *maintaining* involves ongoing evaluation and control through continual guidance and support (Reardon, Reardon & Rowe, 1998).

RESTRUCTURING AND HRM ISSUES

As mentioned earlier in this chapter, restructuring is one of the most common examples of organisational change in the twenty-first century. Compared

FIGURE
Five phases of radical
change
2.5

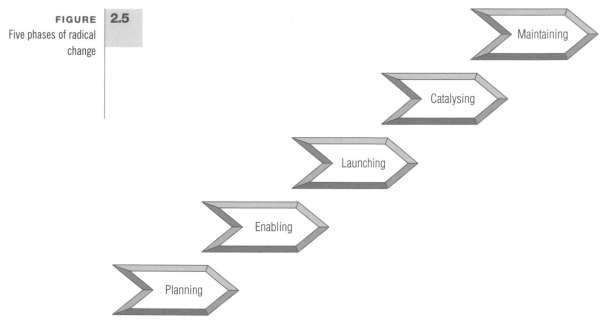

Source: Adapted from Reardon, Reardon & Rowe (1998).

to 50 years ago, when the business environment was stable and predictable, we now live in a world of turbulent change and unpredictable behaviour. Fierce competition and intense globalisation have forced companies to adopt innovative and efficient methods for remaining competitively and financially viable. This is why restructuring is such a popular and effective (at least in the short term) method for business survival. **Restructuring** is the reorganisation of a company to increase efficiencies and adapt to, and enter, changing markets. In recent years, companies such as Telstra, Coles Myer and the ANZ Bank have restructured to maintain their competitive edge in the Australian market.

restructuring
The reorganisation of a company to increase efficiencies and adapt to, and enter, changing markets.

Of course, when any change occurs within an organisation this impacts on the role of the HRM department. Just as some people are self-motivated and others are not, some people embrace change while others fear it. Human behaviour is unpredictable; however, one thing is certain: humans tend to avoid change unless they believe they can change successfully or that it is necessary to change to avoid a worse fate. So when radical change, like restructuring, occurs, how do employees react and what are the implications for HR managers?

RESISTANCE TO CHANGE

Have you ever gone through a major change in your life? For most people, the move from secondary school to university is an exciting, but scary, change. However, once you adapt to the new surroundings and become familiar with the university, the change does not seem that daunting after all. The same concept applies to other changes, including restructuring.

Resistance to change is any barrier that impedes a change from occurring. Lewin (1951) referred to these barriers as restraining forces. In organisational contexts, these can be lack of resources (including employee skills and abilities), an opposing organisational culture or simply the unwillingness to change. In direct contrast to these restraining forces are driving forces, such as the need to survive, a new CEO or the willingness to change. Rather than increase the driving forces as a method of change, Lewin proposed decreasing the restraining forces and, thus increasing the success of permanent change through reduced resistance (Elsass & Veiga, 1994). So how is resistance decreased? Any management scholar will advise that communication is the key. Employees need to recognise the *need* for the change so that they understand and accept it. Once it is accepted, restraining forces decrease and the driving forces move the organisation from its original state to its desired one (see Figure 1.8 in Chapter 1).

resistance to change
Any barrier that impedes a change from occurring.

Unfortunately, managing resistance to change is not as easy as it appears in theory. As mentioned earlier, some people embrace change while others fear it. And with that fear comes resistance. Employees may display their fear in different ways, for example through negative emotions (i.e. avoidance, negative talk), poor or dysfunctional coping (i.e. lack of confidence, ill health, poor concentration) and counterproductive behaviour (i.e. sabotage). It is important to understand that negative emotions do not necessarily translate to resistance to change. Emotional responses (whether positive or negative) are normal manifestations of coping with the way the change is being managed, rather than irrational responses on the part of employees.

HRM STRATEGIES FOR CHANGE

For HR managers, there are several strategies for managing organisational change. First and foremost, managers have to realise that change, and the adaptation to the change, is a dynamic and unfolding process. It takes time. To assist, HR managers are encouraged to provide support and training that enable employees to develop appropriate problem-focused and emotion-focused strategies for coping with the changing workplace. Second, HR managers must ensure that communication channels are open and honest. This means that the CEO, or decision maker, needs to share information that will assist in the acceptance of the change. It also requires that these change agents maintain sensitivity and understanding. Third, a culture of emotional awareness should be cultivated. Emotions are not solely products of individuals. Rather, they are the product of individual emotional characteristics interacting with environmental characteristics. An HR manager therefore needs to be aware of their own, and others', emotion management skills. These are the displayed ability to recognise and manage one's own and other peoples' emotions in such a way that it leads to healthy outcomes for the individuals involved and the organisation (Härtel, Gough & Härtel, 2006). It is also important to remember that when sufficient support and coping strategies are available, employees facing change can find satisfaction, self-esteem and even joy in the new change. Figure 2.6 provides a checklist for designing effective change interventions.

FIGURE 2.6

Checklist for designing effective organisational change interventions

DO	DO NOT
✓ Foster a culture of emotional awareness	✗ Blame resistance on the individual
✓ Maintain open and quality communication	✗ Equate negative emotions with negative outcomes
✓ Provide opportunities for stakeholder input into planning	✗ Overlook the role of the change intervention or implementation in employee response to change
✓ Safeguard a history of positive change efforts	✗ View emotions as irrational
✓ Ensure that decision makers display interpersonal sensitivity	✗ Assume that people will fear change
✓ Monitor emotional reactions in change stakeholder groups	✗ Leave people to fend with the change themselves
✓ Identify perceived causes and consequences behind the emotions	✗ Withhold information about the effect of the change on personal goals
✓ Match intervention to the results of the emotional reaction analysis	✗ Ignore the emotional states of stakeholders of change
✓ Acknowledge the emotional requirements of jobs	✗ Enter the counsellor domain
✓ Put in place support mechanisms for negative emotional events or hassles (e.g. supervisor support, EAP, training and development, breaks)	✗ Ignore the fact that emotional events occur
✓ Develop an ethical framework for what is and is not appropriate regarding emotions management and educate all in it	✗ Use activities that are personally intrusive

It is obvious, then, that emotions play a major role in organisational change. Again, some people display emotions freely and openly, while others suppress them. In the past decade emotional intelligence has been recognised as a critical skill for managing people's emotion at work (Jordan, Ashkanasy & Härtel, 2003). **Emotional intelligence** is the ability to perceive and experience emotions which then guide emotional responses and promote intellectual growth. This can be applied at the intrapersonal (e.g. own emotion), the interpersonal (e.g. co-workers or clients' emotion) and the organisational (e.g. emotional climate at work) level (Härtel, Zerbe & Ashkanasy, 2005). In the past (and perhaps still today), emotionality was regarded as the antithesis of rationality, that is, it was thought that emotion (negative emotion in particular, such as anxiety, fear and anger) prevented organisations from achieving their business strategy, objectives, mission and vision in a rational and objective manner (Ashforth & Humphrey, 1995). However, leading academics in this emerging managing field concur that there are a number of performance areas where emotional intelligence is helpful. Furthermore, empirical studies conclude that emotional intelligence plays a significant role in life satisfaction, self-esteem, and individual success and wellbeing (Härtel, Zerbe & Ashkanasy, 2005). Coupled with the increasing popularity of teamwork, emotional intelligence at the intrapersonal, inter-personal and organisational levels can contribute to building trust, cooperative identity and efficacy that leads to overall high organisational performance (Druskat & Wolff, 2001). For example, Härtel, Gough & Härtel (2006) showed that teams whose members possessed high levels of emotion management skills also had a more positive emotional climate which contributed to both employee and customer satisfaction.

emotional intelligence
The ability to perceive and experience emotions which then guide emotional responses and promote intellectual growth.

Contemporary SHRM Application Tool

As the SHRM Application Tool depicts, instead of constraining emotions, organisations should treat them as integral to the process of achieving the bottom line (e.g. high productivity, high customer satisfaction). Strategic management that fosters positive emotions (i.e. quality of heart) and use of talents (i.e. quality of head) therefore enhances group cohesiveness and positive organisational climate (Pizer & Härtel, 2005) (see Figure 2.7).

FIGURE 2.7
The SHRM Application Tool: opportunity – motivation

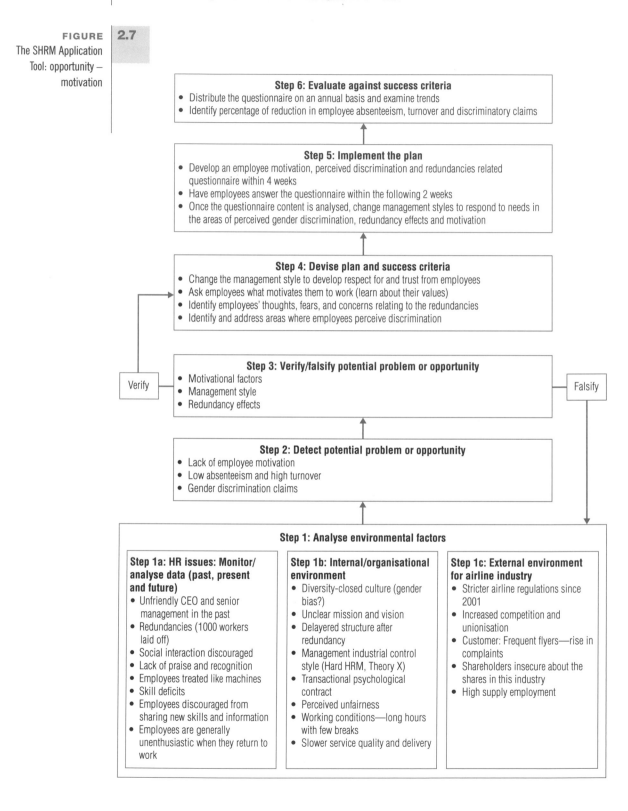

Step 6: Evaluate against success criteria
- Distribute the questionnaire on an annual basis and examine trends
- Identify percentage of reduction in employee absenteeism, turnover and discriminatory claims

Step 5: Implement the plan
- Develop an employee motivation, perceived discrimination and redundancies related questionnaire within 4 weeks
- Have employees answer the questionnaire within the following 2 weeks
- Once the questionnaire content is analysed, change management styles to respond to needs in the areas of perceived gender discrimination, redundancy effects and motivation

Step 4: Devise plan and success criteria
- Change the management style to develop respect for and trust from employees
- Ask employees what motivates them to work (learn about their values)
- Identify employees' thoughts, fears, and concerns relating to the redundancies
- Identify and address areas where employees perceive discrimination

Step 3: Verify/falsify potential problem or opportunity
- Motivational factors
- Management style
- Redundancy effects

Verify

Falsify

Step 2: Detect potential problem or opportunity
- Lack of employee motivation
- Low absenteeism and high turnover
- Gender discrimination claims

Step 1: Analyse environmental factors

Step 1a: HR issues: Monitor/ analyse data (past, present and future)
- Unfriendly CEO and senior management in the past
- Redundancies (1000 workers laid off)
- Social interaction discouraged
- Lack of praise and recognition
- Employees treated like machines
- Skill deficits
- Employees discouraged from sharing new skills and information
- Employees are generally unenthusiastic when they return to work

Step 1b: Internal/organisational environment
- Diversity-closed culture (gender bias?)
- Unclear mission and vision
- Delayered structure after redundancy
- Management industrial control style (Hard HRM, Theory X)
- Transactional psychological contract
- Perceived unfairness
- Working conditions—long hours with few breaks
- Slower service quality and delivery

Step 1c: External environment for airline industry
- Stricter airline regulations since 2001
- Increased competition and unionisation
- Customer: Frequent flyers—rise in complaints
- Shareholders insecure about the shares in this industry
- High supply employment

The acquisition manages an integration   A view from the field

The events preceding the acquisition of a company are unsettling for employees and managers of that organisation. Speculation in the business press is usually rife; rumours abound on the corporate grapevine and general uncertainty makes this period uncomfortable for all concerned. Individual employees understandably become focused on fundamental issues of safety and security; these issues become primary concerns and motivators. Consider the further impact on employees of an integration of another company some weeks after the acquisition has been finalised. No, not a corporate nightmare, but a corporate reality for National Foods Limited during 2005.

San Miguel acquired National Foods Limited, the Australian milk and dairy food company with an annual turnover of A$1.3 billion, in July of 2005. The San Miguel Corporation is Southeast Asia's largest publicly listed food, beverage and packaging company. It was founded in 1890 as a brewery and now has over 100 facilities in the Philippines, Southeast Asia, China and Australia.

The acquisition followed many months of uncertainty for the 2000 employees at National Foods as San Miguel and Fonterra, the New Zealand-based multinational dairy company (turnover of NZ$12.3 billion), considered the acquisition of National Foods. Speculation was rife as to which company would purchase it and when. David Clark, Head of Human Resources and Communication and part of the executive reporting to the CEO at National Foods, concedes that this was a torturous time for employees. The uncertainty created by speculation in the marketplace during a possible acquisition causes employees to feel vulnerable. Inevitably this results in employees considering their options, in an effort to relieve the uncertainty and to address those fundamental issues of safety and security. This may mean that they will move on to other organisations and that valuable executives are more likely to be susceptible to approaches by the circling head hunters. The retention of talent can become a major problem. Mr Clark acknowledged 'we were proactive in talking to our key personnel and putting in place retention strategies to ensure we did not lose talent during this period of uncertainty'.

Clear and honest communication to employees was critical during this time. This is a powerful strategy which assists in containing the impact of the uncertainty, which given the circumstances was the most that could be achieved. This situation could be one faced by many organisations facing merger or acquisition discussions or waiting for the outcome of a major contract renegotiation. No one in National Foods knew what would happen and in some ways the uncertainty was a fact of life during that period. Mr Clark explained, 'This time was particularly difficult as we often didn't have anything to tell employees. The Chief Executive Officer (CEO) and all the Executive team made a conscious effort to get out and about, visiting sites and talking to people. It was essential that we kept communication lines open even if it were to say there was no news'.

In an environment where employees are concerned about fundamental issues such as their ongoing employment which impact on their safety and security, their ability to pay mortgages, school fees and other living expenses, thoughts and energies are likely to be focused on resolving this issue rather than driving business performance. The executive team at National Foods needed to try and contain the fear and uncertainty and help employees understand the link between continued performance and future viability. Mr Clark adds, 'another vital part of the message the CEO and Executive needed to make absolutely clear was the critical nature of sustained business performance. It was in fact key to the future of the company and to the viability of jobs at National Foods.'

When there was information of significance to be communicated, National Foods maximised the power of the communication by using a number of vehicles including, all-site phone hook ups with the CEO, employee briefings, news items on the corporate intranet and email bulletins. Mr Clark believes this regular and honest flow of information established the credibility of the executive team. 'Our people believed if there was something of significance happening we would tell them.'

It appears that some of these strategies paid dividends as over the period running up to the acquisition by

San Miguel, National Foods experienced low levels of employee turnover. Further, operating performance remained at a high level and as a result the share price of National Foods remained steady.

Soon after the acquisition San Miguel made a decision to integrate with National Foods the operations of another Australian group, Berri, a fruit juice company of 1000 employees with an annual turnover of A$600 million. As San Miguel did not have specific operations in Australia it chose to run the integration out of National Foods.

The executive team of National Foods was faced with a significant challenge. A plan for the integration was developed, and the agenda was ambitious with an aim to finalise the integration within 100 days. The view was very much that speed was of the essence. This was yet another unsettling experience for employees at National Foods, but at least this time National Foods was controlling the change. Constant change is a fact of organisational life; however, the extent and protracted nature of the change for National Foods' employees was likely to exacerbate further concerns around safety and security.

The situation presented very differently to Berri employees who were being integrated into the San Miguel National Foods operation. The integration meant wide-ranging changes, potential redundancy or ongoing employment with a different entity, a changed role, office closures, site relocations and a number of new conditions to deal with. The aim was again to contain the disruption for Berri and National Foods' employees alike and move with speed to a resolution which allowed people to feel more certain and shift their focus and energies to achieving business goals.

David Clark has had extensive experience in the area of acquisitions and divestments in former roles with Southcorp and ACI and based on that experience believes success is partially due to the speed of execution. 'The longer employees are left uncertain and speculating about the future, the greater the loss of engagement with the organisation and the greater the impact on productivity of the company. It is critical to get the change moving and new structures in place. This allows people to get on with their lives and the business to move forward.'

After considerable analysis of the two companies' operations with particular focus on the duplication of head office and sales functions, a new structure was identified and some 600 positions were opened up for selection, with approximately 150 potential redundancies resulting. The HR and Communication Group Executive team led by Mr Clark again needed to draw on the communication strategies which were so effective during the period running up to the acquisition by San Miguel and now extend these into the Berri organisation.

The first major communication to employees in both organisations was a plan for the integration process. It provided a broad picture of the plan for the next 90 days, details of the structure and organisation charts, the recruitment and selection process and the roll out and the ongoing communication plans.

During the implementation of the integration a minimum of one major communication bulletin was sent out to employees each week. This provided information on the progress of the integration. The CEO and executive team also continued their pre-acquisition period practice of all-site phone hook ups and regular site visits, extending that to Berri sites as well.

A decision was taken to advertise all available positions starting from the most senior and cascading through the organisation. Again speed was of the essence with the executive team giving an undertaking that the process would be completed in 90 days. This presented quite a challenge to David Clark and his HR and Communication team. He engaged the support of an international search firm to assist with the executive roles and an international recruitment firm for all other positions. At the same time two international firms were engaged to provide outplacement services to those who elected to take a redundancy or found themselves without a position.

The process for recruitment and selection was communicated to employees of both organisations. Positions would be advertised on Monday on the corporate intranet(s) and applications made online. Positions would close on Friday and the selection process be completed midway through the following week with announcements regarding appointments made at the end of that week. Monday of the next week the process would be repeated for the next level within the organisation.

National Foods had analysed closely the HR policies of Berri, particularly in the area of remuneration and benefits. Existing Berri employees were concerned that they may be disadvantaged by the integration process and the requirement to adopt National Foods standards. Mr Clark commented that the policies were not far apart; however, where there was a difference National Foods chose to adopt the better of the two policies. This decision was communicated very early on in the process to all employees and was well received.

The emphasis on speed of execution was extended to those employees who found themselves unsuccessful in obtaining a role in the new structure. Mr Clark explains 'we extended them the same courtesy, making the calculation of their redundancy quotations and introduction to an outplacement provider a priority. We acknowledged their right to make informed judgements about their future and be supported in implementing their plans. This approach is in line with National Foods' values of respect for people and operating with integrity'.

Reflecting on the process of integration, Mr Clark comments, 'not too much went wrong, there was very little noise about the whole process. We lost 3 or 4 people we would have preferred to keep but given the scale of the change that is a good outcome. The challenge in the longer term is to keep people engaged'.

National Foods planned to conduct a survey of its employees in May 2006. The Hewitt Associates Employee Engagement survey (see www.hewitt.com) will be used to gather information on employees' attitudes towards working at National Foods. The Hewitt survey aims to uncover 'what drives people, what engages them in their work and what makes them want to stay and provides organisations with information to assist them in taking action to improve their employees' ability to contribute to sustainable success and long term growth'. National Foods last conducted this survey in 2004. Mr Clark expects to gain greater insight into employees' perceptions of the impact of the acquisition and integration and the effectiveness of efforts by the executive team to manage those changes.

To a certain degree the job is done in National Foods; however, new challenges emerge as San Miguel is a much larger entity with its own agenda and strategic direction. In 2006 Mr Clark sees the task of sustaining the change as a challenge. 'We have sales employees training in new product areas underway; many have never sold juice or milk and dairy foods. Our new teams are established on paper, however, there are team development efforts in the pipeline; as well we have identified leadership development as a priority across the organisation and will commence programs in this area early in 2006.'

Discussion questions

1. The integration of Berri was a commercial deal with a focus on maximising the value of the investment in an acquisition. What role if any should HR play in this undertaking?

2. All change brings threats and opportunities. What are the threats and opportunities that mergers, acquisitions and integrations present to employees? How might such threats and opportunities affect the way employees feel, the way they think about the organisation and their career, and the actions they take?

3. Judge the effectiveness of the National Foods' executive's management of the period of acquisition and the integration process from the perspective of an employee. Then consider how effective Mr Clark and his HR and Communication team were in implementing the executive's decisions. What were the activities that were effective? Were there other activities that should have been undertaken? Explain your answer.

4. Not all organisations include the head of human resources on the executive (i.e. the group directly reporting and working with the CEO). In the case of National Foods, however, Mr Clark, as head of the HR and Communications group, was. Would it have made any difference to the effectiveness of the integration if Mr Clark did not have a seat on the executive? Explain your answer.

Source: Adapted from <http://www.sanmiguel.com>, accessed 28 December 2005; <http://www.natfoods.com.au>, accessed 27 December 2005; <http://was4.hewitt.com/hewitt/services/talent/subtalent/ee_engagement.htm>, accessed 30 December 2005.

A manager's challenge

A rare case of successful organisational change through employee empowerment

Organisational restructuring was highly popularised in the 1990s as many companies strived to stay competitive through various reorganisations of businesses or business units. The success of such change initiatives, however, was not always evident, as the majority of reorganisation efforts fell short of their desired objectives. In such circumstances, the highly successful restructuring and re-engineering project carried out at Mobil Oil Australia (MOA) in the 1990s provides invaluable insight to a rare case of successful organisational change.

In the 1990s, MOA conducted an enterprise-wide review of the company to increase profitability and change in its organisational culture. Consequently, a radical business unit organisation structure was designed, populated and implemented. In the immediate year after the change, the company's net income was six times higher than the previous year, while the return on capital employed increased from 2 per cent to 7 per cent. The project's success was clearly visible from a re-energised company.

The project, which was named Phoenix, consisted of six distinct phases: (1) initiation; 2) diagnosis; (3) process re-engineering; (4) organisation design; (5) implementation; and (6) post-implementation review. The organisational change was spearheaded by a senior Australian Mobil executive who had in-depth understanding of the business. A distinct feature in the change process at Mobil was its encouragement of employee participation throughout all six phases of change. In fact, the managing director of the company sent a memo asking all employees 'to share your ideas and contribute . . . to this crucial review'.

The change process was initiated and implemented based on the notion that ongoing strategic change requires the empowerment of individuals. Such a view was operationalised through various means. For instance, employee team members were nominated from departments and locations in Australia and at different levels in the company with the rationale of giving 'voice' to the employees in the change process and a stake in its outcome. Teams were further empowered by a decision by the managing director to implement 90 per cent of the recommendations suggested by these teams. Employees were given the pride of owning up to the results of the change initiative which, in turn, generated much energy, enthusiasm and motivation towards the successful outcome of the change effort.

In the workplace restructuring scheme at Mobil Adelaide Refinery, such movements of empowering employees for the long term were achieved through the granting of in-plant testing to be carried out by the local technicians, and minor maintenance work to be carried out by refinery technicians. Essentially, the level of supervision was reduced and the role of 'supervisor' was transformed from a controller to a facilitator. Furthermore a competence-based training program was initiated and technical staff were made responsible for condition monitoring of their own units. The concept of self-managed work teams was also introduced as a part of the process, as it was in the change agenda of the company since the restructuring commenced.

A post-implementation review of the change at MOA revealed that teams of employees who were earlier involved in the project became advocates in convincing others of the need for change and the opportunities that Phoenix created. Although stressful, the reorganisation unleashed energy and action at Mobil, galvanising the employees in the new structure, thus making the case of organisational change at Mobil Oil Australia truly exemplary.

Source: Adapted from Dawson, P. (1995), 'Redefining human resource management: Work restructuring and employee relation at Mobil Adelaide Refinery', *International Journal of Manpower*, vol. 16, no. 5/6, pp. 19–66; Martin, I. & Cheung, Y. (2002), 'Change management at Mobil Oil Australia', *Business Process Management Journal*, vol. 8, no. 5, pp. 447–61.

Summary

This chapter highlighted the importance of engaging and motivating employees in the SHRM process. Organisations are composed of people who display cognitive and affective-driven (e.g. emotions) behaviour at work. Thus, in order to ensure organisational long-term success, SHRM should proactively represent the employees' voice in its strategy formulation and implementation. With the ever increasing pressure to deliver profit organisations face the ethical dilemma of pursuing business survival at the cost of humanity. The material covered in this chapter provides a basis for ensuring the wellbeing of workers while at the same time enabling organisational survival.

This chapter began with a discussion on why people work, highlighting the development of the protestant work ethic personality variable. The reasons why people work can generally be categorised as either focal or discretionary behaviour and it is the role of management to understand motivating factors behind employee involvement in the workplace and align individual and organisational goals. There are several theories of motivation that an HR manager can use to understand and encourage people to work. These include content and process theories. Content theories suggest that people are motivated differently because they have different needs, wants and desires and their behaviour is therefore influenced by their environment. Conversely, process theories highlight the thought patterns that predict employee behaviour. Despite the benefit of these theories, it is imperative that HR managers are aware of the possible downfalls and, as such, a critique of these theories was also discussed.

Psychological contracts form an important part of employee motivation and of the employment relationship. These are informal contracts perceived by employees which provide direction and guidance regarding the employment relationship. There are three broad categories of psychological contracts, namely, transactional, relational and ideological. It is also important for HR managers to be aware of the impact that the turbulent business environment has on an employee's perception of their psychological contract, and the role of ethics and organisational justice.

Motivation is closely linked with HRM through the adoption of either hard or soft HRM. Hard HRM, which views human resources as costs, is usually depicted through redundancies and branch closures. On the other hand, soft HRM, a very different style of HRM, focuses on gaining employee commitment through flexibility and adaptability rather than authoritarian management control. The latter HRM style is advocated in this chapter and indeed throughout the book as the most effective way of viewing and managing a company's human resources.

The chapter concluded with a discussion on motivating during times of organisational change. This is when motivation becomes a critical factor as restructuring and mergers (two examples of planned organisational change) occur frequently today and can impact significantly on employees' motivation levels. Resistance to change, which includes any barrier to implementing and adopting change, presents serious consequences for management and must be managed appropriately to ensure that the change adopted is beneficial for all. Motivation therefore plays an important role in the management of human resources.

Key terms

collectivists	incremental change	psychological contracts
conditioning	individualists	radical change
conflict	industrial organisation	resistance to change
content theories	approach	restructuring
discretionary behaviours	motivation factors	sociological approach
emotional intelligence	organisational change	soft HRM
focal behaviours	planned change	work motivation
hard HRM	process theories	workplace diversity
hygiene factors	protestant work ethic	

Review questions

2.1 Why is the combined use of hard HRM and soft HRM valid for today's workforce? Discuss.

2.2 What is the psychological contract? How has the environment changed the characteristics of today's psychological contract? Use examples in your answer.

2.3 Describe the difference between planned and unplanned change, and incremental and radical change. How can HR managers manage resistance to change?

2.4 Why does SHRM take a vital role in business ethics? In your answer, provide case studies of organisations that have used redundancy as a cost-cutting method.

2.5 What does the term emotional intelligence mean? How can it lead to overall high organisational performance?

Exercises

2.1 Visit the website of one organisation (or think of your employing organisation) and identify their soft and hard aspect of HRM. Which aspect is more evident in the organisation? How would you improve the current HRM system if you were an HR manager of the organisation?

2.2 Investigate exemplary companies (i.e. Telstra, IBM, Westpac and Ford) and identify their alternative downsizing strategies. Are they effective?

2.3 Select one organisation you or your associates have worked in. Was there a psychological contract? What was the nature of this contract? What environmental factors affected the nature of contract? Discuss.

2.4 Screen today's newspaper to see how emotions are integrated into the strategic management process of various organisations. Describe the emotions and how they were managed. How would you manage those emotions if you were the HR manager of these organisations?

References

Ackers, P. (2001), 'Employment ethics', in *Contemporary Human Resource Management*, eds T. Redman & A. Wilkinson, Prentice Hall, London.

Adams, J. S. (1963), 'Toward an understanding of inequity', *Journal of Abnormal and Social Psychology*, vol. 67, pp. 422–36.

Alderfer, C. P. (1969), 'An empirical test of a new theory of human needs', *Organizational Behavior and Human Performance*, vol. 8, pp. 142–75.

Ashforth, B. E. & Humphrey, R. H. (1995), 'Emotion in the workplace: A reappraisal', *Human Relations*, vol. 48, no. 2, pp. 97–125.

Atkinson, C. (2002), 'Career management and the changing psychological contract', *Career Development International*, vol. 7, no. 1, pp. 14–23.

Axtell, C. A. & Parker, S. K. (2003), 'Promoting role breadth self-efficacy through involvement, work redesign and training', *Human Relations*, vol. 56, no. 1, pp. 113–31.

Beer, M. & Nohria, N. (2000), 'Cracking the code of change', *Harvard Business Review*, vol. 78, no. 3, pp. 133–41.

Berl, R. L., Williamson, N. C. & Powell, T. (1984), 'Industrial salesforce motivation: A critique and test of Maslow's hierarchy of need', *Journal of Personal Selling and Sales Management*, vol. 4, no. 1, pp. 33–9.

Buhler, P. (1988), 'Motivation: What is behind the motivation of employees', *SuperVision*, vol. 50, no. 6, pp. 18–20.

Bunce, D. & West, M. (1994), 'Changing work environments: Innovative coping responses to occupational stress', *Work and Stress*, vol. 8, no. 4, pp. 319–31.

Collinson, D. L. (2003), 'Identities and insecurities: Selves at work', *Organization*, vol. 10, no. 3, pp. 527–47.

Druskat, V. U. & Wolff, S. B. (2001), 'Building the emotional intelligence of groups', *Harvard Business Review*, vol. 79, no. 3, pp. 81–90.

Elsass, P. M. & Veiga, J. F. (1994), 'Acculturation in acquired organizations: A force-field perspective', *Human Relations*, vol. 47, pp. 431–53.

Fujimoto, Y., Härtel, C. E. J. & Panipucci, D. (2005), 'Emotional experience of individualist-collectivist workgroups: Findings from a study of 14 multinationals located in Australia', in *Emotions in Organizational Behavior*, eds C. E. J. Härtel, W. J. Zerbe & N. M. Ashkanasy, Lawrence Erlbaum Associates, Mahwah.

Greenberg, J. (1990), 'Organizational justice: Yesterday, today and tomorrow', *Journal of Management*, vol. 16, pp. 399–432.

Guest, D. E. (1976), 'Motivation after Maslow', *Personnel Management*, vol. 8, no. 3, pp. 29–32.

Guest, D. E. (1987), 'Human resource management and industrial relations', *Journal of Management Studies*, vol. 24, no. 5, pp. 503–21.

Härtel, C. E. J. & Fujimoto, Y. (2004), 'Culturally specific prejudices: Interpersonal prejudices of individualists and intergroup prejudices of collectivists', *Cross Cultural Management*, vol. 11, no. 3, pp. 54–69.

Härtel, C. E. J., Gough, H. & Härtel, G. F. (2006), 'Provider's emotional competence and workgroup emotional climate predict customer and provider satisfaction with service encounters', *International Journal of Work Organisation and Emotion*, vol. 1, no. 3.

Härtel, C. E. J., Gough, H. & Härtel, G. F. (in submission), 'Work group emotional climate, emotion management skills, and service attitudes and performance', *Asia Pacific Journal of Human Resources*, submitted 15 June 2005.

Härtel, C. E. J., Zerbe, W. J. & Ashkanasy, N. M. (2005), *Emotions in Organizational Behavior*, Lawrence Erlbaum Associates, Mahwah.

Herzberg, F. (1968), 'One more time: How do you motivate employees?', *Harvard Business Review*, January–February, pp. 53–62.

Hofstede, G. (1980), *Culture's Consequences*, Sage, Beverly Hills.

Jordan, P. J., Ashkanasy, N. M. & Härtel, C. E. J. (2003), 'The case for emotional intelligence in organizational research', *Academy of Management Review*, vol. 28, no. 2, pp. 195–9.

Kamoche, K. (1991), 'Human resource management: A multiparadigmatic analysis', *Personnel Review*, vol. 20, no. 4, pp. 3–14.

Kirkman, B., Shapiro, D., Novelli, L. & Brett, J. (1996), 'Employee concerns regarding self-managing work teams: A multidimensional justice perspective', *Social Justice Research*, vol. 9, pp. 47–67.

Kissler, G. D. (1994), 'The new employment contract', *Human Resource Management*, vol. 33, no. 3, pp. 335–51.

Kusum, S. (2003), 'Survivors' reactions to downsizing: The importance of contextual factors', *Human Resource Management Journal*, vol. 13, no. 4, pp. 56–75.

Legge, K. (1989), 'Human resource management: A critical analysis', in *New Perspectives in Human Resource Management*, ed. J. Storey, Routledge, London.

Legge, K. (1998), 'The morality of HR', in *Strategic Human Resource Management: A Reader*, eds C. Mabey, G. Salaman & J. Storey, Sage/Open University Press, London.

Lewin, K. (1951), *Field Theory in Social Science*, Harper and Row, New York.

Locke, E. A. (1968), 'Toward a theory of task motivation and incentives' *Organizational Behavior and Human Performance*, vol. 3, pp. 157–89.

Locke, E. A. & Latham, G. P. (2002), 'Building a practically useful theory of goal setting and task motivation: A 35-year odyssey', *American Psychologist*, vol. 57, no. 9, pp. 705–17.

McClelland, D. (1955), *Studies in Motivation*, Appleton-Century-Crofts, New York.

McGregor, D. (1960), *The Human Side of Enterprise*, McGraw-Hill, New York.

Maguire, H. (2002), 'Psychological contracts: Are they still relevant?', *Career Development International*, vol. 7, no. 3, pp. 67–180.

Maslow, A. H. (1954), *Motivation and Personality*, Harper and Row, New York.

Mirels, H. L. & Garrett, J. B. (1971), 'The protestant ethic as a personality variable', *Journal of Consulting and Clinical Psychology*, vol. 36, no. 1, pp. 40–4.

Mudrack, P. E. (1997), 'Protestant work-ethic dimensions and work orientations', *Personality and Individual Differences*, vol. 23, no. 2, pp. 217–25.

Noon, M. & Blyton, P. (2002), *The Realities of Work*, Palgrave Macmillan, Basingstoke.

Ojuka Onedo, A. E. (1991), 'The motivation and need satisfaction of Papua New Guinea managers', *Asia Pacific Journal of Management*, vol. 18, no. 1, pp. 121–9.

Paterson, J. M. & Härtel, C. E. J. (2002), 'An integrated affective and cognitive model to explain employees' responses to large-scale change', in *Managing*

Emotions in a Changing Workplace, eds N. M. Ashkanasy, C. E. J. Härtel & W. J. Zerbe, M. E. Sharpe, Armonk.

Pavlov, I. P. (1927), *Conditioned Reflexes: An Investigation of the Physiological Activity of the Cerebral Cortex*, translated and edited by G. V. Anrep, Oxford University Press, Humphrey Milford.

Petersen, A. H., Boer, H. & Gertsen, F. (2004), 'Learning in different modes: The interaction between incremental and radical change', *Knowledge and Process Management*, vol. 11, no. 4, pp. 228–38.

Pizer, M. & Härtel, C. E. J. (2005), 'For better or worse: Organizational culture and emotions', in *Emotions in Organizational Behavior*, eds C. E. J. Härtel, W. J. Zerbe & N. M. Ashkanasy, Lawrence Erlbaum Associates, Mahwah.

Ployhart, R. & Ryan, A. M. (1998), 'Applicants' reactions to the fairness of selection procedures: The effects of positive rule violation and time of measurement', *Journal of Applied Psychology*, vol. 83, pp. 3–16.

Ramlall, S. (2004), 'A review of employee motivation theories and their implications for employee retention within organizations', *Journal of American Academy of Business*, vol. 5, no. 1/2, pp. 52–61.

Reardon, K. K., Reardon K. J. & Rowe, A. J. (1998), 'Leadership styles for the five stages of radical change', *Acquisition Review Quarterly*, Spring, pp. 129–46.

Richard, O. C. (2000), 'Racial diversity, business strategy, and firm performance: A resource based view', *Academy of Management Journal*, vol. 43, no. 2, pp. 164–77.

Shelton, C. D. & Darling, J. R. (2004), 'From chaos to order: Exploring new frontiers in conflict management', *Organization Development Journal*, vol. 22, no. 3, pp. 22–42.

Silverthorne, C. (2004), 'The impact of organizational culture and person–organization fit on organizational commitment and job satisfaction in Taiwan', *Leadership and Organization Development Journal*, vol. 25, no. 7/8, pp. 592–9.

Skarlicki, D. & Folger, R. (1997), 'Retaliation in the workplace: The roles of distributive, procedural, and interactional justice', *Journal of Applied Psychology*, vol. 82, pp. 434–43.

Skinner, B. F. (1953), *Science and Human Behavior*, Macmillan, New York.

Skinner, B. F. (1961), *Cumulative Record*, 3rd edn, Prentice Hall, Englewood Cliffs.

Taylor, M. S., Tracy, K., Renard, M. & Carroll, S. (1995), 'Due process in performance appraisal: A quasi-experiment in procedural justice', *Administrative Science Quarterly*, vol. 40, pp. 495–523.

ter Bogt, T., Raaijmakers, Q. & van Wel, F. (2005), 'Socialization and development of the work ethic among adolescents and young adults', *Journal of Vocational Behavior*, vol. 66, no. 3, pp. 420–37.

Thite, M. (2001), 'Help us but help yourself: The paradox of contemporary career management', *Career Development International*, vol. 6, pp. 312–17.

Thompson, J. A. & Bunderson, J. S. (2003), 'Violations of principle: Ideological currency in the psychological contract', *Academy of Management Review*, vol. 28, no. 4, pp. 571–86.

Trigg, A. B. (2004), 'Deriving the Engel curve: Pierre Bourdieu and the social critique of Maslow's hierarchy of needs', *Review of Social Economy*, vol. 62, no. 3, pp. 393–406.

Truss, C., Gratton, L., Hailey, V., McGovern, P. & Stiles, P. (1997), 'Soft and hard models of human resource management', *Journal of Management Studies*, vol. 34, no. 1, pp. 53–73.

Whiteley, A. (1995), *Managing Change: A Core Values Approach*, Mcmillan Education Australia, Melbourne.

Wiley, C. (1997), 'What motivates employees according to over 40 years of motivation surveys', *International Journal of Manpower*, vol. 18, no. 3, pp. 263–80.

Vroom, V. H. (1964), *Work and Motivation*, Wiley, New York.

PART 2

Issues, challenges and theoretical developments in strategic human resource management

Chapter 3

Knowledge, innovation and developing a learning culture

INTRODUCTION

A lack of knowledge is a serious problem for today's organisation. The nature of human capital is the focus of this chapter, specifically the link between strategic knowledge management and SHRM. To be successful in the strategic knowledge management process, SHRM must deal effectively and efficiently with a complex compilation of organisational resources such as culture, technology, organisational infrastructure, tacit and explicit knowledge and employees' discretionary behaviours.

This chapter focuses on the contemporary issues that arise in relation to SHRM, such as knowledge management and the learning organisation. The SHRM Application Tool introduced in Chapter 1 is used to illustrate how each issue is analysed, addressed and turned into a source of competitive advantage.

Objectives

The primary objective of this chapter is to introduce the contemporary issues that arise in relation to SHRM and knowledge management.

After reading this chapter you should be able to:

- understand what knowledge is and why it is an important issue for HR managers;
- define what knowledge workers are and discuss their place in the twenty-first century;
- identify the congruence between knowledge and HRM;
- understand how knowledge is managed and the implications of knowledge management for HR managers;
- demonstrate the link between organisational culture and the learning organisation;
- discuss the difference between innovation and creativity;
- understand the key contemporary knowledge management issues for HR managers.

Knowledge and knowledge workers

Today, with an increasingly dynamic and fast-changing technological, political and socioeconomic society, tangible assets (e.g. technology, product and financial resources) can no longer provide a competitive edge. Based on the theories of the resource-based view (RBV) and SHRM (discussed in Chapter 1), employees are the *key* to gaining a competitive edge in the twenty-first century. Specifically, the human capital (i.e. knowledge, skills and abilities) developed and retained by employees is expected to provide a sustainable competitive advantage for organisations. To understand how this is achieved, knowledge and its relationship to HRM needs to be examined.

WHAT IS KNOWLEDGE?

knowledge
The holistic combination of experiences and information which provides insight to make decisions, develop opinions and direct future behaviour.

When we think of knowledge we know that it is an intangible and powerful source. We can't physically touch or feel it, yet we are aware of its magnitude and importance in daily life. **Knowledge** refers to the holistic combination of experiences and information which provides insight to make decisions, develop opinions and direct future behaviour. It is more than just information. Information is 'potential knowledge' which needs to be received, analysed, understood and applied before it becomes knowledge. For example, the information learnt from university lectures provides insight into new topics, which are then used in essays to further educational development and enable future employment opportunities. The ability to apply learnt information means it has become knowledge.

Although knowledge is not a new phenomenon it is important that HR managers understand its relevance in energising employees to reach their potential at work. By doing this effectively, managers can create a win–win situation for the employee and employer, and realise the goal of obtaining (and maintaining) a competitive advantage through their human resources. Knowledge, therefore, is a commodity which can either be organisational or individual.

There are two types of organisational knowledge: tacit and explicit. Tacit knowledge is generally abstract, embedded in individual experiences and difficult to communicate unless through active involvement (Dhanaraj *et al.*, 2004; Kelloway & Barling, 2000). For example, HRM involves tacit knowledge because, although HR theories provide the foundation for how to manage people, every organisation is different and the easiest way to teach is through demonstration and participation. In contrast, explicit knowledge is easier to communicate and understand than tacit knowledge. It involves formal language and standardised procedures. For example, installing a new DVD player demonstrates explicit knowledge as there are clear step by step instructions and active involvement is not necessary to comprehend the installation.

There is often confusion and debate surrounding knowledge, its definition and what actually constitutes knowledge. After all, isn't it just information and something that every organisation just 'has'? Often, professionals external to the HRM department do not embrace the importance of this concept because they cannot see the value it adds to the bottom line. Indeed, this is one of the biggest challenges for HR managers because, unlike other departments such as production and sales, HRM does not contribute a *tangible* profit. The benefit of HRM is spread across the organisation in the form of improved job satisfaction and organisational culture (to name a few benefits). With this in mind, De Long and Fahey (2000) classify knowledge into three categories, which we refer to as individual knowledge. Figure 3.1 illustrates how this aligns with tacit and explicit knowledge.

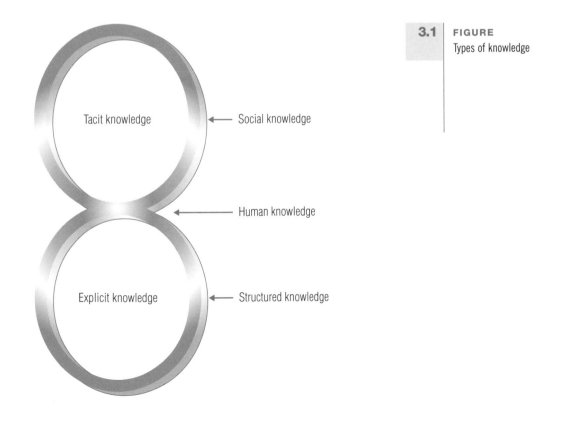

3.1 | FIGURE
Types of knowledge

1. *Human knowledge.* This includes what people know or know how to perform, and usually includes both tacit and explicit knowledge. For example, it may be understanding the organisation's culture (tacit/abstract) or completing a recruitment form (explicit/formal).
2. *Social knowledge.* The knowledge we learn from relationships is called social knowledge, and this may result from both individual and group associations. As such, this type of knowledge tends to be tacit and develops as the relationship develops, for example the culture within a group of friends. There are no rules of how to interact; it just develops as the group forms.
3. *Structured knowledge.* This comprises structured and formalised rules, procedures and routines ingrained within organisational settings. Consequently, this knowledge is explicit. For example, for the HR manager this may include procedures for disciplining inappropriate employee behaviour.

KNOWLEDGE WORK

knowledge work
Behaviour which results in the end product of knowledge being delivered.

Understanding what knowledge is isn't enough to satisfy goals. In organisational contexts knowledge becomes more complex. In fact, it shifts from being known as knowledge to *knowledge work*. In general terms, **knowledge work** is the behaviour which results in the end product of knowledge being delivered. More specifically, knowledge work has been classified into three categories (see Figure 3.2).

FIGURE 3.2
The various categories of knowledge work

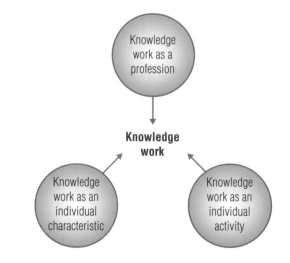

KNOWLEDGE WORK AS A PROFESSION

Some scholars believe that knowledge work defines the type of work that is performed and its association with high technology. For example, in this new economy age where knowledge is a sought after asset, industries such as information technology (IT) and science are depicted as leaders in the pursuit and achievement of knowledge acquisition (Kelloway & Barling, 2000). On the other hand, scholars have also identified education level and organisational hierarchy as characteristics of knowledge work (Bentley, 1990). In this instance, the output of a doctoral student would be classified as knowledge work as it is the highest level of tertiary education possible. Or, in the case of organisational hierarchy, senior managers, such as chief executive officers (CEOs), would be viewed as producing knowledge work.

Viewing knowledge work as a profession makes sense because it is high-quality knowledge that is being produced, and organisations benefit greatly from this. The higher the quality, the greater the strategic benefits and the more likely it is that a competitive advantage will be achieved. However, there are implications for HR managers in viewing knowledge work as such. For example, consider Bentley's (1990) definition of knowledge work. It implies that the higher an employee is in the organisation, the more their work is viewed as knowledge (as opposed to simply information). Yet, clearly that is inaccurate and unfair. What about employees not in management ranks? Is their work not just as important and useful? Kelloway and Barling (2000) claim that Bentley's perspective aligns with Taylorism, where management develops work procedures and employees are simply told what to do. It excludes lower-level employees in the creation of new ideas and decisions, which is incongruent with participatory management theories. Just because an employee is not a manager doesn't mean that they are unable or unwilling to contribute to innovation and creativity. Some of the best ideas and solutions come from such employees because they are the ones actually performing the task, as opposed to managers who oversee the functioning of the organisation.

Another implication that this view has for HRM is the qualification of credentials as quality (Kelloway & Barling, 2000). Although, in theory, higher education translates to higher knowledge, in reality this isn't always the case. For example, an undergraduate degree in business management might provide students with the foundation for how to be a good manager; however, it doesn't necessarily mean that they can enter any company and instantly apply what they learned (i.e. be a manager). Whereas someone who has been working in a company (rather than getting a degree) may be well positioned to be a manager, yet they do not have the certification. Basing knowledge work on a credentialist criterion therefore can be misleading.

KNOWLEDGE WORK AS AN INDIVIDUAL CHARACTERISTIC

The second aspect of knowledge work is defining it as an individual characteristic. In short, this means that the individual, not the job (or profession), contributes value. This is based on the creative and innovative characteristics that the individual possesses (Tampoe, 1993, cited in Kelloway & Barling, 2000). In addition, Ahmad (1991) includes egotistical and sensitivity characteristics in this classification of knowledge work, stating that these individuals prosper from the public attention they receive from eliciting knowledge. Other descriptors in this realm include the fact that the individual creates intangible assets, adding value to both products and services (Harris & Vining, 1987; Harrigan & Dalmia, 1991, both cited in Kelloway & Barling, 2000). Examples are an artist or a movie director as they elicit creativity and innovativeness.

Despite Kelloway and Barling's approval of this definition (in comparison to knowledge work as a profession), it is not without its limitations. Although it considers what an individual actually contributes, it negates the fact that not everybody has the opportunity to be creative and innovative in an organisation. This is attributed to the hierarchical structures of most organisations (e.g. government institutions). However, in rebuttal, we note here that there is a clear trend towards streamlining organisations, removing middle managers and, hence, creating more organic companies. Nevertheless, there are, and always will be, Weberian-style organisations.

HR managers also need to be aware of the role that personalities play. For example, some people are innately quiet, yet it does not mean that they lack creativity or innovation. Furthermore, these employees may also be intimidated by egotistical colleagues who enjoy being in the limelight. National culture may also play a role in that it socialises people as to how they interact within a group and whether their priority is harmony seeking (i.e. agreement) or individuality. Therefore, HR managers should consider motivational factors and culture (as discussed in Chapter 2) and their impact on the display of knowledge work.

KNOWLEDGE WORK AS AN INDIVIDUAL ACTIVITY

The third, and final, classification of knowledge work is as an individual activity. Put simply, this implies the work that employees perform with their head (opposed to their hands). In essence, this aligns closely with the 'profession' view of knowledge work in terms of education level and organisational hierarchy. It also assumes that blue-collar workers do not produce knowledge work, and that only white-collar employees do (Kelloway & Barling, 2000). Peter Drucker (1999), whose seminal research in the 1980s inspired the fruition of knowledge work theory, concurs with this view in that work done with the 'head' produces creativity and innovation. Therefore, if most employees use their head (because they are in management, have education, are creative and innovative or fall within the white-collar sector), then these employees all produce knowledge work.

However, isn't this contradictory? Kelloway and Barling (2000, p. 291) question the relevance, then, of classifying work as knowledge work when it really is just work; '. . . if we are all knowledge workers, then there is no need to use the term [knowledge workers] – simply referring to "workers" would imply "knowledge workers"'.

Please read
Kelloway, E. K. & Barling, J. (2000), 'Knowledge work as organizational behavior', *International Journal of Management Review*, vol. 2, no. 3, pp. 287–304.

KNOWLEDGE WORKERS

knowledge workers
Employees who produce knowledge work.

If we understand what knowledge work is, then it is easy to define **knowledge workers**. These are simply employees who produce knowledge work, such as IT or scientific technicians, CEOs, marketing executives or professors. These all fall within the categories discussed earlier. They certainly use their 'head', are innovative and creative and work within the white-collar segment of the workforce. But remember, there are differing schools of thought on what really constitutes knowledge work. In this book, we believe that *every* individual produces

Knowledge work

Knowledge work

knowledge work, whether by using their head or their hands (see Figure 3.3). Therefore, all human resources are knowledge workers, from junior employees, mid-level managers and even maintenance staff. They all contribute to improving the way their job is performed; for instance, if gardeners find a new appliance for trimming hedges, it might save time and money for the organisation, despite their position as a blue-collar worker. This increases efficiency and effectiveness and, when streamlined with HRM functions, achieves *strategic* HRM in addition to financial goals.

So how is knowledge work created? This is an important question because HR managers manage people; therefore, they also manage knowledge. Knowledge is what makes the company grow, prosper and gain a competitive edge. The implication for HR managers is that they need to motivate employees to see the benefit that knowledge, and knowledge creation, has for them and for the company. If employees produce quality knowledge, they enhance their employment power and the company will see the value they add and want to retain them (i.e. through additional remuneration). Organisations benefit from this too. However, as Drucker (1999, p. 84) asserts, the output knowledge workers produce must be *quality*:

> In judging the performance of a teacher, we do not ask how many students there can be in his or her class. We ask how many students learn anything – and that's a quality question.

HOW IS KNOWLEDGE CREATED?

Knowledge workers can create knowledge in five steps: sharing tacit knowledge, creating concepts, justifying concepts, building a prototype and cross-levelling of knowledge (Nonaka & Takeuchi, 1995).

1. *Sharing tacit knowledge.* Knowledge creation begins with the tacit knowledge held by organisational members. This individual knowledge then becomes organisational knowledge.

2. *Creating concepts.* This involves tacit knowledge being transferred into words and phrases that reflect explicit concepts (i.e. verbalised mental models).
3. *Justifying concepts.* Here, managers need to determine whether the concepts developed will actually satisfy organisational and individual needs.
4. *Building an archetype.* This involves the concept being transformed into a tangible product or service (i.e. prototype).
5. *Cross-levelling of knowledge.* Organisational knowledge is a continual, infinite process. New knowledge is always being developed and integrated into existing knowledge. The cross-levelling of knowledge, which is interactive, occurs both intra- and inter-organisationally.

These steps also prove our belief that everyone can become a knowledge worker if they embrace the concept of knowledge, not just if they have a degree or management position. Of course, this is just one way that knowledge can be created (see the article below).

> ## Please read
> Tirpak, T. M. (2005), 'Five steps to effective knowledge management', *Research Technology Management*, vol. 48, no. 3, pp. 15–16.

THE LINK BETWEEN KNOWLEDGE AND HRM

So far, this chapter has defined and discussed knowledge, knowledge work and knowledge workers. We have presented contemporary literature and debate surrounding this emerging issue with a view to increasing *your* knowledge. We have shown that knowledge can be broadly grouped into organisational and individual knowledge. **Organisational knowledge** is formed through individual interaction between organisational visions, cultures, strategies, technologies and people whereas **individual knowledge** is formed in an individual's mind (Bhatt, 2001, cited in Yahya & Goh, 2002). But how does this relate to HRM? In short, organisational knowledge is largely influenced by the strategic management process and, more specifically, by the strategic management of knowledge. HR managers should leverage organisational knowledge to achieve organisational flexibility and versatility to cope with the dynamic environment (Rodriguez & Ordonez de Pablos, 2002). However, this is easier said than done. According to Hislop (2003), the link between knowledge and HRM is acknowledged by academics and practitioners, but rarely researched because it is a difficult and ongoing debate. Despite this, scholars agree that there *is* a clear link between these two concepts and that it depends on the willingness and motivation of employees, and their congruence with HRM policies and practices (Robertson & O'Malley Hammersley, 2000). Therefore, if knowledge management relies on people, and HRM is the process of managing people, we can understand the link between these concepts.

organisational knowledge
Formed through the interaction between organisational visions, cultures, strategies, technologies, and people.

individual knowledge
Knowledge formed in an individual's mind.

Knowledge management

Managing knowledge might seem like a strange concept. If knowledge is simply information one can apply, then how can you manage something that you physically cannot touch? Information we can apply changes so frequently, even from one minute to the next. How can that be controlled? Despite its perceived difficulties, knowledge management can be achieved but first it must be defined. **Knowledge management** refers to the process of developing and controlling the intellectual capital of employees, in other words, their work-related knowledge. Knowledge management activities include cultivating a learning environment where employees gather knowledge that benefits organisational performance and ensuring available knowledge gets to the relevant tasks in the organisation. But this is difficult because we cannot actually touch their knowledge; it is stored in their minds and employees are distributed across the organisation.

knowledge management
The process of developing and controlling the intellectual capital of employees.

Knowledge might be the 'know-how' of how to produce IT programs, provide solutions to financial problems or maintain a complex filing system. But organisational knowledge doesn't just come from employees. It also resides in policies and procedures (i.e. instruction manuals), technology (i.e. email and software) and organisational behaviour and culture (Alavi & Leidner, 2001). Therefore, knowledge is both tangible and intangible, depending on the source used. Further, it is imperative that HRM be aware of how to manage knowledge because most organisational knowledge resides in the minds of employees. Figure 3.4 demonstrates the link between knowledge management and HRM.

3.4 | FIGURE
The link between knowledge management and HRM

HRM practices	HRM impacts	Knowledge management (KM) outcomes
High commitment management	Employee commitment	Positive response to KM initiatives
Tailoring HRM to knowledge workers	Motivation and retention of knowledge workers	Improved knowledge worker performance
Internal and external fit of HRM practices	Linking KM and HRM to business strategy	Codification and personalisation business strategies
HRM practices to foster social and human capital	Development of capabilities and intellectual capital	Long-run strategic advantages in flexibility and innovation
Developing and sustaining learning within the organisation	Creation and maintenance of communities of practice	Improved sharing of learning and tacit knowledge across the organisation

Source: Carter, C. & Scarbrough, H. (2001), 'Towards a second generation of KM? The people management issue', *Education and Training*, vol. 43, no. 4/5, p. 221.

The notion of knowledge management emerged in the 1970s and gained momentum in the 1980s with the introduction of Total Quality Management (TQM) and Business Process Re-engineering (BPR), which are quality-driven initiatives. There was a clear shift again towards the end of the millennium where Drucker (1999) noted that the twentieth century's greatest assets were *machinery*, whereas the twenty-first century will value *knowledge workers* and their output. He asserted that more focus should be placed on HRM to reflect this in management styles and techniques. In essence, the goal of effective knowledge management is for the organisation to learn, evaluate, transfer and institutionalise knowledge, constantly filling any gaps between the strategic management process (e.g. strategies, goals, cultures, structures), dynamic environmental needs (e.g. knowledge economy, state of art technology) and HRM systems (e.g. rewarding, recruitment, performance management). Like other areas of HRM activity, knowledge management needs to be taken seriously and be linked with the organisation's objectives and goals, and not simply be paid 'lip service'.

Source: <http://www.iaea.org/km/pages/trieste2004/L02(Heigl).pdf>, accessed 10 October 2005. Copyright United Features Syndicate Inc.

Knowledge management is performed in a variety of ways. First, HR managers need to be aware of *what* knowledge already exists and *where* it resides within the organisation. There is no point reinventing the wheel, but at the same time it might be difficult to locate information that can be applied to a given activity. Employees might store it in electronic format or in hard copies, and the physical location of it may vary from employee to employee, branch to branch and country to country. Second, it is the responsibility of HRM to ensure that once an employee gains new knowledge it is embedded within organisational systems. By doing so, it is safeguarded so that if the employee leaves the company the knowledge stays. After all, the knowledge gained from training and development is paid for by the company, therefore they 'own' that knowledge. If an employee departs the company without storing that new knowledge, then the company has wasted valuable time and money which equates to inefficient and ineffective management. Third, companies need to have a mechanism which enables the delivery of knowledge to where it is needed. Mediums such as face to face, email or conferences may be optimal, depending on the type of knowledge being transferred and geographical and communication barriers (including language).

Of course, for this to work organisations must know what knowledge the organisation has and where it is located so it can retrieve the knowledge quickly and transfer it where needed.

Employees also play a significant role in knowledge management, not just HR managers. For instance, Drucker (2005) advocated that employees have to learn to develop and situate themselves where they can have the greatest value to organisations, in essence, make themselves indispensable through their own self-management (see Figure 3.5). According to Drucker, there are several problems associated with this. First, organisations in the twenty-first century are not managing their employees' career development. This may be due to changes in the workforce and the lack of employee loyalty, evidenced through employment casualisation and the increase in temporary assignments. Second, most people don't know how to manage their own careers because they are unaware of their own strengths and how to correlate this with their abilities and the possible career paths available.

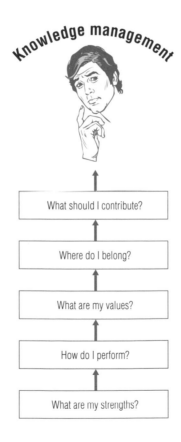

3.5	**FIGURE**
	How employees can manage their own knowledge

Source: Adapted from Drucker (2005).

Please read

Drucker, P. F. (2005), 'Managing oneself', *Harvard Business Review*, vol. 83, no. 1, pp. 100–9.

So, how is knowledge actually transferred? Knowledge transfer and knowledge management are two different concepts. While knowledge management is about coordinating and facilitating the processed information held by employees, knowledge transfer is about transporting this from one place to another. Therefore, **knowledge transfer** can be defined as the movement of information, skills and ideas from one entity to another as depicted in Figure 3.6. This can either be a formal or informal process, and does not simply involve the human element (i.e. skills and ideas held by organisational members) but also the technical element (i.e. procedures and documents), as mentioned earlier. Boardroom meetings, working lunches and conference attendance are all examples of knowledge being transferred.

knowledge transfer
The movement of information, skills and ideas from one entity to another.

FIGURE 3.6
Knowledge management and knowledge transfer

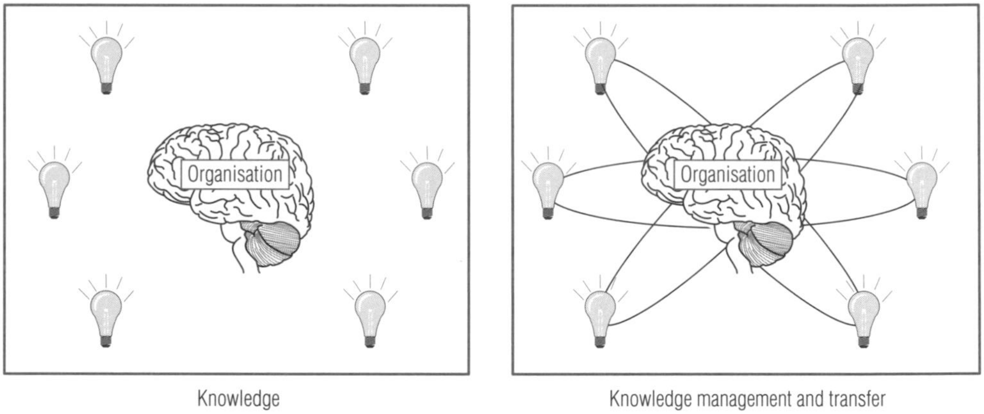

Knowledge

Knowledge management and transfer

STRATEGIC KNOWLEDGE MANAGEMENT

In Chapter 1 we discussed the difference between HRM and SHRM. Likewise, this section of the chapter discusses the difference between strategic management and strategic *knowledge* management. **Strategic management** refers to the planning and achieving of organisational goals with a long-term focus. This type of management is critical to the company's longevity as it ties all aspects of the business together; in a sense, it is a bird's-eye view of the entire company to ensure that each department is moving in the same direction and contributing to the overall organisational goal. Strategic management is usually performed by senior management but in conjunction with departmental managers, such as HRM, Production and Marketing. Within the HRM department, this might include human resource planning (HRP), which is forecasting the required number, and skill requirements, of employees needed by the company. This would be done in consultation with the Production and Marketing departments if, for example, a new product was to be launched. HR managers would anticipate the growth in sales, realise more employees would be required and hire them. It is imperative that every organisation scan its external environment regularly and develop strategic plans to remain competitively viable.

strategic management
The process of managing with a long-term focus, and which is largely composed of strategy formulation and strategy implementation.

Strategic management alone is not enough to maintain a business successfully. Remember, an organisation's greatest and most valuable asset is its human resources (and their knowledge). However, strategic *knowledge* management focuses specifically on the management of knowledge, and falls within the realm of HRM, although the HRM department is not solely responsible for it. Senior management, line managers and employees must also take responsibility. **Strategic knowledge management** refers to a long-term process that uses both tacit and explicit knowledge to cultivate organisational learning, which is then shared among organisational members to achieve the strategic goal. Again, as with strategic management, there is an overall organisational goal which is to be achieved; this makes the concept of knowledge management *strategic*.

strategic knowledge management
The long-term process that uses both tacit and explicit knowledge to cultivate organisational learning, which is then shared among organisational members to achieve the strategic goal.

Based on the RBV of the firm, strategic knowledge management can reap a sustainable competitive advantage when it successfully enhances organisational learning through the management of: (1) technology; (2) organisational infrastructure; (3) corporate culture; (4) knowledge (i.e. human capital); and (5) people (i.e. discretionary behaviours) (Yahya & Goh, 2002) (refer to Table 3.1).

TABLE **3.1** **Characteristics of strategic knowledge management**

Technological infrastructure	The IT tools (i.e. hardware, software) that enable any form of electronic encoding and exchanging of knowledge, which tends to enhance the explicit knowledge
Organisational infrastructure	The way employees are organised into teams; interaction within teams; the set of roles and goals of each team and how they relate to organisational strategy
Organisational culture	The shared values and norms, ethics and practices in the organisation, which tend to influence the tacit knowledge through the explicit means (e.g. information technology).
Knowledge	Includes both tacit and explicit knowledge
People	Includes both the external and internal stakeholders of an organisation who demonstrate discretionary behaviours

Source: Adapted from Yahya & Goh (2002).

Please read

Yahya, S. & Goh, W. K. (2002), 'Managing human resources toward achieving knowledge management', *Journal of Knowledge Management*, vol. 6, no. 5, pp. 457–68.

What, then, is organisational learning?

ORGANISATIONAL LEARNING

Organisational learning is a concept that many have questioned, just like knowledge management. Again, it is an intangible yet crucial element to organisational success. As Drucker (1999) stated, it is no longer production equipment that is the most valuable company asset, but rather *people* and more specifically knowledge workers. So, how is their knowledge *strategically* managed?

organisational learning
A system-wide approach to learning.

Organisational learning has been defined as a system-wide approach to learning. It has also been defined as an organisation-wide change process which identifies a perceived gap in current and desired performance (Argyris & Schön, 1996) (see Chapter 2 for further information on organisational change). Another definition states that organisational learning 'is the process by which managers become aware of the qualities, patterns and consequences of their own experiences and develop mental models to understand these experiences' (Appelbaum & Gallagher, 2000, p. 41). Organisations learn in a similar fashion to individuals; put simply, organisational learning is an elaboration of knowledge transfer. Specifically, this includes the process of knowledge acquisition, information distribution, information interpretation and organisational memory (Huber, 1991).

1. *Knowledge acquisition.* This is the process of collecting knowledge and determining the type of learning required (i.e. self, group, experimental).
2. *Information distribution.* This relies on each source sharing information, which then leads to new information and knowledge development.
3. *Information interpretation.* This involves the information or knowledge being converted into a commonly understood form.
4. *Organisational memory.* Learning is a dynamic process and it is only effective when the acquisition of knowledge is permanent. Organisational memory is the process of storing knowledge for a future use.

Is it really necessary for organisations to learn? Undoubtedly, organisational learning is important in the current competitive climate. The complexity of globalisation and international management advocates the requirement to compete aggressively and research has shown that organisational learning results in improved performance and customer satisfaction (Gómez, 2004). The new knowledge that comes with learning provides companies with the ideas and skills to perform better than competitors, satisfy consumer demands faster and to a higher quality, and get the most value from employees. If an organisation can successfully achieve this, they can ensure effective learning in the workplace:

> Learning is at the heart of a company's ability to adapt to a rapidly changing environment. It is the key to be able both to identify opportunities that others might not see and to exploit those opportunities rapidly and fully . . . In order to generate extraordinary value for shareholders, a company has to learn better than its competitors and apply that knowledge throughout its business faster and more widely than they do . . . Anyone in the organisation who is not directly accountable for making a profit should be involved in creating and distributing knowledge that the company can use to make a profit (Prokesch, 1997, p. 148).

Please read

Appelbaum, S. H. & Gallagher, J. (2000), 'The competitive advantage of organizational learning', *Journal of Workplace Learning: Employee Counselling Today*, vol. 12, no. 2, pp. 40–56.

Some scholars debate the ability for organisations to 'learn'; organisations are entities that do not think or feel like people, so how can they learn? The fact is, organisations comprise individuals and because individuals can learn, so too can organisations. It is a similar concept to individual and organisational knowledge (discussed earlier in this chapter) where knowledge is transferred from employees to the company. However, there is a difference between individual and organisational learning. Essentially, individuals learn from gaining knowledge and experimenting, and once they share (or transfer) that knowledge within the organisation (or when new organisational members are employed), new knowledge is gained and the organisation grows and develops its learning capacity. Hence, it learns.

WHY SOME ORGANISATIONS DO NOT LEARN

Despite the various tools and models scholars advocate as methods for facilitating organisational learning, there is no cure-all for successful organisational learning. Further, some companies lack the capacity or desire to learn. Vaill (1991, cited in Galer & van der Heijden, 1992, p. 6) proposed several reasons to explain why organisations *do not* learn:

- lack of awareness of the world outside the company or industry;

- using traditional frames of reference ('mental models') which have become outdated;

- pressure of time, resulting in too much fire fighting (reacting to short-term demands rather than focusing on priorities);

- shortage of resources to make the necessary analyses, or to embed the learning of individuals;

- executive politics;

- managing by copying others, rather than by appreciating the special circumstances of one's own position;

- scepticism about the value of strategic thinking;

- 'algorithmism' (i.e. believing that there is a magic formula to fix every problem);

- turbulence in the business environment, leading to confusion in interpreting the vital 'weak signals'.

In addition, for organisations to learn, individuals must also be willing and able to learn. Yet not everyone falls into this category. For example, there is some evidence to suggest that older individuals do not like change and require different learning programs from the younger generation. However, it is not just the older generation that HR managers need to contend with. According to Argyris (1991), a pioneer in the theory of individual learning, intelligent people find it the most difficult to learn. He defines these as people who are professionals in key management positions, with high education levels and who demonstrate both high power and high commitment to their modern organisation. In essence, they are knowledge workers. Despite these employees' enthusiasm to discuss critically clients' downfalls, they are less inclined to discuss their own and often display defence mechanisms when attention turns to them. These mechanisms include:

- embarrassment and feeling threatened when critically analysing and discussing their own performance within the organisation;
- avoiding responsibility by projecting blame for their poor behaviour on unclear goals, unfair leaders and unintelligent clients.

Argyris also asserts that these intelligent employees do not enjoy discussing their feelings of embarrassment, threat or blame laying, whether or not they are currently occurring.

Interestingly, Scott-Ladd and Chan (2004) discuss the positive impact that *emotionally intelligent* individuals have on organisational learning and change. They state that the emerging trend between emotional intelligence and organisational results is due to the recognition by these employees that they *and* the company can benefit from increased participation in the decision-making process, including continuous learning techniques (see Chapter 2 for a definition and discussion of emotional intelligence).

HOW ORGANISATIONS LEARN

It is, therefore, the task of HR managers and individual employees to motivate themselves and each other to learn in the work environment. This can be achieved through ongoing training, although training alone does not constitute organisational learning. Learning must be continuous; it is a never ending cycle and in the process of such learning each organisation will usually develop their own learning techniques to complement their unique organisational characteristics. The most effective way of becoming a learning organisation is to build capacity by thinking and acting in new ways, based upon acquiring new knowledge (Redding & Catalanello, 1994). Specifically, organisations learn in a variety of ways:

1. Reflection on what practices are working and why and what practices are not working and why.

2. Experimenting with new practices and learning through trial and error.

3. Learning from others within and external to the organisation by observing and seeking advice.

4. Researching practices of other organisations and academic literature on the topic.

A learning environment must be encouraged for learning to take place. This includes a supportive workplace where senior management actively lead by example; promoting truthfulness and openness where employees think 'outside the square' and view mistakes as learning curves; encouraging participation and decision making at all organisational levels; creating a community atmosphere to reduce barriers and learn from each other; and cultivating a 'learning culture' which aligns with the strategic knowledge management and SHRM of the company.

Despite the benefits of organisational learning, this concept has been subject to criticism. First, many people (especially senior management) find it difficult to grasp the concept given that it is intangible. They view it as 'fuzzy', with no clear guidelines on how it can be achieved (or its success guaranteed), and therefore it is often referred to as another management fad (akin to TQM in the 1980s). Second, there has been no extensive acceptance of any model (or theory) of organisational learning (Fiol & Lyles, 1985). Third, organisational change does not necessarily imply learning, and often it is difficult to measure what has been learnt (i.e. cognitive or behavioural) and how that impacts on the bottom line (Fiol & Lyles, 1985). Fourth, conflicts of interest might result in employees not sharing all information (politics), too much information (i.e. information overload) due to time constraints (i.e. competitive pressure) or the wrong information (i.e. environmental misalignment and/or uncertainly about outcomes) (Easterby-Smith, 1997). Fifth, organisational learning is still in its infancy in terms of empirical research and there is very little critical discussion on the topic (Contu, Grey & Örtenblad, 2003), therefore its validity remains questioned in some circles.

Please read

Easterby-Smith, M. (1997), 'Disciplines of organizational learning: Contributions and critiques', *Human Relations*, vol. 50, no. 9, pp. 1085–1113.

For a final word on organisational learning, we offer a checklist which we believe will guide an organisation to implement learning successfully in their company. An organisation must have:
* a culture amenable to learning;
* a degree of goal divergence, tolerance of dissent, openness to outside ideas and desire to do better;
* freedom to experiment, tolerance of errors;
* commitment, expressed as observable action, by management to learning as an objective;
* planning and action organisationally close to each other;
* follow up to initiatives, capturing of lessons learnt;
* trust in the judgement of colleagues;
* leaders who are able to assist employees to cope constructively with negative emotions;
* coordination through effective organisational conversation (Galer & van der Heijden, 1992, p. 11).

It is the first point on culture which is particularly important for organisational success. As with any company initiative (especially organisational change), the culture must support and align with the desired direction of the organisation. Organisational culture and how it links with the learning organisation is discussed in detail next.

ORGANISATIONAL CULTURE

Culture plays a significant role in the success of knowledge management and organisational learning. Indeed, pertinent management scholars, such as Edgar

culture
The shared values, assumptions, beliefs and perceptions which guide the behaviour of organisational members.

Schein (1996), claim that managing and aligning culture is the *key* to organisational learning. Without an appropriate and supporting organisational culture which aligns with internal and external cultures, he claims that organisational learning will either be hindered or simply fail. **Culture** can be defined as the shared values, assumptions, beliefs and perceptions which guide the behaviour of organisational members. It also identifies the characteristics of relationships, emotional experiences, emotional expression and emotion management in organisations (Pizer & Härtel, 2005).

Culture has both *visible* and *invisible* dimensions. Visible dimensions include uniforms/clothing, décor and office layout. For example, an open office plan indicates open communication and knowledge sharing. In contrast, the invisible dimension of culture refers to the implicit core values of the organisation that guide people's behaviours. This dimension is not explicitly spoken or seen; however, it is manifested in how the established organisational members act, speak and interpret daily issues at work, affecting the tacit knowledge pool. Thus, if the organisation possesses core values which embrace knowledge sharing, the consequent behaviours of employees will be to engage actively in this behaviour. Effective knowledge management entails a balance of the visible and invisible dimensions of culture; that is, visibly demonstrating the significance of sharing knowledge and building on the invisible core values (McDermott & O'Dell, 2001).

As organisations pursue a knowledge management system, they must often make major cultural changes and behavioural adjustments. SHRM should be a proactive change agent by facilitating an effective learning and networking culture to achieve the continual improvements of products and services to cope with the dynamic changing environment (Ulrich, 1998). Therefore, the learning should be both **single-loop learning** (i.e. improving the company by identifying solutions) and **double-loop learning** (i.e. identifying *why* the problem might be occurring, as well as *how* to solve it). Although single-loop learning is effective for providing solutions, double-loop learning is the more thorough and effective method for organisational improvement as it addresses the root of the problem, not just the symptoms. A number of diagnostic techniques, such as the SHAPE method, are available to help practitioners identify the root causes of problems (Härtel, Härtel & Barney, 1998). This method demonstrates how problem identification may be enhanced through the use of a five-step process, namely, **s**crutinise symptoms, **h**ypothesise solutions, **a**nalyse proposed solutions, **p**erform modifications and corrections and **e**valuate results (SHAPE). Research indicates that individuals employing the SHAPE decision-making process are faster and more accurate in problem identification than individuals relying on their intuitive decision-making approach. In essence, if organisations successfully and wholly embrace double-loop learning, then knowledge workers are embracing a learning environment and a learning organisation is born.

single-loop learning
Improving the company by identifying solutions.

double-loop learning
Identifying why the problem might be occurring, as well as how to solve it.

Please read
McDermott, R. & O'Dell, C. (2001), 'Overcoming cultural barriers to sharing knowledge', *Journal of Knowledge Management*, vol. 5, no. 1, pp. 76–82.

THE LEARNING ORGANISATION

There has been much debate surrounding the existence of the learning organisation. The learning organisation, a term coined by Peter Senge (1994) in his seminal book *The Fifth Discipline*, is different from organisational learning, although the two do relate. A **learning organisation** is simply a *type* of organisation which has the ability to change and adapt continuously to new environments and circumstances, through the acquisition of new knowledge. However, as with organisational learning, it is not just a matter of stating that you are a learning organisation; there needs to be a fundamental mindshift (which requires a culture shift) that goes beyond simply training and development, to individual and organisational learning. In general, there are three characteristics of a learning organisation as shown in Figure 3.7. These characteristics enable the organisation to become skilled at knowledge acquisition, transfer and management, through problem solving, experimentation and learning from their own and others' experiences.

learning organisation
A type of organisation which has the ability to change continuously and adapt to new environments and circumstances, through the acquisition of new knowledge.

3.7 | **FIGURE**
Three characteristics of a learning organisation

Source: Adapted from Porth, McCall & Bausch (1999).

According to Senge, who pioneered this concept, a learning organisation must obey five rules, which he referred to as practising five disciplines.

1. *Building a shared vision.* Employees must be empowered to embrace learning and understand their important contribution to the process. This ensures that they visualise the strategic goal of the company and how it is to be achieved; it provides focus and energy for learning.

2. *Team learning.* Just as organisational knowledge is greater than individual knowledge, so too is team learning. Within this stage, members learn from each other and knowledge is transferred throughout the organisation. Everyone learns from the teams' mistakes and successes.

3. *Mental models.* Mental models are Mind Maps® that guide people's behaviour (see Chapter 1 for a discussion on Mind Mapping). They are an image of how they believe things work, and what can or cannot be done. Often, organisational change encounters resistance because people have a picture in their mind of how things are to be done, and resist the change when this is incongruent. Successful team learning eventuates when members are open to constructive feedback and challenge each others' mental models, thus creating a shared vision of the new mental model.

4. *Personal mastery.* Learning is continuous and all members must continually assess the gap between their current and their desired skills. This phase is achieved when employees have the self-esteem and confidence to take on new challenges.

5. *Systems thinking.* Systems thinking has been argued to be the cornerstone of the learning organisation. It asserts that things don't happen in isolation; the organisation and its employees are part of a greater system where everything is connected to everything else. This enables coherence and development towards a common goal. This phase is also dependent on the other four disciplines to develop and realise the potential of the learning organisation.

'Learning to learn' is a key factor in becoming a learning organisation. Learning must be aligned with HR practices and procedures and a culture that values continual learning. Only then will a competitive advantage be obtained (and retained) from continual knowledge acquisition and development. Initiatives that encourage a learning environment include developing strategic goals, open communication, ongoing training, self-managing teams and motivational systems which encourage continual learning and experimentation. Learning organisations need to develop the capacity for obtaining, developing and transferring knowledge and become skilled at changing their behaviour to reflect new insights. Once this has been achieved, the organisation becomes more efficient internally and more effective externally through customer satisfaction, thus gaining the elusive competitive edge that all companies strive for in the twenty-first century. Examples of successful learning organisations include Toyota Motor Corporation Australia, Honda, Corning and General Electric (Garvin, 1993; Sohal & Morrison, 1995).

However, not every company should, or can, become a learning organisation. Learning requires time, financial commitment and human resources to execute the learning effectively. In some companies or industries these resources are not plentiful so learning is impeded. In other situations the philosophy of a learning organisation is not recognised or embraced, therefore becoming a learning organisation is not warranted or is ill advised. For example, while learning is crucial in knowledge-driven or turbulent industries such as research and development, low innovation or stable industries may not always benefit from becoming a learning organisation. In the latter case, the challenges and requirements of becoming a learning organisation may be an unnecessary drain on resources.

DOES THE LEARNING ORGANISATION REALLY EXIST?

Despite the obvious benefits (and necessity) for becoming a learning organisation, there remains much scepticism and debate over this emerging management concept. The most profound argument against the learning organisation is that it can never actually exist (Nyhan *et al.*, 2004). If the underlying notion of a learning organisation is that learning is continuous and infinite, then an organisation can never really reach the end state of becoming 'a learning organisation'. Other scholars debate the validity and usefulness of the learning organisation; have labelled it another management fad (due to the lack of support from the educational community); and believe that differentiations between organisational learning, and adaptation and learning, are unclear (Jankowicz, 2000; Nyhan *et al.*, 2004). Despite these criticisms the learning organisation can exist and it is to the benefit of management and employees alike to work towards developing and sustaining a learning environment.

Please read

Fischer, M. 2003, 'Challenges and open questions raised by the concept of the learning organisation', in *Facing up to the Learning Organisation Challenge – Volume II: Selected European Writings*, eds B. Nyhan, M. Kelleher, P. Cressy & R. Poell, Cedefop Reference Series, Office for Official Publications of the European Communities, Luxembourg.

INNOVATION AND CREATIVITY

To create a learning environment organisations need to foster innovation and creativity. Only through innovation and creativity can organisations truly learn, for example through experimentation, encouragement to 'think outside the square' and viewing mistakes as opportunities from which to learn rather than being embarrassed by them. In this sense, **innovation** is defined as the introduction of a new process or system which ultimately provides benefits at the individual, team or organisational level. Innovation aligns with organisational change; however, as change is not always beneficial to company stakeholders the two are not synonymous. Examples of innovation include mobile phones, space shuttles and the Internet.

innovation
The introduction of a new process or system which ultimately provides benefits at the individual, team or organisational level.

Innovation in business is achieved in many ways and is often aligned with the learning organisation and TQM. Formal methods of achieving innovation include research and development for large-scale innovations (i.e. ground-breaking scientific research such as medical research). However, smaller innovations may be developed through informal methods, such as on-the-job training and practice (i.e. more efficient work procedures, such as reducing the amount of time spent on completing paperwork). Innovation and creativity add fresh life to a company, embracing vibrancy and diversity as core values from which they differentiate themselves. Extending from Drucker's (1999) belief that companies need to place more value on their *people*, not their machines, innovation and creativity allow new thoughts and processes which would otherwise have been stifled. This new age of intense globalisation and competition allows all employees to thrive in their own way of working. Employees are no longer viewed as homogeneous as asserted by Taylorism; they have different ideas, experiences, needs and wants which make them, and the way they work, heterogeneous. They are unique.

HOW CAN INNOVATION BE MANAGED?

Innovation is an important factor for the organisation as it can lead to a competitive edge, and it is imperative that it is managed carefully and individually. There isn't a handbook for managing innovation. Obviously, innovative people are quite different and, as such, a different approach is required for all. There are three factors that need to be addressed before innovation can be effectively managed and achieved: type of innovation, type of person, and work environment. When these three factors are aligned with HRM policies and practices, then the essence of a learning organisation is created.

First, the *type of innovation* needs to be determined. This is important because some innovation is fairly low key and not earth shattering, while other types are of major consequence and produce large-scale change. The type of innovation determines how it is to be managed and the individual requirements of employees. According to Tidd, Bessant and Pavitt (2005), there are four types of innovation:

1. *Product innovation.* This includes low-key innovation, such as minor changes on existing products, for example new handles on refrigerators or larger doors on washing machines. In marketing terms, this is also referred to as 'just noticeable difference'.
2. *Process innovation.* This includes improving the efficiency of processes which is aimed at decreasing time and financial resources used. For example, many financial institutions in Australia claim that you will have an answer in two minutes regarding whether you can be granted a home loan. In general terms, these efforts are designed to streamline processes and improve efficiency, which leads to increased effectiveness.
3. *Positioning innovation.* This includes positioning a product or service in a different industry or within a new market, for example outdoor clothing shops repositioning themselves into the mainstream clothing market as trends change, such as army-style clothing and footwear.
4. *Paradigm innovation.* This is the greatest of innovations, and includes ground-breaking innovation, for example the development of the automobile in the 1900s and the introduction of television in the 1950s.

Second, the *type of person* needs to be determined. In general, there are two types of innovative people: adapters and innovators. Kirton developed a theory of adaptation and innovation in 1976, which proposed that people have different styles of decision making, problem solving and creativity (see also Kirton & McCarthy, 1988). At one end of the spectrum, adapters approached problem solving only within existing structures and paradigms, and generally viewed problem solving as 'how things could be done better'. They are characterised by reliability, safety, discipline and efficiency. An example is administrative employees who work within set boundaries. They may adapt to new changes within the workplace, but generally operate through routine. At the other end of the spectrum, innovators viewed problem solving by 'doing things differently' and are characterised in the opposite way to adapters, for example by disarray, jeopardy and risk. They thrive on being an individual and approach work tasks as such. Not only do they 'think outside the square' but they also work outside the square. Examples of innovators are artists or movie directors; they have a unique way of performing their job and enforcing routine would not align with their personal style of achievement.

Third, the *work environment* needs to be designed to fit the innovation and person. There are several issues that this includes. First, the job design, such as what hours are required and the physical location of the job. For example, adapters prefer routine and therefore working 9 am to 5 pm with 30 minutes for lunch suits them. However, innovators do not work with such routine. When artists are 'in the flow' of creating they often work days at a time, throughout the night and live in chaos until they are satisfied with the outcome. The same applies for writers; often they write in the country or an exotic location that inspires them. But then they might not write for weeks at a time when they have 'writers block'. Job design also includes job fit, which is improved through effective recruitment, selection and training. For example, a receptionist wouldn't necessarily work well in a job designed for an artist.

The second issue is organisational structure. There are various types of structures such as bureaucratic, matrix, organic and cellular. While bureaucratic structures tend to suit large organisations that require control (i.e. universities), flatter organic structures suit small to medium-sized businesses which desire decentralisation for greater participation and shared responsibility in decision making. Sometimes organisations need to function according to what project they have at hand. In these situations, organisations form project teams with members representing different departments. Structures accommodating such project teams are termed matrix structures where emloyees often report to two superiors: (1) their project leader and (2) the respective departmental leader. Alternatively, Acer adopted a cellular structure whereby the company was divided into business units which were responsible for specific aspects of the business (i.e. servicing, selling) although they still collaborated with the wider network from which to borrow designs or problem-solving techniques (i.e. from Acer America). Therefore, each unit was responsible for its own destiny but also for the strategic survival of the parent company.

Third, rewards and recognitions are important in designing the work environment. These may be in the form of intrinsic or extrinsic rewards, which need to be aligned with motivation (discussed in Chapter 2). Different people are motivated differently and for different reasons, therefore it is not possible to predict that adapters prefer intrinsic rewards and innovators prefer extrinsic, or vice versa. This is the task of the HR manager to determine and monitor.

The final issue is the climate for innovation. There are some companies where paradigm innovation is not needed, such as the local grocery store. Yet companies that are operating in fast-changing industries (e.g. IT) are more inclined to require and rely on product, process and paradigm innovation (as do Nokia and Sony Ericsson). A method for measuring the climate for innovation is to analyse the company's vision, participation levels, task orientation and support for innovation.

An example of an organisation that adopted an innovative strategy of improving business is Semco, a Brazilian-based manufacturing company. Their innovative performance management techniques have rescued the company from bankruptcy and transformed Semco into one of Brazil's most successful companies. At Semco, employees choose their salary, what days they work and when they take vacation leave. The senior managers, called Associates, work only a few months a year on a rotating roster. Yet, despite the lack of bureaucratic and authoritarian control, the company reports overwhelming success, both financially and in the form of employee satisfaction.

HR managers need also to be mindful that organisational cultures, although intangible, do change over time. This is dependent on the climate for innovation and the type of innovative employees currently within the company. Therefore, HRM needs to ensure that recruitment and selection policies, in conjunction with human resource planning need to be congruent with the strategic management of the company. Another factor to consider is that homogeneity hinders the creation of new ideas, so a mix of adapters and innovators is required for the right balance, depending on the type of organisation senior management wishes to create.

MANAGING CREATIVE PEOPLE

Despite the perceived similarities between innovation and creativity, the two are quite different. While innovation focuses on the introduction of new processes or systems, creativity is the development of those new systems. **Creativity** can be defined as the generation of ideas, including diverse, abstract and novel ideas. Creative employees need to be managed uniquely; traditional management methods work poorly for them. There is no step by step guide on how to manage creative people but there are certain factors that can be implemented to assist in the process, and management, of creativity.

creativity
The generation of ideas, including diverse, abstract and novel ideas.

It is vital that HRM realises that not everyone is creative, and that not all employees understand or can work with creative people. Most creative and highly innovative people are also very intelligent and, in some cases, they are also eccentric. Think of some highly creative people that you know, such as famous people. Albert Einstein is a good example: it is said that he never wore socks. Elvis Presley visited cemeteries and morgues during the night and collected sheriff badges. Vincent Van Gogh, a Dutch painter and self-confessed psychopath, was also eccentric. He cut off his own ear and later shot himself in the chest. These people were all brilliant at their work but their eccentricity set them apart from their 'traditional' colleagues.

Not everyone can work with creative people (whether eccentric or not), and vice versa. Creative people can, at times, be in a world of their own and their irregular way of working can appear chaotic and inefficient. Others might view this as undisciplined, rude or selfish, but it is the way they work best. Therefore, for creative people to work effectively they must have an understanding support network. So, how can HRM ensure that creative people have this? One tool that can be used to predict vocational interest (and personality type) is Holland's (1985) Self Directed Search (SDS). He asserts that there are six types of characteristics by which people can be classified: realistic, investigative, artistic, social, enterprising or conventional. By using the SDS to characterise people, HR managers can group similar people together, such as investigative and artistic, or realistic and conventional.

However, sometimes creative people prefer to work alone. This is a challenge for HR managers because, although they should do what they can to accommodate creative employees (for the benefits it brings to the organisation), they also need to learn methods to ensure the employees are still performing well, meeting budgets and working in an ethical manner. It is important for HRM to implement systems to monitor and control employees, for example train them how to manage their own budget and work within organisational policies and procedures. It is also important that others understand their creativity and uniqueness through, for example, diversity training. Another important issue to consider in the management of creativity is the emotional climate of the workgroup. Research shows that playfulness aids creativity while sadness diminishes it (Härtel, Zerbe & Ashkanasy, 2005).

Knowledge management and HRM issues

As all organisational knowledge arises from people who make the discretionary choice to exchange and share their knowledge, SHRM plays a significant role in achieving learning. This is especially important during the process of knowledge creation, knowledge transfer and knowledge institutionalisation. Although IT significantly contributes to the implementation of knowledge management initiatives, for example Internet forums, IT is weak in knowledge creation (i.e. information interpretation) and knowledge transfer (i.e. high-level face to face communication).

In theory, knowledge management, organisational culture, innovation and creativity are easily managed. But the world is unpredictable. We no longer live and work in a stable environment like in the 1950s. As such, managers need to be aware of the HRM issues and implications of managing people today.

IMPLICATIONS FOR THE PSYCHOLOGICAL CONTRACT

Earlier in this chapter we highlighted that increasing strategic control over employees (rather than employees' commitment) can lead employees to perceive a violation of the psychological contract, which in turn results in uncommitted employees. The psychological contract (defined and discussed in Chapter 2) is an important, intangible aspect of the employment relationship. While organisations emphasise the importance of the knowledge management initiative, uncommitted employees provide a significant drawback to knowledge management initiatives. SHRM, therefore, faces a challenge of effectively managing employees' discretions (i.e. willingness and motive) to create, share and institutionalise their tacit knowledge through explicit means. To achieve this, managers are encouraged to adopt soft HRM as this advocates that employees are the foundation of organisational knowledge.

Please read

Hislop, D. (2003), 'Linking human resource management and knowledge management via commitment: A review and research agenda', *Employee Relations*, vol. 25, no. 1/2, pp. 182–202.

RETAINING EMPLOYEES AND KNOWLEDGE CAPITAL MANAGEMENT

Another implication of knowledge management is how it can be retained by the employer. In fact, this is the *key* problem that organisations face today. With the decrease of job security and the rise of changing employment conditions and expectations (discussed in Chapter 1), job loyalty seems to be quickly disappearing. Whereas employees would have once experienced their entire working life in just one company, nowadays employees move from job to job without a second thought at being loyal to one company. Of course, this is just a generalisation; not everybody is like this. But this seems to be the case for the younger generation and for individualists (as opposed to collectivists) as they tend to consider to their own needs before others' needs.

So how can knowledge be retained? The answer is simple: by retaining employees. If a machine broke down in the organisation, what would we do? We wouldn't throw it out because we could repair it, but it might mean spending some time and money fixing it. The same principle applies to employees. If they become 'broken' or want to leave the organisation, it is their responsibility, as well as HRM, to renegotiate remuneration and fix the problem. This might include specialised training so they can focus on their career development, such as moving into a management position. Or it might include increased responsibility, a more emotionally supportive work environment, more challenging tasks or an increase in their salary. It is worth HRM efforts to retain that employee because any additional negotiation will cost less (both in dollar terms and also in the impact it may have on the organisational culture) than the costly and time-consuming process of advertising, recruiting, selecting and training a new employee.

Another implication for knowledge management is how it can be measured. As with all HRM processes, knowledge management does not contribute a tangible dollar amount to company profit. So, how can you convince senior management that it is being done, and being done effectively? The best way to prove this is to look at other factors, such as job satisfaction (Are employees happy? Do they trust others enough to share their knowledge?), organisational culture (Is the culture one of sharing or is it a competitive culture?) and profit (Has the profit increased since knowledge management was implemented? How does this compare with training and development costs?). Another way that this can be done is to receive feedback from stakeholders, such as customer and employee surveys, performance appraisals or suggestion boxes.

A further implication is the transfer of knowledge. This is simple for most small organisations as vertical and horizontal communication is facilitated freely. For example, it may be a matter of asking if your colleagues have already written the procedures for interviewing candidates for a particular client. But for larger organisations it presents a problem, especially for multinational corporations where communication, including language, presents a barrier. In this case, the company must decide how to store the knowledge, and in what form, so that it is easily accessible to all employees regardless of their language. There may also be competition between departments, or the unwillingness to share based on a competitive or unfriendly corporate culture. If you were working in a Melbourne office and someone from the New York branch asked for the interviewing procedures that you spent valuable time developing, would you be willing to share? To solve this problem, the organisational culture needs to be aligned with the strategic knowledge management goals to ensure that a learning environment is fostered, and that information sharing and exchange occurs for the benefits of individual and organisational goals.

The storing of knowledge also presents an issue. Before correct knowledge management procedures are developed, most employees would store their knowledge in unique ways, formats and locations. This presents a further problem of finding and interpreting the information when it is required. As such, knowledge management techniques need to be developed as early as possible, and the methods of doing so clearly communicated to all staff, including new staff. It is important that the benefits of doing so are communicated clearly to all staff, so they too embrace the learning environment of which they are a fundamental part.

Contemporary SHRM Application Tool

Imagine you are an HR manager of a multinational telecommunication company. The HR challenge you face is to ensure that every single technical support engineer adequately knows about newly developed technology for providing accurate and quick answers to customers on the phone. You have 400 technical support engineers scattered in 10 call centres worldwide, answering approximately 7000 questions every month about the company's products. You are, however, facing a problem since you acquired a few companies. As engineers from the acquired companies joined, they were reluctant to share their knowledge about the products they had been supporting. Further, service delivery has slowed down and quality decreased over the past two years. Although your company has an online service where customers could search for frequently asked questions, you need a better knowledge management system. The SHRM process model demonstrates how you could brainstorm this problem and create plans for improvement, implementation and evaluation (see Figure 3.8).

FIGURE 3.8

SHRM Application Tool:
problem – knowledge
management

Step 6: Evaluate against success criteria
- Has the profit increased since knowledge management was implemented?
- Look at the customer complaint statistics and determine whether they have decreased by a significant degree
- Has the number of service deliveries increased?
- Has the collective knowledge of the organisation's employees increased?

Step 5: Implement the plan
- Structure engineers into level 1, level 2 and level 3 to provide a fast and orderly knowledge transfer (training) and customer service
- Facilitate engineers to make use of knowledge base to foster knowledge creation and transfer between 10 call centres worldwide
- Give incentives half yearly to engineers who submit their knowledge online and train other engineers to respond to customers with a wider range of knowledge

Step 4: Devise plan and success criteria
- Percentage of engineers' half yearly incentives on the amount of knowledge they submitted online
- Incentives given for facilitating mentoring and training other engineers
- Create an ongoing knowledge base for the latest solutions to customers' product and systems problems
- Structure the knowledge workers into level 1 (simple queries), level 2 (intermediate queries) and level 3 (advanced queries)

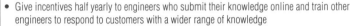

Step 3: Verify/falsify potential problem or opportunity
- Lack of knowledge transfer
- Slower customer service and lower quality
- Lack of knowledge-based incentives

Verify

Falsify

Step 2: Detect potential problem or opportunity
- Lack of knowledge-sharing culture
- Lack of training or structure to share knowledge
- Lack of recognition placed on knowledge sharing and transfer
- Customer complaints

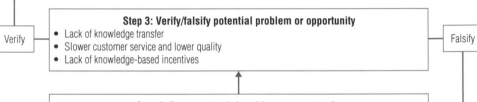

Step 1: Analyse environmental factors

Step 1a: HR issues: Monitor/ analyse data (past, present and future)
- New engineers hesitant to share their technical knowledge
- Acquisition of new companies
- Lack of service speed and quality
- Lack of incentives to transfer knowledge
- Lack of motivation to share new skills and information

Step 1b: Internal/organisational environment
- Unwillingness to share based on insecure culture
- Acquisition
- Lack of knowledge management
- Lack of strategic link between knowledge and business objectives (e.g. accurate, speedy and high-quality customer service)
- Inadequate knowledge creation strategy
- Inadequate knowledge transfer structure

Step 1c: External environment
- IT industry regulation on intellectual property
- Increased competition in IT industry
- Customer: worldwide increased complaints
- Low employee substitutability

Connecting people to people and people to knowledge

Professional services organisations sell their knowledge and expertise. Their employees are clearly knowledge workers, and these organisations face unique challenges in harnessing the knowledge of their employees and communicating and leveraging that knowledge for the benefit of clients. The ability to maximise and transfer knowledge is truly the competitive advantage of a professional services organisation. Consequently, this issue is attracting a great deal of attention in this industry.

Knowledge management is referred to in the chapter as the process of developing and controlling the intellectual capital of employees. Knowledge management activities include creating a learning environment where employees gather and share knowledge that benefits the performance of the organisation, and making sure the knowledge is readily available and transferable. The effective management of knowledge incorporates the identification, capture and transfer (or retrieval when required) between individuals within the organisation. To be a truly effective strategy, employee cooperation, clear direction, management support and appropriate human and technological organisation systems are required to create the right environment and organisational culture for sharing knowledge.

The catch cry for knowledge management at GHD, a privately owned international professional services company, is 'Connecting People to People and People to Knowledge'. GHD employs around 4500 people in a network of offices throughout Australia, New Zealand, Asia, the Middle East and the Americas. Its team of architects, engineers, drafters, planners, scientists, management consultants and economists serve the global market sectors of infrastructure, mining and industry, defence, property and buildings, and the environment. Projects range widely. A small sample is the design and development of moving sightscreens for the Melbourne Cricket Ground, master plans for manmade islands in Dubai, designing noise attenuation resulting in the world's quietest Caterpillar truck for a mine in the Hunter Valley (in New South Wales, Australia) and the development of a National Flood Management Strategy for China.

GHD was established in 1928 and today is ranked in the world's top 30 engineering and architecture companies. Annual turnover for the year 2004/05 was AUD$401.9 million, an increase of 28 per cent on the previous year. Growth has been mainly organic despite acquisitions in Australia, New Zealand and the Middle East, and staff numbers have increased by 1000 in the last 12 months. The company recruited a record number of graduates, over 140, in 2005, an increase of 75 on the preceding year.

Formalising a knowledge management plan (KMP) for GHD is seen as an integral part of responding to and managing this phenomenal growth in business and record numbers of new staff. GHD's Corporate Knowledge Manager, Steven Young, is a civil engineer who has been with GHD for 17 years. Mr Young has worked on and managed GHD's input into a range of civil infrastructure projects and has always had an interest from the application of business systems to enhance GHD's position. Says Mr Young, 'The scale and geographic spread of the company's operations, and the diversity of services provided by our people, now requires more systems when it comes to knowledge management. Historically, this is something we have done well at GHD through a combination of informal and formal systems. Our people have understood where the skills and experience lie and have been able to access people and records in an effective way. The parameters have shifted now that we employ more than 4000 people globally, with 1000 of those joining in the last year.'

GHD's formal matrix structure is intentionally based around the development of GHD informal communities of shared interest, where people share knowledge and experiences in the course of their work.

The company structure is built around 18 geographically spread Operating Centres. The Operating Centres' key roles are to foster and maintain GHD's brand and relationships with clients, manage and develop its employees' business and technical skills, maintain a forward workload by bidding for client project consultancy services and deliver successful project outcomes for clients. Each project requires the establishment of a project team drawing the right mix of GHD's resources to define, manage and deliver a knowledge-based outcome to meet client needs. Says Mr Young, 'There is an ongoing requirement to look for creative and innovative solutions to meet the Operating Centre and project needs'.

To achieve these outcomes, employees are grouped into Service Group teams of 10 to 30 people, according to a combination of work functions, market areas, client relationships and employee skill sets, to deliver these Operating Centre outcomes. Typically, there may be 50 or more projects being delivered concurrently by a larger Service Group.

The matrix-based structure also sees GHD people belonging to Service Lines, which are communities of staff with practice-based and technical experience. There are 58 Service Lines associated with the development of technical experience and capability across GHD's global operations. Each Service Line has a leader and a network of technical specialists in the Operating Centres to guide and mentor the development of staff and to advance their careers in these technical areas.

Finally, 16 Business Streams overlay the operations, reflecting the key markets which GHD provides knowledge-based services. A Business Stream Leader has the role of promoting GHD's profile in the market, driving the strategic business development activities and coordinating the management of strategic client relationships across multiple operating centres.

This structure sounds complex but on a day-to-day basis it functions very effectively and almost seamlessly for clients and staff, facilitating the movement of knowledge ideas and experience across the organisation.

A further unique feature of GHD's structure is the fact that it has no head office, rather, senior executives are located in their home office and travel regularly for meetings and to keep in touch with the different Operating Centres' management teams and staff, again facilitating the exchange of knowledge. GHD's rapid growth and increased size has necessitated the establishment of corporate management roles in disciplines such as people, information services, marketing, knowledge and risk. These are needed to support the operations and to provide the focus and resources required to enhance capabilities across Operating Centres.

The KMP, along with other initiatives such as the GHD Business School, a virtual school that provides training and development to all employees, was launched to support GHD's structure as described above and GHD's five-year strategy plan, *Strategy Towards 2010*. When announcing the strategy, GHD Chairman Clive Weeks commented, 'The focal points of *Strategy Towards 2010* are Clients, People and Performance. These focal points recognise that our business is about our clients, their stakeholders and our people, and how they work together to achieve outstanding performance.'

The KMP acknowledges that GHD's business is based on its people's collective knowledge and experience which enables them to deliver services to meet clients' needs, and the many different ways all GHD people contribute to the business. The KMP takes informal and effective systems and encourages people to continue these practices, while embedding them further in more formal systems and supporting them with technology. The KMP is designed to become an integral part of working at GHD, not an onerous chore. As Mr Young comments, 'The anticipated outcome will be the ability to source information held by our people to explore resources and experiences available to respond to clients' needs and create opportunities for GHD people'.

The approach to the implementation of the KMP at GHD has been carefully staged and managed. Mr Young explains, 'The roll-out of the KMP is an important part of developing our people's understanding of what this initiative means to them. As part of our staff induction process we explain the KMP, and explain that as a company we are leveraging a more common approach for the benefit of our people and our clients. We also acknowledge existing efforts of our people to share knowledge and information, and explain the KMP and discuss what it means to them, to give them the confidence to apply the practices and invite their further cooperation in this important initiative. Key takeaway messages from the briefings include, "everyone has a role to play" and "if it is good enough to keep, then it is good enough to share".'

At the end of the briefing, staff are invited to reflect on how they can contribute to knowledge management as part of their day to day work. Mr Young explained that the intention of this was to acknowledge and encourage people's current efforts.

The professionals employed by GHD to develop and deliver wide-ranging and innovative projects around the world clearly bring diverse skills and experience. The broader philosophy and values of GHD encourage and promote a learning environment where employees' skills and knowledge are valued, and where they formally and informally share their knowledge and experience. A stated organisational goal is to establish a culture of shared responsibility for the harnessing of people's skills and experience, and for overall knowledge management. The inclusion of the KMP as a key tool assists with the delivery of the company's five-year *Strategy Towards 2010*, and clearly signals the intent to use knowledge management as a tool to harness this knowledge more effectively to deliver results for GHD's clients and people.

Discussion questions

1. How does GHD's matrix structure contribute to the management of knowledge across this organisation?
2. Imagine you are the newly appointed HR manager of a firm of architects with offices in Australia (four offices) and Indonesia (two offices). Your managing director has asked you to make suggestions about ways of improving the transfer of knowledge between staff across offices. Use the case study to assist you in making some broad suggestions.
3. Review GHD's approach to knowledge management described above. How could it contribute to an HR strategy to attract and retain staff?

Easy-going Australian managers 'just get the job done'   **A manager's challenge**

An international study has found that Australian managers are more easy-going than their overseas counterparts, encouraging workers to 'just get the job done'. This phenomenon seems to undermine seriously the knowledge management philosophy of innovation and creativity as the focus is on job completion, rather than fostering a learning environment. The findings suggest that the time spent correcting poor performers is influenced by a country's management style. Despite their autonomous technique, Australian managers were found to be increasingly suspicious of strong leadership and vision, and spent more time (approximately 12 per cent of their work time) correcting others' mistakes than did their international colleagues in Sweden, the USA and the Netherlands. British managers were found to share similar traits to Australians, but with a higher priority on developing employees' competence.

The Australian Prime Minister John Howard warns that Australia is experiencing a shortage of skilled workers to drive the economy, and calls for Australian managers to be more proactive in valuing, rewarding and developing high achievers. There needs to be a fundamental culture shift to recognise the value of managing human resources effectively rather than just getting the job done.

Source: Adapted from Gettler, L. (2005), 'Our bosses not so bossy, but the job gets done', *The Age*, 10 February, p. B3.

Summary

This topic examined the SHRM role of knowledge management, organisational culture and innovation and creativity. SHRM should be integrated into this strategic management process in order to create, transfer and institutionalise organisational knowledge. There are several ways that this can be achieved. First, however, it is important to recognise the different types of knowledge that exist within an organisation. These include tacit, explicit, human, social and structured knowledge. Once this knowledge has been recognised, it is imperative to understand what knowledge work is, which is simply the discretionary behaviour that results in the end product of knowledge being delivered.

Employees, or knowledge workers, develop knowledge work. This might include scientists, professors or gardeners and, as such, includes both white- and blue-collar employees. Knowledge has an important and strategic link to SHRM because knowledge is influenced by strategic organisational processes. HR managers need to leverage organisational knowledge to achieve organisational flexibility and versatility to cope with the dynamic environment.

Knowledge management, which is another key function of HRM, is the process of developing and controlling the intellectual capital of employees. This is critical to survival in the twenty-first century where the focus of valuable assets has changed from machinery to people. However, knowledge isn't easily managed and it is important that knowledge management be aligned with the strategic goals of the company to ensure that the entire company is moving in the same direction. One way to develop knowledge is through continual learning, or becoming a learning organisation. This is a type of organisation which has the ability to change and adapt continuously to new environments and circumstances, through the acquisition of new knowledge. To truly become a learning organisation, the organisational culture must reflect and foster the desire to learn, supported by senior management and the HRM department. However, despite the benefits of becoming a learning organisation, not all organisations are required or have the capacity to become one. Innovativeness and creativity play an important role in this quest. Finally, this chapter addressed some of the implications and issues for knowledge management, such as cultural differences, how to retain knowledge and the impact knowledge has on the psychological contract.

Key terms

creativity

culture

double-loop learning

individual knowledge

innovation

knowledge

knowledge management

knowledge transfer

knowledge work

knowledge workers

learning organisation

organisational knowledge

organisational learning

single-loop learning

strategic knowledge
    management

strategic management

Review questions

3.1 Briefly describe the different types of knowledge, citing examples for each within the realm of HRM.

3.2 What is one of the biggest challenges for HRM departments regarding knowledge?

3.3 Are both blue- and white-collar employees 'knowledge workers'? Give examples to support your answer.

3.4 Define strategic knowledge management. Why is it so significant in today's workforce? How does SHRM facilitate strategic knowledge management?

3.5 What is the difference between organisational learning and the learning organisation? Can the learning organisation ever really exist?

3.6 What are some HRM issues and implications for managing knowledge? How might these be overcome?

Exercises

3.1 Think of a time when you have learnt how to do something. Using the five steps of knowledge creation, describe each step in relation to your example. If there are some steps which were skipped, explain why and the impact (if any) this had on the knowledge creation.

3.2 Critically evaluate how one organisation manages organisational learning through the following factors: (1) technology; (2) organisational infrastructure; (3) corporate culture; (4) knowledge; and (5) people. If you were the HR manager of this company, how would you enhance the learning?

3.3 What kind of visible and invisible dimensions of culture can you interpret or perceive from your tertiary institution? How do these compare with other organisations you have encountered?

3.4 Tony, the branch IT manager at Ardski, recently developed a new system for streamlining online transactions. Shortly afterwards, he was headhunted by a rival company. As HR manager at Ardski, how would you control Tony's knowledge management? In your answer, discuss some of the issues associated with strategic knowledge management.

3.5 Assume that you are the CEO of a major international corporation. Your HR manager has just been to a seminar on learning organisations and wants your company to become one. Devise a strategy for becoming a learning organisation, taking into consideration some of the implications of this transition.

3.6 Referring to Figure 3.5, use the five questions to test your knowledge management. Base your answers on a task you perform well or are familiar with.

References

Alavi, M. & Leidner, D. E. (2001), 'Review: Knowledge management and knowledge management systems: Conceptual foundations and research issues', *MIS Quarterly*, vol. 25, no. 1, pp. 107–36.

Appelbaum, S. H. & Gallagher, J. (2000), 'The competitive advantage of organizational learning', *Journal of Workplace Learning: Employee Counselling Today*, vol. 12, no. 2, pp. 40–56.

Argyris, C. (1991), 'Teaching smart people how to learn', *Harvard Business Review*, vol. 69, no. 3, pp. 99–109.

Argyris, C. & Schön, D. A. (1996), *Organizational Learning II: Theory,*

Method, and Practice, Addison-Wesley, Reading.

Bentley, T. (1990), 'The knowledge workers', *Management Accounting–London*, vol. 68, no. 3, p. 47.

Carter, C. & Scarbrough, H. (2001), 'Towards a second generation of KM? The people management issue', *Education and Training*, vol. 43, no. 4/5, pp. 215–24.

Contu, A., Grey, C. & Örtenblad, A. (2003), 'Against learning', *Human Relations*, vol. 56, no. 8, pp. 931–52.

De Long, D. W. & Fahey, L. (2000), 'Diagnosing cultural barriers to knowledge management', *The Academy of Management Executive*, vol. 14, no. 4, pp. 113–27.

Dhanaraj, C., Lyles, M. A., Steensma, H. K. & Tihanyi, L. (2004), 'Managing tacit and explicit knowledge transfer in IJVs: The role of relational embeddedness and the impact on performance', *Journal of International Business Studies*, vol. 35, no. 5, pp. 428–42.

Drucker, P. F. (1999), 'Knowledge-worker productivity: The biggest challenge', *California Management Review*, vol. 4, pp. 79–94.

Drucker, P. F. (2005), 'Managing oneself', *Harvard Business Review*, vol. 83, no. 1, pp. 100–9.

Easterby-Smith, M. (1997), 'Disciplines of organizational learning: Contributions and critiques', I, vol. 50, no. 9, pp. 1085–1113.

Fiol, C. M. & Lyles, M. A. (1985), 'Organizational learning', *Academy of Management Review*, vol. 10, no. 4, pp. 803–13.

Galer, G. & van der Heijden, K. (1992), 'The learning organization: How planners create organizational learning', *Marketing Intelligence and Planning*, vol. 10, no. 6, pp. 5–12.

Garvin, D. A. (1993), 'Building a learning organization', *Harvard Business Review*, vol. 71, no. 1, pp. 78–91.

Gettler, L. (2005), 'Our bosses not so bossy, but the job gets done', *The Age* (Business Section), 10 February, p. 3.

Gómez, C. (2004), 'The influence of environmental, organizational, and HRM factors on employee behaviors in subsidiaries: A Mexican case study of organizational learning', *Journal of World Business*, vol. 39, no. 1, pp. 1–11.

Härtel, C. E. J., Härtel, G. F. & Barney, M. F. (1998), 'SHAPE: Improving decision-making by aligning organizational characteristics with decision-making requirements and training employees in a metacognitive framework for decision-making and problem-solving', *Training Research Journal: The Science and Practice of Training*, vol. 4, pp. 79–101.

Härtel, C. E. J., Zerbe, W. J. & Ashkanasy, N. M. (2005), *Emotions in Organizational Behavior*, Lawrence Erlbaum Associates, Mahwah.

Hislop, D. (2003), 'Linking human resource management and knowledge management via commitment: A review and research agenda', *Employee Relations*, vol. 25, no. 1/2, pp. 182–202.

Holland, J. L. (1985), *Making Vocational Choices: A Theory of Vocational Personalities and Work Environments*, 2nd edn, Prentice Hall, Englewood Cliffs.

Huber, G. P. (1991), 'Organizational learning: The contributing processes and the literatures', *Organization Science*, vol. 2, no. 1, pp. 88–115.

Jankowicz, D. (2000), 'From "learning organization" to "adaptive organization" ', *Management Learning*, vol. 31, no. 4, pp. 471–90.

Kelloway, E. K. & Barling, J. (2000), 'Knowledge work as organizational behavior', *International Journal of*

Management Reviews, vol. 2, no. 3, pp. 287–304.

Kirton, M. J. (1976), 'Adaptors and innovators: A description measure', *Journal of Applied Psychology*, vol. 61, no. 5, pp. 622–9.

Kirton, M. J. & McCarthy, R. M. (1988), 'Cognitive climate and organizations', *Journal of Occupational Psychology*, vol. 61, pp. 175–84.

Lehr, J. K. & Rice, R. E. (2002), 'Organizational measures as a form of knowledge management: A multitheoretic, communication-based exploration', *Journal of the American Society for Information Science and Technology*, vol. 53, no. 12, pp. 1060–73.

McDermott, R. & O'Dell, C. (2001), 'Overcoming cultural barriers to sharing knowledge', *Journal of Knowledge Management*, vol. 5, no. 1, pp. 76–82.

Nonaka, I. & Takeuchi, H. (1995), *The Knowledge-Creation Company: How Japanese Companies Create the Dynamics of Innovation*, Oxford University Press, New York.

Nyhan, B., Cressey, P., Tomassini, M., Kelleher, M. & Poell, R. (2004), 'European perspectives on the learning organisation', *Journal of European Industrial Training*, vol. 28, no. 1, pp. 67–92.

Pizer, M. & Härtel, C. E. J. (2005), 'For better or worse: Organizational Culture and Emotions', in *Emotions in Organizational Behavior*, eds C. E. J. Härtel, W. J. Zerbe & N. M. Ashkanasy, Lawrence Erlbaum Associates, Mahwah.

Porth, S. J., McCall, J. & Bausch, T. A. (1999), 'Spiritual themes of the "learning organization"', *Journal of Organizational Change Management*, vol. 12, no. 3, pp. 211–20.

Prokesch, S. E. (1997), 'Unleashing the power of learning: An interview with British Petroleum's John Browne', *Harvard Business Review*, vol. 77, no. 5, pp. 147–68.

Redding, J. C. & Catalanello, J. C. (1994), *Strategic Readiness: The Making of the Learning Organization*, Jossey-Bass Publishers, San Francisco.

Robertson, M. & O'Malley Hammersley, G. (2000), 'Knowledge management practices within a knowledge-intensive firm: The significance of the people management dimension', *Journal of European Industrial Training*, vol. 24, no. 2–4, pp. 241–53.

Rodriguez, J. M. & Ordonez de Pablos, P. (2002), 'Strategic human resource management: An organisational learning perspective', *International Human Resource Management*, vol. 2, no. 3/4, pp. 254–9.

Schein, E. H. (1996), 'Three cultures of management: The key to organizational learning', *Sloan Management Review*, vol. 38, no. 1, pp. 9–20.

Scott-Ladd, B. & Chan, C. C. A. (2004), 'Emotional intelligence and participation in decision-making: Strategies for promoting organizational learning and change', *Strategic Change*, vol. 13, pp. 95–105.

Senge, P. M. (1994), *The Fifth Discipline: The Art and Practice of the Learning Organization*, Random House Australia, Sydney.

Sohal, A. & Morrison, M. (1995), 'TQM and the learning organization', *Managing Service Quality*, vol. 5, no. 6, pp. 32–4.

Tidd, J., Bessant, J. & Pavitt, K. (2005), *Managing Innovation: Integrating Technological, Market and Organizational Change*, 3rd edn, John Wiley & Sons, Chichester.

Ulrich, D. (1998), 'Intellectual Capital = Competence x Commitment', *Sloan Management Review*, vol. 39, no. 2, pp. 15–16.

Yahya, S. & Goh, W. K. (2002), 'Managing human resources toward achieving knowledge management', *Journal of Knowledge Management*, vol. 6, no. 5, pp. 457–68.

Chapter 4

Technology and strategic human resource management

INTRODUCTION

This chapter examines the strategic synergy between technology and SHRM, and how managers can utilise technology to manage human resources more efficiently and effectively. Part 1 of this textbook identified a number of significant changes that we face in the twenty-first century, such as increased competition, globalisation, diversity and technological advancements. Although all of these issues are equally important for managers to examine, this chapter focuses on the role of technology in this information era, and how it impacts on SHRM. Specifically, it examines the benefits and drawbacks of interfacing IT with HRM practices, and the role of creating, developing and maintaining human resource information systems (HRISs), which are a vital component for business survival. This chapter draws from previous chapters and examines how human resources can be leveraged through the strategic capability of IT, which acts as a catalyst for achieving a competitive advantage.

Objectives

The primary objective of this chapter is to introduce you to the important relationship between technology and SHRM.

After reading this chapter you should be able to:

- identify how technology plays a vital part in today's SHRM process;
- distinguish between the various types of HRM technology and the role of communication within each;
- describe online learning processes and how they can be used by HR managers;
- understand how an HRIS may be developed and utilised by HRM to achieve strategic goals;
- identify benefits and implications of technology integration with SHRM.

The technology era

As the world rapidly changes we are increasingly aware that we are now living in the technology era. IT has transformed the way we do business and, consequently, the way we manage our human resources. The days of a paper-based society are slowing fading and the emergence of an exciting and fast-paced technology era is upon us. Technology can help us to achieve goals faster and more efficiently and effectively than our competitors. However, many senior managers ask 'How is technology integrated with HRM? What is the price that organisations and employees pay?' Most importantly, 'Is it worthwhile?'. This chapter addresses these questions and discusses some of the implications for the new relationship between technology and SHRM.

Following on from Part 1, which discussed the importance of SHRM in today's competitive business environment, this chapter focuses on the relationship between technology and SHRM. It is imperative to understand how technology and SHRM can provide a highway for organisational human capital by fostering the learners (i.e. individuals, groups and organisations) to learn faster and smarter through leveraging human capital (i.e. knowledge, skills and abilities). For technology to reap human capital it needs to be well integrated with the planned strategic management process. So, how is this achieved?

HOW CAN HRM BE LEVERAGED THROUGH TECHNOLOGY?

Activists of HRM strongly promote the notion that we are living in a transient world and that future technology is paving the way for a very different HRM from what we once knew. This new HRM, referred to as **virtual HRM**, implies that computer technology is used to recruit, train, develop and monitor human resources. How and why this technology is used is dependent on the organisation: its culture, resources, size, strategic fit and, of course, its human resources. Unlike virtual HRM, e-HRM is 'a way of implementing HR strategies, policies, and practices in organizations through a conscious and directed support of and/or with the full use of web-technology-based channels' (Ruël, Bondarouk & Looise, 2004, p. 365). This involves developing and maintaining HRM within organisations. According to Wright and Dyer (2000), there are three ways that e-HRM can be integrated into a company (see Figure 4.1).

virtual HRM
Computer technology used to recruit, train, develop and monitor human resources.

1. *Transactional activities*. These include general HRM administrative responsibilities, such as payroll and compensation administration. For example, HR managers can either pay employees via a cheque (paper based) or by directly depositing into a bank account (technology based).
2. *Traditional activities*. These refer to the functional areas of HRM, such as recruitment and selection, training and development, performance management, appraisal and rewards. For example, advertisements for vacant positions may be advertised in newspapers (paper based) or on websites (i.e. company websites or online agencies such as seek.com or careerone.com) (technology based). These traditional activities consume a substantial amount of an HR manager's time and energy.
3. *Transformational activities*. These include strategic HRM functions such as culture and knowledge management, and organisational change and renewal. For example, employees attending training seminars can either store new knowledge in hardcopy (paper based) or soft copy (technology based). These high-value activities are the most important aspect of a manager's job, yet due to time and resource constraints, very few HR managers dedicate sufficient time to transformational activities.

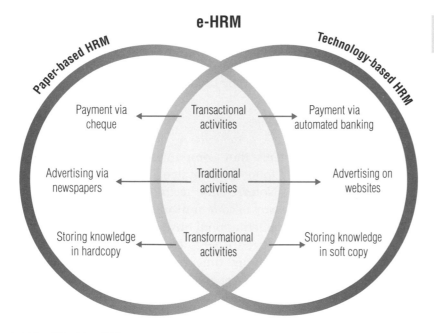

4.1 FIGURE
How e-HRM can be integrated into a company

Source: Adapted from Wright & Dyer (2000), p. 58.

HRM technology

Information technology is not a new phenomenon. Everywhere we look, technology surrounds us. Computers, which once took up the space of a small room, are now so compact and innovative that they fit into the palm of your hand. Mobile phones, which were once large and bulky, are now incredibly small, yet have a myriad of additional uses, such as camera, email and Internet functions. Even cars have benefited from technology; smaller, lightweight cars with bigger engines are being built all the time, with advanced safety mechanisms and computer-generated assistance such as global positioning systems (GPS). Technology has advanced so far and so quickly in the past decade that things we only ever dreamed of are now reality. But what actually constitutes technology in HRM?

The degree and type of technology differs across industries. Scientific, manufacturing, engineering and agricultural industries all use different types of technological equipment. Quite often this includes large machinery and specialised technology to enable mass production or conduct scientific research, such as within laboratories. However, to manage human resources, different types of technology are used. These do not include mass-producing machinery and are usually technologically based to improve communication and efficiency. Hence, when used appropriately, HRM technology is a mechanism for organisational effectiveness.

Although HRM technology is relatively straightforward (in comparison to high-tech machinery used in other industries), it forms an integral part of the organisation. Three decades ago, companies would not have heard of email or the Internet, yet today we wonder how they ever lived without them. Technology provides us with a world of knowledge and enables goals to be achieved faster, better and smarter than ever before but only if used in a way that fits the organisation's situation and objectives (i.e. SHRM Application Tool thinking). It changes the way we approach work tasks and our interaction with others. As technology continues to evolve, so too does the organisation.

The types of HRM technology used by organisations are depicted in Figure 4.2 and are discussed in detail below.

EMAIL

There are various email systems that companies can use to communicate. Companies can choose either tailor-made systems or generic brands, such as Microsoft Outlook® and Lotus Notes®. HRM technology includes email because this is an efficient and effective way to communicate. There are several benefits of using email. First, in this era of international business, diminishing geographical borders mean that business is not restricted to traditional working hours. Hence, emails can be sent and received at any time, regardless of where the business is being conducted. This is a significant benefit for international colleagues as they are unhindered by time differences which can make communication problematic. Second, because emails can be stored in the system, they allow knowledge recollection at any time. In fact, email storage is one example of knowledge management (discussed in Chapter 3). This is a significant advantage as it improves effectiveness through accurate data collection and knowledge retention, whereas verbal communication (i.e. face to face or via the telephone) relies on memory, which increases the likelihood of error. Third, email is an efficient way of communicating with a large number of people at once. This is especially useful when company-wide messages are distributed. For example, at Deakin University, updates on Enterprise Bargaining Agreements (EBAs) are emailed by HR managers to all staff regularly, which saves time and effort. In addition, copies of

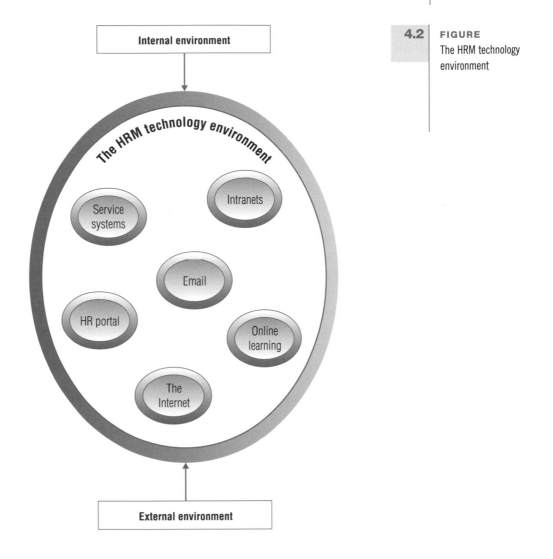

4.2   FIGURE
The HRM technology
environment

one email may be sent to several staff members through carbon copy (cc) and blind carbon copy (bcc). This is valuable when emailing an important message to functional managers (i.e. marketing, accounting, finance) and sending a carbon copy to the CEO so they are aware of what message was distributed, when it was sent and who received it.

However, there are a number of disadvantages with email. The primary disadvantage is that it can be perceived as impersonal. It is difficult to convey emotion (except by using specific wording) and because there is no personal contact the receiver is often unaware of the sender's tone, and vice versa. One way to combat this is by using capital letters to emphasise a point. In technical terms, capital letters imply the sender is 'yelling' so the emotion conveyed is anger, frustration or a sense of urgency. Other variations include inserting a 'smiley' face (i.e. ☺) or other caricatures to personalise the message.

In addition to the impersonality of email, it is also difficult to know whether the message has been read or received successfully. Often, email addresses become invalid when employees leave the company. Likewise, error probability is quite high; just one incorrect or missing letter will cause the email to fail or 'bounce' back. The benefit of this is that the sender knows the email hasn't been received and can try an alternative address or communication mode. An additional function on modern email systems is the request of a 'return receipt', which sends an automatic email when the reader has opened the email, thus senders know when their email is received. However, systems such as Eudora give the reader the option of not sending this receipt or sending it later, so it is at the discretion of the receiver to formalise receipt confirmation and, hence, effective communication. A further disadvantage is an over-reliance on email. Quite often employees send an email to colleagues who are within close proximity rather than simply walking over to them. HR managers need to encourage staff to communicate face to face for minor matters and develop a culture of open and appropriate communication.

THE INTERNET

Since its conception in the 1980s, the Internet has become an excellent source of communication between organisations and their customers. Today, most companies have their own website which promotes their mission and vision, as well as the products and/or services that are on offer. In essence, company websites are another marketing tool as they are an external network. They provide enormous benefit to both the company and customer alike; it is low-cost advertising, yet customers around the world can log on at any time and view the website. In addition to self-promotion, some websites encourage further communication with customers through customer feedback options (which are emailed directly to the company) and other contact information including local representatives and international branches.

A further benefit for HRM is that potential employees can use the Internet to gather information about the company before applying for job vacancies or being interviewed. They can discover the structure and culture of the company, the type of work they might be doing and who they might be working with, and future job opportunities, such as career advancements and international consignments. HRM can also use the Internet to profile key employees, such as those in graduate or senior management positions, to promote mentoring programs.

A downfall of Internet sites is that they require continual maintenance. Outdated information displayed on websites appears unprofessional, and customers may link this to the quality of service provided, which results in a poor reputation. For example, job advertisements need to be removed once applications have closed and an employee recruited. Likewise, 'What's New' sections need to be updated regularly; for instance, if a staff training program is advertised as 'new', yet occurred years earlier, customers may begin to wonder what the company has invested in since then.

Organisations also need to ensure that websites are attractive and user friendly. An attractive and exciting website increases the likelihood of repeat visitation, thus enhances advertising. Likewise, if the website is simple to navigate, customers will be satisfied with their experience and view the organisation positively. Alternatively, if it is not user friendly, or they cannot locate required information, then they will be unhappy, unsatisfied and frustrated with the system and possibly not return to it again. However, it isn't just customers who log on to websites. All stakeholders do, including suppliers, competitors and potential employees. Quite often, websites are the first point of contact for the organisation so they must emanate professionalism and an accurate account of the organisation.

INTRANETS

Unlike the Internet, which is an external system, **intranets** are internal networks which can only be accessed by organisational members. They contain company information only, such as new announcements, daily reminders and company-specific policies, practices and documentation. Essentially, the intranet has replaced the old company newsletter, thus enhancing the speed, efficiency and effectiveness of organisational communication.

Intranets offer the same benefits as the Internet; employees can view company information at any time and from any location, as long as it is updated knowledge and they have access to a computer. They can also discover future employment opportunities that are only advertised internally, thus gaining a competitive advantage over external job applicants. However, there are additional benefits that the intranet provides for HRM: HR portal, online learning and service systems.

intranets
Internal networks which contain company information and can only be accessed by organisational members.

HR PORTAL

Most intranets have an HR portal. This is the link to all HR-related matters, including personnel information and personal information. Personnel information includes employee contact details, including emergency contacts. Rather than complete forms to update contact information, employees can log on to the HR portal, using their password, and update the information. The benefits of this include: time saving, as there is no time wasted on completing and entering paperwork unnecessarily; error reduction, as the employee is changing the details themselves; and instantaneous update. Personal information refers to online payslips and leave information (such as holiday or conference leave). This provides a significant benefit to employees as leave may be applied for, calculated and approved online, and staff may view remaining leave at any time.

However, an HR portal not only lists employee information, but also company-preferred suppliers and their contact details. As is often the case, strategic alliances are developed with preferred suppliers because they offer the company a special discount. In order to streamline HRM and financial resources, managers should always refer to the HRIS for policies and procedures on organisational alliances.

ONLINE LEARNING

Online learning refers to virtual training and development which does not take place at a specific location, but rather when and where employees choose. It is the process of acquiring and developing new knowledge via computer-based systems (such as intranets). For this to occur, the employee simply logs on to the HR portal and clicks on the required training and development as determined by HRM or their manager. This will be different for each individual as not everyone is

online learning
Virtual training and development – the process of acquiring and developing new knowledge via computer-based systems (such as intranets).

required to complete all training and development. For instance, companies are often required to offer occupational health and safety (OHS) training to meet legal requirements. In this case, employees would receive an automatic email advising that they need to complete this training online, and giving specific dates when the training will be available (including deadlines). Employees then log on to the HR portal, complete the training (i.e. reading required materials and completing electronically submitted questions) and, once it is complete, both they and HRM receive an email stating that the employee has successfully completed this training component. This is then automatically recorded on the staff member's personal file.

Online learning has become very popular in recent years due to its proven success in reducing organisational costs and improving efficiency. It offers the company a standardised and efficient procedure for learning and fosters a culture of continual learning. Further, because it requires less paperwork, data entry and employee control (all of which are done via technology), and fewer HR staff are required, resulting in cost savings. For example, a large company might once have employed several staff in the training and development department to conduct, analyse and report the training to senior management. However, with the introduction of IT, training and analysis is automatically conducted online, and reports are generated to determine who completed the training, their result and suggested areas for improvement. This data is then fed back to the managers of trainees who use this information in performance appraisals. Therefore, the function of training and development becomes streamlined with other HRM functions, which improves the efficiency and effectiveness of the entire organisation.

Employees also benefit from online learning. Today, there is a trend for employees to work longer hours than the traditional 9 am to 5 pm. Travel (both national and international) is also often integrated into the employment contract. Therefore, because learning is conducted at a time and location which is convenient for them, employees are more willing to participate in training, which reduces resistance and increases the likelihood that the learning will be both successful and effective. This is especially useful for expatriates who often feel neglected and 'left out of the loop' with respect to their home company's activities. If employees feel happier and more satisfied in the workplace, then productivity increases and individual and organisational goals become a reality.

Successful e-learning companies such as ANZ, IBM and Qantas have productively utilised online learning to achieve strategic needs. Notably, ANZ's success with online learning is shown by their comprehensive ongoing strategic development that underpins the continual online learning agenda. In support of online learning, SHRM should assess all possible internal and external environmental factors affecting the implementation of online learning in HRM systems. Table 4.1 illustrates examples of these environmental factors.

Please read
Härtel, C. E. J. & Tilton, P. (2005), 'Australia and online learning: Lessons for effective implementation', in *Skill Formation and Globalisation*, ed. M. Powell, Ashgate Publishing, Aldershot.

TABLE 4.1	Environmental factors impacting on the implementation of online learning

Internal factors	External factors
Emerging strategies	Emerging technologies
Employee values and attitudes	Sociocultural influences
Organisational structure	Political influences
Organisational culture	Government agendas

SELF-SERVICE SYSTEMS

One of the biggest hurdles management faces is learning *how* to interface technology with HRM functions. One way that this can be accomplished is through self-service systems, which are located within the HR portal. A **self-service system** is a virtual HR menu where organisational members can make changes or additions to their personal details or access company policies or documents. There are two types of self-service systems: **employee self-service systems** (ESS) or **manager self-service systems** (MSS). The difference between the two is simply what information each requires. An ESS allows employees to access their own personal details, whereas an MSS allows managers to view and update employee records such as enrolment in training courses (see Figure 4.3).

In a recent international study analysing the effectiveness of e-HRM, companies such as Ford and IBM reported a significant increase in organisational performance and communication through the use of intranets. For example, the HR intranet at Ford was rated the most visited internal website, with 80 per cent of employees declaring the intranet the primary source for HRM. In another example, IBM reported a cost reduction of 57 per cent through e-HRM and improved organisational culture for factors such as climate for change, flexibility, enhanced communication and support for innovation and risk taking (Ruël, Bondarouk & Looise, 2004). Therefore, despite the time and cost involved in developing and maintaining intranets, the strategic benefits for the organisation far outweigh the detriments. Technology is also one way that HRM can have a tangible impact on the company's bottom line, as cost benefits are real and visible.

self-service system
A virtual HR menu where organisational members can make changes or additions to their personal details or access company policies or documents.

employee self-service systems
Allow employees to access their own personal details.

manager self-service systems
Allow managers to view and update employee records.

Human resource information system

Undoubtedly, the strategic integration of technology has facilitated more efficient and effective HRM. As the role of HRM evolves with environmental changes, so too does its capability. Today, HRM is a fully integrated organisational department, equipped with valuable resources to obtain and sustain human resources. Its role in a company is viewed as vital and it is a strategic partner contributing to overall organisational success. However, HRM hasn't always been viewed this way. Traditionally, this department was referred to as 'personnel management' and its main focus was purely administrative. Personnel staff were employed simply to

FIGURE 4.3
Self-service systems:
ESS and HSS

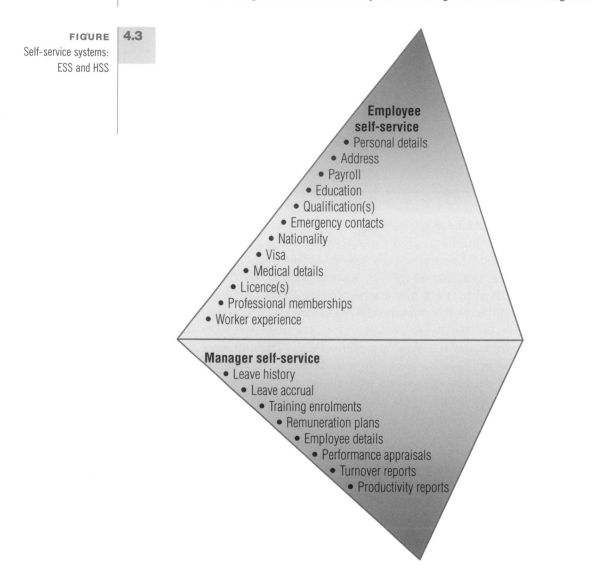

recruit new staff and process salaries. There was very little, if any, focus on career development, training and development, performance appraisals and continuous learning. Employees were simply a means to an end. The focus was on task completion as managers employed bureaucratic management styles; employees were 'seen but not heard'.

However, the rise of knowledge management and the sociocultural paradigm shift from viewing people as costs to viewing them as assets changed this view. Nowadays, managers realise that employees are an organisation's most valuable asset. Companies are willing to invest in their human resources as they understand the unique advantage employees provide. They cannot be imitated by competitors. However, unlike other resources (i.e. financial and technical), human resources can depart the company at any time, therefore they warrant special attention. The HRM function, which was once merely an administrative function, now offers a wide range of products and services to organisational members. It is impossible to provide such vast and comprehensive service effectively without the use of technology. IT enables greater access, accumulation, dissemination and control of these services. Specifically, within the realm of HRM, this technology is referred to as a human resource information system (HRIS).

FUNCTIONS OF AN HRIS

An HRIS (also referred to as computer-based human resource information systems (CHRIS)) provides the structure for all HRM functions through the use of technology. In short, it is the backbone of an organisation's HRM department. An **HRIS** is defined as an integrated technological system which accumulates, stores, maintains and analyses all data relating to a company's human resources. This includes information on the employees, and organisational policies, procedures and knowledge required to manage them effectively. Managers can use the HRIS to track staff development, from their employment history to the training they participated in. Their knowledge, skills and abilities can be checked at any time, allowing a manager to conduct skill audits to monitor individual performance and obtain important information on their progress at any time. In short, the functions of an HRIS include skill audits, performance management, recruitment, retention, training and development, project management and rewards and recognition. This improves the overall efficiency and effectiveness of SHRM. For example, Applied Business Systems, a human, payroll and financial systems consulting company, have alliances with leading HR software vendors to develop systems which have created significant cost and flexibility benefits for clients.

> **HRIS**
> An integrated technological system which accumulates, stores, maintains and analyses all data relating to a company's human resources.

To get the most out of an HRIS, the technology needs to be integrated with every HRM function. The shift from a paper-based to a technology-based system is imperative if the HRIS is to be utilised at its full capacity. Table 4.2 lists these functions and the corresponding data that is stored within the HRIS. It is clear from this table that the HRIS essentially stores all employee employment details. For example, when a new employee is recruited, it is imperative to keep e-copies of their résumés, cover letter, referee checks and test results. Managers then have this information on hand and can refer to it at any time, on a 'need to know' basis. This is especially useful when data retrieval is required quickly because all information is stored in soft copy and can be accessed at any time by authorised personnel. For instance, a manager can see if an employee has the relevant qualifications or experience when applying for promotions, or whether they have completed training courses to determine if their skills need updating. Storing data in the HRIS also facilitates the management of international staff as there are no geographical borders hindering the access and input of data onto the system. Again, this is especially useful for managing expatriates as the efficacy of the process is enhanced.

HRIS IMPLEMENTATION

Before an HRIS can be implemented there are two factors that HR managers need to consider. First, the phases of the implementation process and, second, what role HR plays in this process.

TABLE **4.2** **HR process stored within an HRIS**

HR process	Description
Employee history	Previous employment, including company, tenure and position(s) held
Recruitment	Résumé and cover letter
	Experience and qualification(s)
	Tests
	Referee and/or police checks
Selection	Who was on the selection panel
	Why the applicant was chosen
	Contract, including tenure and commencement/termination dates
Payroll	Banking and superannuation information
Job evaluation	Position description
Performance appraisals	Employee, employer and peer appraisals
	Final signed copy of performance review
Training and development	Training undertaken, including dates, duration and location
	Certification/qualification achieved
Remuneration	Salary
	Bonuses and commission (if applicable)
	Rewards and recognition
Career development	Previous roles within the company
Pension planning	Superannuation contribution (employee and employer)
	Retirement plans

THE PHASES OF HRIS IMPLEMENTATION

As with any organisational change, a carefully developed plan forms the foundation for success; 'if you fail to plan, you plan to fail'. The same principle applies to the implementation of an HRIS. People, as creatures of habit, generally dislike any new change as it disrupts current processes and presents 'fear of the unknown'. However, once employees recognise the need for the HRIS, and how it will benefit them and their job, they are likely to embrace the change, paving the way for successful implementation of an HRIS. A carefully tailored plan needs to be designed to enable this.

There are six phases that are required for the effective implementation of an HRIS (see Figure 4.4). First, a detailed plan needs to be designed by the potential users of the HRIS. This includes information such as who will use the HRIS, what tasks it needs to complete, the volume of data, the organisational size, resource constraints (i.e. human, technical and financial) and the structure and culture of the organisation. In some cases, an HRIS may not even be necessary for the company, although it may be desired. Therefore the degree of necessity needs to be ascertained.

The second phase is most crucial to the HRIS implementation. Here, a SWOT analysis is conducted. This involves analysing the strengths, weaknesses, opportunities and threats of an HRIS. Will it help the company achieve a competitive advantage? At what price? What are the benefits, detriments and implications of buying, installing, using and maintaining the HRIS? Most importantly, what is the dollar value? Senior management will generally look more favourably on the HRIS if it can clearly see the return on investment.

Third, before the process proceeds any further, approval must be sought. Usually this will be decided by senior management who either approves or disapproves the implementation of the HRIS. To do this, it will want to see a business case outlining the advantages, disadvantages, risks and opportunities associated with the HRIS, which is why a plan and SWOT analysis is necessary. In the proposal, it is essential to specify how the HRIS will contribute to organisational goals. It is not enough simply to state that it will 'improve efficiency and effectiveness'. Tangible results are necessary and these may be linked to organisational goals for added benefit. Once approval is received, the next phase begins. However, if approval is not given, this may mean going back to phases 1 and 2 and reanalysing the need and SWOT analysis, or not proceeding with the HRIS at all. This will be dependent on senior management's comments.

The fourth phase involves searching for an HRIS supplier and design. The supplier can either be in-house (internal) or a professional HRIS/IT supplier (external). Managers need to consider the needs of the organisation (and the stakeholders) and match these needs to the capability of the HRIS. Once an HRIS supplier has been found, the specific HRIS needs to be determined. Each supplier will usually suggest a few different types of HRIS, each with different functions and capabilities. A list of possible HRISs is then generated.

The fifth phase aligns the plan and the HRIS list, and considers any resource and budget constraints. Essentially, this phase examines the practicality of an HRIS. A panel of key organisational members, including senior management, HRM managers, IT and project managers (if necessary) discuss the pros and cons of each HRIS, and vote for the one which would best serve the needs of company.

The final phase is the physical implementation of the HRIS. This involves installation and staff training. Employees need to be aware in advance that the HRIS is being implemented so that resistance may be managed. However, there are no concrete timeframes as each organisation is different. Generally, the change needs to be communicated to staff as soon as senior management has approved the HRIS. It may be communicated via emails, memos, on the HR portal or in departmental seminars which clearly explain why it is necessary, how it will impact on employees and their jobs and give a timeframe (even if it is a rough estimate). It is imperative in these seminars to allow employees to voice their concern and provide feedback to management.

Although there are six phases in the implementation of an HRIS, the process is never complete. It is a continuous cycle. Constant maintenance and updating is necessary, especially as the internal and external environments change. Therefore, at any point in the process it is possible to go back to an earlier stage. Indeed, this happens after the final stage of installation as it is necessary to have a re-examination of stakeholder needs every three to six months, and also of new threats and opportunities. It is necessary during pre- and post-HRIS installation for senior management's support and commitment to continue if the HRIS is to reach its full potential.

FIGURE **4.4**
The implementation
process of an HRIS

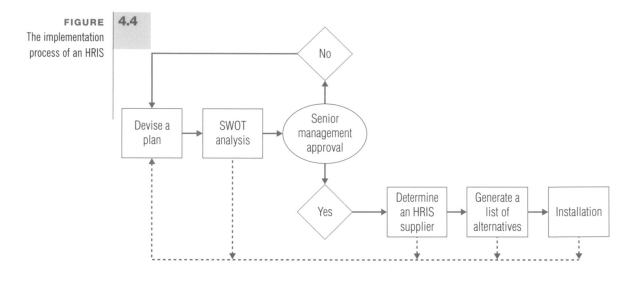

THE ROLE OF HR SPECIALISTS

HR specialists (also referred to as change agents) may take one of the following roles during the HRIS process: reactive, supportive or proactive (Martinsons & Chong, 1999). These roles infer the degree of HR involvement in the strategic formulation and implementation stages.

- *HR reactive role.* The role of HR specialists is limited to the actual installation of the new HRIS (rather than participating in the planning and designing stages). HR specialists tend to manage the consequences of the implementation, such as dissatisfaction, stress, complaints and ineffective performance, rather than the implementation itself. This approach tends to lead to negative behavioural results as managers are often entering the situation long after the problems have begun, instead of acting earlier to prevent them. This is likely to harm the integrity of HRM.

- *HR supportive role.* HR preventative policies can be developed through the anticipation of people problems. For example, appropriate support and training could be planned at specific stages of the HRIS development process. The job descriptions and reporting relationship structure may be developed to help employees' adoption of the change within anticipated timeframes.

- *HR proactive role.* HR managers are involved from the very first stage, where they determine plans which consider human factors at all stages and consequential processes of the HRIS. Senior management can obtain an ideal work structure balancing technical and HR perspectives, increasing the possibility of successful IT adoption by employees.

These three roles are depicted in the technology and SHRM model (see Figure 4.5).

Please read

Martinsons, M. G. & Chong, P. K. C. (1999), 'The influence of human factors and specialist involvement on information systems success', *Human Relations*, vol. 52, no. 1, pp. 123–52.

4.5 FIGURE
Involvement in the
implementation of
an HRIS

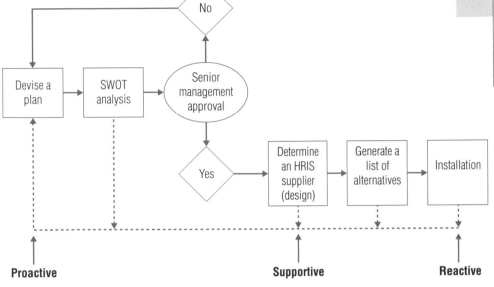

Source: Adapted from Martinsons & Chong (1999), p. 133.

BENEFITS OF AN HRIS

A well-implemented HRIS can provide numerous benefits to an organisation. However, the key is *implementation*. If an HRIS is institutionalised effectively and appropriately in the company, the benefits can be not only substantial but also long lasting.

STANDARDISATION

One of the principal challenges an organisation faces when expanding is how and when to standardise procedures. Quite often, business opportunities happen so quickly and unexpectedly that employees spend their time frantically seizing these opportunities, with little concern as to how to manage them. It isn't until after the fact that they realise how and where they stored information is inconsistent, which presents difficulties when colleagues need to access that information. An HRIS provides uniformity through templates and predetermined procedures for uploading data and downloading reports. It also means that data retrieved and viewed is in a format that is easily identifiable and user friendly. Therefore, consistency is automatically enforced. Despite differing geographical locations, it is imperative that all company offices (either national or international) adhere to the same HRIS as this expands the applicability of the data and enhances the delivery of successful SHRM.

KNOWLEDGE MANAGEMENT

An HRIS is an excellent example of a knowledge management system. As discussed in Chapter 3, knowledge management is a crucial element in successful HRM. To achieve a sustainable competitive advantage, organisations must cultivate a learning environment which forms part of the firm's culture and structure. However, cultivating such an environment is meaningless unless systems have been installed to store knowledge acquisition.

In this sense, an HRIS can house important information on the various aspects of an employee's history within the company. For example, when they commenced, the various training courses completed (i.e. OHS, first aid, diversity management) and when and where this training took place. Managers in differing departments can then access the HRIS (through the MSS) to determine where their staff can do similar training and any feedback on the usefulness of it.

HRIS IMPLICATIONS

As discussed earlier, an HRIS is an integral part of e-HRM. Coupled with other HRM technology, it allows management to facilitate more efficient and effective ways of managing staff and obtaining a competitive advantage. Not only does this benefit the company, but employees are more satisfied because of the streamlined system. Waiting for weeks for leave approval is now a thing of the past. Bureaucratically challenged HRM has shifted to an employee-focused service. However, not all HRISs are successful. There are several factors that need to be considered before, during and after HRIS implementation.

First, the HRIS needs to meet the needs of all stakeholders. This includes employees, employers, suppliers, customers, the government and any other party that affects (or is affected by) the company. To do this, managers must adopt a holistic approach to e-HRM by acknowledging and aligning the people, culture, structure, processes and HRM technology. Each of these components needs to be *strategically* aligned with the overall purpose of the organisation to ensure that all efforts and contributions move in the same direction as company goals (see Figure 4.6). Only then will the HRIS be fully implemented, accepted and successful.

As with all technology, people need to be trained in how to use the HRIS. This includes inputting, retrieving and updating data. Those who need to be trained are HRM management and staff. Ideally, they will be trained by the installers (and developers) of the HRIS, although this is dependent on who installs and develops the HRIS. For instance, if the HRIS is developed and installed in-house by the

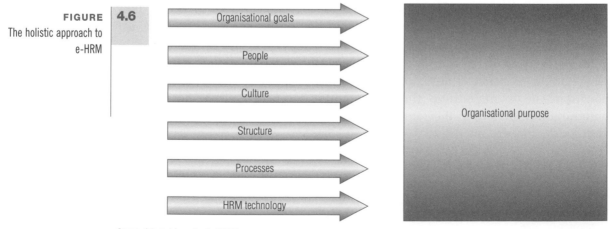

FIGURE 4.6
The holistic approach to e-HRM

- Organisational goals
- People
- Culture
- Structure
- Processes
- HRM technology

Organisational purpose

Source: Adapted from Beatty (2005).

IT department, then it will train staff. Alternatively, external HRIS vendors (who sell HRIS products) will simply install the HRIS and provide training to HR staff. Examples of HRISs used within companies include Oracle, PeopleSoft and SAP. Whether to choose an internal over an external supplier can be problematic although there are advantages of choosing one over the other (see Table 4.3).

Another consideration is the size of the organisation. Different-sized companies require different HRIS capabilities which meet their specific requirements and financial constraints. In general, smaller companies tend to use generic software such as Microsoft Access® as the foundation of their HRIS. As an HRIS is essentially a large database, Microsoft Access® sufficiently stores all data for smaller companies. However, its capacity is limited and it also acts independently of other HRM technology and systems. Despite this limitation, Microsoft Access® is a viable option for smaller companies.

For larger companies, a more sophisticated system is necessary as the amount of data, and number of people accessing the system, become more complex. In this instance, it is more efficient and effective to adopt a specialised HRIS which can be integrated with other technology. For example, an Australian company which offers HRIS solutions is Frontier Software, located in Western Australia. Frontier Software ensures that the HRIS is integrated with other IT, such as email and the Internet, and is accessed via the company's intranet. Depending on specific organisational needs, the HRIS is customised to meet all stakeholder requirements, while ensuring that confidential data is protected through appropriate security measures (Frontier Software, 2003).

As with any technology input, incorrect data entry is always a concern. While due care is taken to ensure this never occurs, it is usually caused by human, rather than technical, error. As such, no HRIS can prevent this from happening; however, systems can be put in place to guide the user. For example, rather than typing in employee details such as their preferred title, a 'drop down' box can be installed. While this does not prevent the user from choosing an incorrect title (e.g. Ms instead of Mr), it ensures that spelling mistakes, which look unprofessional, are avoided.

TABLE **4.3**   **Internal and external suppliers of HRISs**

Internal suppliers	External suppliers
• Limited expertise in HRIS development and installation	• Professionals in HRIS development and installation
• HRIS implementation is just one aspect of their job	• Usually have a passion for HRIS implementation
• Inexpensive	• Expensive
• Extensive knowledge and understanding of organisational culture	• Limited knowledge and understanding of organisational culture
• May be biased	• Unbiased
• Understand power structure	• No knowledge of power structure
• Continual post-implementation support	• Continual post-implementation support dependent on guarantee
• Long-term interest in the company	• Short-term interest in the company
• Immediate assistance	• Assistance delays possible

The difficult aspect of an HRIS is that not all staff have access to the same part of the HRIS. For example, authorised personnel may be able to view and modify data, whereas others may only be allowed to view it. This is advantageous as it reduces the likelihood of errors; if everyone had authorisation to modify data then the likelihood of errors would be high. So it allows control over the data. However, when errors are detected authorised personnel need to be notified so they can change them. This is especially problematic within large companies, such as Telstra and Westpac. Quite often minor errors, such as incorrect postcodes, are entered in customer profiles. To correct this involves completing forms and then sending the form to an authorised personnel department to amend. This is a very convoluted process for fixing such a small error and frequently, because of the nature of large, bureaucratic firms, these minor mistakes still take a long time to fix, or never are.

Most companies have now captured some aspect of the international market and hence cross-cultural implications are more prevalent now than ever before. This must be factored into a company's HRIS. For most of the Western world, using technology (and especially the Internet and intranet) is second nature. However, in comparison, people in Eastern Europe, Latin America, the Middle East and Africa have significantly less access to and use of technology, but this is changing (see Table 4.4). This needs to be taken into consideration when designing, implementing and training staff in the HRIS. For example, multinational companies may implement an HRIS that can be viewed in different languages, to suit the needs of international users. Further, additional training and computers may be purchased for offices with limited computer access and knowledge. Alternatively, smaller offices may maintain a paper-based HRIS, while larger ones utilise a technology-based HRIS.

A final implication of the HRIS is that the implementation is never final. Maintenance is continuous as the HRIS must be updated with new data, software and hardware. Staff need to be trained with every new change, as do newly employed staff. However, it is not just continual training that is the issue. Organisational and stakeholder needs constantly change, and when they do the HRIS needs to be reanalysed to ensure that it still meets their needs. Modifications are necessary and companies need to ensure that they have sufficient personnel and financial support to update the HRIS successfully.

TABLE   4.4   **Proportion of Internet use by world region**

Region	2000	2005
North America	43.2%	30.2%
Western Europe	25.1%	27.9%
Asia–Pacific	20.6%	24.8%
Latin America	5.6%	7.3%
Eastern Europe	3.1%	5.9%
Middle East/Africa	2.3%	3.8%

Source: *The Industry Standard*, 14 February 2000, cited in DeFidelto & Slater (2005), p. 278.

Please read

Hendrickson, A. R. (2003), 'Human resource information systems: Backbone technology of contemporary human resources', *Journal of Labor Research*, vol. 24, no. 3, pp. 381–94.

HRM implications

Despite the benefits, technology and SHRM are not without their limitations. Undoubtedly, e-HRM has reduced the administrative workload required by HR managers, so that this function has now changed from a 'personnel' focus to developing and maintaining an organisation's most valuable assets: human resources. However, systems have to be in place for technology and SHRM to work effectively and HR managers need to analyse the culture, structure and overall strategic vision of the company to ensure technology will be accepted and benefit the organisation in the way it was intended.

WHAT DOES ORGANISATIONAL CULTURE HAVE TO DO WITH IT?

As with any change within an organisation, the implementation of technology needs to be understood by employees if they are to adopt it successfully. There can be a lot of hype associated with new technology, but not all technology is necessary in companies. For example, high-tech telephone systems to replace older models may be advantageous, although not always essential. Further, when these new systems are installed, staff need to be educated in how to use them. In some cases, because staff are unaware of the need for newer systems, they revert to using the same phone functions they always have and avoid learning additional functions. Hence, it is a waste of financial and technical resources. If new technology is to be implemented, it must be supported with appropriate training.

The climate for change also needs to be open to new technology. Put simply, the culture and technology need to align. For this to occur, the company strategy, structure and culture may need to be revised once the technology is implemented. For example, if the culture implies that employees are afraid of new technology (as is generally the case with older-generation employees) then HR managers need to consider whether it is worth installing. The first step is to conduct a gap analysis and determine what restraining forces are impeding the technological change, such as employee resistance or lack of training. HR managers then need to address these factors by actively reducing restraining forces, rather than increasing driving forces (see Chapter 1 for a definition and discussion of gap analysis).

STRATEGIC INTEGRATION

The key to successful HRM technology is strategic integration. A recent report by the Australian Auditor General found that many federal government agencies were relying on independent, manual systems and were not realising the full potential of their HRIS (Australian National Audit Office, 2004). The implementation of IT must be aligned with future goals and resources to ensure it will impact positively on the growth and goal achievement of the organisation. IT systems that are poorly planned, developed and executed can impede individual, group and organisational effectiveness. As such, technology failure within HRM is attributed to human, rather than technical, factors (Jones & Brown, 2004). This highlights the importance of an active and participative approach by HR managers in IT implementation. Quite often, unsuccessful IT ventures are the result of managers' late involvement in the process which leads to resistance to change, an unsupportive culture and an expensive underutilised technology system.

An Australian survey recently revealed that many HRIS users are unsatisfied with their system. Only 20 per cent of respondents reported that their HRIS was a valuable investment, with 17 per cent of respondents reporting that the HRIS helped them achieve over three-quarters of their goals, and 56 per cent stating that they would invest in another HRIS. However, only 44 per cent have integrated their HRIS with other systems, such as payroll and finance (Ogier, 2003). These findings indicate that unless the HRIS is implemented strategically with the company's structure, culture and processes there is a high probability that it will yield less than satisfactory results.

THE IMPACT OF TECHNOLOGY
In addition to a supportive culture and the strategic integration of technology, there are other implications for HRM regarding IT implementation. The most important factor is that the goal of technology implementation is clear to everyone. It must fit the needs of employees, employers and customers, and HRM must take an active role in ensuring that their needs are met. Goals that are unclear, unrealistic or too technology driven will affect the success of the technology implementation (Ruël, Bondarouk & Looise, 2004).

FLOW-ON EFFECTS OF TECHNOLOGY IMPLEMENTATION
One of most pressing issues is the impact IT has on unemployment. The introduction of new, streamlined IT systems (whether it is in the HRM department or otherwise) results in a decreased need for employees to perform jobs that are now being done by technology. In e-HRM, this is particularly the case where administrative procedures become automated, thus reducing the requirement for administrative staff. In other organisational areas, such as production and engineering, more technology and machinery replace the human element and again the HR department has the responsibility of deploying or retrenching these employees. All of this must be conducted with the utmost sensitivity and understanding of how the change has affected employees, with a view to flow-on effects such as decreased organisational commitment and productivity. Any restructuring of jobs, including retrenchments, must adhere to organisational procedures and legal requirements.

Although technology is a cost saving for the company, managers also need to be aware of the possible impact this may have on organisational culture, job satisfaction and job security, all of which may be negative. In the long term, this may affect strategic goals and organisational effectiveness. Therefore, before any IT is implemented companies need to conduct an organisational analysis to ensure that the type of technology is appropriate for individual and organisational needs, and that it will have a positive return on investment.

IT ACCESS

Another issue to consider is the fact that not every employee has access to technology. Not all employees work at a desk, or have computer and/or Internet access. In some cases, a computer may be available but with limited, shared access. This reduces the possibility that staff can use and access the different types of HRM technology mentioned above, such as email, HR portals and the HRIS. In this case, management must consider whether it is worthwhile adopting such technology. For example, construction sites would benefit from other technology, such as machinery, rather than the installation of a new email system from which they will obtain little value. In this instance, HRM should consider alternative HRM communication modes, such as a combination of paper-based systems (for employees) and technology-based systems such as email, the Internet, intranet and an HRIS (for HRM).

PRIVACY ISSUES

In Australia current privacy laws have changed the way companies store and disseminate employee and customer information. In particular, this relates to personal details such as private contact addresses and phone numbers, employment history, performance evaluations and financial information (i.e. salary and banking details). It is imperative, therefore, that HR portals contain sufficient security measures so that staff feel safe when accessing personal information via the portal.

It is also important to consider who should have access to confidential information within the HR department. Specifically, managers need to determine who has access to this data and is able to use it. Again, security measures need to be in place and, depending on the type of information, only senior management should have access to highly confidential information. Employees who do not feel confident with the technology will be reluctant to use it and it will be an effective drain on resources.

Please read

Ruël, H., Bondarouk, T. & Looise, J. K. (2004), 'E-HRM: Innovation or irritation. An explorative empirical study in five large companies on web-based HRM', *Management Revue*, vol. 15, no. 3, pp. 364–80.

SHRM AND INFORMATION SYSTEM MANAGEMENT

Strategic information systems, of which an HRIS is an example, are increasingly being recognised as a value-adding component to organisational success. Indeed, information systems, if integrated correctly with HRM, are one way that companies can gain the elusive competitive advantage that is necessary for survival in the twenty-first century. Technology, however, could destroy individual and/or group performance if it is poorly planned, developed and implemented by the organisation. In other words, senior management needs to comprehend the interdependent role of the end-users (i.e. employees) and the information systems which fall under the auspices of SHRM.

SHRM can contribute significantly to implementing information system management by fostering a healthy relationship among managers, IT specialists and end-users. Today, information systems are not just being managed by technical experts. The emergence of personal computers (PCs), friendlier commercial software and multi-user networks has led to the fact that information systems can be managed at the individual, group and organisational level. In order to succeed in multifaceted strategic information system management, SHRM plays a vital role in managing the social, structural and psychological (i.e. cognitive and affective behaviours) issues addressed by information systems. The recruitment and selection, performance management and compensation policies based on the IT competencies; training and development on IT applications; occupational health and safety in IT handling; organisational and job design based on information system management (e.g. virtual teams) all contribute to effective information system management (Martinsons & Chong, 1999).

Research findings repeatedly indicate that poor SHRM can hinder information system implementation. The common causes of failure are documented as HR issues, namely, organisational culture, performance management, change management and conflict resolution processes (see Martinsons & Chong, 1999). Despite these findings, in practice, the role of SHRM as part of the information system management process (i.e. planning, development and implementation) has been given little attention to date.

An HR change agent role is necessary as IT is assimilated into the organisation. Technological change tends to evoke employee fears and anxiety about job insecurity, loss of work control and deskilling. HR managers can assist IT-phobic individuals (typically older, senior-level employees) to assimilate themselves into the technology-related world. As technology assimilation and change take place simultaneously, HR managers can strategically develop an appropriate sequence of change activities based on sound behavioural principles. The SHRM Application Tool (see Figure 4.7) identifies how technology takes a vital part in today's organisations.

Contemporary SHRM Application Tool

Imagine that you are an HR manager in one of the world's largest consulting companies specialising in infrastructure development for the energy, water, information and government markets. Your company values employees as its greatest asset and aims to maintain an international reputation for excellence based on the application of high human intelligence. In order to compete against other internationally reputable consulting companies, top management recognises the significance of recruiting the best and brightest employees to provide the best and fastest consulting services to clients. Integrating with such a strategic direction, you see an opportunity to utilise the HRIS to capitalise on the global talent pool the company has worldwide. How could the hiring manager from different subsidiaries in different departments, geographical locations (including both nations and states) and even functional divisions collaborate in real time ensuring the same hiring quality (refer to Figure 4.7)?

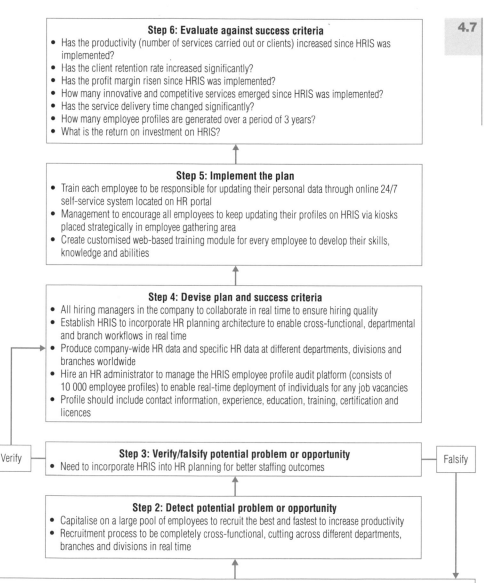

4.7 | FIGURE

SHRM application tool: opportunity — technology

Step 6: Evaluate against success criteria
- Has the productivity (number of services carried out or clients) increased since HRIS was implemented?
- Has the client retention rate increased significantly?
- Has the profit margin risen since HRIS was implemented?
- How many innovative and competitive services emerged since HRIS was implemented?
- Has the service delivery time changed significantly?
- How many employee profiles are generated over a period of 3 years?
- What is the return on investment on HRIS?

Step 5: Implement the plan
- Train each employee to be responsible for updating their personal data through online 24/7 self-service system located on HR portal
- Management to encourage all employees to keep updating their profiles on HRIS via kiosks placed strategically in employee gathering area
- Create customised web-based training module for every employee to develop their skills, knowledge and abilities

Step 4: Devise plan and success criteria
- All hiring managers in the company to collaborate in real time to ensure hiring quality
- Establish HRIS to incorporate HR planning architecture to enable cross-functional, departmental and branch workflows in real time
- Produce company-wide HR data and specific HR data at different departments, divisions and branches worldwide
- Hire an HR administrator to manage the HRIS employee profile audit platform (consists of 10 000 employee profiles) to enable real-time deployment of individuals for any job vacancies
- Profile should include contact information, experience, education, training, certification and licences

Verify

Step 3: Verify/falsify potential problem or opportunity
- Need to incorporate HRIS into HR planning for better staffing outcomes

Falsify

Step 2: Detect potential problem or opportunity
- Capitalise on a large pool of employees to recruit the best and fastest to increase productivity
- Recruitment process to be completely cross-functional, cutting across different departments, branches and divisions in real time

Step 1: Analyse environmental factors

Step 1a: HR issues: Monitor/ analyse data (past, present and future)
- One of the top international consulting firms for over a decade
- Facing more competition. Lost some major clients to competitors over the past 3 years
- Need to capitalise on technology to compete

Step 1b: Internal/organisational environment
- Value employees as the greatest asset
- Aim to maintain international reputation for excellence based on the application of high human intelligence
- Employees are servants to clients by seeking tough assignments, producing best and fastest results, achieving high levels of client satisfaction
- Widely spread global talent pool

Step 1c: External environment
- Highly competitive consulting industry
- Regulation of intellectual property
- Customer: enterprises
- Low employee substitutability

A view from the field

e-Learning as a force multiplier

A **force multiplier** is a military term referring to a factor that dramatically increases (hence, 'multiplies') the combat effectiveness of a given military force. Sometimes this factor may apply more or less under different circumstances. Some common force multipliers are:

- Technology
- Geographic features
- Recruitment through diplomacy
- Morale
- Weather
- Training

Source: 'Force multiplier', *Wikipedia, The Free Encylopedia*, <http://en.wikipedia.org/w/index.php?title=Force_multiplier&oldid=18064068>, accessed 9 December 2005.

Consider a group of well-armed infantry soldiers. The group will make a certain impact moving through enemy territory; however, the use of air support such as a helicopter will accelerate their movement and impact on the battlefield.

Technology applications in learning are likened to force multipliers in military terms. Fifteen classroom trainers and three instructional designers providing learning services to an organisation of 5000 employees can only do so much. The introduction of technology can maximise the impact of learning programs and allow resources such as classroom trainers to be redirected to other high-value activities.

Scott Mahoney is Managing Director of Omni Asia Pacific Pty Ltd, one of Australia's leading learning technology, courseware development and consultancy firms in the relatively new online learning or e-learning industry. Scott defines e-learning 'as a situation where any element of learning or the learning process is created, managed, undertaken with or controlled by any electronic means in whole or in part'. He has a clear view on how strategic human resources managers can make the most of the 'force multiplier' opportunities available through the application of technology to learning. 'HR professionals need to develop an understanding of e-learning and its potential. They don't need to become technologists overnight. The key is to develop an understanding of the technology and then explore where and how it can be used to maximum advantage.'

Technology offers the opportunity for the HR function to connect closely to business imperatives contributing to the resolution of key business challenges and reducing costs. The application of technology to HR processes is widespread; the introduction of technology in areas such as payroll, leave records and collection and maintenance of employee personal information demonstrates its potential to reduce costs, introduce efficiencies and allow more emphasis on higher value activities.

So where do HR professionals begin when trying to explore the possibilities in the world of e-learning? The point of leverage seems to be identifying a compelling business benefit in the development of e-learning infrastructure. What business issue or problem will it address? What opportunity or differentiation will it provide to a company in its marketplace?

In the Australian financial services sector, for example, the introduction of a new regime of government regulation and reporting presented a substantial challenge for organisations. The new regulations required organisations to provide their staff with specified levels of training prior to allowing them to sell financial products (including credit cards and investment accounts) to customers. It also required the maintenance of records of that training and the ability to report the levels of staff accreditation to the regulator at nominated times. The penalties for failing to meet these standards were significant, including substantial fines and an ultimate penalty of loss of a banking licence. These new regulations were confronting for large and small players in the industry. Financial services organisations were concerned about the costs associated with the development and delivery of training and the onus of record keeping and few had the infrastructure to support the demands of these regulations.

Is it reasonable for HR managers to inherit responsibility for addressing this major business issue? As is often the case with these types of issues a significant component is related to the human factor surrounding, in this case, the training of existing staff and the ongoing management of the provision of training to meet regulatory compliance requirements. Certainly this places the issue squarely within the realm of HRM. Scott comments that the widespread use of e-learning as a solution to the regulatory challenges in the financial services sector is no surprise. 'Savvy HR Managers saw the potential of e-learning to assist with delivery of training in a "just in time" fashion to (in many cases) large and geographically dispersed workforces, with the added benefit of comprehensive data management and reporting that supported the detailed regulatory compliance reporting requirements. Used in this manner, e-learning systems offered genuine cost efficient solutions to these major business challenges. The benefits didn't end there. For example, organisations that "cut their teeth" on the initial compliance driven e-learning initiatives have seen their e-learning systems continue to return benefits on the significant investment as they have been used to respond to a very competitive marketplace, which demands new and innovative financial products (bank accounts, credit cards and loans) offered to customers. E-learning systems help with the delivery of up to the minute training and accreditation on new products to staff in a flexible and efficient way, ensuring that time to competence regarding new products and services is not an inhibitor to sales.'

The value of e-learning systems is not limited to this application. Many HR professionals use e-learning for a multitude of purposes – everything from supporting business projects, through supply and value chain training, to creating virtual online communities centred on learning cultures. Some HR professionals even use e-learning to generate revenue streams from supply of courses to customers or intermediaries to offset some of the cost of content development. The use of e-learning as a force multiplier is only limited to an organisation's desire and need to satisfy its strategic and tactical objectives with a cost-effective, robust and scalable 'non traditional' means of delivery.

Creating an e-learning force multiplier through an initial driver such as the regulatory requirements faced by the financial services sector is only half the battle. Achieving initial management support and sponsorship for an e-learning initiative can be achieved through qualifying and quantifying objectives in a way the business finds compelling and then through solid execution of the system. Scott observes, 'Many HR professionals have found, to their chagrin, ensuring consistent support of your e-learning initiative is only achieved through establishing governance structures, policies and processes. These support your business as people within develop an under-standing of the ways in which e-learning can be leveraged to achieve tangible business results. HR professionals can play a key role in creating and managing the total e-learning force multiplier environment through provision of an organisation wide, focal point for expertise and the management of e-learning infrastructure and projects.'

In trying to maximise the potential of e-learning, HR professionals do not need to manage the physical technology, or even content development, rather they need to manage in a robust, consistent and value-based manner the way that business requests for e-learning projects are treated from inception through to delivery.

Support for learners and content is also a critical component of the success of e-learning. Scott has observed the failure to provide this support as one of the key reasons for the failure of any e-learning initiative. The lack of a robust and effective support environment for learners will potentially disenfranchise the users and other stakeholders, making future projects difficult to initiate due to lack of cross-organisational support.

Success breeds success, so the use of an effective evaluation mechanism to assist in quantifying the value and effectiveness of e-learning is vital. A marketing strategy will also assist greatly with managing positive expectations of business stakeholders and thereby generate ongoing support for e-learning initiatives. In Scott's view, HR professionals often fail to wear a sales cap and neglect to share their success with key stakeholders and the wider business. This failure is an opportunity missed. Success can be used as a springboard for the introduction of other applications and to generate ongoing support for e-learning initiatives.

The argument for the use of e-learning as a force multiplier is compelling. So why do some HR professionals resist? Scott believes three things hold HR professionals back. First, denial, believing more of the same will work (it doesn't). Technology has had an impact in all areas of our lives – the way we shop, communicate and manage our holiday plans and the options available for learning. The traditional ways of delivering learning opportunities are under challenge and the new ways create all sorts of possibilities. The second reason is ignorance of technology in general and of its potential in this area of HRM. Finally, fear of what the change might bring and what it might expose. E-learning statistics and reporting capabilities can show up inefficiencies and highlight the potential for savings in the delivery of learning.

Clearly e-learning systems offer enormous potential for HR managers to demonstrate their relevance to the business they support. The systems offer efficiencies which can free resources to be redeployed to other learning and development efforts or simply reduce the costs of training. The technologies also embed the governance of the training function, requiring standardisation of processes and identifying where the activity is focused.

Discussion questions

1. Choose a well-known retail outlet you enjoy shopping at, for example a clothing or electronics group. How could that chain make use of e-learning as a force multiplier in training staff?
2. How can you as an HR professional develop your skills and knowledge in the area of e-learning?
3. You are the HR manager of a company with 2000 employees. Your company operations are spread over two states; 150 people are located in Head Office with the remainder scattered across a total of 15 metropolitan and regional outlets. The company is about to introduce a new accounting system which 90 per cent of your staff will need to be fully trained in. The Chief Accountant has asked what you know about e-learning. She is wondering whether it would be useful in this situation. Use the information above to assist you to frame your advice.

A manager's challenge

E-recruitment at Coles Myer

Retail giant Coles Myer recently launched its own company career website to accommodate recruitment for its ever-expanding staff. The company, which is Australia and New Zealand's largest employer with 170 000 staff, was until this time using a decentralised, paper-based recruitment system to manage staffing for its 22 brands, including Target, Kmart, Myer, Megamart and Officeworks.

The shift to e-recruitment eventuated after the company centralised its recruitment process in a bid to streamline HRM and increase the efficiency, effectiveness and professionalism of the recruitment process. Within seven weeks of the program's installation (powered by PageUp People), Coles Myer received 110 000 applications for job vacancies across 1900 stores! This, according to Josephine Thompson, recruitment strategy manager at Coles Myer, is an excellent result. 'The cost savings on paper and postage alone is $300 000 annually, not to mention all of the intangible savings', says Thompson.

The system is really very simple. Applicants simply log on to the Coles Myer careers website (http://careers.colesmyer.com) or browse seek.com, a partner career website. Applicants then receive emails or short message services (SMS) detailing information on the recruitment tracking or interview reminders. Apart from cost savings, these two communication modes are instantaneous and convey both professionalism and style, which appeals to a wide range of the company's target employee market.

The program, which is expected to pay for itself within a year, has an outstanding success rate for filling job vacancies. 'We had 70 IT job vacancies and filled 80 per cent of them within three weeks of the site going live', says Thompson. The new program is expected to increase efficiency over busy periods too, such as in the months leading up to Christmas. On average, around 3000 vacancies are advertised each week. Other program functions include psychometric testing and interview scheduling.

With this efficient e-recruitment process, HRM at Coles Myer is expected to supersede their competitors', making this retail giant one of the most successful in Australia and the world.

Source: Adapted from Simmons, L. (2003), 'E-recruitment drivers', *Technology and Business Magazine*, September, pp. 115–18.

Summary

This topic discussed the vital role of SHRM in the strategic information management process. As the world becomes more technologically advanced, and IT systems are put in place to increase efficiency and effectiveness, it is imperative that HRM adopt IT systems that complement its processes. HRM is leveraged through technology via virtual HRM which implies that computer technology is used to recruit, train, develop and monitor human resources. However, how and why this technology is used is dependent on the organisation – its culture, resources, size, strategic fit and, of course, its human resources. There are three ways that technology (specifically e-HRM) is integrated in a company: through transactional, traditional and transformational activities. Although all of these activities are important to the development of IT and HRM, transformational activities include high-value-adding activities which result in significant organisational benefits, yet are also the activities that most senior managers have the least amount of time for due to time and resource constraints.

The type of technology used to manage human resources is different from other technology. For example, scientific, manufacturing, engineering and agricultural industries tend to used large machinery and specialised technology to achieve work goals. However, within HRM, the technologies are mainly used to increase communication, efficiency and effectiveness. These technologies include email, the Internet, intranets, HR portal, online learning and service systems (including ESS and MSS).

One specific technology used within HR is an HRIS. This is the backbone of an organisation's HR department as it accumulates, stores, maintains and analyses all data relating to a company's human resources. An HRIS is similar to a large database and authorised personnel use it to obtain employee information, such as employee skill audits, performance management details and information on rewards and recognition. Functional management relies on HRIS capabilities to help it achieve business goals.

To get the most out of an HRIS the technology needs to be integrated with every HRM function. It also needs to be implemented effectively, led by the HR manager who assumes the role of a change agent. There are six phases of HRIS implementation: devise a plan; SWOT analysis; senior management approval; determine an HRIS supplier (design); generate a list of alternatives; and installation. However, the implementation process is discontinuous, and constant re-examination is necessary to ensure that the HRIS continues to meet the needs of all stakeholders. The SHRM Application Tool provides one way to perform such re-examination.

The role the HR manager adopts in the implementation process is crucial to the success of the system. Although there are three roles (reactive, supportive and proactive), managers need to adopt a proactive role which emphasises planning, communication and the prevention of mistakes. Their support, motivation and guidance during the process are of the utmost importance. Although the other two roles may be adopted, they focus more on maintaining and sustaining effective HR support after the planning process and address the cure rather than the prevention.

A well-implemented HRIS can result in various organisational benefits, such as the standardisation of information storage, which creates efficient means to read and report data. In addition, an HRIS is an ideal knowledge management system which is crucial to SHRM success. Despite these benefits, there are also several implications associated with an HRIS. It must meet the needs of all stakeholders (both internal and external to the company), staff need continual training for how to input and output data, including new employees; data entry error may occur, which may look unprofessional; security measures need to be well developed, with only authorised personnel having access to the HRIS; and organisations also need to consider cross-cultural barriers, such as language barriers and the limited access to computers in some parts of the world. A further consideration is the company size. In general, smaller companies require less sophisticated systems than larger ones, although this also depends on the overall organisational goal as the technology must align with people, processes, culture and structure if it is to be viewed as a holistic approach to people management.

Technology also exerts general implications on HRM, not just on an HRIS. The organisational culture must facilitate the use of technology. Techno-phobic employees, such as older or senior employees, may contribute negatively to the institutionalisation of new IT. An assessment must be conducted to determine the openness to change and to analyse the degree of resistance before any new technology can be implemented. Further, once the culture is accepting of IT, the technology must be strategically integrated with the company's overall values, mission and vision to ensure they are aligned and working together to achieve overall goals. Failure to do so may result in the poor design, development or implementation of the technology. Flow-on effects of this include decreased job satisfaction and security and, ultimately, productivity. Of further consequence is who has access to confidential information, such as that contained in the HR portal or in the MSS, as privacy issues and legal requirements must be adhered to. In conclusion, an HRIS is expected to increase its strategic value in order to reap the full potential of geographically and organisationally dispersed human capital. However, as with all technology, managers must be aware of the risks, benefits and implications of embracing new IT within the organisation.

Key terms

employee self-service systems	intranet	self-service system
human resource information system	manager self-service systems	virtual HRM
	online learning	

Review questions

4.1 What is e-HRM? How can it be integrated into a company's HRM functions?

4.2 Define and describe each of the HRM technologies. Support your answer with an example for each.

4.3 What is meant by the term 'online learning'? Why has it become popular in recent years?

4.4 An HRIS is said to be the backbone of an organisation's HRM department. Briefly define what an HRIS is, how it can benefit organisations, and some of the important implications it has for HRM.

4.5 During the implementation of information systems (IS), there are several roles that the HR manager can adopt. Define and describe each of these. Which is the preferred role and why?

4.1 Imagine you are the HR manager of a large international firm. The company's market share has recently decreased due to new competition entering the market. Design a strategy for implementing an HRIS, taking into consideration some of the cultural implications of designing and using the HRIS. How will the HRIS help the company increase its market share and profitability?

4.2 Access the workforce management website (www.workforce.com) and conduct a content search on HRIS. Examine the way different organisations utilise various HRISs to improve their operations.

4.3 An HR portal is an important component of HRM technology. Using the tables below, list some of the benefits and implications for the e-HRM functions of recruitment and performance appraisal.

Recruitment

Features	Benefits	Implications
Employee referral		
Interview availability		
Online assessment		
Induction program		
Online applications		
Applicant tracking		
Letter of acceptance/rejection		

Performance appraisal

Features	Benefits	Implications
360° feedback		
Key performance indicators		
Career development		
Professional development		
Online performance appraisals		
Email reminders		
Online performance management forms		

References

Australian National Audit Office (2004), *The Use and Management of HRIS in the Australian Public Service*, The Auditor General Report No. 49 (2003–2004), Commonwealth of Australia, Canberra.

Beatty, B. D. (2005), 'A framework for transforming your HR function', in *Web-Based Human Resources*, ed. A. J. Walker, McGraw-Hill, New York.

DeFidelto, C. & Slater, I. (2005), 'Web-based HR in an international setting', in *Web-

Based Human Resources, ed. A. J. Walker, McGraw-Hill, New York.

Frontier Software, 'Welcome to the Frontier Software Website' (2003), <http://www.frontiersoftware.com>, accessed 25 October 2005.

Härtel, C. E. J. & Tilton, P. (2005), 'Australia and online learning: Lessons for effective implementation', in *Skill Formation and Globalisation*, ed. M. Powell, Ashgate Publishing, Aldershot.

Hendrickson, A. R. (2003), 'Human resource information systems: Backbone technology of contemporary human resources', *Journal of Labor Research*, vol. 24, no. 3, pp. 381–94.

Jones, R. A & Brown, K. A. (2004), 'Human resource management professionals: Their perspective on successful information systems implementation', *International Journal of Human Resource Development and Management*, vol. 4, no. 4, pp. 375–89.

Martinsons, M. G. & Chong, P. K. C. (1999), 'The influence of human factors and specialist involvement on information systems success', *Human Relations*, vol. 52, no. 1, pp. 123–52.

Ogier, J. (2003), 'Are you a tech wreck?: Trouble with HRIS', *HR Monthly*, September, pp. 18–24.

Ruël, H., Bondarouk, T. & Looise, J. K. (2004), 'E-HRM: Innovation or irritation. An explorative empirical study in five large companies on web-based HRM', *Management Revue*, vol. 15, no. 3, pp. 364–80.

Simmons, L. (2003), 'E-Recruitment drivers', *Technology and Business Magazine*, September, pp. 115–18.

Wright, P. M. & Dyer, L. (2000), *People in the e-Business: New Challenges, New Solutions*, Working Paper 00-11, Centre for Advanced Human Resource Studies, Cornell University, Ithaca.

Chapter 5

Workforce diversity, work life demands and strategic human resource management

INTRODUCTION

The workforce today is becoming increasingly diverse. Organisations are made up of people with a variety of individual differences. Race, age, gender, life experience, disabilities and religious beliefs are all examples of how people differ. The diverse aspect of human life and behaviour, coupled with disappearing geographical borders, has fostered today's diverse workforce. To manage an organisation's human resources effectively managers need to be aware and understand what diversity is, how it impacts on employees and the implications it has for individual, group and organisational goals.

This chapter addresses the issue of workforce diversity as it is a significant challenge HR managers face in the twenty-first century. Diversity management changes the way people think, act and behave in organisations, and policies and practices need to be in place to manage organisational members effectively and legally. This chapter identifies how and why people respond to diversity by drawing on key theories, and encourages an understanding of workforce diversity and individual acceptance through applied processes in the SHRM Application Tool.

Objectives

The primary objective of this chapter is to highlight issues arising from an increasingly diverse workforce and how these can be managed. In particular, careful consideration is given to diversity-oriented SHRM, which covers the management of employees as well as managers and leaders.

After reading this chapter you should be able to:

- understand the effect of workforce diversity on individual, group and organisational outcomes;
- identify the key theories of diversity and how they can be applied in organisational settings;
- understand the relationship between diversity management and SHRM, and the implications of this relationship;
- discuss ways in which individual differences can be managed as well as ways in which a group manager/leader can manage diversity;
- identify some issues surrounding diversity and how these can be effectively managed.

Definition of workforce diversity

Like many concepts within the realm of management, there is not a single definition of workforce diversity. In essence, workforce diversity is based on group identity and individual differences and includes all aspects which make us different, such as race, age, gender, sexuality, interests, needs and desires. Because we are all unique, we are all diverse. However, within the realm of HRM, diversity encompasses much more than just these differences. This is because diversity within HRM is specified as *workforce diversity*. Therefore, under the workforce diversity umbrella, aspects such as educational level, disabilities, work experience, perceptions, attitudes towards others (and towards employment), psychological and contractual expectations and values and perception are included. It is evident then that diversity consists of many attributes, all of which can significantly affect individual, group and organisational outcomes such as performance, job satisfaction, absenteeism, turnover and strategic transformation.

The definition of diversity is, therefore, multifaceted. However, it is often categorised as having two dimensions: observable and underlying differences (Milliken & Martins, 1996). Observable differences include differences in race/ethnic background, nationality, gender, age and verbal/non-verbal behaviours. The underlying (or less observable) differences include values/beliefs (i.e. cultural values, work/social orientation), sexual orientation, skills/knowledge and organisational cohort differences. The two dimensions can then be categorised into the following five types of diversity that influence the processes and outcomes of organisations:

1. *Group identity diversity*. This includes race, nationality, gender and age.
2. *Values and beliefs diversity*. This includes cultural values, work style orientation values and social values (such as valuing diversity).

3. *Skills and knowledge diversity.* This includes specialisation, and experience in the area and the industry.
4. *Verbal and non-verbal behavioural diversity.* This includes verbalised and non-verbalised discussions and behaviour.
5. *Organisational cohort diversity.* This includes group tenure and employment status.

Despite the various definitions of diversity, in this chapter **workforce diversity** is based on group identity and individual differences and is defined as any visible or invisible difference between organisational members, such as race, age, gender, sexuality, religion, educational level, work experience, disability, language, perceptions, attitudes, interests, lifestyle, expectations, values, needs and desires.

workforce diversity
Any visible or underlying difference between organisational members.

Please read

Milliken, F. J. & Martins, L. L. (1996), 'Searching for common threads: Understanding the multiple effects of diversity in organizational groups', *Academy of Management Review*, vol. 21, no. 2, pp. 402–33.

HOW DOES DIVERSITY ENTER THE WORKFORCE?

Significant changes in the composition of the workforce in Australia are taking place, with organisations becoming increasingly more diverse due to a large number of individual differences. Gone are the days when the labour force of Australia was predominantly made up of white males. As indicated above, today's organisations are likely to be made up of people who differ in terms of such things as gender, national origin, race, ethnicity and culture as well as sexual orientation, physical ability, educational level and their basic values, attitudes and beliefs. A number of factors have been put forward as leading to this increased workforce diversity including migration, which is changing the ethnic composition of the population as a whole, the globalisation of trade, legal and moral stances for diversity as well as the business cases for diversity, increased female participation in the workforce and the increase in use of such things as cross-functional teams.

One of the most significant reasons why diversity is entering the workforce is the fact that Australia is increasingly becoming a multicultural society. Long gone are the days when we could pinpoint what a 'typical' Australian looked like. From our early British and Irish immigrants to the influx of immigrants from Mediterranean countries such as Italy and Greece, and now to the wave of migrants from Middle Eastern, African and Asian countries such as Iraq, Sudan and Indonesia, Australia is a country with an increasingly diverse cultural heritage (see Figure 5.1 and Tables 5.1 and 5.2). As would be expected, this diversity has moved into the workforce meaning that people who come from vastly different backgrounds and perspectives must work with one another.

As Australia is becoming increasingly more diverse due to the large number of individual differences between people, organisations are also creating increasingly more diverse workforces based on three 'cases' for diversity. These are the legal, moral and business cases for diversity.

FIGURE 5.1
Percentage of overseas
born Australians

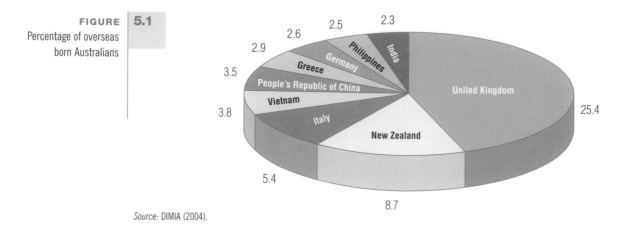

Source: DIMIA (2004).

TABLE 5.1 Australian population birthplaces which have significantly increased (1996–2001)

Country	Number of people	Percentage increase
Sudan	4,911	105%
Afghanistan	11,264	93%
Somalia	3,726	82%
Bangladesh	9,077	79%
Iraq	24,819	77%

Source: Data from DIMIA (2004).

TABLE 5.2 Australian population birthplaces which have significantly decreased (1996–2001)

Country	Number of people	Percentage decrease
Latvia	6,701	17%
Estonia	2,797	16%
Lithuania	3,689	13%
Poland	58,093	11%
Portugal	15,407	10%

Source: Data from DIMIA (2004).

The underlying motive for embracing diversity is not always a genuine concern for employees' welfare, or because senior management realise the value of a diverse firm. Sometimes, against their will, companies are required to adopt diversity-friendly policies due to regulatory and legislative regulations such as equal employment opportunity (EEO) and affirmative action (AA) policies created by the government to try to ensure that organisations have fair employment policies. When this is the situation, it is referred to as the **legal case for diversity**. Examples of Australian Commonwealth legislation relating to employment include the *Racial Discrimination Act 1975*, *Sex Discrimination Act 1984*, *Human Rights and Equal Opportunity Commission Act 1986*, *Disability Discrimination Act 1992* and the *Equal Opportunity for Women in the Workplace Act 1999*. Rather than punishing organisations for something they did, the legal case for diversity punishes those who do not participate. For example, failure to abide by EEO laws results in serious consequences for companies, such as a warning or a fine. In this situation, the legality does not alleviate the problem or benefit the organisation (Schneider & Northcraft, 1999), but rather makes it 'fair' for minority groups (i.e. women, people with disabilities, Aborigines and, in Australia, Torres Strait Islanders).

legal case for diversity
When companies are required by law to adopt diversity-friendly policies such as equal employment opportunity and affirmative action.

The second case is the **moral case for diversity**. This is where diversity is embraced for the purpose of equity creation and diverse employees are integrated throughout the organisation and rewarded without regard to their dissimilarity.

moral case for diversity
When diversity is embraced for the purpose of equity creation where diverse employees are integrated throughout the organisation and rewarded without regard to their dissimilarity.

There are two ways that the moral case develops (Glastra *et al.* 2000). The systematic approach analyses how ethnic groups are socially classified within an organisation in comparison to other organisational members and seeks to balance this classification between all organisational members. Here, diversity is only employed with the *genuine* intention of gaining equality. The second approach, called the discrimination approach, is more controversial. This involves targeting sources of discrimination and inequality, and implementing strategies to reduce prejudice, racism and exclusion, for example through diversity and prejudice awareness programs.

The final case is the **business case for diversity**. The underlying notion in this situation is that diversity initiatives have been sidetracked from their original intention, which was to improve opportunities and experiences for previously excluded minority groups. By increasing the viewpoints and contributions of these groups, employees and employers benefit from a variety of differing opinions and ideas, and are able to deal more effectively with dynamic environments (Lineehan & Konrad, 1999).

business case for diversity
The improvement of opportunities and experiences for previously excluded minority groups which aims to improve overall organisational capability.

The business case for diversity forms the foundation and focus of this chapter as it should be the underlying motive for implementing diversity in organisations.

How and why people respond to diversity

People respond to diversity in a variety of ways. The reaction will differ from person to person, and can depend on national culture, personal values, expectations and experience with dissimilar people. However, negative emotional and behavioural consequences of diversity are largely explained by three theories: the similarity attraction paradigm, social identity theory and social categorisation theory, as discussed below.

SIMILARITY ATTRACTION PARADIGM

similarity attraction paradigm
States that humans are inclined to be attracted to others they perceive to be similar.

The **similarity attraction paradigm** states that humans are inclined to be attracted to others they perceive to be similar. For example, intelligent people tend to be attracted to other intelligent people, and Caucasians tend to be attracted to other Caucasians. However, this attraction means that dissimilar others (or those perceived as dissimilar) are excluded. In essence, this exclusion can also be referred to as discrimination.

This theory, which is one of the key diversity theories, is evident in certain workplaces and communities. For example, in diverse organisations people from similar cultures tend to socialise together because they have similar backgrounds and understand each other better than dissimilar others do. Examples are people lunching together or sharing rides to work. Likewise, around Australia there tend to be communities of similar cultures or backgrounds in the same location. Darwin has the largest population of Aborigines in Australia, and Queensland is where retirees tend to live; not only is the nice weather appealing but retirees share similar interests and, subsequently, are attracted to each other on that level.

discrimination
Any difference or preference based on race, gender, colour, religion, political beliefs or nationality which results in disadvantageous or unfair treatment regarding employment, occupation or status.

One significant implication of this theory is that the attraction of similar others automatically excludes dissimilar others, resulting in discrimination. **Discrimination** is defined as any difference or preference based on race, gender, colour, religion, political beliefs or nationality which results in disadvantageous or unfair treatment regarding employment, occupation or status. In Australia, there is a variety of state and federal legislation pertaining to discrimination (see Table 5.3). This legislation is at the very core of HRM and it is the responsibility of HR managers to know each of these laws, and regularly update organisational policies and procedures with new information.

direct discrimination
A policy or certain behaviour which purposely treats one group less favourably than another.

indirect discrimination
A policy which appears to be non-discriminatory at the outset, but in practice results in discrimination.

Direct discrimination (also referred to as overt discrimination) occurs when a policy or certain behaviour purposely treats one group less favourably than another, for example when an employee makes derogatory comments about the appearance of another employee. However, **indirect discrimination** (also referred to as covert discrimination) occurs when a policy appears to be non-discriminatory at the outset but in practice results in discrimination. For example, if a job advertisement advertises for people over 180 cm, this is indirect discrimination unless the job could not be performed by people shorter than this height. In this case, discrimination is based on the grounds of gender or race (as most women and some ethic groups would be physically unable to meet this criterion). The latter discrimination occurs within the similarity attraction paradigm. It should be noted that, despite good intentions, both types of discrimination are illegal and can result in legal action being taken against the discriminating party. Therefore, it is imperative that managers and employees are provided with the correct training resources to distinguish between the two types of discrimination and ensure that they do not occur. In the event of discrimination, there are three steps that a company and/or employee can take:

• Discuss the issue with the person responsible and/or a manager.
• Seek advice from the Equal Opportunity Commission in your state. They provide free and confidential advice on your rights and the possible actions you may pursue. Alternatively, advice may be sought from the HR or EEO manager within your company.

- Present the complaint to the Equal Opportunity Commission in your state. The commission will examine the complaint and attempt to resolve it confidentially and impartially. If a resolution cannot be reached through conciliation, it may be referred to a tribunal which has the power to make a decision (such as the Victorian Civil and Administrative Tribunal in Melbourne).

SOCIAL IDENTITY THEORY

Social identity theory expands on the similarity attraction paradigm as another negative consequence of diversity. Drawing on the work of Tajfel and Turner (1986), **social identity theory** states that group members attempt to achieve or maintain a positive self-image as a result of a favourable comparison between their social category and other groups. In short, this means that group members will exert favouritism towards their own members. However, there is a catch; the favouritism only applies to majority group members (such as white males) and minority group members (e.g. black males, women and Aborigines) are excluded.

Given that workforce diversity is on the rise, this theory is commonly observed in action in today's organisations. Group (or team) formation theories indicate that diverse teams yield more effective results than homogeneity. Therefore, it is

social identity theory
States that group members attempt to achieve or maintain a positive self-image as a result of a favourable comparison between their social category and other groups.

TABLE **5.3** **Discrimination legislation in Australia**

Jurisdiction	Legislation
Federal	Equal Opportunity for Women in the Workplace Act 1999
	Disability Discrimination Act 1992
	Human Rights and Equal Opportunity Commission Act 1986
	Workplace Relations Act 1996
	Racial Discrimination Act 1975
	Sex Discrimination Act 1984
	Crimes Act 1914 (s. 85ZV)
New South Wales	Anti Discrimination Act 1977
	Criminal Records Act 1991
Victoria	Equal Opportunity Act 1995
Queensland	Anti Discrimination Act 1991
	Workplace Relations Act 1997
	Criminal Law (Rehabilitation of Offenders) Act 1986
South Australia	Equal Opportunity Act 1994
	Racial Vilification Act 1996
Western Australia	Equal Opportunity Act 1984
	Criminal Code Chapter XI
	Spent Convictions Act 1988
Tasmania	Anti Discrimination Act 1998
Australian Capital Territory	Discrimination Act 1991
Northern Territory	Anti Discrimination Act 1992
	Criminal Records (Spent Convictions) Act 1992

Source: Adapted from CCH Australia Limited (2000), *Human Resources Management*, vol. 10, no. 530, pp. 3621–33.

likely that group members will experience what social identity theory describes at some point of their group involvement. For the majority group member, this suggests they will enjoy a greater allocation of rewards and support, and will generally be admired. Their positive attributes will be highlighted. However, for the minority group member the consequences are not so encouraging. They will generally experience increased stress, anxiety and negative identification with the social group. This can lead to job dissatisfaction, decreased job security, a feeling of hopelessness and, ultimately, poor productivity (Fujimoto, Härtel & Panipucci, 2005).

As a manager, there are several implications of this theory. Obviously, the first step is to allocate group members appropriately to ensure that there is a fair distribution of majority and minority group members. Ideally, groups should comprise no fewer than 20% minority members in order to give the minority members a good chance at voicing their opinions and maintaining equality. Managers also need to allocate a suitable group leader who is impartial and unbiased. This leader needs to be well versed in discrimination and diversity policies and legislation, and actively practise them. Leadership by example is imperative and is a useful way of setting standards and expectations. The leader also needs to monitor group performance and ensure that the subculture (i.e. the norms, values and attitudes of the group) conforms to the organisational culture, and to the long-term values and goals of the firm. Any behaviour deemed unacceptable (i.e. discrimination or favouritism) needs to be immediately acknowledged and appropriately dealt with (Ayoko, Härtel & Callan, 2002). Although the method of sanction is contingent on the situation, employees must know the consequences of their actions. After all, there is no room for discrimination in the workplace.

SOCIAL CATEGORISATION THEORY

social categorisation theory
States that people tend to categorise themselves and others into various social categories, namely 'in group' and 'out group' membership.

Social categorisation theory is consistent with the similarity attraction paradigm. **Social categorisation theory** derives from the research of Turner and Oakes (1989) and states that people tend to categorise themselves and others into various social categories, namely 'in groups' and 'out groups'. An in group is a group whose members perceive themselves to be similar. They belong to the same group for motivational, emotional and value significance. Conversely, an out group is a perceived dissimilar group to which individuals do not belong (Triandis, 1994). Within this theory, people tend to form a group with others they perceive to be similar and differentiate themselves from dissimilar others.

Consistent with the theories of similarity attraction and social identity, the behaviour suggested by social categorisation theory also results in negative organisational attitudes. When distinctions between groups (and people) are made (i.e. when in groups are formed), negative consequences are evoked. These consequences, which appear in the form of stereotypes and prejudice, cause members to make biased attributions. Generally, there is a tendency for members to support their in-group colleagues through congruent values and behaviour, and to emphasise this image as being more desirable and dominant than that of the out groups.

The formation of in groups is highly likely when people conform to **groupthink**. This is often evident in highly cohesive groups and occurs when people publicly agree with the group, yet privately do not. This is generally the case when members' loyalty to the group is high and people tend to agree for the sake of agreeing; they do not want to 'rock the boat'. Therefore, it is often difficult for these members to disagree publicly or question the group (or a members') decision, opinion or idea. This is disadvantageous because a group is most effective when members are encouraged to share viewpoints not withhold them.

groupthink
When people publicly agree with the group, yet privately do not.

The management implications of social categorisation are similar to those of social identity theory. That is, managers need to ensure that an unbiased and impartial group leader is appointed to control such behaviour. However, as this theory suggests, it is a *social* categorisation, which implies that the in and out groups are not necessary work oriented. They are usually social groups formed within organisational boundaries. This presents a new dilemma for management as the control of social groups is somewhat more difficult than work groups. However, it is possible (see Panipucci & Härtel, in press).

One way that management can prevent in and out groups from forming is through diversity training and awareness. This allows employees to realise that the formation of such groups results in discrimination against out-group members, and for this they may be legally liable. The company must also clearly articulate company-specific policies, such as anti-discrimination, and distinguish between direct and indirect discrimination. This is important as some members may not realise they are discriminating against dissimilar others and therefore they must be taught correct behaviour before they can exercise it. In other cases, they may be discriminating when conforming to groupthink, or because they are intimidated by dominant group members and fear that if they oppose such behaviour they will then become out-group members. Whatever the situation, management must exercise discretion and prevent such behaviour before it escalates out of control.

Effects of diversity in the workplace

Although the interaction among the array of differences within the workplace makes it difficult or impossible to disentangle what aspect of diversity affects individuals, groups and organisational outcomes (Major & Crocker, 1993), diversity has generally been recognised as having both positive and negative outcomes (Milliken & Martins, 1996). It is important to consider and understand some of these outcomes before the recruitment of diverse individuals so that the company has the appropriate skills and resources to deal with the impact of diversity effectively. Poorly handled diversity can result in further negative outcomes and be disastrous for both the employees and the organisation involved. Diverse attributes differ from person to person; they are part of who we are. Therefore, any positive or negative outcomes as a result of our diversity affect us on a *personal* level. Unsatisfied employees, poor reputation and even sabotage can occur if diversity is inappropriately handled. It is the responsibility of HRM to manage diversity and teach other managers and employees what their role in diversity is.

POSITIVE EFFECTS OF DIVERSITY

On the positive side, diversity produces cognitive benefits through knowledge creation, innovation, higher quality decisions and flexibility to advance the business. The cognitive benefits can provide the organisation with a competitive edge by responding to today's increasingly diverse volatile environment (e.g. diverse labour market and customers) coupled with the advancement of a knowledge economy.

Specific examples of positive diversity effects include:

- *Innovation.* If diverse individuals are embraced, then their diverse ideas, knowledge and opinions foster innovation that may otherwise not have developed. For example, when launching a new product, it is wise to consider how that product will impact on different kinds of people. Sometimes the people developing the product are too close to the project and cannot understand or perceive how it might affect people who are dissimilar to them. Recruiting diverse individuals for product development allows innovation to occur.

- *Empowerment.* Individuals who are excluded because of their diverse quality (i.e. gender, sexuality, disability, age) become discouraged and unsatisfied with their work and the work environment. They generally feel unhappy and sometimes even unsafe at work. As a result, they do not feel compelled to work to the best of their ability. However, when people are included and treated with respect by others (i.e. colleagues *and* management) their perspective changes. They feel happier and more confident at work, knowing that they have the support and respect of their peers. They feel empowered and rise to challenges and increased responsibility. In essence, they are satisfied with their job.

- *Information sharing.* People can learn from each other, and the more diverse a workforce is the more there is to learn. The greater the information that is shared, the greater the organisational knowledge. Hence, better ideas are stored through knowledge management. Unlike other forms of data, knowledge multiplies when it is shared, rather than simply being transferred from one source to another. This adds significant value to the firm.

- *Group decision effectiveness.* Diverse members have different ways of doing things, which allows the group to 'think outside the square' and develop unique, inimitable solutions. Whereas similar group members will generally develop the same solutions, diverse members increase the probability of broader alternatives and thus the overall decision is more effective.

- *Openness to dissimilarity.* A diverse workplace teaches people that diversity needs to be embraced, rather than avoided or shunned. Just because people are different doesn't mean that they are less important or less capable of performing tasks. For example, people with intellectual disabilities may be unable to develop a strategic marketing plan, yet they may have outstanding skills in other areas, such as invention or attention to detail. At the Caulfield campus of Monash University in Melbourne, some of the grounds-keeping staff have Downs Syndrome (an intellectual disability) but perform an excellent job of maintaining the gardens. They have very friendly personalities, genuinely enjoy their job and are able to interact with both staff and students. Although there are companies who specifically employ intellectually disabled people (such as community shelters) there is no reason why disabled people are unable to work in 'normal' organisations. It also boosts their self-esteem and confidence and allows them to be a part of mainstream society.

Likewise, physically disabled people are also able to work in 'normal' jobs. This is especially important to consider when people have been injured at work. Quite often, employees' motivation decreases after work injuries, and one way of combating this is to give them different jobs while they are healing. Not only does their motivation increase, but they can keep earning a salary and experience a different part of the workplace (multiskilling) and it can assist physical and mental healing. By making things as normal as possible, both the individual and the organisation benefit greatly.

Additionally, in Australia we live in a multicultural society. As a country, we benefit from the variety of cultural activities, food and resources/skills that now make up Australia. In turn, this provides companies with a competitive edge. Australians of all national heritages need to be open to accepting others who are dissimilar to them.

- *Productivity*. There is no doubt that diverse organisations are more productive. Employees who are more innovative, empowered and open to difference are more likely to be happier and hence more productive at work. Different people have different information to contribute to idea development and crisis solutions. Therefore, decisions will undeniably be more effective.

Diversity, if implemented and embraced by all, is a catalyst for a competitive advantage. However, not all diversity effects are positive.

NEGATIVE EFFECTS OF DIVERSITY

Sometimes, diversity can directly or indirectly have negative consequences on individuals, groups and/or organisations. One explanation of this is because, in practice, there is a gap between the organisations' recognition of the benefits of diversity and the action to reap the benefits. They simply do not have the understanding or knowledge of how to manage diversity effectively to get the most out of it. Therefore, negative effects prevail.

Research has shown that diversity is often associated with negative affective and behavioural outcomes. Diverse workers tend to exhibit negative emotions (e.g. stress, anxiety and depression), are likely to be less satisfied with their jobs, more likely to leave, more often absent and experience more communication difficulties (Fujimoto, Härtel & Panipucci, 2005). These findings reveal that the potential cognitive benefits of diversity in organisations are being outweighed by affective and behavioural costs.

Specific examples of negative diversity effects include:

- *Discrimination*. As humans, people tend to fear others who are different from themselves. In particular, certain communities or societies tend to act this way, such as the tendency for Australians not to trust foreigners (Mackay, 1993). The problem isn't that we fear the people, but rather the *difference*, such as the religion, behaviour, beliefs or manner of working. Simply because it is unknown or dissimilar, others tend to treat the difference as unequal and discriminate against it.

Discrimination is more likely to occur when there is an increased diversity of people. The type of discrimination will depend on the culture of the workplace (i.e. the norms, values and attitudes of organisational members). Historically, minority groups have been discriminated against simply because their representation in the workplace is minimal. However, this isn't always the case. For example, five years ago there was a recorded case of discrimination based on sexual preference at a prominent state-owned Victorian organisation. A heterosexual employee who had been on maternity leave returned to find her desk moved to the very corner of the office. Because a majority of employees in this workplace were gay, they discriminated against this employee's heterosexuality and the employee was compensated for her colleagues' inappropriate and discriminatory behaviour.

When people are discriminated against they feel less secure at work, and their motivation, satisfaction, commitment, loyalty, productivity and even feelings of self-esteem decrease. It is the company's responsibility to implement diversity awareness and training, such as through posters, seminars and reprimand. Failure to do so will result in the *company* being liable for the discrimination (not the employee(s)) and possibly involve litigation. A flow-on effect of this is, of course, a poor reputation with all stakeholders, including clients and potential high-quality employees. These employees may choose another firm over the so-called 'discriminatory' company and thus the company's competitive advantage will vanish.

- *Communication.* With a variety of diverse individuals comes a variety of verbal and non-verbal behaviour. This can cause communication problems in the workplace and be extremely frustrating for all involved, especially if people fail to understand the differences. One way to help managers and employees understand cultural differences is by looking at a framework for the dimensions of national culture. In 1980, Geert Hofstede conducted a study on the broad differences in national cultures and the management implications of these. His data, accessed through an IBM database, revealed that the degree of impact depended on four dimensions. The fifth dimension, time orientation, was subsequently added in later research.

power distance
The degree to which people accept an equal or unequal distribution of power in organisations and society.

The first dimension is **power distance**. This is the degree to which people accept an equal or unequal distribution of power in organisations and society. For example, countries such as the Philippines display high power distance between those with and without authority, both in organisations and in society. This is evident by the large gap between the poor and the rich in society, and between government officials and public servants. On the other hand, countries such as Australia exert low power distance as there is a much more equal power distribution in society and in organisations. Therefore, how and when people communicate with high- or lower-level employees will differ.

uncertainty avoidance
The degree to which society takes risks or tolerates uncertain or ambiguous situations.

Uncertainty avoidance is the second dimension. This refers to the degree to which a society takes risks or tolerates uncertain or ambiguous situations. For example, Greek nationals tend to tolerate more risk and uncertainty than do Singaporean nationals, who tend to desire structure and continuity. Countries such as Japan and Australia, however, are somewhere in between.

This is important to understand because it can affect the way people communicate with each other and also communicate risk levels. What is deemed not risky by one person may be perceived as very risky by another.

The third dimension is *individualism versus collectivism* (see Chapter 2 for key term definitions). Individualism, which is common in Western societies, infers that people tend to look after their own needs and put these before others. In contrast, collectivism, which tends to occur in Eastern societies, is when people put the needs of the group (or community) above their own. For example, in an organisation collectivists may communicate openly with each other, yet may shield this from those not within their group. Likewise, individualists compete against each other and tend to communicate primarily to better their position over others' (See chapter 2 for a further discussion on individualism and collectivism).

Masculinity versus femininity is the fourth dimension. Similar to individualism versus collectivism, this dimension refers to the degree of masculine characteristics (i.e. material success and assertiveness) as opposed to feminine characteristics (i.e. concern and feelings for others and for relationships). This dimension features prominently in the communication aspect as it may be considered appropriate or inappropriate to display certain characteristics. For example, in masculine societies such as Japan, Australia and the USA, displaying feminine characteristics is a sign of weakness. Whereas in feminine societies, such as Sweden, the display of masculine characteristics is often viewed as harsh, abrupt and selfish. This is important as the communication content can be misconstrued if not effectively understood.

masculinity versus femininity
The degree of masculine characteristics (i.e. material success and assertiveness) as opposed to feminine characteristics (i.e. concern and feelings for others and for relationships).

The final dimension is **time orientation**, which is the degree to which long- or short-term consequences are considered. Western societies tend to have short-term orientations, for example when they are conducting business meetings. Work always seems to be rushed and they tend to get straight to the point as an answer was needed 'yesterday'. However, Eastern societies are much more relaxed in the pursuit of business. It is very important to them that they get to know a person before they begin negotiation and, as such, it is quite common for a potential business partner to socialise with them before business matters are addressed. This socialisation may include dinner with their family or visits to a cultural site. This is difficult for a Westerner to comprehend because they do not conduct business like this. However, if they wish the business to be successful they must understand how important this is to Easterners.

time orientation
The degree to which long- or short-term consequences are considered.

- *Power play*. Certain individuals communicate and behave differently, according to their national culture. The way they treat others, their expectations of self and others and their perceived status all impact on how power is distributed and exhibited within organisations. For example, men may think they have more power than women because they view women as the weaker sex. This may particularly be the case with men from the Middle East as women are largely controlled by men in such societies. Therefore, men may have difficulty adopting new behaviours when working with women in the workforce. On the other hand, gender may not be the issue. Any difference may be viewed as weak or powerful, depending on how it is perceived. For example, intellectually disabled people, young employees or Hispanic staff may be viewed as weak by others and hence treated as such. However, the perception of 'weak' is only a *perception* and management should monitor any inappropriate power plays to ensure that employees are not unfairly treated.

- *Conflict*. As with communication problems, the more diverse individuals who are employed, the more conflict is inevitable. This is simply because people do not understand why others think, act or behave a certain way, and the manner in which this is conducted is probably different from what we expect or understand. For example, Indonesians place a high value on family responsibilities and attend to these as a priority. Therefore, they will often arrive late and leave early from work. This is where training in Hofstede's cultural dimensions is useful because it allows employees to be aware of differences so that even if they do not agree or know how to react, they at least understand *why* others are acting that way and a compromise can be reached.

- *Control*. One of the most difficult factors in employing a diverse workforce is that it needs to be controlled. Ineffective control which allows mechanisms such as discrimination, power plays and conflict to arise can have significant negative consequences on individuals, groups and the organisation as these factors foster negativity and, in time, decreased performance. It is imperative that management adopt diversity initiatives to teach all stakeholders (including clients and suppliers) that it is a diversity-friendly organisation and that discrimination or negative behaviour will not be tolerated.

Please read
Richard, O. C., Kochan, T. A. & McMillan-Capehart, A. (2002), 'The impact of visible diversity on organizational effectiveness: Disclosing the contents in Pandora's black box', *Journal of Business and Management*, vol. 8, no. 3, pp. 265–91.

Diversity management

Diversity management is a critical management issue in the twenty-first century and one of the most important challenges HR managers face. To this end, diversity management is closely associated with HRM policies and practices. Australia is becoming an increasingly diverse nation and the way in which diversity is managed can either make or break a company. Diversity management isn't just about employing diverse staff or recognising that different people have different skills. It is much more complicated and important than that.

Historically, Australia has emanated a racist image. This stems from a variety of factors, one of which is Australia's isolation from the rest of the world, particularly British and European colonies. Since the 1950s, however, Australia has attempted to eliminate its racist image by removing the White Australian policy. This policy essentially excluded all non-white people from entering Australia and was evident even up until the 1970s. Despite the eradication of this policy, the level of prejudice and discrimination has continued and experts caution it may even be on the rise. The terrorism attacks on the USA (2001), Indonesia (2002 and 2005) and London (2005) have further fuelled vilification towards people of Islamic or Arabic backgrounds. Unfortunately, despite the importance of diversity management, many Australians fail to recognise its importance and leave racial tensions unaddressed in the workplace (James & Heathcote, 2002). The problem is that Australians perceive themselves to be open to other cultures, races and ethnicities, yet in practice are not. There still needs to be a mind shift regarding diversity openness. Therefore, organisations not only *desire* diversity management, but now *require* it if all organisational members are to embrace, understand and utilise diversity effectively to achieve a competitive advantage.

Diversity management refers to the planning, organising and controlling of diversity-friendly policies and practices, and is reflected in an open-minded organisational culture and climate. It aims to include all employees regardless of background in both the formal and informal structures of the organisation, therefore diversity management may be viewed as a systematic commitment by an organisation to employ, develop and promote a diverse range of employees. Diversity management differs from the equal employment opportunity and affirmative action equity policies used by organisations in the past in that, while these policies were employed by organisations in accordance with legal and regulatory requirements, diversity management is a managerial initiative within the organisation.

diversity management
The planning, organising and controlling of diversity-friendly policies and practices, which is reflected in an open-minded organisational culture and climate.

Diversity management is seen as both more effective and less ambiguous than the management of diversity through legislative and equity policies. A key reason for this is that, rather than valuing the broad range of diversity features of the workplace, these policies tend to focus on one group such as racial minorities or women which is only one segment of today's diverse workforce. Diversity management, on the other hand, is the development of a strategy which facilitates the inclusion of the full range of diverse employees in an organisation to allow them to perform to their maximum potential, which, in turn, ensures the maximum productivity for the organisation.

Successful management of diversity develops within an organisational environment where no one is perceived as advantaged or disadvantaged, and in which the core causes of the problems that can arise from diversity, for example prejudice and inequality, are dealt with. This ensures that all employees have the opportunity to work in an environment which will allow them to contribute unhindered by group identities such as race or gender and develop their capabilities further. Successful diversity management leads to positive outcomes for both individuals and organisations.

When working in an organisation with a diversity management strategy employees report having an improved work life, citing higher cohesion between employees, which is linked with increased productivity and greater commitment and loyalty to the organisation. In turn, this creates higher returns for the organisation. Furthermore, well-managed diversity can be a competitive advantage to an organisation. Organisations who exclude potential human resources in their recruitment and development processes due to their diversity are reducing their pool of employees and potentially denying themselves valuable resources. On the other hand, organisations who practise diversity management have access to a greater pool of unique and valuable human resources which leads the way to developing a competitive advantage. In order to achieve this competitive advantage, diversity management should be incorporated into all the functional areas of the organisation, which includes the HRM system.

INDIVIDUAL DIFFERENCES

A great deal of research has been undertaken that has looked at workforce diversity and a common finding has been that problems tend to arise when there is a failure to integrate and utilise diverse employees, which can have significant implications for both the organisation and the employee. At the group and organisational levels, there is a failure to utilise these employees' capabilities and, hence, productivity is decreased. At an individual level, exclusion can be harmful to the employee's general wellbeing and result in low levels of job satisfaction, commitment and motivation. Consequently, a key aspect of diversity management is the integration and utilisation of diverse individuals. In order to manage diversity effectively and realise the benefits that can be gained from it, individual employees need to be able to manage individual differences effectively. To do this they need both to understand and be open to these differences so that they are able to communicate and integrate across them. Two key skills that assist in the management of individual differences are dissimilarity openness and cultural knowledge.

DISSIMILARITY OPENNESS

Research indicates that individuals will be attracted to those people they perceive to be similar to themselves, which can lead to the exclusion of diverse co-workers, creating a negative impact on organisational processes and performance and even leading to diverse individuals being driven out of the organisation. However, diverse individuals are not always excluded. The extent to which individuals are attracted to people they perceive to be similar to themselves may be moderated by their **dissimilarity openness**.

dissimilarity openness
The extent to which an individual is open to people they perceive to be dissimilar to themself.

The Perceived Dissimilarity Openness Moderator Model (Härtel & Fujimoto, 2000) indicates that people may differ in the way they react to dissimilarity because of differences in their openness to perceived dissimilarity. The more open people are to perceived dissimilarities, the less likely they are to be attracted only to those people they perceive to be similar to themselves and the more likely they are to incorporate difference into work processes in a positive way. A person who is open to dissimilarity is likely to be open to learning from dissimilar others and trying to see things from their point of view. They don't make value judgements based on the degree to which they are similar or dissimilar to another person. Overall, they view difference as positive. On the other hand, individuals who are not open to dissimilarity are not open to learning from diverse colleagues, nor are they willing to try and see things from their point of view. Overall, they view differences as negative.

The importance of dissimilarity openness has been demonstrated in the results of a number of studies that have looked at the impact it can have at the individual, group and organisational levels. For example, it has been found that openness to difference assists with conflict resolution and group cohesion in organisations. Clearly, then, in order for an organisation to operate to its maximum potential the individuals within it need to be able to overcome their predisposition to be attracted to individuals they perceive to be similar to themselves.

CULTURAL KNOWLEDGE

For individuals to manage their relationships effectively with diverse co-workers and in particular co-workers from different cultural backgrounds, they need to be able to communicate properly with them. This can be very difficult as people from different cultural backgrounds have different frames of reference or ways of thinking about things and can ascribe different meanings to behaviours. Consequently, they may interpret messages differently from one another. The best way to overcome these problems and lower barriers to communication is with knowledge and understanding of cultural factors. Hence, cultural knowledge is another key skill for managing individual differences effectively.

Cultural knowledge is knowledge of things such as social norms and beliefs and frames of reference used by people from different cultural backgrounds. The amount of cultural knowledge an individual has will shape the way they think about things and is a key determinant of their effectiveness in interacting with diverse colleagues. The more knowledge a person has about different cultures, the less influence their own cultural background and frames of reference will have on the way they interpret information and interactions with culturally diverse colleagues.

cultural knowledge
Knowledge about such things as cultural practices and beliefs of cultures other than one's own.

A person with high cultural knowledge will have a better understanding of the frames of reference that diverse individuals use and hence the way they think. Therefore, when they are acting with colleagues from diverse cultural backgrounds they are less likely to misinterpret information or non-verbal signals, meaning their interactions are far less likely to be subject to the problems that cultural and behavioural differences can create. A person with low cultural knowledge, on the other hand, is likely to face serious challenges when they are interacting with colleagues from diverse cultural backgrounds. It is likely that productivity will suffer as a result of misunderstandings and conflict which can arise as a result of a failure to interpret accurately the messages and behaviours of culturally diverse colleagues.

Two key ways in which cultural knowledge can be acquired are through training and through experience. Overall, interacting with people from different cultural backgrounds is one of the most effective ways of developing cultural knowledge, therefore the more 'international experience' an employee has, the higher their cultural knowledge is likely to be. It is important to recognise that 'knowing how culturally different people think and act does not make one a member of that culture nor does it guarantee that one will successfully think and act like them' (Mamman, 1995, p. 99).

GROUP/LEADER MANAGEMENT

Effective leadership is a key component of successful diversity management. Managers play a crucial role in shaping an organisation's environment as well as an employee's skills and abilities through the provision of coaching, feedback and management in all organisations. In organisations with a diverse employee base the complexities of the relationships between individuals is even greater hence the role of the manager is even more crucial and it is important that organisations have managers who can manage diverse workgroups effectively. These managers need to understand the different frames of references that their employees use that shape their attitudes, feelings and behaviours as well as interpersonal and group processes. They also need sound communication skills and the ability to maintain cooperative relationships with and between employees. Overall, three key leadership skills which are important for managing diversity can be identified: conflict management skills, emotion management skills and openness to dissimilarity.

CONFLICT MANAGEMENT

A key barrier to organisations with a diverse employee base maximising their productivity is conflict. For this reason, good conflict management skills are essential for managing diversity. Three main types of conflict can occur in workgroups: relationship conflict, which is personal disagreement not related to work; task conflict, which is conflict about the work being undertaken by the group; and process conflict, which is conflict about the strategy for doing the work such as the delegation of duties and resources (Jehn & Chatman, 2000).

conflict management skills
Involve an understanding of not only how to manage conflict but also how other people manage conflict.

Good **conflict management skills** involve understanding not only the way you manage conflict but also the way that others manage conflict. Cooperation, collaboration, avoiding, compromise and competing are five conflict management strategies that people may employ and which managers should understand. In diverse groups, a cooperative rather than a competitive approach to conflict management is best. The reason for this is that a competitive approach to conflict can lead to perceptions of prejudice and intimidation and to group segregation, while a cooperative approach encourages more positive behaviours that facilitate group cohesion.

In diverse groups, it is also important for managers to realise that an individual's cultural background can have a significant impact on their perceptions of conflict as well as their reactions and strategies for dealing with conflict. For this reason, managers need to be sensitive to cultural cues which suggest the need for the use of a different conflict management strategy and they need the ability to implement a variety of different conflict management strategies and tactics appropriate to the situation.

EMOTION MANAGEMENT

While social conflict is unrelated to work tasks it can have a considerable emotional toll on employees and a crippling effect on an organisation. There are two main reasons for this. First, instead of doing the tasks they are employed to do, employees are focusing their efforts on dealing with the social conflict. Second, emotions related to social conflict often lead to people being unable to obtain and take in all relevant information when doing a task. For this reason, emotion management skills are a second key skill in diversity management.

Four significant components of **emotion management** are discussed by Jordan, Ashkanasy and Härtel (1997). These include dealing with your own emotions, which includes being aware of and displaying your own emotions as well as controlling the emotions you feel; dealing with other people's emotions, which includes being aware of and empathising with others' emotions as well as being able to manage other people's emotions; using emotions in decision making; and using emotions in problem solving.

emotion management
Dealing with your own and others' emotions as well as using emotions in decision making and problem solving.

Emotion management capabilities are important as successful emotion management allows people to deal with such things as social conflict and focus their energies and attention on more important issues such as the task at hand. People differ in their emotion management abilities, yet with effort and training their abilities can be changed and enhanced. This is important as good emotion management skills help people process information more effectively and they are thus able to motivate, plan and achieve better. For this reason, leaders of diverse groups need to be able to monitor both their own emotions as well as the emotions of their employees to facilitate positive organisational outcomes.

DISSIMILARITY OPENNESS

As well as being important for the management of individual differences, dissimilarity openness is also an important attribute for managers of diverse teams to possess. As indicated in the previous section on managing individual differences, people tend to be attracted to people they perceive to be similar to themselves. This can be problematic in the manager–employee relationship in diverse groups as leadership theories indicate that mangers will typically develop a closer relationship with a small group of employees, who are given greater influence and benefits in exchange for their assistance and commitment. Their relationship with other employees is significantly different and in a diverse group this can become particularly problematic.

According to the Perceived Dissimilarity Openness Moderator Model (Härtel & Fujimoto, 2000), managers who are open to dissimilarity will be less likely to make distinctions between those people they perceive to be similar to themselves and those they perceive as dissimilar. For this reason, openness to dissimilarity is a particularly important trait for leaders of diverse groups as their making fewer distinctions between group members will reduce the levels of conflict in the group as well as increase their conflict management skills. Overall, it can be said that a manager's openness to and treatment of diverse group members is critical to the cohesion and outcomes of the group.

Please read

Dass, P. & Parker, B. (1996), 'Diversity: A strategic issue', in *Managing Diversity: Human Resource Strategies for Transforming the Workplace*, eds E. E. Kossek & S. A. Lobel, Blackwell Business, Cambridge, Mass.

Diversity-oriented HRM

While diversity management has the potential to create a competitive advantage for an organisation, it is dependent upon the effectiveness of the HRM policies and practices employed by the organisation. In other words, to realise this potential competitive advantage the organisation needs to match its HRM policies and practices with its employees to facilitate the development and maximisation of their abilities. **Diversity-oriented HRM** refers to HRM policies and practices that aim to attract, employ, develop and promote high-potential diverse employees who will be able to assist the organisation to meet the challenges of today's diverse marketplace.

As the impact of diversity on individuals, groups and organisations is complex and unpredictable, diversity-oriented HR functions, including recruitment, performance appraisals, development programs and remuneration packages, will assist in minimising the potential negative effects of diversity and contribute to the organisation realising the potential benefits of a diverse workforce. One organisation that has capitalised on the implementation of diversity-oriented HRM policies and practices is IBM. At IBM, recruitment, training and development, evaluations and promotions are based on individual merit alone. The success of this organisation globally indicates that these practices are paying off. Diversity is here to stay, therefore the integration of diversity-oriented HRM policies and practices is essential if an organisation wants to be successful in the long run.

diversity-oriented HRM
HRM policies and practices that aim to attract, employ, develop and promote high-potential diverse employees.

DIVERSITY-OPEN RECRUITMENT AND SELECTION

The aim of **diversity-open recruitment and selection** is to recruit and select the most suitable person(s) for the job regardless of diversity attributes such as gender, race, age or religion. Diversity-oriented recruitment and selection require an organisation to be proactive. This can be done in a number of ways. One example is through the establishment of diverse selection committees and recruiters. This is important to ensure that applications are not excluded based on irrelevant criteria. Another way an organisation can be proactive is by placing advertisements that clearly indicate that the organisation is diversity oriented. This will attract individuals from a range of diverse backgrounds as well as individuals wishing to work in an organisation with an inclusive environment. A third example of proactive diversity-oriented recruitment and selection is the establishment of minority recruitment goals, which have been shown to have positive outcomes for organisations.

diversity-open recruitment and selection
Recruiting the person(s) most suitable for the job regardless of diversity attributes.

Organisations who fail to practise diversity-open recruitment and selection will find themselves disadvantaged for a variety of reasons including:
1. Without a diverse workforce an organisation will not have the human resources necessary to meet the challenges of today's diverse marketplace.
2. Having a diverse workforce will facilitate the effective marketing of an organisation towards its diverse customers.
3. Diversity-open recruitment and selection practices assist an organisation in the development of a good public image.
4. Employing a diverse range of individuals increases innovation, creativity and the quality of ideas that an organisation will produce.
5. It is against the law to allow prejudice to influence employee recruitment and selection.

Clearly, diversity-oriented recruitment and selection are steps towards an organisation developing a sustainable competitive advantage. However, it cannot create this advantage alone and research indicates that the problems associated with workforce diversity are related less to the recruitment and selection of diverse employees and more to their development, promotion and retention. Therefore, in order to support diversity-open recruitment and selection, an organisation must also have diversity-open training and development as well as performance evaluations and appraisals.

DIVERSITY-OPEN TRAINING AND DEVELOPMENT

Training is essential for the development of an organisation's workforce. It is of particular importance for organisations with a diverse workforce as it may be necessary to assist individuals to manage their differences and work together effectively. Furthermore, **diversity-open training and development** have been shown to have a substantial positive impact on employee attitudes toward diversity as a whole as well as increasing employees' perceptions of management's actual concern and commitment to diversity issues (Ellis & Sonnenfeld, 1994). Another distinct advantage of diversity-open training is that it can stop employees inaccurately perceiving that minority employees have been hired because of their minority status or that they receive too much attention or special treatment from management due to it.

diversity-open training and development
Training and development that will foster understanding between all employees as well as provide all employees with equal opportunities to enhance their skills.

Diversity-open training and development can be both formal and informal. Formal educational programs may be established to educate employees about the diversity existing in their workplace. For example, training programs to facilitate attitudinal changes in employees could be established to increase their awareness and understanding of differences. This would prevent negative perceptions related to stereotyping which hinder employee interactions. Another example of formal diversity-open training is intercultural communication training to improve employees' intercultural communication abilities. Effective communication between employees is essential, therefore communication training that not only teaches employees communication skills (e.g. active listening techniques) but also provides them with information related to the norms of communication in different cultures will facilitate improved communication.

Informal diversity-oriented training can be just as important as formal diversity-oriented training. The reason for this is that it sets the tone for the type of behaviour expected of employees. An example of informal diversity training is in the communication practices of an organisation. For example, if an organisation incorporates diversity-related issues into things such as newsletters or its marketing, it provides employees with the perception that diversity is valued in the organisation and assists in developing a diversity climate of openness.

Overall, both formal and informal diversity-open training and development should:

1. provide employees with information that will help them to understand one another better so that they are able to overcome their dissimilarities, manage individual differences effectively and create a diversity climate of openness;
2. assist in the development of interpersonal skills to reduce unnecessary misunderstandings and conflicts between colleagues;
3. develop team working skills to facilitate cooperation and cohesion as well as facilitate diverse group learning;

4. have the support of senior management as this is the best predictor of training success.

It should be noted that diversity-open training and development should be provided for managers as well as employees. This is essential as it is the leaders within an organisation who set the tone. Consequently, many organisations provide their senior managers with diversity training to ensure that they understand the importance of developing a diverse workforce to meet the diverse needs of the marketplace.

DIVERSITY-OPEN PERFORMANCE EVALUATIONS FOR APPRAISAL, PROMOTION AND COMPENSATION: ACCOUNTABILITY FOR MANAGERS' BEHAVIOURS

diversity-open performance evaluations
Achieved by including diversity criteria in organisational objectives and the evaluations of individual managers.

Diversity-open performance evaluations are essential to the motivation, retention and promotion of diverse individuals. The aim of diversity-open performance evaluations and appraisals is to evaluate performance based on job-related characteristics rather than irrelevant characteristics of the individual. It is in this area that numerous organisations have suffered in the past as is evident from research showing the operation of prejudice in performance appraisals. While performance evaluators are not always conscious of allowing prejudice to influence their evaluations, it can impact considerably on the minority employees being appraised. As well as creating barriers to their advancement in the organisation, it can also create feelings of resentment, which generally results in reduced commitment and productivity.

To ensure that performance evaluations for appraisal, promotion and compensation are diversity open, organisations need to:

1. incorporate diversity into organisational objectives;
2. hold individual managers accountable for the performance appraisals they conduct by including diversity criteria in the performance evaluations of the individual managers.

Managers can be assessed to see the extent to which they are meeting organisational diversity objectives, for example providing mentors or training for minority employees. This can be done through such things as employee surveys or 360-degree reviews. Implementing these criteria in manager evaluations will make it difficult for managers to allow bias to influence their performance evaluations of employees. It also clearly indicates to employees that diversity is valued within the organisation and that minority status will not hold them back from achieving. It also assists in the development of a diversity climate of openness and is likely to motivate employees to perform to their maximum potential.

Please read

Kossek, E. E. & Lobel, S. A. (1996), 'Introduction: Transforming human resource systems to manage diversity: An introduction and orienting framework', in *Managing Diversity Human Resource Strategies for Transforming the Workplace*, eds E. E. Kossek & S. A. Lobel, Blackwell Business, Cambridge, Mass.

Issues related to workforce diversity

While in the past the workforce was predominantly made up of white males, today, as this chapter has demonstrated, there are people from many backgrounds and with vastly divergent values, attitudes and beliefs working together. While this chapter has considered the positive and negative impacts that these differences can have upon individual, workgroup and organisational outcomes there are other issues that increased workforce diversity raises. These include but are not limited to things such as work–life balance and having the freedom/facilities to practise one's religious beliefs.

A BALANCED WORK LIFE

In Australia, women account for 42 per cent of the workforce meaning that female participation in the workforce has increased 20 per cent in the past decade, reflecting society's changing view regarding the role of women at home and in the workplace. Far more women with children are working full time than in the past and women and men are both working longer hours than they were a decade ago. Additionally, many households today have increased responsibilities such as financial pressures or caring for elderly relatives and it is likely that these pressures are only going to increase in the future. Consequently maintaining work–life balance can be very difficult and stressful. Over half of the active labour force in Australia identifies this pressure as negatively impacting on their personal/ family life. This stress can translate into decreased productivity or alternatively the difficulty in maintaining work–life balance can lead employees to look for alternative, more flexible or family-friendly employment. It is therefore important that the organisations of the future employ HRM policies and practices that will assist employees in maintaining a balanced life.

There is a variety of HRM policies and practices which organisations can utilise to help their employees maintain a healthy work–life balance. Examples of these practices and why they are important include:

- The provision of childcare facilities or childcare assistance. This is one of the most commonly provided programs. The reason for this is likely to be due to high demand as in a majority of families with children both parents are employed.
- Considering that we have an ageing population, another program likely to gain popularity in the future is the provision of assistance of care for older family members. This is likely to be of particular importance for employees with an Asian cultural background as it is the custom in many Asian countries to care for the elderly at home.
- Many organisations have introduced flexible work practices to allow employees to meet both their work and home obligations. These include practices such as job-sharing arrangements that allow employees to share the responsibility of their job with another person and work part time only.
- Telecommuting and remote work arrangements are increasingly being used by large organisations. With the state of technology today it is possible for employees to work effectively from a home office, allowing them to meet both their work and home obligations.

Providing HRM policies and practices which facilitate employees maintaining a work–life balance allows an organisation to retain the knowledge and abilities of highly skilled staff who would otherwise seek employment elsewhere. The reason for this is that organisations which offer flexible work practices are generally seen as employers of choice and attract high-quality employees. Furthermore, employees in organisations offering these policies and practices tend to have higher levels of motivation and lower levels of absenteeism which has been estimated to lead to a $2 to $6 return for every $1 spent on these programs by the organisation.

ACCOMMODATING RELIGIOUS PRACTICES

While the major religion in Australia today is Christianity, all major religious groups are represented with Hinduism, Buddhism, Islam and Judaism the religions experiencing the greatest increase. Each of these religions has different practices, traditions and holidays hence with increased workforce diversity comes the need to accommodate religious practices in the workplace.

Christians celebrate such religious occasions as Easter and Christmas, for which Australia has public holidays, while Hanukah is an important religious celebration on the Jewish calendar and Ramadan is an important religious celebration on the Muslim calendar. Furthermore, while Sunday is the day of the week that Christians predominantly go to church, people of the Jewish faith attend synagogue on Saturdays and Muslims have Friday afternoon prayers at the mosque. In addition, many Muslims pray five times a day. It is important that, as far as possible, organisations allow employees to meet their religious commitments.

Organisations which provide flexible work arrangements so that their employees are able to meet their religious commitments are more likely to attract and retain high-calibre employees from a range of religious backgrounds than organisations which do not. Ways in which employers can do this include:
• Providing flexible work arrangements through the use of flexible scheduling or voluntary substitutions and allowing employees to make up time taken for things such as prayer at other times.
• Providing a space in which employees are able to undertake their prayers.
• Scheduling important events such as interviews, evaluations and training at times/dates which will not conflict with significant religious commitments.

Contemporary SHRM Application Tool

Businesses facing a labour shortage have been urged to hire marginalised workers such as mature aged and people with disabilities. Imagine that you are an HR manager of a large multinational IT company, leading the way in recruiting people with disabilities. Even before the new government regulation encouraging recruitment of people with disabilities, your company has always been actively looking for ways to capitalise on people of all differences. Due to today's significant skill shortage and changing labour market, your company is facing an opportunity to promote diversity openness to a large number of clients and to sell accessible technology software to them. Accessible technology is a term used to refer to technology which has been developed to give disabled individuals access comparable to those without a disability. This may be achieved by functions built into the product, software available to assist with using the product or specialty technology products (e.g. Braille labeller). The SHRM Application Tool demonstrates how you can put this opportunity into innovative practice (refer to Figure 5.2).

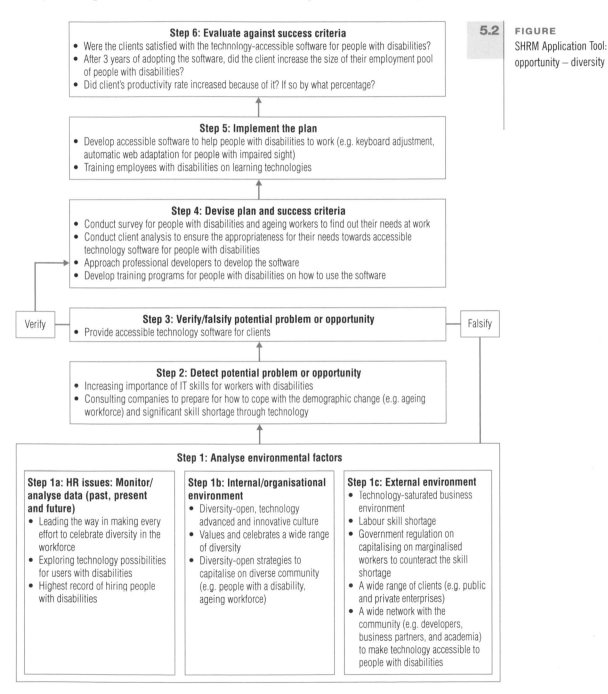

5.2 FIGURE
SHRM Application Tool: opportunity – diversity

Step 6: Evaluate against success criteria
- Were the clients satisfied with the technology-accessible software for people with disabilities?
- After 3 years of adopting the software, did the client increase the size of their employment pool of people with disabilities?
- Did client's productivity rate increased because of it? If so by what percentage?

Step 5: Implement the plan
- Develop accessible software to help people with disabilities to work (e.g. keyboard adjustment, automatic web adaptation for people with impaired sight)
- Training employees with disabilities on learning technologies

Step 4: Devise plan and success criteria
- Conduct survey for people with disabilities and ageing workers to find out their needs at work
- Conduct client analysis to ensure the appropriateness for their needs towards accessible technology software for people with disabilities
- Approach professional developers to develop the software
- Develop training programs for people with disabilities on how to use the software

Verify

Step 3: Verify/falsify potential problem or opportunity
- Provide accessible technology software for clients

Falsify

Step 2: Detect potential problem or opportunity
- Increasing importance of IT skills for workers with disabilities
- Consulting companies to prepare for how to cope with the demographic change (e.g. ageing workforce) and significant skill shortage through technology

Step 1: Analyse environmental factors

Step 1a: HR issues: Monitor/ analyse data (past, present and future)
- Leading the way in making every effort to celebrate diversity in the workforce
- Exploring technology possibilities for users with disabilities
- Highest record of hiring people with disabilities

Step 1b: Internal/organisational environment
- Diversity-open, technology advanced and innovative culture
- Values and celebrates a wide range of diversity
- Diversity-open strategies to capitalise on diverse community (e.g. people with a disability, ageing workforce)

Step 1c: External environment
- Technology-saturated business environment
- Labour skill shortage
- Government regulation on capitalising on marginalised workers to counteract the skill shortage
- A wide range of clients (e.g. public and private enterprises)
- A wide network with the community (e.g. developers, business partners, and academia) to make technology accessible to people with disabilities

A view from the field

Work–life balance as a diversity strategy

The critical mass in the population, a bubble known as baby boomers (those born between 1946 and 1964), is moving towards traditional retirement age. How can we, in organisations, deal with this large group potentially exiting the productive workforce? The answer may be work–life balance.

Work–life balance presents in different ways to different age groups occupying the workforce. What is important to baby boomers may be insignificant to generation X's (those born between 1965 and 1980). Therefore, work–life balance options are many and varied and present much potential in an organisation's attempt to address diversity.

According to Australian Bureau of Statistics research, population ageing is occurring on a global scale, with faster ageing projected for the coming decades than has occurred in the past. Between the years 1950 and 2000, the median age of the world's population rose just three years (from 23.6 to 26.4). In contrast, from 2000 to 2050, the median age is projected to increase by 10 years, to reach 36.8 years. Globally, the population aged 60 years and over is projected to nearly triple by 2050, while the population aged 80 years and over is projected to experience a more than fivefold increase.

This global trend presents enormous challenges for organisations as they plan to meet the demand for skills in the future. The talent pool available in the labour market is shrinking and its makeup is certainly changing. The Australian demographic profile reflects this global trend as it is clearly ageing. Those currently available in the labour market are certainly getting older, and fewer younger workers joining the workforce compound the problem. The Australian government's Intergenerational Report indicates that there are approximately five people of working age for every Australian over 65. That figure will be halved by the middle of the century as the baby boomers age.

The Australian Minister for Workplace Relations, Mr Kevin Andrews, highlighted these issues in a recent address. He stated that, 'Our changing demographic profile is caused by two factors: firstly we are living longer (an average of 20 years longer than our ancestors a century ago) and, secondly, our fertility rate has fallen below replacement level for more than 30 years'.

Many commentators are calling for increased levels of immigration to bolster the Australian workforce, particularly in trade areas. Others are advocating the further application of technology to low-value, transactional processes, allowing the shift of labour resources to high-value activities. These solutions may assist in the short term; however, the bigger issue of population trends across the globe looms large. These trends call for innovative responses.

One strategy currently being explored by the Australian government is the possibility of increasing workforce participation rates and encouraging Australians to extend their working lives. As part of this strategy, the government's Department of Employment and Workplace Relations advises employers to:

1. Change their mindset to be open to recruiting experienced workers, removing real or imagined barriers.
2. Use creative employment strategies to inspire experienced workers to want to continue working longer.

The department highlights flexible employment strategies as a key to retaining high-value employees as they age and minimising the loss of valuable skills to retirement or other life choices. It recommends an environment supporting work life balance, such as part-time work, longer holiday options and phased retirement. In order to maximise the benefit of these initiatives, organisations will need to take a strategic view of the acquisition and retention of their employees. It will be necessary to review traditional approaches to the structuring of work, conditions of employment and incentives.

In 2003 the Business Council of Australia (BCA) released a report entitled '50+ age can work'. Dr John Schubert, President of the BCA, highlighted the critical nature of Australia's response to the challenges associated with an ageing population. Australia's capacity to respond will depend significantly on the ability and willingness of older Australians to participate in the workforce. The report also highlighted the impact the changing age profile will have on consumption patterns. It indicates that, over the next decade, spending of those aged over 55 years will grow at twice the national average. This group will be powerful and influential in consumption trends and, consequently, organisations should seek to align their workforces better with this profile.

The report also highlighted the need for individuals to maintain and improve their skills and employability over time. Employers and employees share responsibility for this investment in individual and collective skill bases.

Organisations large and small are testing new approaches to address the issues of an ageing population. In September 2005, the ANZ Banking Group, one of Australia's largest banks with a strong presence in Asia and the Pacific, announced a new policy that confirmed its commitment to providing opportunities for older workers by guaranteeing over 55s the right to work. The policy offers existing ANZ staff the opportunity to explore a range of working options including part-time work and a move to less demanding positions allowing for a better work–life balance.

In announcing the policy, ANZ highlighted this strategy as a further step in developing an environment where staff are highly engaged and valued for their work, and also encouraged to achieve the right balance between work and home life. Further ANZ HRM policies were highlighted in the announcement. These included: doubling maternity leave to 12 weeks which is available to all staff without a qualifying service period; priority access to childcare facilitates with salary sacrificing available for childcare payments; and flexible work practices such as job sharing, telecommuting and flexible hours.

ANZ further strengthened its commitment to the advancement of diversity within its workforce with the announcement in November 2005 of the appointment of a Head of Advancement of Diversity and Women reporting to the Group General Manager of People Capital. The appointee, Fiona Krautil, is a former Director of the Equal Opportunity for Women in the Workplace Agency (EOWA). EOWA is the Australian government agency responsible for developing and promoting policies and programs designed to address issues faced by women in the workplace.

Another company that has implemented diversity initiatives for the ageing population is Noni B, a women's retail fashion outlet catering for women in the 40 plus age group. Currently, the company employs 920 staff and has benefitted from exploring work–life balance issues with its employees. More than 50 per cent of Noni B's employees are aged over 45 and the majority of employees (98 per cent) are women. The company has a highly flexible approach to its staffing structures with many employees electing to work permanent part-time to accommodate work–life balance.

Staff surveys have provided Noni B with feedback which led to an examination of existing employment conditions and the introduction of options designed to provide optimum flexibility to employees. As a consequence, a number of employees have altered their working arrangements, with significant growth in the number electing to work in a permanent part-time capacity, from 10 per cent to 35 per cent of total staff numbers. Approximately 40 per cent of the remaining staff are permanent full-time employees with the balance being casual staff. This flexibility has also made employment with Noni B an attractive proposition and is one of the factors which has contributed to a reduction in staff turnover from 40 per cent to 16 per cent over three years, assisting with the retention of valued employees.

Bob Critchley is Chairman of Noni B's Board. He comments, 'The ability to accommodate the life choices of our employees has been a key influence on the reduction of turnover in Noni B. We have found that staff are delighted with the flexible employment options on offer. The employment flexibility has made a significant difference to our ability to attract and retain quality staff'.

Global population ageing is a significant social and economic issue worldwide. Governments and organisations are searching for options and solutions to address the significant challenges this phenomenon presents.

Work–life balance and diversity present opportunities to encourage and extend workforce participation to contribute towards addressing the labour market challenges.

Discussion questions

1. Identify the issues ANZ may face in managing a workforce made up of many different age groups. How would you try to address these concerns?

2. ANZ and Noni B have explored diversity as a strategy to maximise the potential of the talent available in the labour market. How can the experiences of these companies be applied to other organisations?

3. Imagine you are the Head of Human Resources for an organisation experiencing significant growth. You are required to recruit 300 staff for a new facility. What would you do to ensure that a diversity-open recruitment and selection process was applied?

Source: Adapted from Australian Government (2002), *Intergenerational Report*, Budget Paper no. 5, <http://www.budget.gov.au/2002-03>, accessed 1 June 2005; Department of Employment and Workplace Relations (2005), *Attract and Retain People?*, Commonwealth of Australia, Canberra; ANZ (2005), 'ANZ guarantees over 55s the right to work part time', *Media Releases*, <http://www.anz.com>, accessed 19 September 2005; Business Council of Australia (2003), '50+ age can work', *Reports*, <http://www.bca.com.au>, accessed 5 January 2005.

A diverse workplace sets IBM apart

Led by the notion of 'One Team—Many People', IBM Australia's Diversity, Equal Employment Opportunity (EEO), Anti Discrimination and Anti Harassment Policy has made the company one of the most sought after employers in the world. In 2002, IBM received the Diversity@Work Award for the most Outstanding Organisation, in recognition of its inclusion of people with disabilities. In 2003, IBM was again the joint winner of this award for large organisations. In 2004, Philip Bullock, the CEO of IBM Australia & New Zealand, and also the chairperson of IBM's Diversity Council, was awarded the 'Leading CEO for the Advancement of Women award' by the Equal Opportunity for Women in the Workplace Agency (EOWA). Moreover, IBM Australia is a partner sponsor of the 2005 Diversity@work Leadership in Diversity awards.

Philip Bullock says, 'At IBM, one of the core values of the organisation is that people are our strength – and this has not changed since the inception of the company. Our commitment to diversity gives the company access to the brightest and best in the workplace: it engenders loyalty; it builds our reputation for good corporate citizenship and enables us to compete more effectively in the marketplace'. The fact that IBM's efforts in maintaining a diverse workforce have been spearheaded by its CEO has rendered serious regard and direct managerial support for its diversity policy. IBM's Diversity Council ensures that differences of employees from diverse backgrounds are recognised and their contributions valued. The company also has Diversity Contact Officers, who are permanent employees of the company who serve as conduits on information relating to diversity and who are also trained as work life balance coaches. Such officers include men, women, ethnic minorities, people with disabilities and people who are gay or lesbian, transgender or bisexual. Congruent with its diversity and EEO policy, IBM also facilitates diversity networking groups, networking events and diversity champion awards.

IBM Australia has 26 per cent of its technical jobs filled by women and is proactively seeking more female participation in the area of IT, in which women are largely underrepresented. The company runs programs that promote female mentoring and work–life balance. As a part of this initiative, IBM also offers a range of flexible work options such as the School Speakers Program (NSW/VIC) where female employees of IBM, together with university students, visit schools in New South Wales and Victoria to enlighten students with regards to studies and careers in the field of IT. Another such program aimed at encouraging more school girls to take up IT was initiated by IBM at Melbourne's Monash University in 2000, named 'Go Girl Go for IT!'.

IBM also seeks to employ people with disabilities and enhance the capacity to accept such individuals as valued employees within the company. It provides workplace modifications and adjustments in relation to specific individual needs and also the option of working from home. When IBM won the Prime Minister's employer of the year award in 2002, Rebecca Adam, Product and Service Manager of IBM Australia, who herself has been profoundly deaf from birth, stated, 'When I joined IBM I was looking at an organisation that valued the individual and was not taken aback in employing a person who is profoundly deaf . . . my manager treats me just as any member of the team. He has the same expectations and provides the same advice. He has always believed I could do the job whether I was deaf or not.' In this respect, IBM has not denied itself valuable human resources due to certain disabilities in people, rather it has succeeded in seeing and developing the abilities of this part of the population.

Due to its commitment to have diversity represented at the workplace, IBM has created not only a more holistic employee base but also one that is representative of the customers it is serving.

Source: Adapted from Anonymous (2002), 'Rebecca's talents are a big plus for big blue – Prime Minister's Employer of the year awards: A special advertising report', *The Weekend Australian*, 31 August, p. 40; IBM Australia official website, <http://www.ibm.com/au>, accessed 19 November 2005.

Summary

This chapter has highlighted the importance of workforce diversity in the SHRM process. Organisations are composed of people from vastly different backgrounds, with differences in race, culture, ethnicity, religion and sexual orientation. These differences lead to dissimilarity in basic values, attitudes and beliefs which, if misunderstood, can lead to significant problems for organisations. Thus, in order to ensure long-term success organisations need to implement diversity-oriented policies and practices which facilitate employees to have a better understanding of one another as well as provide equal opportunities for all employees. This, in turn, will facilitate the development of a competitive advantage for the organisation.

This chapter began with a definition of workforce diversity, which refers to visible or invisible difference between organisational members, such as race, age, gender, sexuality, religion, educational level, work experience, disability, language, perceptions, attitudes, interests, lifestyle, expectations, values, needs and desires. Although the definition is multifaceted, it is generally categorised as having two dimensions: observable and underlying differences.

The fact that most countries are becoming increasingly multicultural has resulted in the introduction of diversity into many organisations. However, the reasons that workforces may choose to adopt diversity depends on the 'case' they put forward. These cases are referred to as the legal, moral and business cases for diversity and different organisations will choose different cases depending on their recognition, acknowledgement and genuine desire for a diverse workplace.

People respond to diversity in either positive or negative ways. However, although the positive response is beneficial for employees and the organisation alike, there are three theories of diversity which specifically align with negative responses: the similarity attraction paradigm, social identity theory and social categorisation theory.

In addition to the positive and negative responses to diversity that stakeholders may react to, HR managers also need to consider the value that diversity brings to an organisation. The positive effects of diversity include innovation, empowerment, information sharing, group decision effectiveness, openness to dissimilarity and increased and improved productivity. However, the negative effects include discrimination (both direct and indirect) and problems associated with communication, power play, conflict and control. As a means of managing the negative effects of diversity, HR managers may employ diversity management. This refers to the planning, organising and controlling of diversity-friendly policies and practices, and is reflected in an open-minded organisational culture and climate, therefore diversity management may be viewed as a systematic commitment by an organisation to employ, develop and promote a diverse range of employees. For diversity management to be successful, managers need to consider the impact of individual differences (such as openness to dissimilarity and cultural knowledge). However, it is also important for managers to be effective leaders as they play a crucial role in shaping an organisation's environment as well as an employee's skills and abilities through the provision of coaching, feedback and management in all organisations. Managers also need to develop and maintain effective conflict and emotion management skills.

Diversity is a concept that is here to stay, therefore the integration of diversity-oriented HRM policies and practices is essential if an organisation wants to be successful in the long run. Diversity-oriented HRM refers to HRM policies and practices that aim to attract, employ, develop and promote high-potential diverse employees who will be able to assist the organisation to meet the challenges of today's diverse marketplace, and it includes recruitment and selection, training and development, and performance evaluations. Some implications and issues relating to diversity include ensuring employees have a balanced work life (such as the provision of childcare facilities, implications of an ageing population and flexible work practices) and accommodating religious practices (such as accommodating religious holidays and prayer schedules).

Key terms

business case for diversity
conflict management skills
cultural knowledge
direct discrimination
discrimination
dissimilarity openness
diversity management
diversity-open performance
    evaluations

diversity-open recruitment
    and selection
diversity-open training and
    development
diversity-oriented HRM
emotion management
groupthink
indirect discrimination
legal case for diversity
masculinity versus femininity

moral case for diversity
power distance
similarity attraction paradigm
social categorisation theory
social identity theory
time orientation
uncertainty avoidance
workforce diversity

Review questions

5.1 What is meant by the term 'workforce diversity'? List some of the observable and underlying differences between members in your classroom.

5.2 Imagine you are the HR manager of an organisation employing a diverse range of staff. How would you handle the negative effects of diversity? In your answer, apply Hofstede's cultural dimensions to the negative outcomes of diversity. How might these be overcome?

5.3 What is discrimination? How do direct and indirect discrimination differ? Give examples for each in your answer.

5.4 Drawing on the three key diversity theories discussed in this chapter, define and explain each of the theories, and the implications for management.

5.5 Diversity management can have considerable benefits for an organisation. What are they? Describe the diversity-oriented HRM policies and practices that will help an organisation to create a competitive advantage.

Exercises

5.1 Referring to Tables 5.1 and 5.2, explain why certain birthplaces have either increased or decreased immigration during the years of 1996 and 2001. What world events have impacted on this? What future trends do you anticipate regarding Australia's immigration?

5.2 Hofstede's theory of cultural dimensions is a good guide for understanding diversity; however, it has been subject to much criticism. Conduct research using academic journals and books to discover these criticisms. What are they and how might they be overcome?

5.3 Think of a large Australian-based company. Log on to their website and search for their diversity management programs. Do they mention EEO and AA? Compare this with a small Australian-based company. How do they differ? Conduct the search again, this time for a company based in Asia or the Middle East. Do they have the same type of diversity programs? Why/why not? What role does culture play in this?

References

Ayoko, O. B., Härtel, C. E. J. & Callan, V. J. (2002), 'Resolving the puzzle of productive and destructive conflict in heterogeneous workgroups: A communication accommodation theory approach', *The International Journal of Conflict Management*, vol. 13, no. 2, pp. 165–95.

Dass, P. & Parker, B. (1996), 'Diversity: A strategic issue', in *Managing Diversity: Human Resource Strategies for Transforming the Workplace*, eds E. E. Kossek & S. A. Lobel, Blackwell Business, Cambridge, Mass.

DIMIA (2004), *Population Flows: Immigration Aspects*, Department of Immigration and Multicultural and Indigenous Affairs, Economic and Demographic Analysis Section (Migration Branch), Commonwealth of Australia, Canberra.

Ellis, C. & Sonnenfeld, J. (1994), 'Diverse approaches to managing diversity', *Human Resource Management*, vol. 33, pp. 79–109.

Fujimoto, Y., Härtel, C. E. J. & Panipucci, D. (2005), 'Emotional experience of individualist–collectivist workgroups: Findings from a study of 14 multinationals located in Australia', in *Emotions in Organizational Behavior*, eds C. E. J. Härtel, W. J. Zerbe & N. M. Ashkanasy, Lawrence Erlbaum Associates, Mahwah.

Glastra, F., Meerman, M., Schedler, P. & De Vries, S. (2000), 'Broadening the scope of diversity management: Strategic implications in the case of the Netherlands', *Relations Industrielles*, vol. 55, no. 4, pp. 698–721.

Härtel, C. E. J. & Fujimoto, Y. (2000), 'Diversity is not a problem to be managed by organisations but openness to perceived dissimilarity is', *Journal of Australian and New Zealand Academy of Management*, vol. 6, no. 1, pp. 14–27.

James, D. & Heathcote, A. (2002), 'Race gets the silent treatment', *Business Review Weekly*, April, pp. 70–3.

Jehn, K. A. & Chatman, J. A. (2000), 'The influence of proportional and perceptual conflict composition on team performance', *International Journal of Conflict Management*, vol. 11, no. 1, pp. 56–73.

Jordan, P. J., Ashkanasy, N. M. & Härtel, C. E. J. (1997), 'Emotional intelligence in work teams: Construct definition and measurement', paper presented at the *Second Biennial Industrial and Organisational Psychology Conference: Best Paper and Abstract Proceedings*, Melbourne, Australia.

Kossek, E. E. & Lobel, S. A. (1996), 'Introduction: Transforming human resource systems to manage diversity: An introduction and orienting framework', in *Managing Diversity Human Resource Strategies for Transforming the Workplace*, eds E. E. Kossek & S. A. Lobel, Blackwell Business, Cambridge, Mass.

Lineehan, F. & Konrad, A. M. (1999), 'Diluting diversity: Implications for intergroup inequality in organizations', *Journal of Management Inquiry*, vol. 8, no. 4, pp. 399–414.

Mackay, H. (1993), *Australia Reinvented: The Mind and Moods of Australia in the 90s*, Angus & Robertson, Sydney.

Major, B. & Crocker, J. (1993), 'Social stigma: The consequences of attribution ambiguity', in D. M. Mackie & D. L. Hamilton (eds), *Affect, Cognition and Stereotyping: Interactive Processes in Group Perception*, Academic Press, Orlando, FL.

Mamman, A. (1995), 'Socio-biographical antecedents of international effectiveness: The neglected factors', *British Journal of Management*, vol. 6, no. 2, pp. 97–114.

Mamman, A. (2000), Strategic human resource and workforce diversity: A theoretical framework and practical implications', *Management Development Forum*, vol. 3, no. 2, pp. 9–34.

Milliken, F. J. & Martins, L. L. (1996), 'Searching for common threads: Understanding the multiple effects of diversity in organizational groups', *Academy of Management Review*, vol. 21, no. 2, pp. 402–33.

Panipucci, D. & Härtel, C. E. J. (in press),

'Positive disobedience: When norms prescribe the exclusion of dissimilar others', in *Dimensions of Well-Being. Research and Intervention*, ed. A. Delle Fave, Franco Angeli, Milano.

Richard, O. C., Kochan, T. A. & McMillan-Capehart, A. (2002), 'The impact of visible diversity on organizational effectiveness: Disclosing the contents in Pandora's black box', *Journal of Business and Management*, vol. 8, no. 3, pp. 265–91.

Schneider, S. K. & Northcraft, G. B. (1999), 'Three social dilemmas of workforce diversity in organizations: A social identity perspective', *Human Relations*, vol. 52, no. 11, pp. 1445–67.

Tajfel, H. & Turner, J. C. (1986), 'The social identity theory of intergroup behaviour' in *Psychology of Intergroup Relations*, eds S. Worchel & W. G. Austin, Nelson Hall, Chicago.

Triandis, H. C. (1994), *Culture and Social Behavior*, McGraw-Hill, New York.

Turner, J. C. & Oakes, P. J. (1989), 'Self-categorization theory and social influence', in *Psychology of Group Influence*, ed. P. B. Paulus, Lawrence Erlbaum Associates, New Jersey.

6 Chapter

Ethics and the law: employee rights and employer responsibilities

INTRODUCTION

Ethics and the law provide the foundation for strategic HRM. They coexist in an important relationship which sets the boundaries of effective management and strategic achievement. HRM is not just about employing the right staff, providing training and development and rewarding employees. It is a complex web of functions, bound together by ethical and legal frameworks. The failure to comply with these frameworks often results in serious and significant consequences, both for the employee and employer.

Despite the serious consequences of unethical or unlawful behaviour, many companies still test the boundaries of the HRM framework. Although most people know 'right from wrong', they still choose to act unethically when it comes to business. The recent demise of Enron is a perfect example. Fifteen years ago, Enron, a trading and energy company based in Texas, was losing money at a substantial rate. Company directors decided to restructure in a bid to save the company and the next decade saw Enron's wealth radically increase through its marketing and promotion of power and unique communications commodities. It worked, and Enron was named 'America's Most Innovative Company' by *Fortune* magazine for six consecutive years (1996 to 2001). In 2000, it was even on *Fortune*'s '100 Best Companies to Work for in America', and was considered elite even among the top employees in the financial world.

Then it all came falling down.

Rumours of bribery, political pressure and scandals surrounding questionable accounting procedures plagued the company. Insider trading, offshore entities and undisclosed financial partnerships eventually led to the demise and bankruptcy of Enron. It is one of the largest unethical business cases in history and court battles are still being pursued today. No doubt they will continue well into the future.

So what happened? Quite simply, what was once a very powerful and successful company quickly eroded through corporate greed and selfishness.

Unethical and illegal behaviour became the norm. As a result, the company has now dissolved.

Despite being an American company, Enron is an important example for Australian managers to learn from. This chapter introduces the need for organisational stakeholders (particularly employees and employers) to be aware of possible dilemmas they may struggle with regarding their ethical and moral behaviour. These dilemmas are likely to occur when their values conflict with their employing organisation and the society within which they work. In particular, the chapter introduces the need to identify and develop an ethical perspective and an awareness of the context in which ethical and illegal dilemmas arise, and appropriate employee and employer responses to these.

Objectives

The primary objective of this chapter is to introduce the relationship between ethics and the law. Unlike previous chapters, the concepts discussed in this chapter will provide you with an understanding of employee and employer responsibilities in the workplace, and the legally binding implications of these. Above all, the purpose of HRM is to ensure that employees and employers create, maintain and sustain a 'fair' and socially just workplace, fostering a win–win situation. Ethics and the law provide the foundation for this to occur.

After reading this chapter you should be able to:

- define ethics and discuss some of the ethical issues in business today;
- explain the reasons behind the relevant legislation pertaining to HRM;
- understand the reasons why unions exist and why employees join them;
- discuss the bargaining process and the goals and strategies of unions and employers;
- understand and explain the reason for occupational health and safety legislation;
- describe what management can do to provide a safe and healthy workplace;
- explain the negotiation process and the practical aspects of union negotiation;
- discuss the impact of the changing workforce on union growth and survival.

Ethical issues in business today

There is no doubt that ethics play a vital role in business today. Dilemmas involving discrimination, harassment, fraud, contractual breaches, favouritism and inconsistent policies regarding pay, rewards and discipline are common occurrences in many organisations. So who is responsible for managing ethics, and how does it impact on employee satisfaction and organisational productivity? These are important questions that all managers, especially HR managers, need to address in order to foster and encourage an ethical business environment. However, despite the moral perception and expectation that businesses should operate ethically, not all organisations do, as is evident by the recent Enron scandal. The following subsection defines business ethics and identifies the ethical stance that organisations may adopt, which doesn't always translate into ethical behaviour!

BUSINESS ETHICS

As children, we learn ethical behaviour from our parents and teachers. Treating others with respect, not stealing, cheating or lying and avoiding hurting others are simple examples that most elders teach children. However, different people have different interpretations of ethical behaviour depending on how they were raised and their environmental (i.e. cultural and religious) influences. What is considered ethical in one country may not be considered ethical in another. For example, in Mexico, bribery is part of the culture and it is expected that police and government officials use this behaviour to reach resolutions. Mexicans consider this normal behaviour. If this were to occur in Australia, however, it would be a very different story! This presents dilemmas for managers when dealing with employees of different cultural and religious backgrounds, and also for employees (including expatriates) who are dealing with organisations in different countries as each has its unique interpretation of ethical guidelines from which professional work stems.

Another implication for managers is that the ethics we develop at a young age generally stay with us for life, although they may change over time. Therefore, managers must be aware of ethical differences, and be prepared for individual views on what constitutes ethical behaviour. However, it is not just culture and religion which impact upon ethical values. Past experiences, family beliefs, personal values, external pressures and peer expectations all affect the ethical stance which is adopted. One thing is for certain: employees' ethics enter an organisation when they do, and this can present unexpected and difficult consequences for all organisational members.

In essence, ethics are simply what we use to distinguish 'right from wrong'. However, in a business sense it can be expanded to include intentions, behaviours, attitudes, perceptions and expectations which are both verbal and non-verbal. Therefore, **business ethics** are defined as the stance and standard of behaviour concerning morals and ethics that an organisation may adopt. This includes determining what is right and wrong, and good and bad, and is the view held by senior management as drivers of the company. It is usually congruent with the mission and vision of the company.

business ethics
The stance and standard of behaviour concerning morals and ethics that an organisation may adopt.

ETHICAL PERSPECTIVES

Business ethics can be examined from three different perspectives. Each demonstrates who the organisation is obligated to and, in meeting these obligations, ethical behaviour is achieved. The first perspective, called the **traditional perspective**, states that an organisation's primary obligation is to its shareholders. Organisational responsibilities should be directed towards serving shareholder needs (i.e. return on investment) as shareholders maintain business survival, therefore they are the most important stakeholder. In short, this perspective asserts that business should be conducted in ways which increase shareholder wealth. This might include cutting corners in production or using lower quality supplies. It does not consider long-term consequences but rather focuses on short-term financial gain. It is argued that the traditional approach is the reason organisations exist and therefore it would be unethical not to accommodate stakeholders' needs.

traditional perspective
The perspective that an organisation's primary obligation is to its shareholders.

Cigarette companies adopt the traditional perspective. Their primary focus is on increasing shareholder wealth, and they do whatever they can (within legal boundaries) to achieve this. Despite numerous protests and campaigns highlighting the dangers of smoking, cigarette companies continue to make products that are harmful to humans. Why? Because they sell. The profits they reap are enough to keep investors happy and guarantee future investment opportunities. They believe it is not a company's responsibility to be concerned with what happens to the product or consumer after the product is purchased.

The second perspective focuses on employees. The **human resource perspective** views people as an organisation's most valuable asset. It states that all business operations should consider employee implications and consequences because without employees the business would not exist. Quite simply, all organisational efforts are directed at recruiting, developing and maintaining a high-quality workforce, which in turn results in greater generation of innovation and creativity, increased production and more profit. By looking after the needs of employees, an organisation can ensure business survival and longevity, including secure and ongoing employment for staff. Therefore, it has acted ethically. This perspective builds on the resource-based view (RBV) of a firm, as discussed in Chapter 1, and considers long-term consequences.

> **human resource perspective**
> Views people as an organisation's most valuable asset and states that all business operations should consider employee implications and consequences because without employees the business would not exist.

There are many companies that *believe* they adopt this perspective. However, in reality, not all companies do. While management understands the benefits of the human resource perspective, rarely does it *genuinely* practise it. In most situations, it pays lip service to it because it knows that it is important to communicate its commitment to employees and other stakeholders. This is a disappointing reality. However, on the other hand, there are some companies that genuinely adopt the human resource perspective. Many small companies know that without their employees the business would not survive. Therefore, they honestly do put employee needs above all others.

The final perspective, the **societal perspective**, is based on obligations to society. Within this view, an organisation carefully considers societal impacts before it makes a decision. This might include impacts on the environment i.e. people, animals and land) and on the general wellbeing of society (i.e. the political and economic environments). This long-term perspective is usually embraced by pressure groups, such as Greenpeace, who assert that it is unethical not to consider societal impacts. After all, if the world is not looked after then it may cease to exist and no amount of shareholder wealth or employee recruitment and selection will change that.

> **societal perspective**
> States that an organisation should carefully consider societal impacts before decisions are made.

ETHICAL RESPONSIBILITIES

Ethical issues are not purely the responsibility or concern of managers. All stakeholders play a role in the management of ethics. However, it is the responsibility of managers to communicate accepted and unaccepted ethical behaviour and control unethical behaviour. Generally, most companies communicate ethical guidelines in a **code of conduct**. This is a company policy outlining company expectations and formal rules surrounding ethics, including legal implications and disciplinary action. A code of conduct also includes specific

> **code of conduct**
> A company policy outlining company expectations and formal rules surrounding ethics, including legal implications and disciplinary action.

information on how employees, employers and other stakeholders should professionally conduct their business and contains specific behavioural requirements written in generalised language. It is important that all organisational members receive a copy of this, and any updated information (such as amendments to laws and how they impact on individuals and the organisation). Failure to do so may result in the company being liable for unethical or illegal behaviour performed by employees. A good idea is for the code of conduct to be placed on the company intranet, which facilitates communication although does not ensure that all employees have read and understood it.

There are five items which are generally addressed in codes of conduct (Wiley, 2000).

1. *Legality*. This includes all information pertaining to laws and legislation in the state and/or country of business operation.
2. *Confidentiality*. This states that all people have the right to have privileged information protected. In Australia, this is protected by legislation (*Privacy Act 1988* and the *Privacy Amendment Act 2000*).
3. *Integrity*. This states that organisational members will operate and work with high levels of honesty, integrity, fairness and professionalism.
4. *Proficiency*. This includes maintaining and improving professional competence. Companies can encourage this through regular training and development, including professional development.
5. *Professional loyalty*. This states that organisational members support the profession and ensure that professional associations and affiliations are strictly and appropriately for professional use only. They must not be used for personal gain.

Please read

Wiley, C. (2000), 'Ethical standards for human resource management professionals: A comparative analysis of five major codes', *Journal of Business Ethics*, vol. 25, pp. 93–114.

ETHICAL DECISION-MAKING MODELS

While managers might understand the importance of ethical decision making in organisations, how do they actually make those decisions? What guidelines and policies help them make such important decisions pertaining to ethical values of their organisations? Although the resources, knowledge, skills and expectations of each company differ, there is a variety of models which can provide guidance for making ethical decisions in organisations. All of these models cover different elements of decision making, including behaviour, and also incorporate individual and organisational factors which influence the decision-making process.

REST'S (1986) MODEL FOR INDIVIDUAL ETHICAL DECISION MAKING AND BEHAVIOUR

Rest's (1986) model presents a strong basis for individual ethical decision making and behaviour by underscoring moral issues. The four-component model asserts that an entity (i.e. person or organisation) must progress through a series of moral decisions: recognising the issue, making a moral judgement, establishing moral intent and engaging in moral behaviour (see Figure 6.1). Rest asserts that each of the four phases are conceptually separate from one another and that success in one phase does not necessarily result in success in another. Although this model is theoretically sound, as it provides a basis for ethical decision making, it fails to take into consideration other factors which may also impede the process, such as situational, interpersonal and organisational aspects. It is, therefore, a limited model for ethical decision making.

6.1 FIGURE
Rest's (1986) model for individual ethical decision making and behaviour

Source: Adapted from Rest (1986).

JONES' (1991) ISSUE-CONTINGENT MODEL OF ETHICAL DECISION MAKING

This model of ethical decision making expands upon the model developed by Rest by incorporating two factors: moral intensity and organisational factors (see Figure 6.2). According to Jones (1991), Rest's model provides a good foundation for ethical decision making which is simple and easy to use. By adding the extra elements, it is clear to see how decisions are affected by moral intensity (i.e. the magnitude of the problem, the probability of effect, proximity and social consensus) and organisational factors (i.e. group dynamics, authority and socialisation attributes). This model provides a solid foundation for ethical decision making, and is easy for managers to understand and use. However, despite this, it lacks consideration of other factors such as individual beliefs and perceptions of ethical behaviour, as addressed in Trevino's model.

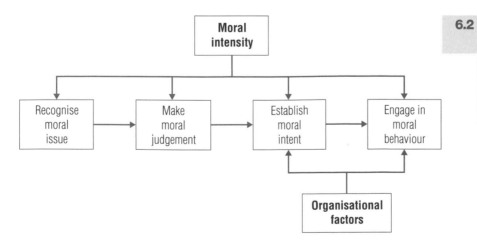

6.2 FIGURE
Jones (1991) issue-contingent model of ethical decision making

Source: Jones (1991), p. 379. Reproduced with permission of Academy of Management in the format textbook via Copyright Clearance Center.

TREVINO'S (1986) INTERACTIONAL MODEL OF ETHICAL DECISION MAKING

Trevino's (1986) model of ethical decision making adopts an interactional angle. Here, the decision begins with an ethical dilemma and then proceeds through the stages of moral development. In essence, it implies thought processes (or cognitions) regarding the dilemma. However, her model, which is not purely linear like Rest's model, has a variety of external factors influencing the decision-making process (see Figure 6.3). These include individual moderators such as ego strength and locus of control.

locus of control
The perceived control over individual behaviour.

internal locus of control
Implies that people control their own destiny through their decisions and actions.

external locus of control
The belief that our destiny is controlled by external forces, such as fate or luck.

Locus of control refers to the perceived control over individual behaviour. People with an **internal locus of control** believe that they control their own destiny through their decisions and actions. However, people having an **external locus of control** believe that their destiny is controlled by external forces, such as fate or luck. The locus of control is an important factor in this model as it depicts the degree to which people control their decisions and, consequently, accept responsibility for them. Trevino's model also incorporates situational moderators such as the organisational culture and the job characteristics and context. The final phase in this model is the outcome of ethical or unethical behaviour.

This model expands on the models by Rest (1986) and Jones (1991) by adding more depth and detail to factors which may influence the ethical decision-making process and, hence, the outcome of ethical or unethical behaviour.

DUBINSKY AND LOKEN'S (1989) ETHICAL DECISION MAKING MODEL

This model of ethical decision making, developed by Dubinsky and Loken (1989), addresses decision making from the theory of reasoned action and within the

FIGURE 6.3
Trevino's (1986) interactional model of ethical decision making

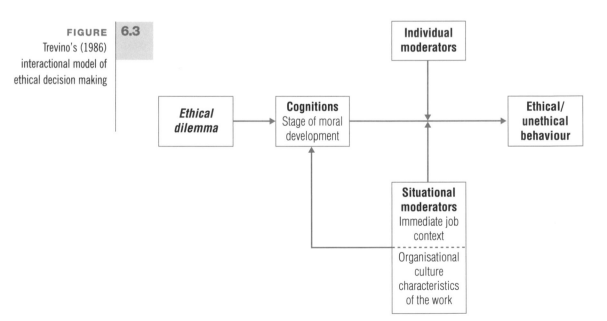

Source: Adapted from Trevino (1986). Reproduced with permission of Academy of Management in the format textbook via Copyright Clearance Center.

realm of marketing (see Figure 6.4). The model is initially divided into two sections. The first analyses behavioural beliefs (i.e. the likelihood that ethical behaviour will lead to certain outcomes) and outcome evaluations (i.e. the 'goodness or badness' of ethical behaviour), the result of which leads to attitudes towards ethical or unethical behaviour. The second section analyses normative beliefs (i.e. the likelihood that referent others think the person should perform ethical behaviour) and motivation to comply (i.e. the willingness to acquiesce to referent others), the result of which leads to a subjective norm toward ethical or unethical behaviour. The next section analyses the likelihood that the individual will engage in unethical behaviour (i.e. their intention), which leads to the final decision of whether or not ethical behaviour is adopted.

A strength of this model is that it considers ethical and unethical behaviour individually, rather than as one component. It also considers the decision in light of seven different factors, clearly taking into consideration the entire aspect of the decision. However, the model has one major implication: it does not take into consideration variables such as the individual's past experience, norms or culture (e.g. religious beliefs). These can significantly impact on the process of ethical decision making.

BOMMER, GRATTO, GRAVANDER AND TUTTLE'S (1987) MODEL OF ETHICAL DECISION MAKING

The final model discussed is that developed by Bommer et al. (1987). It provides a process of ethical decision making from an environmental perspective. Here, the

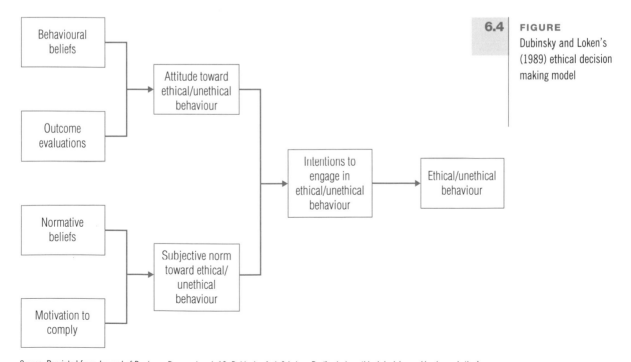

6.4   **FIGURE**
Dubinsky and Loken's (1989) ethical decision making model

Source: Reprinted from Journal of Business Research, vol. 19, Dubinsky, A. J. & Loken, B., 'Analyzing ethical decision making in marketing', pp. 83–107, copyright 1989, with permission from Elsevier.

model considers internal and external environmental factors which influence or impact upon an ethical decision. The perception and degree of influence for each environmental factor is considered in relation to the influence that the decision process has on the factor, and the degree of influence that the factor has on the decision process (see Figure 6.5).

Internal factors include the personal environment and individual attributes, such as the moral level, personal goal and life experience. External factors include the professional, work and social environments, and the government/legal environment. The decision-making process itself consists of information, cognitive processes and perceived rewards and losses. Once all of these factors are considered, a decision is then made which is either ethical or unethical.

This model, which considers major influencing factors, is highly detailed; however, there is no clear guidance on which factor has priority over another, or in which order these should be considered. Essentially, it is simply a process of listing the pros and cons of each factor in the decision process and weighing up the benefits of each decision. Therefore, although detailed, it provides no clear guideline of how to make an ethical decision.

FIGURE 6.5

Bommer, Gratto, Gravander and Tuttle's (1987) model of ethical decision making

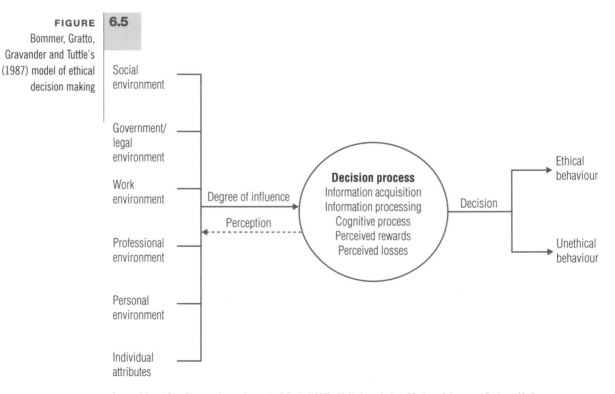

Source: Adapted from Bommer, Gratto, Gravander & Tuttle (1987) with kind permission of Springer Science and Business Media.

All of the above models make a significant contribution to the field of ethics by identifying the stages of ethical decision making. However, they fail to state explicitly how an ethical decision can be made. Of course, there is no answer to this and the models are simply a guide to how ethical decisions can be determined. What the models do provide, however, is the identification of multiple factors that can influence the process, all of which managers need to be aware of before they make decisions surrounding ethics.

Please read

Jones, T. M. (1991), 'Ethical decision making by individuals in organizations: An issue-contingent model', *Academy of Management Review*, vol. 16, no. 2, pp. 366–95.

WHY PEOPLE ACT UNETHICALLY

As previously mentioned, individuals' ethical stance may differ depending on their cultural and religious beliefs. However, this is not always the case. Despite cultural and religious convictions, there is still a myriad of other reasons why people act unethically. They can be summarised into three major reasons: the level of cognitive moral development; the ethical climate; and national culture.

LEVEL OF COGNITIVE MORAL DEVELOPMENT

Every person exerts different degrees of moral and ethical behaviour. This depends on the **level of cognitive moral development** of each individual and may be explained as an individual's perception of what is right and wrong cognitively (i.e. what they *think*). Some people refer to this as a 'gut feeling'. People with high levels of cognitive moral development will behave very ethically and morally. They will always think about the consequences of their actions and consider whether their behaviour is 'the right thing to do'. When they are confronted with peer pressure to act unethically, they will avoid conforming to the pressure even when doing so evokes anxiety or fear in them. For example, the hotel manager portrayed in the movie *Hotel Rwanda*, Paul Rusesabagina, demonstrated the highest level of cognitive moral development. Faced with a civil war between two African tribes and personal danger, Paul refused an offer of salvation for him and his family and instead remained in the village to help prevent his people from being slaughtered. He did not have to stay and risk the lives of his young family, yet because he had reached the highest level of moral cognitive development (a stage reached by very few people), Paul felt it was the right course of action – to leave would have been morally and ethically wrong to him.

> **level of cognitive moral development**
> An individual's perception of what is right and wrong cognitively (i.e. what they think).

Conversely, people with low levels of cognitive moral development will find it difficult to behave in ethical and moral ways. When confronted with pressure to act unethically they will usually conform, not only because of the pressure or their fear of being rejected or hurt, but because they cannot recognise what is wrong with the behaviour. They find it easy to rationalise their behaviour.

There are six stages of moral cognitive development (Kohlberg, 1984) (see Figure 6.6). These stages are divided into three levels and it is important to understand these levels before examining the six stages. The first level is the *preconventional* moral level and relates mostly to the level of children (i.e. those under nine years of age, some adolescents and many criminal offenders who are either adults or adolescents). The second level is the *conventional* moral level, which relates to most adolescents and adults. The final level, the *postconventional* moral level, relates to adults who accept and understand societal rules and the

FIGURE | 6.6
The stages of moral
cognitive development

Stage 6
Universal ethical principles
Following ethical principles determined and chosen by the self; obeying these ethical principles when these conflict with laws; universal principles of justice include respect for others and the equality of human rights
Stage 5
Social contract or utility and individual rights
A sense of obligation to the law; realising how rules impact on the group and form part of the social contract; realising that life and liberty rights and values must be obeyed regardless of majority opinion
Level III: Postconventional moral level

Stage 4
Social system and conscience
Fulfilling agreed duties and adhering to laws (except in rare circumstances where these conflict with predetermined social duties); contributing to organisations, groups and society
Stage 3
Mutual interpersonal expectations, relationships and interpersonal conformity
Living up to role model expectations; showing concern for others; valuing trust, loyalty, respect and gratitude
Level II: Conventional moral level

Stage 2
Individualism, instrumental purpose and exchange
Compliance with rules to satisfy personal interests and allowing others to do the same; fair and equal agreements (i.e. deals)
Stage 1
Heteronomous morality
Avoidance of punishment; compliance with rules only for personal interests; avoidance of physical damage to others and property
Level I: Preconventional moral level

Source: Adapted from Kohlberg (1984), pp. 174–6.

general moral principles which underpin these rules; however, a majority of adults (i.e. those over the age of twenty) do not reach this level.

Although the range of employees in an organisation is likely to include a mix of high and low cognitive moral development, it is imperative that leaders have high cognitive moral development. This is crucial if they are guiding and motivating employees and are representing the company. If leaders, such as senior management, do not act ethically, then others will follow suit, believing that it is acceptable for everyone to act unethically. Leadership by example is a powerful tool. Furthermore, employees should not only want managers to have high cognitive moral development; they should expect it. Such behaviour then shapes organisational culture and impacts upon all stakeholders.

ETHICAL CLIMATE

Within an organisation the ethical climate shapes the behaviour of employees. This extends from the managers' moral development and penetrates the company to shape organisational behaviour and expectations. In essence, it becomes part of the company's culture and forms the attitudes, values and expectations of organisational members. A **positive ethical climate** implies that the organisational culture encourages members to behave ethically and morally. Long-term consequences are considered and employees are guided by the ethical values of senior management. However, a **negative (or poor) ethical climate** implies that unethical behaviour is tolerated by organisational members, including management. This behaviour then forms part of the culture and, consequently, becomes a norm. When this occurs, often employees fail to recognise that they are acting unethically; because they are so used to doing so, they may not even realise they are doing it.

positive ethical climate
Implies that the organisational culture encourages members to behave ethically and morally.

negative ethical climate
Implies that unethical behaviour is tolerated by organisational members, including management.

NATIONAL CULTURE

The final reason that people behave unethically may be attributed to national culture. As mentioned earlier, ethical norms are shaped by a country's culture and religion. These include legislation, bribery, corruption and religious beliefs and expectations. National culture, therefore, is distinct from organisational culture.

Most Western countries, such as Australia and New Zealand, display high ethical values. State and federal legislation provides ethical boundaries for organisations to work within, and failure to comply with these results in discipline (such as fines, dismissal and even imprisonment). However, this doesn't necessarily mean that all companies within these countries act ethically. Rather, the national culture *guides* ethical behaviour. If the general consensus is the provision of ethical behaviour, then most companies act this way. Remember, national culture is only one reason why people do (or do not) act unethically. It differs for every individual, group and organisation.

Other countries, such as the aforementioned Mexico and even Bangladesh, have higher incidents of unethical behaviour because this has become the culture of such countries. Bribery and corruption are the norm and because solutions are only reached using these methods people tend to conform. The more they feel compelled to conform, the more it becomes general practice and part of their personal value system. However, it is not just national culture that shapes ethical behaviour. Religious beliefs have an extremely powerful hold over individuals. Certain beliefs are taught at a very young age, coupled with routine religious attendance, and these also influence the degree of ethical behaviour adopted by people. For example, most religions condemn homosexual relationships.

Therefore, engaging in a homosexual relationship would be considered unethical, although not illegal. As an HR manager, codes of ethical conduct must be implemented to ensure that people are not discriminated against as a result of their sexual preference, or any other difference (see Chapter 5 for a discussion on discrimination and diversity).

A serious management implication arising from national culture is how this impacts on international business operations. National culture is easy to adopt when it is the home country of the organisation; however, what happens when a new branch opens in an international location? There are three options for organisations in this situation: (1) attempt to retain ethical business practices; (2) conform to cultural practices; or (3) compromise. For most companies, the reason they relocate to international locations is because the host country's ethical practices are so lax. Relaxed ethical practices, such as cheap labour and long working hours, entice management to improve productivity at a low cost. Despite protests for protecting the rights of poorer nations who succumb to poor working conditions, most multinational companies continue to operate in international locations because financially it presents costs savings. They justify this by saying they are looking after the welfare of shareholders, who have a vested interest in the business and to whom their primary obligation is (according to the traditional perspective). While there is no doubt that these companies will continue to prey on poorer nations (because they are operating within legal guidelines), they should also consider the extent to which they can compromise for a fairer solution.

So, how can ethical outcomes be achieved in unethical cultures? The answer is simple: if companies are going to continue operating in international locations they need to make the conditions as fair as possible. It is not enough simply to conform wholly to unethical practices because 'that's the way things are done here'. By doing that, companies are only adding to the problem instead of possibly reducing it. Richer nations have the knowledge and resources to improve poor nations and they should, from a sense of societal obligation, contribute towards solving the issue. Developing education programs, designing systems and structures and implementing regulation can improve working conditions and make them bearable for employees.

For example, in Thailand child labour is endemic. Unfortunately, despite the outcry from the rest of the world, child labour continues. Many children in Thailand are made to work by their parents because they are so desperately poor and the income is needed for survival. While child activists condemn multinational companies for employing children, the alternative for most children is to conduct other work, such as prostitution. While child labour is unsavoury, the reality is that children are forced to work either in factories or prostitution. This situation is not going to change in the near future. However, given the options, it is better for children to work in factories (such as those provided by Nike) than become illicit sex workers. Despite this, companies can compromise and implement systems which provide better working conditions for children, such as more frequent breaks, shorter working days and the provision of education, all of which needs to be regulated.

This poses an important question: do boardrooms think of the ethical implications of their business decision or just dollar amounts? (see 'Is Ethics a Dirty Word?' in 'A manager's challenge' at the end of this chapter).

Employment law

A key role of legal frameworks is to enforce certain ethical notions through the use of specific 'criteria' audits and penalties for breaches. The **employment relationship**, which is the working relationship between employees and employers, is a fundamental relationship in workplaces and it will, to a certain degree, determine the ethical standards within the organisation. The way the employment contract is negotiated and its content both impact on the psychological contract and therefore it affects the perceptions of justice and fairness which build or diminish commitment, job involvement, organisational citizenship behaviours and work attitudes (see Chapter 2 for a discussion on psychological contracts).

employment relationship
The working relationship between employers and employees which is a fundamental relationship in workplaces.

EMPLOYMENT LAW AND WORKPLACE REFORM: THE EXAMPLE FROM AUSTRALIA

In 2005, employment law in Australia saw radical changes in workplace reform. A new workplace relations system called WorkChoices replaced a variety of workplace agreements and simplified the system to make it fairer and more flexible for employees and employers. According to the WorkChoices booklet released by the Australian government, the new policy has streamlined over 130 pieces of industrial relations legislation, over 4000 different awards and six different workplace systems that were operating in Australia. They claim this was done with the aim of creating more workforce flexibility, in alignment with the changing workforce as discussed in Chapter 5, such as the trend for more part-time and casual employees and the desire to balance work and family life. The Australian government also asserts that more work opportunities have been created for women and school leavers in the past ten years, and the new workplace relations system will further benefit the economy, employers and employees. Tables 6.1 and 6.2 list the changes under the new system and what hasn't changed.

TABLE 6.1	**Government claims regarding the workplace relations system**

- One simpler national system
- Simplified workplace-agreement-making processes
- Establishment of the Australian Fair Pay Commission to protect minimum and award classification wages
- Introduction of the Australian Fair Pay and Conditions Standard to protect workers' wages and conditions in the agreement-making process
- Protection of a set of minimum conditions in federal legislation for the first time
- Provision of modern award protection for those not covered by agreements
- Ongoing role for the Australian Industrial Relations Commission (AIRC)
- Protection against unlawful termination
- Better balance of the unfair dismissal laws

Source: Adapted from Commonwealth of Australia (2005), p. 6. Copyright Commonwealth of Australia, reproduced by permission.

TABLE   6.2   **Existing protections under the workplace relations system**

- Minimum wages and award classifications will not be cut
- Protection against unlawful termination will not be removed
- Awards will not be abolished
- The right to join a union will not be removed
- The right to lawful industrial action when negotiating an agreement will not be removed
- Union agreements will not be outlawed
- The Australian Industrial Relations Commission will not be abolished

Source: Adapted from Commonwealth of Australia (2005), p. 7. Copyright Commonwealth of Australia, reproduced by permission.

Despite this government initiative, who *really* benefits from workplace reform? Did the Australian government implement this system for their advantage, or for employers, employees, or both? These are the sorts of questions that surround any workplace policies because the employment relationship is a fundamental relationship in workplaces. By sustaining a fair workplace relationship, employees and employers benefit from increased job security, increased job satisfaction and, consequently, increased productivity. Therefore, it is a positive system for Australian society.

Employment law sets the minimum standards and conditions for employment in a given region. The International Labour Organisation (ILO) is an attempt at getting a particular set of minimum standards and conditions adhered to across the globe. Due to the variety and complexity of employment options in Australia, it is important that all stakeholders in the employment relationship have a current and accurate understanding of employment law.

LEGAL OBLIGATION

legal obligation
The legal responsibility that an employer has towards employees and vice versa.

While employment law in Australia has changed focus recently, the legal obligation that an organisation, and its members, has has not changed. The **legal obligation**, or the legal responsibility an employer has towards employees and vice versa, varies for the two parties in the employment relationship. For employers, there are four relevant legal obligations. First, the employer must ensure employees are paid their lawful salary or wage and that general expenses are covered by the company during the course of employment (i.e. office supplies, tools, uniforms). Second, an employer is obligated to create a safe working environment, and must cover expenses to ensure that this environment is created, for example ensuring that floors are not slippery, dangerous areas are clearly designated and appropriate clothing is worn on worksites. Third, for any workplace injury, employees must be compensated for medical expenses and loss of income. This also includes the responsibility of employers to keep employees working (if possible) by changing their work tasks. For example, if a staff member is physically injured, they may still be able to conduct office work or the like, thereby sustaining their employment to ensure a win–win situation. The final obligation is that employers create a fair working environment which enhances the employment relationship, increasing cooperation between the two parties. Although this has not traditionally been the case for managers and unions in Australia, it remains a legal obligation for employers.

Although some people believe that only an employer has a sense of legal obligation to their staff, employees also have a responsibility to ensure they contribute towards a fair and equitable workplace. The first of their four obligations is to ensure they conduct their work demonstrating knowledge, skill, competency and professionalism. They should take pride in their work as they are representing the company, by which they are being paid. Second, they should comply with their employers' work-related requests, assuming that these are reasonable and relevant to the task at hand. Senior managers have a holistic view of the company and therefore will set tasks that will contribute to the overall goals of the organisation. Third, they are obligated to work in good faith; that is, not to accept bribes, conform to corruption or work for competitors. Finally, employees must foster and embrace a fair working environment and not take action or adopt behaviours which potentially damage the employment relationship.

These obligations can, in fact, be legally binding and grounds for dismissal may apply. For example, bribery, embezzlement and corruption entail serious legal consequences. Therefore, all organisational members need to ensure they are addressing these needs in a mutually beneficial employment relationship.

HRM LEGISLATION

Building on the diversity-related legislation discussed in Chapter 5, it is important to identify other Australian legislation which relates to the employment relationship. Without a positive relationship, works tasks may not be completed as efficiently and effectively as they could be. When this occurs a competitive advantage is lost. Therefore, it is imperative that both parties genuinely and honestly embrace the relationship to create a beneficial outcome for all.

At the Commonwealth level in Australia there are several Acts which relate specifically to employment. Although this list is not exhaustive, it does cover the major Acts under Commonwealth law. These include:

- *Workplace Relations Act 1996*
- *Workplace Relations Amendment (Termination of Employment) Act 1996*
- *Privacy Amendment (Private Sector) Act 2000*
- *National Occupational Health and Safety Commission Act 1995*
- *Occupational Health and Safety (Commonwealth Employment) Act 1991*
- *Safety, Rehabilitation and Compensation Act 1988*
- *Superannuation Guarantee (Administration) Act 1992*

At the state level in Australia there are also several Acts which relate to employment. Again, this list is not exhaustive but it is clear to see that a range of employment conditions are covered including:

- *Industrial Relations Act (Queensland) 1999*
- *Workplace Video Surveillance Act (New South Wales) 1998*
- *Workplace Health and Safety Act (Queensland) 1999*
- *Long Service Leave Act (Victoria) 1992*
- *Workers Compensation Act (New South Wales) 1987*

These Acts, which fall under state and federal law in Australia, should be thoroughly known and understood by HR managers. In addition to the Acts relating to diversity (such as discrimination and EEO), these Acts are a fundamental component of employment law in Australia and form the foundation for effective HRM.

RISK MANAGEMENT

In all workplaces there is an element of risk associated with business operations. Risks are essentially anything that could potentially damage the organisation or cause problems for it and for organisational members. The most problematic and concerning of all is financial risk because it largely determines the fate of an organisation. However, there are other types of risks that management need to consider, such as knowledge management risks, insurance risks and strategic management risks (i.e. when the company is expanding or diversifying into new business areas). Put simply, anything that is affected by, or affects, the business is a potential organisational risk and managers need to be aware of these risks and how to manage them effectively.

risk management
The process of measuring and assessing risk and developing systems to manage the risk successfully.

Risk management is the process of measuring and assessing risk and developing systems to manage the risk successfully. It includes various management techniques such as business diversification, purchasing insurance and maintaining cash reserves and flexibility in the company. Risk management is a decision-making process which requires a holistic approach. This means that risk cannot be measured or assessed in isolation; it must be considered as a strategic component of organisational operations, and how risk impacts on all sectors regardless of how many sectors are initially affected must be assessed. As with most areas of business management, what occurs in one section will undoubtedly affect other sections. Risk management is no exception.

The process of managing risk involves six phases: assess current and future business opportunities; identify current and future resources; identify internal

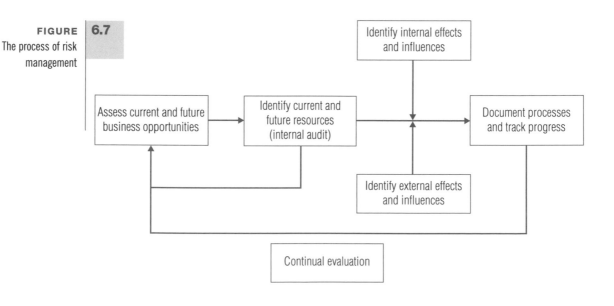

FIGURE 6.7
The process of risk management

effects and influences; identify external effects and influences; document processes and track progress; and continual evaluation (see Figure 6.7). These are discussed in more detail below.

- *Assess current and future business opportunities.* This involves performing a SWOT analysis to determine the strengths, weaknesses, opportunities and threats that may impact on the business in its current or future state (see Chapter 1 for how to conduct a SWOT analysis). New business opportunities should be highlighted and considered for venture.

- *Identify current and future resources (internal audit).* Before any new ventures can be adopted it is imperative to identify current and future resources. In this sense, resources include financial, technical and human resources. Questions such as 'Do we have enough resources?', 'Will we have an excess of resources?' and 'Do we have the right resources?' need to be addressed. In terms of financial resources, managers should call on the knowledge of accountants and financial analysts to provide an estimate of future financial needs. In terms of technical resources (which include everything that is physically needed to conduct business, such as buildings, technology, machinery and office supplies), managers should liaise with individual departments and accountants to determine current and future needs. Finally, in terms of human resources, HR managers should conduct human resource planning (HRP) to forecast current and future needs, and segment their workforce accordingly (see Chapter 8 for a discussion on HRP). At this stage of the risk management process, if there are insufficient (or an excess of) resources, the process should not proceed until appropriate systems have been put in place to balance the resource allocation.

- *Identify internal effects and influences.* The internal environment of an organisation is made up of people, processes and structures. Essentially, these may collectively be referred to as organisational culture. One element of culture is the degree of risk organisational members are willing to take. This will differ for every organisation. Some companies, such as financial investment firms, thrive on risk taking: the more they risk, the higher the return. Other companies, such as smaller firms, tend to avoid risk because they do not have the knowledge or the financial resources to cover their base should the risk turn out to be unfavourable. The adoption of risk is also dependent on the company values and overall mission, which need to be aligned with the organisational culture. If employees are not used to risk taking, or are opposed to it, then this will severely impact on the risk management decision making.

- *Identify external effects and influences.* There are a variety of external factors that influence or impact on (and vice versa) a business. These include all factors in the external environment, such as the government, laws and legislations, politics, the economy (e.g. interest rates and taxes), pressure groups, demographics (e.g. baby boomers, workforce diversity), technology, customers, suppliers and competitors. It is especially important to consider the legal implications or restrictions of laws and legislation, and the likely effect these would have on the firm. In addition, a risk influenced by a law might also impact on workforce diversity which, in turn, might impact on the company's reputation and future customers. This demonstrates the holistic approach to risk management that must be embraced.

- *Document processes and track progress.* It is always wise to keep a record of everything that is conducted in the business in case it ever needs to be referred to in the future. This is especially important in relation to human resources for performance management and performance appraisal purposes, to ensure that appropriate steps were taken by the organisation, complying with legal requirements.
- *Continual evaluation.* Risk management is a continuous process. It does not simply end when one aspect of risk is solved but rather continues in a cyclical fashion. Continual evaluation makes the process more effective.

Although risk management applies to all aspects of a business, it is important for managers to consider the specific HR implications. In terms of HRM, risks such as unfair dismissal, discrimination, negligent recruitment and selection, favouritism and bias and general standards for safety can impact significantly on the organisation and its members. In particular, knowledge management creates serious consequences for risk management as knowledge is an important organisational asset, yet an intangible. This presents problems for management regarding who 'owns' the knowledge and appropriate systems must be implemented to protect employee and employer rights. However, in the case of knowledge management, the employer owns the knowledge as it was created during employment hours and using company resources, despite the fact that employees retain that knowledge and take it with them when they leave the company. Therefore, it is crucial for managers to be aware of laws and legislation which serve to protect employees and employers, and are a source of risk management.

What if a manager does all they can to avoid risk yet it still occurs? Depending on the type of risk, there are several employees who can assist in the resolution of this problem. If it is a financial risk, then financial managers and accountants can help. However, it becomes more complex when it is a risk associated with human resources because, unlike money, people cannot be dealt with easily. There are all sorts of complexities, including laws, and physical and emotional distress. One avenue that may be sought is conciliation and arbitration. **Conciliation** involves an independent moderator who mediates a meeting between the two parties, and together they determine a solution. **Arbitration** also involves an independent moderator but arbitrators have the authority to make decisions after they have discussed both sides of the issue with relevant parties.

conciliation
Involves an independent moderator who mediates a meeting between the two parties and together they determine a solution.

arbitration
Involves an independent moderator who mediates a meeting between the two parties and has the authority to make decisions.

RISK MANAGERS

In reality, however, it is unlikely that a manager will be able to conduct all of their business *and* analyse risk assessments effectively. A risk manager may be appointed to assist managers in all aspects of risk management, whether it is in relation to financial matters, legislation or HRM. The role of a risk manager is to have a thorough understanding of the business' operations (i.e. goals, mission, vision, policies and procedures) and have outstanding leadership and communication skills. A risk manager must also have a thorough understanding of risk management and how it applies to every section of the business.

A risk manager will usually conduct training in risk management. This allows employees to gain an understanding of what constitutes a risk and the process for assessing and evaluating whether it is worth pursuing that risk. Training will usually be conducted in conjunction with HRM and legal counsel. For example, negligent recruitment and selection poses several risks for the company, although HR managers may be unaware of them. By outlining what possible risks a company faces and the consequences of them, a company can dramatically reduce the possibility of poor risks.

RISK MANAGEMENT AND HRM

As a final note regarding this important management issue, it is necessary to provide some guidelines on how liability can be reduced in the workplace. According to Jarret (2003), there are several steps that a risk manager can take to reduce employment practices liability:

- Establish hiring practices that comply with state and federal laws.
- Ensure that employee handbooks (i.e. codes of conduct) clearly and concisely outline company policies and procedures. Jargon should be avoided as should ambiguous statements.
- Provide formal, published policies regarding all forms of discrimination. Both state and federal Acts need to be included and should be updated regularly. Any reported discrimination needs to be investigated seriously and professionally, with full documentation of processes and outcomes.
- Make EEO and affirmative action documents readily available. Posters should be displayed in prominent positions around organisational workplaces.
- Conduct performance appraisals at least annually. Where corrective behaviour is necessary, more frequent reviews may be required.
- Document the termination policy in compliance with state and federal laws. In the event of a termination, the policy must be strictly adhered to.
- Conduct and document exit interviews properly.
- Ensure thorough, truthful annual reviews are conducted and documented.

Please read

Clardy, A. (2004), 'Toward an HRD auditing protocol: Assessing HRD risk management practices', *Human Resource Development Review*, vol. 3, no. 2, pp. 124–50.

Industrial relations

As discussed earlier in this chapter, employment law sets the minimum standards and conditions for employment in a given region and it is important for all stakeholders in the employment relationship to have an accurate understanding of this law. Employment law falls under the umbrella of **industrial relations**, which refers to the formal relations between management, employees, unions and the government through work rules and agreements. The most difficult aspect about industrial relations is that it is constantly changing (i.e. new laws, policies and agreements are developed which supersede old ones) and these changes are specific to particular regions. For example, in Australia there are different

industrial relations
The formal relations between management, employees, unions and the government through work rules and agreements.

industrial relations Acts in most states, making it difficult for HR managers to stay afloat of correct laws and agreements; hence, they often experience difficulty in resolving industrial relations disputes in a timely and correct manner.

Traditionally, industrial relations in Australia have been fostered by a strong trade union presence and the perception and expectation of conflicting values between managers and employees. This aligns with 'hard' HRM which views employees as costs and emphasises control-based strategies for managing people. For example, such control can be achieved through workplace agreements and laws which are supported by the government and which serve to sustain working environments fairly but formally. However, this traditional view of industrial relations assumes that the employment relationship can only be resolved through strict rules and hierarchy, imposed by third parties, such as the **Australian Industrial Relations Commission** (AIRC), whose role is to act as a mediator to resolve conflicts between management and employees. This traditional view therefore contrasts starkly with the new industrial relations, which also aligns with 'soft' HRM and focuses on gaining employees' commitment through quality of work life and is based on the belief that employees need to be cared for, motivated and self-directed through flexibility and adaptability, rather than being controlled by management (see Chapter 2 for a discussion of the hard and soft HRM paradox). To this end, Legge (2005) proposes that the traditional view of industrial relations and HRM are, in fact, perhaps incompatible, which poses a dilemma for HR managers, employers and employees alike. However, Legge (2005) also proposes that the new industrial relations accepts the soft perspective of HRM and that employers and employees can work together in a mutually beneficial employment relationship, without the need for hierarchy and strict forms of control.

So, if society is moving towards the new industrial relations, with mutually beneficial working arrangements, how can HR managers ensure that their information and resources are up to date? The easiest way to access this information is to determine what area of industrial relations is relevant and then contact regional (or state) government agencies to obtain this data. Table 6.3 lists some possible websites for industrial relations matters in Australia. It is important as an HR manager to be familiar with these sites and regularly refer to them to keep abreast of changes.

Australian Industrial Relations Commission
A third party whose role is to act as mediator to resolve conflicts between management and employees.

Occupational health and safety

In the last decade the Australian government has increased awareness of occupational health and safety (OHS) in the workplace. Legislation, at both the state and federal level, has forced companies to consider the welfare of employees in the workplace and, consequently, policies have been implemented to combat the rise and aftermath of injury at work. **Occupational health and safety** refers to the health, safety and welfare of employees in the workplace. It is the effort to improve workplace conditions to prevent accidents and injury occurring at work, and developing systems to deal with rehabilitation and compensation. Like all aspects of this chapter, a knowledge of OHS is imperative for HRM and for organisational productivity and effectiveness.

occupational health and safety
The health, safety and welfare of employees in the workplace. It is the effort to improve workplace conditions to prevent accidents and injury occurring at work, and developing systems to deal with rehabilitation and compensation.

TABLE 6.3   **Websites for industrial relations matters in Australia**

Entity	Website	Details provided on the website
Australian Industrial Relations Commission (AIRC)	www.airc.gov.au	A government-based website which provides information on the AIRC and its role in dealing with employment issues such as resolving conflicts, unfair dismissal and determining wages and conditions for the Australian workforce
Australian Council of Trade Unions	www.actu.asn.au	The ACTU is a national centre which represents the Australian workforce. The website includes details about union membership, minimum wages, employee rights and Helpline contacts
WageLine (Australian federal wages and conditions of employment)	www.wagenet.gov.au	A government-based website which provides information about wages and conditions regarding employment in Australia for work that is covered by federal awards and agreements
Employment and workplace relations services for Australians	www.workplace.gov.au	A government-based website with factual information for both employers and employees regarding contracts and agreements (i.e. the *Workplace Relations Act 1996*, enterprise bargaining and award restructuring), entitlements, responsibilities, employment incentives (i.e. for employing Indigenous Australians and wage assistance), salaries and wages and training

There are many hazards in a workplace which may contribute to a workplace injury. A **workplace injury** is an injury or illness sustained: (1) as part of work activities; (2) in transit to or from the place of employment; or (3) by aggravation of pre-existing conditions where employment contributed to the injury. The hazards contributing to these can either be physical or psychological, and include:

workplace injury
An injury or illness sustained: (a) as part of work activities; (b) in transit to or from the place of employment; or (c) by aggravation of pre-existing conditions where employment contributed to the injury (ABS, 2001).

- *Physicality.* This includes noise, lighting, vibration, extreme or excessive temperatures, physical labour, repetition and speed. This can result from manual labour, laser technology and poor air-conditioning systems.
- *Hazardous commodities.* These include dangerous chemicals in the workplace such as poisons, toxins, pollutants, petrol, asbestos, oil, mercury, dust and any chemical that can cause a reaction when placed in contact with other surfaces, including the human body.
- *Physical harm.* This includes violence or physical harm from other organisational members in the workplace such as pushing, hitting, fighting and involuntary movement (i.e. being coerced into undesirable positions or locations).
- *Psychological harm.* This includes stress, job burnout, tension, bullying and depression. It also includes any workplace occurrence, such as organisational restructuring or job redesign, that results in employee responses such as alcohol or drug abuse.

Workplace injuries in Australia

Although workplace injuries are a serious concern for companies, how often do they really occur? What is the cost that Australian employees and employers pay? According to the Work Related Injuries Survey conducted by the Australian Bureau of Statistics (ABS) (2001), an overwhelming number of workplace accidents and injuries are reported every year. According to the ABS, in the year ending September 2000, 477 800 people were reported to have experienced a work-related injury or illness that was sustained as a result of their work activities (this included the aggravation of pre-existing conditions at work and injuries sustained on the journey to and from work). Although the injuries varied across Australian states, South Australia and Tasmania reported the highest occurrences (65 per 1000 and 58 per 1000 respectively), with the Northern Territory and Victoria reporting the lowest rates (both 42 per 1000).

This survey also revealed the difference between the number of injuries reported by males and females. Men reported twice as many injuries as females, with 28 per cent of people being aged between 35 and 44, 24 per cent between 25 and 34 and 9 per cent being 55 and over. Interestingly, males between 35 and 44 reported the highest occurrence of workplace injuries.

What is the cost of a workplace injury? Managers deal with workplace injuries every day and the costs are not just those of an injured worker but include financial costs as well. First, there are compensation costs. Of the 477 800 people who reported a workplace injury in the ABS survey, 325 400 received financial assistance. Of these, 21 per cent received sick leave provided by the employer and 20 per cent received Medicare benefits. It should also be noted that over half (54 per cent) who did not apply for compensation did not receive any financial assistance for that injury or illness.

Although compensation costs, which are covered wholly by either the employer and/or WorkCover, are easily accounted for, there are other costs associated with injured employees. A manager needs to consider all of these and the impact they have on all organisational members, including employees, customers, suppliers and, of course, the employer.

- *Replacing injured employees.* When an employee is injured in the workplace the first thing a manager must consider (after the injured employee has received medical attention) is who is going to replace that employee. How is the job going to get done? How quickly is it necessary to obtain a replacement? Can the company afford to wait days, weeks or months before locating a substitute? This will depend on the nature of the job and whether a replacement is essential or if colleagues are willing and able to do the injured employee's tasks while they heal. In some cases, job redesign may be necessary. For example, if the injured employee is unable to move physically, an option would be for them to swap with a colleague who performs less physical work in the interim. However, where this is not the case, the process of advertising, interviewing, checking referees and skills, selecting and training a new employee often presents additional and unexpected costs, both in time and money. Line managers, HR managers and senior management are all involved in this process, so time is deducted from everyone's work, possibly creating stress and frustration. Even if co-workers are prepared to share the workload in the interim, the impact on them is sometimes less than fair, and can result in more problems, as discussed further in this section.

- *Impact on colleagues.* An injured employee impacts upon their colleagues in a number of ways, both physically and psychologically. The physical ways include the fact that the job of the injured employee still has to get done. Whether that involves manual labour, administration or laboratory assistance, someone still has to perform that job. However, most staff are not multiskilled and therefore additional training may be required, taking up more time in an already busy schedule. Usually, this will lead to psychological effects, such as stress, burnout, worry, pressure and even resentment towards the injured employee. Distracted employees are also more likely to have a workplace accident. For managers, this means dealing with additional OHS issues . . . for the already injured employee's colleagues! It is also important to remember that sometimes the people who are closest to the employee will be affected the most, and HR managers need to develop soft HRM skills to manage this effectively and professionally (refer to Chapter 2 for a discussion on hard and soft HRM practices).

- *Quality of product/service.* When just one employee loses the ability to work, and colleagues take on an additional workload, the quality of the product or service can suffer. Lack of time, increased pressure and overall job stress can result in tasks being rushed or not completed thoroughly. It can also result in staff not paying enough attention to the task at hand, which can lead to further workplace accidents and injuries. When the quality of work begins to suffer, other organisational units that rely on that work feel this impact, as well as external stakeholders such as customers. Therefore, the replacement of an injured worker needs to be viewed holistically and questions such as 'How might additional work impact upon company members?' and 'What systems can be implemented to deal with additional work effectively?' need to be addressed before injuries take place.

- *Relationships with stakeholders.* As a result of reduced quality, the employee–stakeholder relationship can also suffer. In this sense, stakeholders may be customers, suppliers or any party that has a vested interest in the organisation. Reduced quality (in the product or service), poor or limited communication and unprofessional business manners (i.e. being rude or rushed) could lead to the stakeholder either making a complaint or, more likely, taking their business elsewhere. This also includes the relationships employees have with each other. Quite often, an injured employee's absence will affect the entire department, not just the immediate area that the employee worked in. Therefore, line managers need to manage this adequately, which may involve actually helping employees perform tasks rather than purely supervising. Employees will appreciate the gesture and will develop a sense of trust and respect for their managers, creating a positive, supportive culture.

- *Job satisfaction.* **Job satisfaction** refers to the level of contentment an employee associates with their job. For the injured employee, reduced job satisfaction may result when they return to work because they may have lost clients to

job satisfaction
The level of contentment that an employee associates with their job.

other colleagues or not have the ability to perform as well or in the same way as they did prior to the injury. For their co-workers, reduced job satisfaction is likely if they feel their workload has increased too much and is a source of tension, pressure or stress. Unsatisfied workers are less productive as the level of contentment with their job has decreased; they become unhappy workers and this feeds into the organisational culture breeding negativity.

- *Turnover.* Employees who feel less satisfied with their job and/or with the company are likely to have low levels of loyalty. For organisations, this means they are likely to terminate their employment and resign. The cost of employee turnover places great financial and physiological stress on employees and the company, exacerbating the initial problem of replacing an injured worker. The recruitment, selection and training process becomes an infinite cycle within the organisation.
- *Organisational outcomes.* All of the above factors ultimately lead to one thing: outcome. If these factors are not dealt with effectively and promptly, organisational productivity and outcomes will suffer as a result. Declining market share and return on investment, increased OHS costs, negative organisational culture and employee turnover are the realities of poorly handled OHS processes.

CURRENT ISSUES IN HEALTH AND SAFETY

While OHS has now reached most boardroom discussions in companies across the globe, there are some new issues surrounding this HRM concept. Traditional OHS issues include wearing appropriate safety clothing, the use of protective materials (such as gloves, laboratory coats and eyewear) and ensuring safety harnesses are used and correctly fitted on worksites. The focus was primarily on the blue-collar workforce as this was where a majority of manual labour was performed and where accidents were a common occurrence. However, injuries have also emerged in white-collar workforces such as offices. With the introduction of new technology in a fast- paced global environment, new safety hazards in all types of workplaces are emerging. In fact, according to the International Confederation of Free Trade Unions (ICFTU), there are two million fatalities worldwide that occur on the job each year (5000 deaths per day) and an overwhelming 270 million occupational accidents yearly (ICFTU, 2004).

VISUAL IMPAIRMENT

The introduction of computers in the 1980s made a significant change to the way business was conducted. They allowed work to be performed better, faster and in a more efficient and effective way than ever before. However, 25 years on, the effects of computer use are revealed. Impaired eyesight is a common OHS issue that computer users experienced. More and more people are developing the need for glasses as they sit for hours on end staring at a computer screen. One way to combat this, however, is to ensure staff regularly take a break from using the computer. Simple exercises to regenerate eyes can prevent or minimise the need for glasses.

REPETITIVE STRAIN INJURY

Another OHS issue from the use of computers is repetitive strain injury (RSI). In the workplace, this usually occurs in wrists or arms from excessive computer use without breaks. It results from repetitive work tasks such as continual typing or data entry where the body part's movement is limited. RSI can be very painful, causing swelling and aches to occur, and it can prevent work from occurring if the pain if significant. However, this injury is not just related to the use of computers. Any employee who does one task repetitively runs the risk of getting RSI. For example, gardeners using a shovel for long periods of time may also experience pain in their wrist, arms or shoulders, as might carpenters holding a specific tool for extended periods. As with the prevention of visual impairment, RSI can be avoided or minimised with regular breaks and exercises to stretch and relax the muscles. With computer use, employees may purchase a gel pad, which either sits near the keyboard or the mouse, on which the wrists rest while typing. For blue-collar workers, job sharing may be required with colleagues, and appropriate materials should be provided to rest against when using devices for long periods at a time.

BACK INJURIES

Back injuries, which have been reported as an OHS issue for years, not only relate to physical labour but are also associated with computer use. It is important to maintain a correct posture when using computers, with an ergonomic chair and footrest to ensure that the body is not strained. If requested, companies are required to provide correct seating and footrests for employees as part of their commitment to OHS and employee wellbeing. Again, regular breaks and exercises are necessary to prevent back injuries from occurring.

MOBILE PHONES

In the mid-1990s, reports investigating the harmful use of mobile phones surfaced. This is a serious OHS concern as most employees use mobile phones as part of their work-related communication. In fact, about 75 per cent of the Australian population have mobile phones for personal and professional use. Professional employees tend to use mobile phones to maintain contact with customers and to be accessible at any time. This is the reality of the 'mobile office'. Mobile phones, which have significantly decreased in size due to advanced technology, may cause a myriad of health problems. These include exposure to radiation and the growth of cancers in the immune system. It is also a danger for employees to use phones while driving or near flammable chemicals such as petrol.

Despite telecommunications companies' reassurance that mobile phones are safe to use, effective OHS policies advise the use of 'hands-free' equipment to minimise the effects of radiation and also to comply with traffic laws. In Australia, it is against the law to drive while talking on a mobile phone unless a hands-free device is attached. People found breaking this law will receive a $135 fine and the loss of three demerit points.

ENVIRONMENTAL HAZARDS

If you look carefully around most workplaces, OHS hazards are easily spotted. Untidy computer cables, wet surfaces and poor air-conditioning systems and photocopier ventilation are some examples of environmental hazards found in offices. Employees and employers alike must continually keep an eye out for unsafe conditions or hazards that could potentially lead to injury. For example, teachers must ensure that students' school bags are placed under desks and not left lying in aisles, waiting for someone to trip over them. Even small items that may not be considered dangerous, such as whiteboard markers, need to be used for short periods and in rooms with sufficient ventilation as the fumes from these can be harmful.

STRESS

stress
Tension people experience when they are under considerable physical and psychological demand.

Another common OHS issue evident in today's organisations is stress. Stress, which was once perceived as an individual weakness, has subsequently been recognised as a significant OHS issue warranting serious management attention. Rapidly changing workplaces, increased consumer demand and a competitive business environment has increased stress levels in firms around the globe. Worldwide, a reported 30–40 per cent of adults report extreme stress at work. **Stress** is defined as tension people experience when they are under considerable physical and psychological demand. This may be exhibited in forms of frustration, anger, bad moods and even violence. However, not all stress is detrimental.

There are two forms of stress: positive and negative. For employees to maintain motivation and a competitive edge, a certain amount of positive stress is needed. This enhances stimulation and encourages employees to achieve goals. However, positive stress needs to be managed to ensure it doesn't spiral into negative stress. Negative stress has an adverse effect on individual and organisational productivity and goal achievement. In essence, it prevents work from being completed effectively, creates disruptions and leads to job dissatisfaction and job burnout. HR managers should be aware of the symptoms of job stress, which include absenteeism or tardiness, personality changes and conflicts, differing work habits and job burnout (Fujimoto, Härtel & Panipucci, 2005).

For an HR manager to deal with this OHS issue effectively they need to understand the sources of stress. How is stress created? There are three main sources of organisational stress (Anderson & Pulich, 2001). *Job-related stress* includes work overload, organisational change and restructuring, and lack of control or autonomy. *Role-related stress* includes role conflict and role ambiguity. Finally, *group-related stress* includes intragroup demands and intergroup demands. However, there are additional sources of stress, such as poor communication, shift work, short-term contracts, new technology, job insecurity, poor training, family commitments and conflicting individual, group and organisational goals. In this sense, stress is very closely associated with job burnout.

The effect of stress   When stress isn't managed well the employee, employer and the employee's friends and family can suffer as a result. Employees can experience breakdowns, depression, personal conflict (such as divorce), professional conflict (such as resigning from the job) and even develop alcoholism or addiction to drugs. For employers, the negative effects of stress include absenteeism, low morale and job satisfaction, poor quality of work and working relationships, difficult industrial relations, higher occurrences of accidents and litigation. Family and friends of stressed employees will also experience negative effects from the stressed person such as mood swings and poor communication, which will usually test their friendship and levels of toleration. All of these factors can further exacerbate the already dire situation.

Dealing with stress in the workplace   As with all OHS issues faced by organisations today, it is strategically more effective to implement policies on prevention rather than on cure. Stress is no exception. With the increased reporting of stress in the workplace across the globe, it is evident that this OHS issue is not going to disappear quickly. However, there are factors which can minimise the negative consequences of stress.

First, companies need to consider how stress can be prevented. Policies and training on the prevention of stress need to be implemented and reviewed on a regular basis. For example, if an employee feels they are getting stressed, they should have the option to seek advice from a counsellor (either internal or external to the company), thus preventing stress from occurring. This counsellor, incidentally, should be provided and paid for by the organisation. Alternatively, colleagues should look out for stressed signals (such as frustration, mood swings, depression) and raise the issue immediately with an appropriate person. This includes colleagues looking out for managers and vice versa. In fact, the highest reporting of work-related stress is of senior managers, an epidemic which is sweeping the globe and which explains why some senior managers feel the quickest and easiest way of managing is to act unethically.

Wellness programs are another way that stress can be prevented, minimised or relieved. This involves employees taking an active role in the workplace regarding OHS and stipulates the sources of stress, why they may occur and how they can be managed. This enables employees to understand the issue holistically, thereby allowing them to address the cause of the problem, not just the symptoms. Quite often, wellness programs advocate dealing with stress in a variety of ways such as regular exercise, healthy diets and sufficient breaks (both during work hours and also holidays). Large organisations, such as Coles Myer's head office in Melbourne, even have a gymnasium within the building which members can access before, during or after work, hence actively promoting exercise and stress alleviation. Other companies have joined the trend in providing employees with regular massages during lunch breaks, to rest the mind and body and stimulate energy. According to these employees, the massages really do work and employees feel more energised to continue working in the afternoon (when most people begin to feel tired).

As a final word of caution, it is not enough simply to implement policies or have a program on stress. Companies also need to take a proactive role. When a stress incident is reported in the organisation, this should be documented by the HR manager and a solution found in the event that this occurs again. Over time, not only will stress reduce but the company and its employees will feel the positive effects of a stress-free environment.

JOB BURNOUT

Job burnout has gained much recognition in the workplace and media in recent years due to the significant health issues it poses for employees. **Job burnout,**

job burnout
Exhaustion experienced by employees as a result of their work efforts.

which is a particularly popular topic in HRM circles, refers to exhaustion experienced by employees as a result of their work efforts. More specifically, it is defined as having three components (Maslach, 1982):

1. *Emotional exhaustion.* This is characterised by a lack of energy and the distinct feeling that emotional resources have been fatigued. Frustration and tension are common symptoms, as is the feeling of dread at the thought of work.
2. *Depersonalisation.* This is evident when people feel like they are treated as objects not humans, and employees become emotionally detached and often cynical towards all organisational members. This is also referred to as dehumanisation.
3. *Diminished personal accomplishment.* This is characterised by employees lacking self-confidence and developing a negative opinion about the self. Job competency and achievement decline, as does their interaction with others.

In today's busy and transient workplaces, employees find themselves working harder and faster: work relationships become strained, overworked employees have less time to devote to quality and everything seems to be needed 'yesterday'. This is typical of Western workplaces. As a result, people become exhausted, less effective and eventually tired and cynical.

There are six reasons why job burnout occurs (see Figure 6.8). The first, *work overload*, occurs when there is simply too much work to do than can be reasonably expected. Employees feel under pressure and unable to cope effectively with the workload. Therefore, a decline in productivity results, causing them to experience even more stress. A *lack of control* occurs as a result of companies implementing policies in a bureaucratic fashion, centralising control with senior management. Therefore, lower-level employees are left with no control over work choices, resource allocation and procedures in completing work tasks. *Insufficient rewards* relate back to the theory of motivation discussed in Chapter 2. Different people are motivated differently, either intrinsically or extrinsically, and HR managers need to determine ways to satisfy individual members to ensure that they feel sufficiently rewarded. A *breakdown of community* occurs when the work community (i.e. department or organisation) becomes disparate. For instance, negative influences such as a loss of job security or lack of collegial support are examples of breakdowns. When people do not feel a sense of belonging (which is related to Maslow's hierarchy of needs theory discussed in Chapter 2), they often feel very isolated and alone. This can lead to job burnout. An *absence of fairness* can also lead to stress, distrust and job burnout. Workplaces that foster positive, equitable cultures with trust and respect tend to experience less employee job burnout than those which don't. Although open and honest communication is a key factor in fairness, being able to trust top management is also highly important. Finally, *conflicting values* are another important factor in the creation of job burnout. Employee, departmental and overall organisational values and goals need to be congruent for individual, group and organisational success. This is the main argument in the development of SHRM, for HRM can only be strategic when all organisational members' goals are aligned.

If not effectively managed, job burnout can have serious effects on the organisation. High rates of absenteeism, increased employee turnover, decreased

FIGURE
The six causes of job burnout

productivity, costly mistakes, reduced job and organisational commitment and declining morale and job satisfaction are the realities of ineffectively managed job burnout.

It is clear, therefore, that job burnout presents a serious OHS risk to employees and a potentially damaging risk for organisations. But what can be done about it? Naturally, training should be provided to prevent it from occurring in the first instance. However, in situations where job burnout is evident, there are several steps employees and managers can take to manage it.

- Clearly define employee and manager roles and responsibilities. Updated job descriptions are necessary which also comply with correct HR procedures.
- Ensure that workloads are equitable and aligned with employee capabilities and organisational resources.
- Improve communication channels. While managers need to dictate work tasks to a certain degree, employees should also be able to voice their opinions and be involved in decision making, encouraging a sense of empowerment.
- Establish work schedules that are conducive to employees' external commitments and responsibilities, including the option for part-time or casual employment due to family or lifestyle commitments.
- Develop a policy on job burnout which is easily accessible to all employees, outlining what it is and how it can be prevented and managed. Taking sufficient breaks, going for a walk, listening to music and meditation are examples of activities that will reduce the effects of job burnout.
- Ensure employees have the opportunity to share fun experiences. Positive emotions help people recharge emotionally.
- Actively support and look out for employees displaying symptoms of job burnout. Counselling should also be available.

BULLYING

An OHS issue which has gained much attention over the past decade is workplace bullying. **Bullying**, which usually leads to job stress, is an OHS issue when it is performed in the workplace by colleagues, line managers, senior managers and

bullying
Undesirable, unfavourable and inappropriate treatment experienced by employees within the workplace.

organisational stakeholders such as customers and suppliers. It is defined as undesirable, unfavourable and inappropriate treatment within the workplace. Although bullying is usually thought of as a physical behaviour it can also be emotional and both forms are serious health and safety issues. Deplorable acts of bullying have been reported in Australian workplaces for years; however, the problem was that bullying became part of the culture for manual labourers. They experienced bullying as means of intimidation or as part of initiation rights when they were young apprentices and so the culture developed. Even some line managers participated in and encouraged the bullying and those who complained were tainted as weak and were subsequently ostracised. Since the introduction of new legislation and OHS standards, fewer accounts of bullying have been reported and the bullying culture is slowly diminishing.

It is important to remember that even though there are numerous potential accidents and injuries at all types of workplaces, most of these can be prevented or at least minimised through some caution and a little common sense.

Please read
Angerer, J. M. (2003), 'Job burnout', *Journal of Employment Counseling*, vol. 40, no. 3, pp. 98–107.

GOVERNMENT REGULATION
Occupational health and safety is covered under government regulations and it is the responsibility of all employers to know the laws relating to employee wellbeing in the workplace. As these laws are constantly changing, HR managers are advised to locate the source of this information and stay informed of any updates or changes to make certain they are adhering to legislation and providing a safe and responsible working environment. In Australia, these laws differ at the state and federal levels; however, a useful website for all Australian companies on OHS regulation is <www.worksafe.gov.au>. This is an Australian government website under the Department of Employment and Workplace Relations (Office of the Australian Safety and Compensation Council) which provides information on national standards, codes of practice, research, and statistics on OHS. Specific contacts for workplace safety at the state and territory level are also available via this website (see Table 6.4) and these can provide valuable OHS information within desired regional areas. For example, Victorian Acts containing OHS requirements for workplace safety are listed in Table 6.5.

MANAGING HEALTH AND SAFETY
Historically, the health and safety of employees was viewed as the joint responsibility of union representatives and the personnel department. Even during the 1970s and early 1980s, it was perceived as the union's responsibility to stand up for employee rights with regard to OHS; management simply continued to conduct business until complaints were lodged with the union. Consequently, managing health and safety was not a management priority. However, the shift from personnel management to human resource management in the late 1980s saw a radical modification in OHS. The establishment of health and safety

| TABLE | **6.4** | **State and territory contacts for workplace safety** |

NSW Workcover Authority	www.workcover.nsw.gov.au
Victorian Workcover Authority	www.workcover.vic.gov.au
Worksafe Western Australia	www.safetyline.wa.gov.au
South Australian Workcover Authority	www.workcover.com
Workplace Services South Australia	www.eric.sa.gov.au
Queensland Division of Workplace Health & Safety	www.dir.qld.gov.au/workplace
Workplace Standards Tasmania	www.wst.tas.gov.au
Northern Territory Work Health Authority	www.nt.gov.au/ntg/indrels.shtml
ACT Workcover	www.workcover.act.gov.au

Source: <http://www.worksafe.gov.au/OtherRelatedSites/australiansites>, accessed 3 December 2005.

| TABLE | **6.5** | **Victorian Acts containing OHS requirements** |

Accident Compensation Regulations 2001

Accident Compensation (Self-Insurers' Contributions) Regulations 1999

Dangerous Goods (Explosives) Regulations 2000

Dangerous Goods (High Consequence Dangerous Goods – HCDG) Regulations 2005

Dangerous Goods (Storage and Handling) Regulations 2000

Dangerous Goods (Transport by Rail) Regulations 1998

Equipment (Public Safety) (Incident Notification) Regulations 1997

Equipment (Public Safety) (General) Regulations 1995

Occupational Health and Safety (Asbestos) Regulations 2003

Occupational Health and Safety (Certification of Plant Users and Operators) Regulations 1994

Occupational Health and Safety (Confined Spaces) Regulations 1996 (S.R. No. 148/1996)

Occupational Health and Safety (Hazardous Substances) Regulations 1999

Occupational Health and Safety (Issue Resolution) Regulations 1999

Occupational Health and Safety (Lead) Regulations 2000

Occupational Health and Safety (Major Hazard Facilities) Regulations 2000

Occupational Health and Safety (Manual Handling) Regulations 1999

Occupational Health and Safety (Mines) Regulations 2002

Occupational Health and Safety (Noise) Regulations 2004

Occupational Health and Safety (Plant) Regulations 1995

Occupational Health and Safety (Prevention of Falls) Regulations 2003

Road Transport (Dangerous Goods) (Licence Fees) Regulations 1998

Road Transport Reform (Dangerous Goods) Regulations 1997

Source: <http://www.workcover.vic.gov.au/vwa/home.nsf/pages/so_regs>, accessed 3 December 2005. The Victorian WorkCover Authority website should be accessed for more information and future updates on the references used.

regulations and legislation around the world, including Australia, coupled with conscious company efforts to engage in the responsibility of its workers, gave light to a new management era. Managers finally began to realise the insufficiency of fixing problems after they occur and they began focusing on prevention techniques in line with new government legislation.

Today, workplace safety is not only a hot topic, but one that has reached the priority lists of boardroom meetings. The costs of workplace injury, as discussed earlier, dictate that it is far wiser for a company to focus on prevention rather than cure. In the workplaces of today, with modern features and high-tech equipment, OHS is more important than ever before. But how can safety and health in the workplace be managed? Fortunately, there are several systems a manager can put in place to deal with OHS effectively.

The primary responsibility for a company is to ensure that state and federal OHS laws are complied with. It is not enough for management to be aware of these; employees need to know and understand what factors fall under the umbrella of OHS and the company policies and procedures which complement these. For example, an executive entering a worksite might not know that it is a legal requirement to wear steel-capped boots. Therefore, signs should be placed for employees entering the site and appropriate safety clothing provided (i.e. steel-capped boots, hard hat and so on). Communicating the legislation to organisational members might also be done via training or information seminars, emails, memos, posters and on the company intranet.

An OHS officer also needs to be appointed. Usually, this will either be a staff member within the HRM department, or a union representative. It is the officer's responsibility routinely to check and inspect the workplace to ensure that it is safe, and to report dangerous or suspicious activities. They must also liaise with management and union representatives when a report (or complaint) has been lodged, and it is their duty of care to investigate this seriously and thoroughly. The officer is also responsible for promoting awareness of OHS matters throughout the organisation, including developing new training programs specifically to target problem areas. For example, this may include the use of medical facilities or using appropriate protective clothing. Traditionally, OHS officers were called 'inspectors' which implies that the company might get caught acting unsafely. However, nowadays an officer's role is to support, encourage and create systems to ensure that workplace safety is a priority and becomes second nature in the job.

It is also the OHS officer's responsibility to develop contingency plans. This needs to be done in conjunction with senior managers and will ensure that, should anticipated problems occur, there will be appropriate action. This is an ideal way to ensure that the company looks into the future and acknowledges possible problems, supported with possible action plans. It avoids chaos and panic, and allows the problem to be solved faster and more efficiently than without such plans. This may be useful if, for example, a disease broke out within the building, or there were multiple accidents at once if technology and machines broke down.

A final responsibility of the OHS officer is to develop rehabilitation and compensation packages. This must be done in accordance with law, but it is also influenced largely by the culture of the organisation and senior management's commitment to OHS (which should be strong). By having a standard rehabilitation and compensation package, it is clear to employees and employers what they are entitled to and what the process of rehabilitation and/or compensation entails. This is especially useful because all workplace injuries are unplanned and often leave the employee feeling helpless and depressed if they are no longer able to work as effectively as they once could. It is important to remember that, to most people, their job is a significant part of their life and once that is removed psychological stress can set in, which can snowball into a variety of other illnesses.

Along with training in OHS laws, employees also need to be trained in how to prevent workplace injuries. This involves monitoring work activities and work areas and actively taking initiative to prevent possible accidents from occurring. If the employee is unable to prevent an accident or injury (i.e. if it involves a large machine or they do not have the authority), they must report it to the line manager and OHS officer immediately.

It is, of course, imperative that managers lead by example and not only follow the laws but also set examples by working safely in the workplace and encouraging staff to look out for unsafe work activities or areas. Workplace safety is everybody's responsibility.

Managing the employment relationship: healthy organisations

The employment relationship is the foundation of work. Employers and employees alike need to work together cooperatively to achieve goals efficiently and effectively in order to obtain and sustain a competitive advantage. When this advantage is achieved, all stakeholders benefit; employees have increased job security, customers have higher quality products at competitive prices and shareholders have increased returns on investment. However, the employment relationship should not be wholly governed and regulated by law. It is possible (and more beneficial) for employers and employees to have common goals, with minimised levels of conflict traditionally inherent in typical employment relationships. When common goals are pursued, the employment relationship is described as **unitarist HRM**. This is the approach that most organisations today are striving to achieve, realising that it is not always necessary for law to enact amicable behaviour and control in the workplace. Traditionally, unitarism has been reflected in the HRM practices of Malaysian and Singaporean companies. Conversely, **pluralist HRM** occurs when conflict between employers and employees is perceived as inevitable, favouring strong union involvement. Traditionally, pluralism has been reflected in the HRM styles and practices of Western companies such as those in Australia and the United Kingdom.

So, how can management control employee behaviour and ensure it is ethical and legal without relying heavily on the law? The control of social behaviour needs to be addressed to ascertain this answer.

unitarist HRM
An employment relationship where employers and employees assume common goals.

pluralist HRM
The perceived inevitable conflict between employers and employees, favouring strong union involvement.

WHERE THE LAW ENDS: THE SOCIAL CONTROL OF BEHAVIOUR

The control of social behaviour is imperative to the development of a healthy organisation. The law cannot be relied upon for every conflict employers and employees experience; the company and its stakeholders must take the initiative and responsibility for their own actions and attempt to resolve issues fairly and professionally. The fact that many companies are demonstrating a harmonious relationship with employees has resulted in the decline of trade unionism, proving that it is possible (and certainly more desirable) to increase the use of communication and problem-solving techniques between employer and employee, without third-party intervention.

However, the employment relationship and the control of employee behaviour have not always been amicable. Historically, the control of employees' behaviour in the workplace was performed through authoritarian management styles such as Taylor's (1911) scientific management and Weber's (1904) organisational theory of bureaucracy. Employees tended to be coerced through strict supervision and regulation, where capitalism and discipline reigned. Nowadays, modern organisations control social behaviour very differently. The processes of command and control do not suit many modern organisations as they shift from authoritarianism to a culture of collegiality and mutual agreement (Mastenbroek, 2000). There is a trend toward implicit rather than explicit control of behaviour, a term Mastenbroek (2000) refers to as 'controlled decontrolling'. This implicit control implies that although there is more relaxed formal control and social behaviour in the workplace, this in effect places greater demands on people in that they need to detect the appropriate cultural norms and practices governing a given workplace. Employees may not, however, possess sufficient skill to detect or appropriately adapt to these implicit norms; nonetheless, it is expected that they possess this capacity and thus are deemed in control of their behaviour. This example explains this paradox (Mastenbroek, 2000, p. 29):

> Never, ever come into a place in a hurry. Better to walk in cool and collected and be ten minutes late, than being on time and out of breath. Panting indicates: this person does not have his affairs under control. Whatever you do, don't take too many notes. Writing a lot indicates: this person is afraid to forget things. Or: this person has no authority, he/she has to report back in detail.

So, what implications does this have for management? Although less visible, the modern organisation continues to control employees through culture.

Negotiating in the workplace

Negotiation is a critical component of personal and organisational life. In our personal lives, we begin negotiating when we are very young and our skills and knowledge of the negotiation process develop from our experiences. In the workplace, however, negotiations are a focal point of the employment relationship and are therefore an important aspect for employees, employers and HR managers to handle. **Negotiation** refers to the process of resolving disputes or conflicts between two or more parties. It entails interaction between the parties, usually in the form of a face to face meeting and at a neutral location. However, because the negotiation process involves questioning, explanation, requests and compromise, it is often considered a stressful and contentious process.

Negotiations typically arise in the workplace when conflict occurs and agreement cannot be reached. A negotiation meeting is scheduled and appropriate parties, including their legal representation (if necessary) contribute to civil discussions to reach a solution. Negotiations can occur on a formal or informal basis, between employees, employers, customers and suppliers. However, for the purpose of this chapter and its focus, negotiations (also called collective bargaining) between employees and employers only will be addressed to the extent that they play a significant role in industrial relations and the law.

To comprehend negotiation fully, including managerial implications, it is necessary to discuss the negotiation hierarchy and the negotiation process.

PERSPECTIVES IN NEGOTIATION

According to negotiation theory, people approach negotiation from one of two perspectives: cooperative or competitive. The cooperative perspective emphasises trust, flexibility and cooperation and a win–win goal in the negotiating relationship, while the competitive negotiating relationship emphasises power, control and competition between parties (Olekalns & Smith, 2005). Traditionally, negotiations between unions and employers tended to be competitive as they viewed the employment relationship from a pluralist perspective, although towards the end of the millennium this view shifted and a unitarist perspective has since been adopted.

It is important that HR managers are aware of the power differences that exist in the workplace and the influence they have on the negotiation process, for example the power that managers have because of their hierarchical status, or the collective power of trade unions. Rather than persist with power struggles and political games, HR managers need to shift the focus to win–win outcomes and ensure that those in positions of power use their influence fairly to create healthy workplace relationships and environments. Negotiation strategies need to be devised that ensure the inappropriate use of power is avoided and that all parties involved aim for an amicable and mutually beneficial outcome which ultimately benefits all stakeholders and increases the strategic focus and competitive advantage of the organisation.

THE NEGOTIATION PROCESS

Individuals perceive the negotiation process uniquely. This is because mental models shape values, beliefs and expectations which, in turn, affect behaviour and how outcomes are constructed. **Mental models**, which are representations of events, interpretations and behaviours, are an important aspect in the negotiation process. There are many factors that influence a person's mental model, such as their ethical stance, national culture, personal and professional experiences and religious or political beliefs. Figure 6.9 depicts the relationship between negotiation perspectives and mental models and the overall negotiation outcome.

mental models
Representations of events, interpretations and behaviours.

In effect, negotiation is a decision-making process which involves six steps, from the conception of the conflict to its formal documentation. These six steps are described in detail below.

FIGURE **6.9**

The relationship between
negotiation perspectives
and mental models

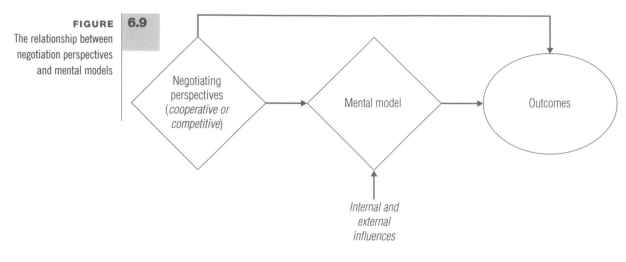

Source: Adapted from an article by M. Olekalns & P. L. Smith in *The Australian Journal of Management*, vol. 30, no. 1, June 2005, p. 58, published by The Australian Graduate School of Management.

1. *Identify the conflict.* A conflict is identified when the parties involved cannot reach an agreement or compromise about an outstanding issue. The conflict needs to be clearly identified and agreed upon by all parties involved.

2. *Identify parties involved.* Precautions must be taken when identifying the parties involved in the conflict. More often than not, problems become out of control and others seek to join the conflict, taking sides. This is usually the case in negotiations as pressure groups (such as trade unions) seek to expand the issue. However, only the actual parties involved should proceed with negotiations.

3. *Listen to each party's opinion.* At a neutral location, each party should rationally, formally and professionally voice the benefits and detriments of the problem at hand, listening to each other. This step may be conducted in a similar way to a debate whereby each party receives several opportunities to voice their opinions and state their concerns in a constructive and professional manner.

4. *Develop a list of alternatives.* After the problem has been clearly identified and each party has sufficiently highlighted their concerns, the parties need to develop cooperatively a list of possible alternatives to solve the problem. Depending on the dynamics of the group, people may work solely in their group (i.e. each party in their own group) or they may work together as a larger group. The alternatives can range from taking no action to a fully integrated approach, and can be as far fetched as possible because at this point the alternatives are simply listed. For the parties, this step is about writing a wish list although some degree of compromise is needed to reach a solution that satisfies all parties.

5. *Select one of the alternatives.* This step is where the true negotiations begin and parties should be prepared for a lengthy process. Usually, this in an iterative process between steps 4 and 5 and parties will need to go back and forth between the alternatives developed until an appropriate alternative that all agree upon is developed and selected. During this stage, parties need also to agree upon the selection criteria to ensure that the solution satisfies those involved, taking into consideration the implications of the decision reached.

6. *Formally document the decision.* Once a final decision has been made and agreed upon by the parties involved, formal documentation confirming the solution needs to be signed (and witnessed) by all parties and kept on file should it need to be referred to in the future.

JUST NEGOTIATIONS

The negotiation process draws on the need to adopt win–win frameworks to encourage and facilitate fair, or 'just', negotiations. When the process is viewed as fair by all parties involved, the employment relationship is enhanced and a community of equity and harmony is born, resulting in individual and organisational benefits.

Organisational justice, which is a concept closely linked to organisational change, focuses on individual reactions to organisational processes and outcomes, for example how people are treated during company restructuring, whether they maintain their employment or are made redundant, and whether or not they perceive this to be a fair outcome. For 'just' negotiations to occur, the principles of procedural, distributive and interactional justice need to be adopted from the realm of organisational justice theory. This theory proposes that people evaluate important situations according to the fairness of the procedures used to make decisions (procedural justice), the treatment they receive from decision makers (interactional justice) and the actual outcomes of the decisions (distributive justice).

Procedural justice is concerned with the fairness of organisational procedures and how employees were treated during that time, including frequency and quality of communication. This is important because it allows employees to have a sense of control over the process and outcomes of decisions, and their strategic perceived fairness (Paterson, Green & Cary, 2002). *Interactional justice* distinguishes between the nature of formal procedures conducted by the company and the way they are enacted within the company. This type of justice proposes that employees use this distinction to determine how fairly they were treated by decision makers. For example, characteristics such as honesty, courtesy and respect help justify decisions. *Distributive justice* proposes that people make a comparison between their own work and those of relevant others, and seeks to ensure that the work input and outcomes are fair (i.e. that they match).

Organisational justice and change management theories are important determinants of employee acceptance during large-scale change, such as industrial relations reform or the implementation of new procedures such as OHS legislation. Managers who attempt to install new changes may encounter strong resistance (stemming from procedural, distributive or interactional injustices) which may result in reduced job security, morale and productivity, and increased turnover and resentment. Further, it could jeopardise other HR functions such as the recruitment of new staff and reduce overall organisational effectiveness. Therefore, HR managers need to consider individual and group thoughts and feelings about change efforts as these will determine, to a significant degree, the success of organisational change (see Figure 6.10 for tips on how to create successful negotiations).

organisational justice
Focuses on individual reactions to organisational processes and outcomes.

FIGURE   6.10
How to create successful
negotiations

✓ Build the future with creative solutions
✓ Enter negotiations incredibly well prepared
✓ Create and claim a fair 'piece of the pie' for each party
✓ Understand different negotiation styles and influences
✓ Master the negotiation process through awareness of verbal and non-verbal behaviour
✓ Build strategic alliances through networking
✓ Embrace lifelong learning

Source: Adapted from McRae (2005), p. 1.

Contemporary SHRM Application Tool

Imagine that you are an HR manager for a medium-sized company specialising in software engineering, re-engineering and maintenance. Your employers are under legal obligation by the Victorian *Occupational Health and Safety Act 2004* to ensure that your workplace is safe and without risks to health. Nowadays, people spend most of their working hours in front of computers and are at risk of developing musculoskeletal injuries such as back, neck and wrist injuries. The severity of this problem is indicated in recent multi-million dollar lawsuits against keyboard manufacturers. Last year, your company's OHS-related compensations and complaints increased significantly and you are now concerned about OHS issues for your employees (software engineers in particular) and for the future business operation. Is your company currently meeting all its OHS legal obligations? The accompanying SHRM Application Tool demonstrates how OHS issues are monitored, planned, implemented and evaluated in this company (refer to Figure 6.11).

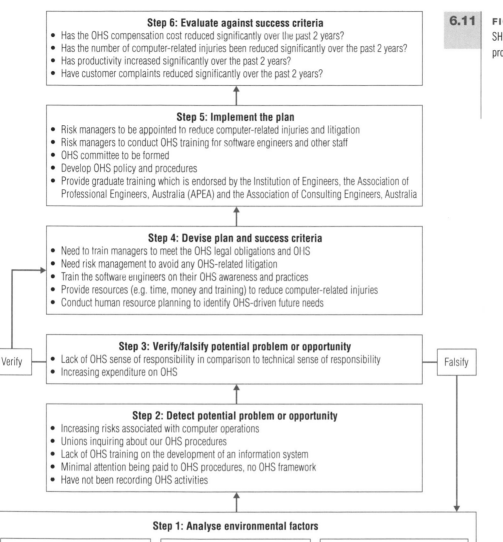

Step 6: Evaluate against success criteria
- Has the OHS compensation cost reduced significantly over the past 2 years?
- Has the number of computer-related injuries been reduced significantly over the past 2 years?
- Has productivity increased significantly over the past 2 years?
- Have customer complaints reduced significantly over the past 2 years?

Step 5: Implement the plan
- Risk managers to be appointed to reduce computer-related injuries and litigation
- Risk managers to conduct OHS training for software engineers and other staff
- OHS committee to be formed
- Develop OHS policy and procedures
- Provide graduate training which is endorsed by the Institution of Engineers, the Association of Professional Engineers, Australia (APEA) and the Association of Consulting Engineers, Australia

Step 4: Devise plan and success criteria
- Need to train managers to meet the OHS legal obligations and OHS
- Need risk management to avoid any OHS-related litigation
- Train the software engineers on their OHS awareness and practices
- Provide resources (e.g. time, money and training) to reduce computer-related injuries
- Conduct human resource planning to identify OHS-driven future needs

Step 3: Verify/falsify potential problem or opportunity
- Lack of OHS sense of responsibility in comparison to technical sense of responsibility
- Increasing expenditure on OHS

Verify

Falsify

Step 2: Detect potential problem or opportunity
- Increasing risks associated with computer operations
- Unions inquiring about our OHS procedures
- Lack of OHS training on the development of an information system
- Minimal attention being paid to OHS procedures, no OHS framework
- Have not been recording OHS activities

Step 1: Analyse environmental factors

Step 1a: HR issues: Monitor/ analyse data (past, present and future)
- Company's OHS expenditure and complaints increased significantly in the last 3 years
- Sufficient technical training so far; however, lack in OHS training
- Many challenges facing graduate engineers in managing OHS issues in system development (e.g. reducing human errors, resulting in a safer, more efficient work environment)

Step 1b: Internal/organisational environment
- Software engineering company consisted of 100 software engineers
- Innovation and quality excellence in technical/software engineering, meeting the quality assurance standard ISO 9001 and ISO 14001
- Create basic software for large-scale systems and networks for government agencies, financial, insurance and securities industries

Step 1c: External environment
- Information technology era
- Increased demand on software engineering in all business sectors
- Government (e.g. National Occupational Health and Safety Commission (NOHSC)), laws, legislation (e.g. Victorian *Occupational Health and Safety Act 2004*)
- Pressure groups (e.g. Australian Council of Trade Unions (ACTU))
- Customers: mainly government agencies, financial, insurance and securities industries

A view from the field — Controversy over proposed *WorkChoices* reform

Peak bodies of every type – employer, employee, churches, women's groups and other organisations – have been making representations to government and the broader public on proposed changes to Australia's framework of workplace relations regulation. David Gregory, the Victorian Employers' Chamber of Commerce and Industry's (VECCI) General Manager for the Workplace Relations Policy, made a presentation espousing the merits of the reform at a forum involving the Minister for Industrial Relations, Rob Hulls, and Bill Shorten, Federal Secretary of the AWU in November 2005. What follows is adapted from David Gregory's presentation.

The new WorkChoices legislation currently before the federal parliament seeks to introduce significant changes to the current framework of workplace relation's regulation. These changes are of particular significance when viewed in the context of Australia's century-old framework of industrial relations/workplace relations regulation that has been in place in this country since 1904.

While we have seen a series of changes over the past fifteen years, from both ALP and Coalition governments – changes designed to place more emphasis upon outcomes developed in individual workplaces and tailored to the needs of that workplace and its employees – these changes have been evolutionary; the current proposals are of a different order of magnitude. They do take one much larger and more significant step along the path that we have been pursuing: a move away from our traditional centralised system to a more decentralised framework.

These changes include:

- *New arrangements for setting minimum wages and conditions with the Australian Fair Pay Commission taking over the traditional role exercised by the Australian Industrial Relations Commission. It is perhaps likely that the new commission will operate more like the Reserve Bank does now in terms of its role in setting and adjusting interest rates with the new Fair Pay Commission to decide how it wants to gather information and inform itself about how it conducts its wage-setting and adjustment role.*
- *A different role for awards, a different constitutional basis for the award-making powers, as well as an ongoing emphasis upon rationalising/simplifying both individual awards and the overall framework of existing award coverage.*
- *A different process for making agreements, with different procedures, different standards to be satisfied in terms of moving from award to agreement coverage, which will see a break in the nexus that has existed up until now between awards and agreements through the operation of the 'no disadvantage' test.*
- *Changes to the framework of unfair dismissal regulation with employees in many businesses now to be precluded from accessing that jurisdiction.*
- *Driving the development of a national workplace relations framework across this country, in particular, to simplify the complicated framework of national and state-based regulation that now exists, particularly in states other than Victoria.*

While it is apparent that there is a general agreement about the significance of what is now being proposed, it is less likely that broad agreement can be reached at this time about the need for these changes.

So why does VECCI, as a peak body representing employers, support ongoing change and reform in the context of our workplace relations framework? The imperative for change in this country needs to be seen in the context of changes occurring in the global economy and the impact and the potential impact that these trends are having on Australia. For example, one need only look at the loss of Australian jobs in the manufacturing industry, as a result of moves to off shore locations, to understand the impact of this global competition. In our view, the pressure of global competition poses a far greater threat to employees than any new workplace relations legislation. It poses real threats to jobs and to the standards of living that we have come to value and expect in this country.

In response, we need to look at a whole range of areas in order to address these challenges – better infrastructure, enhanced export capacity, a better-skilled workforce, better Commonwealth–state relations, tax changes among others – as well as changes to our workplace relations framework, to explore how we can do things differently and more effectively.

Specifically, in focusing on workplace reforms we believe that there are a number of actions which can and should be initiated. First, it does make sense to move to initiate the development of a single national workplace relations system – to work around the constitutional limitations that have created a complicated federal system, but also enabled state systems to operate and be sustained at the same time. The recent experience in Victoria has already shown how a single system can be developed and demonstrated the benefits which flow from that streamlined approach.

Second, it does make sense in our view to continue to develop a framework that allows working conditions, working arrangements and work relationships to be developed and agreed upon, based on the needs of individual workplaces and the employers and employees working in those locations. The parties to those relationships should in turn assume a greater responsibility for dealing with and resolving disputes that might subsequently arise in that workplace.

It makes sense therefore for some limitations to be imposed upon the powers exercised by the Australian Industrial Relations Commission, and upon the scope of awards, to enable in turn greater focus upon agreement making and workplace-based outcomes.

There are further areas that warrant attention in this discussion. The practices and behaviour in the building industry in the past, particularly in Victoria, have been identified and highlighted in many forums. Historically, the industrial relations system has not been effective in dealing with those issues.

The ability to take protected or legal industrial action, a relatively recent addition to the framework of regulation, arguably also requires amendment. Many employers believe that those rights have not operated in a balanced way, and that under the current system it has been too easy for unions to be able to put themselves in a position where they can take protected industrial action. Proposals to introduce cooling-off periods, third-party intervention and secret ballots all have the potential to introduce greater balance into the system.

The operation of the unfair dismissal laws has also been another area where business has experienced concern. Many employers and others have long believed that the system has not operated in a balanced way, that it has protected those who are not performing or behaving in an acceptable way. There has also been the perception that the operation of the system has hindered job creation in this country. The proposed changes will assist in addressing those issues.

It also should be mentioned briefly that pattern bargaining approaches are seen as working against the objective of legitimate enterprise-based outcomes. The legislative change will seek to prevent these pattern outcomes being imposed across entire industry sectors.

Finally, it is worth putting the current WorkChoices proposals into some perspective. Here in Victoria we have been something of a melting pot in terms of change to the framework of industrial relations regulation. In the mid-90s, in particular, a previous Victorian government introduced probably the most radical deregulation of an industrial relations system that we have ever seen in this country. It brought to an end the operation of the state-based industrial relations system and the operation of some 230 plus awards that had been created by that system, and had been in operation in some cases for decades.

Certainly, those changes left open avenues to move into the federal system, and many unionised areas of the workforce took that option, but at the same time many Victorian firms and businesses remained within that deregulated framework.

We know from working with and talking to many firms and businesses that were part of that process of change and deregulation that many were able to grow and prosper, to employ and to develop a whole range of more diverse working arrangements. These outcomes were not achieved by using employees as cannon fodder, or by driving employment conditions down to rock bottom levels. Contrary to the logic and rationale that seems to be the basis of many of the arguments being pursued at the moment, the overwhelming majority of employers do not seek to gain an improvement in their business operations only by corresponding loss and detriment being suffered by their employees. Most understand that achievement occurs because of arrangements that provide mutually beneficial outcomes for both the employer and the employees.

Time will tell whether the details of WorkChoices are on the mark in terms of the outcomes that David Gregory predicts will be delivered. In contrast to those opposing the direction the WorkChoices reform is taking, VECCI supports in general terms the continued shift toward a more decentralised system based upon outcomes determined by agreement in an individual workplace reflecting the needs of that particular workplace and its employees.

Discussion questions

1. What implications would the proposed issues described by Mr Gregory have for organisations negotiating new or changed employment arrangements with their staff?
2. What are the implications of these changes for employee representatives (such as trade unions)? What strategies might they employ to maintain their current level of influence in society?
3. What are the implications for individuals and organisations in the change from the AIRC to the Fair Pay Commission?

Is ethics a dirty word?   A manager's challenge

Ethics. According to recent Australian research, this word is enough to send a chill down the spine of Australia's top companies. The research, conducted by the Australian Council of Superannuation Investors (ACSI), found that while ethics are firmly on the agenda of top Australian companies, in practice these companies are putting their investors' interest above all other concerns. These other concerns, which include community, environmental and consumer interests, have been crossed off the priority list in boardroom discussions.

This response is disappointing given the number of Australian businesses recently caught in ethical controversies. Issues such as price fixing, boycotts, misuse of market power, exclusive dealing and resale price maintenance have been associated with high-profile Australian companies such as Telstra, Coles Myer, Woolworths, Boral, Visy Industries and Rural Press. In fact, according to ASCI, an overwhelming majority of boards in Australia's top companies are failing to monitor unethical business practices such as price fixing, bid rigging, insider trading, secret commissions and kickbacks.

The report found that 83 per cent[1] of companies had no formal processes controlling bad business practices. Although 52 per cent of companies had codes of conduct, they did not confront responsible marketing and promotion issues and truth in advertising. More than half did not publicly disclose information about protecting consumer privacy, nor did they disclose policies protecting whistleblowers (46 per cent). Product safety training (including the handling of hazardous material) also failed to be mentioned by 46 per cent of companies, perhaps indicating that this wasn't conducted.

The ASCI report comes only one year after international research on ethical countries was conducted. According to this research, performed by Transparency International in 2004, Australia is the eleventh most honest country in the world. The company, who used a variety of methods to rank corruption in countries, rated Finland as the most honest country, with New Zealand in third place, followed by Britain (tenth) and the USA (sixteenth).

Despite these findings, unethical business behaviour does still occur in Australia and overseas. The problem is that it isn't always easy to detect. People tend to behave unethically in business when three factors coincide: opportunity, pressure and rationalisation. A recent American survey revealed that 65 per cent of employees admitted witnessing high levels of unethical behaviour but that 96 per cent refused to report ethical problems because they feared repercussions and ostracising. The solution, according to an American academic, is that companies need to teach people the difference between right and wrong, and help them develop the courage to stand up and challenge unethical behaviour in business.

So, what is the final word on ethics in business? Erik Mather, the Head of BT Governance Advisory Service, said it was in the best interests of company directors to promote ethics. 'Companies that actively promote business ethics and implement systems, codes of conduct, training programs and whistleblower policies are best placed to avoid potential costs and reputation damage caused by poor business ethics', Mr Mathers said.

Let's hope that Australia's top companies start following this advice.

Source: Adapted from Gettler, L. (2005), 'Funds blow whistle on ethics', *The Age*, 25 June, p. B2; Hunter, C. (2004), 'Call to arms on corporate fraud', *The Canberra Times*, 12 August, p. 23; Lampe, A. (2005), 'Boardroom ethics aren't for everyone', *The Sydney Morning Herald*, 22 October, p. 48.

---

[1] This figure refers to companies listed on the S&P/ASX Index.

Summary

The focus of this chapter was on the relationship between ethics, the law and SHRM. These three concepts are bound together in a complex web and must be managed effectively by HR managers, employers, employees and other stakeholders such as trade unions and the government. Ethical dilemmas in the workplace involve discrimination, harassment, fraud, contractual breaches, favouritism and inconsistent policies regarding pay, rewards and discipline and it is the responsibility of all stakeholders to uphold the law and conduct business in an ethical and professional manner. This is often difficult as ethics are instilled in humans at a young age and it can be difficult to change ethical and moral values displayed by adults in workplace settings. Nevertheless, ethics and the law are important for business practice, HRM and for achieving a competitive advantage.

Business ethics refer to the stance and standard of behaviour concerning the morals and ethics that an organisation may adopt and may be examined from three different perspectives. The traditional perspective states that an organisation's primary obligation is to its shareholders. The human resource perspective views people as an organisation's most valuable asset. Finally, the societal perspective states that organisations need to consider societal effects carefully before making decisions.

Despite these different ethical perspectives, ethical issues are the responsibility of all stakeholders. Employers and employees alike need to obtain specific information relating to ethical standards. This may be sourced via codes of conduct, which are company policies outlining company expectations and formal rules surrounding ethics, including legal implications and disciplinary action. Often, codes of conduct are available on a company intranet, which facilitates communication and access to information although it does not ensure that all employees have read and adequately understood the material.

Companies may adopt a variety of ethical decision-making models to assist in the decision regarding an ethical dilemma. The range of models discussed in this chapter varied in content. For example, some focused on moral judgements and behaviour, cognitive processes and the external environmental influence, while others included the effect of moral intensity and organisational factors. Also covered was the perception of locus of control (internal or external), and although no one model was considered 'the best' they all provide guidance on how to make ethical decisions.

Despite the importance of ethical values in the workplace, people differ in their perception and definition of ethical behaviour, which has implications for HRM. There are several reasons why ethical behaviour may differ between people, such as the level of cognitive moral development, ethical climate and national culture. For example, countries such as Mexico and Bangladesh have higher incidence of unethical behaviour than most other countries because such behaviour has become part of the culture. This impacts significantly on the management of employees in international business operations and HR managers need to determine the most suitable method for conducting business. In most cases, a compromise needs to be reached which is mutually beneficial.

So, what is the relationship between ethics and the law? A key role of legal frameworks is to enforce ethical notions through the use of specific 'criteria' audits and penalties for breaches. This is underpinned by the employment relationship, which is the working relationship between employees and employers, and this affects the perceptions of justice and fairness (through employment and psychological contracts) which build or diminish commitment, job involvement, organisational citizenship behaviours and work attitudes.

Although employment law sets the minimum standards and conditions for employment in a given region, it is frequently modified and it is the responsibility of HR managers to stay abreast of these changes and the impact on their organisation. There is a variety of Acts, at state and federal levels, which specifically focus on employment conditions, including the *Industrial Relations Act 1999* (Queensland) and the *Workers' Compensation Act 1987* (New South Wales), to name two. Although the Acts listed in this chapter are not exhaustive, they form the foundation for effective HRM and therefore it is important for HR managers to be aware of them.

Legally, risk management also presents implications for HRM. Each organisation needs to consider the types of risks that the company may encounter such as knowledge management risks, insurance risks and strategic management risks. Risk management involves measuring and assessing risk and developing systems to manage the risk successfully and it includes various management techniques such as business diversification, purchasing insurance and maintaining cash reserves and flexibility in the company. As a guide for HR managers, the process of risk management involves six phases: assess current and future business opportunities; identify current and future resources; identify internal effects and influences; identify external effects and influences; document processes and track progress; and continual evaluation. In case that risk does occur, companies can seek resolution through conciliation and arbitration although it is the responsibility of the risk manager to ensure that all company risks are minimised or avoided.

Another important aspect for HRM regarding the law is industrial relations. This refers to the formal relations between management, employees, unions and the government through work rules and agreements. Traditionally, industrial relations in Australia have been fostered by a strong trade union presence and the expectation of conflict between employers and employees (aligning with the hard view of HRM). However, a shift in relations and employment relationships has resulted in a 'new' view of industrial relations which is congruent with the soft view of HRM and illustrates mutually beneficial outcomes with minimal involvement from third parties, such as the AIRC.

In alignment with legislation, safety in the workplace should be a priority for all stakeholders. Occupational health and safety (OHS) refers to the health, safety and welfare of employees in the workplace and companies should focus on preventing workplace injuries from occurring (rather than curing them). In addition to the physical liability they present, accidents in the workplace can also impact on employee morale and employer finances. The cost of workplace injuries to the employer includes: replacing injured employees, impact on colleagues, quality of product/service, relationships with stakeholders, job satisfaction, turnover and organisational outcomes. Some of the current issues in OHS include visual impairment, repetitive strain injury (RSI), back injuries, mobile phones, environmental hazards, stress, job burnout and bullying. It is the core responsibility of the OHS officer to check and inspect the workplace routinely to ensure that it is safe, and to report dangerous or suspicious activities. They also need to be aware of workplace safety laws to ensure that they are acting in accordance with them for the benefit of the entire organisation.

Managing the employment relationship is important for the development of healthy organisations. When employers and employees share common goals the employment relationship is described as unitarist HRM. In contrast, when goals misalign and conflict is inherent and expected between parties, the employment contract is described as pluralist. At this stage, it may be necessary for HR managers to control the social behaviour of employees through increased communication and social norms that foster a healthy and mutually beneficial working relationship.

One way for managers to increase communication and fairness is through negotiation. This refers to the process of resolving disputes or conflicts between two or more parties and, although the aim is to reach a compromise, negotiation often involves questioning and explanation and is therefore often considered a stressful and contentious process. As a decision-making process, negotiation involves six steps, from the conceptualisation of the conflict to the formal documentation of the process and outcomes for legal purposes and obligations. However, not all negotiations have favourable outcomes for all parties and it is imperative that the concept of organisational justice is considered in the process as it is closely linked with individual reactions, such as resistance to change, which can foster negativity between employers and employees and create further complications for HRM, such as reduced job security, morale and productivity and increased turnover and resentment.

Key terms

arbitration	internal locus of control	occupational health and
Australian Industrial Relations	job burnout	safety
Commission	job satisfaction	organisational justice
bullying	legal obligation	pluralist HRM
business ethics	level of cognitive moral	positive ethical climate
code of conduct	development	risk management
conciliation	locus of control	societal perspective
employment relationship	mental models	stress
external locus of control	negative ethical climate	traditional perspective
human resource perspective	negotiation	unitarist HRM
industrial relations		workplace injury

Review questions

6.1 What are the three ethical perspectives discussed in this chapter? Which perspective do you think managers should adopt and why? Use Asia–Pacific workplace examples to support your answer.

6.2 What impact does national culture have on the ethical stance that people may adopt? What other factors influence unethical behaviour? How might the ethical behaviour of Australians differ from that of Mexicans?

6.3 How can HR managers adopt a holistic approach to industrial relations? List some important elements that employers and employees need to consider in the industrial relations process.

6.4 Occupational health and safety is an important issue for all workplaces, and both employers and employees need to take responsibility for OHS in their organisation. Devise a list of possible OHS issues in each of the following workplaces: (a) a laboratory, (b) a building site, (c) a hospital and (d) your classroom.

6.5 Recall an ethical dilemma that you have recently experienced (either first or second hand). Using Kohlberg's six stages of moral cognitive development, which stage did your response to the dilemma represent? Compare this to another ethical dilemma you experienced. Explain any differences in stage developments, taking into consideration the severity of the issue, consequences to yourself and others and your level of involvement.

Exercises

6.1 Conduct a class debate using the following topic: 'Trade unions in contemporary organisations are obsolete'.

6.2 Visit the website for Australia's workplace relations system (www.workchoices.gov.au). How does the new system differ from the old and what are the advantages of the new system? Do employees or employers benefit more from the new system? In your answer, consider the impact this new system will have on white- and blue-collar workforces.

6.3 Organisational justice is an important issue in the acceptance of organisational change efforts. However, justice theories are not the sole concern for profit companies.

Not-for-profit companies also manage justice issues in an international context. Visit the website for Human Rights Watch (http://www.hrw.org) and navigate to the section on Interactional Justice. Click on one of the many issues and relate the content to the principles of organisational justice theory discussed in this chapter.

6.4 In small groups, scan a recent newspaper to locate an article where a conflict or issue was being discussed. Using this article, divide the group into two opposing parties and work through the six steps of the negotiation process to resolve the issue, recording each step as you work through it.

References

Anderson, P. & Pulich, M. (2001), 'Managing workplace stress in a dynamic environment', *The Health Care Manager*, vol. 19, no. 3, pp. 1–10.

Angerer, J. M. (2003), 'Job burnout', *Journal of Employment Counseling*, vol. 40, no. 3, pp. 98–107.

Australian Bureau of Statistics (2001), *'Work-Related Injuries, Australia*, Cat. No. 6324.0, Australian Bureau of Statistics, Canberra.

Bommer, M., Gratto, C., Gravander, J. & Tuttle, M. (1987), 'A behavioural model of ethical and unethical decision making', *Journal of Business Ethics*, vol. 6, pp. 265–80.

Clardy, A. (2004), 'Toward an HRD auditing protocol: Assessing HRD risk management practices', *Human Resource Development Review*, vol. 3, no. 2, pp. 124–50.

Commonwealth of Australia (2005), *WorkChoices Booklet*, The Australian Government, Canberra.

Dubinsky, A. J. & Loken, B. (1989), 'Analyzing ethical decision making in marketing', *Journal of Business Research*, vol. 19, pp. 83–107.

Fujimoto, Y., Härtel, C. E. J. & Panipucci, D. (2005), 'Emotional experience if individualist–collectivist workgroups: Findings from a study of 14 multinationals located in Australia', in *Emotions in Organizational Behavior*, eds C. E. J. Härtel, W. J. Zerbe & N. M. Ashkanasy, Lawrence Erlbaum Associates, Mahwah.

International Confederation of Free Trade Unions (ICFTU) (2004), *Final Resolution – A 21st Century Approach to Occupational Health and Safety for Trade Unions*, 18th World Congress, Miyazaki, 5–10 December, <http://congress.icftu.org/displaydocument.asp?Index=991220328&Language=EN>, accessed 16 November 2005.

Jarret, J. G. (2003), 'Reducing employment practices liability', *Risk Management*, vol. 50, no. 9, pp. 20–3.

Jones, T. M. (1991), 'Ethical decision making by individuals in organizations: An issue-contingent model', *Academy of Management Review*, vol. 16, no. 2, pp. 366–95.

Kohlberg, L. (1984), *The Psychology of Moral Development: The Nature and Validity of Moral Stages*, Harper & Row, San Francisco.

Legge, K. (2005), *Human Resource Management: Rhetorics and Realities*, Palgrave Macmillan, Hampshire.

Maslach, C. (1982), *Burnout. The Cost of Caring*, Prentice Hall, Englewood Cliffs, NJ.

Mastenbroek, W. (2000), 'Organizational behavior as emotion management', in *Emotions in the Workplace: Research, Theory, and Practice*, eds N. M. Ashkanasy, C. E. J. Härtel & W. J. Zerbe, Quorum Books, Westport.

McRae, B. (2005), 'The seven strategies of master negotiators', *Ivey Business Journal Online*, May/June, p. 1.

Olekalns, M. & Smith, P. L. 2005, 'Cognitive representations of negotiation', *Australian Journal of Management*, vol. 30, no. 1, pp. 57–76.

Paterson, J. M., Green, A. & Cary, J. (2002), 'The measurement of organizational justice in organizational change programmes: A reliability, validity and context-sensitivity assessment', *Journal of Occupational and Organizational Psychology*, vol. 73, pp. 393–408.

Rest, J. R. (1986), *Moral Development: Advances in Theory and Research*, Praeger, New York.

Taylor, F. W (1911), *The Principles of Scientific Management*, Harper, New York.

Trevino, L. K. (1986), 'Ethical decision making in organizations: A person–situation interactionist model', *Academy of Management Review*, vol. 11, no. 33, pp. 601–17.

Weber, M. (1904), *Die Protestantische Ethik und der Geist des Kapitalismus*, Archiv fur Sozialwissenschaft und Sozialpolitik, band XX, XXI.

Wiley, C. (2000), 'Ethical standards for human resource management professionals: A comparative analysis of five major codes', *Journal of Business Ethics*, vol. 25, pp. 93–114.

Chapter 7

Strategic human resource management in a global context

INTRODUCTION

There is no denying that the world is operating more and more on a global basis. The merging of national cultures has resulted in overwhelming diversity the world over and people have to adapt to this emerging societal trend. Some countries have managed to deal with this successfully while others have not. For instance, since the terrorist attacks in 2001 against the USA, the vast clash of cultures and mix of religions around the world has sparked much fury and debate. Although the media have preyed on these events for newsworthy coverage, the issue remains unsolved and teeters on the edge of disaster, with the potential to spiral out of control and impact upon hundreds and thousands of people.

Consequently, today's global environment, which includes cross-national environmental issues (including political, cultural, legal and sociopsychological issues), affects both our personal and professional lives, necessitating adaptation to these changing conditions and implementation of systems to manage business adequately on a global, not local, scale. This chapter addresses this strategic and continuous HR issue, examining the SHRM Application Tool from a global perspective. To deal with this unremitting reality, global organisations should aim to apply their human capital to the international market effectively, efficiently and flexibly to gain a sustainable competitive advantage.

The success of strategic international human resource management (SIHRM) is predominantly determined by senior management's strategic international management processes. This chapter examines the global challenges and opportunities of SIHRM and discusses the role of SIHRM in relation to the resource-based view of HRM.

Objectives

The primary objective of this chapter is to highlight issues raised for SHRM when operating in a global context (i.e. SIHRM). In particular, strategic international HRM, which is the management of employees on a global scale, is discussed and examined in detail.

After reading this chapter you should be able to:

- understand what strategic international human resource management (SIHRM) is and identify the three key approaches organisations may adopt when developing their international SHRM strategies and practices;
- identify some factors which will influence the SIHRM approach that an organisation adopts;
- explain the benefits and downfalls of globalisation and its relationship with international business operations;
- understand some challenges to successful implementation of SIHRM strategy and practices;
- discuss how the resource-based view (RBV) of SIHRM creates a sustainable competitive advantage.

Strategic international HRM

strategic international management
Global strategic formulation and global strategic implementation.

strategic international HRM
The management of employees in more than one country.

Globalisation is a reality in today's business environment making it necessary for many organisations to operate globally in order to succeed. For organisations operating in a global context HRM is an issue of considerable importance and can be a critical factor in their success or failure. It is widely believed that SHRM can be used as a means of achieving a sustainable competitive advantage when competing on a global scale. The **strategic international management** (SIM) process refers to global strategic formulation (i.e. global vision, mission and objectives) and global strategic implementation (i.e. global structuring of organisations, job design and training). To cope with the dynamic and volatile global environment, the SIM process includes **strategic international HRM** (SIHRM), which refers to the management of employees in more than one country. It involves performing the responsibilities of domestic SHRM, including recruitment and selection, training and development, performance management and reward management as well as the responsibilities and issues typical of global operations. These may include such things as the expatriation and repatriation processes, language training and translation services, international taxation and host government relations. Additionally, an SIHRM system refers to 'the set of distinct activities, functions, and processes that are directed at attracting, developing, and maintaining MNCs' [Multinational corporations'] human resources' (Taylor, Beechler & Napier, 1996, p. 960). The relationship between SIM and SIHRM effectively interrelates three factors:

- the SIHRM system;
- heterogeneous human capital (i.e. cognitive ability); and
- heterogeneous employee behaviour (i.e. cognitively and affectively driven discretionary behaviour) (see Chapter 2 for a discussion on discretionary behaviour).

The process of developing and implementing SIHRM strategy and practices is more complex than that of developing and implementing SHRM in one country. This is because there are numerous contextual factors that need to be taken into consideration. These contextual factors are often country-specific which makes it difficult to prescribe a strategy and set of practices that can be applied across a range of countries. As it is clear that SHRM has an impact on organisational performance overall, those organisations which are able to identify the best approach to developing SIHRM strategy and practices are likely to be more successful when operating in a global environment that those which are not.

Approaches to SIHRM

The key question HRM practitioners working in a global context need to address is, 'What is the most suitable approach to adopt when devising SIHRM strategies and practices'? The challenge in answering this question is that while an SIHRM approach that is consistent across an organisation will assist in the maintenance of a corporate identity, when operating in a global context the approach used also needs to be effective at a local level (Laurent, 1986).

An organisation may choose to adopt one of three dominant approaches. The first possible approach that an organisation may adopt is a globalised approach whereby the same HR strategy and practices, generally those of the parent organisation, are used in all locations. The second possible approach that an organisation may adopt is a localised approach whereby HR strategy and practices are adapted to the local context. The third possible approach that an organisation may adopt is an adaptation approach whereby either HR strategy or HR practices are adapted to the local context (Lloyd & Härtel, 2004).

When an organisation adopts a **globalised approach to SIHRM** they use the SIHRM strategy and practices of the parent company globally. This approach allows the organisation to maintain a certain level of internal consistency. Further, it also allows for a higher level of resource sharing across the organisation which can decrease overall costs. An example of an organisation that uses a global approach to SIHRM is any international fast-food restaurant, such as McDonald's. This can be seen when you enter any McDonald's store in the world: the stores are designed similarly as is the training of staff. This is a deliberate strategy to ensure familiarity for international customers.

A **localised approach to SIHRM**, on the other hand, is when an organisation adapts its HRM strategy and practices to the local environment. This approach is often used when the home and host countries of an organisation are so different that the parent company SHRM strategy and practices would be ineffective in the host country. It is also often used by organisations who believe they will get the most out of their human capital by having SHRM strategy and practices developed locally. For example, this strategy is likely to be preferred by organisations working in highly regulated industries, such as in the financial sector.

The third key approach which can be adopted by an organisation is an **adaptation approach to SIHRM**. This approach may take one of two forms depending on whether SIHRM adaptation is required at the macro level (strategy)

globalised approach to SIHRM
The use of the parent company's HR strategy and practices globally.

localised approach to SIHRM
The development of HR strategy and practices to suit the local environment.

adaptation approach to SIHRM
The use of either a globalised HR strategy and localised practices or a localised HR strategy and globalised practices.

or the micro level (practices). In the first instance an organisation may adopt a globalised strategy while localising practices. Alternatively, they may localised HR strategy while globalising practices. Organisations will adopt one of these two approaches when, for example, it is necessary for them to implement global uniform resource deployment while at the same time realising the need to have context-sensitive SHRM strategies or practices (Lloyd & Härtel, 2004). This strategy is gaining in popularity as it allows organisations to maintain some consistency across their operations while allowing the subsidiaries to have the level of flexibility required to meet the needs of the markets in which they operate. Examples of organisations which would be likely to employ this type of approach would include organisations in the automobile industry such as Ford or Toyota. While the nature of these organisations is consistent across countries, country-specific factors would require some adaptation.

SELECTING THE RIGHT APPROACH FOR YOUR ORGANISATION

An organisation will need to take a number of factors into account in order to select the right approach to SIHRM. These include both organisational factors such as the organisation's orientation toward staffing practices in its global operations, and country-specific factors such as local laws, regulations and culture.

ORGANISATIONAL ORIENTATION

The type of SIHRM approach an organisation uses in its global operations can be largely influenced by its overall approach toward management and staffing practices. Perlmutter (1969) identified three orientations toward management, ethnocentric, polycentric and geocentric, which multinational corporations (MNCs) may have. A fourth orientation, regiocentric, was conceptualised by Heenan and Perlmutter (1979). While quite some time has passed since these orientations were identified, little seems to have changed in the literature and these four orientations are still recognised as the possible management strategies which an MNC may employ.

ethnocentric management orientation
When employees from company headquarters fill key managerial positions and power and decision making are centralised at the head office.

An **ethnocentric management orientation** is generally the result of a 'home country attitude'. When an organisation uses an ethnocentric approach, power and decision making is centralised at the head office. Key management positions both at home and in overseas subsidiaries are filled by people from organisational headquarters and headquarter standards are applied in the evaluation and control of employees and performance. SIHRM practitioners in these organisations have the responsibility of identifying employees who will be able to perform successfully on expatriate assignments. This is not an easy task, as to be successful expatriates need to possess skills above and beyond those of the general managerial and technical skills of a manager working in their country of origin as they need to build a company culture that reflects that of the parent company (Caligiuri & Stroh, 1995).

polycentric management orientation
When local managers are used to fill key managerial positions.

A **polycentric management orientation** is likely to be used by organisations which are less concerned about maintaining a common corporate culture. To this end, organisational headquarters give more control to subsidiary organisations and subsidiaries are managed by managers from the host country but with guidance from headquarters on the direction that the organisation should be taking. Managers in these organisations are given autonomy in determining the most suitable strategy and practices for the subsidiary. Consequently, the standards for evaluation and control of employees and performance are determined locally.

A **regiocentric management orientation** is similar to a polycentric management orientation. It is likely to be used by organisations which are less concerned about maintaining a common corporate culture and organisational headquarters give more control to their subsidiary organisations. Where these orientations differ is that, as well as being managed by home-country nationals, these organisations may also be managed by third-country nationals. This is because these organisations are divided into regions, for example Asia–Pacific or the Middle East, and managers are selected and developed within the region. When using this management orientation subsidiary managers are given control to determine the most suitable strategy and practices for the subsidiary. It is important, however, that the MNC has highly developed communication and integration systems in order to maintain some level of control (Caligiuri & Stroh, 1995).

The fourth management orientation that an organisation may use which will influence the SIHRM approach the organisation employs is a **geocentric management orientation**. This orientation is generally adopted by MNCs aiming to develop a fully integrated organisation with a worldwide corporate culture. In these organisations managerial positions are filled by the best person for the job regardless of whether they come from the home, host or third-country branch of the organisation. To this end, these organisations have a highly unified corporate culture but this is not necessarily dictated by the home country (Caligiuri & Stroh, 1995). While subsidiaries within this organisation are given discretion to determine the most suitable strategy and practices for them, the unified corporate culture tends to lead to a certain level of integration.

> **regiocentric management orientation**
> When organisations are broken into regions and host-country or third-country nationals are used to fill key managerial positions.

> **geocentric management orientation**
> When the best person for the job, regardless of whether they are a home-country, host-country or third-country national, is used to fill key managerial positions.

NATIONAL CULTURE

National culture is defined as 'the collective programming of the mind that distinguishes the members of one group or category of people from another' (Hofstede, 2001, p. 9). The fact that it has an impact on overall management practices and HRM strategy is undeniable. The values, attitudes and beliefs that people from different cultures have vary. As identified in Chapter 5, there are five key dimensions on which cultures can vary, specifically individualism–collectivism, masculinity–femininity, uncertainty avoidance, power distance and time orientation. These dimensions will affect: (1) the degree to which the parent company is willing and able to adapt its strategy and practices to suit the conditions in the subsidiary country; (2) the degree to which it may be necessary to adapt parent company strategy and practices to suit the conditions in the subsidiary countries; and (3) the degree to which the parent company strategy and practices will be effective in subsidiary countries.

To address the first point, organisations whose headquarters are based in countries which rank highly on the dimension of uncertainty avoidance are less likely to be comfortable adapting organisational strategy and practices to local conditions than organisations whose headquarters are based in countries that rank low on the dimension of uncertainty avoidance. For this reason, they would be more likely to adopt a globalised approach to SIHRM. At a minimum they will want to maintain some degree of control. This is why subsidiaries whose parent company is based in high uncertainty avoidance cultures such as the Japanese-based MNC Toyota have managing directors from the home country in Australia.

To address the second point, the degree to which the culture of the home and host country differs will impact upon the degree to which it may be necessary to adapt SIHRM strategy and practices. Countries such as Australia and New Zealand can be said to have 'similar' cultures. For example, both countries have cultures deemed to be individualistic and masculine and rank relatively low on the power distance and uncertainty avoidance dimensions. Consequently, it could be expected that the SHRM strategy and practices of an Australian MNC operating in New Zealand would require relatively little adaptation to work effectively in New Zealand. In contrast, the culture of a country such as Thailand, which is deemed to be collectivist and ranks highly on the power distance dimension, is very different from the culture of a country such as Australia. For this reason, the effectiveness of the SHRM strategy and practices used by an Australian MNC in Australia may be quite limited when applied in Thailand, and thus they will require considerable adaptation.

The above example indicates that the SHRM strategy and practices used in one location successfully may not have the same impact in another location. Consequently, differences in culture between the home and host country will determine how effective parent company SHRM strategy and practices will be in subsidiary countries. To this end, a great deal of research which has looked at the area of IHRM indicates that HRM practices tend to vary owing to differences in national culture. To put this into a practical perspective we will use the example of reward and recognition schemes. In an individualistic culture, publicly acknowledging and rewarding an employee for their achievements would be a source of pride for the employee and is likely to bring them some satisfaction. In contrast, publicly acknowledging and rewarding an employee for their achievements in a collectivist culture is likely to be a source of embarrassment to the employee. The reason for this is that they view their work as a group effort and put the good of the group above that of an individual within it. Consequently, it is important to take account of differences in national culture when designing and implementing SIHRM strategy and practices.

COUNTRY-SPECIFIC FACTORS

When an organisation is determining the SIHRM approach it will implement, it is necessary for it to take into account a number of factors specific to each country it operates in. These will include such things as the economic system, government mandate, the regulatory/legal environment, political stability, labour groups such as unions, public opinion, employment and industrial relations frameworks, labour market skills and education, language and cultural differences.

These factors will impact on the degree to which IHRM strategy and practices are transferable and acceptable in a global context. For example, while negotiating employment conditions and remuneration packages with union groups may be an effective (and necessary) strategy in a country with high union membership, it is likely to be ineffective in a country with low union membership and representation. Similarly, while the industrial relations framework in one country might allow for individual employees to negotiate their contract, in another country this may not be possible. From another perspective, while providing individual recognition and reward for good work through, for example, employee of the month schemes may be highly valued in one country, differences in cultural values could see it being a potential liability in another, with employees making an effort not to stand out, hence damaging the productivity of the firm.

The role country-specific factors play is a major factor and it can underpin the success or failure of an organisation. For example, an organisation is more likely to adopt a localised approach when required by government laws and regulation, when there is a high degree of dependency on local resources or when they are highly visible (Lloyd & Härtel, 2004; Rosenzweig & Nohria, 1994).

Please read

Caligiuri, P. M. & Stroh, L. K. (1995), 'Multinational corporation management strategies and international human resource practices: Bringing IHRM to the bottom line', *The International Journal of Human Resource Management*, vol. 6, no. 3, pp. 494–507.

Globalisation and international business operations

In order to meet changing demands and expand into the dynamic global business environment, organisations need to globalise their business progressively. This is achieved through a process called **globalisation**, which refers to the removal of geographical borders when conducting business so that cultural and distance barriers become obsolete as national markets fuse into one global market. It is a very important aspect of international management as it allows companies to expand their business from a *local* to a *global* perspective, thus capturing a larger market segment and fostering a competitive advantage.

globalisation
The removal of geographical borders when conducting business so that cultural and distance barriers become obsolete as national markets fuse into one global market.

WHAT IS GLOBALISATION?

Globalisation means different things to different people, depending on their work environment, responsibilities, tasks and field of trade. For example, scientists may view globalisation differently from engineers, accountants and academics. Globalisation is a common term in today's society and, as such, there is little agreement about the definition of *globalisation*, except that it refers to an increase in international business and the flow-on effects of this. Accountants may refer to it in terms of international trade and foreign investment accounts whereas management academics refer to it in terms of disappearing geographical borders and the impact of differing cultures, values and perceptions on the way business is conducted.

In this chapter, we expand on our earlier definition of globalisation (which refers to the removal of geographical borders when conducting business) to assert that 'Globalisation is a process whereby worldwide interconnections in virtually every sphere of activity are growing. Some of these lead to integration/unity worldwide; others do not. . . The result is blurred boundaries within and between organisations, nations, and global interests' (Parker, 2005, p. 5). This definition is particularly poignant in today's sociopolitical climate where the increase of globalisation (especially differing political beliefs) has impacted heavily on sociocultural boundaries, and significant conflicts between cultures are occurring on a worldwide scale. Therefore, in the business sense, it is imperative that HR managers understand and manage the issue of globalisation better. One way to do this is to identify the drivers of globalisation.

There are many reasons why globalisation has gained momentum in recent years and will continue to do so. In fact, according to advocates of the concept, globalisation has now reached the stage where it is unstoppable; the effects of it are cascading into a powerful force that dominates the global business arena. Globalisation creates opportunities for societies that would otherwise be unreachable, thereby creating new business avenues that are attainable on a global scale. In general, there are four drivers of globalisation: *market*, *cost*, *governments* and *competition* (Yip, 1995). The decision for organisations to embrace globalisation will depend on each of these four drivers.

Market drivers for globalisation include examining the global market and consumer needs, wants and expectations. The most important factors to consider within the market perspective are whether there is an international (or global) market for the product and/or service, and whether the product/service is transferable across markets. It is also necessary to consider the influence of the economy and the amount of disposable income people have and are willing to spend. Do they place priority on other products? Will the product or service offend people (such as conflicting religious beliefs)? Careful consideration should be given to cultural, political, technological and socioeconomic transferability of the product and the impact this may have on human resources. For example, will it require expatriation of staff to develop and/or maintain the product and market overseas, with the consequent set-up costs associated with this and the potential impact on the employees' careers and the organisational culture.

Cost drivers for globalisation are particularly important for HR managers to consider. These include determining the cost of producing the product in a different country, and the influence of global environments upon production. More importantly, cost drivers include examining the cost of labour in different locations. For example, unskilled labour in China and Thailand is considered quite cheap, although there are ethical and legal implications of tapping this resource. Also, what about the cost and availability of highly skilled employees in these countries? In contrast, in Germany there is an abundance of highly skilled workers, although the cost of employing them is significant. Other cost considerations include the cost of materials (to develop, transfer and market the product) and whether there is an international market for the product. Therefore, companies need to consider carefully the cost of 'going global' as this plays a substantial role in the success or failure of international business.

Government drivers for globalisation also play a significant role as they present legal and political barriers to globalisation. Companies need to consider the political relations between the home and host countries and the impact these can have on the desire to operate in the host country's market. Taxes, tariffs, quality control and import/export restrictions are also important governmental influences. For example, it may be more beneficial to conduct business with some countries and not others, especially taking into consideration past political events and ethical/legal beliefs for how business is ideally and realistically conducted. For instance, although New Zealand is a relatively small country with a small international market scope, its close proximity to Australia and the free-trade agreement between the two neighbouring countries makes it an obvious and easy choice for international trade. On the other hand, when Australians deal with the Chinese, there is a myriad of complex cultural considerations (as well as regulations and restrictions) which often impede successful business transactions there. For HR managers, the importance of government drivers when determining which factors impact on the business and how they can be managed necessitates the need for skilled and experienced employees to locate information on these before international business strategies are devised.

Competition is the final driver for consideration in the emergence of globalisation. This driver tends to cover two important aspects: competitors' strategies and the volume of imports/exports in the industry. Senior managers, in consultation with the marketing department and possibly an international business consultant, need to examine the marketing strategies employed by competitors and whether they are competing in the same global market. For example, do they also compete in other international markets or remain in local markets, and to what extent will this influence their competitors' success and market share in that market? Second, organisations need to consider how much of their product they can import/export, and whether this is enough to be a significant player in the industry (i.e. is it worthwhile entering and competing). Managers need to consider the loyalty consumers may already have to existing 'local' suppliers and the acceptance of foreign products and companies. In many cases, the product will need to be adapted to suit the new international market, which means adapting it for every different international market it enters. Again, this implies that HR managers need to select and recruit employees to assist, including experts who have specific knowledge and 'know-how' of specific markets which can prove particularly advantageous.

So, now that a definition of globalisation has been discussed and the drivers of globalisation have been identified, how do organisations actually 'go global'?

INTERNATIONAL BUSINESS OPERATIONS

The decision to enter a global market is an important and strategic decision which impacts upon SIM and HRM in a variety of ways. Consequently, it also impacts on the SIHRM of a company as this forms part of the SIM focus. Determining a suitable skill base for employees, identifying cultural, political and legal influences on current and potential employees and analysing international recruitment and selection techniques are some things that HR managers need to do before, during and after an organisation has embraced globalisation.

In order to 'go global', an organisation needs to consider the extent to which they participate in international markets and competition. These levels of participation, which include *domestic*, *international*, *multinational* and *transnational operations*, are useful in understanding the role and need for HRM in the international arena (McWilliams, Van Fleet & Wright, 2001) (see Figure 7.1).

FIGURE | **7.1**
Levels of international business operations

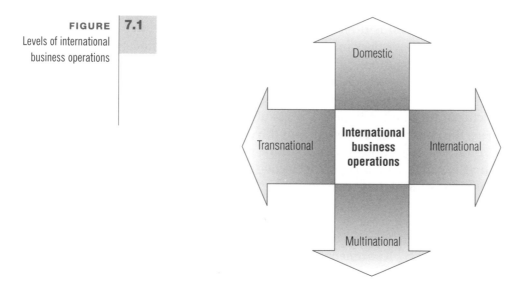

Source: Adapted from McWilliams, Van Fleet & Wright (2001), pp. 2–4.

DOMESTIC OPERATIONS

For most companies, commencing operation in the domestic market is the norm. This is because it is considered easier and safer to begin business in countries and markets with which you are familiar, in terms of national culture, legal, political and economic systems, human resources (and their values, beliefs and expectations) and the sociocultural environment. Although domestic influences may vary in geographical regions, they are generally very similar and offer some familiarity for the company's operations. Therefore, domestic operations are concerned only with HRM in the domestic environment as they have not yet entered the international arena.

INTERNATIONAL OPERATIONS

Once the organisation has saturated the domestic market, it can choose to operate at the international level. To do this companies often build facilities (such as offices or factories) in another country, thereby allowing them to compete in an international market. Despite their international presence, the company's head office still maintains tight control over certain elements, such as marketing and production strategies. Although international operations are regarded as simply an extension of the domestic market (Bartlett & Ghoshal, 1998), there are significant HRM implications involved, for example, the recruitment, training and performance management of foreign staff, and their conflicting or differing work ethics, values and perceptions, such as their perception of the psychological contract. During their expansion into international markets, companies need also to consider the quality and quantity of international staff (which may be estimated through human resource planning) and the impact of cost and government drivers upon international operations and HRM.

MULTINATIONAL OPERATIONS

Multinational operations are very similar to international markets; however, instead of building *one* new facility in an international market, *several* new facilities in *several* international markets (i.e. countries) are built when operating at the multinational level. This level of operation is also commonly referred to as 'global' and the key advantage of this is economies of scale, therefore a low-cost strategy is adopted. This is generally achieved by opting to maintain consistency and standardisation by offering the product in its original form to all locations; to customise would in fact increase costs, negating the style of operation. This also allows the company to transfer production from high-cost to low-cost locations to take advantage of the standardised and transient level of operation. However, although the HRM implications are similar to those experienced in international operations, they are far more varied and complex due to the increased number of countries the firm is operating within. Therefore, the influence of culture, legal, political and economic systems, human capital and the sociocultural environment is quite high because they are so varied and impact significantly on business operations.

TRANSNATIONAL OPERATIONS

Transnational operations are the final level at which organisations can operate globally. At this level, the main focus is on exploiting local markets and maximising the benefits of global learning by using high-tech equipment and producing top-quality products at low costs. Products are mass produced at locations which provide the most efficient and effective operations, allowing congruency to be created from cultural differences and with the overall strategic goals of the company. Although production and research and development tend to be controlled centrally to maximise economies of scale, HRM tends to be decentralised, taking advantage of local cultural aspects and employee management. Unlike international and multinational companies, which view cultural, political and legal differences as possibly having an adverse effect on their global operations, transnational organisations view these as an advantage and actively seek to identify how these can assist the company in developing a unique competitive advantage.

In general, a company can determine if they are operating within the global arena by looking at four characteristics (Parker, 2005):

1. Increased and continuous worldwide connections
2. Rapid, turbulent and discontinuous development
3. A growth in the number and diversity of stakeholders (including employees, customers, suppliers and pressure groups)

4. Increased organisational complexity, such as strengths, weaknesses, opportunities and threats and the implications of each.

Please read
McWilliams, A., Van Fleet, D. D. & Wright, P. M. (2001), 'Strategic management of human resources for global competitive advantage', *Journal of Business Strategies*, vol. 19, no. 1, pp. 1–24.

THE COST OF GLOBALISATION

For many years the strategy for companies seeking to expand their business has been through the process of globalisation. This is due to the unprecedented opportunities globalisation offers a company and the potential growth and profit that are derived from such a venture. Consider the opportunities a developing company has in a localised region such as Auckland. Then imagine expansion into national markets (New Zealand), then into the Asia–Pacific region (such as Australia, Singapore, Malaysia and Papua New Guinea) and then into the international arena (Asia, Africa, Europe, America and Antarctica). The opportunities are endless! However, it is easy to get caught up in the excitement of business expansion without carefully considering the implications of globalisation.

Globalisation is a very strong and powerful force that is sweeping the international business world. According to many, the force is so powerful that it is considered unstoppable (refer to Table 7.1). Although globalisation has been subject to much criticism, it is necessary to determine objectively its benefits and detriments.

The benefits of globalisation are, in essence, increased business opportunities through a wider customer base. This is further achieved through free-trade agreements, integrated global economies, limited barriers and disruptions (for immigration and international transportation), uniform principles and standards for taxation and industry regulation (which promotes streamlined and organised market functioning), competitive leadership strategies and cooperative and

---

TABLE 7.1 **Why globalisation is unstoppable**

- Leaders around the world have concluded that capitalism and open markets are the best means for achieving economic wellbeing
- As global market forces gain momentum, national governments become less significant in international affairs and are, therefore, less likely to interfere with international commerce
- The spread of democracy promotes international harmony because democratic governments don't go to war with each other
- Technology advances – particularly involving media and communications – foster cross-border linkages
- Globalisation serves the purposes of powerful Western political and economic interests, notably those of the United States

Source: Allen & Raynor (2004), p. 17.

peaceful international and intercultural relations (Allen & Raynor, 2004). Companies such as Nokia, Heinz and Coca-Cola have successfully entered and operate within the international market.

Yet globalisation has also been the topic of much debate, with sceptics arguing that this irreversible force gives organisations much more than they bargained for or can adequately handle. The most pressing issue is that although globalisation offers a wider range of consumers, business opportunities and alliances, it also offers intense, international competition. Instead of simply competing within the national arena some organisations struggle to compete with larger, stronger, more powerful and well-equipped companies. Quite often, smaller firms simply cannot compete on this scale because larger companies are more dominant and have a seemingly endless supply of resources to enable them to compete. It is the classic case of the rich getting richer and the poor getting poorer. So, what specific HRM implications and costs of globalisation should a company consider?

There are two major factors that directly impact on the management of human resources. The first is *competition*, as briefly identified earlier. Organisations should conduct an analysis of the industry to determine the likelihood of their success and level of competition. For example, companies should identify barriers to entry, threats of substitutes, supplier power, buyer power and intensity of rivalry (Porter, 1980). One useful tool for identifying areas to address is Porter's five forces model (see Figure 7.2). In using this model, it is necessary to first identify the characteristics of each force (i.e. barriers to entry, threat of substitutes, supplier power, buyer power and degree of rivalry) in the new country. Second, it is necessary to identify the HR implications of each of these forces. Third, strategies must be designed to address any implications identified. It is imperative to acknowledge strategies for managing these before any global strategy can be actioned, otherwise the effort is destined to fail.

HR managers need to consider the level at which international competition is being played and whether the existing human resources will adequately satisfy international assignments. Human resource planning (HRP) is a tool used to forecast organisational HR requirements and, based upon the results, companies may need to begin recruitment and selection prior to globalisation so that they have an adequate number of staff to compete in global markets. This requires determining appropriate training and development for these staff also (i.e. Do they have the skills at the appropriate level?), which impacts on the company's financial resources. Alternatively, if it is projected that fewer employees will be required (due to downfalls in sales or increased competition) then staff cutbacks may be necessary, such as retrenchments and transfers within the company. It is clear, then, that delving into international markets cannot be achieved overnight. It takes plenty of time and planning in order to pave the way for success.

The second major factor affecting HRM in international business operations is *cultural differences*. This includes analysing existing and future markets and identifying any cultural differences in and between these markets. Cultural differences play a significant role in international business and companies need to be aware of and understand the role and impact of culture (such as values, expectations, customs and perceptions), as well as different legal, political and

FIGURE **7.2**
Porter's five forces
and HRM

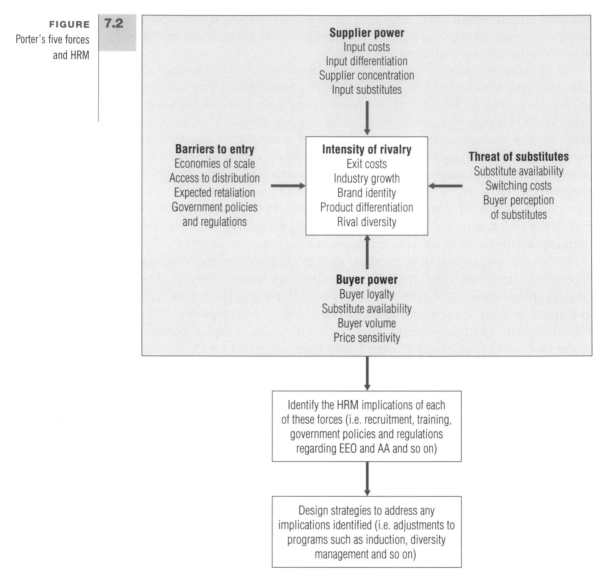

Source: Adapted from Porter (1980).

socioeconomic norms and environments. In Chapter 6, for example, a comparison of the ethical values of Mexicans and Australians was made. The difference in ethical values raised significant and serious issues for management to consider; if Mexicans were employed by an Australian company (or vice versa), they may need to be managed, trained and performance managed differently from Australians. Other cultural differences to consider are religious beliefs, health and hygiene, safety issues, languages and expectations and values about work and how these influence employee behaviour. For example, in some religions, family values and responsibilities have priority over work tasks and flexibility may be required with the working hours and delegated breaks of these employees. It is important to remember that, as HR managers, it is not simply enough to be *aware* of the cultural differences; you must *actively* manage them and learn to compromise as well as to assist employees to work harmoniously with others. After all, employees are an organisation's most valuable resource and they must be looked after if they are to provide a company with a competitive advantage.

It is evident, therefore, that 'going global' has significant business and HRM benefits and downfalls. Critics of globalisation cite the downfalls as labour exploitation, intense and unmanageable competition where larger companies dominate, financial instability, environmental disruption and damage, increased terrorist activity, tainted international relations, disintegration of cultures and Western domination. In fact, some critics go so far as to argue that companies should be implementing strategies to halt globalisation, a concept they refer to as *deglobalisation* (Allen & Raynor, 2004). This implies that companies should scale back their international business before the pitfalls of globalisation become a harsh reality and focus on national relations only. For example, countries are advised to raise trade barriers and regulations to make it more difficult for companies to enter international markets and form strategic alliances with national partners to increase national power and wealth. Therefore, the reality of deglobalisation is that companies would find it increasingly challenging to enter global markets and develop international businesses, including the importing and exporting of goods and services. Firms could benefit from the advantages of deglobalisation and enjoy decreased competition in their country, a far cry from the risk of overseas ventures which may become jeopardised by dynamic international conflicts and a changing business environment. Companies would experience increased security and protection from foreign alliances and possibly develop new commercial interests, with a view to gaining a competitive advantage.

Is globalisation good or bad for society? Castillo Peraza, a Mexican intellectual and politician, provides an insightful answer to this question by distinguishing between the Latin meaning of the words 'globe' and 'world'. The globe he notes refers only to the physical or, in other words, to the actual planet, while the world refers to the human element, in other words, to such things as nations and people (Bharadwaj, 2003). If globalisation is only about the physical, the material, then surely it will lead to harm. But if globalisation is worldisation, then it will think about the effects and wellbeing of all the people in all parts of the globe.

Major challenges to SIHRM

In addition to the issues of increased competition and cultural differences discussed in the previous section, there are two further issues which warrant significant management attention in relation to SIHRM. These are issues of expatriation and repatriation.

The process of SIHRM involves developing and setting up business expansion in the international arena. In order to do this, companies need to allocate human capital to global business ventures. Staff can be recruited from two sources in businesses: the home countries or the host country. However, how do you know when to employ which staff? Are home or host employees better? Which one can provide a company with a competitive advantage? This is an issue which plagues many international ventures and assignments as the choice of location for human capital can significantly impact upon the success or failure of the business. While employing home-country staff is favourable because of their knowledge of the organisation (i.e. its systems, structures, culture, politics and familiarity with other staff), host-country staff often offer more leverage in international operations. This is because they can offer a wide variety of information about operating in the foreign country, with advice and know-how about the specific cultural, political, legal, technical and socioeconomic environments and influences. This is a significant advantage as home-country staff (viewed as outsiders) often find it difficult to get this information because local people will frequently only divulge it to other locals. They don't trust foreigners and hence home-country staff experience significant difficulties when living and working in foreign countries. So, what other difficulties might home-country staff experience, and what are some key factors for successful international assignments?

expatriation
The process of sending a home-country national to a foreign country to work.

Expatriation is the process of sending a home-country national to a foreign country to work. This is often the choice for companies who adopt an ethnocentric approach to cross-cultural management as they view expatriates as a means to maintain control over international operations by head office staff. Currently, almost 80 per cent of mid- to large-sized companies send employees on expatriate assignments (Black & Gregersen, 1999). The most difficult aspect about the expatriate process is international adjustment. Not only do they need to adapt to a new country, but to a new culture as well.

The experience of living in a different culture is often referred to as 'culture shock' and the degree to which this is experienced will depend on how different the culture is from the home country. For example, people moving from Australia to New Zealand experience very little culture shock as the two cultures are relatively similar, as evidenced in the following quote: 'I also found no appreciable difference between the Australian and New Zealand workforces in terms of their workplace culture and demographics. There was literally no culture shock in the Trans Tasman relocation. Moving from Queensland to New Zealand is about the same as moving from Queensland to Victoria. Of course, some things were different, but only to the extent that they are a different shade of grey' (Panipucci et al., 2004, p. 18). However, moving from Singapore to Germany or from Japan to Africa would entail far more culture shock as these cultures differ significantly and therefore this impacts on the expatriate's experience. When dealing with culture shock companies need to consider the effect of the following:

- Language
- Work ethics and priorities
- Social customs and social events
- Transport
- Religious beliefs and expectations (including prayer time and clothing)

- Food differences (including the availability and quality of certain types of food)
- Attitudes toward women and other races and ethnicities.

Another factor when employing expatriates in international operations is how they cope with working in foreign operations. Even though they are working for the same company, and are familiar with organisational policies and systems, they are no longer working with familiar people or in familiar surroundings. Everything and everyone is new to the expatriate, including a new organisational culture. Communication barriers might hinder the expatriate's ability to manage the international operation effectively, and their motivation and morale could decrease because they feel isolated or lonely at work.

A final crucial effect of the expatriate process is the impact it has on expatriates' personal relationships. Depending on the length of assignment, expatriates may choose to take their family or partner with them. In this situation, those accompanying the expatriate need to adapt to new surroundings, including finding a place to live, settling children in school and organising work. Again, it is important to remember that the family or partner will undoubtedly experience some degree of culture shock and this needs to be dealt with appropriately.

Once an expatriate has completed their assignment, their return home is known as **repatriation**. This is where the expatriate undergoes a process of acclimatising to their home country and organisation. Repatriation is an important and sensitive process as employees have to reorientate themselves to the home organisation. The problems associated with repatriation will, in part, depend on the length of time the expatriate has spent abroad. The longer the overseas assignment the more difficult repatriation becomes. Feelings of reversed culture shock may be experienced, as well as emotional responses such as isolation and an inability to fit back in to the home culture. Traditionally, companies have had a tendency to focus more energy on expatriation and have had the perception that repatriation is easy because employees are 'coming back home'. However, this is not the case.

repatriation
The process of acclimatising an expatriate to their home country and organisation.

Repatriates often discover that, while they were away adjusting to a new environment and life abroad, the home organisation and society as a whole have changed. They also notice that they too have changed, and fitting back into their old life is not as easy as they think. They often find themselves lost between two worlds and struggle to gain a sense of identity. They can also experience a disengagement with previous colleagues and social groups, and they need to 'find their grounding' once again, forming new social groups and readjusting to new work tasks. In some cases, a loss of power and status will often result upon the return home, along with a relocated office or shift in organisational structure. The repatriation process, which is perceived as being a relatively easy transition, then becomes daunting and confusing. In fact, 10–25 per cent of expatriates terminate their employment within one year of returning home (Black, 1989 and O'Boyle, 1989, cited in Black, 1992).

KEY FACTORS TO SUCCESSFUL EXPATRIATION AND REPATRIATION

One of the key factors to successful expatriate assignments is the use of in-country adjustment. This is where the expatriate (and their family) receive training prior to departure for the international venture. This training may include language lessons, learning about new cultures and the impact they have on work and personal lives, developing support networks in the host country (such as where to seek housing assistance, enrol in schools and find partner employment) and implementing mechanisms to cope with change (such as counselling).

It is also important for expatriates to learn the signs of culture shock and how this can be managed, for example, how to deal with feelings of frustration, loneliness, role identity and family conflict. This is imperative because most expatriate failures are, in fact, not caused by job-related factors (McEnery & DesHarnais, 1985) but rather personal problems with adjusting to the new environment. A key way to avoid expatriate failure – the expatriate not being able to perform their job effectively and being terminated or recalled back home – is to be aware of the warning signs of culture shock (see Table 7.2) and address them before they spiral out of control.

TABLE 7.2 The warning signs of culture shock

- Feelings of anxiety, confusion, frustration, stress, impatience, anger, disappointment, hopelessness and embarrassment
- Loss of control and a loss of perceived ability to perform the job
- Physiological responses such as restlessness, sleeplessness, headaches, stomach aches and trembling hands
- Feelings of being rejected by members of the new company branch and local community
- Fatigue, tension, hostility, excessive concern about hygiene, an obsession about being cheated, withdrawal into or away from expatriate-associated activities (such as work, family and the expatriate community), unhealthy use of alcohol and/or drugs
- Feelings of loss, loneliness and isolation
- A confused sense of personal and professional roles, values and identity
- Feelings of an inability to cope in the new environment

Source: Adapted from Sappinen (1993), p. 4.

The expatriate also needs to maintain contact with the home branch so that they feel they are still a part of the home organisation. This can be encouraged through technology such as email, the intranet and teleconferencing. Such contact allows the expatriate to 'stay in the loop' with home matters, such as new staff appointments, policy changes and company restructuring, which decreases the likelihood of isolation and feelings of loneliness emerging. It also assists in the repatriation process because the expatriate is already familiar with company developments and changes and doesn't experience intense culture shock upon their return.

Finally, it is important for the expatriate to return home on a regular basis. This is especially a concern if the expatriate has left their family or a partner at home for the duration of their assignment. Regular visits, paid for by the company, allow the expatriate face to face contact with their colleagues, clients and, of course, family and friends. It is evident, therefore, with in-country adjustment training, the cost of relocation and return travel home, expatriation is a costly business and companies need to prepare adequately for such assignments to ensure their success.

In terms of repatriation, companies need to understand expatriate difficulty returning back home, both physically and psychologically. It is important to begin repatriation training before the employee makes the final voyage home, by communicating what their new job will be, where they will be located and their key responsibilities and tasks. This is why it is so important for the expatriate to remain in frequent communication with home organisation colleagues throughout the expatriate process, to minimise the detrimental effects of being abroad and losing contact. It is also advisable for the repatriate to ease into their new work life, for example by working part time initially or having a vacation. After all, they may need to locate housing, schooling and employment for their family. It is also a good idea for the company to arrange social events to reintroduce the expatriate (and their family) to the country and to the organisation. Again, counselling may be required as children and parents alike get used to their old environment and cope with feelings of confusion and disillusion.

Please read

Black, J. S. (1992), 'Coming home: The relationship of expatriate expectations with repatriation adjustment and job performance', *Human Relations*, vol. 45, no. 2, pp. 177–92.

SIHRM: A source of sustainable competitive advantage

A resource-based view of SIHRM expects heterogeneous human resources under SIM to have the highest probability (of all the resources such as financial and technical) of being the source of sustainable competitive advantage. Heterogeneous human capital must be strategically managed by well-trained, experienced and educated culturally diverse senior management. Coupled with the international HRM system, this provides a strong infrastructure that produces human capital which is valuable, rare, inimitable and non-substitutable.

Unlike other departments within an organisation, the HR department is in constant communication with a wide range of diverse employees. Consequently, SIHRM should work in conjunction with other areas of management and adopt change agent and business partner roles to create a strong competitive global culture (Schell & Solomon, 1997).

SIHRM should:

- proactively forecast global HR issues;
- select employees with global values;
- set diversity-open initiatives (revisit Chapter 5);
- offer globally competitive pay, good health benefits and a flexible family-friendly work environment;
- develop and retain the globally best talented employees who support and foster the organisation's strategic goals.

Once the most highly talented global employees are selected and motivated to work for the organisation, their learning capability, flexibility and transferability across a variety of technologies, products and markets provide a sustainable *global* competitive advantage. Based on the theory discussed in this chapter, the SHRM Application Tool addressed in the following section has been modified to include a global dimension.

Contemporary SHRM Application Tool

Imagine that you are an HR manager for a Japanese car company which has attracted international recognition for delivering high-quality cars for the past 10 years. The company has specialised in exports since 1990, expanded its export markets since 1995 and began localising manufacturing plants since 1998. In order to grow international operations further in the face of intensified global competition in the car industry, you are facing the challenge of how to develop further international operations in spite of the increasing complexity of managing different subsidiaries worldwide. The SHRM Application Tool is completed for this scenario in order to demonstrate how you can monitor the environment, verify the HR opportunity, and plan, implement and evaluate the HR implementation for this company (refer to Figure 7.3).

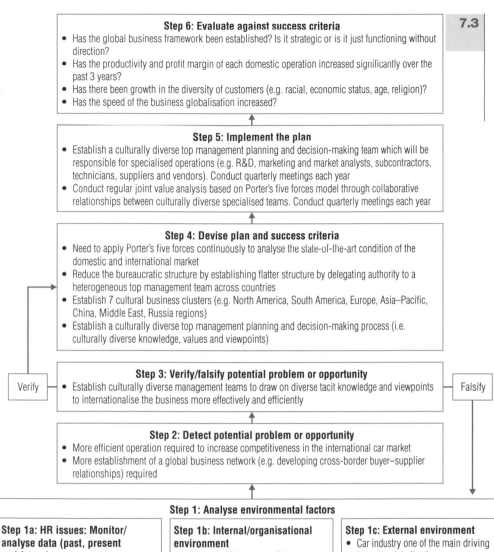

7.3 FIGURE

SHRM Application Tool: opportunity – globalisation

Step 6: Evaluate against success criteria
- Has the global business framework been established? Is it strategic or is it just functioning without direction?
- Has the productivity and profit margin of each domestic operation increased significantly over the past 3 years?
- Has there been growth in the diversity of customers (e.g. racial, economic status, age, religion)?
- Has the speed of the business globalisation increased?

Step 5: Implement the plan
- Establish a culturally diverse top management planning and decision-making team which will be responsible for specialised operations (e.g. R&D, marketing and market analysts, subcontractors, technicians, suppliers and vendors). Conduct quarterly meetings each year
- Conduct regular joint value analysis based on Porter's five forces model through collaborative relationships between culturally diverse specialised teams. Conduct quarterly meetings each year

Step 4: Devise plan and success criteria
- Need to apply Porter's five forces continuously to analyse the state-of-the-art condition of the domestic and international market
- Reduce the bureaucratic structure by establishing flatter structure by delegating authority to a heterogeneous top management team across countries
- Establish 7 cultural business clusters (e.g. North America, South America, Europe, Asia–Pacific, China, Middle East, Russia regions)
- Establish a culturally diverse top management planning and decision-making process (i.e. culturally diverse knowledge, values and viewpoints)

Step 3: Verify/falsify potential problem or opportunity
- Establish culturally diverse management teams to draw on diverse tacit knowledge and viewpoints to internationalise the business more effectively and efficiently

Verify

Falsify

Step 2: Detect potential problem or opportunity
- More efficient operation required to increase competitiveness in the international car market
- More establishment of a global business network (e.g. developing cross-border buyer–supplier relationships) required

Step 1: Analyse environmental factors

Step 1a: HR issues: Monitor/ analyse data (past, present and future)
- Specialised in export since 1992, expanded export (1995–1999), and localising manufacturing plants since 1998. Excellent just-in-time delivery records
- Expanding business into multinational operations through partnership with foreign companies
- Has seen a growth in the number and diversity of stakeholders
- Increasing complexity of managing different subsidiaries worldwide
- Developing a fully integrated worldwide corporate culture to mirror the international customer base
- Challenged to reduce the Japanese cultural characteristic of uncertainty avoidance culture and expand into an international business

Step 1b: Internal/organisational environment
- High collectivist culture (high uncertainty avoidance)
- Bureaucratic structure where major decisions are made in the HQ in Japan
- De-segmented international markets
- Vision is to produce cars that satisfy diverse needs of local customers
- Established modern communication technologies to set up international logistics in 1994

Step 1c: External environment
- Car industry one of the main driving forces in globalisation
- Intense globalisation
- Dynamic changing global environment associated with diverse political, cultural, legal, and socioeconomic national environments
- Saturated status of the domestic car market and tougher trade barriers placed by developed countries
- Diverse pressure groups (e.g. different industrial relations frameworks)
- Exposure to intense international competition

A view from the field

International business operations at Bosch

Strategic human resource management in a global context is complex and multifaceted, and this impacts on a range of HRM functions. For example, laws regarding taxation and employment conditions vary widely, making the application of consistent remuneration and benefits practices a real challenge. Cultural specifics of each host country also require consideration when developing and operationalising HRM policies and systems to support global strategic direction.

Robert Bosch (Australia) P/L (RBAU) is a regional subsidiary of the global Bosch Group, one of the world's largest private industrial corporations, with 242 000 employees in 260 production locations and a sales revenue of €40 billion (AUD$66 billion dollars) in 2004.

Headquartered in Clayton, Victoria, and employing some 1600 people representing over 60 nationalities, RBAU manufactures automotive products and supplies and distributes power tools, gas hot water systems and Blaupunkt car audio and navigation equipment. In 2004, RBAU's Australian annual sales revenue was nearly AUD$1 billion.

RBAU has a 50 year history of engineering and manufacturing know-how in Australia. It has high levels of domestic market share and a high dollar content represented in Australian-produced cars. The Australian arm of RBAU has a well-qualified and flexible workforce which includes 280 engineers (178 of which are employed in the research and development field).

The HR function at RBAU operates holistically as part of a very large organisation in a fiercely competitive sector driven by cost imperatives and fast-moving technology developments. Pat Tucker joined RBAU after a diverse HRM career with large, multifunctional organisations including the University of Melbourne and the Victorian state government's Ministry of Education. As the General Manager of Human Resources and a member of the Board of Management of RBAU, Mr Tucker has a great opportunity to influence the broader business agenda. In his 10 years with the organisation he has experienced increased pressure on costs and an increased emphasis on technology and its application to operations. International competition and the significant changes to the automotive industry in Australia have driven a major restructure of nearly all its operations to ensure long-term viability.

Mr Tucker explained that Bosch's worldwide human resource systems (known as BHS) are modelled on lean manufacturing principles. HR practices match business requirements through six key principles considered valid across the global organisation. Each part of the company must apply these principles within the host-country-specific legislative frameworks, allowing for some modification to suit local culture.

The six key principles are:

- International executive development
- Leadership development with a local focus
- Competitive organisation and cost structures
- Competence development
- Motivation focus
- Process focus

These principles are supported by standardised systems, terminology and databases which allow for transfer of knowledge and best practice around the global operation. Mr Tucker's responsibility in the Australian operation is to communicate and operationalise the six BHS principles and to respond to specific local issues. He says 'the key is to value-add to the core business and as a consequence earn the right to partner with the business'. Over the past five years, the RBAU HR budget (staff and projects) has reduced by 20 per cent. The reduction has coincided with increased demand from the business for HR services and specific projects.

The RBAU HR team delivering services is well qualified, focused on understanding the business and contributing to its success. Mr Tucker says, 'There are no bells and whistles; our aim is to mirror the lean profile of support services across the automotive industry world wide. Clearly as a cost to business operations, we are subject to close scrutiny and are required to demonstrate return on investment'.

Speed of innovation, testing and trialling new ideas and the ability to replicate these across the global operation rapidly are critical to competitive advantage in manufacturing. Bosch looks to apply this discipline and rigour to all areas of its operations. The Bosch Group HR structure and a peak HR Council support this intention.

The peak HR Council, made up of representatives of Bosch regions, oversees the Bosch Group Worldwide BHS, designed to match business requirements and to be valid worldwide. Mr Tucker commented, 'What we do here in Australia is similar to Bosch operations in China, Turkey or the USA, although obviously we optimise the principles to suit local requirements'. The council is the global link that converts business strategies in HR actions and provides general orientation for the function. Any initiatives rolled out from the council or the central HR department are fully endorsed by the Bosch Board of Management, ensuring that HR matters are taken seriously and professionally by the organisation.

In 2006, the HR Council is proposing to introduce a standard worldwide measurement and application of processes. This will involve the use of a balanced scorecard and maturity model evaluations which will be applied to HR functions and broader business activities in each country in the Bosch Group.

Mr Tucker points to the implementation of the BHS principles, specifically number six, *process focus*, which requires a focus on lean services geared to what the company needs rather than just the latest HR fad, as a key driver for the HR function at RBAU. The application of technology to paper-based activities has greatly improved efficiency and allowed resources to be reallocated to strategic and project-based work. Pat runs what he refers to as the 'Resources Ledger' which allows him to monitor the activities of his HR team. He aims for optimum applications of 25 per cent to transactional activity and 75 per cent to value-add efforts, either operationalising the BHS principles or responding to business-specific requests. This split has allowed Mr Tucker and his team to demonstrate better a very close connection between HR activity and the business priorities.

The inclusion of the General HR Manager as a member of the Board of Management of RBAU is significant for the profile of the function. This inclusion acknowledges the role of HRM as integral to the successful Australian operation. A seat at the board table allows the HR function to contribute expertise to key business decisions and engage the senior leadership team as partners and sponsors of HR activity. For instance, the recently implemented leadership development program, *LeaD*, has a different board member sponsoring each of the six modules, thereby creating high-level links to HR activities and communicating a clear message about the importance of this development activity.

Success on a number of fronts has contributed to the high profile of the RBAU HR function. In October 2004, RBAU won the right to become a self-insurer in workers' compensation in Victoria. This initiative has already resulted in significant savings against annual premiums and assisted with improved management of people issues associated with claims. The new approach contrasts sharply with the rather more arm's length model of paying premiums to a insurance company annually, which RBAU had grown accustomed to. 'We now manage the risk, pay the costs of injury and the absolute responsibility for rehabilitation and return to work of injured employees'. This is a very tangible example of HR's ability to support the business in its drive to reduce costs and continue to be a viable player in a very competitive marketplace.

The *LeaD* program, an experiential modular development program designed for first-time leaders, has also been very well received. It supports BHS principle number two, *leadership development*, with a local focus and is based on competencies and requirements defined by the HR Council. RBAU is seeing significant behavioural changes in participants as they deal with their leadership and management responsibilities in a refreshingly positive way. The success of this program has generated interest in, and requests for, leadership programs from other levels within RBAU. The HR team is currently developing programs for senior managers and team leaders in response to this demand.

The size and scale of the Robert Bosch Group Worldwide is such that it would be no surprise to see terms dictated to the relatively small Australian operation. Pat agrees that 'some could see the Group-wide BHS principles as constraints; quite to the contrary they offer enormous challenge and opportunities to leverage frameworks and get on with supporting the Australian business'. He concludes, 'Like most other companies in the automotive components business in Australia, RBAU is facing some tough challenges but I am very confident that the HR function is making a significant contribution to enable RBAU to achieve its goals and objectives by providing world class HR people management strategies and services'.

Discussion questions

1. Review the experience of RBAU in operating within the Robert Bosch Group HR agenda. What are the features and clues to the success of Pat Tucker and his team?

2. Examine the RBAU case and consider ways in which a country's HR group could influence the broader SHRM agenda of its global parent.

3. What are some of the potential issues associated with a SHRM agenda developed without reference to the local issues you face in your country of operation?

Western MNCs in Asia A manager's challenge

With the increasing expansion of companies into international markets, the management of new-age organisations should transcend geographical as well as cultural barriers. In instances where parent- and host-country cultures are particularly incompatible, decisions regarding human resource policies and corporate culture become crucial aspects of management. Recently, two Australian construction companies operating in Malaysia have addressed these issues from contrasting perspectives of operation.

Unlike multinational manufacturing firms that are operating in many of the developing countries to gain cost advantages in their supply chain, foreign construction companies seek to cater more to a domestic market. As the industry's core product is inherent to a particular demographic area and therefore non-transferable, construction companies require a local presence and acceptance more than their counterparts in the manufacturing sector. Attesting to this, 86 per cent of construction companies (in contrast to just 46 per cent of manufacturing firms) identify their work as 'domestic only'. Further, the industry is characterised by subcontracting and networking with a multitude of domestic producers. Hence, it can be a challenging task for foreign construction companies to maintain corporate culture and policies imposed by headquarters amid the pressure of local environmental factors. In such circumstances, the two Australian construction firms operating in Malaysia, Concrete Construction Group (CCG) and Leighton Asia, have taken differing management stances on the same issue of internationalisation of their strategic human resource functions, policies and practices.

Managers of CCG act from the stance that the company represents Western know-how, technology and skill and therefore they strive to maintain its image as a Western company that caters to a niche market. The CEO of CCG argued his point in relation to vital HR decisions: 'Concrete will never have a local CEO. It has to do with the philosophy of leadership. The people [in Malaysia] don't have the skills overall. It was the plan to provide Australian expertise – this negates the possibility of local leadership. Expats are good for putting forward the values of the company internationally.' CCG's corporate culture is based on Western best practices (and is its point of differentiation) and therefore this gives it a competitive edge over its rivals. Congruent with this viewpoint, the company's human resource values are based on Western cultural attributes such as employee empowerment, leadership and innovation.

Similarly, Leighton Asia emphasises the innovation, quality, cost and safety of its operations; however, in stark contrast to CCG, Leighton Asia has embraced the Asian aspects of business. Its Asian-based parent company stresses its commitment to the region and maintains its local presence as a main differentiating factor of the company. Leighton Asia believes local leadership enhances the local acceptance of the company, hence Leighton Asia's operations in Hong Kong are managed by the Chinese. As the company's local presence is higher than its rivals, the need to market its international image or Western corporate values is not considered a vital ingredient to its success.

When comparing the two companies, CCG's resistance to the 'Asianisation' of corporate values has kept the company under the strict control of its head office, whereas Leighton's maturity in the Asian region has encouraged its senior managers to accommodate Asian business practices. The difference is further highlighted in the perceptions the two companies hold regarding the ideal length of stay for its expatriates. CCG claims that beyond three years expatriates tend to be acculturated into local ways of practice and lose their competitive edge of 'thinking outside the box'. Conversely, Leighton's General Manager in Malaysia argues that three years is a minimum requirement to have a sound understanding of the Asian way of doing business. Why are both companies currently thriving in Asia despite their vastly different SIHRM approaches? What conditions would change the success of their strategies?

Source: Adapted from McGrath-Champ, S. & Carter, S. (2001), 'The art of selling corporate culture: Management and human resources in Australian construction companies operating in Malaysia', International Journal of Manpower, vol. 22, no. 4, pp. 349–67.

Summary

The global environment is an important aspect for all organisations to incorporate into their strategic HRM. This chapter explored the SHRM Application Tool from a global perspective, beginning with a discussion on strategic international management (SIM) and strategic international HRM (SIHRM), the latter of which refers to the management of employees in more than one country. There are three approaches to SIHRM and organisations need to consider which one is most appropriate and suitable for them. The approaches include a globalised approach, a localised approach and an adaptation approach.

Selecting the right approach for a company is crucial to the success of the firm. The first factor which may impact upon this is the organisational orientation. There are four management orientations: ethnocentric, polycentric, geocentric and regiocentric. These can all influence the management approach and staffing practices. The second factor is the national culture, which affects the overall management practices and HRM strategy. Here, a company needs to consider the influence of home and host country and cultural practices which impact on the success or failure of SIHRM. The third factor is country-specific factors such as the economic system, government mandates, the regulatory/legal environment, political stability, labour groups, public opinion, employment and industrial relations frameworks, labour market skills and education, language and cultural differences and the like. These factors will impact on the degree to which HRM strategy and practices are transferable and acceptable in a global context.

A key word which sparks many debates in international business is globalisation. This refers to the removal of geographical borders when conducting business so that cultural and distance barriers become obsolete as national markets fuse into one global market. Most companies shift from a local to a global context to take advantage of increased opportunities and economies of scale; however, there are some downsides to globalisation. These include the difficulty of managing across borders and the rapid transformation of today's global economy. In essence, there are four drivers of globalisation: market, cost, governments and competition. Managers need to consider these drivers when they are operating in international markets. The level of operation can either be domestic, international, multinational or transnational and every company needs to operate at the level most suitable for it.

The chapter also discussed the challenges of SIHRM. Specifically, the challenges identified were expatriation and repatriation. Expatriation refers to the process of sending a home-country national to a foreign country to work, whereas repatriation refers to the acclimatisation of an expatriate to their home country. The most difficult aspect about both processes is international and national adjustment, which affects not only the expatriate but also their families and work colleagues.

The chapter concluded with a discussion on how a global workforce can provide a sustainable competitive advantage. This is achieved through the effective management of human capital through international HRM which provides a strong infrastructure that produces human capital which is valuable, rare, inimitable and non-substitutable. If human resources are effectively managed a company can develop a competitive advantage not only in the national arena but also in the global business environment.

Key terms

adaptation approach to SIHRM

ethnocentric management orientation

expatriation

geocentric management orientation

globalisation

globalised approach to SIHRM

localised approach to SIHRM

polycentric management orientation

regiocentric management orientation

repatriation

strategic international HRM

strategic international management

Review questions

7.1 What is meant by the term 'strategic international HRM'? Describe the key factors that will influence an organisation in selecting the right approach to SIHRM for it.

7.2 There are three approaches to SIHRM. Identify and describe each of these approaches, drawing on international examples. Which approach do you believe is the most effective for international business?

7.3 How does an ethnocentric orientation differ from a regiocentric orientation? Do you think transnational operations might adopt either orientation?

7.4 The world is clearly becoming globalised. What are some potential issues of globalisation and how can they be managed?

7.5 What are the major challenges associated with expatriation and repatriation? In your answer, draw up a table listing the problems associated with each. Are they similar? What are some key initiatives an HR manager can take to resolve these problems?

Exercises

7.1 Conduct a search in your local newspaper for issues related to globalisation. Briefly summarise these issues and the intensity of them. Now conduct a separate search in a state or nationwide newspaper. How do these issues compare to the ones located in the local newspaper? Provide an explanation for the difference in issues and intensity.

7.2 Imagine you are the HR manager of a small company based in Malaysia. The CEO has recently announced that a new branch office will be developed in France. How will you choose an expatriate for this assignment? Devise a list showing the possible training you can give them before and after their international venture.

7.3 Search the Internet for companies that began operations in one country and track their expansion into international markets. Which level of international operation did they adopt (i.e. domestic, international, multinational and transnational) and after how many years of operation did they expand? What impact do you think this would have had on their human capital and how it was managed? In your research, determine whether their international venture was successful and the influence it had on their overall strategic HRM.

References

Allen, D. & Raynor, M. E. (2004), Preparing for a new global business environment: Divided and disorderly or integrated and harmonious?, *The Journal of Business Strategy*, vol. 25, no. 5, pp. 16–25.

Bartlett, C. A. & Ghoshal, S. (1998), *Managing Across Borders*, Harvard Business School Press, Boston.

Bharadwaj, P. N. (2003), 'Making globalization globally advantageous', *Advances in Competitive Research*, vol. 11, no. 1, pp. i–v.

Black, J. S. (1992), 'Coming home: The relationship of expatriate expectations with repatriation adjustment and job performance', *Human Relations*, vol. 45, no. 2, pp. 177–92.

Black, J. S. & Gregersen, H. B. (1999), 'The right way to manage expats', *Harvard Business Review*, March–April, pp. 52–61.

Caligiuri, P. M. & Stroh, L. K. (1995), 'Multinational corporation management strategies and international human resource practices: Bringing IHRM to the bottom line', *The International Journal of Human Resource Management*, vol. 6, no. 3, pp. 494–507.

Heenan, D. A. & Perlmutter, H. (1979), *Multinational Organizational Development: A Social Architectural Approach*, Addison-Wesley, Reading.

Hofstede, G. (2001), *Cultures Consequences*, 2nd edn, Sage, Beverly Hills.

Laurent, A. (1986), 'The cross-cultural puzzle of international human resource management', *Human Resource Management*, vol. 25, pp. 91–102.

McEnery, J. & DesHarnais, G. (1985), 'Culture shock', *Training and Development Journal*, April, pp. 43–7.

Lloyd, S. L. & Härtel, C. E. J. (2004), 'Predicting IHRM strategy and practice decisions: Development of the IHRM orientation typology', *Cross Cultural Management: An International Journal*, vol. 11, no. 4, pp. 60–76.

McWilliams, A., Van Fleet, D. D. & Wright, P. M. (2001), 'Strategic management of human resources for global competitive advantage', *Journal of Business Strategies*, vol. 19, no. 1, pp. 1–24.

Panipucci, D., Habib, M., Strybosch, V. E. & Appo, D. (2004), 'From Australia to New Zealand: A trans Tasman experience', *Doing Business Across Borders*, vol. 3, no. 1, pp. 17–23.

Parker, B. (2005), *Introduction to Globalization and Business: Relationships and Responsibilities*, Sage, Thousand Oaks.

Perlmutter, H. (1969), 'The tortuous evolution of the multinational corporation', *Columbia Journal of World Business*, vol. 4, no. 1, pp. 9–18.

Porter, M. E. (1980), *Competitive Strategy: Techniques for Analyzing Industries and Competitors*, Free Press, New York.

Rosenzweig, P. & Nohria, N. (1994), 'Influences of human resource management practices in multinational corporations', *Journal of International Business Studies*, vol. 25, no. 2, pp. 229–51.

Rowden, R. W. (2002), 'The strategic role of human resource management in developing a global corporate culture', *International Journal of Management*, vol. 19, no. 2, pp. 155–60.

Sappinen, J. (1993), 'Expatriate adjustment on foreign assignment', *European Business Review*, vol. 93, no. 5, pp. 3–11.

Schell, M. S. & Solomon, C. M. (1997), 'Global culture: Who's the gatekeeper?', *Workforce*, vol. 76, no. 11, pp. 35–8.

Taylor, S., Beechler, S. & Napier, N. (1996), 'Toward an integrative model of strategic international human resource management', *Academy of Management Review*, vol. 21, no. 4, pp. 959–85.

Yip, G. S. (1995), *Total Global Strategy*, Prentice Hall, Englewood Cliffs.

PART 3

Implementation of strategic human resource management

Chapter 8

Staffing models, recruitment and selection

INTRODUCTION

Recruitment and selection are crucial functions of SHRM because they provide the foundation for a competitive advantage through effective and efficient human resources. Because they are two of the first activities in the HRM process, it is imperative that they are performed with a strategic view and in alignment with other HRM functions and organisational goals. Congruent with the resource-based view (RBV) of HRM, companies can develop and maintain a competitive position in national and international markets if they focus their strength on appropriate recruitment and selection techniques. Although there is a variety of techniques for the recruitment and selection of employees, in reality HR practitioners are often overwhelmed by the literature and research on these topics, and they fail to adopt the most appropriate methods. This chapter aims to simplify these techniques and discuss some implications of recruitment and selection, in conjunction with some solutions to guide HR managers to develop a competitive advantage through their human resources.

One of the biggest challenges facing organisations today is the ability to obtain and retain the 'best' human resources. Companies are continually realising that financial and technical resources, while valuable to the firm, are no longer the determinants of a competitive advantage. Instead, time and money must be spent on attracting and retaining human resources which will add value to the company. However, although many may perceive recruitment and selection to be a straightforward process, it can be quite complex and demanding. Pressures to attract the best staff, 'weed out' unsuitable or problem candidates and meet stringent time and budget constraints can make this process a very perplexing task for HR managers. Therefore, consideration should be given to ensure that the available information is valuable, rather than a hindrance, for managers to work with.

This chapter begins with an introduction of human resource planning and job analysis, which are the foundation of recruitment and selection. These are important because they assist an HR manager in determining current and future HR needs, which assists with meeting strategic organisational goals. Next, the contemporary staff model is discussed, followed by detailed discussions on strategic recruitment and selection and the implications of each. The chapter concludes with an example of the SHRM Application Tool.

Objectives

The primary objective of this chapter is to discuss the fundamental staffing issues involved in implementing strategic human resource management (SHRM).

After reading this chapter you should be able to:

- define human resource planning and its practical application in contemporary contexts;
- define and describe job analysis and job design;
- explain the key features of strategic recruitment and their advantages and disadvantages;
- explain strategic selection and its methodologies in the light of validity, reliability and legality issues.

Human resource planning

In today's dynamic environment, organisations constantly struggle to survive by employing adaptable processes and strategies, especially when dealing with human resources. Not only is it imperative that companies develop these processes and strategies to compete aggressively, but the attainment of human resources is quickly becoming a vital ingredient in strategic organisational success. Therefore, there needs to be a clear link between organisational strategies and resources. One way that this may be achieved is through **human resource planning** (HRP).

human resource planning
A dynamic planning process which involves ongoing environmental scanning and an analysis of organisational objectives, strategies and policies in order to ascertain the right quantity and quality of employees when and where necessary.

HRP assists managers in determining how the organisation should move from its current staffing position to its desired staffing position, both in the long and short term. As such, HRP is a dynamic planning process, which involves ongoing environmental scanning and an analysis of organisational objectives, strategies and policies in order to ascertain the right quantity and quality of employees when and where necessary. An easy way to conceptualise HRP is to think of it as forecasting human resources; that is, identifying how many employees an organisation currently has and how many it will need in the future. Although forecasting usually results in a growth in human resources, it may also require a culling of them. This is especially the case in today's business environment where mergers, acquisitions and bankruptcies are becoming common occurrences due to intense competition, making it even more important for HR managers to strive to obtain the best employees. Further, skill shortages around the globe (and especially in Australia) are crippling the effects of effective HRM (refer to Chapter 9 for a discussion of skill shortages).

As indicated in Figure 8.1, human resource planning should activate organisational objectives by closing the gap between the present staffing position

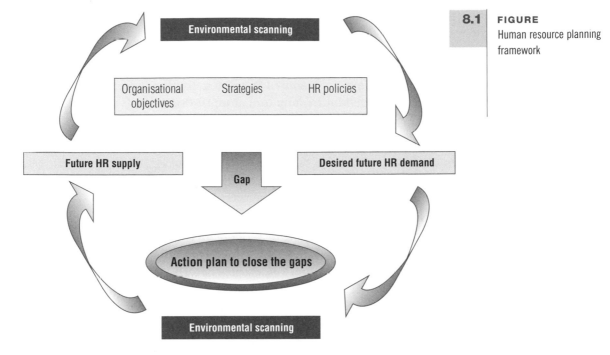

FIGURE
Human resource planning
framework

Source: Adapted from Thomason (1988).

and the future HR supply and demand (Thomason, 1988). However, HRP is not purely concerned with the *number* of human resources required, it also involves planning and developing programs to ensure that companies have the right mix of employees who are equipped with the right skills to achieve organisational goals. As such, HRP should be closely aligned with SHRM to ensure that the objectives of both are congruent and that they are working towards the same goals.

THE EVOLUTION OF HRP

To date, HRP has evolved through three distinctive phases (Ulrich, 1987). First, it was a regulatory mechanism. Traditionally, the role of HRP was to ensure legal compliance with laws relating to industrial relations, minimum wages and salaries and employment conditions. In addition, HRP was viewed as a means to control individual and organisational behaviour and, consequently, focused on operation rather than strategic practices. This regulatory phase of HRP dominated much of the 1960s, 1970s and 1980s.

Second, HRP was a control mechanism to align individuals' behaviours with organisational strategies. As recognition and popularity for SHRM grew towards the late 1980s, HRP focused on developing and maintaining control strategies through reward systems such as performance management which were designed to control individual behaviour. Strategic plans were implemented by a team of HR professional and strategic planners, and control was exercised to meet these plans.

Finally, HRP has evolved to a contemporary mechanism which is designed to create a competitive advantage through strategic HR planning. As such, HRP is not viewed as a regulatory or control mechanism but rather the HR plans developed shape organisational behaviour and create strategic unity. The mission and vision of the company is shared by all stakeholders who, as a result, strive for an alignment of individual, group and organisational goals.

Please read
Ulrich, D. (1987), 'Strategic human resource planning: Why and how?', *Human Resource Planning*, vol. 10, no. 1, pp. 37–56.

ENVIRONMENTAL INFLUENCE ON HRP

It is evident, from the evolution of management, that HRP today is viewed as a strategic component of SHRM. This emphasises a proactive role for the HR manager. Yet what factors impact upon effective HRP?

HRP's strategic orientation aims to transform HR *inputs* from the environment into better HR *outputs* (i.e. better goods and services delivery). It also translates strategic objectives into desired and measurable quantitative and qualitative skill requirements. Consequently, HRP must be based on the most accurate information available. In a dynamic environment, frequently updated information about the internal and external environment is critical in order to reduce the risk associated with the surplus or shortage of particular skills, knowledge and abilities. Managers identify these gaps using systematic environmental scanning, which is a continual analysis of whether the current knowledge, skills and abilities in the organisation are sufficient to achieve its strategic plan. If any human resource gaps are identified, managers need to develop an action plan to recruit new employees and/or train and develop current employees to fill the gap.

Environmental scanning should take place in the internal and external environments and is the starting point of HRP.

INTERNAL SCANNING

internal scanning
Involves analysing the internal environment of an organisation.

Internal scanning, as the name suggests, involves analysing the internal environment of an organisation. This includes information about the staff (past and current) and the organisation's climate and culture. This is performed to determine what current knowledge, skills and abilities employees have and whether they will be sufficient to achieve the organisation's strategic goals. In order to conduct internal scanning organisations should possess a current internal HR inventory to identify the current HR strengths and weaknesses. This inventory, also commonly referred to as a human resource information system (HRIS), should contain updated employee information which may be further analysed at two levels: micro and macro (Idris & Eldridge, 1998).

micro internal HR information
Includes the current number of employees, their job-related skills, demographic characteristics, performance level, management skills and work attitudes.

Micro internal HR information includes the current number of employees, their job-related skills, knowledge and abilities, demographic characteristics, performance level, management skills and work attitudes. This information should be located within the HRIS (refer to Chapter 4 for a discussion on the HRIS).

However, although an HRIS is valuable, outdated information kept on such a system can severely impact on the effectiveness of HRP as the HR needs predicted, and required, may differ significantly from those of the past. However, it is very time consuming to update employee records continually and, in reality, a majority of HR managers do not perform this task well. To streamline the process and overcome this problem, companies should automatically update the HRIS after the employee's induction and yearly performance appraisals which may be done online via the company's intranet (ensuring that only HR have access and authority to update this information).

In contrast, **macro internal HR information** includes the organisational culture, climate, philosophy and structure. Information on the company structure, philosophy, mission and vision may be obtained from company documents. However, the culture and climate is generally intangible and this may be obtained from personal accounts or feedback from stakeholders, such as customer and staff surveys. The macro internal HR information may also have been documented over time, so HR managers can compare past and current analyses and contrast this with other data to obtain any correlations which provide insights into the current environment of the company. All information obtained, whether from the micro or macro environment, is crucial to HRP and should be analysed in view of strategic HR and organisational goals.

macro internal HR information
Includes the organisational philosophy, culture, climate and structure.

EXTERNAL SCANNING

Since the 1980s there has been an unprecedented amount of external environmental change which has had an inevitable influence on the flexibility and decentralisation of HRP. **External scanning** involves the systematic identification and analysis of key trends in the external environment and the monitoring of their impact on HR strategies. This is required to optimise HR output at any given time. This is conducted by identifying and analysing the external environment, which includes the government, political/legal climate, technology, socioeconomic factors, consumer, customer and pressure group environments. Specifically, examples of contemporary external environmental effects are globalisation and the increase in diverse people with differing skill standards, skill migration, ageing workforces and changing consumer legislations relating to competency-based skills, which are all used to forecast the HR demand and supply. Realistically, HR managers cannot perform this alone as it is time consuming and involves constant environmental scanning at local, national and international levels. Therefore, experts may be employed to assist, such as financial managers (for economic factors), political advisers (for government changes), and statisticians to collate and analyse the data and present it in layperson terms.

external scanning
Involves the systematic identification and analysis of key trends in the external environment and the monitoring of their impact on HR strategies.

In essence, the internal and external environmental scanning of HRP determines the organisation's adaptability and capability to respond and compete within a dynamic environment, thus planting the seed for a competitive advantage.

APPROACHES TO HUMAN RESOURCE PLANNING

When considering HRP, managers need to take into account when the planning will be conducted and who takes responsibility for it. As a general rule, planning is usually conducted on a yearly basis, towards the end of the year. For example, towards the end of 2005, HR planning should be conducted for 2006 and beyond. Therefore, planning involves long- and short-term plans, depending on the needs and strategic capability of the company. It is performed towards the end of the year because most budget meetings occur in October, and it is then that the company will know budget and resource constraints and can work with such information to determine HR needs. It is important to remember, however, that budgets are merely a guideline for staff to work with, and any unexpected negative influences on the company (such as the effect of terrorism on the airline industry) will usually result in budget cuts. Therefore, although HRP officially takes place once a year, modifications could be made at any time. Unfortunately, the HR department is usually the first department to feel the impact of such influences and it is the victim of cost-cutting exercises. This is because many senior executives fail to see the link between HR department activities and the company bottom line.

HRP is usually performed by HR managers, in consultation with line and senior managers. The level of involvement by various managers will depend on the needs and strategic focus of the company. For example, short-term staffing solutions will generally require the assistance of the line manager to determine what tasks need to be done and how quickly the position needs to be filled. In this case, a temporary employee may be required. However, if a new division is opening up within the company, entire departments will need to be staffed on a long-term basis and this will involve an intense strategic focus coordinated with senior management. Now that HRP has been defined and discussed in detail, it is necessary to identify *how* it is conducted.

As a strategic process, HRP has three major steps:

1. Demand forecasting
2. Supply forecasting
3. Filling the gap between demand and supply to ensure skill optimisation.

DEMAND FORECASTING

demand forecasting
Involves estimating the quantity and quality of employees required to meet organisational objectives.

HR **demand forecasting** involves estimating the quantity and quality of employees required to meet organisational objectives. Forecasting techniques can range from highly sophisticated computer simulations to simple trend models, depending on the size of the organisation, its structures, level of expertise and environmental vitality factors. However, demand forecasting is restricted by the quality and quantity of HR availability in the external labour market. For example, recent years have witnessed a decline in 17–25 year olds entering the workforce. Consequently, this indicates that there will be a greater skill shortage and competitiveness in recruiting skilled young employees. Hence, availability in this segment has declined and this impacts upon supply and demand.

trend projection
A time series analysis where past information about the number of people hired (or requested) by the organisation over time is plotted on a graph so that HR trends and requirements can be forecast into the future.

Demand forecasting may be undertaken quantitatively (i.e. using numbers) and/or qualitatively (i.e. using words). The *quantitative* approach uses statistical and mathematical techniques to analyse HR data. Two such common techniques include trend projection and multiple regression. **Trend projection** is a time series analysis where past information about the number of people hired (or requested) by the organisation over time is plotted on a graph so that HR trends and requirements can be forecast into the future (see Figure 8.2). This technique provides easily interpretable data to managers, but it overly simplifies forecasting and assumes that future HR demand will follow the trends of the past, which isn't always the case. Therefore, managers using trend projection need to be wary of this downfall.

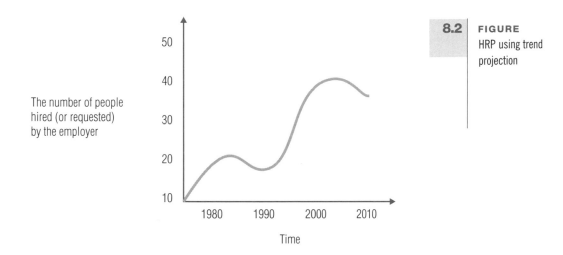

8.2 FIGURE
HRP using trend projection

Multiple regression is a mathematical technique used to relate HR demand to several independent variables, such as sales output, product mix or per capita productivity. This technique analyses the association between several independent variables and HR demand, which increases the complexity of the analysis and is a more efficient use of the available data in the organisation. The accuracy of the HR forecast is increased by adding more independent variables. Despite these advantages, multiple regression requires a large sample size, can be mathematically complex and relies on past data, which is not always suitable in a rapidly changing environment. In recent years, it was anticipated that HR software packages such as Peoplesoft® and SAP® would improve the process of workforce planning; however, they have been slow and somewhat cumbersome to implement, thereby diminishing their usefulness (Kossek *et al.*, 1994).

multiple regression
A mathematical technique used to relate HR demand to several independent variables, such as sales output, product mix or per capita productivity.

While the quantitative approach to demand forecasting relies on statistical data analysis, the *qualitative* approach draws the HR demand forecast from key stakeholders of HR trends (e.g. employees, supervisors, managers and organisational experts). In contrast to quantitative forecasting, qualitative forecasting relies on words rather than numbers to obtain information, such as interviews and focus groups. Two common techniques of qualitative forecasting include the Delphi technique and the nominal group technique.

The **Delphi technique** extracts the forecast from a group of experts who exchange several rounds of HR estimates, normally without meeting face to face, to increase the breadth of the HR forecast. All of the expert responses and feedback

Delphi technique
Extracts the forecast from a group of experts who exchange several rounds of HR estimates, normally without meeting face to face, to increase the breadth of the HR forecast.

are collated and returned to each individual to 'fine-tune' their independent estimate. The process continues until a consensus is reached between the experts. This is a very economical technique as experts may be located in differing geographical locations, and it also avoids common problems with expert panels such as personality conflicts and groupthink.

nominal group technique
A group process where a small number of experts meet face to face.

Alternatively, the **nominal group technique** (NGT) is a group process where a small number of experts meet face to face. After open discussion and private assessments, they reach a consensus concerning the future HR demand. The strength of the NGT is that it involves expert participants at one location which facilitates the efficiency of problem solving; however, it is not always a cost-effective method and can result in group conflict.

The benefit to demand forecasting of these qualitative approaches is the involvement that it requires of key decision makers, who will ultimately be affected by the subsequent HR decisions. However, the NGT can be time consuming, highly subjective and costly.

SUPPLY FORECASTING

Once a manager quantitatively and qualitatively forecasts the HR demand, they must then assess the internal and external HR supply needed to meet that demand. That is, once they have determined how many employees the company will require in the future (whether that be in one, five or ten years' time), they then need to fill those positions, either from internal or external sources.

internal labour supply
Comprises all employees currently employed with the company.

The **internal labour supply** is composed of all employees currently employed with the company. The HR department can use these employees to fill current and future staffing vacancies through promotions or transfers. However, because the internal supply of labour can be quite large, how can managers obtain such information as which staff have qualified skills for promotions or which ones have expressed a desire for a transfer? The quickest way to determine this information is via a **skills inventory form**, which is a system which keeps track of employee skill development. For example, this may be a form employees complete on an annual basis (i.e. as part of their performance appraisal) which details their work experience, education (including new courses), areas of expertise and professional association memberships. Companies can then ensure updated information is on their HRIS, which facilitates effective HRP. A skill inventory represents a useful starting point to assess the internal HR supply. The inventory is also useful in meeting the quantitative approach to demand forecasting by establishing cross-functional work teams, multiskilling programs and career development options for employees.

skills inventory form
A system which keeps track of employee skill development.

external labour supply
Any person not currently employed with the company.

If there is no matching internal candidate, organisations need to look outside the organisation for their HR supply. The **external labour supply** refers to any person not currently employed with the company. As this definition is quite broad, it is often divided into categories, such as employed, unemployed, retired, full-time students and those over the legal age to work (i.e. in Australia the legal age a person can begin work is 14¾ years). Managers should regularly monitor current and potential environmental changes (e.g. ageing workforce due to the baby boomers, a casualised workforce and company closures which would significantly increase the external supply of labour) to assess their qualitative and quantitative effect on the external HR supply. Specifically, baby boomers, which refer to people born between 1946 and 1964, play a significant role in the external labour supply. Although most people in this category are still working, they are heading towards retirement in the next decade or so (i.e. 2015), hence there will be a shortfall of candidates in the internal and external labour supplies, although this may be compensated for by the baby boomers' children. Nevertheless, there will be an age and skill gap between the two which organisations will need to contend with. Numerous monitoring services are available through government research agencies such as the Bureau of Statistics, the National Centre for Vocational Education Research (NCVER) and, specifically in Australia, Centrelink.

The final step is filling the gap between demand and supply to ensure skill optimisation. To do this, managers need to analyse the supply and demand and forecast appropriately.

PRACTICAL CRITICISM OF HRP

As today's rapidly changing environment affects managers' HR decisions (e.g. downsizing and restructuring), it inevitably influences the nature of HRP. As highlighted earlier in this chapter, HRP should take an emergent strategic approach to ensure the organisation has the optimal quality and quantity of HR output despite the emergence of unforeseeable environmental changes. Due to the emergent, flexible and networked nature of the work environment today, staffing is increasingly being defined by people organising themselves rather than people being organised according to a formal plan (Stewart & Carson, 1997). However, it is important to note that some scholars reject the 'anti-planning perspective of HRM' and argue that coping with a dynamic environment requires more planning rather than less (Wilson, 1994). In other words, continuous learning and flexible HR planning is a significant competitive advantage within the dynamic environment.

Despite this, it is also important to note that such environmental volatility places great demands on the abilities of HR managers to conduct environmental analyses practically and effectively. In fact, Huselid (1993) argues that environmental volatility affects organisations' adoption of HRP or SHRM. He concluded from his research that companies in highly stable or highly dynamic environments were much less likely to adopt HRP and SHRM than those experiencing moderate levels of volatility. Therefore companies need to be aware of this effect and ensure systems are developed to make the best possible use of HRP and SHRM for individual and organisational effectiveness.

Please read

Huselid, M. A. (1993), 'The impact of environmental volatility on human resource planning and strategic human resource management', *Human Resource Planning*, vol. 16, no. 3, pp. 35–51.

Job analysis

Once an organisation has sufficiently undergone the process of HRP, and before employees can be hired, promoted or transferred within the company, a job analysis needs to be conducted. This is to ensure that employees are moving into appropriate positions which have been carefully designed to ensure they will contribute to the strategic goals of the company. It is important that job analysis is conducted before an employee accepts the position because it is very difficult to change it once they are in that position. Companies who attempt to change job descriptions after an employee has signed a contract may experience legal ramifications, or be perceived as being negligent or breaking the psychological contract, and it may cause irreparable damage to the morale and culture (which could extend beyond the individual to other employees). Therefore, it is imperative that HR managers conduct job analysis carefully prior to HRP.

job analysis
A systematic analysis of the tasks, duties and responsibilities of a job as well as the necessary knowledge, skills and abilities a person needs to perform the job adequately.

Job analysis is a systematic analysis of the tasks, duties and responsibilities of a job as well as the necessary knowledge, skills and abilities a person needs to perform the job adequately. It also includes any physical or manual labour required, and may specify a geographical location for the position to be undertaken (i.e. if the job involves travel or international assignment). Some job analyses, depending on the nature of the work, may also list the type of tools, equipment, software, training and social environment an employee could expect to experience as part of the job. These are all important because they contribute to whether an employee is willing and able to perform the job given its requirements, and form part of the criteria for recruitment and selection. More importantly, a job analysis is a critical aspect of HRM because it forms part of legal requirements. That is, employees should be hired, promoted, transferred, trained, developed and performance managed based on *job-related* aspects, not personal criteria. Failure to do so may result in discrimination for which the company is held liable.

A job analysis comprises three components: job description, person specification and job context (see Figure 8.3). Each of these is discussed in detail next.

JOB DESCRIPTION

job description
Outlines the broad nature of a job.

A **job description** (also referred to as a position description, or PD) outlines the broad nature of a job. Usually, a job description will include the job title, the department the job falls within, who the job reports to and, in some cases, the staff who report to the job. It also contains a list of the key tasks the employee

FIGURE **8.3**
Components of job analysis

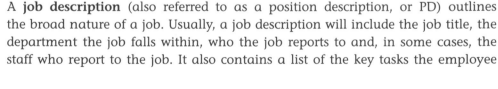
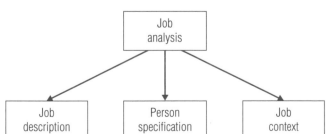

Job Description

Incumbent name: Samantha C. Jones   **Job title:** Human Resources Assistant
Job classification: HRM-25902   **Starting date:** 1 January 2007
Department: Human Resource Management   **Contract end:** 31 December 2010
Branch: Adelaide CBD

Reporting
The position of Human Resources Assistant reports directly to the HRM Manager.

Qualifications required
- The incumbent should have a Bachelor of Business or higher qualification with a major in management, human resource management or commerce.

Responsibilities
- The key responsibility is to assist the HRM Manager.

Key tasks
- Coordinate advertisements for vacant positions.
- Analyse and update job descriptions.
- Prepare and update induction manuals.
- Conduct screening interviews with candidates and present preliminary results for the HRM Manager.
- Assist in the preparation of training and development programs, including diversity awareness, EEO and AA.
- Ensure that safety equipment is updated and regularly checked (i.e. first aid kits, fire hydrants) and that fire wardens and safety officers are regularly trained.
- Observe policy changes to state and federal laws regarding occupational health and safety.
- Maintain the human resource information system (HRIS) with regard to all personnel information.
- Liaise with the Information Technology Department to update the company intranet.
- Assist the HRM Manager to prepare for monthly board meetings.

is expected to perform, their duties and/or obligations, the qualifications or prerequisites required to perform the job (also referred to as job specifications) and the job responsibilities. Figure 8.4 illustrates a sample job description for a human resources assistant.

PERSON SPECIFICATION

Person specification falls under the umbrella of the job description. It outlines the knowledge, skills and abilities a person requires to perform the job adequately. It will usually list the specific training and/or qualifications that are required and the level at which the employee should be competent. For example, most HR positions are required to hold a Certificate in Assessment and Workplace Training. In other cases, job descriptions will be quite specific in identifying the type and level of qualifications required, such as a Diploma in Business Management, Bachelor of Law (Honours) or a Doctorate of Philosophy (PhD).

person specification
The knowledge, skills and abilities a person requires to perform the job adequately.

JOB CONTEXT

The final component of job analysis is the **job context**. This refers to the situational and supporting information regarding the job, such as work climate,

job context
The situational and supporting information regarding the job, such as work climate and unspoken rules.

reporting relationships and unspoken rules. It may also list budgetary information and incentives, as well as physical and psychological requirements. For example, the job context for a mining position should state that the incumbent would be required to work underground and in confined spaces for lengthy periods of time. Likewise, the job context for a call centre operator may state that the position may be associated with serious complaints, verbal abuse, threat of physical abuse and time pressure.

Overall, the purpose of a job analysis is to assist managers to plan staffing strategies and to provide job-related HR procedures such as training, selection, compensation and performance appraisal. For example, after redefining the job description and person specification of a sales representative, a different sort of customer service training may emerge.

JOB ANALYSIS METHODS

Job analysis is important because it identifies the purpose of a job, when and where it is to be performed, the skills required by the incumbent and the working conditions associated with the position. The difficult aspect of this is that environmental and organisational conditions are constantly changing and people often enter and leave positions without much thought as to whether the job needs to be reanalysed. Therefore, there are a number of methods HR managers can employ to analyse jobs effectively and ensure that the right job is designed to contribute to the achievement of strategic goals. An HR manager needs to consider the objective of the job analysis, the type of information that needs to be collected, the source of the information (i.e. the incumbent, supervisor, peers, HR files), the method of data collection and who will analyse the data and how. Therefore, the methods described next are only one step in the job analysis process.

The most common method of collecting data is through the use of *interviews*. These can be used to collect a variety of information from an incumbent or the manager of an incumbent by asking them to describe the incumbent's tasks and duties. A specific type of interview which is a useful tool is a critical incident interview, whereby the incumbent is asked to recall several incidents that resulted in them excelling or underperforming on a job objective (SHL Group, 2001). The interview can also obtain information about unobservable aspects of a job (such as the organisational culture); however, the information provided in interviews is subjective and only as good as the judgement of the interviewee.

Structured questionnaires are another common method of data collection. These are usually completed by the incumbent, the incumbent's line manager and others who are regularly associated with the job, such as their peers. In a similar vein to interviews, structured questionnaires are also subjective. Consequently, a

360-degree feedback
A type of appraisal which collects views from people both in the job and holding jobs hierarchically above and below the position being analysed, providing a multifaceted view.

method such as a **360-degree-feedback** questionnaire is recommended to reduce subjectivity. This type of appraisal collects views from people both in the job and holding jobs hierarchically above and below the position being analysed, providing a multifaceted view. Although 360-degree feedback is gaining popularity due to its ability to improve individual and organisational effectiveness, this method is not commonly used in Australian companies

(Nankervis & Leece, 1997). Nevertheless, questionnaires are still a viable method of data collection relating to job analysis and the use of technology (i.e. making the questionnaire available on the company intranet) facilitates the likelihood of stakeholders adopting this method.

An incumbent can also be asked to provide a *diary* of their day to day work activities. This involves documenting their job-related activities, thus helping an HR manager to determine whether the job description needs to be amended. Alternatively, the *direct observation* of an incumbent performing their job enables the job analyst to gather first-hand information about the job. This observation method is suited for those jobs where work behaviours are observable (e.g. machine operator, police officer, flight attendant and craft workers). In comparison to interviews and questionnaires, which produce indirect information and subjective errors such as omissions or exaggerations, direct observation provides first-hand objective job information. However, the act of observation may cause the incumbent to alter their normal work behaviour, thus unobtrusive observation is important. Of course, this method is unlikely to be appropriate for jobs that demand a high level of concentration and mental effort.

Job analysts can also combine methods to obtain more accurate information about the job and the person best fitted for the job. The set of information that a job analyst draws upon needs to:

- be manageable (i.e. not too many competencies);
- be defined behaviourally (to be specific and observable);
- identify accurately independent competencies; and
- be comprehensive, accessible and compatible with an organisation's visions, goals and culture (SHL Group, 2001).

Although the aforementioned methods of job analysis are useful for HR managers in designing and analysing jobs, they are subject to criticism and HR managers should be aware of the possible downfalls of such methods before employing them (see Table 8.1).

JOB DESIGN

The establishment of excellent HRM practices relies on a foundation of well specified jobs and accurate job analysis. **Job design** refers to the way that an entire job is organised and categorised and, unlike job analysis, which focuses on the needs of the organisation, job design focuses on the needs of the incumbent. It includes creating an alignment between individual and organisational goals, and considers how much the incumbent is willing and able to perform (i.e. identifying what is expected and individual limitations), work processes which aid the completion of tasks and finally any psychological issues such as favourable working conditions and achieving a work life balance. Job design is usually grouped into the following four categories: job specialisation, job enlargement, job rotation and job enrichment.

Job specialisation involves employees performing standardised, repetitive tasks so that analysts can record what the job involves and how long it takes to perform each task. This category of job design aligns closely with scientific management as employees are closely monitored and the results of the job

job design
The way that an entire job is organised and categorised; focuses on the needs of the incumbent.

job specialisation
Involves employees performing standardised, repetitive tasks so that analysts can record what the job involves and how long it takes to perform each task.

TABLE **8.1** **Advantages and disadvantages of job analysis methods**

Job analysis method	Advantages	Disadvantages
Interviews	• Flexibility • Ability to clarify details immediately • Establishment of trust and rapport • Interviewee is involved in the data collection	• Time consuming (i.e. organising a time, date and location as well as pre-interview preparation) • Costly • Interviews can easily go 'off track' • Interviewee may become irritable, bored, tired or lose concentration • Subjective errors such as omissions or exaggerations • Data needs to be analysed qualitatively
Structured questionnaires	• Ability to obtain detailed information • Questionnaires may be completed in the incumbent's own time and location • Unsupervised so the incumbent does not feel intimidated • Cost effective for the job analyst	• Time consuming (i.e. preparing the questionnaire) • Printing and distribution costs (although these may be reduced by placing the questionnaire on the intranet) • Subjective errors such as omissions or exaggerations • Poor response rate
360-degree feedback	• Ability to obtain detailed information • Cost effective • Information from all viewpoints is obtained	• Incumbent may feel threatened or intimidated by others • Peers may feel intimidated about their comments for fear that they will be put in similar positions in the future • Time consuming
Diary	• Flexibility • Cost effective	• Time consuming for the incumbent • May be biased • Subjective errors such as omissions or exaggerations
Direct observation	• First-hand information	• May be obtrusive and intimidating • Time consuming

specialisation will specify the most efficient method for performing that task. As such, it is a rational analysis that provides management with standardised procedures which usually equate to cost savings, fewer errors and minimal training. However, not all employees are motivated by being told how to perform a job and enjoy the flexibility of using their initiative, therefore this approach to job design may also result in decreased morale and the employment of low-skilled staff (see Chapter 1 for a discussion on scientific management).

job enlargement
The horizontal expansion of a job by allocating to it a variety of similar-level skills and new responsibilities.

Job enlargement involves the horizontal expansion of a job by allocating to it a variety of similar-level skills and new responsibilities. This is a concept adopted by many companies today as organisational restructuring and downsizing is a common cost-saving mechanism, thus fewer people are retained within the company but they have more responsibility and tasks to perform.

Although advantageous for the company in the short term, it can lead to overloading staff, job burnout, resentment and poor quality work due to increased demand.

Job rotation involves increasing task variety by shifting employees from one task to another task. This is generally employed by companies for two reasons. First, to increase the variety of tasks to ensure employees do not become bored with their job. This is important because boredom can lead to a lack of concentration and can result in poor quality, high error rate and injuries in the workplace (see Chapter 6 for a discussion on workplace injuries). Second, job rotation can foster multiskilling, which benefits both employees and the organisation, leading to increased morale. Further, different staff members can develop new and better ways of performing the job which enhance overall efficiency and effectiveness. The main problem with job rotation is continuous training as new members need to learn how to perform each job. This may disrupt productivity and decrease efficiency, although this would only be in the short term. Despite this, it can be tiresome and frustrating for line managers or trainers to be continually training different staff to do the same job.

Job enrichment involves the vertical expansion of a job by increasing the amount of employee control or responsibility, such as providing more decision-making or planning responsibilities. Often this is achieved by combining tasks and is economically viable for the company although employers need to consider whether staff want their job enriched (as it means extra responsibility) and whether there are additional consequences of this for the company, such as altering job descriptions, increased union involvement and competition between staff.

The success of many HR initiatives is contingent upon effective job analysis and its evaluation. **Job evaluation** is the final stage of job analysis and refers to an analytical tool which determines the relative worth of the job with the aim of providing fair and objective pay. It can help job analysts or managers identify the appropriate level of grades or pay ranges as well as the relative differences between them. This concept is explained further in Chapter 10, on performance management, and Chapter 11, on reward management.

job rotation
Involves increasing task variety by shifting employees from one task to another task.

job enrichment
Involves the vertical expansion of a job by increasing the amount of employee control or responsibility.

job evaluation
An analytical tool which determines the relative worth of the job with the aim of providing fair and objective pay.

PRACTICAL CRITICISM OF JOB ANALYSIS

Despite the significance of job analysis, some scholars argue that the rational staffing process of choosing applicants based on a specific job description and person specification is no longer viable for the contemporary workforce. To cope with dynamic environmental changes, such as advanced technology and increased diversity, employees are often called upon to perform more than is stated in their job description, requiring them to perform many tasks at once, using cross-functional skills (Stewart & Carson, 1997). This can lead to emotional and physical exhaustion, resentment, decreased morale and overall ineffectiveness.

Today, companies can monitor work behaviours and employee attributes by using O*NET, a flexible database that contains information on personality and cognitive and situational variables regarding employment. Organisations can use O*NET to understand occupational features better so that they can distribute work tasks and ensure that jobs are designed to suit individual and organisational needs, without overloading human resources (Petersen *et al.*, 1999).

Furthermore, the increasing popularity of humanistic HR approaches (i.e. soft HRM) in organisations is creating shared power structures such as self-managed work teams (SMWT) where staffing decisions are made by teams rather than individuals. Thus, job descriptions are increasingly being formulated, evaluated and determined by applicant stakeholders (e.g. co-workers, managers and customers), the consequences of which need to be closely monitored by HR managers and senior management.

Strategic recruitment

At the beginning of the chapter HRP and job analysis were highlighted as the foundation of recruitment and selection. Not only do they provide a strategic forecast of HR needs, but they also ensure the knowledge, skills and abilities of future staff will meet job and organisational requirements. Taken together, these benefits underpin the development of a competitive advantage through having the 'best' human resources for the firm's needs.

recruitment
The process of generating a pool of qualified candidates for a particular job who can contribute best to the strategic objectives of the organisation; involves identifying what jobs need to be filled and how the most suitable candidates will be attracted.

Once the planning of human resources has been established, and job analysis and job design are completed, it is necessary to begin recruiting employees. **Recruitment** is the process of generating a pool of qualified candidates for a particular job who can best contribute to the strategic objectives of the organisation. It involves both the organisation and the applicant having a clear understanding of the nature of the job, in terms of identifying *what* jobs need to be filled and *how* the most suitable candidates will be attracted. Recruitment is a crucial function of SHRM because it determines the quantity and quality of future employees and, consequently, it also determines the type of organisation created and the organisational capability to achieve success. It is important that companies carefully plan the recruitment process to ensure that they obtain the 'best' pool of candidates; poorly planned recruitment initiatives may result in too many applicants with the incorrect skills or too few applicants. Both of these outcomes can be financially expensive and time consuming especially if the company decides to conduct another recruitment drive to compensate for the poor results of the initial drive.

When an organisation is devising its recruitment strategy, it is imperative that the recruitment activities are aligned with the business strategy and company culture to ensure a 'good fit' with the organisation. For example, HR managers should consider the overall business strategy, such as its purpose, goals and the way business is conducted, and ensure recruitment initiatives attract people who have the capabilities to contribute to the achievement of the organisation's strategic goals. Likewise, the type of people recruited should have the same or similar values to the company (i.e. ethical values) and be able to fit into the organisational culture (i.e. innovative, risk taking or team based). It is also vital to recognise that recruitment strategies are influenced by the dynamic external environment, such as volatile labour markets, intense competition and pressure groups.

So, how do companies commence the recruitment process? There is a variety of options for HR managers in the determination of where to locate applicants. Broadly, these may be classified as internal and external attraction activities.

INTERNAL ATTRACTION ACTIVITIES

Depending on the company needs and the organisational strategy assumed, **internal attraction activities** provide an effective and efficient solution for employee recruitment. These involve the organisation looking internally for its human resource needs. The benefits of internal attraction activities include:

- Cost effectiveness (i.e. minimal, if any, advertising costs).
- Time effectiveness (i.e. less time required to train employees).
- Familiarity of the candidate with the organisational structure, culture, stakeholders and politics, and with company policies and processes.
- Familiarity by the company with the employee's knowledge, skills, attitudes, personality and work ethics and being able to determine, to a large degree, whether that employee will 'fit' into the vacant position.
- Increased morale and motivation for employees.
- Higher probability of success due to a holistic and thorough understanding of the candidate's knowledge, skills and abilities.

Examples of internal attraction activities to recruit applicants include advertising on the company intranet, in company newsletters, on noticeboards and via job bidding. In addition, HR managers can access data available on the HRIS, such as management and skill inventories. Hence they can match current employees to vacant positions by performing automated searches on the HRIS to identify employees with the appropriate skills or those eligible for a promotion.

However, although there are many advantages of internal attraction activities, there are also some negative implications companies and employees need to consider. These include inbreeding; political infighting for promotions; low morale for those not promoted; limited pool of applicants; limited knowledge, skills and abilities (and the inability to bring new, fresh ideas into the company); and the time involved when HR managers conduct equitable and fair performance appraisals.

> **internal attraction activities**
> An organisation looking internally for its human resource needs.

EXTERNAL ATTRACTION ACTIVITIES

In contrast to internal attraction activities, **external attraction activities** look outside the organisation for a pool of candidates. Usually, companies would conduct an internal search initially, to determine if a suitable candidate could be found among current employees, thus saving time and money on advertising and recruitment costs. However, if a suitable applicant was not found, the company would then adopt external recruitment activities, which include some of the following benefits:

- Larger talent pool.
- Acquisition of new knowledge, skills and abilities for the organisation.
- Increased knowledge creation and innovation.
- Reduced subjectivity (i.e. no perceived biases or favouritism from inside the company).

> **external attraction activities**
> An organisation looking externally for its human resource needs.

- More compatibility to equal employment opportunity (EEO) and affirmative action (AA) concepts by increasing the recruitment pool to be much more diverse.

Examples of external attraction activities include using the Internet (e.g. seek.com, careerone.com, company and professional association websites), newspapers and magazines to advertise, in addition to job fairs (such as those at universities), recruitment agencies and word of mouth.

In the past decade the trend to use recruitment agencies has increased dramatically as they streamline the recruitment process and increase efficiency. **Recruitment agencies** are external companies who supply human resources. In effect, they ease the HR manager's responsibility by conducting the initial stages of recruitment, such as advertising, interviewing, testing and culling of candidates. Recruitment agencies, which are hired and paid for by the company, then present a shortlist of candidates for the HR manager to peruse and conduct final interviews. A once-off fee applies for all successful job placements. The trend to use such agencies is largely due to the time efficiency as HR managers today deal with a complex variety of additional responsibilities, such as EEO, AA, diversity management and changing employment laws.

A comparative study across Australia, New Zealand and South Africa found that non-standard forms of employment (e.g. increased recruitment agency labour, home-based work and subcontracting) were an increasingly important feature of the contemporary workforce. This type of non-standard employment comprises about one-third of the Australian and New Zealand workforce, and one-eighth of the South African workforce (Hall, 2000) and may be attributed to work–life balance issues and the casualisation of the workforce. Contemporary HR managers should, therefore, take advantage of this trend and (where financially viable) employ recruitment agencies to help source the 'best' candidates.

However, managers should also be aware of some negative implications of external attraction activities. These include lower morale, firm commitment, productivity and trust of agency staff as they may not be considered a 'true' member of the organisation (or may be temporary); transaction, monitoring and management costs associated with recruitment agencies; loss of control of the recruitment process; labour cost premiums; candidates who are unfamiliar with the company's internal processes, structure, strategies and culture; additional effort required for orientation and training; resentment from internal candidates who were 'passed over'; and difficulty in assessing the candidates' true credentials (at least until they have worked for some time).

TECHNOLOGY IN RECRUITMENT

As discussed in Chapter 4, technology is an invaluable tool for HRM. Technology not only can streamline the processing of employee data and facilitate organisational communication, but is also useful in the recruitment process. **E-recruitment** (or online recruitment) refers to the process of recruiting via the intranet (internal) and Internet (external). A survey of managing directors of Australia's leading recruitment firms found that job recruiters are advertising 50 per cent more of their available positions on the Internet than in print. The same survey by the Internet job advertisement service, Seek Communications,

recruitment agencies
External companies who supply human resources.

e-recruitment
The process of recruiting via the intranet (internal) and Internet (external).

also found that recruiters expect the number of available positions advertised on the Internet to rise from 71 per cent to 90 per cent within 12 months. More than 80 per cent of recruiters now see the Internet as important to their recruitment strategy (IRS, 2001).

The key potential benefits of e-recruitment are:

- *Reach.* There is unlimited exposure of advertisements for local, national and international markets.
- *Cost.* The lack or lessening of advertising costs in the usage of online recruitment agencies such as seek.com or career.com.
- *Speed and accessibility.* The immediate advertisement of job vacancies which can be accessed 24 hours a day, at the convenience of the candidate.
- *Flexibility.* The unlimited length of advertising material (unlike newspapers which are very costly for small advertisements).
- *Interaction.* Employer and candidate can interact utilising online communication devices.
- *Integrating the recruitment system with other computerised HR functions.* For example, integrating it with payroll and employee databases (via the HRIS) which allows operations to be streamlined.

Many companies around the globe have adopted e-recruitment, such as Optus in Australia, which was awarded the 2002 *Insite Gold Award* for Best Practice in e-Recruitment, and Coles Myer (refer to 'A manager's challenge' in Chapter 4). Despite this, e-recruitment is still at a developmental stage for most employers and findings from the latest annual study of recruitment practices conducted for the Chartered Institute of Personnel and Development showed that national newspapers are still the preferred medium for recruitment advertising (IRS, 2001).

The key potential costs of e-recruitment are a large number of unsuitable or unqualified applicants; poor candidate matching (as it is often computerised); the possible lack of employer confidentiality; the posting of non-existent jobs; non-compliance with ethical and legal procedures (i.e. discriminatory or politically incorrect statements); and general IT problems such as the need constantly to update websites, 'unavailable' web pages, forms that are difficult to download and computer 'freezing' during the application process. To date, the potential downfall of e-recruitment implies that it should be used to complement, rather than replace, traditional recruitment methods.

Please read

Stewart, G. L. & Carson, K. P. (1997), 'Moving beyond the mechanistic model: An alternative approach to staffing for contemporary organizations', *Human Resource Management Review*, vol. 7, no. 2, pp. 157–84.

Strategic selection

Once the recruitment process has been completed, the next phase of HRM is selection. As with all aspects of SHRM, the selection process should be conducted with a strategic focus and should be congruent with overall organisational objectives and plans. Essentially, selection begins where recruitment ends: with the applicant pool. Consequently, the success and quality of selection is significantly affected by the recruitment strategies employed. Therefore, it is important that HR managers adopt a holistic view of SHRM, taking into consideration how functions influence each other.

selection
The identification of candidates who can best contribute to the strategic objectives of the organisation and help in the quest to obtain a competitive advantage.

Selection is an integral part of SHRM as the selection processes identify those candidates who can best contribute to the strategic objectives of the organisation and help in the quest to obtain a competitive advantage. To select the most suitable person for an organisation, three essential questions must be answered (Caruth & Handlogten, 1997):

1. What is the candidate's *can do* ability (i.e. human capital) (refer to Chapter 3)?
2. What is the candidate's *will do* ability (i.e. discretionary behaviours) (refer to Chapter 2)?
3. How well will the applicant *fit* into the organisation?

HR managers need to consider these three questions before, during and after the selection process. For example, before selection approaches begin, it is wise to consider what knowledge, skills and abilities are *essential* for the job and what is *desired*. Job descriptions should include such information. During the selection process, managers should consider these three questions when they are reviewing résumés and interviewing applicants. Finally, continual evaluation (such as performance appraisals) should be conducted after the selection process to ensure that the applicant still has the right knowledge, skills and abilities. If they do not, training programs may need to be designed specifically to address this. One common problem that employees experience is that they no longer 'fit' into the organisation, either culturally or skillwise. Often this occurs to employees who have been with the same company for a long time and have seen the company grow, restructure and change orientations. When this occurs, employees are encouraged to discuss their personal goals with HR managers in an attempt to align them with organisational goals once more or reach a compromise.

SELECTION METHODS

Selection is a process of measurement, decision making and evaluation, in which organisations must use reliable and valid measures of job applicant characteristics. A good selection process should be fair to all applicants and take into consideration ethical and legal requirements (see Chapter 6 for a discussion of ethics and employment law).

There are various selection methods available. Selection methods include application forms, résumés, interviews, psychological tests (e.g. cognitive ability or personality tests), assessment centres, biographical information blanks, references, polygraphs (lie detector test), integrity tests, graphology and medical examinations. Depending on the nature of the work, different employers will adopt different selection methods and will usually use a combination of methods. For example, polygraph and/or integrity tests might be used for police or military staff, whereas medical examinations might be used for laboratory staff. Application forms and résumés will almost always be used as the basis of the selection, with specific tests being used to gain more detailed information. Some tests, such as personality tests, are usually conducted at the beginning of the selection process, whereas specific tests (such as medical tests or reference checking) are usually conducted as a final step in the process, and usually as a matter of clarification before the job is offered. It is important to keep in mind that selection methods vary in their validity or accuracy in capturing the knowledge, skills and abilities that define success for a given position. The primary selection methods that are commonly employed by companies are discussed in detail next followed by a consideration of testing issues and obligations.

INTERVIEWS

Interviews are one of the most common selection methods employed by HR managers. They are formal or information-guided discussions between a candidate and an organisational representative. Typically, they involve an exchange of information about the job and the candidate's ability to perform the job and are purposeful. That is, the purpose is for the interviewer to make a decision about whether or not to hire the candidate. However, employees can also benefit from the interview as they may use it to determine whether they would want to work for the company. They can get a 'feel' for the company by viewing the working environment and the people, and also from the professionalism of the interviewer's technique (i.e. did they conduct the interview ethically and legally). For example, it is illegal under Australian law to ask a candidate if they are married, have children or are planning on having children.

interviews
Formal or information-guided discussions between a candidate and an organisational representative.

Unlike cognitive or personality tests, interviews are designed to assess many different candidate attributes, such as values and beliefs. There are many different types of interviews a company can choose to adopt.

* *Structured interviews.* These involve a predetermined list of questions and generally focus on assessing cognitive (i.e. thinking) factors. Structured interviews mainly comprise situational or behavioural interviewing, whereby applicants are asked to describe what they have done, or would do, in a particular situation.
* *Unstructured interviews.* These involve a few open-ended questions which enable the interviewer to pursue the applicant's responses in depth. Consequently, they may be used to assess affective (i.e. feeling) and personality factors.
* *Panel interview.* This involves more than one organisational member interviewing one applicant. Usually, a panel interview will be conducted as a second or third round of interviews, when the applicants have been shortlisted, and will usually involve the HR manager, line manager and a senior manager. In some situations it may also involve a colleague. This allows interviewers an opportunity to view how the applicant will contribute to all organisational goals and reduces the possibility of bias as multiple perceptions are gained at once.
* *Group interview.* As the name suggests, this involves a group of candidates who are interviewed at the same time. This method is adopted for comparative purposes and allows the interviewer to compare candidate responses and interactions, thus allowing them to see how the group may interact with potential colleagues. This is especially useful for determining competitive behaviours and also to identify dominating or submissive personalities and decide whether they will fit into the organisational culture.

Interviews are beneficial because they allow the interviewer and interviewee to meet face to face and develop rapport. They are also flexible, especially if they are semi-structured or unstructured, and allow the interviewer to clarify details immediately. However, the disadvantages include high preparation and conducting time, the ability to go 'off track' easily, the interviewee may become irritable, bored, tired or lose concentration, the interview may be dominated by one party, the interview goals may be unclear, premature judgement may occur, or the interviewer may not be adequately prepared or trained for the interview purposes.

APPLICATION FORMS AND RÉSUMÉS

Although most selection processes begin with application forms and résumés, these are, in fact, the second most frequently used method of selection after interviews (Robertson & Smith, 2001). These selection methods provide a crucial first contact point for the candidate and the potential employer. Application forms are generally made available when the position becomes vacant and include information for the candidate to complete about themselves (i.e. their contact details, qualifications, work experience and training programs completed). They are usually accompanied by résumés (or shorter versions of résumés, called curriculum vitaes (CVs)), which provide more detailed information about the candidate. Application forms and résumés are beneficial as they provide a brief insight into the candidate's working experience and qualifications, thereby allowing the HR manager to select an initial shortlist for interviewing based on those details. However, managers need to be aware of the possibility of false statements being included in the documents. It should also be noted that the inclusion of competency statements and a photograph in the résumé is highly correlated with an invitation to an interview (Earl, Bright & Adams, 1998; Watkins & Johnson, 2000).

EMPLOYMENT TESTS

employment tests
Standardised tests in which applicants perform a selected set of actual tasks that are physically and/or psychologically similar to those performed on the job (Ployhart, Schneider & Schmitt, 2006).

Employment tests are standardised tests in which applicants perform a selected set of actual tasks that are physically and/or psychologically similar to those performed on the job (Ployhart, Schneider & Schmitt, 2006). Tests are employed to determine whether candidates are able to perform as listed in their résumé and, consequently, the likelihood that they will be able to perform their job successfully. Examples of tests include typing and mathematical tests.

psychological test
A test designed to provide insight into human behaviour.

Psychological tests are very common in many organisations today and help companies determine whether candidates 'fit' into the organisation's psychological context. A **psychological test** is designed to provide insight on human behaviour in areas such as perception, learning, human development, individual differences in ability, personality, attitude formation and change and group relationships (Oakland, 2004). Psychological tests are broadly classified as *affective* tests (i.e. I feel happy when . . .), which include personality, interest and attitude tests, or *cognitive* tests (i.e. Which of the following is not a type of flower . . .), which include intelligence, aptitude and achievement tests. For example, the Myers-Briggs Type Indicator (MBTI) is a popular psychological test which may be used to identify personality types, such as extraversion or introversion, and thinking or feeling. The results of this are then used to determine whether the candidate will fit into the organisational culture. In recent times, however, researchers and practitioners have shown interest in emotional intelligence, which is the ability to perceive and experience emotions which then guide emotional responses and promote intellectual growth (refer to Chapter 2 for a detailed discussion on emotional intelligence).

ASSESSMENT CENTRES

Assessment centres are generally used to gain insight into problem-solving and team-based activities. They involve a range of activities such as group discussions, games and exercises where people are assessed (generally by a group of assessors who monitor activities) and candidates are graded on their performance by assessors. This information is then passed on to the HR manager who adds the results to those from other selection methods to make an informed selection decision.

Assessment centres are beneficial for HR managers as they allow candidates to be placed in mock situations which represent real business situations. Therefore, these simulations are indicative of how candidates might feel, behave and react in the organisation, and whether their strategy aligns with the culture and strategy of the company. However, this type of selection method is also time consuming and expensive, and the results obtained could potentially be obtained with cheaper selection methods, such as psychological tests (Robertson & Smith, 2001).

assessment centres
A selection technique comprising problem-solving and team-based activities where people are assessed and graded on their performance based by assessors.

BIOGRAPHICAL INFORMATION BLANKS

Biographical information blanks (BIBs) (also referred to as biodata) refer to any type of information collected regarding an applicant's personal history, experience or education. This selection technique asks candidates questions that reflect weighted success criteria (e.g. attitudes, hobbies, and sales experiences). For example, a sample question might be:

What kind of hobby most interests you?
(a) Basketball
(b) Sewing
(c) Bungy jumping
(d) Painting or drawing
(e) None – I don't have any hobbies

HR managers then use the answers to determine two factors. The first is the type of employee they want in the company. Using the above example, those who chose basketball indicate they like team-based activities; sewing indicates they prefer independent activities; bungy jumping indicates they are daring and like a challenge; painting or drawing indicates they have an artistic flair; and none indicates perhaps they lack initiative or drive. Second, managers can compare the results to highly productive employees and hire those who rank similarly in the hope that this correlates positively with the candidate's job success.

Although beneficial, BIBs also have drawbacks. As with assessment centres and interviews, they can be time consuming and costly to prepare (e.g. the

biographical information blanks
Any type of information collected regarding an applicant's personal history, experience or education.

construction of scales), and empirical methods are required to analyse the data, which is usually done by experts. In addition, analysts should consider the generalisability of the results.

CONTEMPORARY SELECTION METHODS

Today's dynamic business environment changes the way people and organisations work and consequently this influences selection techniques. Whereas once selection techniques were based on the task, there has now been a shift away from *task*-centred approaches to *person*-centred approaches. For example, in order to reflect the dynamic environment (coupled with the increasing popularity of work teams), selection criteria have shifted from focusing on specific technical skills to a person's generalised ability to fit into a group (Werbel & Johnson, 2001). Similarly, candidates with personality attributes such as having a 'flexible approach' and being 'quality driven' are now highly sought after by employers.

SELECTION CRITERIA

In addition to choosing an appropriate selection method, it is important to develop **selection criteria**, which are the key work-related factors used to make the decision to hire or not to hire a person (e.g. qualifications, experience, special skills and abilities). For example, the selection criteria for a job might be that the incumbent must have five years' experience, relevant tertiary education and the ability to work in a team environment. Selection criteria are important for HR managers to be aware of and understand because the accuracy and quality of the selection process is dependent upon them. The criteria should therefore be carefully developed because once employees matching the criteria have been hired it is very difficult to fire them if the criteria were not appropriately developed to match the job requirements.

selection criteria
Key work-related factors in making the decision to hire or not to hire a person.

Selection criteria should be established based upon two areas of performance: task and contextual.

Task performance relates to an individual's ability to perform tasks that are associated with the job, and which contribute to the achievement of organisational goals. For example, employees working in a café should be able to perform the task of making coffee using the cappuccino machine. Incumbents who fail to satisfy this criterion would not be able to perform their job effectively, which would hinder the achievement of company goals. Task performance is usually contained in a job description, which has perhaps been overemphasised in developing criteria (Robertson & Smith, 2001).

Contextual performance relates to an incumbent's behaviour at work which promotes a positive working environment. This may include organisational citizenship behaviour (i.e. acting in ways which protect and promote the welfare of individuals, groups and the organisation) and also displaying altruism, courtesy and constructive feedback to others (Robertson & Smith, 2001).

These criteria are predicted to change as the environment and business management fashion changes, hence it is the responsibility of employees and employers alike to update task and contextual performance to ensure that employees are satisfied in the workplace and strategic goals can be achieved.

Furthermore, increasing emphasis on globalisation, work teams, communication and service orientation would increase the importance of criteria based on factors relating to teamwork, cross-cultural relations and expatriate assignment (Robertson & Smith, 2001).

> ## Please read
> Robertson, I. T. & Smith, M. (2001), 'Personnel selection', *Journal of Occupational and Organizational Psychology*, vol. 74, pp. 441–72.

IMPLICATIONS OF SELECTION METHODS AND CRITERIA

Because of the importance of selection methods and criteria in the development of an HR-focused competitive advantage, the practicality of selection methods have been subjected to extensive research and scrutiny by industrial and organisational psychologists (Hough & Oswald, 2000). The areas of concern relate to three important issues: reliability, validity and legality.

RELIABILITY

Reliability refers to the degree to which interviews, tests and other selection procedures produce comparable data over a period of time and the degree to which two or more methods produce similar results or are consistent. For example, inter-rater reliability may be employed, whereby two raters code data and then compare results until all discrepancies have been resolved. This may be employed when a candidate completes a qualitative test (i.e. written) or when an interview is conducted and notes are taken which need to be analysed. Reliability is even more important in qualitative (i.e. words) work than in quantitative (i.e. numbers) work because words are open to interpretation and there is a higher risk of error due to subjectivity. Thus, the data is then reliable and may confidently contribute to selection decisions.

reliability
The degree to which interviews, tests and other selection procedures yield comparable data over a period of time and the degree to which two or more methods yield similar results or are consistent.

VALIDITY

Reliability and validity tend to go hand in hand. Hence, **validity** refers to the extent to which something measures what it claims to measure. This is important when candidates are completing tests to ensure that the correct behaviour, knowledge or ability is being measured as it will contribute to the selection decision of that candidate. There are various types of validity that HR managers need to consider in the development and use of selection methods (see Table 8.2). Reliability and validity are vital for determining future candidates' success and to achieve strategic business objectives.

validity
The extent to which something measures what it claims to measure.

LEGALITY

A selection method should also be assessed against current employment legislation, particularly with respect to employment opportunities legislation. Selection is a venerable process under law because it involves judgements about people that tend to evoke perceptions of fairness/unfairness (Caruth &

TABLE **8.2**　**Types of validity**

Type of validity	Definition
Construct-related validity	The degree to which a selection method actually reflects the theoretical construct it is designed to assess
Content-related validity	The extent to which a selection method (e.g. interview) adequately tests the knowledge, skills and abilities required for a particular job
Criterion-related validity	The extent to which the result from a selection method (e.g. résumé) adequately predicts or correlates with job performance criteria (e.g. customer satisfaction)
Concurrent validity	Involves assessing a sample of existing employees on the criterion predictor (e.g. cognitive test) and if the scores employees obtained on the criterion predictor correlate with performance (e.g. sales output), the criterion predictor is regarded as usable in the selection process of new employees. This type of validity falls under criterion-related validity
Predictive validity	Involves assessing all applicants on the criterion predictor; however, the scores are ignored when making a hiring decision. If, after a specified period, a correlation exists between the criterion predictor (e.g. interview decisions) and the criterion (e.g. customer satisfaction), the criterion predictor is regarded as usable in the future selection process. This type of test falls under criterion-related validity

Handlogten, 1997). Perceptions are very important for HR managers to consider in all aspects of SHRM, not just in selection, because individuals perceive things differently. For example, what an interviewer perceives to be unethical behaviour may be perceived by the candidate as ethical. Therefore, especially with regard to selection, HR managers need to ensure that organisational representatives involved in the selection process are well trained in legal matters.

Among HRM activities, selection has been most exposed to discrimination charges and lawsuits (Caruth & Handlogten, 1997). If the selection decision is in the candidate's favour, the procedure is likely to be viewed as fair, avoiding the possibility of costly litigation. However, organisations should carefully plan, choose and implement their selection methods in order to increase their perceived fairness by all candidates.

Organisations tend to avoid a legal challenge if the selection method has the following four characteristics:

1. Job relatedness
2. An opportunity for the candidate to demonstrate ability
3. Sympathetic interpersonal treatment
4. Questions that are not perceived as improper.

Contemporary SHRM Application Tool

Imagine that you are an HR manager of a large-sized petroleum company with more than 100 000 employees across diverse operations in 100 countries. Today, Australian employers are working hard to retain their top talented employees in their competitive respective labour markets. The record low unemployment and shortage of skilled workers have made retention and development of high-calibre employees the top priority of managers. Your company is no exception. In the petroleum industry, recruitment of female engineers (electronic engineers in particular) has been a major challenge. However, you find an opportunity in the midst of this. After monitoring your business environment (internal and external) and current trends, you have decided to create an HR recruitment strategy leveraging on the existing core company value of a discriminatory-free environment where human rights and work–life balance are emphasised. You are just about to take action to recruit a potential minority target group – female engineers. The SHRM Application Tool helps you with the appropriate decision-making steps (refer to Figure 8.5).

FIGURE 8.5
SHRM Application Tool:
opportunity – recruitment

Step 6: Evaluate against success criteria
- Did the recruitment strategy result in attracting more female engineers?
- How many more % of female engineers return to work after maternity leave?
- Did the recruitment strategy result in more % of female managers
- Did the recruitment strategy result in more innovation and productivity after 3 years of its implementation?

Step 5: Implement the plan
- Establish flexible work initiatives allowing women to work part time for up to 4 years
- Across all engineers, flexible hours to be applied
- Company sponsored crèche close to the office
- Establish childcare fees out of pre-tax income
- Incentives to pay for nanny in the case of interstate or international business travel
- Conduct an information session for female engineers (both graduate recruitment and internal promotion)
- Preferred mix of salary and approved non-salary benefits

Step 4: Devise plan and success criteria
- Recruit (internal or external) at least 10 electronic engineers from female target group every year in each branch
- Make all staff aware of company openness towards general equality through intranet, website, newsletters and posters
- Specific recruitment (attraction) strategy to ensure that the female target group is informed of the different work options available
- Create female-friendly workplace
- Promote minority recruitment agenda (e.g. gender, race and disability)

Step 3: Verify/falsify potential problem or opportunity
- Recruitment of female electronic engineers to find ourselves a competitive edge in the competitive 'engineer' labour market

Verify | Falsify

Step 2: Detect potential problem or opportunity
- High-calibre electronic engineers being poached by competitors
- Attracting best and brightest electronic engineers – especially female
- Attracting other minority group members such as Asians, South Africans and Middle Eastern employees

Step 1: Analyse environmental factors

Step 1a: HR issues: Monitor/analyse data (past, present and future)	Step 1b: Internal/organisational environment	Step 1c: External environment
• Staff development and retention as organisation's highest priority • Attracting suitable employees as second highest priority • Increasing investment on the retention of skilled workers • Recruitment of high-tech females has been a challenge due to people's view of electronic engineering as a male-oriented career	• 'Creativity, innovation and motivation' is our business slogan • Commitment to human rights • Respect each employee's need to work–life balance • Fair and open working environment where discriminatory behaviours are unacceptable • Fairly hierarchical structure due to large-sized enterprise	• Record low unemployment • Diminishing pool of qualified workers including electronic engineers • Other petroleum companies try to poach our top talent (position-filling battle going on) • Shift in the wage structure from award-based to individual-based contract. Possible reduction in engineers' wages • Multicultural labour market

The recruitment and selection challenge – a creative approach

A major Australian rural city council has taken a creative approach to the recruitment and selection of homecare staff.

At first glance, recruitment and selection for a home carer seem a simple task for the council. The work itself is relatively straightforward. It requires the home carer to visit a client's home regularly to provide basic household cleaning, prepare and cook meals and assist with banking and transport to medical appointments. The client relationship can be ongoing for either a long- or short-term period, depending on the client's need. This certainly presents as a straightforward exercise. However, surprisingly, the recruitment and selection process was fraught with problems!

Each time job opportunities were advertised the council received hundreds of applications of varying quality. Many applicants did not address the selection criteria, despite this requirement being made very clear in all advertisements. The large number of applications and the failure by many applicants to address the selection criteria made the screening and shortlisting process administratively heavy. The council was also concerned that the failure of some candidates to address the selection criteria might result in their applications not being given fair consideration, thereby compromising its commitment to equity and fairness in the selection process.

This rural city, like many in Australia, has been badly affected by 10 years of drought. Employment opportunities are limited, therefore many residents and ratepayers are interested in these job vacancies. The process for selection of candidates was, as a consequence, subject to close scrutiny by the local community. The council needed to ensure information was readily available and opportunities were extended to all interested parties. The selection process also needed to be easily understood, transparent and defendable if subject to criticism.

A further complication was the fact that a high proportion of newly recruited staff left in a relatively short timeframe. Twenty per cent of new employees left within three months of commencing their jobs. This trend worsened despite interventions, including the provision of induction training and the support of a 'buddy' system during the first two weeks of employment. Exit interviews revealed that many of those leaving found that 'the job was not what they expected'. Anecdotal information suggested that the new employees had not clearly understood the demands of the job. Comments such as 'I know I can clean and cook but it is hard to do that in someone else's house' and 'I don't like working with the oldies' were reported back to the council.

The council had benchmarked the cost of recruiting and selecting new staff and estimated that filling each vacancy cost around 30 per cent of a home carer's annual salary. When a new starter left within six months, the entire process was repeated, which meant that cost was doubled. There was clearly a need to improve the return on investment for these recruitment and selection exercises. Client relationships were also seriously affected by this turnover rate. Homecare is a personal service, providing invaluable assistance to housebound elderly or vulnerable clients. The service is both physical (i.e. cleaning) and personal (i.e. social interaction) and generally both of these components are important to clients. The issues of continuity and relationship are also imperative when considering a client's experience of the service and overall assessment of the quality.

The Aged and Disability Services Manager and her team decided it was time to try some innovative strategies to combat this recruitment problem. They developed a multifaceted approach to the recruitment campaign and selection process.

Advertising

The team developed an alternative approach to traditional recruitment strategies. Jobs were announced through advertisements in local newspapers and on library and community centre noticeboards. Potential candidates were invited to attend an information session to learn more about the opportunities in the homecare area.

Information sessions

The information sessions were offered in time slots suited to the potential candidate pool. Many of the current staff, and those traditionally interested in the positions, had family responsibilities or commitments, such as morning and evening milking on dairy farms. As a consequence, the sessions were offered mid-morning (while children were at school or kindergarten) and early evening (after milking was finished) to ensure they were accessible to all interested applicants.

The sessions were carefully planned to explain the nature of the work, hours, pay and the selection process. The Aged and Disability Services Manager and a team leader spoke about council's homecare service, expectations of staff and the selection process. Two homecare workers also participated in the information sessions, discussing what the work would entail and their experience as home carers. At the conclusion of the sessions, potential candidates were served refreshments and invited to talk informally to council staff.

Information pack

An information pack was prepared and made available at the end of the session. The pack included general information on the council, the homecare service, a job description and an application form. This pack was also available online, via council's website and in hardcopy from council offices. The information pack signalled clearly that further questions would be welcomed and key contact details were provided.

The outcomes

This new strategy generated some expected and unexpected outcomes.

The process of advertising, preparing information packs, scheduling and conducting information sessions was time consuming; however, the Community Services team believed it was worthwhile because of the efficiency it created in other areas.

As a result of the new approach, the council found it was receiving a smaller number of applications for vacant roles. Those received were, however, of a higher quality and the use of a structured application form forced most candidates to address the selection criteria. As a consequence, the process of shortlisting was much more streamlined and less time consuming.

The goodwill that the council generated among the local community (by investing such effort in communicating widely the opportunities and explaining the work and selection process) was a bonus; it certainly was not anticipated. Previously, many potential candidates found the formality and perceived bureaucracy of the council to be daunting. The information session allowed real people, the 'home carers', to talk about the work in a very straightforward and down to earth fashion. An improved understanding helped on a number of levels; some people decided that (based on information provided) this was not the job for them. The real-life examples made others really enthusiastic about pursuing the opportunity. Those charged with the selection decisions found they had more suitable candidates than positions available, which was a welcome change! After discussions with the Aged and Disability Services Manager and team leaders, the selection panel approached a number of unsuccessful candidates to explore their interest in becoming part of a relief pool of temporary carers who could cover peak periods and relief commitments of existing staff.

At this stage, it is too early to judge the effect of the new approach on turnover in the homecare area. However, the team believe that new staff have a much clearer understanding of the work and its demands and hope that they will see fewer resignations as a result of 'the job not being what they expected'.

Only time will tell!

Discussion questions

1. Imagine you are the CEO of the council. You have three vacancies for civil engineers (graduate entry level). Civil engineers are scarce and there is fierce competition for new graduates. How could you apply the learnings from this case study to the recruitment of engineers? What else would you do?

2. How could the information sessions be used to communicate the culture of the organisation and explore the psychological contract?

3. How realistic was the council's benchmark of the costs of recruitment and selection? Identify the direct and indirect costs of recruitment and selection. Use these to make a judgement about the accuracy of the council's benchmark.

4. Identify an organisation you have worked for or one you know well. Could this approach be used to address a recruitment and selection challenge in that organisation? What internal and external difficulties might it encounter?

Virgin's wings clipped over discrimination case — A manager's challenge

Virgin Airlines were left red faced over a successful discrimination claim by eight former Ansett flight attendants. Eight mature-aged women filed for discrimination after they were disqualified from the initial round of interviews for Virgin Blue Airlines between 2000 and 2002. The women, aged 36 to 56, claimed that they had been rejected for consideration for the positions due to their age by assessors who favoured 'young and beautiful' women. The rejection of the eight early on came despite significant work experience from Ansett Airlines, one of the women having accrued 37 years in total from the now defunct airline.

The interviews required applicants to exhibit theatrical flair by singing and dancing, effectively targeting young and beautiful employees. The selectors also emphasised the 'Virgin flair', which was stated to be a willingness to embrace fun in interactions with customers. The eight complainants outlined the role of youth and beauty in the selection of applicants, claiming that applicants fulfilling these criteria were eagerly accepted during first-round interviews.

The case was heard by the Queensland Anti-Discrimination Tribunal with seven of the women awarded compensation for economic loss, and another, Alma Frank, receiving $5000 compensation for 'hurt, humiliation and the like'. The tribunal found that the criteria were fair, but judged that the method of recruitment involved unconscious discrimination on the part of selectors. Tribunal member Douglas Savage criticised the selection officers, composed of mostly young people lacking significant experience. Mr Savage claimed they unconsciously favoured applicants of similar social class and age, resulting in a homogenous selection that ignored people over 36 years.

Virgin Airlines spokeswoman Heather Jeffrey rejected the findings, claiming that her employment as a woman over 40 proved Virgin was not averse to employing mature-aged women. However, during a two-year period the number of flight attendants over 36 employed by Virgin numbered only one, which Ms Jeffrey claimed was due to a low percentage of this age group applying for the positions. Yet, the number of people at or over 36 who applied was found to be close to 750. The case effectively put pressure on the interview and selection process at the airline. Theresa Stewart, one of the complainants, claimed the eight women were not the only people who emerged victorious, with the number of cabin crew aged over 36 employed by the company having increased in recent years. The desire to glorify a particular image of youth and beauty has proven to be costly for Virgin, which is now looking to the future with a more mature, experienced and balanced workforce.

Source: Adapted from Gregory, J. (2005), 'Virgin rapped over age discrimination', *Herald Sun*, 11 October; Meade, K. (2005), 'Women win age case against Virgin', *The Australian*, 11 October; Todd, M. (2005), 'Virgin Blue loses age discrimination case', *The Age*, 10 October.

Summary

This chapter highlighted the importance of strategic recruitment and selection for HR managers. For organisations to obtain a competitive advantage there needs to be a clear link between organisational strategies and resources. This may be achieved through human resource planning (HRP), which is the first step in recruitment. It involves ongoing environmental scanning and an analysis of organisational objectives, strategies and policies in order to ascertain the right quantity and quality of employees when and where necessary. In other words, it is forecasting HR needs to ensure that the organisation has the right amount of human resources when they require them. This is an important, proactive approach because when new markets emerge or the company expands, organisations that have conducted HRP will have the right number of skilled employees when they need them. A failure to plan will result in companies becoming preoccupied with obtaining, culling or training staff, by which time their competitors would have achieved both their market share and a competitive advantage. HRP involves scanning the internal and external environment to determine what skills current employees have and what are required (in response to market changes), and has evolved over time from a regulatory mechanism to a control mechanism and, finally, to a contemporary mechanism designed to create a competitive advantage through strategic HR planning.

As a strategic process, HRP has three major steps. *Demand forecasting* involves estimating the quantity and quality of employees required to meet organisational objectives; however, it is restricted by the quality and quantity of HR availability in the external labour market. Demand forecasting may be undertaken quantitatively (i.e. using numbers) and/or qualitatively (i.e. using words). Examples of quantitative approaches include trend projection and multiple regression, whereas examples of qualitative approaches include the Delphi technique and the nominal group technique (NGT).

Supply forecasting determines the current supply of human resources in the labour market, which may be determined by searching internally (i.e. within the company) or externally (i.e. outside the company). For example, an HR manager can use the skills inventory form to determine the internal supply of labour, such as the number of staff qualified for a vacant position and whether they are eligible for a promotion. The final step is *filling the gap between demand and supply to ensure skill optimisation*. To do this, managers need to analyse the supply and demand and forecast appropriately.

Once HRP has successfully and thoroughly been conducted, job analysis should be conducted. This is a systematic analysis of the tasks, duties and responsibilities of a job as well as the necessary knowledge, skills and abilities a person needs to perform the job adequately. A *job analysis* comprises three components: job description, person specification and job context. A *job description* (also referred to as a position description, or PD) outlines the broad nature of a job. It also contains a list of the key tasks the employee is expected to perform, their duties and/or obligations, the qualifications or prerequisites required to perform the job and the job responsibilities. A *person specification* outlines the knowledge, skills and abilities a person requires to perform the job adequately. *Job context* refers to the situational and supporting information regarding the job, such as work climate, reporting relationships and unspoken rules. There are various methods for analysing jobs, such as structured questionnaires, 360-degree feedback, a diary and direct observation.

After job analysis has been performed, and HR managers are satisfied with the results, a job needs to be designed. This refers to the way that an entire job is organised and categorised and it focuses on the needs of the incumbent. It includes *job specialisation* (the process of employees performing standardised, repetitive tasks so that analysts can record what the job involves and how long it takes to perform each task), *job enlargement* (the horizontal expansion of a job by allocating to it a variety of similar-level skills and new responsibilities), *job rotation* (increasing task variety by shifting employees from one task to another task), *job enrichment* (the vertical expansion of a job by increasing the amount of employee control or responsibility) and *job evaluation* (an analytical tool which determines the relative worth of the job with the aim of providing fair and objective pay).

The chapter then focused on the HRM functions of strategic recruitment and selection. Once the planning of human resources has been established, and job analysis and job design are completed, it is necessary to begin recruiting employees. Recruitment is the process of generating a pool of qualified candidates for a particular job who can contribute best to the strategic objectives of the organisation and involves both the organisation and the applicant identifying *what* jobs need to be filled and *how* the most suitable candidates will be attracted. People can be recruited from two sources. *Internal attraction activities* involve the organisation looking internally for its HR needs and include using search mechanisms involving the company intranet, company newsletters, noticeboards and job bidding or the human resource information system (HRIS). *External attraction activities* focus on developing a pool of candidates from outside the organisation and include using search mechanisms such as the Internet (e.g. seek.com, careerone.com, company and professional association websites), newspapers and magazines to advertise, in addition to job fairs (such as those at universities), recruitment agencies and word of mouth. However, managers need to be aware of the drawbacks of these sources and take them into consideration when using them.

The use of technology in recruitment has increased due to the increased ease and efficiency technology provides for the recruitment process. E-recruitment (or online recruitment) refers to the process of recruiting via the intranet (internal) and Internet (external) and is advantageous because of the unlimited exposure (vast reach of potential candidates); the lack or lessening of advertising costs; the immediate advertisement of job vacancies which can be accessed 24 hours a day; the unlimited length of advertising material (flexibility); and the integration of the recruitment system with other computerised HR functions, such as payroll and employee databases.

The next phase after recruitment is to select strategically employees to fill vacant positions. Selection is the process of identifying candidates who can best contribute to the strategic objectives of the organisation, and it involves three questions to be addressed by HR managers: What is the candidate's *can do* ability?, What is the candidate's *will do* ability?, How well will the applicant *fit* into the organisation? These questions can be answered by analysing a variety of selection methods such as application forms, résumés, interviews, psychological tests (e.g. cognitive ability or personality tests), assessment centres, biographical information blanks, references, polygraphs (lie detector test), integrity tests, graphology and medical examinations. Generally, most companies use application forms, résumés and interviews, although other methods employed will be dependent on the type of job. Commonly, a variety of selection methods are used to complement each other and provide a more thorough selection process.

Once the selection methods have been conducted, it is important to develop the selection criteria. This refers to key work-related factors used in making the decision to hire or not to hire a person, for example the qualifications, experience, special skills and abilities of the incumbent. Selection criteria should be established based upon two areas of performance. *Task performance* relates to an individual's ability to perform tasks that are associated with the job, and which contribute to the achievement of organisational goals. In contrast, *contextual performance* relates to an incumbent's behaviour at work which promotes a positive working environment, for example organisational citizenship behaviour, being courteous and providing constructive feedback to others.

Finally, this chapter discussed some implications of selection methods and criteria. These may be classified into three issues. *Reliability* refers to the degree to which interviews, tests and other selection procedures produce comparable data over a period of time and the degree to which two or more methods produce similar results or are consistent. *Validity* refers to the extent to which something measures what it claims to measure (refer to Table 8.2 for a list of the different types of validity). Lastly, the legality of the selection process needs to be considered. HR managers should consider whether the process is fair, equitable and conducted within legal requirements to avoid legal ramifications. In doing so, they must also consider how different behaviour may be perceived differently by people, such as what constitutes ethical behaviour. As a guide, organisations may avoid a legal challenge if the selection method has job relatedness, an opportunity for the candidate to demonstrate ability, sympathetic interpersonal treatment and questions that are not perceived as being improper.

Key terms

assessment centres	interviews	multiple regression
biographical information blanks	job analysis	nominal group technique
	job context	person specification
Delphi technique	job description	psychological test
demand forecasting	job design	recruitment
employment tests	job enlargement	recruitment agencies
e-recruitment	job enrichment	reliability
external attraction activities	job evaluation	selection
external labour supply	job rotation	selection criteria
external scanning	job specialisation	skills inventory form
human resource planning	macro internal HR information	360-degree feedback
internal attraction activities		trend projection
internal labour supply	micro internal HR information	validity
internal scanning		

Review questions

8.1 What is human resource planning (HRP)? Explain the three steps in HRP, using examples for each.

8.2 Job analysis is an important concept for HR managers to be aware of before recruitment and selection can be conducted. What is the difference between job analysis,

job description, person specification and job context? Are all of these processes performed by HR managers?

8.3 What is job design? Briefly identify and discuss each of the five processes in job design and include an example for each using the job of a café waitress/waiter.

8.4 Devise a list of the benefits and disadvantages of recruiting internally and externally. Which one would you use if you were the HR manager of a (a) large multinational company and (b) small, local company?

8.5 What are the three questions that HR managers need to consider when selecting incumbents for vacant positions? Describe, using examples, some selection methods that are used by HR managers. Which ones are most common and why?

Exercises

8.1 Visit the O*NET website at <http://online.onetcenter.org> and examine the examples of contemporary job analyses. Write down a list of key points you learn from this and compare these with others in your class.

8.2 Imagine you are the HR manager of a local florist on the Gold Coast in Queensland which employs one full-time employee, two part-time staff and one delivery driver. Industry experts are forecasting a surge in sales over the next five years as holiday makers plan visits to the Gold Coast. Devise a human

resource plan to accommodate for the supply and demand, taking into consideration the fact that it is a very busy time for Queensland in the summer holidays, but not as busy over the winter.

8.3 Tsutomu Tanaka is the owner of Devine Sushi, a sushi café in Melbourne. The café is expanding and Tsutomu needs to hire a new employee to prepare and make sushi. Write up a job description which demonstrates the knowledge, skills, ability and relevant experience required for this vacant position. (Hint: Refer to Figure 8.4.)

References

Caruth, D. L. & Handlogten, G. D. (1997), *Staffing the Contemporary Organization: A Guide to Planning, Recruiting, and Selecting for Human Resource Professionals*, Praeger, Westport.

Earl, J., Bright, J. F. H. R. & Adams, A. (1998), '"In My Opinion": What gets graduate résumés short-listed?', *Australian Journal of Career Development*, vol. 7, pp. 15–19.

Hall, R. (2000), 'Outsourcing, contracting-out and labour hire: Implications for human resource development in Australian organizations', *Asia Pacific Journal of Human Resources*, vol. 38, no. 2, pp. 23–34.

Heneman, H., Judge, T. & Heneman, R. (2000), *Staffing Organizations*, McGraw-Hill, Boston.

Hough, L. M. & Oswald, F. L. (2000), 'Personnel selection: Looking toward the future–remembering the past', *Annual Review of Psychology*, vol. 51, pp. 631–64.

Huselid, M. A. (1993), 'The impact of environmental volatility on human resource planning and strategic human resource management', *Human Resource Planning*, vol. 16, no. 3, pp. 35–51.

Idris, A. R. & Eldridge, D. (1998). 'Re-conceptualizing human resource planning in response to institutional change', *International Journal of Manpower*, vol. 19, no. 5, pp. 343–57.

IRS, (2001), 'E-recruitment: Online express or delayed arrival?', *IRS Employment Review*, vol. 734, pp. 10–12.

Kossek, E., Young, W., Gash, D. & Nichol, V. (1994). 'Waiting for innovation in the human resource department: Godot implements a human resource information system', *Human Resource Management*, vol. 33, no. 1, pp. 135–59.

Nankervis, A. R. & Leece, P. (1997), 'Performance appraisal: Two steps forward, one step back?', *Asia Pacific Journal of Human Resources*, vol. 35, no. 2, pp. 80–92.

Oakland, T. (2004), 'Use of educational and psychological tests internationally', *Applied Psychology: An International Review*, vol. 53, no. 2, pp. 157–72.

Petersen, N. G., Mumford, M. D., Borman, W. C., Jeanneret, P. R. & Fleishman, E. A. (1999), *An Occupational Information System for the 21st Century: The Development of O*NET*', American Psychological Association, Washington.

Ployhart, R. E., Schneider, B. & Schmitt, N. (2006), *Staffing Organizations: Contemporary Practice and Theory*, Lawrence Erlbaum Associates, Mahwah.

Robertson, I. T., Baron, H., Gibbons, P., MacIver, R. & Nyfield, G. (2000), 'Conscientiousness and managerial performance', *Journal of Occupational and Organizational Psychology*, vol. 73, pp. 171–80.

Robertson, I. T. & Smith, M. (2001), 'Personnel selection', *Journal of Occupational and Organizational Psychology*, vol. 74, pp. 441–72.

SHL Group (2001), *Guidelines for Best Practices in the Use of Job Analysis Techniques*, SHL Group, Surrey.

Stewart, G. & Carson, K. (1997), 'Moving beyond the mechanistic model: An alternative approach to staffing for contemporary organizations', *Human Resource Management Review*, vol. 7, no. 2, pp. 157–84.

Thomason, G. F. (1988), *A Textbook of Human Resource Management*, Institute of Personnel Management, London.

Ulrich, D. (1987), 'Strategic human resource planning: Why and how?', *Human Resource Planning*, vol. 10, no. 1, pp. 37–56.

Watkins, L. & Johnston, L. (2000), 'Screening job applicants: The impact of physical attractiveness and application quality', *International Journal of Selection and Assessment*, vol. 8, pp. 76–84.

Werbel, J. & Johnson, D. J. (2001), 'The use of person–group fit for employment selection: A missing link in person–environment fit', *Human Resource Management*, vol. 40, no. 3, pp. 227–40.

Wilson, I. (1994), 'Strategic planning isn't dead – it changed', *Long Range Planning*, vol. 27, no. 4, pp. 12–24.

Chapter 9

The training and development of employees

INTRODUCTION

In order to survive in today's fiercely competitive business environment, organisations need to develop systems to improve employee performance. This is one of the key responsibilities of HR managers and it may be achieved via the HRM function of training and development. Companies that effectively train and develop their human capital experience reduced costs, improved product and/or service quality, enhanced innovation and knowledge management techniques, increased productivity and, as a result, high consumer loyalty, customer satisfaction and return on investment (ROI).

However, in reality, the training and development process is a complex task with a variety of HRM implications. For example, despite Australian government training initiatives (e.g. financial investment and the increased recognition of the importance of training for the Australian economy), Australia still suffers from a skills shortage in certain professions, such as nurses and chefs. In fact, Australian immigration policies have recently been adjusted to encourage qualified chefs to migrate to Australia because of the visible skill shortage. Although such policy changes have not been implemented for nurses, the current skill shortage, which is especially evident in mental health nursing, is expected to increase in the future. This has many implications for the competitive position of the Australian economy. Organisations need to retain skilled workers through effective training and development if they are to survive and compete in the international arena. Therefore, training and development are not just desired components of SHRM, but rather vital pieces of the complex HRM puzzle.

This chapter focuses on training and development as indispensable tools that allow organisations to bridge the gap between actual performance and desired performance (e.g. knowledge, skills and abilities). Specifically, an understanding of training and development is a crucial aspect of applying the SHRM application tool to advance employees' contributions toward continuous organisational development. This chapter focuses on the importance of training and development for the holistic growth of the organisation by identifying emerging learning theories, the practical steps of training and its delivery, and significant aspects of employee development.

Objectives

The primary objective of this chapter is to enable you to apply the SHRM Application Tool by using your knowledge of training and development. The concept of training and development is important for HR managers and employees to consider as it forms part of the overall HRM function and enables the strategic achievement of organisational goals.

After reading this chapter you should be able to:

- understand the significance of training and development for the Australian workforce;
- understand the aim of employee learning and the two orientations to learning;
- explain the contemporary learning approach;
- understand the link between learning and training;
- identify the four fundamental steps of the training systems approach;
- distinguish between training and development;
- understand the links between development, the employee orientation process and the career development process;
- explain how training and development activities contribute toward organisational development.

Significance of training and development

In 2005 the Australian job market permanently lost an estimated 50 000 skilled workers, with a further 170 000 workers leaving the country for more than 12 months to obtain higher pay in the American and European markets (Anon, 2005). This loss is devastating for the Australian economy as the loss of a substantial number of skilled employees in effect increases the competitive advantage of its competitors! Hence it is imperative that HR managers recognise the importance of training and retaining skilled employees to ensure that Australian organisations remain globally competitive.

Over time, organisational emphasis moved from manufacturing to the management of information, knowledge and human capital. This was heightened by the shift from the industrial evolution to the information era of the 1990s, and knowledge management has become a core competency for most firms. As such, this focus of training has transferred from manual skills to the development of conceptual and innovative skills which foster continuous learning (through training and development) and lead to the development of a learning organisation (see Chapter 3 for a discussion on knowledge, organisational learning and the learning organisation). However, while conceptual and innovative skills are important for the strategic survival of a company, they provide a holistic approach to training and development only and it is necessary to maintain focus on the technical skills required by a majority of employees to achieve work tasks. As such, this chapter will address training and development in this realm, beginning with a discussion of employee learning, which forms the foundation of this important HRM function.

Employee learning

The aim of training and development is to maximise employees' learning of new skills, knowledge, attitudes and behaviours to cope with the demands of a dynamic environment; consequently, an understanding of learning theories and practices is crucial. **Learning** is defined as a *lifelong change* in attitudes, behaviours and cognition as a result of one's interaction with the surrounding environment (Merriam & Caffarella, 1998).

> **learning**
> A lifelong change in attitudes, behaviours and cognition as a result of one's interaction with the surrounding environment.

A number of factors affect the way each individual learns, for example past experiences, cultural influences, level of resilience, perceptions and preferred approaches to learning. Some people prefer to learn from practical application (i.e. actually performing the task), others learn visually (i.e. reading instruction manuals or watching videos) and others learn cognitively (i.e. by thought). As such, HR managers and trainers need to consider how each individual learns best (also referred to as the 'learner-based approach') as this underscores the training and development process.

Bloom's (1956) taxonomy identifies three domains of employee learning which inform the training and development process: the cognitive domain, the affective domain and the motor skill domain. First, the *cognitive domain* refers to mental skills. This includes knowledge, comprehension, application, analysis, synthesis, evaluation and problem-solving skills (e.g. knowledge of organisational or departmental cultures, norms and policies, or the innovation of new products and services). Second, the *affective domain* refers to feelings, values, appreciation, enthusiasm, motivation and attitudes. This includes how employees receive and respond to phenomena according to their value system toward a particular object, event or behaviour. Finally, the *motor skill domain* refers to manual or physical skills. The development of this skill requires hands-on practice and is measured in terms of speed, precision, distance, procedures and techniques (e.g. performing a sequence of steps in a manufacturing process, using a personal computer or repairing a leaking pipe).

Orientations to learning

There is no doubt that employee learning underpins the process of training and development. However, managers need to understand how employees actually learn. There are two distinctive theories (or orientations) which guide trainers in the workplace: the *behavioural* orientation to learning and the *cognitive* orientation to learning. These theories should be used by managers and training practitioners to apply the learning objectives to training session goals, plans, design and delivery. Once trainers understand how people learn, they can then develop a learner-centred training approach which increases the likelihood of training success and, consequently, the likelihood that a higher return on training investment (ROTI) will be achieved.

THE BEHAVIOURAL ORIENTATION TO LEARNING

behavioural orientation to learning
Emphasises changing behaviour through reinforcement and punishment and is advocated by a number of behavioural psychologists.

The **behavioural orientation to learning** emphasises changing behaviour through reinforcement and punishment and is advocated by a number of behavioural psychologists. For example, call operator instructors often coach trainees by praising any actions which are close to the desired behaviour. As the trainee becomes more competent, however, the instructor will praise only those behaviours that are precisely accurate.

This orientation to learning is illustrated by Pavlov's (1927) classical conditioning and Skinner's (1975) operant conditioning experiments. Both Pavlov's and Skinner's behavioural studies, outlined next, demonstrate the importance of external stimuli to learning and also reveal the observable and measurable behaviours that substantiate learning outcomes.

CLASSICAL CONDITIONING

The concept of classical conditioning was first described by Russian psychologist Ivan Pavlov. Pavlov discovered this type of learning by accident while conducting research into the digestive system of dogs. While conducting his research, Pavlov noticed that the dogs would begin to salivate prior to being presented with food, for example when the person who was going to feed them entered the room. Exploring this phenomenon further, Pavlov began pairing a bell sound with feeding the dogs and found that, eventually, even when the dogs were not presented with any food, they would begin to salivate simply upon hearing the bell. To summarise, the key concepts related to classical conditioning can be identified as:

- *Unconditioned stimulus.* A stimulus that will naturally elicit a response such as the smell of food or touching a hot object.
- *Unconditioned response.* The response which is naturally elicited by a stimulus, such as salivating at the smell of food or pulling your hand away from a hot object.
- *Conditioned stimulus.* A stimulus which is paired with a naturally occurring stimulus, such as the ring of a bell with the smell of food or the sounding of an alarm when touching a hot object.
- *Conditioned response.* A response learned through the pairing of a conditioned stimulus with an unconditioned stimulus, such as salivating when a bell rings or pulling your hand away from an object when you hear an alarm.

The findings of Pavlov's studies (along with further research into the phenomenon of classical conditioning) indicate that people learn to develop a response to a stimulus that is not naturally occurring. For example, this might include a song or a smell triggering a memory. In an organisational context, classical conditioning indicates that organisations can use an external stimulus or conditioning to encourage learning.

OPERANT CONDITIONING

Operant conditioning was developed by Skinner (1975) in the attempt to further Pavlov's classical conditioning research. The key principle of operant conditioning is the use of rewards and punishments to encourage desirable behaviours and to discourage undesirable behaviours. There are four types of operant conditioning that trainers need to be aware of when training employees.

Positive reinforcement occurs when behaviour is strengthened as a consequence of experiencing a positive condition. For example, in laboratory settings a mouse may press a lever and receive food. If the mouse presses the lever a second time it receives food again. As such, the mouse's behaviour is strengthened as a result of the positive condition experienced and it will continue to press the lever as long as behaviour is rewarded.

Negative reinforcement occurs when behaviour is strengthened as a consequence of avoiding or terminating a negative experience. For example, if the laboratory mouse presses a lever and receives an electric shock (instead of food) and presses the lever again and the shock discontinues, then the mouse's behaviour is strengthened by the consequence of being able to avoid or terminate the negative experience.

Punishment refers to when behaviour is weakened as a consequence of experiencing negative conditions. Drawing on the previous example, if the mouse receives an electric shock every time it presses a lever (instead of food), then it quickly learns to avoid pressing the lever as it results in a negative experience. Hence the behaviour is weakened in response to the negative condition experienced.

Extinction refers to the situation where behaviour is weakened as a result of (1) not experiencing a positive condition or (2) terminating a negative condition. For example, if the mouse presses the lever and nothing happens, the mouse is likely to press the lever again to check whether a response (i.e. food or electric shock) is received. When still no response results, the mouse's behaviour is weakened by no experience of positive conditions or the terminating of negative conditions.

Behavioural orientations to learning are criticised as being 'determinist' because of their overemphasis on conditioning individuals' behaviours through environmental stimuli alone (Hampshire, 1950). Despite criticism, the operant conditioning concept has contributed significantly to the development of learning theory, indicating the importance of external stimuli (e.g. trainers' feedback or the learning environment) in achieving desired training outcomes.

THE COGNITIVE ORIENTATION TO LEARNING

Unsurprisingly, the behavioural orientation is disinterested in investigating the process of learning. It may be scientifically rigorous but it does not further our understanding of what happens inside the mind of a learner. Conversely, cognitive psychologists investigate precisely the mental or cognitive learning processes that occur through the learners' participation and motivations. Chapter 3 confirms that the workforce consists of knowledgeable and creative workers who, when properly managed, enable a learning organisation. Consequently, the **cognitive orientation to learning** emphasises changing behaviour through giving people information and the opportunity to process it mentally so they understand what correct behaviour is and how to perform it. Several researchers

cognitive orientation to learning
Emphasises changing behaviour through giving people information and the opportunity to process it mentally so they understand what correct behaviour is and how to perform it.

supported this orientation to learning, including Bandura (1989), Bruner (1961), Ausubel (1963) and Gagné (1985), as discussed next.

Bandura (1989), a social cognitive theorist, advocated that people's cognitive processes are engaged through their attention to the environment and behavioural modelling, which highlights the importance of having a role model upon which to base one's behaviour. His work bridged the gap between the behavioural orientation to learning and the cognitive orientation to learning.

Bruner (1961) argued that a categorisation in the mind is the principal activity involved in the learning process of a learner. Categorisation reduces the complexity of the environment and allows us to simplify situations, contexts and experiences. Burner suggested that this 'discovery learning' technique allows individuals the flexibility to maximise learning.

Ausubel (1963) and Gagné (1985) further developed the work of Bruner by stressing the important role of the trainer in reducing the inefficient use of time associated with the discovery learning approach, particularly in the case of learning complex concepts. In addition, Hartley (1998) outlined some key principles of cognitive learning as illustrated in Table 9.1.

TABLE 9.1   Key principles of cognitive learning

Instruction should be well-organised.	Well-organised materials easier to learn and to remember.
Instruction should be clearly structured.	Subject matters are said to have inherent structures (logical relationships between key ideas and concepts) which link the parts together.
The perceptual features of the task are important.	Learners attend selectively to different aspects of the environment. Thus, the way a problem is displayed is important if learners are to understand it.
Prior knowledge is important.	Things must fit with what is already known if it is to be learnt.
Differences between individuals are important as they will affect learning.	Differences in 'cognitive style' or methods of approach influence learning.
Cognitive feedback gives information to learners about their success or failure concerning the task at hand.	Reinforcement can come through giving information, a 'knowledge of results', rather than simply a reward.

Source: Hartley (1998).

It is evident, therefore, that the behavioural and cognitive orientations to learning differ. Trainers, in consultation with HR managers, need to determine the most appropriate orientation for their participants. This may be influenced by the trainers' own beliefs and style of preferred training, the purpose of training and the organisational culture. Despite the orientation chosen, some considerations for trainers which draw on both orientations include:

- People respond to external stimuli and reinforcement.
- A key feature of any training design should be a learner's orientation to learning.

- Information should be organised to facilitate learning.
- Training should move from simple concepts to more complex concepts.

THE CONTEMPORARY LEARNING APPROACH

Within the organisational context, trainers should view trainees as adult learners. Based upon the cognitive school of thought, adult learning advocates the experiential learning nature of employees. Adults are capable of organising, coordinating and synthesising their experiential knowledge into new skill sets and differ from children because, unlike children, adults *choose* to learn (Knowles, 1970). Consequently, organisations are advised to provide their employees with maximum opportunities to learn and develop their skills, abilities and knowledge. Therefore trainers need to account for several factors when developing training programs. These include *the role of the self* (e.g. being prepared for learners to make suggestions), *experience* (e.g. selecting activities that encourage learners to organise the knowledge from their personal experiences and create knowledge) and *facilitation* (e.g. being intelligently aware of the capacity, needs and past experiences of learners, as adults can link their past and present experiences through a thought analysis and a consideration to act more intelligently in the future).

Implicit in the contemporary learning approach is the concept of **experiential learning cycles**, which view individuals as self-directed learners who learn by trial and error. Experiential learning theory copes with rapidly changing environments by overcoming the slowness of traditional 'one-off' training deliveries (Kolb, 1984). Figure 9.1 explains the experiential learning cycle as a four-stage process of experiencing, reviewing, concluding and planning (Mumford & Honey, 1992). To illustrate this process using a training and development example, imagine an employee is using a new software program recently installed by the company. The employee begins learning the program by experiencing it; that is, they actually use the program to complete work tasks. The next stage of the learning is reviewing the experience whereby the employee evaluates whether the experience of using the program was, for example, positive, negative, easy, difficult, useful or valuable. Based upon this review, the employee proceeds to the next stage of learning which is concluding from the experience. In this stage, the employee determines what they could do to improve the use of the program. For example, if the experience was negative because they experienced many problems, then they may conclude that further assistance is required from the program developer or information technology (IT) consultant. The final stage involves the planning required to improve the learning experience for future use. Here, the employee acts on their suggested improvements by contacting the program developer or IT consultant for further guidance using the program.

It is therefore evident that experiential learning is an active, rather than passive, approach to learning. It is the ongoing daily process of acquiring knowledge, skills and abilities by 'doing' and is often termed action learning (McGill & Beaty, 1995), reflection learning (Seibert, 1999) or action reflection learning (Daudelin, 1996). All of these terms suggest the principle of a full learning cycle as well as some interplay between the action and reflection of a learner.

experiential learning cycles
View individuals as self-directed learners who learn by trial and error.

FIGURE 9.1
The experiential learning cycle

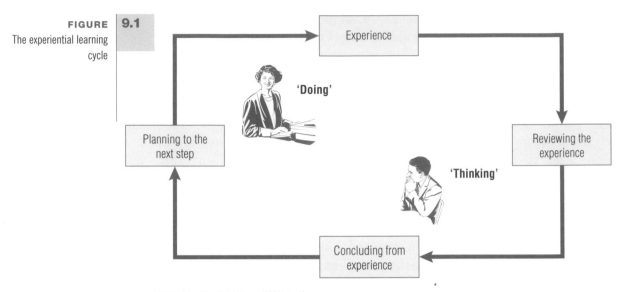

Source: Adapted from Mumford & Honey (1992), p. 10.

In today's rapidly changing business environment, the experiential learning cycle model illustrates the importance of trainers allowing individuals (and managers in particular) to reflect on their knowledge, skills and abilities in order to advance their work attributes. The trainer's role is to facilitate adult learners to find the gaps in their job-related knowledge, skills and abilities and then to fill that gap through relevant training and development activities. Trainers can further apply this theory to adult learners by including experiential activities in training programs and facilitating trainees to question and reflect on their actions.

The experiential learning cycle further asserts that there are two major styles of learning: those that 'do' believe in the concept of 'nothing ventured, nothing gained' and those that 'think' prefer to ponder and proceed more cautiously based on the belief of 'looking before you leap'. The learning cycle suggests that the combined learning attributes of doing and thinking produce a balanced learner who can engage in all four stages of the learning cycle, thereby achieving the maximum gain of new knowledge, skills, abilities, attitudes and behaviours.

Learning modes

Learning modes reflect the widely accepted belief that people generally remember or learn only 10 per cent of what they read, 20 per cent of what they hear, 30 per cent of what they see, 50 per cent of what they see and hear and 90 per cent of what they say and do (Treichler, 1967). Consequently, training by reading, hearing and seeing represents passive training, which is most suited to passive learners (Skinner, 1975). In contrast, training by saying and doing represents active training, which is most suited to active learners (Saettler, 1990). Depending on individual and organisational preferences, trainers should use multiple training methods to cater for both active and passive learners (see Figure 9.2).

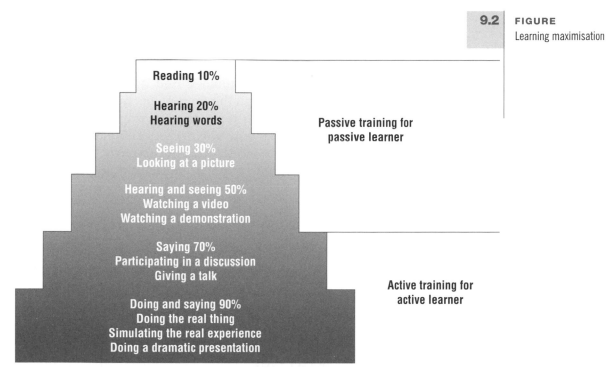

Reading 10%

Hearing 20%
Hearing words

Seeing 30%
Looking at a picture

Hearing and seeing 50%
Watching a video
Watching a demonstration

Saying 70%
Participating in a discussion
Giving a talk

Doing and saying 90%
Doing the real thing
Simulating the real experience
Doing a dramatic presentation

Passive training for
passive learner

Active training for
active learner

Source: Adapted from Treichler (1967) and Dale (1969), p. 107.

As mentioned earlier, learning forms the foundation for the HRM function of training and development. The training and development process plays a significant role in bridging the performance gap of the organisation's employees (i.e. their lack of knowledge, skills, abilities and positive motivation). This gap is identified in the gap analysis, to cope with identified threats and opportunities, as well as strengths and weaknesses (see Chapter 1 for a discussion of gap analysis).

Training and development is an integral part of the overall SHRM process and relates to other HRM concepts discussed previously: strategies to engage and motivate employees (Chapter 3), help employees adapt to new technology (Chapter 4), manage diversity (Chapter 5) and ensure employees are prepared to meet their ethical and legal responsibilities within the organisation (Chapter 6). Consequently, this chapter's focus now turns to training and development, demonstrating the importance of employee development to organisational development.

From learning to training

Given the dynamic nature of the international business environment, human capital is becoming an increasingly valuable and critical component of organisational competition. Globalisation, advances in technology, demanding consumers and decreased product life cycles are encouraging organisations to look beyond technical resources to improve competitive position and acknowledge the value of human capital. However, for human resources (i.e. resource-based view of HRM) to remain strategically viable, companies need to invest in the continuous training and development of employees.

training
The deliberate activities planned by an organisation to increase employee knowledge, skills and attitudes; occurs at particular times and in particular locations.

Training refers to the deliberate activities planned by an organisation to increase employee knowledge, skills and attitudes, and it occurs at particular times and in particular locations. Although the training of employees is usually coordinated by line and HR managers (in terms of what employees need to be trained in), employees should also take responsibility to identify which areas or skills of task performance they need to be trained in or improve upon. The HR manager then organises the appropriate training (either in house or external) depending on the specific requirements and demand for the training (i.e. if demand is high, then group training is an efficient option) and the qualified staff to teach the training, all, of course, within financial constraints. In many instances, in-house training is the financially preferred option as it is considerably more cost effective than external training. For example, if an employee is required to use Adobe®PageMaker® as part of their job, managers have two choices: ask another employee who is competent in this program to train their colleague (which does not cost the company additional dollars) or hire a consultant to train the employee. On average, external consultants charge between $1000 and $2500 per day to train employees, depending on the training content. As there are advantages and disadvantages for each option, HR managers need to consider training options carefully before embarking on them.

Training can take place in a variety of forms. For example:

- *Formal training.* This includes planned and structured training sessions such as learning about a new diversity policy. This type of training is usually documented on employee records (i.e. for performance management purposes) and is proactive.
- *Informal training.* This includes unplanned and unstructured planning such as showing a colleague how to format a document. Unlike formal training, this type of training is not documented as it occurs on a casual basis and it is usually (although not always) reactive.
- *On-the-job training.* This involves training which takes place within organisational settings. This type of training can either be formal or informal.
- *Off-the-job training.* This involves training which takes place externally to the organisation and is usually classified as formal training.

In addition to these four types of training, training can specifically take place in a variety of forms including: lectures, forums, videos, field trips, role plays, brainstorming sessions, coaching, computer-based learning, question and answer discussions, video and teleconferencing and simulations (refer to Step 3 of the training system approach discussed later in this chapter). All of these can also either be at the organisational, group or individual level and, in most situations, a variety of forms will be adopted to reiterate the training content.

TRADITIONAL AND CONTEMPORARY TRAINING

Recent data from the Australian Bureau of Statistics (ABS, 2003) reveals that 81 per cent of all Australian employers provide some form of training to their employees, therefore it is evident that training is a core component of business management. Further, research from the ABS (2003) indicates three predominant reasons for providing training:

1. to meet specified industry standards (specifically ISO 14000 for environmental management and ISO 9000 for quality management);
2. for organisational advancement; and
3. for the improvement of the quality of goods or services.

However, the provision of training is not just related to 'traditional' technical skills, such as manual labour. HR managers need to adopt a holistic approach to training and view it as one of the many HRM functions that contribute to strategic performance. This traditional view of training, referred to as competency-based training (CBT), identifies standards (or competencies) that should be reached for an employee to be able to perform a job effectively and Australian workplace training has relied upon CBT since the late 1980s. The key feature of CBT, which in Australia encompasses standards identified in the National Training Reform Agenda (NTRA) is that it allows employees to attain and demonstrate industry specified skill standards rather than an individual level of achievement relative to others in the group.

However, in today's dynamic environment traditional training is inadequate to manage the Australian skill shortage effectively and maximise organisations' international competitiveness. CBT has been criticised as an extremely narrow, rigid and atomised approach which ignores the human element of judgement, reflection, changing behaviours and the continual reconstruction of knowledge. Its checklist approach to industry specified performance criteria has been considered too simplistic, demotivating and encouraging of a minimum level of industry competency rather than a standard of excellence. While this form of training may be efficient in the short term, it disadvantages the Australian economy through a lack of diversity and competency development in the long term.

An alternative solution, according to Mckay (2004), is to approach training from a broader perspective, taking into consideration the changing nature of work and organisational diversity. Rather than simply focus on training employees in the skills required to perform their job *technically* (i.e. the manual skills), a proactive diversity management model should be adopted which goes beyond industry-determined competencies and which capitalises on diverse individuals' knowledge, skills, abilities, behaviours, personalities and values, thereby equipping employees with a diverse range of skills actively and behaviourally to work in a global arena.

Please read

Mckay, H. (2004), 'Locating the fault line: The intersection of internationalisation and competency based training', *International Education Journal*, vol. 4, no. 4, pp. 203–11.

A training system approach

Training involves multifaceted considerations including a training needs analysis (TNA), the learning environment features, the characteristics of the learners, the trainer's qualifications, the delivery methods, the learning outcomes, the time duration, adult learning principles, the cost of training and the learning objectives. To prevent trainers from omitting components of effective training or trainees from experiencing uncertainty regarding their directions and goals, a systematic training process was introduced by von Bertalanffy (1968). The systematic training process comprises four major steps: (1) training needs analysis; (2) training input; (3) the training process; and (4) training output (see Figure 9.3). It is designed to establish structural training in which training activities encompass a predetermined plan with a specified rigorous content. Each of these steps is discussed in detail below.

FIGURE 9.3
Training system process model

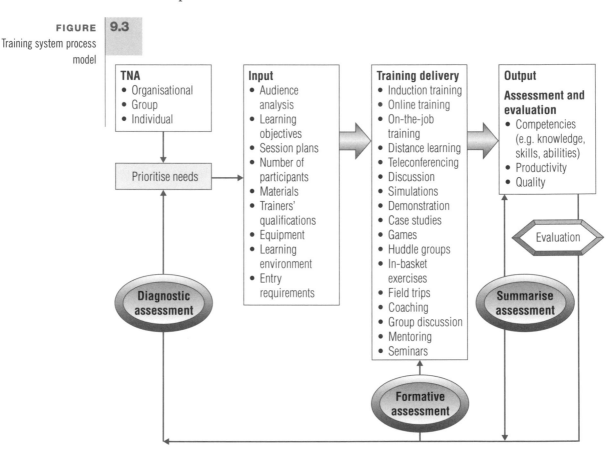

STEP 1: TRAINING NEEDS ANALYSIS

training needs analysis
A tool used to identify the gap between the actual performance and the desired performance in the organisation.

It is important for a TNA to be conducted first so that the training process can be started correctly. **Training needs analysis** is a tool used to identify the gap between the actual performance and the desired performance in the organisation. Training needs may be identified using a variety of methods such as direct observation, interviews, information searches, focus groups and inventory methods. TNA is usually broken into three levels of analysis: the organisational, operational and individual levels (McGehee & Thayer, 1961).

The **organisational level of analysis** refers to the analysis of training needs from an organisational point of view. For example, a taxi service might identify a performance gap shown by the high number of customer complaints about their call centre representatives. As a result of the analysis, training needs could be ascertained in relation to the handling of customer needs under stressful and time-intensive conditions. The organisational data for the analysis includes organisational goals and objectives, job turnover, absenteeism rates, organisational culture and climate and efficiency measures such as labour costs, quality assurance and production process time.

organisational level of analysis
The analysis of training needs from an organisational point of view.

The **operational level of analysis** refers to the analysis of training needs from a job or operational perspective. The analysis entails a systematic collection of job-related information to find the gap in incumbents' skills, knowledge and abilities to perform the job. The operational data for the analysis includes job descriptions, person specifications, performance criteria, 360-degree feedback, on-the-job market analysis and a literature review about the job.

operational level of analysis
The analysis of training needs from a job or operational perspective.

The **individual level of analysis** refers to an analysis of training needs from an individual's perspective, based on how well they perform their job. The analysis measures the individual's current performance against the desired performance. The data for the analysis includes performance appraisal data, critical incidents, job diaries, interviews, direct observations and attitude surveys. These three levels of analysis should yield information that can be used to increase synergistically overall organisational performance.

individual level of analysis
An analysis of training needs from an individual's perspective, based on how well they perform their job.

STEP 2: TRAINING INPUT

Following on from step 1 is the training input phase which represents the design of the training program. The key features of this phase include the learning objectives and the session plan.

LEARNING OBJECTIVES

It is important for any training program to have observable and measurable learning objectives. Training can have a wide range of results and expectations. Consequently, clear and measurable training objectives are important so that everyone's expectations can be met (trainers, trainees, managers and customers). The learning objectives state the precise learning requirement to provide both trainers and trainees with clear direction and goals, which in turn allows trainees to meet their manager's expectation for performance and for serving the customers' best interest. Learning objectives consist of three elements: (1) a performance; (2) a condition; and (3) a standard (Mager, 1975).

A **performance** states what trainees should be able to do at the end of training. It is recommended that a performance uses action words that are not open to interpretation and are measurable and observable, such as 'add', 'calculate', 'collect', 'identify', 'illustrate', 'translate', 'solve' and 'compute'. Trainers should avoid interpretative words such as 'know', 'understand', 'believe' and 'grasp the significance of'. For example, the performance element of an

performance
To accomplish, execute or carry out an ordered task or assignment.

objective could read: 'At the end of the session, the trainee will create and edit a document using a word processing program'.

Conditions should be stated under which the performance is to take place. A performance can be specified to occur within a certain environmental condition (e.g. using instructional manuals, tools, the instructor's assistance or under customer pressure). For example, a condition element of an objective could read: 'Without assistance from others' or 'Given all necessary tools, equipment and instruction manuals'.

A **standard** states the expected criteria of performance (e.g. quality, quantity or timeline). In other words, trainers should ask how well a trainee will be expected to perform at the end of the training. For example, a standard element of an objective could read 'Within 20 minutes', 'Without error', or 'Ten units of sales output per hour'.

In summary, a complete learning objective might read: 'At the end of a training session, a trainee will be able to type 200 words (performance) in a quiet working environment (condition) without any error (standard)'.

standard
The expected criteria of performance (e.g. quality, quantity or timeline).

SESSION PLAN

Within the context of instructor-led training, a session plan is an indispensable tool for instructors. A **session plan** is a blueprint of the training program, which typically includes a particular skill and how it will be taught. In other words, a session plan should include all the key aspects of the training so that a third party could use the session plan to run the exact training session that the trainer had in mind. A session plan should therefore include every aspect of the input resources, namely, the learning objectives, materials required, trainers' qualification level, entry-level requirements, number of participants, timelines, equipment (if required) and assessment and evaluation method.

session plan
A blueprint of the training program, which typically includes a particular skill and how it will be taught.

As it is underpinned by cognitive learning theories, the session plan should have a task breakdown to distinguish between simple and complex tasks. Task breakdowns assist trainers to perform effective, efficient and organised training delivery using the most logical sequence of tasks and timelines across stages. Figure 9.4 provides a sample session plan. The sample session plan indicates how different learning styles can be combined to achieve the maximum learning results.

STEP 3: THE TRAINING PROCESS

The training process refers to the delivery of the training program. There are various training methods available. Choosing an appropriate delivery method requires skill in the area and a sound knowledge of: (1) the content or task itself; (2) the learning objectives; (3) the learners' characteristics; and (4) the time and cost requirements. Training method approaches can vary across a spectrum from *instructor/trainer led* to *learner led* (Tovey & Lawlor, 2004, p. 227). Figure 9.5 displays the various training methods available. The spectrum of training also indicates the application of underpinning learning theories; instructor-led training tends to be underpinned by the behavioural school of thought while learner-led training tends to be underpinned by the cognitive school of thought.

Title: Assisting with customer queries and complaints
Learning objectives: By the end of this training session, employees will be able to:

      (1)   Deal with customer complaints themselves without supervisory assistance.
      (2)   Handle customer abuse in friendly manner under stressful circumstances within ten minutes.

Number of participants: 30 employees
Duration: 1 hour and 15 minutes
Equipment required:
(1) Designated training room
(2) Chairs and tables for 30 employees
(3) PowerPoint projector
(4) Papers and pens
(5) Complaint form
(6) Role-play handout
(7) Assessment form

Time	Content	Training technique	Training activity	Equipment
15 mins	Welcome employees to the training session Explain learning objectives and explain the job description in detail	Lecture	Listening and seeing	PowerPoint slides PowerPoint projector
15 mins	Split into 3 people per group. Facilitate a discussion by asking employees for any real-lite situation of dealing with customer complaints. Ask the participant to jot it down on a piece of paper	Small-group discussion	Active participation	Papers and pens
15 mins	Distribute the 'customer complaint sheet' and work the participant through by explaining the key principles of dealing with customer complaints	Lecture	Listening and seeing	PowerPoint slides PowerPoint projector
15 mins	Experiential activity. Split into pairs to practise the key principle, using a role-play handout	Role-play	Active participation	Role-play handout
15 mins	Conclude the session. Ask for any questions to discuss. Ask the participants to complete the assessment form	Lecture and discussion	Listening, seeing and discussion	PowerPoint slides PowerPoint projector Assessment form
Following week	Observation by supervisors			

Although many training methods are self-explanatory (e.g. lecture, demonstration, reading and games), some methods use training jargon that requires clarification. Extensive clarification of training methods is beyond the scope of this textbook, but a few common methods are outlined below.

- *Case studies* present job-related cases to be worked through by learners which is usually provided in a printed format.
- *Critical incidents* refer to past real-life situations that facilitate the learners' development of better skills to deal with such situations the next time they occur.
- *In-basket exercises* are simulation exercises where learners pick an item and are asked to solve typical job-related problems without assistance or resources.
- *Buzz groups* refer to small groups given a specific topic to be discussed intensively. Groups are asked to provide solutions or recommendations for the issue.

FIGURE 9.5
Training methods

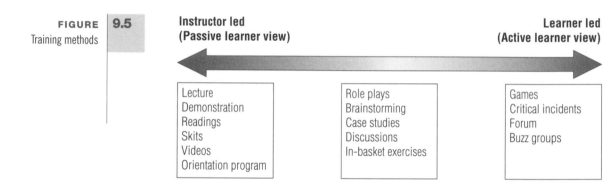

Source: Tovey & Lawlor (2004), p. 228. Reproduced with the permission of Pearson Education Australia, © Pearson Education Australia (a division of Pearson Australia Group Pty Ltd) 2004.

STEP 4: TRAINING OUTPUT

Training output refers to the assessment and evaluation of training programs. While **assessment** is used to determine the success of trainees, **evaluation** is used to determine the success of the training program itself. Assessment is designed to test the trainees' competencies (e.g. knowledge, skills and abilities) at different stages of the training system process as demonstrated in Figure 9.3. Assessment can be categorised as diagnostic, formative and summative (Ramsay, 1991).

assessment
Used to determine the success of trainees and can be categorised as diagnostic, formative and summative.

evaluation
Determining the success of the training program.

DIAGNOSTIC ASSESSMENT

Diagnostic assessment refers to the audience analysis within the TNA. However, this assessment is specific to the particular audience needs after the completion of TNA to determine the learning style approach and trainees' interest level. Diagnostic assessment should also recognise the prior learning of trainees.

diagnostic assessment
Audience analysis within the training needs analysis.

FORMATIVE ASSESSMENT

Formative assessment occurs during the training delivery to give trainees regular feedback on the task (rather than the person). Providing affirmative statements such as 'Yes, you are operating this machine correctly so far' provides greater accuracy in the audience learning process rather than no feedback at all.

formative assessment
Occurs during the training delivery to give trainees regular feedback on the task (rather than the person).

SUMMATIVE ASSESSMENT

Summative assessment refers to a holistic assessment of the trainees' competencies at the end of a training session. Usually, trainers will conduct a test or distribute questionnaires to ascertain the accomplishment of particular skills. For example, at the end of a training session a trainer asks the trainees to operate a particular machine by themselves and gives them a score on how well they operated the machine.

Evaluations analyse the worth of a training program using a systematic process of gathering relevant information including the TNA, the training design, the training delivery, the participants, the trainers, training methods, resources, materials, equipment used and the outcomes of the training (e.g. competencies, productivity and quality).

summative assessment
A holistic assessment of the trainees' competencies at the end of a training session.

Employee development

While training is concerned with gaining job-related skills and the knowledge to do a particular job, **development** is concerned with the holistic growth of individuals in work and non-work roles as well as learning, adapting and handling the organisation's culture, policies and procedures. The focus of development tends to be on the *learner*, not the *learning*, as the aim of development is to improve organisational performance through the enhancement of jobs and employee abilities (Garavan, Barnicle & O'Suilleabhain, 1999). Therefore, as development tends to focus initially on employee development (and organisational development is reached as a consequence), the benefits of development may be realised at individual, group and organisational levels. These include enabling employees to become resilient and gain the ability to adapt to new changes and challenges, the creation of a supportive and participative organisational culture and a more cooperative and harmonious relationship between managers and employees.

development
The holistic growth of individuals in work and non-work roles as well as learning, adapting and handling the organisation's culture, policies and procedures.

As with training, development can also take place in a variety of forms, both internal and external to the company. These include in-house or external development programs, mentoring, job rotation, performance appraisals and management, career development, international assignments, training centres, workshops, coaching, action learning, self, peer and group training and management development programs (i.e. those designed to enhance leadership and confidence).

Employee orientation processes and career development processes are fundamental tools for achieving maximum employee development. For example, Figure 9.6 emphasises an overarching relationship between organisational development, employee development and time-specific training activities. From this figure, it is evident that as employee development increases over time (through specific training activities which increase the skills, knowledge and abilities of staff), so too does the development of the organisation. Hence, organisations can reach their strategic capabilities through continued employee training and development.

FIGURE 9.6
Organisational development and training framework

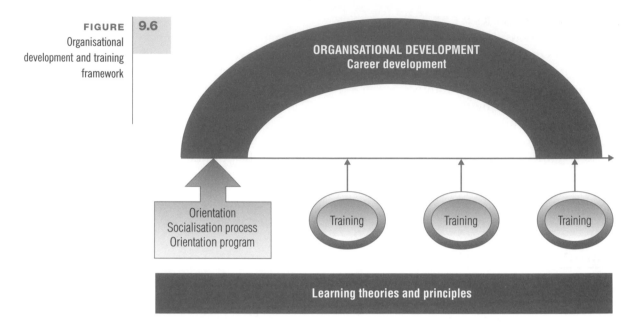

ORIENTATION PROCESS

Employee development begins when employees join an organisation. It is incorporated into the orientation process and continues throughout the duration of employment. The orientation process generally focuses on the adaptation and assimilation of new recruits into the organisational culture, rather than job-specific knowledge, skills and abilities. This is a crucial process as new recruits' perceptions, attitudes and beliefs about the organisation are largely shaped when they begin a new job or swap to a new department within the organisation (Feldman, 1981).

Figure 9.7 depicts an employee socialisation process that is typically represented by three transformational phases: anticipatory socialisation, encounter and settling in.

ANTICIPATORY SOCIALISATION

As employees' adjustment and assimilation into the organisation begins before and during the recruitment and selection process, so anticipatory socialisation occurs prior to a new job beginning. This phase establishes employees' impressions and expectations of their company, job, working conditions and relationships. Impressions and expectations are developed through various means such as rumours, printed material, advertisements, the media, the Internet, recruiters and prospective peers both before and during recruitment. For example, IBM uses the media to reflect its openness to diversity and also displays media releases on its website.

realistic job preview Provides new employees with complete and accurate information about the job and the organisation to avoid a mismatch between the employee's expected and actual work experience.

During this phase, it is important for the organisation to promote realistic expectations of the job, something known as the **realistic job preview** (RJP). An RJP provides new employees with complete and accurate information about the job and the organisation so as to avoid a mismatch between the employees' expected and actual work experience.

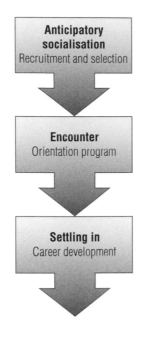

ENCOUNTER

When new employees enter an organisation they need to become familiar with their job tasks and receive appropriate training so that they understand organisational practices and procedures. This phase is referred to as the encounter, that is, the beginning of a new job. In this phase it is crucial for managers to develop quality relationships with their recruits and to assist employees to resolve any work–life or role conflicts and working relationship issues, clarify the necessary policies and outline any unspoken norms and rules (inherent in the organisational culture). As a general rule, the active involvement of managers, supervisors and experienced employees who are willing to guide and encourage new employees is regarded as crucial for encountering success. Further, the **orientation program** is a type of specific training program which assists new entrants as they encounter new job, workgroup, cultural, organisational, departmental and miscellaneous information. Table 9.2 provides an example of orientation program content. Getting new employees started in the right frame of mind is important to reduce their stress and anxiety levels as well as subsequent turnover and negative attitudes (Wexley & Latham, 2002).

orientation program
A type of specific training program which assists new entrants as they encounter new job, workgroup, cultural, organisational, departmental and miscellaneous information.

SETTLING IN

In this phase employees start to feel comfortable with their new job, working relationships, work policies, norms and values. Once organisations have successfully anticipated and encountered new recruits, employees are expected to be satisfied, internally motivated and committed to their job. From this stage, however, ongoing performance appraisals and training and development activities become essential tools for employees to keep developing their knowledge, skills, abilities, values and attitudes.

TABLE **9.2** **Orientation program content**

I. Company-level information

Company history, philosophy, values and missions
Organisational structure or charts
Key policies and practices
Compensation benefit package
Employee and union relations (if any)
Organisational physical layout
Summary of performance appraisal or management system
Career development information (e.g. succession planning)

II. Departmental-level information

Job description and person specification
Job-specific information
Departmental structure and working relationships
Policies, procedures, spoken and unspoken rules
Departmental tour

III. Miscellaneous

Housing
Employee assistant programs
Occupational health and safely
Dress code (e.g. Jeans Friday)
Informal activities (e.g. sports day, multicultural day, green day)

Source: Adapted from Schwarz & Weslowksi (1995).

CAREER DEVELOPMENT

Once new employees are successfully socialised into an organisation they are free to focus on developing their career. A **career** refers to a series of work-related experiences over one's life. **Career development** is, therefore, the series of work-related training activities, experiences, tasks and relationships an employee undertakes. Within the organisational context, an employee's career development is underpinned by the employee's own initiatives (or career planning) and employer's initiatives (or career management). Thus, organisations are expected to succeed at employee career development when they master the career development equation indicated below:

$$\text{Career development} = \text{Career planning} + \text{Career management}$$

Career planning is an employee's deliberate process to understand and to plan their work. It involves becoming aware of the 'self' by conducting a SWOT analysis and identifying one's own values and career-related goals, which can be supported by external assistance from peers, family members, education, training activities and experiences. When planning a career, one should question their strengths, weaknesses, opportunities and threats in relation to the organisation as well as the external environment (e.g. family and educational background,

career
A series of work-related experiences over one's life.

career development
The series of work-related training activities, experiences, tasks and relationships an employee undertakes.

career planning
An employee's deliberate process to understand and to plan their work.

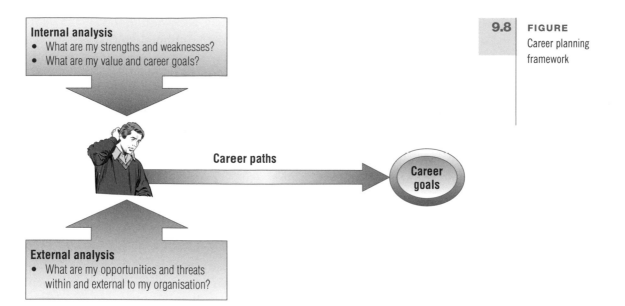

9.8 FIGURE
Career planning framework

colleagues, religion and nationality) (refer to Chapter 1 for a discussion of the SWOT analysis). Having conducted a SWOT analysis of the 'self', career paths should be planned. Figure 9.8 outlines the career planning framework.

Career management refers to an organisation's management activities aimed at helping employees with preparing, implementing and monitoring their career planning process. It includes training and development activities to help individuals develop and carry out their career plans. The career planning tool includes employee self-assessment instruments such as career planning workshops, self-led workbooks, corporate seminars, corporate success planning, skills inventories and regular performance appraisals.

career management
An organisation's management activities aimed at helping employees with preparing, implementing and monitoring their career planning process.

CAREER DEVELOPMENT IN THE CONTEXT OF NEW EMPLOYMENT RELATIONSHIPS

Individuals and organisations must be flexible and adaptable to succeed in a highly volatile and uncertain environment. Today, an organisation's competitive advantage is becoming more reliant on highly qualified and adaptive 'knowledge workers'. The present environment is characterised by a flatter, leaner and decentralised organisational structure, which presents fewer promotional opportunities. Simultaneously, the new psychological contract depicts employees' perception of themselves as free agents. Therefore, increasing importance is placed on the mutual involvement of both career planning and career management to ensure that skilled employees are retained and developed (refer to Chapter 2 for a discussion on psychological contracts and to Chapter 3 for a discussion on knowledge workers).

CAREER DEVELOPMENT MODEL

The series of stages often referred to in career development is underpinned by Levinson's life stage view of adult development (Levinson, 1986). Levinson categorises the adult life into three seasons, namely, early adulthood (17–45 years old), middle adulthood (40–60 years old) and late adulthood (>60 years), which helps employees to plan and develop their career. Managers can use this sequence of life events to help identify the development needs of their employees.

The early adulthood exploration stage (17–45 years) often represents organisational entry and one's early career. It is often a period of great energy and stress, where employees strive to achieve their life goals. Typically, the age of 30 is a significant transition point in life, as people have typically resolved their life goal ambiguity and made a firm commitment to their life goals (or dreams).

Middle adulthood (40–60 years) represents a reaffirmation or modification of the dream. This phase tends to be associated with a mid-career crisis engendered by being laid off, a career plateau and skill obsolescence. A **career plateau** refers to the low probability of an employee receiving significant job responsibilities or advancement. **Skill obsolescence** refers to reduced employee competence resulting from a lack of knowledge and skills to perform new work responsibilities, techniques and technologies. At this stage, career counselling and outplacement counselling are important tools for employers to help middle-aged employees develop their career further.

Late adulthood (>60 years) refers to employees in the workforce representing those aged 60 and upwards. Employees in this category occupy a significant number of positions in today's ageing workforce (i.e. baby boomers). As older employees are often role models or mentors for developing younger employees, it is important for employers to encourage staff in this phase to develop a sense of belonging to the organisation and so they work to become company sponsors. A sponsor provides direction to other employees through their organisational expertise, represents the organisation to customers and makes important organisational decisions. In this stage of late adulthood, employers should also help employees develop a greater sense of balance between work and non-work activities.

Organisational development

Organisational development is a planned organisational intervention to increase the effectiveness and wellbeing of employees in order to bring about meaningful and lasting organisational change. Based on Kurt Lewin's change process discussed in Chapter 2, this chapter introduces the concept of organisation-wide transformation through the implementation theory below.

Implementation theory focuses on specific intervention strategies that are designed to induce changes. There are four intervention strategies: the human processual intervention strategy; technostructural intervention theory; sociotechnical systems design; and organisation transformation change (DeSimone, Werner & Harris, 2002).

THE HUMAN PROCESSUAL INTERVENTION STRATEGY

The **human processual intervention strategy** focuses on changing behaviours by modifying individual attitudes and values (Argyris, 1970). This strategy is concerned with improving organisational culture by improving interpersonal

career plateau
When the likelihood of an employee receiving significant job responsibilities or advancement is low.

skill obsolescence
Reduced employee competence resulting from a lack of knowledge and skills to perform new work responsibilities, techniques and technologies.

implementation theory
Focuses on specific intervention strategies that are designed to induce changes.

human processual intervention strategy
Focuses on changing behaviours by modifying individual attitudes and values.

inter- and intra-group relationships. Commonly, attitude surveys (e.g. cultural diversity attitudes survey), team-building exercises and continuous committee meetings on particular interpersonal and intergroup issues (e.g. diversity committee) are used to improve organisational attitudes, spirit and morale.

TECHNOSTRUCTURAL INTERVENTION THEORY

Technostructural intervention theory focuses on improving work content, work method and work flow with the aim of lowering costs by replacing inefficient work practices, designs, material, methods and equipment with technologies (Friedlander & Brown, 1974). Human resource information systems (HRISs) (which were covered in Chapter 4) are an example of how replacing traditional SHRM practices with technologies can enhance knowledge capital management.

> **technostructural intervention theory**
> Focuses on improving work content, work method and work flow with the aim of lowering costs by replacing inefficient work practices, designs, material, methods and equipment with technologies

SOCIOTECHNICAL SYSTEMS DESIGN

Sociotechnical systems (STS) design aims to find innovative ways of increasing productivity and worker satisfaction through redesigning workflow structures, work methods and work content (Nicholas, 1982). Quality circles, Total Quality Management and self-managed workteams are all innovative ways of increasing work satisfaction and productivity.

> **sociotechnical systems design**
> Aims for innovative ways of increasing productivity and worker satisfaction through redesigning workflow structures, work methods and work content.

ORGANISATION TRANSFORMATION CHANGE

Organisation transformation change views organisations as complex human systems that consistently face new challenges (Beckhard & Harris, 1987). To meet new environmental challenges, managers are required to develop the habit of constantly examining and analysing internal organisational issues (e.g. organisational culture, underpinning value systems or work structures) and external organisational issues (e.g. the impact of multiculturalism or technology). The learning organisation concept, covered in Chapter 3, partially explains this change initiative.

> **organisation transformation change**
> Views organisations as complex human systems that consistently face new challenges.

Implications of training and development

Despite organisational benefits of undertaking the training and development of employees, there are some HRM implications which should be considered. The first implication addresses senior management's perception of the competencies they require employees to perform effectively. This is important because senior managers are drivers of the company and their knowledge, skills and abilities are crucial to the strategic success of the organisation and its human resources. Hayes, Rose-Quirie and Allinson (2000) note that there is a variety of development programs (such as action learning) that can be integrated into the development programs of senior managers to increase their awareness of such variety and help them develop, test and improve their development to become and remain competent managers. As such, HR managers need to liaise with senior managers to design effective development programs which are tailored to meet individual needs, and to ensure that managers are truly competent at their job. This includes the ability to self assess and receive constructive feedback to improve performance and continually develop as key strategic employees.

The increase in diversity, as identified and discussed in Chapter 5, results in many implications for training and development. This depends on the level of diversity integration in the company. According to Moore (1999), there are four perspectives on diversity and each has implications for training and development. If an organisation has adopted the *diversity blindness* perspective (i.e. diversity is not regarded as an issue), the training implications are that diversity training is simply ignored in the design and development of organisational training programs. If an organisation adopts the *diversity hostility* perspective (i.e. diversity is viewed as negative), the organisation proactively avoids (and even suppresses) diversity issues and attempts in training programs are made to create and foster homogeneity. Organisations adopting the *diversity naiveté* perspective (i.e. diversity is viewed as positive) acknowledge in training interventions that they welcome diversity, but they are unlikely specifically to tackle potential problems associated with diversity. A further implication with this perspective is that it can give false hope and unrealistic expectations to diverse groups. The final perspective, *diversity integration* (i.e. the outcomes of diversity are neither automatically positive or negative, and diversity needs to be effectively managed and integrated into all business activities), has several implications for training. These include proactive training of diverse organisational members; the development of skills for all organisational members to manage diversity; the management of problems and opportunities arising from diversity and a diverse workforce; and the development of effective communication between all organisational members.

Some other HRM implications arising from training and development are direct costs of training design and delivery, indirect costs of training such as time taken from employees to attend training and how the process can be integrated with the performance appraisal and career development of each employee. Further, qualification level of trainers and trainability of target employees also need to be considered. Although these implications are not exhaustive, they are congruent with SHRM and the contemporary issues many organisations face, such as the emergence of globalisation.

Contemporary SHRM Application Tool

Since the deregulation of the financial industry several years ago, competition has intensified between banks. Imagine you are an HR manager for one of Australia's major banks. With the advent of the service era, your bank has experienced a dramatic change in the role of tellers. They are expected to change from being mainly cash handlers to being proactive salespeople. Due to the lack of training in developing their customer skills and knowledge of requirements based on the recent Financial Services Reform Act (FSRA) and new sales opportunities, employee morale has been rather low. As an HR manager, you see a need to train the tellers on how to serve today's customers. The SHRM Application Tool walks you through the current environment and HR trends of your company (refer to Figure 9.9). It is clear that sales volume needs to be increased in order to remain competitive in the industry. What training do you need to implement based on your organisational, operational and individual analysis?

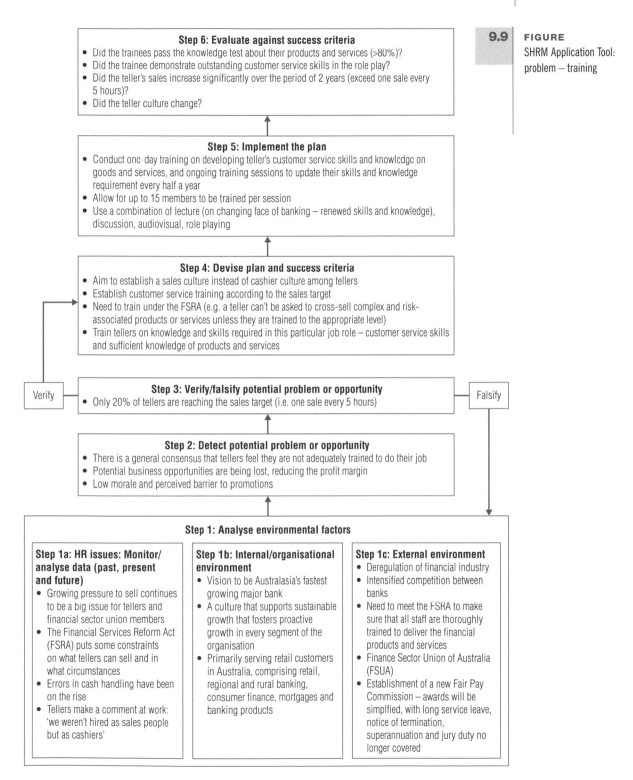

9.9   FIGURE
SHRM Application Tool:
problem – training

Step 6: Evaluate against success criteria
- Did the trainees pass the knowledge test about their products and services (>80%)?
- Did the trainee demonstrate outstanding customer service skills in the role play?
- Did the teller's sales increase significantly over the period of 2 years (exceed one sale every 5 hours)?
- Did the teller culture change?

Step 5: Implement the plan
- Conduct one-day training on developing teller's customer service skills and knowledge on goods and services, and ongoing training sessions to update their skills and knowledge requirement every half a year
- Allow for up to 15 members to be trained per session
- Use a combination of lecture (on changing face of banking – renewed skills and knowledge), discussion, audiovisual, role playing

Step 4: Devise plan and success criteria
- Aim to establish a sales culture instead of cashier culture among tellers
- Establish customer service training according to the sales target
- Need to train under the FSRA (e.g. a teller can't be asked to cross-sell complex and risk-associated products or services unless they are trained to the appropriate level)
- Train tellers on knowledge and skills required in this particular job role – customer service skills and sufficient knowledge of products and services

Verify

Step 3: Verify/falsify potential problem or opportunity
- Only 20% of tellers are reaching the sales target (i.e. one sale every 5 hours)

Falsify

Step 2: Detect potential problem or opportunity
- There is a general consensus that tellers feel they are not adequately trained to do their job
- Potential business opportunities are being lost, reducing the profit margin
- Low morale and perceived barrier to promotions

Step 1: Analyse environmental factors

Step 1a: HR issues: Monitor/ analyse data (past, present and future)
- Growing pressure to sell continues to be a big issue for tellers and financial sector union members
- The Financial Services Reform Act (FSRA) puts some constraints on what tellers can sell and in what circumstances
- Errors in cash handling have been on the rise
- Tellers make a comment at work: 'we weren't hired as sales people but as cashiers'

Step 1b: Internal/organisational environment
- Vision to be Australasia's fastest growing major bank
- A culture that supports sustainable growth that fosters proactive growth in every segment of the organisation
- Primarily serving retail customers in Australia, comprising retail, regional and rural banking, consumer finance, mortgages and banking products

Step 1c: External environment
- Deregulation of financial industry
- Intensified competition between banks
- Need to meet the FSRA to make sure that all staff are thoroughly trained to deliver the financial products and services
- Finance Sector Union of Australia (FSUA)
- Establishment of a new Fair Pay Commission – awards will be simplfied, with long service leave, notice of termination, superannuation and jury duty no longer covered

A view from the field   Induction introduces lifelong learning at World Vision Australia

World Vision was founded in the USA by Bob Pierce during the 1950s after a life-changing trip to China and Korea in 1947. Bob was a missionary and he saw that words alone were not necessarily good news to those without food, clothing, shelter or medicine. Bob's concern for children was strengthened by his experiences in Korea during the Korean War (1950–54).

In the 1960s, World Vision expanded its operations to meet the needs of refugees in Indochina and of people recovering from disasters in Bangladesh and in several African countries. Where long-term assistance was needed, children began to be sponsored by America, Australia and other countries worldwide. In 1966, World Vision Australia (WVA) officially began operations.

World Vision has traditionally been known for its work in the area of child welfare and, most particularly, as an avenue for child sponsorship. Disasters (both natural and those caused by humans), afflict millions of people each year. In 2002, severe drought spread across the southern part of Africa putting 14 million people at risk and 2.4 million children in serious danger. World Vision International provided 19 000 tonnes of food per month to 1.2 million people. WVA responded, raising over $2.2 million from the Australian public. More recent disasters such as the tsunami in 2004 and the Pakistan earthquake in 2005 have brought aid organisations such as WVA into the spotlight as a channel to contribute to relief efforts.

WVA is Australia's largest overseas aid and humanitarian organisation. More Australians donate money to World Vision than any other charity in the country. World Vision International employs 23 000 staff in 90 countries around the world. Specifically in Australia, WVA employs 450 staff across Australia and it communicates a very clear vision to its Australian staff, partners and donors: 'Our vision for every child, life in all its fullness; our prayer for every heart, the will to make it so'.

Andrea Pink is Head of People, Culture and Learning for WVA. She joined the organisation after 17 years in the private sector. Andrea comments: 'It is critical that all our staff understand our vision, the strategy and culture which bring it to life. Our induction program is the first step on the path to understanding; and working effectively to contribute to the fulfilment of our vision'.

She elaborated further: 'The majority of the people who join WVA do so because of a strong commitment to the humanitarian cause. We welcome that commitment and their choice to apply their skills and energy to WVA's efforts. It helps that we share beliefs and a commitment to address the causes of poverty. However, other considerations are also important; WV is a complex operation and we need to bring the 'best practice' practices into our operations. There is close scrutiny of the income generated in this field and donors want to be assured that their contributions are being used to maximum impact. In many ways we face the same pressures a commercial business does; we need to provide maximum return on investment (and benefit to those we seek to assist) or our donors, like shareholders, will take their investment elsewhere.'

The WVA induction program provides the opportunity to provide new staff with tools and knowledge which will help them do their work effectively. Importantly, it also provides an understanding of what World Vision is about, the causes of poverty and the work WV does to try to alleviate it. Armed with this knowledge and information, new people are equipped to contribute by doing their job and understanding the important part they play in the broader WV agenda. They are also able to advocate externally for the fight against poverty, spreading the message among family and friends and the broader Australian community.

The message delivered as part of induction is very clear. 'At WVA people are expected to take personal responsibility; be accountable for outcomes and share ownership of the organisation. Our induction program is the first stage of a journey. It reinforces our request that a staff member needs to be engaged with and contributing to the whole organisation (not just "my bit")'.

A new staff member first learns about the induction program in the pack which includes the offer of employment. The staff member is provided with a checklist to assist them in building the best program to suit them. The manager also has a checklist of induction requirements to ensure that all the required elements are included in the initial induction.

WVA's induction program was designed to support and develop the desired culture. Careful planning and consideration went into its structure and mode of delivery. It is delivered over 12 months with a 'just in time' intention to provide people with information and learning to assist with a smooth entry into WVA and their new role. The induction program moves steadily from fundamentals required for new starters – systems, remuneration, occupational health and safety (first three months – to programs which engage staff in all aspects of the work. An example is the program 'Why is that child poor?'. It is designed to ensure that all staff understand the causes of poverty and activities and operations of WVA designed to address these issues. Staff will understand their part in the overall operation and be able to advocate proudly for World Vision.

The design and the 'self-paced' nature of the induction program models WVA's request to new people to 'Be accountable and take responsibility' by asking them to take responsibility for themselves and their learning. It also encourages them to work in partnership with their manager. Finally, it flows seamlessly into 'lifelong' learning at WVA.

New staff are given the opportunity to meet the CEO and the rest of the leadership team as part of the induction. That meeting takes the form of a no frills, bring your own lunch where new staff converse freely with the management team. According to Andrea, there is something very levelling about sharing your brown paper bag lunch with others. Barriers such as levels within the organisation and titles melt away. At this session, staff are asked to share with the leadership team their reasons for joining World Vision and their hopes for their time there. In return, the CEO and other leaders share their own stories, hopes and vision for the organisation. This interaction builds on the WVA sense of community and allows new people to connect with the driving personal commitment of senior people.

The induction program flows seamlessly into the WVA Learning Framework which is designed to extend the focus on continuous learning. It recognises that people have different learning styles and that much learning occurs in the context of working. Staff are offered a variety of suggestions about how to learn and practise key skills.

The WVA Learning Framework takes the capabilities identified as crucial to World Vision and describes the skills, knowledge and behaviours which need to be displayed by staff to achieve successful performance. The Learning Framework reinforces the principle within WVA that development planning is a joint responsibility of the employee and their manager, designed to ensure that people develop the competencies required to meet current and future business needs. Managers and staff are encouraged to link learning objectives directly to desired organisational outcomes.

A number of vehicles for learning are offered through the Learning Framework:

- Access to the MyAIM database. The database covers an extensive collection of 3650 full text periodicals such as *Harvard Business Review*, *Sloan Management Review*, *California Management Review* plus indexing and abstracts for more than 4100 periodicals covering all aspects of business, leadership, management and learning, country economic and political reports from EIU, CountryWatch, WEFA and the ICON Group and detailed company profiles for the world's largest 5000 companies.
- 360-degree assessment tool. This tool enables staff to undertake an assessment of their performance against the competencies in the Learning Framework and to identify areas for further development.
- Self-assessment questionnaires and information are available to enable staff to identify their learning styles and how this can be used to enhance the effectiveness of their development.
- Self-guided reflective activities.

- Work-based assignments.
- Shadowing, partnering and mentoring.
- Suggestions on how to choose appropriate training courses or workshops for your learning need.

WVA encourages staff to take personal responsibility by making the framework available via Info Central, WVA's intranet. Staff and managers design learning to suit business and personal needs and aspirations. HR staff provide a facilitative resource, providing advice and ensuring materials are current and tailored to WVA needs.

At WVA, it is clear that the induction process is actively used to assist new staff to engage with WVA and its vision and culture. The clear message about personal responsibility is reinforced and further learning is invited through the accessibility of the Learning Framework.

Discussion questions

1. What are the advantages and disadvantages of the learning design utilised in World Vision Australia's induction program?
2. What longer-term value does World Vision Australia's induction program provide to the organisation?
3. How scalable and transferable is the approach to induction taken by World Vision Australia? What changes might need to be made to adapt it to a large, publicly listed corporation?

Skills shortage crippling the backbone of the Australian workforce

Australia's economy is reeling from the impact of an acute skills shortage, but it is not just trade careers that are crippling Australia's suffering economy. With the perception of trade jobs as being low paid and 'dead end' careers, how is the Australian economy expected to survive? Trades requiring skilled workers, from plumbing to carpentry, have traditionally provided strength to the Australian economy. Yet, apprenticeships are currently in an enormous slump, with the average age of workers across the sector sitting at 50, a figure which is surprisingly quite old. So, where have all the young tradespeople gone?

The industry is finding it increasingly difficult to attract young people to trades, with the perception of such jobs as low paying and reflecting low status, coupled with shrinking apprenticeships across all trades and a lack of enthusiasm by career advisers and parents. This assumption is refuted by Adam Furphy, a business owner and contributor to the Victoria Summit, convened by the Victorian Employers Chamber of Commerce Industry (VECCI). Furphy, who claims that trades can provide lucrative incomes for individuals and provide stable, prosperous careers, stated that 'Parents and career advisers view the metal trades as dirty, low-paid jobs that don't have a future. In reality, the pay in some of them is very good, and they certainly have a future.'

Despite advocates of trade careers, skilled workers remain few and far between in the Asia–Pacific region. There has been a warning of a dismal economic forecast in the wake of reduced skilled workers in the Australian workforce as this shortage extends beyond traditional trades into almost every industry, from engineering and agriculture to medicine and accounting. The shortage is believed to be responsible for an escalation of average annual wages of up to 4 per cent, and contributes towards increasing inflation, both circumstances potentially positioning Australia's economy for a nosedive if they continue. Pressure on Australia's economic stability is the only certainty if these figures continue to rise, which is inevitable if skills shortages continue.

Immediate measures are vital to reverse the shrinking skilled workforce, as our population continues to age and the baby boomers work towards retirement. One such measure the Australian government has introduced is the encouragement of skilled workers from overseas into Australia. The government expects 50 000 skilled immigrants to take up residency in Victoria over a period of four years from countries such as England, India, Singapore, China and South Africa. There are also plans for Australian trade colleges based offshore in the Pacific. While providing people from nations such as Papua New Guinea and Fiji with Australian qualifications that will give them access to citizenship, these graduates will also provide Australia with valuable skilled workers. Yet, the lack of Australian skilled workers continues to need addressing.

The government has begun to implement steps that are necessary to quell fears of a looming economic crisis. Regional areas have received a funding boost, with $43 million pledged towards curtailing the skills shortage in regional areas. This will include measures such as vocational training, marketing to induce skilled workers to move to regional areas and assisting unemployed people to 'skill up' in order to gain employment. The Chamber of Commerce and Industry has also urged the government to implement further measures in addition to increased skilled migration, including increased funding for trade training, marketing trades as a career, beginning apprenticeships at a younger age and opening up apprenticeships to people of all ages. Addressing the need for qualified workers is a first step to improving Australia's long-term financial forecast.

Source: Adapted from Colebatch, T. (2005), 'No furphy, trades are dying', *The Age*, 9 November, p. 8; Dowling, J. (2005), '$400m boost for regions', *The Age*, 13 November, p. 7; Hartcher, P. (2005), 'Solving problems that don't exist', *The Sydney Morning Herald*, 18 November; Shanahan, D. (2005), 'Fighting fires with faith and reason', *The Australian*, 28 October, p. 14.

Summary

The concept of training and development is a key factor in the quest for a sustainable competitive advantage through SHRM. This chapter began with a discussion on the significance of training and development. In Australia, a significant number of skilled workers leave every year to obtain higher pay in American and European markets, which has a devastating impact on the Australian economy. As such, managers need to recognise the importance of training and retaining skilled workers to enhance individual, group and organisational development.

The aim of training and development is to maximise employees' learning of new skills, knowledge, attitudes and behaviours to cope with the demands of a dynamic environment. Learning refers to lifelong changes in attitudes, behaviours and cognition as a result of one's interaction with the surrounding environment. Although there are many reasons why people learn differently, Bloom (1956) identified three domains of employee learning: cognitive, affective and motor skills. These domains cover the type of skills employees may use when learning new tasks.

As employee learning underpins the process of training and development, two distinctive theories (or orientations) to learning were identified in this chapter. The behavioural orientation to learning emphasises changing behaviour through reinforcement and punishment and is advocated by a number of behavioural psychologists, while the cognitive orientation to learning emphasises changing behaviour through giving people information and the opportunity to process it mentally so they understand what correct behaviour is and how to perform it. Although the two orientations differ, there are several factors for managers to consider which can be drawn from both orientations, such as organising information to facilitate learning and ensuring that training moves from simple to complex concepts.

Within an organisation, trainers should view trainees as adult learners (as distinct from children). Adults are capable of organising, coordinating and synthesising their experiential knowledge into new skill sets and differ from children because, unlike children, adults *choose* to learn. Adults learn via the experiential learning cycle model which illustrates the importance of trainers allowing individuals (and managers in particular) to reflect on their knowledge, skills and abilities in order to advance their work attributes (Seibert, 1999). The trainer's role is to facilitate adult learners to find the gaps in their job-related knowledge, skills and abilities and then to fill these gaps through relevant training and development activities.

Extending from employee learning is the notion of training. This refers to the deliberate activities planned by an organisation to increase employee knowledge, skills and attitudes, and it occurs at particular times and in particular locations. The four main types of training are formal, informal, on the job and off the job. In addition, there is a variety of modes of training such as lectures, field trips, brainstorming sessions and simulations. As most people learn differently, HR managers are encouraged to use a variety of types and modes to meet all participant needs.

In Australia, traditional training refers to the training of manual skills (also known as competency-based training, which is the level employees should reach before being able to perform a task effectively). However, in today's changing and competitive business environment, training in traditional skills alone is not enough. Makay (2004) argues that companies need to train employees in other 'soft' skills such as diversity management. Specifically, this type of training capitalises on diverse individuals' knowledge, skills, abilities, behaviours, personalities and values, thereby equipping employees with a diverse range of skills to work actively and behaviourally in a global arena.

An approach which organisations can use to train employees is referred to as the training system approach, which comprises four steps. The first step is *training needs analysis* (TNA), which is a tool used to identify a gap between the actual performance and the desired performance in the organisation. This analysis may be conducted at the organisational, operation or individual level, and the data for the analysis includes performance appraisal data, critical incidents, job diaries, interviews, direct observations and attitude surveys. The second step is the *training input*, which features the learning objectives and the session plan. It also takes into consideration the performance, condition and standard which comprise the learning objective. The third step is the *training process*, which refers to the delivery of the training program. For this step to be effective, appropriate training methods should be adopted. These may include lectures, demonstrations and games. The final step in the training system approach is the *training output*, which refers to the assessment (i.e. diagnostic, formative and summative) and evaluation of training programs.

While training is concerned with the growth of job-related skills and the knowledge to do a particular job, development refers to the holistic growth of individuals in work and non-work roles as well as learning, adapting and handling the organisation's culture, policies and procedures. Development can take place in a variety of forms, such as mentoring, performance management and international assignments. The process of development occurs prior to when employees join the organisation (i.e. anticipatory socialisation) and continues when they begin the job (i.e. encounter) and throughout their career with the company (i.e. settling in). Career development refers to the series of work-related training activities, experiences, tasks and relationships an employee undertakes, and is composed of career planning and career management (Greenhaus, Callanan & Godshak, 2000). Career planning is an employee's deliberate process to understand and to plan their work, whereas career management refers to an organisation's management activities aimed at helping employees with preparing, implementing and monitoring their career planning process. The age of an employee will influence their career development and HR managers need to be aware of this influence. For example, the early adulthood exploration stage (17–45 years) often represents organisational entry and one's early career. It is often a period of great energy and stress, where employees strive to achieve their life goals. In contrast, employees in the late adulthood stage (60 years and over) will be seeking a greater balance between work and non-work activities as they work towards retirement.

The process of employee training and development contributes to overall organisational development which is a significant reason for organisations to encourage and promote this important HRM function. Implementation theory focuses on specific intervention strategies that are designed to induce changes in a company. There are four intervention strategies: human processual intervention strategy; technostructural intervention theory; sociotechnical systems design; and organisation transformation change. Such interventions increase the effectiveness and wellbeing of employees in order to bring about meaningful and lasting organisational change and development.

This chapter concluded with a discussion on some training and development implications. The first implication focused on senior management's perception of the competencies they require to perform effectively. HR managers need to liaise with senior managers to design effective development programs which are tailored to meet individual needs, and to ensure that managers are truly competent at their job. This includes the ability to self-assess and receive constructive feedback to improve performance and continually develop as key strategic employees. The second implication was the increased penetration of diversity in the workforce. Companies may adopt different levels of diversity awareness and each impacts significantly on the design of training programs. Therefore, it is imperative that HR managers are aware of diversity initiatives and develop training programs which are congruent with organisational goals.

Key terms

assessment
behavioural orientation to
    learning
career
career development
career management
career planning
career plateau
cognitive orientation to
    learning
development
diagnostic assessment
evaluation

experiential learning cycles
formative assessment
human processual
    intervention strategy
implementation theory
individual level of analysis
learning
operational level of analysis
organisation transformation
    change
organisational level of
    analysis

orientation program
performance
realistic job preview
session plan
skill obsolescence
sociotechnical systems design
standard
summative assessment
technostructural intervention
    theory
training
training needs analysis

Review questions

9.1 What are the three learning domains that guide trainers to develop employees' knowledge, skills and attitudes? How might they be used in different situations?

9.2 What is the difference between the behavioural orientation to learning and the cognitive orientation to learning? List some considerations for trainers that draw on both orientations.

9.3 What is the difference between training and development? Are there any implications that HR managers need to be aware of when designing training and development programs?

9.4 Referring to Figure 9.3, define and describe each of the four steps in the training system approach.

9.5 How do career planning and career management contribute to career development? Illustrate your answer with relevant examples within an Australian context.

9.6 Describe the four elements of implementation theory underpinned by organisational development. Use examples in your answer to demonstrate your depth of understanding.

Exercises

9.1 View the website of the National Training Information Service (http://www.ntis.gov.au) to find the industry-specific competency standards and some examples of training packages. Discuss and compare the differences between these training packages.

9.2 Look through the newspaper and conduct a training needs analysis for one company. Use the method discussed in this chapter to write this up.

9.3 Write down the learning objectives for the following activities.
(a) Using Microsoft® Word.
(b) Making a cappuccino.
(c) Developing EEO policies.

References

Anonymous (2005), 'Creative solutions to HR headaches', *The Canberra Times*, 24 June.

Argyris, C. (1970), *Intervention Theory and Method: A Behavioural Science View*, Addison-Wesley, Reading.

Australian Bureau of Statistics (2003), *Employer Training Expenditure and Practices, Australia, 2001–02*, Cat. No. 6362.0, ABS, Canberra.

Ausubel, D. (1963), *The Psychology of Meaningful Verbal Learning*, Grune & Stratton, New York.

Bandura, A. (1989), 'Social cognitive theory', in *Annals of Child Development*, ed. R. Vasta, Jai Press, Greenwich.

Beckhard, R. T. & Harris, R. (1987), *Organizational Transitions: Managing Complex Change*, Addison-Wesley, Reading.

von Bertalanffy, L. (1968), *General System Theory: Foundations Development Applications*, George Braziller, New York.

Bloom, B. S. (1956), *Taxonomy of Educational Objectives*, Longman, London.

Bruner, J. S. (1961), 'The act of discovery', *Harvard Educational Review*, vol. 31, pp. 21–32.

Dale, E. (1969), *Audio-Visual Methods in Teaching*, Dryden, New York.

Daudelin, M. W. (1996), 'Learning from experience through reflection', *Organizational Dynamics*, vol. 24, no. 3, pp. 36–48.

DeSimone, R. L., Werner, J. M. & Harris, D. M. (2002), *Human Resource Development*, Harcourt, Fort Worth, TX.

Feldman, D. C. (1981), 'The multiple socialization of organization members', *Academy of Management Review*, vol. 6, pp. 309–18.

Friedlander, F. & Brown, L. D. (1974), 'Organization development', *Annual Review of Psychology*, vol. 25, pp. 313–41.

Gagné, R. M. (1985), *The Conditions of Learning*, Holt, Rinehart and Winston, New York.

Garavan, T. N., Barnicle, B. & O'Suilleabhain, F. (1999), 'Management development: Contemporary trends, issues and strategies', *Journal of European Industrial Training*, vol. 23, no. 4/5, pp. 191–207.

Greenhaus, J. H., Callanan, G. A. & Godshak, V. M. (2000), *Career Management*, Dryden Press, Forth Worth, TX.

Hackman, J. R. & Oldham, G. R. (1976), 'Motivation through the design of work: Test of a theory', *Organizational Behaviour and Human Performance*, vol. 16, pp. 250–79.

Hampshire, S. (1950), 'Critical notice of Ryle, the concept of mind', *Mind*, vol. 59, pp. 237–55.

Hartley, J. (1998), *Learning and Studying: A Research Perspective*, Routledge, London.

Hayes, J., Rose-Quirie, A. & Allinson, C. W. (2000), 'Senior managers' perceptions of the competencies they require for effective performance: Implications for training and development', *Personnel Review*, vol. 29, no. 1, pp. 92–105.

Knowles, M. S. (1970), *The Modern Practice of Adult Education: Andragogy versus Pedagogy*, Association, New York.

Kolb, D. A. (1984), *Experiential Learning: Experience as the Source of Learning and Development*, Prentice Hall, New Jersey.

Levinson, D. J. (1986), 'A conception of adult development', *American Psychologist*, vol. 41, pp. 3–13.

Mager, R. F. (1975), *Preparing Instructional Objectives*, Pitman, Belmont.

McGehee, W. & Thayer, P. W. (1961), *Training in Business and Industry*, John Wiley, New York.

McGill, I. & Beaty, L. (1995), *Action Learning: A Guide for Professional, Management and Educational Development*, Kogan Page, London.

Mckay, H. (2004), 'Locating the fault line: The intersection of internationalisation and competency based training', *International Education Journal*, vol. 4, no. 4, pp. 203–11.

Merriam, S. & Caffarella, R. (1998), *Learning in Adulthood: A Comprehensive Guide*, Jossey-Bass, San Francisco.

Moore, S. (1999), 'Understanding and managing diversity among groups at work: Key issues for organisational training and development', *Journal of European Industrial Training*, vol. 23, no. 4/5, pp. 208–17.

Mumford, A. & Honey, P. (1992), 'Questions and answers on learning styles questionnaire', *Industrial & Commercial Training*, vol. 24, no. 7, pp. 10–13.

Nicholas, J. M. (1982), 'The comparative impact of organization development interventions on hard criteria measures', *Academy of Management Review*, vol. 7, pp. 531–42.

Pavlov, I. P. (1927), *Conditioned Reflexes*, Oxford University Press, Oxford.

Ramsay, H. (1991), 'Reinventing the wheel? A review of the development and performance of employee involvement', *Human Resource Management Journal*, vol. 1, no. 4, pp. 1–22.

Saettler, P. (1990), *The Evolution of American Educational Technology*, Libraries Unlimited, Englewood.

Schwarz, J. L. & Weslowski, M. A. (1995), 'Employee orientation: What employers should know', *Journal of Contemporary Business Issues*, p. 48.

Seibert, K. W. (1999), 'Reflection-in-action: Tools for cultivating on-the-job learning conditions', *Organizational Dynamics*, vol. 27, no. 3, pp. 54–65.

Skinner, B. F. (1975), 'The steep and thorny way to a science of behavior', *American Psychologist*, vol. 30, pp. 42–9.

Tovey, M. & Lawlor, D. (2004), *Training in Australia*, Pearson Education Australia, Sydney.

Treichler, D. G. (1967), 'Are you missing the boat in training aids?' *Film and Audio-Visual Communication*, vol. 1, pp. 14–16.

Wexley, K. N. & Latham, G. P. (2002), *Developing and Training Human Resources in Organizations*, Prentice Hall, New Jersey.

Chapter 10

Strategic performance management

INTRODUCTION

Today's growing intensity of global competition and relentless advancements in technology constantly pressure organisations to produce innovative and high-quality goods and services at a globally competitive standard and in a timely manner. Hence, managers are constantly engaged in a quest to find better ways of managing to improve organisational performance. Some innovative ideas that have revolutionised workplace performance include practices such as Total Quality Management, just-in-time management, learning management systems, computer-aided manufacturing and high-performance work systems.

This chapter addresses the issues HR managers face regarding performance management in the twenty-first century. It is believed that in order to manage performance effectively managers need first to understand what 'performance' means and how it should be managed. Like the SHRM Application Tool discussed in this book, performance management can be viewed as a process that starts with a plan which is then implemented and reviewed at the individual, group and organisational level. Performance appraisal is also explained distinctively in this chapter as part of the performance management process, and considered in light of conventional and contemporary methods. Overall, this chapter demonstrates the significant contribution of the performance management process to organisational survival and success.

Objectives

The primary objective of this chapter is to understand the significant role of performance management in SHRM.

After reading this chapter you should be able to:

* define performance and performance management;
* understand the essential building blocks of the performance management process;
* understand performance appraisal as part of the performance management process;
* understand conventional and contemporary methods of performance appraisal and their potential implications.

The annual 'fiasco' of the performance review

Organisations today are engaged in a relentless quest to outdo one another and redefine industrial standards of operating in the global arena. Success in such a context can become a shortlived phenomenon which can only be achieved through continuous improvements in organisational performance. Hence, the concept of performance management has gained widespread recognition since its introduction by Beer and Ruh in 1976. However, in practice, full advantage is yet to be taken of performance management as a useful management tool. Often this is the case in organisations where employees regard performance review as the 'annual fiasco' of the company. An underlying reason for such a negative attitude towards performance management initiatives has been the failure to visualise the link between performance reviews and future performance improvements in organisations. From a managerial perspective performance management is considered to be vital by many senior executives; however, what is regarded as challenging is the 'open and honest dialogue' that is required in a performance review. For instance, an international survey conducted on 10 000 employees found that 50 per cent of the respondents thought their managers were unclear or incomplete in their performance reviews, while more than 90 per cent claimed that they would welcome the opportunity for a 'real dialogue' about their performance (Pickett, 2003).

From a more general stance, recall an instance where your marks for a subject were not as good as you expected. Did you want to know exactly what level of performance your lecturer expected? What was wrong with your approach towards the subject? Or did you wish that your lecturer had given you more constructive feedback along the way? Similarly, in organisations, employees seek honest and accurate information that can provide them with guidance to perform their jobs to the best of their ability so they can reach their full potential. Such information may include knowing what is expected of them in their given job roles, what to do and how to do it; what is expected of them by superiors; how they are progressing; what their manager honestly believes about their performance; what competencies they need to develop; what learning and development opportunities exist; and whether they are genuinely valued in the workplace. As employees' discretionary behaviours largely contribute to organisational success, understanding how organisations should manage employees' discretion to perform is a significant HRM issue (refer to the psychological contract in Chapter 2). Hence, this chapter highlights how performance appraisal (as a function of overall performance management) can make a significant contribution to the way in which employee performance is managed. However, it is first essential to build a conceptual understanding of performance and performance management.

What is performance?

Performance is usually approached as a two-dimensional concept that consists of task performance and contextual performance. Of the two, **task performance** represents the technical know-how, organisational knowledge repositories and skill base needed to engage in the core business of goods and/or service production. In contrast, **contextual performance** refers to the behaviours that are discretionary, yet capable of nurturing the sociopsychological environment within which the core business operates. Such contextual performance may include volunteering, collaboration with other employees and the cohesive creation of a supportive working environment.

Broadly defined, **performance** is to accomplish, execute or carry out an ordered task or assignment. Applied in a business context, the definition of performance encapsulates two factors: output and input. **Output** refers to the accomplishment of target levels of productivity (e.g. number of units sold, customer satisfaction and profit margin), whereas **input** refers to the source materials of the output, such as labour hours, raw materials, land and capital. Ingrained in the notion of input are also the elements of contextual performance which include applying one's skills, capabilities and knowledge to their full potential, and incorporating personal values and personal traits to accomplish organisational goals in the best way. Although it is important for HR managers to be aware of both task and contextual performance when performance managing staff, research has revealed that motivated employees have much higher task performance and contextual performance than less motivated employees, in addition to also displaying higher organisational commitment and job satisfaction at work (Klein *et al.* 1999).

In another attempt to conceptualise performance, Campbell *et al.* (1993) conducted a study on employee performance. The study resulted in a taxonomy of eight major performance components through the analysis of 275 entry-level jobs. The performance components they identified were:

1. job-specific task proficiency (e.g. software engineering skills and auditing skills);
2. non-job-specific task proficiency (e.g. integrity, accountability and business ethics);
3. written and oral communication task proficiency;
4. demonstrating effort (e.g. performance beyond the call of duty and the willingness to work under adverse conditions);
5. maintaining personal discipline (e.g. punctuality, meeting deadlines);

task performance
The technical know-how, organisational knowledge repositories and skill base needed to engage in the core business of goods and/or service production.

contextual performance
Behaviours that are discretionary, yet capable of nurturing the supporting sociopsychological environment within which the core business operates.

performance
To accomplish, execute or carry out an ordered task or assignment.

output
The accomplishment of target levels of productivity.

input
Source materials of the output such as labour hours, raw materials, land and capital.

6. maintaining peer and team performance;
7. supervision/leadership; and
8. management and administration.

Performance management

Performance can be conceptualised in a multitude of ways. However, the task of managing such a multidimensional phenomenon can be an onerous task for HR managers approaching performance management. Although the management literature is replete with definitions of performance management, it is commonly referred to as the management of organisational and employee performance, or as an integration between the two. In this chapter, **performance management** is defined as a collective range of activities conducted by an organisation aimed at enhancing individual, group or unit-level performance with the overarching purpose of improving organisational performance in the long term (refer to Figure 10.1).

It is important when discussing performance management to highlight its relationship with organisational performance. In general, organisational performance is measured in terms of return on investment (ROI), profit margins, market share, brand value and the quality of goods and services. However, advocates of sustainable development have introduced the concept of the 'triple

performance management
A collective range of activities conducted by an organisation aimed at enhancing individual, group or unit-level performance with the overarching purpose of improving organisational performance in the long term.

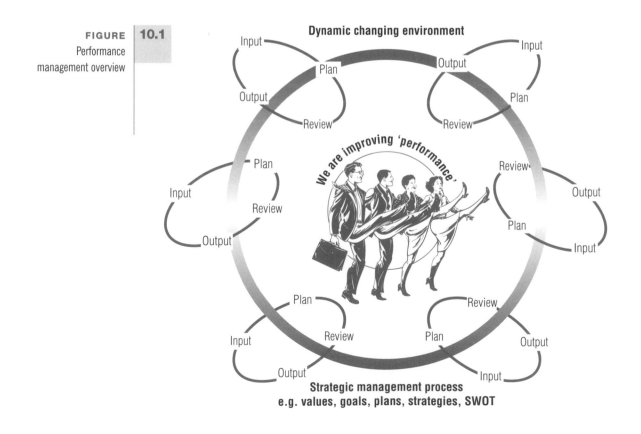

FIGURE 10.1
Performance management overview

Dynamic changing environment

We are improving 'performance'

Strategic management process
e.g. values, goals, plans, strategies, SWOT

bottom line', which states that measurement of organisational performance should not only include fiscal terms but also incorporate environmental and social company performance. Irrespective of the performance assessment method utilised by HR managers, individual and group performance contributes to overall organisational performance.

PERFORMANCE MANAGEMENT AND TEAMS

Performance management has also been influenced by the increased popularity of teams in organisations. For example, cross-functional and self-managed work teams (SMWTs) have given group performance a new meaning in organisations. As a **group** is commonly referred to as a collective body of individuals striving towards a common objective guided by an overarching organisational framework, therefore *group performance* essentially involves the process of individuals interacting in a group, and the outcomes of such a process.

group
A collective body of individuals striving towards a common objective guided by an overarching organisational framework.

Performance in groups is often dependent on a number of aspects. These include a shared purpose, group norms, hidden and espoused goals, member roles, communication, available resources and group cohesion. A well-functioning group is expected to meet both the task and social needs of the group in the accomplishment of a goal. For example, social norms include the socialisation and interaction of the group, whereas task needs include the purpose or goals of the group (e.g. to develop a new product).

PERFORMANCE MANAGEMENT AND INDIVIDUALS

Despite the increased popularity of teams in today's workforce and managing through group performance, individual performance should always be the focal point for HR managers, for example managing the performance of employees' knowledge, skills and ability. So, why is this important? After all, wouldn't it be easier for managers to manage a group of employees at once? Although this is a logical approach, in practice this would be ineffective because people have different levels of knowledge, skills and abilities, as well as attitudes, values and beliefs (as discussed in Chapter 5). Therefore, managing an individual or group depends on each employee and the task at hand, in addition to the HR manager's capabilities (i.e. availability of time).

Monitoring individual performance is a critical determinant of organisational performance, which is why it is important for HR managers to conduct performance management at this individualised level. Individual performance tends to be conducted via performance appraisal, which is discussed later in this chapter.

In order to gain an understanding of how to improve organisational performance (via group and individual performance), it is first necessary to grasp the characteristics of performance management.

CHARACTERISTICS OF PERFORMANCE MANAGEMENT

As depicted in Figure 10.1, performance management is a process of continuous input and output management, in addition to planning and reviewing. The overall aim of performance management is to establish whether performance has been or is being improved, and implementing strategies to ensure it is. Such a process requires the participation and involvement of both employers and employees, and is certainly not considered a set of activities that is limited to the senior management or HRM department of an organisation. As such, there are five characteristics of performance management that HR managers need to consider before conducting performance reviews (see Figure 10.2). These are explained in detail next.

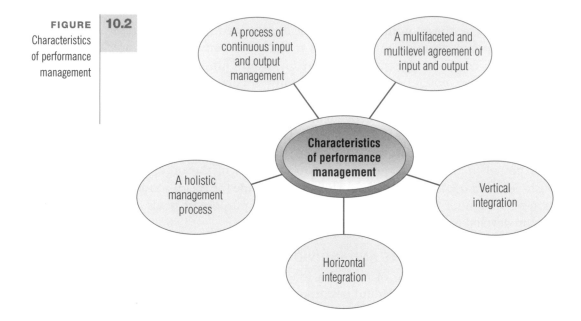

A PROCESS OF CONTINUOUS INPUT AND OUTPUT MANAGEMENT

The need for continuity for a performance management initiative is a crucial element in an ever-changing business environment. In order to achieve sustainable performance growth amid environmental volatility, companies need to devise plans based on inputs followed by production of output, and evaluate these continuously in a systematic manner. For this to occur, performance management requires a coherent systematic review of performance against organisational objectives and strategic plans, including HR goals and objectives. For example, in a hospital the HR objective is to attend to 1000 patients a month. In order for this to be achieved every doctor would have to attend to 50 patients a week.

A MULTIFACETED AND MULTILEVEL AGREEMENT OF INPUT AND OUTPUT

As stated in the previous characteristic, performance management requires a comparison between actual performance and strategic organisational objectives and plans. Therefore, this process requires a multifaceted and multilevel agreement of inputs and outputs in an organisation. For example, using the hospital example above, the output would refer to the agreed numerical target (i.e. 1000 patients per month) and the input would refer to time allocated for each patient (i.e. 15 minute appointments). Essentially, this implies that performance management is a process requiring vertical and horizontal integration in an organisational system.

VERTICAL INTEGRATION

Performance management involves the interpretation of strategic objectives in terms of group and individual objectives and alignment of those objectives to achieve the long-term strategic intention of the organisation. For example, consider an information technology (IT) company with a strategic intention of 'striking an optimum balance of IT opportunities and IT business requirements to deliver state-of-the-art IT services to business enterprises'. Cascading down from the overall organisational goal, group objectives can be set, such as, 'Achieve 10 outstanding projects per year', or 'Reduce client complaints by 25 per cent'. Cascading further down to the individual level, employees can be given personal goals, for example 'Produce one outstanding IT innovation or a productivity improvement technique per year'. Therefore, **vertical integration** is defined as the integration of individual, group, functional and organisational objectives.

> **vertical integration**
> The integration of individual, group, functional and organisational objectives.

HORIZONTAL INTEGRATION

Along with the vertical integration of performance targets, it is necessary to ensure that HRM practices are congruent with organisational objectives. In this respect, strategic objectives should also be reflected in an organisation's performance appraisals, recruitment and selection practices, rewarding, training and development and job design. Hence, **horizontal integration** refers to the integration of HRM functions.

> **horizontal integration**
> The integration of HRM functions.

The set of HRM practices an organisation uses to achieve its strategic objectives is known as a high-performance work system (HPWS) (MacDuffie, 1995). An HPWS is a central aspect of performance management as it sends a powerful message to employees concerning an organisation's seriousness in investing in its employees. Importantly, HRM practices within the set should complement one another in terms of strategy and focus (as a part of the horizontal integration) and thereby collectively strive to improve organisational performance in a holistic manner.

However, there are a few issues that could constrain the relationship between HR practices and organisational performance. These may include internal contextual factors (e.g. weak financial capabilities), external contextual factors (e.g. the degree of workforce unionisation), factors relating to employee demographics (e.g. age, gender and level of education) and issues relating to job preference (e.g. job type) and level of autonomy.

A HOLISTIC MANAGEMENT PROCESS

As previously emphasised, performance management is a holistic management process that amalgamates individual, group and organisational performance into achieving short- and long-term organisational objectives. In order for performance management to be a holistic endeavour, the process should be characterised by double-loop learning. This type of learning facilitates the rationale of the decision process and thereby encourages employees to review, debate and even modify current business objectives if necessary (refer to Chapter 3 for a discussion on double loop learning). A holistic approach to performance management improves the performance of a system as a whole, while ensuring the performance levels of individuals and subsystems make a substantial contribution to the overall improvement. Another important aspect of performance management is the ongoing communication. It is necessary for managers and employees to maintain open lines of communication based on acceptable ethical standards such as mutual trust, respect, fairness and transparency. Channels of communication should also be open to divergent parties of stakeholders such as shareholders, employee unions, customers, suppliers, government and the wider community.

THE PERFORMANCE MANAGEMENT PROCESS

Despite organisational knowledge of the strategic role of performance management, most companies fail to identify the link between performance management and organisational strategy. Therefore, it is crucial for organisations to identify the gap between performance management and strategic management, the latter term referring to the process of managing with a long-term (or strategic) focus. Once the gap has been identified, one should be able to establish the performance criteria to achieve a given business strategy.

Based on this view, Aguilar (2003) has identified some critical dimensions of performance management.

1. *Strategic planning.* This is normally performed by a small team of senior executives in consultation with middle management and external consultants. The strategic planning process involves developing long-term plans for the company and begins with an internal and external analysis of the firm. An **external analysis** involves the evaluation of the environment in which the company operates. Such an evaluation takes into account the political, economic, social and technology-related aspects that are external to the organisation. This process is followed by an **internal analysis**, which is an audit of a company's core competencies, strengths, weaknesses, opportunities and threats (i.e. a SWOT analysis). The results of both analyses provide the basis for organisational goal setting and subsequent strategy formulation. Strategies are then translated into actionable business plans and goals. Once the planning team develops the actionable goals, the goals are then cascaded down the company (i.e. vertical integration). Performance management links these organisational goals to individual performance targets, establishing clear links between corporate objectives and daily employee activities. However, as Table 10.1 indicates, despite the recognition of the importance of strategic planning, senior management often experience a lack of validity in the planning process.

---

external analysis
The evaluation of the environment in which the company operates.

internal analysis
An audit of a company's core competencies, strengths, weaknesses, opportunities and threats.

TABLE 10.1   Factors leading to ineffective planning

CEOs are asked what factors are causing their planning process to lack validity	
Lack of well defined strategy	57%
Lack of a link between strategy and action plan	53%
Lack of individual performance accountability	45%
Lack of meaningful performance criteria	34%
Lack of reward based on performance	21%
Lack of appropriate information	21%

Source: The Conference Board.

2. *Performance criteria and measures.* Determining what constitutes good performance, and how the different aspects of high performance can be measured, is a critical part of any performance management process. Recently, the balanced scorecard has gained popularity in the assessment of employee performance (refer to Chapter 1 for a discussion of the balanced scorecard). According to Tarantino (2003), the balanced scorecard evaluates performance in four key functional areas: (1) external customer satisfaction, (2) internal operations (e.g. sales volume), (3) people's growth and learning (e.g. the research and development of new products and services), and (4) financial targets (e.g. a 50 per cent increase in the profit margin). Since the balanced scorecard is of particular use in translating organisational goals into departmental, group and individual actions, its value as a contemporary management tool in performance management is noteworthy.

3. *Taking action.* The core activities of organisations tend to include product manufacturing, service provision and customer service. Knowing how to improve these core activities doesn't, however, necessarily translate into any improvements. For example, many organisations today suffer from a 'knowing–doing gap', where the action plans and knowledge are in abundance but there is minimal translation of knowledge into action (Pfeffer & Sutton, 1999). It is of utmost importance that organisations identify such a gap between plan and action, and bridge that proactively. Further, commitment and support by the senior management is crucial in transferring such plans into actions as they have the ability to harness organisation-wide support (through employees) towards a commonly articulated strategic direction.

4. *Organisational culture.* Organisational culture encapsulates corporate values and norms which dictate appropriate behaviours and attitudes at work. It is often considered a difficult task to conceptualise, as every aspect in an organisation is affected by it and, in turn, the culture is moulded by all aspects of an organisation. However, it is important for an organisation to have a healthy, performance-oriented culture which rewards and fosters continuous performance improvements.

Please read

Tarantino, D. P. (2003), 'Using the balanced score card as a performance management tool', *Physician Executive*, vol. 29, no. 5, pp. 69–72.

Performance appraisal

performance appraisal
A formal and mutually agreed upon system of planning and reviewing employee performance.

Performance management requires managers to work cooperatively with their employees. For example, they need to set mutual performance objectives and standards, and continuously measure and review predetermined objectives with actual performance, all of which needs to be conducted with the ultimate aim of positively affecting organisational performance. In the previous chapters, the importance of strategic recruitment and selection, and training and development has been discussed, with the underlying goal of filling organisational performance gaps. **Performance appraisal** is another SHRM tool which is used to fill performance gaps and is defined as a formal and mutually agreed upon system of planning and reviewing employee performance (e.g. skills, abilities, knowledge and attitudes). In general, performance appraisal is regarded as the process whereby an organisation assigns a score to indicate the level of performance of a target person or group. A performance appraisal is an accurate measure of key aspects of employee performance, which is a crucial aspect of the performance management process if the company wants to improve overall organisational performance and achieve a competitive advantage.

PERFORMANCE APPRAISAL VERSUS PERFORMANCE MANAGEMENT

Performance appraisal is both distinct from performance management and a part of it. In other words, performance appraisal is focused on the planning and reviewing of *individual* performance and is a subset of performance management; whereas performance management is concerned with *organisational* performance improvement through various HRM functions and procedures, including performance appraisal. Another distinguishing feature between performance management and performance appraisal is that performance appraisal is a time-specific formal assessment, whereas performance management is a non-time-specific endeavour that is cyclical and ongoing.

Viewed as a part of the performance management process, the performance appraisal process involves a number of steps:

• determining how well individual employees are doing their job;
• communicating this information to employees;
• establishing a plan for performance improvement;
• implementing this plan through the facilitation of self-management;
• training and development.

In short, it is a process of reviewing, evaluating and planning individual or group performance. Performance appraisal is often regarded as a system whereby organisations attempt to measure one's performance by assigning a corresponding 'score' to indicate the level of performance, for example scoring one's performance as 'outstanding', 'very good', 'good', 'average', 'poor', 'very poor' or 'unsatisfactory'.

THE PROBLEM WITH PERFORMANCE APPRAISALS

Despite the benefits of performance appraisals in setting performance objectives for employees, which leads to improved organisational performance, performance appraisals have been subject to criticism. Quite often performance appraisals are approached with animosity as annual or biannual rituals conducted by the HRM department, reflecting the hierarchical bureaucracy in organisations. Therefore, HR managers should be aware of potential employee resentment surrounding the appraisal process and develop methods to ensure that this important process is still effectively pursued and objectives are achieved.

There are a number of critical factors which have led to the negative perception of performance appraisals. First, it has been blamed as being backward looking, subjective and concentrating only on the negative aspects of work. This is because performance appraisals are designed to provide constructive feedback which is often perceived as negative. To combat this, managers should provide positive feedback, followed by constructive (and honest) feedback, and then conclude the appraisal with positive feedback once again to ensure the process ends on a positive note. Managers should also avoid shying away from discussing negative aspects as both positive and negative work aspects should be openly discussed if the employee, and organisation, is to reach its full potential. However, at all times, the parties involved in the process should conduct the appraisal with utmost professionalism.

Second, people fail to see the clear link between their performance appraisal and organisational objectives, due to poor interpersonal communications. Therefore, HR managers need to develop excellent interpersonal skills and learn to use appropriate communication mediums, taking advantage of technology where possible (see Chapter 4 for a discussion on technology and communication). It is also important in the development of communication skills for managers to align performance appraisal with strategic performance management in a bid to achieve strategic business objectives. In this sense, performance management is viewed as a forward-looking developmental process which contributes to work flexibility and is a vital component of organisational survival today.

Third, unfortunately a number of past researchers confirm that both managers and employees alike find formal performance appraisals not particularly useful in developing better organisational performance. For example, Fletcher (2001) argues that if performance appraisals are to be used optimally organisational members need to escape the present static mindset and dynamically apply the outcomes of the appraisal in a positive and constructive manner. While, traditionally, performance appraisals were viewed with much scrutiny, contemporary appraisals should be viewed as a fluid 'process' and not a static 'state'. For instance, by viewing appraisals as a process, performance may be enhanced by:

1. *goal setting:* at both micro (e.g. job description) and macro (i.e. strategic) levels;
2. *performance review:* to assess the task and contextual performance; and
3. *performance planning*: to ascertain training and development needs and reward allocation.

CONSIDERATIONS IN THE PERFORMANCE APPRAISAL PROCESS

As discussed in the previous section, HR managers should adopt the contemporary view of performance appraisals and view it as a dynamic process. However, there are a number of considerations that need to be acknowledged. The most important of all is that, although performance appraisals are conducted on an annual or biannual basis, the outcomes of the appraisal may occur on a day to day level and should be viewed as a holistic approach to performance management. The specific criteria that management should consider are discussed next.

DEFINE THE PERFORMANCE CRITERIA

Performance in the knowledge economy cannot be measured with the traditional performance criteria that were once used. This is because businesses have changed dramatically in the last few decades, with a shift from industrially focused business practices (i.e. machine oriented) to a human resource approach (i.e. people oriented). Therefore, modern-day performance criteria should reflect certain critical business aspects, such as the creation of knowledge, learning and innovation. The internationalisation of business also brought about global work teams that require team members to communicate constructively with culturally diverse members. As such, clear performance criteria help managers to make distinctions between low- and high-potential employees. For example, the performance criteria for academics usually consist of teaching evaluations, publication quality and quantity and professional internal and external services. The degree to which academics achieve this, therefore, will be the distinction between low- and high-potential employees.

key performance indicators
Criteria incumbents should achieve for a particular job to be performed effectively.

Within business contexts, performance criteria are often referred to as **key performance indicators** (KPIs). Therefore, KPIs are the criteria that managers would expect an incumbent to achieve for a particular job to be performed effectively. Specific examples of KPIs for various jobs may be found in Table 10.2.

FACILITATE DISCUSSION REGARDING THE PERFORMANCE REVIEW

The performance appraisal process refers to the re-evaluation of past performance by employees and their managers and discussing of future performance

TABLE 10.2 Key performance indicators

Job	Key performance indicators
Customer relations officer	• Number of reported customer complaints • Customer retention rate • Average response time
Transportation coordinator	• Percentage of timely deliveries • Accuracy of the delivery
Marketing manager	• Percentage of advertising revenue raised • Customer loyalty and retention rate • Market share

development, that is, comparing past and present performance, such as knowledge, skills, abilities and annual retention rates. In short, it is an indispensable tool which identifies the performance gap between past performance and the required performance so that personnel development needs are identified for the future (see Figure 10.3). This also helps managers ascertain future resource needs, such as human, technical and financial resources. This is important if HRM is to be viewed as a strategic organisational function which interrelates with other organisational capabilities and functions.

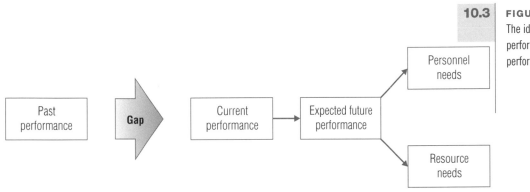

10.3 FIGURE
The identification of performance gaps via performance appraisals

IDENTIFY TRAINING AND DEVELOPMENT NEEDS

Performance appraisals are closely linked to the HRM function of training and development and therefore should not be viewed separately from other functions. For example, performance appraisals are a diagnostic assessment tool which identify the training needs of employees (e.g. negotiation and presentation skills). However, the training needs of employees may also have been identified in the training needs analysis (TNA), which is conducted when determining the training and development needs of individuals, groups or the organisation as a whole. Therefore, line managers need to work cooperatively with training managers to ensure that employees' training needs are identified and appropriately developed. After all, performance appraisals are categorised as a source of training and development of new knowledge and abilities.

REWARD GOOD PERFORMANCE

Rewarding good performance is critical to employee motivation and, ultimately, organisational success. As indicated in Figure 10.4, if performance appraisals are conducted properly they are a valuable tool for effective performance management in both the short and long term. Research in the area shows that performance appraisals are growing in significance as a strategic managerial tool capable of capitalising on human assets in an individualised manner. From the perspective of senior management, performance appraisals provide a great opportunity for superiors not only to uplift employee performance but to also reinforce the corporate climate, values and attitudes, and to harmonise performance appraisals with the strategic direction and improved performance of the organisation.

FIGURE 10.4
The link between
performance appraisals
and improved
organisational
performance

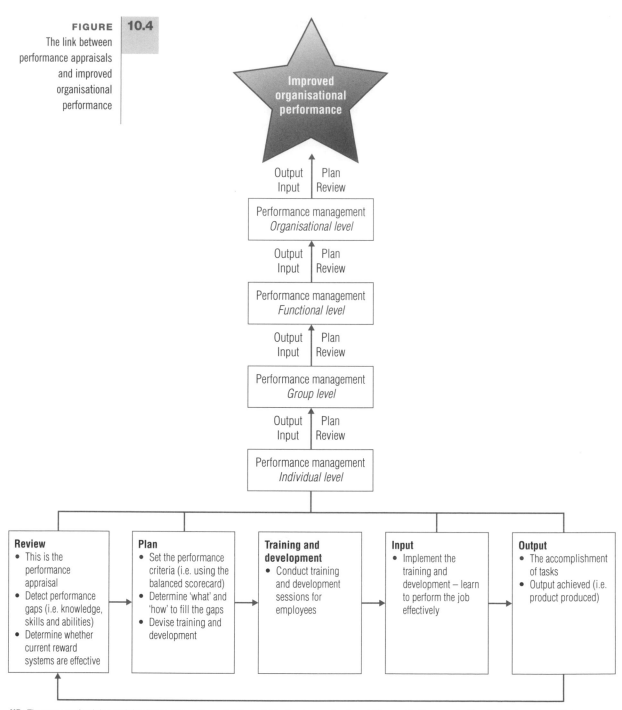

NB: *The process of training and development is performed at the individual and group levels and filters vertically upwards. Therefore it doesn't need to be conducted again at the functional and organisational levels.*

HOW ARE PERFORMANCE APPRAISALS LINKED TO OTHER HRM FUNCTIONS?

As advocated in Chapter 1, for HRM to be considered strategic all HRM functions need to be strategically aligned with organisational objectives. This ensures that all HR-related aspects of the business are working towards the same organisational goals, that is, moving in the same direction. Therefore, performance appraisals should be interrelated strategically with other HRM activities, such as reward allocation, job analysis, workforce planning, training and development, promotion, demotion, transfer and termination (refer to Figure 10.5). Although there is a variety of ways to link performance appraisals to other HRM activities, every organisation will differ due to their uniqueness (i.e. company size, quality and quantity of employees and organisational culture). Therefore, HR managers need proactively to design performance appraisals and performance management to suit each particular company.

REWARDING

As mentioned previously, the outcomes of an appraisal can provide information for organisational reward management, particularly concerning pay for performance. It is important that HR managers recognise that employees' discretionary behaviour is a major determinant of high performance and therefore positive discretionary behaviours should be encouraged (refer to Chapter 2 for a discussion on discretionary behaviours).

The appraisal process can influence an employee's motivation level because it provides an opportunity for management to recognise and reward employees who have been outstanding or have achieved significant performance improvements. (Note: The concept of performance, motivation and reward management is discussed in detail in Chapter 11.)

JOB ANALYSIS

The outputs of a job analysis (i.e. job description and person specification) form the basis of a performance appraisal. In other words, performance appraisals involve a comparison and evaluation of the actual performance of an employee against the performance criteria drawn from the job analysis. However, it is important to note that formulation of such performance criteria requires the participation of employees and employers as it is a mutual process that seeks agreement from all parties concerned. The results of the performance appraisal are, in turn, utilised to reassess the job description and person specifications, which will be used for determining future performance criteria. This procedure of continuous updating is important in today's changing business environment, as job roles and skill requirements should not be standardised over a long period of time (refer to Chapter 8 for a discussion on job analysis).

WORKFORCE PLANNING

Performance appraisals can also be seen as a type of 'performance audit'. That is, they enable an organisation to collect information regarding the overall skills, knowledge and abilities of organisational members. In essence, this is congruent with human resource planning (HRP), which refers to a dynamic planning process involving ongoing environmental scanning and analysis of organisational objectives, strategies and policies in order to ascertain the right quantity and quality of employees when and where needed. Information collected this way may be used to assess the capabilities of the organisation's human resources against the required competencies to attain strategic objectives and a competitive advantage.

TRAINING AND DEVELOPMENT

As mentioned earlier in this chapter, performance appraisals help managers identify an organisation's training and development needs. This is important because the correct identification can enable and foster the ability to achieve and retain a competitive advantage. Further, training and development help to identify individual training needs, in addition to performance gaps at the individual, group and organisational level. In this sense, performance appraisals can contribute to assessing the adequacy of current training and development approaches and programs for achieving individual, group and organisational goals.

PROMOTION, DEMOTION, TRANSFER AND TERMINATION

The outcome of a performance appraisal is actionable and should be so in order for it to be perceived as a process of substantial outcome. This is the joint responsibility of employees and employers alike. For example, if employees view the appraisal process as a constructive employee development tool, then they may take the feedback on board and improve their performance which could result in a promotion. Consequently, if employees are encouraged to adopt feedback proactively, the company will ultimately benefit from overall improved individual performance (as illustrated in Figure 10.5). Therefore, information arising from performance appraisals can be used to formulate decisions to promote, demote, transfer or even terminate employees (if necessary).

PERFORMANCE APPRAISAL 'TIPS FOR SUCCESS'

As discussed at the beginning of the chapter, performance appraisals should not be treated as an annual fiasco but as an ongoing systematic process of review, plan and development of employee performance. In other words, performance appraisals should be a series of time-specific interim information reviews held annually, half-yearly or quarterly. As performance appraisal is an indispensable tool in the process of performance management, some tips for success are highlighted next. These tips are important for managers as they view performance appraisals as a holistic tool. That is, performance appraisals (as a component of performance management) are not considered purely at the time they physically occur, but rather HR managers need to prepare:

1. *before* the performance appraisal meeting;
2. *during* the performance appraisal meeting; and
3. *after* the performance appraisal meeting.

BEFORE THE PERFORMANCE APPRAISAL MEETING

Contrary to popular belief, a performance appraisal requires significant preparation before the meeting can occur. Therefore, managers should allow

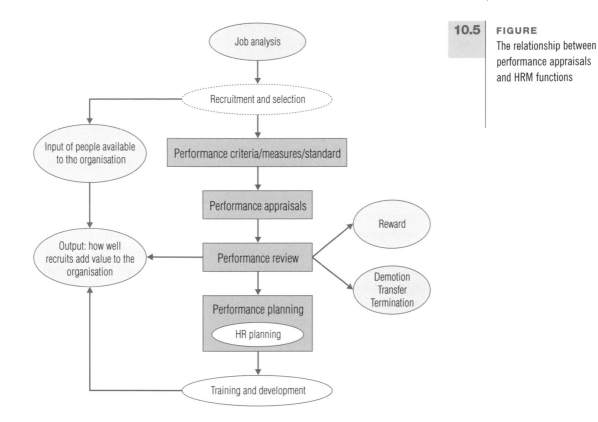

plenty of time before the appraisal to prepare for the meeting adequately. First, the employer needs to consider and decide who should conduct the appraisal. Usually, it is performed by either the line or HR manager, although in some situations peers and senior management may also participate, depending on the appraisal method adopted. Next, employers need to consider the purpose of the appraisal, and have sufficient (and correct) information on hand. This information may include a copy of the previous performance appraisal notes, KPIs, specific performance criteria and training and development undertaken since the last appraisal. If technology has been appropriately integrated with SHRM, most of this information can be easily accessed via the human resource information system (HRIS).

In order to set accurate job-related goals the manager and the employee should have a sound and precise knowledge of the employee's job performance. This would involve obtaining the relevant job description and statistics or outcomes resulting from the employee's performance since the last review, such as the number of products developed, profit and loss statements, customer feedback or the percentage of market share obtained.

One way to determine the purpose of the appraisal is to employ the SMART method of goal setting (i.e. **s**pecific, **m**easurable, **a**greed, realistic and time-bounded performance goals). This will result in performance criteria that can motivate an employee by providing a specific purpose and a direction. In general, the goal of a performance appraisal serves a number of purposes, such as to facilitate the performance review discussion; to identify training and development needs; to distinguish high and low performers; and to determine the reward according to the level of performance. In essence, a performance appraisal has a dual purpose:

1. to facilitate an open, honest and non-threatening discussion where employees are given plenty of opportunity to self-evaluate, and to suggest ways of improving future performance; and

2. to explicate how an employee's performance and goals contribute to the organisational, group or departmental strategic objectives, and devise plans for future performance improvements.

Serving these two purposes can be a challenging task for HR managers as there are constantly changing trends in the workforce and industry. For instance, increased workforce diversity demands a portfolio of rewards (as opposed to homogenous rewards) that can motivate individuals from diverse groups. Further, the emergence of different modes of employment (such as casual labour, telecommuting and self-managed work teams) has imposed the need to create an array of performance management tools that can evaluate each type of labour without potential discrimination or injustice.

However, there are several implications for HR managers in this preparation stage before the appraisal. The sophistication of the performance appraisal can mean little if there is no management commitment to the process. Equipping managers with the required skills, and maintaining the consistency and fairness of the performance management process, is crucial in legitimising it in the organisation. Such systematic procedures and prior preparation by the management will largely determine employees' contextual performance (e.g. commitment to perform) as well as technical performance (e.g. the skills required to perform the job) in organisations. It is a necessity for managers to be well prepared for each performance review they have with an employee and this can be done through advance reviewing of the employee's set performance goals, previous review outcomes and evaluation of the most recent performance records of the employee. Such an evaluation should be analytical in terms of incorporating both strengths and weaknesses of the employee; it should also incorporate potential avenues for the employee to capitalise on their strengths and overcome their weaknesses.

It is also recommended that the interim performance review be kept informal. It is generally a meeting arranged by the manager where the employee is given an insight as to their progression, and may be performed on a daily or weekly basis, for example an informal discussion on the job site. The interim performance review does not lead to any reward allocation or training and development decisions. In contrast, the formal performance review should be given more careful consideration by the manager as they are expected to explain what and how certain ratings were derived, and formally to introduce the development plans and allocate rewards or penalties.

DURING THE PERFORMANCE APPRAISAL MEETING

The review process between the employee and the manager determines the degree of performance improvement that is expected of the employee in the future and what has been achieved since the last appraisal. For example, this is achieved by reviewing the set KPIs and analysing the degree to which they have (or have not) been achieved. In the performance review process, it is also important to reduce any perceptual errors to ensure that the information sent and received is accurate. Therefore, managers should have excellent performance review skills, including communication skills. If they don't this may result in a misconception of feedback and negate the effectiveness of the performance appraisal.

As with most management tasks, conducting a performance review requires a set of specific skills. A failure to develop and utilise these skills (outlined below) often results in performance reviews without any effective action plans.

Elicit input from the employee   A performance review is a mutual process that seeks agreement between the reviewer and the employee. Therefore, employee voice (i.e. opinion and ideas) in a performance review plays a significant role in terms of procedural justice, as well as the acceptability of the review's outcomes. In order to facilitate the input of each employee the appraiser should allow the employee an opportunity for self-evaluation. Hence, it is often suggested that performance reviews be conducted in an informal manner, yet within a formal contextual framework.

Another noteworthy point to consider is that performance reviews should adopt a balanced approach towards both positive and negative aspects of performance, without focusing too much on one and focusing too little on the other. In order to deal effectively with both the positive and negative aspect of performance, it is recommended that managers use probing questions such as 'What kind of difficulties did you go through this year?' and 'Are there any parts of your job that you feel you could perform better in the following year?'.

Strategic communication   For performance management to be successful, performance reviews should allow enough time to discuss how the employee's performance is contributing to the organisational, group and departmental objectives. In order to establish a clear link between employee performance and strategic goals, it is also important to encourage upward review and communication. This means managers should provide an outlet for employees to express their feelings, aspirations and perspectives on their strategic contribution to the improvement of the organisation. This can enhance the mutual understanding of both parties concerned and also provides insight into the training and development needs of employees.

Feedback and performance Giving feedback on performance is an important managerial competency. Part of the skill involves providing both positive and negative information in a constructive manner. Many people find disclosure and confrontation to be stressful, particularly in the case of negative feedback. However, inability to give genuine feedback leads to ambiguous, incomplete and irrelevant appraisals, making performance reviews a source of stress. In this respect, provision of constructive feedback is a crucial aspect of performance appraisal. It is widely acknowledged that effective feedback:

- is specific, rather than general;
- is accompanied by detailed examples;
- is directed toward behaviours, not the person, so that the receiver can do something about it;
- takes into account the needs of the receiver;
- is solicited, rather than imposed;
- involves the amount of information a receiver can use (i.e. take care not to overload or provide too little information);
- concerns what is said or done and how, not why;
- is checked to ensure clear communication.

In order to deal with poor performers and dismissals, the appraiser should:

- identify area(s) of poor performance and objective indicators (which should be incorporated into the performance appraisal form);
- record behavioural incidents with dates and times (in formal documents which are filed);
- systematically record measures of indicators on all employees;
- meet the employee and describe strengths (that are internal to the employee) and weaknesses (based on the behaviour and not on the person);
- seek ideas on ways to improve performance in their area of competence;
- mutually develop a performance plan with set targets, standards and deadlines. This involves taking incremental steps. For example:
  – arranging interim and annual feedback meetings;
  – explicitly stating and documenting rewards (or consequences) of performance and attaching a copy of this to the paperwork (including the KPIs); and
  – ensuring both the employee and the appraiser sign the final document and acknowledge that they understand the stated performance goals, deadlines and implications set forth.

AFTER THE PERFORMANCE APPRAISAL MEETING

Once the performance appraisal has been conducted it is necessary for the manager to ensure that the feedback and outcomes from the meeting are put into practice. For example, this may include developing and implementing training and development for the employee, or encouraging the development of skills, such as communication or technical skills. Unlike the initial preparation for the meeting, which generally occurs once a year, the outcomes of the meeting occur on a daily basis and are continuous, until the employee's performance is reviewed once again.

PERFORMANCE APPRAISAL METHODS

So far, this chapter has identified and discussed a number of issues associated with performance management and performance appraisals. But how are performance appraisals actually conducted? For the appraiser, there are a number of methods that can be adopted; however, it is quite common for appraisers to adopt a combination of methods to conduct the review effectively and thoroughly. The methods chosen will depend on the skills and abilities of the appraiser, as well as organisational and appraiser constraints, such as time and budget resources.

GRAPHIC RATING SCALE

The **graphic rating scale** is the simplest and the most popular performance appraisal method used by managers. It enables each employee to be rated on a bipolar scale (ranging from Unsatisfactory to Outstanding) based on individual traits. Typically, supervisors compare each employee on their job-related skills, knowledge and abilities, and subsequently rank them from being unsatisfactory to outstanding. The major advantage of the graphic rating scale is that is uses simple consistent criteria for all employees who being appraised. However, the rating scale can be inaccurate if the performance traits measure the performance of certain jobs more accurately than others. For example, 'employee creativity' may not be a vastly relevant trait to demonstrate in an accounting job. Therefore, an employee in such a job role may not have the same opportunities to show their creative abilities as a person working in the research and development department. If the two employees are rated on the same performance measurement scale, the result can be potentially misleading. Another potential pitfall of the graphic rating scale is that it is a trait-based measure (not a behavioural measure), and is subject to perceptual errors.

graphic rating scale
Enables each employee to be rated on a bipolar scale (ranging from Unsatisfactory to Outstanding) based on individual traits.

GRADING

Grading encourages supervisors to grade each employee's overall performance at a specific performance level. For example, Superior, Good, Acceptable, Marginal and Unsatisfactory. By pre-empting the percentage of employees who can fall into each grade, the supervisor avoids underrating, overrating or the provision of an average rating for all employees. Like the graphic rating scale, grading does not specify a performance level for each job. Therefore, it is criticised for not providing precise guidance for the performance review and employee training and development.

grading
Rating an employee's overall performance at a specific performance level, such as Superior, Good, Acceptable, Marginal and Unsatisfactory.

In contrast to graphic rating scales and grading, which are both *trait*-based methods of performance appraisal, the following appraisal methods are all *behavioural*-based methods, with the exception of essay descriptions, which may be considered as both.

MANAGEMENT BY OBJECTIVES

Management by objectives (MBO) is a results-oriented method of performance appraisal, where measurable goals or criteria are jointly established by the supervisor and the subordinate (e.g. increase the gross quarterly sales volume by 20 per cent by 30 June 2007). MBO avoids the assumption of standardised appraisal criteria and is, therefore, based on individualised job-specific measurable criteria. This approach significantly reduces subjective perceptual errors of the assessor by measuring objective job-related outcomes. With its job-specific, shared and measurable performance criteria, MBO is considered to be the best appraisal method to support a performance management process. Notably, some organisations employ the SMART approach to setting the performance criteria, which is a form of MBO.

management by objectives
A results-oriented method of performance appraisal, where measurable goals or criteria are jointly established by the supervisor and the subordinate.

CRITICAL INCIDENT METHOD

The **critical incident method** of appraisal involves the documentation of highly effective or highly ineffective instances of performance in a journal designated for

critical incident method
The documentation of highly effective or highly ineffective instances of performance in a journal designated for each employee.

each employee. For this approach to be successful the appraiser must immediately record information as incidents take place. The critical incident method tends to be an objective tool of appraisal, as it is performance oriented rather than person oriented. The appraisal tends to produce a constructively critical report that assists the employee to review, plan and correct behaviours for future performance. An appraiser using the critical incident appraisal, however, needs to be careful of possible recency error effects (i.e. the incidents that have occurred recently having a bigger impact on the rating than the past incidents) when appraising.

BEHAVIOURALLY ANCHORED RATING SCALES

behaviourally anchored rating scales
Produce a numerical rating, anchored by specific narrative examples of behaviours, ranging from very negative to very positive attributes of employee performance.

In a similar vein, **behaviourally anchored rating scales** (BARSs) are also designed to assess job-related behaviours through a critical incident method. However, BARSs produce a numerical rating, anchored by specific narrative examples of behaviours, ranging from very negative to very positive attributes of employee performance. While BARSs produce a job-specific scale of evaluation, they can be very time consuming as the critical incidents of each job need to be identified and analysed separately. Nonetheless, this rating scale format tends to enjoy high acceptance by both raters and ratees as it is developed using input from both groups.

BEHAVIOUR OBSERVATION SCALE

behaviour observation scale
An appraisal tool that measures the frequency of desirable job-related behaviours observed.

The **behaviour observation scale** (BOS) is an appraisal tool that measures the frequency of desirable job-related behaviours observed. The list of desired behaviours is usually developed through critical incident records and is given a rating of observation frequency ranging from 'Almost never' (1) to 'Almost always' (5). BOS has been criticised as giving the appearance of reducing subjectivity because of its use of behaviours rather than traits while, in reality, raters appear to be guided by their subjective evaluation of overall performance when rating behaviour frequencies.

ESSAY DESCRIPTION

essay description
Managers expressing their views on each employee's performance, and suggestions for future development, in their own words.

An **essay description** allows managers to express their views on each employee's performance, and suggestions for future development, in their own words. The major downfall of this approach is the subjectivity of each manager's perceptions regarding each employee's performance. The essay description is also time consuming in practice and therefore is usually not a preferred method in today's fast-paced business environment.

Although these performance appraisal methods are valuable for managers, it is important to remember that the method best suited to one situation may not be suitable for another. In addition, an appraisal method may need modification as an organisation matures, grows, restructures or condenses.

CONTEMPORARY APPRAISAL METHODS

Conventional methods of performance appraisal, such as those discussed in the previous section, emphasise the accuracy of ratings, for example graphic rating scales and behaviourally anchored rating scales. However, contemporary appraisal methods have broadened in scope to ensure that they are not only accurate, but also cover all aspects of an employee's work life. Hence, they address social and motivational aspects of a job, along with job-specific technical skills. Consequently, the content being measured in a performance appraisal today goes beyond task performance to incorporate broader performance capabilities, such as team working capabilities, interpersonal communication skills, cultural awareness and organisational citizenship behaviours.

The changing nature of job roles in today's workplace has blurred the traditional command and control management style, requiring individuals to work in teams and network across multiple levels and units in the organisation. In such a work environment, performance appraisals provided by one's superior only may not be sufficient to gain an all-encompassing evaluation of an employee.

Contemporary performance appraisals have tried to encompass the *360-degree-feedback* method to gain a more holistic performance review of employees. The 360-degree-feedback method is a type of appraisal which collects views from people both in the job and holding jobs hierarchically above and below the position being analysed, providing a multifaceted view. As such, it includes upward appraisal, downward appraisal, peer appraisal and customer appraisal of a single employee. In such a method of appraisal, employees are exposed to evaluation at any time or place. Moreover, as 360-degree feedback provides feedback from multiple perspectives, it lessens the perceptual biases (extreme biases cancel each other out) and increases the objectivity of the appraisal outcome.

The multiple-perspective feedback gained from this procedure helps set self-development goals for the future and ultimately improves individual performance in the organisation. The 360-degree-feedback method is also regarded as an effective tool in developing self awareness, which is a key element of emotional intelligence. Research in Australia indicated that, in 2002, 90 per cent of Fortune 500 companies used 360-degree feedback (Carruthers, 2003). However, this method of performance appraisal should be used carefully so as not to foster a politically negative climate in the organisation.

With the increasing popularity of flatter organisational structures, upward appraisal is recognised as a more accurate measure of performance management. *Upward appraisal* is often used to appraise managers' leadership abilities and their behavioural and attitudinal congruence to the organisation's values and mission statement. The appraisal is typically conducted through the administration of an anonymous questionnaire.

Performance appraisals in the service sector should be different from the product manufacturing sector. In the service sector, customer satisfaction is considered to be a key success indicator. Consequently, *customer appraisal* (or the assessment of employees based upon customer satisfaction or feedback) has become a viable performance indicator. Customer surveys, interviews, recording of sales conversations and using mystery shoppers are popular methods of assessing employees' customer service capabilities.

Moreover, the increasing popularity of cross-functional teams, self-managed work teams and short-term project teams indicates the importance of *team-based appraisals*. Conjoined appraisals of the overall team performance also serve as a basis to determine team rewards and incentive schemes. Nevertheless, good processes do not always guarantee a good outcome and bad processes do not necessarily lead to a bad outcome, although in the long term such associations can be expected. Therefore, specific task performance levels need to serve as benchmarks of team-based appraisals.

IMPLICATIONS OF PERFORMANCE APPRAISAL

As with every aspect of managing, and specifically with HRM, managers need to consider the implications of management processes. Performance management is no exception, and there are a number of factors that should be carefully considered before performance appraisals are conducted. These include contextual performance attributes, culturally appropriate appraisals, technology-based appraisals and performance appraisal errors.

CONTEXTUAL PERFORMANCE ATTRIBUTES

With increasing importance placed on team-based work and effective organisational communication, contextual performance (in addition to task performance) is recognised as a crucial indicator of overall employee performance. As discussed earlier in the chapter, contextual performance refers to non-job-specific behaviours that enhance the climate and effectiveness of the organisation, such as cooperation, dedication, interpersonal facilitation, enthusiasm and persistence. According to Conway (1999), these attributes tend to be associated with the personality and motivational aspects of employees. Conversely, the job-specific performance of an employee tends to be associated with cognitive abilities, skills and experience. In particular, peers tend to emphasise the contextual performance of an employee (e.g. interpersonal facilitation) more so than a supervisor, who would place more emphasis on job-related performance. Finally, contextual performance seems to be best appraised through the 360-degree-feedback method.

CULTURALLY APPROPRIATE APPRAISALS

Cultural differences must be taken into consideration when conducting performance appraisals in a multicultural context at both the organisational and national levels. Considering the nature of internationalised businesses worldwide, cultural diversity in performance appraisal and performance management is an unavoidable topic. In Australia, for example, approximately 25 per cent of the population were born overseas and come from more than 220 nations. Further, it is expected that by the year 2030, 25 per cent of the Australian population will be of Asian origin.

So, how does this affect performance appraisals? It can create implications for HR managers who may need to adopt different methods of appraising. For example, individualistic performance appraisals that tend formally to set individualistic performance goals may be quite distressing for employees with a collectivist background. Hence, they might prefer more informal, group-based performance appraisals that de-emphasise individualism.

TECHNOLOGY-BASED APPRAISALS

Technology plays an increasingly important role in performance appraisals. Technological advancements influencing this area include electronic monitoring of work performance, storage of multifaceted feedback systems and the systematic processing of performance appraisal results for each employee (Sulsky & Keown, 1998). There are many software packages that support the task of corporate performance management (CPM), such as Hyperison Solutions, Cognos and Oracle. In particular, the provision of feedback online is increasing in popularity due to reduced emotional influences in responses, which can decrease any potential biases arising from interpersonal cues. A recent advancement in the field has been a software program called 'e360', which provides greater flexibility in conducting web-based 360-degree-feedback appraisals.

PERFORMANCE APPRAISAL ERRORS

Despite the high recognition of performance appraisal as a strategic tool capable of capitalising on individual performances, research has long confirmed the existence of performance appraisal errors. Employees are highly concerned about the accuracy of rating scales and measurements used in performance appraisals, as the results derived from these lead to serious and substantial career outcomes such as promotions, demotions and even termination of employment. In order to increase the validity and reliability of performance appraisals, managers need to avoid performance appraisal errors as much as possible.

Serious problems with rating include perceptual errors, which refer to the tendency of people to make highly subjective assessments of performance and seek further confirmation of the initial view. Such perceptual errors include the halo effect, leniency/strictness bias, central tendency, prejudices and the recency effect.

The **halo effect** occurs when the assessor believes that an employee is inherently good or bad based upon one job-related factor, regardless of the employee's actual level of performance. For instance, employees with low levels of absence tend to be perceived as high performers notwithstanding the number of errors they may have made while working. This can be a particular concern in regard to graphic rating and grading scales due to the inherent generic nature of evaluation.

Leniency/strictness bias occurs when the assessor tends to rate at one end of the rating scale (i.e. high or low) in a consistent manner. To avoid confrontation and future conflict, an appraiser could rate everyone extremely leniently or be extraordinarily strict and rate everyone extremely strictly. Either way, inaccurate ratings cause confusion for employees, resulting in ambiguous goals and low levels of perceived integrity concerning the performance appraisal.

Central tendency typically occurs when busy and untrained appraisers are attempting to rate everyone in the range of 'satisfactory' or 'adequate' regardless of their actual performance. This can be a common occurrence when the appraiser is unclear about the rating system and purpose of the appraisal.

halo effect
When the assessor believes that an employee is inherently good or bad based upon one job-related factor, regardless of the employee's actual level of performance.

leniency/strictness bias
When the assessor tends to rate at one end of the rating scale (i.e. high or low) in a consistent manner.

central tendency
When busy and untrained appraisers are tempted to rate everyone in the range of 'satisfactory' or 'adequate' regardless of their actual performance.

prejudices
The errors generated as a result of the positive or negative attitude held by the appraiser towards the employee.

recency effect
When the performance appraisal is based on the most recent behaviours rather than the performance over the full review period.

relationship effect
When the performance appraisal is affected by the quality of the supervisor and subordinate's relationship as opposed to the actual work performance.

Prejudices in the context of performance appraisal refer to the errors generated as a result of a positive or negative attitude held by the appraiser towards the employee. For instance, research has found that appraisers tend to give significantly higher ratings to subordinates of their own race (Lefkowitz, 1994). Interestingly, however, research also indicates that appraisers who are open to individual differences are less likely to provide such discriminatory performance ratings (Härtel *et al.*, 1999).

The **recency effect** occurs when the performance appraisal is based on the most recent behaviours rather than the performance over the full review period. Likewise, the **relationship effect** occurs when the performance appraisal is affected by the quality of the supervisor and subordinate's relationship as opposed to the actual work performance.

Contemporary SHRM Application Tool

Imagine that you are an HR manager of a national law firm which specialises in corporate law. In the past 10 years, your organisation has tripled in size and employs about 400 people across the state today. One significant drawback to this organisation is that it did not value the function of human resource management at all. Instead, it relied heavily on the expertise and skills of lawyers and financial development to grow the business. Human resource management was not regarded as an organisational function worth dedicating resources to.

However, due to the lack of human resource management, your organisation has reached a crisis level of extremely low employee morale, high levels of resignation, absenteeism and turnover. Because of this, the CEO has approached you to develop a human resource management strategy that is linked to organisational goals and objectives. After monitoring the culture of your organisation through interviews (with both existing and former employees) and focus groups, you have decided to implement a better performance appraisal process that is focused on motivating employees. The SHRM Application Tool example demonstrates how you could help the CEO make the strategic decision of how to implement a better performance appraisal process in the organisation (refer to Figure 10.6).

10.6 | FIGURE
SHRM Application Tool:
problem – performance
management

Step 6: Evaluate against success criteria
- Has the performance appraisal course significantly reduced the employee resignation, turnover and absenteeism rate over the period of 2 years?
- Has the performance appraisal course contributed to higher employee morale and higher employee performance in both task and contextual areas?

Step 5: Implement the plan
- Conduct interviews through mail and informal discussions with open-ended questions to explore employees' contextual performance problems
- Establish a one-day course to train supervisors on how to run performance appraisals with the aim of fostering employees' motivation and morale
- Course content must include (a) understanding supervisory challenge, (b) importance of performance appraisal to meet business objectives, (c) motivating employees, (d) effective communication, (e) effective leadership
- Performance appraisals to be conducted quarterly in the year with focus on effective leadership daily

---

Step 4: Devise plan and success criteria
- Aim to develop better contextual performance to the same standard as the current task performance
- Invest in employees' discretionary behaviours by developing a friendly and proactive work culture in the long term
- Need to educate supervisors to conduct performance appraisal based more on contextual performance
- Conduct interviews to explore employees' problems (including exit interviews) to identify what kind of supervision is lacking in this organisation
- Prepare performance appraisal training for supervisors in order to develop positive and motivated employees

---

Verify

Step 3: Verify/falsify potential problem or opportunity
- Need to develop effective supervision especially in the area of performance appraisal process

Falsify

Step 2: Detect potential problem or opportunity
- Lack of management of employees' performance
- Lack of contextual performance (e.g. volunteering), which is leading to lack of task performance (e.g. soliciting skills and knowledge)
- Lack of managers' supervisory skills
- Lack of business core value of 'human relations'

Step 1: Analyse environmental factors

Step 1a: HR issues: Monitor/ analyse data (past, present and future)	**Step 1b: Internal/organisational environment**	**Step 1c: External environment**
- Extremely low employee morale - Experiencing high number of resignations, absenteeism and costly turnover - Supervising lawyers are well educated, trained in a successful practice in 'law', not on 'human' aspects - Poor performance management	- Specialised in business law - Develop a reputation for quality client service and provision of practical legal solutions - Portray commitment and sensitivity in meeting business and personal goals - Provide business-related legal services including intellectual property, civil litigation, insurance and insolvency - Ability to work in a fast-paced environment with minimal supervision	- Competitive intelligence for the legal industry requiring competitive techniques and practices - Need to utilise increasingly complex information and legal environment - Law Council of Australia, governments, courts and other federal agencies

A view from the field

The meat in the sandwich

Organisations in the not-for-profit and non-government sectors have moved to introduce contemporary corporate governance strategies. Such measures have been implemented to ensure they are accountable and transparent in their decision making, which includes the allocation of funds provided by both private donors and governments.

Such governance standards have necessitated the review of systems used to develop programs and services and allocate funds. More formal systems have evolved to monitor the standards and performance of those services and financial operations. The rigour required is often a challenge for organisations in these sectors, as many of the principles of governance are drawn from more commercial operations which are driven by profit, rather than values and commitment to a cause.

The board of one particular Australian non-government organisation (NGO) had, over a two-year period, introduced a more comprehensive way of monitoring the performance of the organisation. The results have begun to be published as detailed assessments of the organisational performance biannually. The Chief Executive Officer (CEO) was of the opinion that the same type of system would be valuable in the management of his employees. He had three clear objectives in mind – the system would provide:

1. A vehicle for implementing annual objectives and performance standards throughout the organisation.
2. A way to engage his staff better in the delivery of the organisation's objectives.
3. Better information on the skills available in the organisation.

The Human Resources Manager of this organisation pointed out that it could also provide more formal feedback to staff on their performance and facilitate development discussions – an opportunity many staff were seeking. She was delighted that there was some interest in aligning the HR issues with annual planning and review processes discussed at board level. The current performance appraisal system involved an appraisal interview which was an annual event conducted on the staff member's employment commencement anniversary. It was based on a simple model which required managers to rate general performance and attitudes of staff against a rating between one (very good) and three (unsatisfactory). Managers and staff felt this process added little value to performance management.

After extensive discussions and consideration, the board and the CEO decided to align the performance management system with the annual reporting cycle of the organisation. The CEO and his management team developed an integrated approach. This required unit heads to propose their detailed annual plans, including budget bids and performance targets, to the CEO and management team. The CEO would then propose an annual plan, including budgets, to the board for discussion and sign-off. The agreed plans would then be handed down to managers and staff, allowing staff performance plans and targets to be implemented. Formal reviews of staff performance against these agreed plans would be conducted biannually with the final annual assessment submitted to HRM.

This organisation was in a growth phase and working with many new programs and challenges. The management team suggested that an individual development plan be included in the annual program to help ensure staff were equipped to handle the constantly changing environment. The CEO agreed that this was a positive way to encourage growth in the skill base of the organisation.

The new approach was enthusiastically launched by the CEO prior to the end of the 2004 financial year. It was supported by a new policy and forms which were available on the organisation's intranet. Managers and staff were provided with an hour-long briefing on the new policy, associated forms and timelines. The HR team produced a simple catalogue of development options and reference materials to assist individuals and managers with the development planning process.

Halfway through the year, the HR and Finance teams uncovered a surprising trend. It appeared that the spending on training and development allocations was running at 30 per cent of total budget, which was well below projections. This was a most unusual trend as most years these funds were fully allocated by the third quarter. There seemed to be no obvious reason for the slow rate of expenditure of the training and development budget.

As the end of the year drew near, the HR department sent all managers with responsibility for staff reminders of the due date for finalised performance reviews for the year ending and development plans for the forthcoming year. Finance staff also reminded managers that requests for funds for travel, conferences and other training were due for inclusion in the annual budget cycle.

The HR manager was concerned that there did not seem to be much interest in the review process across the organisation. Anecdotally, staff were reporting that their reviews had not been completed, or for that matter scheduled. The underspending in the training and development budget was continuing; however, this did offer an opportunity. A half-day program on performance management was sourced, and programs for managers and staff were advertised across the organisation. HR staff were pleased when all places were taken up very quickly as this demonstrated an interest in developing further skills in this area, particularly with deadlines for reviews looming.

The first managers' program uncovered some surprises. At the scheduled start time only two of the 20 participants who had enrolled had arrived. After making many follow-up phone calls, HR staff had to apologise to the trainer and proceed with only two participants. The participant-to-trainer ratio made this a very expensive training option. Further investigations revealed that the majority of those scheduled for the second program were now unable to attend and, as a consequence, the second program was cancelled.

The training for staff proceeded with 100 per cent of those scheduled attending. Staff had been asked to bring along their position descriptions and performance plans. The trainer reported some concerns to the HR manager after this training was finalised. The details are provided below.

Training participants were very keen to explore goal setting and the building of measurable performance targets. With few exceptions, they had not been party to the process of establishing goals and targets for performance as part of the new performance management system. In fact, most expected to be reviewed against their current position descriptions and were bemused to hear that the CEO and board believed the new system had been implemented across the organisation.

In an attempt to make the training of value, the trainer worked with the position descriptions of attendees, but many of those were well out of date. Those which were current had pages and pages of duties listed but few (if any) objectives or measurable, outcome-oriented statements. The trainer found that participants were keen to reshape their responsibilities into objectives and measurable outcomes, and most had been required to do this for the programs and services they delivered to internal and external customers.

The trainer was concerned with the lack of connection between the performance management system she had been briefed about and actual practice within the organisation. She tried to explore the gap with training participants. Two key themes emerged:

1. *Managers' skill*. Staff reported that managers did not seem keen to engage in these discussions. Some felt that managers struggled with the need to identify and implement clear objectives and standards. Others believed poor communication skills, in addition to a reluctance to tackle difficult people and conversations, to be the crux of the problem.

2. *Priorities*. There was general consensus that staff performance management was not given the same priority as review of services, programs and budgets. The training program also included a section on career planning designed to assist staff to think through their personal plans and consider development options. The exploration of this issue caused great uproar among training participants in both staff groups. It seemed that over the last year formal and informal training and development opportunities had almost completely ceased. Previously, access to these types of opportunities had been a feature of working in this organisation;

conferences, training programs, professional supervision, secondments, site visits and the like had been integral to staff skill development and the continued improvement of the services and programs. The new performance management system was blamed for the lack of interest in such activities, and staff believed all development activities needed to be integrated into the development part of their performance plan. Development opportunities seemed to have all but disappeared.

Discussion questions

1. Imagine you are the Head of HR in this organisation. Assess the implementation of the new performance management system, including feedback from the trainer. Develop a broad outline for a progress report on implementation to the CEO.

2. Review the implementation process for this new performance management system. What opportunities for identifying more efficient and effective processes exist for other organisations?

3. It seems that managers are the 'meat in the sandwich' in this case. What is (are) the cause(s) of this situation? What can HR do to assist the managers to meet the expectations of those above and below them in the hierarchy?

Performance management at the Australian Public Service and Merit Protection Commission

A manager's challenge

Performance management has been an area of much significance in the private sector, where business plans are outlined with measurable outcomes and each member, unit or department's inputs/outputs are evaluated in terms of their contribution to the organisation's bottom line. However, in the public sector, and even more so in the public service, defining such 'measurable' outcomes can be challenging as the bottom line is often evaluated in terms of social welfare. Nevertheless, Australian Public Service (APS) agencies have striven to apply tools of performance management in a sophisticated manner by linking and aligning individual, team and organisational objectives and results. The performance management scheme executed in the Public Service and Merit Protection Commission (PSMPC) is one such example.

The performance management scheme which was initiated in 1996 on a six-month trial basis is a part of the overall corporate performance planning, management and accountability framework of the PSMPC. It relies on an achievements- and value-based performance appraisal system which aims to develop an organisational culture that is focused on achieving target performance outcomes. According to the PSMPC, a distinctive purpose of the scheme is its vertical integration of individual development planning and corporate-level planning. Through performance management, the PSMPC aims to achieve congruence in individual, team and departmental objectives in a way that leads to the fulfilment of the overall corporate goals.

The performance management scheme at the PSMPC operates on an annual management cycle. All employees are required to participate in the process, with the exception of sessional and temporary staff. The scheme requires employees to have personal performance agreements that articulate expected performance achievements for the next year. These agreements are subsequently linked to the 'Team business plans' of the PSMPC. Individual training and development needs that may have risen in this endeavour are then included in the annual corporate training calendar. As a part of the performance appraisal scheme, employees who demonstrate outstanding skills and knowledge will be given recognition and rewards, while the concerns of the underperforming employees are addressed with remedial plans. The performance management scheme at the PSMPC is also complemented with a 360-degree-feedback process. The outcomes of the 360-degree-feedback process do not directly influence appraisal ratings or remuneration of individuals; nevertheless, they provide a more holistic and less biased preview of individuals and give significant insight to personal development plans.

The performance management scheme at the PSMPC has proved to be effective in linking team performance and corporate goals, and better at articulating individual responsibilities to achieve those team objectives. It also provides a basis for biannual feedback on performance. Moreover, the systematic nature of the scheme fosters fairness in issues such as salary increases, bonuses and career advancements. Attesting to this, a staff survey conducted in 1997 and 2000 has indicated generally positive views of the performance management scheme at the PSMPC.

Source: Adapted from Management Advisory Committee (2001), *Performance Management in the Australian Public Service: A Strategic Framework*, Commonwealth of Australia, Canberra.

Summary

Managing the performance of employees is an important HRM function if a company is to achieve strategically organisational objectives. After all, employee performance leads to organisational performance, therefore employees should receive guidance and encouragement from their managers regarding continual performance improvement. This chapter addressed the issues and implications associated with performance management, and how HR managers can effectively manage this function to achieve and continually foster a competitive advantage through their human resources.

The chapter began with a discussion on why performance reviews are perceived as 'fiascos'. Occurring on an annual or biannual basis, performance reviews are generally viewed negatively by employees and managers alike because they involve open, honest and constructive feedback which some employees may have difficulty receiving, and some managers may experience difficulty articulating. Despite this, they are crucial to the long- and short-term success of individual, group and organisational performance and are therefore a critical component of SHRM.

Performance management refers to the collective range of activities conducted by an organisation aimed at enhancing individual, group or unit-level performance, with an overarching purpose of improving strategic organisational performance. It is concerned with inputs (i.e. materials) and employee outputs (i.e. task accomplishment). However, although performance management has traditionally been conducted at the individual level, the increased popularity of teams in organisations also allows managers to conduct performance management at the group level. The unit level of analysis will depend on individual and organisational requirements and capabilities, all of which need to be aligned with strategic organisational goals.

There are five characteristics of performance appraisals that HR managers need to consider before conducting performance reviews. These include: a process of continuous input and output management; a multifaceted and multilevel agreement of input and output; vertical integration; horizontal integration; and a holistic management process. Although each characteristic is important to the understanding of performance management, the final characteristic is imperative if the process is to be viewed and conducted with a strategic, holistic focus. It is this characteristic which aligns the HRM function with other organisational functions, in a bid to achieve strategic, organisational success.

It is vital for managers to understand and acknowledge the process of performance management. As such, there are some critical dimensions which need to be highlighted. The *strategic planning* process involves developing long-term plans for the company and begins with an internal and external analysis of the firm (i.e. a SWOT analysis). Determining *performance criteria and measures* is a critical aspect of performance management which may be achieved by using the balanced scorecard to measure individual performance. The third dimension is *taking action*, whereby the gap between planning and action needs to be bridged proactively by employees and employers alike. Finally, understanding the influence of *organisational culture* is vital for an organisation to have a healthy, performance-oriented culture which rewards and fosters continuous performance improvements.

Performance management requires managers to work cooperatively with their employees by setting mutual performance objectives and standards, and continuously measuring and reviewing predetermined objectives with actual performance. The method of achieving this is through a performance appraisal, which refers to an SHRM tool which is used to fill performance gaps and is defined as a formal and mutually agreed upon system of planning and reviewing employee performance (e.g. skills, abilities, knowledge and attitudes). However, managers need to be aware of problems associated with performance appraisals, such as the tendency to blame them for being backward looking, subjective and concentrating only on the negative aspects of work. To combat this, HR managers need to take several factors into consideration when conducting performance appraisals. These include defining the performance criteria, facilitating discussion regarding the performance review; identifying training and development needs; and rewarding good performance. In essence, performance appraisals provide a great opportunity for superiors not only to uplift employee performance but to also reinforce the corporate climate, values and attitudes, and to harmonise appraisals with the strategic direction and improved performance of the organisation. Above all, performance appraisals should be interrelated strategically with other HRM activities, such as reward allocation, job analysis, workforce planning, training and development, promotion, demotion, transfer and termination.

Despite the theory surrounding performance appraisals, they can be a difficult and time-consuming task for both managers and employees. Yet, because they are important to the development of individual and organisational performance, it is imperative that they are performed on a regular basis. Therefore, some tips for success were identified in the chapter. These included tips for preparation *before* the performance appraisal meeting (i.e. gathering correct information, revising the performance criteria and having a well-established purpose), *during* the performance appraisal meeting (i.e. eliciting input from the employee, communicating strategically and effectively and providing feedback on performance) and *after* the performance appraisal meeting (i.e. ensuring that the feedback and outcomes from the meeting are put into practice through relevant training and development initiatives).

The chapter concluded with an identification of the traditional and contemporary performance appraisal methods and management implications. Some traditional methods included graphic rating scales, management by objectives, behaviourally anchored rating scales, and essay description, which were classified as either trait- or behavioural-based methods. The contemporary performance appraisal methods include 360-degree feedback, upward appraisal, customer appraisal and team-based appraisals. Finally, some implications that HR managers (or those conducting the appraisal) need to be aware of include contextual, cultural or technology-based implications, in addition to errors such as the halo effect, leniency/strictness bias, central tendency, prejudices, the recency effect and the relationship effect.

Key terms

behaviour observation scale	graphic rating scale	output
behaviourally anchored rating scales	group	performance
	halo effect	performance appraisal
central tendency	horizontal integration	performance management
contextual performance	input	prejudices
critical incident method	internal analysis	recency effect
essay description	key performance indicators	relationship effect
external analysis	leniency/strictness bias	task performance
grading	management by objectives	vertical integration

Review questions

10.1 What is performance? How does performance management enhance employees' overall performance in the organisation?

10.2 What are the characteristics of performance management? Are there any issues that could constrain the relationship between HR practices and organisational performance?

10.3 Are performance appraisal and performance management the same? What is the difference between the two? How are they related?

10.4 If you were the HR manager of an Australian company operating in China, what are some performance appraisal implications you would need to consider? How might they be overcome? Would these implications be different if the company was operating in Mexico? Use examples to illustrate your answer.

Exercises

10.1 Self-appraisal in the performance appraisal process is an important, although sometimes difficult, task. As a student, conduct a self-appraisal of your work in one of your classes. Do you think your teacher would conduct an appraisal with similar results? What factors influenced your appraisal and how could you conduct a fair, honest and constructive appraisal in the future?

10.2 Using the theory of the 360-degree-feedback method, ask your family and friends to conduct an appraisal of you, identifying your strengths and weaknesses. How can you use this information to improve your performance?

10.3 Using the Internet, visit the website of a company you are interested in or familiar with, and search for one of their core values (i.e. mission, vision or future direction). Using this core value, establish vertical and horizontal integration.

References

Aguilar, O. (2003), 'How strategic performance is helping companies create business value', *Strategic Finance*, vol. 84, no. 7, pp. 44–9.

Beer, M. & Ruh, R. A. (1976), 'Employee growth through performance', *Harvard Business Review*, vol. 54, no. 4, pp. 59–66.

Campbell, J. P., McCloy, R. A., Oppler, S. H. & Sager, C. E. (1993), 'A theory of performance' in *Personnel Selection*, eds

N. Schmitt & W. C. Borman, Jossey-Bass, San Francisco.

Carruthers, F. (2003), 'Nothing but the truth', *The Australian Financial Review*, 14 November, p. 78.

Conway, J. M. (1999), 'Distinguishing contextual performance from task performance for managerial jobs, *Journal of Applied Psychology*, vol. 84, no. 1, pp. 3–13.

Fletcher, C. (2001), 'Performance appraisal

and management: The developing research agenda, *Journal of Occupational and Organizational Psychology*, vol. 74, pp. 473–87.

Gallie, D., White, M., Cheng, Y. & Tomlinson, M. (1998), *Restructuring the Employment Relationship*, Clarendon Press, Oxford.

Härtel, C. E. J., Douthitt, S., Härtel, G. F. & Douthitt, S. (1999), 'Equally qualified but unequally perceived: General cultural openness as a predictor of discriminatory performance ratings', *Human Resource Development Quarterly*, vol 10, no. 1, pp. 79–89.

Klein, H. J., Wesson, M. J., Hollenbeck, J. R. & Alge, B. J. (1999), 'Goal commitment and the goal setting process: Conceptual clarification and empirical synthesis', *Journal of Applied Psychology*, vol. 84, no. 6, pp. 885–96.

Lefkowitz, J. (1994), 'Race as a factor in job placement: Serendipitous findings of "ethnic drift"', *Personnel Psychology*, vol. 47, pp. 497–513.

MacDuffie, J. P. (1995), 'Human resource bundles and manufacturing performance', *Industrial Relations Review*, vol. 48, no. 2, pp. 199–221.

Pfeffer, J. & Sutton, R. I. (1999), 'Knowing "what" to do is not enough: Turning knowledge into action', *California Management Review*, vol. 42, no. 1, pp. 83–108.

Pickett, L. (2003), 'Transforming the annual fiasco . . .', paper presented at the Hong Kong Institute of Human Resource Management Annual International Conference, 12–15 November, Hong Kong.

Sulsky, L. M. & Keown, J. L. (1998), 'Performance appraisal in the changing world of work: Implications for the meaning and measurement of work performance', *Canadian Psychology*, vol. 39, pp. 52–9.

Tarantino, D. P. (2003), 'Using the balanced score card as a performance management Tool', *Physician Executive*, vol. 29, no. 5, pp. 69–72.

Chapter

Strategic reward management

One of the most important outcomes people derive from work is compensation, in other words, what people are paid (or receive) for working. As discussed in Chapter 2, money is a significant driver of why people work because people need money to survive. Of course, not everybody works for money, for example volunteer and charity workers. However, for a large percentage of the population money is a significant factor in the employment relationship. The base pay, variable pay, employee benefits and non-financial reward that employees collectively receive for working are critical elements of the reward management system.

Apart from providing financial compensation, reward management also determines, to a large degree, extra discretionary behaviour, absenteeism, turnover and, ultimately, the company's bottom line. For example, if employees are well paid and are satisfied with their financial arrangement, then there is an increased likelihood that they will be more productive and stay with the company. On the other hand, if they are unhappy or dissatisfied with their salary, then they are inclined to be less productive, absent more often and more likely to leave, hence the organisation's productivity and profitability will be negatively affected.

To compete in today's dynamic environment, pay has undergone a tremendous transformation, from a rigid, inflexible and tenure-based pay system to a new flexible pay system that bridges reward and business strategies. Managers need to be more strategic in establishing flexible reward systems to align with a dynamic changing environment.

This chapter emphasises the importance of dynamic strategic reward management for today's managers. While training and development (Chapter 9) and performance management (Chapter 10) fill the performance gap by continually improving performance, reward management plays an indispensable part in reinforcing the 'right' employee behaviours and performance. In essence, reward management, coupled with training and development and performance management, should result in a high-performing successful organisation. This chapter will unfold the reward management process by presenting the components of a reward system, and applying these to the essential 'building blocks' in the reward management process. This chapter concludes by considering contemporary reward strategies to meet individual and organisational needs.

Objectives

The primary objective of this chapter is to demonstrate the significant role that reward management plays in SHRM. This is important for HR managers to consider as it has a significant influence on employee behaviour and organisational performance, including the ability to achieve a competitive advantage.

After reading this chapter you should be able to:

- define reward management and how it has shifted from a transactional system to a human relations approach;
- understand the underlying principles of a reward strategy;
- understand how a reward strategy helps meet organisational and employee needs;
- explain base pay in the Australian context;
- apply the essential building blocks of total reward management to establish a reward strategy;
- explain performance pay and how it is associated with performance management and training and development;
- explain employee benefits and non-financial rewards.

Strategic reward management

Almost every organisation has a system of reward management which is used to increase individual performance and contribute to the achievement of a competitive advantage. However, before reward systems can be designed and implemented strategically with SHRM goals, it is first necessary to define what reward management is and its relationship to other HRM functions.

Reward management is concerned with the strategic formulation and implementation of equitable rewards in a way that aligns with the strategic direction and values of an organisation. It concerns financial and non-financial forms of compensation that employees receive for working, such as a service award, training opportunities, a salary, a wage, bonuses or commission. However, it may also refer to other forms of compensation, such as a notebook computer, mobile phone, new office, corner office or a car. Of course, the type of reward available is unique to the company and will usually depend on the company size, culture and profitability, as well as the incumbent's position. For example, a receptionist would usually receive a salary as a form of reward management. In contrast, a sales assistant might receive a capped salary and a bonus for a percentage of the sales they achieve, while a senior manager might receive a salary, bonus, notebook computer, mobile phone and a car. As a general rule,

reward management
Concerned with the strategic formulation and implementation of equitable rewards in a way that aligns with the strategic direction and values of an organisation.

the higher the position, the more reward management needs to be tailored to the employee.

Reward management deals with the design, implementation and maintenance processes needed to improve organisational, group and individual performance (Armstrong & Murlis, 2004). As its definition suggests, reward management plays a crucial part in the strategic management process. It helps the organisation attract, motivate and retain employees who possess strategic attributes such as knowledge, skills and values that are aligned with the organisation's strategy. Traditionally, reward management was based on the scientific management approach advocated by Frederick Taylor (1911), where it was regarded as a transactional system of simply linking effort to pay. Management and employees alike viewed an individual's output (i.e. productivity) as a determinant of how much they should be paid. Therefore, this encouraged employees to increase productivity: the more they produced, the more they were paid. Although effective in theory, a drawback of this approach was that quality was often sacrificed for quantity.

Reward management today, however, has a human relations approach which is ever changing with the business environment and with an emphasis on continually motivating employees to increase their performance. Rather than focusing on output, HR managers should encourage employees to develop a sense of ownership and pride when completing work tasks, thus emphasising both quality and quantity. Reward management should be viewed as a total integrated strategy (or approach) that utilises every aspect of rewards to achieve performance maximisation. As such, **reward strategy** is referred to as the development, implementation and use of reward systems which enable individuals to complete work tasks that are aligned with organisational goals, structures and strategies.

reward strategy
The development, implementation and use of reward systems which enable individuals to complete work tasks that are aligned with organisational goals, structures and strategies.

While training and development (see Chapter 9) and performance management (see Chapter 10) are tools which foster continuous performance improvement by filling the performance gap, reward management is a crucial integrated strategic implementation tool for continually reinforcing and fostering the right performance.

THE REWARD SYSTEM

When devising reward systems it is necessary to consider what constitutes a reward and from where the reward may be sourced. This is important because different people perceive rewards differently, therefore a manager failing to take this into account may, unknowingly, foster an ineffective company. Therefore, a **reward** is defined as an item (either tangible or intangible) which is received in recognition for behaviour or output. There are two important factors to remember when identifying rewards and designing reward systems. First, rewards can be applied to positive or negative behaviour; that is, for positive behaviour it can be a congratulatory or appreciative mechanism, but for negative behaviour it can be a punishment or control mechanism. Second, rewards are generally categorised as either extrinsic or intrinsic.

reward
An item (either tangible or intangible) which is received in recognition for behaviour or output.

INTRINSIC VERSUS EXTRINSIC REWARDS

Intrinsic rewards are rewards which are sourced from inside, or are internal to, the individual. Generally, intrinsic rewards are intangible although they may sometimes be tangible, for example the pleasure or value received from the content of the work, work motivation and satisfaction (intangible), or a plaque awarded for employee of the month (tangible). Intrinsic rewards tend to be reinforced by:

Non-financial rewards. These include the company's or manager's recognition (e.g. employee of the month, company newsletter or a 'pat on the back'). For example, St George Bank has established Star Awards which seize the opportunity to thank individuals who have gone above and beyond the call of duty in supporting the organisation's customer focus.

First choice. This refers to receiving the first choice (i.e. priority above colleagues) for things such as holiday leave, preferred shifts, training or projects.

Receipt of valued things. This refers to factors that are highly sought after or valued in the workplace, such as the 'best' bus route for a bus driver, the closest parking spot to a building and an office with a window.

Extrinsic rewards are rewards which are sourced outside, or are external to, the individual. Generally, extrinsic rewards are tangible although they may also be intangible. They are also usually financially related. For example, *direct* financial rewards include base pay, performance pay (e.g. profit sharing and stock options) and deferred pay (e.g. superannuation); in other words, they include any form of financial payment for the work performed. In comparison, *indirect* financial rewards include factors such as sick leave, employee assistance programs (EAP), childcare or a car, items that would otherwise have cost the employee additional money for self-purchase. As illustrated in Figure 11.1, direct and indirect (i.e. extrinsic) and non-financial (i.e. intrinsic) rewards are the components of the reward system.

intrinsic rewards
Rewards which are sourced from inside, or are internal to, the individual.

extrinsic rewards
Rewards which are sourced outside, or are external to, the individual.

11.1   FIGURE
Reward management system

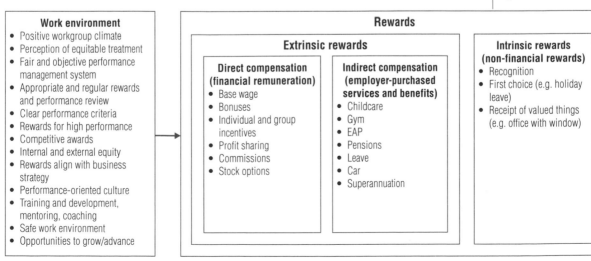

So, which type of reward do employees prefer? As discussed in earlier chapters, the workforce today comprises a vast range of unique and diverse employees who have different perceptions, ideas and values about what constitutes 'work' and the employment relationship. Therefore, it makes sense that these people would also have different opinions about what constitutes a reward and the type of reward they prefer. This is very important to acknowledge because a common problem experienced by managers is that they do not adequately identify *how* employees want to be rewarded. The reward system therefore needs to be tailored to suit the individual. Quite often, a lack of time or experience has resulted in managers' inadvertently rewarding *undesirable* behaviours. Therefore, in order to reward desirable behaviours accurately, managers need be aware of and understand the underlying principles of reward strategy and how they can capitalise on the total reward management process to reward desirable behaviours.

Please read
Kerr, S. (1995), 'On the folly of rewarding A, while hoping for B', *Academy of Management Executive*, vol. 9, no. 1, pp. 7–14.

UNDERLYING PRINCIPLES OF A REWARD STRATEGY
Although many organisations have good business strategies, only a few succeed in their implementation. This is because managers often fail to develop and execute strategies carefully; often they are rushed in response to changing consumer demands and in the race to secure market share before their competitors. Companies also frequently implement strategies but fail to ensure they are correctly designed and continually evaluated. It is the responsibility of HR managers to address the underlying principles of a reward strategy in reward management.

Rewarding is a particularly important aspect of SHRM implementation which involves employee motivation and assists in retaining valuable employees. Thus the underlying principle of a reward strategy is motivation. As defined in Chapter 2, work motivation refers to the stimulation of effort required to achieve, and maintain, organisational goals. Therefore, a reward strategy aims to stimulate the effort and willingness of every employee to work at their full potential by applying the principles of motivational theory. Specifically, content and process theories of motivation will be discussed in relation to reward strategy (refer to Chapter 2 for an extensive discussion on the various theories of motivation).

CONTENT AND PROCESS THEORIES
Content theories suggest that human beings have certain wants and needs that direct their behaviour and these, in turn, are influenced by the environment (see Chapter 2 for a detailed discussion). These theories include Maslow's (1954) hierarchy of needs theory and Alderfer's (1969) existence, relatedness, growth (ERG) theory. Content theories explain *what* rewards motivate individuals. As such, HR managers can employ intrinsic or extrinsic rewards, depending on the individual's preference and the organisation's resource capability. Many organisations use Maslow's hierarchy of needs theory to determine the reward

system. For example, if employees' self-esteem needs are not met, then they may prefer a reward similar to employee of the month, whereby they are acknowledged for their good work, rather than receiving a bonus. It is, however, advisable to examine what rewards are valued by current employees before deciding what to offer. For instance, recent literature suggested individuals differ in the meaning they attach to money. Some people value money and are motivated by monetary rewards (money) more than others.

On the other hand, process theories highlight the thought patterns that underlie the decision of whether or not to engage in certain behaviours (refer to Chapter 2 for a detailed discussion). As such, they may be used to explain the underlying principles behind the formation and implementation of a reward strategy. Process theories infer that employees' motivational processes are, in part, determined by the reward management of the organisation, although the psychological process underlying the reward process should not be ignored (Kohn, 1993). Specifically, there are four process theories which have particular relevance to reward strategy (Mitchell & Mickel, 1999), as discussed next.

Vroom's (1964) expectancy theory suggests that employees should exert greater work effort if they have reason to expect that it will result in a reward that they value. It also suggests that individuals' performance level is dependent upon the expectation they have regarding how their performance will be linked to rewards (Lawler, 1981). As discussed in Chapter 10, on performance management, ongoing performance review is based on specific performance criteria which enables individuals to see the link between their performance and subsequent rewards.

Adams' (1963) equity theory suggests that individuals tend to compare their rewards with the performance/rewards ratio of relevant others. The theory suggests that the perceived inequity in the reward others get for similar performance leads to demotivation and, subsequently, low performance (Gerhault, Minkoff & Olsen, 1995).

Locke's (1968) goal setting theory states that a specific challenging goal or performance criterion tends to motivate employees to increase their performance. Organisations tend predominantly to use goals driving pay to improve employees' focus on achieving business goals and employee's skills, and to focus employees on customer needs.

Skinner's (1953) reinforcement theory suggests that an organisation's reward system should frequently reinforce *desirable* performance criteria (Gerhart, Minkoff & Olsen, 1995). Research suggests that the more closely reward is tied to performance, the more powerful its motivational effect (Guzzo & Katzell, 1987).

Reward experts should consider the process theories discussed here to understand and design reward strategies better. Figure 11.2 illustrates how these theories influence individual performance and therefore how they should be considered in the design of reward strategies. They should use the information described in the theories to strengthen and expand the linkages between an organisation's performance and the individual and group contribution to that performance and to the distribution of rewards. In essence, the content and process theories of motivation should underpin managers' decisions as to how they should formulate and implement a reward strategy.

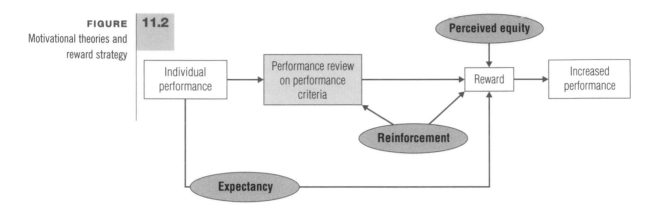

11.2

INDIVIDUAL AND ORGANISATIONAL NEEDS

It is important, when designing, implementing and using a reward strategy, for it to meet individual and organisational needs. Organisationl plans that achieve this are viewed as strategic plans as they ensure that individual and organisational needs align and are congruent. Employees' motivations for working are different and change over time; for example, employees working in the banking industry in Australia 20 years ago might have searched for rewards that satisfy their self-esteem needs, whereas today they search for safety needs as the industry is experiencing much downsizing and restructuring. Based on the underlying principle of motivation, reward strategies should not only meet individual needs but also organisational needs. Therefore, a list of individual and organisational needs is provided below.

Individual needs:
- Meet motivational content and process needs:
  - financial and non-financial rewards
  - perceived equitable treatment
  - a fair and objective performance management system
- provide appropriate reward changes and challenges;
- provide regular rewards and performance reviews.

Organisational needs:
- support the achievement of the organisation's strategic objectives;
- reinforce the key values and the desired culture and behaviours through clear performance criteria (e.g. customer first);
- motivate employees to continue improving their performance by making sure that high performers will be rewarded for their contributions;
- attract and develop the desired quality mix of employees (see Chapter 8 for a discussion on recruitment and selection);
- ensure competitive rewards (i.e. what are your competitors offering?);
- control costs and achieve optimum value;
- reduce unnecessary turnover;
- comply with legal requirements.

Essential building blocks of the total reward management process

Having understood that motivation is the underlying principle of an effective reward strategy, it is necessary to examine in depth the total reward management process. As such, the focus of this chapter now turns to how an effective reward management process can be implemented.

The reward management process plays a crucial role in improving organisational performance by improving individual performance. There are four essential building blocks in the total reward management process and each is explained from a practical application point of view. Specifically, reward management calls for managers to build a reward strategy based on the four building blocks of base pay, performance pay, employee benefits and non-financial rewards.

Figure 11.3 provides an overview of the total reward management process. By examining this figure, it is possible to understand how factors impact on and influence the development of the reward strategy. This is important because this strategy, like all other business strategies, contributes to the overarching business goal. The following discussion highlights, in detail, each of the four essential building blocks that should be used as a guide in establishing the appropriate strategic rewards for employees' desired behaviours.

BLOCK 1: BASE PAY

Base pay refers to the cash amount guaranteed for just turning up for work before any rewards or benefits are added. This is what a majority of full-time employees receive in most work settings. It is generally referred to as a salary or wage. A **salary** is pay that is paid consistently from period to period (e.g. fortnightly) and is not directly related to the number of hours worked by the employee. In some cases, a salary may already include benefits. For example, a hotel manager may earn $65 000 per annum but they may live above the hotel. Therefore, their base pay might be $55 000 and include $10 000 of living expenses. A **wage**, however, is generally used for part-time, casual, temporary or contract employees and refers to hourly, daily or weekly payment based on the time worked. It usually includes rewards and pay incentives. For example, a research assistant in a laboratory may receive $29.75 for every hour worked. If they work overtime they will continue to be paid by the hour as opposed to full-time employees who get paid the same salary regardless of how many extra hours they work.

salary
Pay that is paid consistently from period to period.

wage
Hourly, daily or weekly payment based on the time worked.

BASE PAY IN THE AUSTRALIAN CONTEXT

In Australia the base rate refers to the guaranteed cash amount under state or federal awards, or within enterprise agreements or individual contracts (also referred to as Australian Workplace Agreements (AWAs)). In 2005 Australia underwent major industrial relations reform which significantly changed the base pay design of Australian workplaces. Although Chapter 6 extensively highlighted how industrial relations and employment law has recently changed in Australia, this chapter focuses specifically on how reward strategies are designed based on new workplace agreements and employment law.

FIGURE 11.3
The total reward
management process

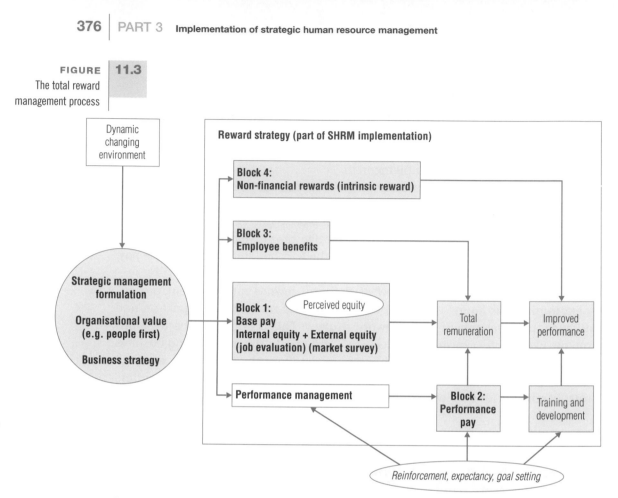

Source: Adapted from Armstrong & Murlis (2004), p. 7.

award
A formal, legally binding
document that provides legal
protection for five minimum
conditions of employment.

An **award** is a formal document, made by federal or state industrial tribunals or authorities in legally enforceable terms, that provides legal protection for five minimum conditions of employment. Under federal government initiatives, the recent industrial relations reforms significantly reduced award considerations to base pay design; that is, the base pay design of a company has gone from an award base to an award-free base. In essence, the reforms emphasise direct pay negotiation between employees and employers, thus increasing the power of corporations to determine pay and conditions and significantly reducing the role of unions and industrial tribunals.

Today, the minimum wage is determined by the newly established Australian Fair Pay Commission (AFPC), headed by an economist appointed by the federal government. The AFPC focuses primarily on the economic effects of minimum wage determinations, rather than considerations of equity. Under the legislative guidelines establishing the AFPC, it is expected that, over time, lower paid workers will receive much less than they would have under the previous system of annual safety net adjustments made by the Australian Industrial Relations Commission (AIRC). This has implications for HRM, such as the increased likelihood of a pluralist employment relationship, where conflicts are viewed as inevitable between employers and employees. Consequently, there is likely to be an increase in the role of HRM as a mediator to resolve disputes and conflicts of interest in order to achieve strategic organisational goals. Although the new laws are advantageous for some stakeholders, it should be noted that these laws are supported by employer groups such as the Business Council of Australia and the Australian Industry Group, but are opposed by the Australian Council of Trade Unions (ACTU), the Australian Labor Party (ALP), the Australian Greens, the Family First Party and various church groups.

Certified agreements (CAs), formally known as enterprise bargaining, are now registered with the Office of the Employee Advocate (OEA) and arise out of collective bargaining (usually involving unions) at the enterprise level to establish terms and conditions of employment, including a base pay. **Collective bargaining** is the process of negotiation between a union and employers to reach agreement on wages and employment conditions. Enterprise agreements set the terms and conditions of employment and are a method of developing, interpreting and administering collective terms and conditions of employment with or without union involvement. It is usual practice for such agreements to be valid for three years. Under the new Australian industrial laws, CAs are no longer the jurisdiction of the AIRC, and no longer have to be subject to a 'no disadvantage test' which ensures that they meet award minimum standards. Again, this has implications for HR managers as they need to ensure that employees and employers alike are satisfied with the agreed working conditions and that any conflict is resolved with minimal disruption to the employment relationship and the achievement of organisational goals. Hence, the role of HRM has increased in light of recent industrial relations reform.

As a result of Australia's change in industrial relations, award-free individual contracts have become a major determining factor of base pay in Australia. An **award-free individual contract** is an agreement, such as an AWA, between an employer and a single employee. Every company and/or industry has a unique AWA that is developed collaboratively between employers, employees and the relevant union(s). For example, the AWAs at Australian universities were developed by the management, staff and the National Teachers Education Union (NTEU). In contrast, a different agreement was developed for national hospitals and the Nurses Federation of Australia (NFA). The individual contracts determine working conditions, expectations and base pay for the employees and are, therefore, an important aspect of the employment relationship.

As a general rule, the greater the employer power relative to employee power in determining base pay, the greater the likelihood of employee controversies. For example, lower paid employees could now face the dilemma of 'sign or be sacked', forcing them to forfeit rights unfairly.

So, how are reward strategies developed in relation to awards such as AWAs? As mentioned above, the first step in developing a reward strategy for employees is to determine what their base pay is, and this is determined largely by their workplace agreement, award or individual contract. Therefore, reward strategies need to be customised for every organisation, presenting further implications for HR managers. It should be noted here that many current management and HRM textbooks state that the establishment of base pay concentrates on award-free situations, which refer to individual contracts of employment between employers

certified agreements
Arise out of collective bargaining (usually involving unions) at the enterprise level to establish terms and conditions of employment, including a base pay.

collective bargaining
The process of negotiation between a union and employers to reach agreement on wages and employment conditions.

award-free individual contract
An agreement, such as an AWA, between an employer and a single employee.

and employees and reflect changing industrial relations laws. However, in establishing 'award-free rewards', managers (usually line and HR managers) should establish base pay by consulting employment law specialists, consultants, researchers, advisers from employer associations and even representatives of government departments and unions to ensure that they are adhering to current workplace laws and practices.

In addition to the implications for HRM discussed above, it is also crucial to consider those arising from reward strategies under award and award-free pay. Reward management under award-based pay tends to be *reactive* (i.e. review a job description and align it with award classifications to ensure award rates are paid to employees), while reward management under award-free pay tends to be more *proactive* and calls for companies to monitor the reward strategies developed by their competitors as the award no longer needs to be aligned with award classifications. As award-free pay has been adopted in Australia, it is necessary for HR managers proactively to develop reward strategies that align with individual and organisational goals in the quest for a competitive advantage. There are several factors that proactive reward management should consider, such as:

1. ensuring compliance with reward-related legislation;
2. ensuring the job worth is consistent with the market worth;
3. frequently updating all job descriptions by reporting all changes in jobs;
4. controlling overtime work and pay; and
5. continually formulating reward policies to align with the business strategy.

So, how is base pay established under an award-free setting? There are two issues which should be considered: internal equity and external equity.

INTERNAL EQUITY

Motivation theory relating to perceived equity is the vital issue to be considered in establishing the base pay. Research has shown that internal (organisational) equity and external (market) equity influence pay-level satisfaction (Bordia & Blau, 2003). **Internal equity** reflects the equity (or relative) value associated with jobs and people within the organisation's internal labour market. For example, the value of the marketing manager would be relatively higher than the value of the sales representative. The significant prerequisite for determining internal equity is a comprehensive job analysis (refer to Chapter 8 for a discussion about job analysis). The internal equity (or relative value of jobs) is assessed through job evaluation. **Job evaluation** is the method of ranking jobs in relation to their worth to the organisation and ensures internal equity. Job evaluation takes place qualitatively or quantitatively.

Qualitative job evaluation includes job ranking and job grading or job classification. Job ranking is one of the simplest job evaluation tools and ranks jobs according to their worth to the organisation. The 'worth' of a job is usually determined by using an accurate job description in relation to the strategic skills, knowledge and abilities required to perform the job. For example, jobs that require supervision, decision-making or independent problem-solving skills (e.g. CEO) would be more highly valued to organisations than apprenticeships or administrative jobs (e.g. secretary or sales assistant positions).

internal equity
The equity value associated with jobs and people within the organisation's internal labour market.

job evaluation
An analytical tool which determines the relative worth of the job with the aim of providing fair and objective pay.

Quantitative job evaluation includes the point system and the factor comparison system. The **point system** calculates a job's worth by assigning points to specific job factors. These job factors are usually categorised into skills (e.g. experience and education), responsibilities (e.g. financial and managerial), effort (e.g. mental and physical) and working conditions (e.g. location, environmental and working hazards and surroundings) (Hay Group, 2005). The **factor comparison system** calculates the relative worth of jobs on a range of job-related factors, such as skills, mental effort and location). In other words, all jobs are calculated independently on each job factor and given an overall ranking (e.g. a secretarial position received 5/10 points for skills and 0.5/10 points for responsibility, whereas a senior management position received 8/10 points for skills and 8/10 points for responsibility). There are commercially available job evaluation systems such as the Hay Guide Chart-Profile Method™.

point system
Calculates a job's worth by assigning points to specific job factors.

factor comparison system
Calculates the relative worth of jobs on a range of job related factors, such as skills, mental effort and location.

EXTERNAL EQUITY

External equity refers to the levels of pay for similar jobs in the external labour market. Put simply, these are the market rates (i.e. what competitors are paying for the same or similar jobs). Information on external equity is collected formally or informally via pay surveys. These surveys ensure external equity by translating job values into dollars relative to similar jobs in other organisations. Formal surveys include pay frameworks established by the Australian Information Industry Association (AIIA) Salary Survey and the Australian Human Resources Institute (AHRI) Salary Survey. Informal surveys, however, examine similar job pay through media, for example via newspapers, magazines and company websites. Generally, the type of information that an HR manager would use to gather pay data would include base pay, salary ranges, incentives/bonuses, employee benefits, working hours and working conditions (Hay Group, 2005).

external equity
The levels of pay for similar jobs in the external labour market.

Once internal and external equities are ascertained, a pay curve should be established to demonstrate graphically the relationship between base pay (currently paid for jobs) and job worth. Figure 11.4 depicts the pay curve coloured in grey. The pay curve in the graph represents one line, but in reality the pay range for a job could by anywhere between the minimum and maximum values (i.e. plus or minus 30% from the midpoint). In recent years, broadbanding has increased in popularity as it increases employees' flexibility and multiskilling to cope with the dynamic environment. **Broadbanding** refers to collapsing a large number of salary grades into a few wide bands where each grade includes a wide range of jobs and salary ranges. Figure 11.4 depicts the broadbanding framework coloured in green.

broadbanding
Collapsing a large number of salary grades into a few wide bands where each grade includes a wide range of jobs and salary ranges.

In summary, the suggested steps of establishing base pay are:
Step 1: Conduct a pay survey to ascertain the job market value.
Step 2: Complete job evaluation and categorising of similar job values into pay grades.
Step 3: Ascertain pay curve.
Step 4: Devise pay range.

At the time of considering base pay, organisations should also establish an appropriate pay strategy according to their core values (see the Southwest Airlines case in Figure 11.5).

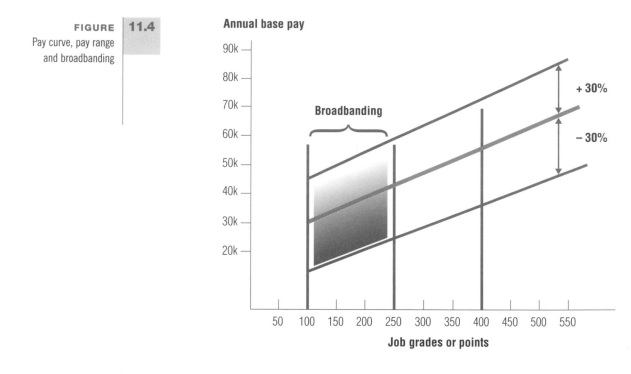

Southwest Airlines is well known as a company that offers excellent perks to its employees. It exhibits exemplary strategic reward management practices, which strategically incorporate both intrinsic and extrinsic rewards. Based on the culture of 'nothing comes ahead of my people' and the business strategy of 'retaining valued employees and securing long-term employment', Southwest views its strategic reward system as a process for supporting and reinforcing the airline's core values and business strategy. Southwest Airlines aims to reduce people conflicts by having its CEO receiving below-market-rate base pay and its employees receiving competitive market-rate base pay. Employee benefits include 'free airfare for employee's family members' and their incentives include profit sharing on a deferral basis (supporting the long-term employment strategy). In addition to offering alluring perks like free flights and profit sharing, Southwest rewards its employees for excellent performance through recognition programs known as 'Heroes of the Heart' and 'Winning Spirit' Awards. Consequently, Southwest Airlines is ranked second in Fortune's *100 Best Companies to Work For*, exhibiting remarkably low turnover, tardiness and absenteeism.

Source: Adapted from Tripp, T. (2004), 'Best Perks: Southwest Airlines', <http://www.vault.com/nr/newsmain.jsp?nr_page=3&ch_id=401&article_id=21007&cat_id=1089>, accessed 13 October 2004.

PAY STRATEGIES

Reward strategy is concerned with whether employees are paid above, below or at the prevailing market rate. Organisations can choose the following pay strategies or policies in making their decision.

Lead–lead policy. A salary leads the market from hiring to retiring. In other words, a salary begins above the market rate and continues to rise above the market rate.

Lead–lag policy. A salary leads the market at hiring, then lags the market at some later point in the career. In other words, a salary begins above the market rate but falls below the market rate over time.

Lag–lead policy. A salary lags the market at hiring, then leads it at a later point in the career. In other words, a salary begins below the market rate but goes above the market rate over time.

BLOCK 2: PERFORMANCE PAY

A central feature of performance pay is the development of a more performance-oriented culture in an organisation (Kessler & Purcell, 1992). **Performance pay** is the pay individuals receive based upon their individual, group and/or organisational performance and is also referred to as variable pay, contingency pay or pay at risk. Performance pay is influenced by the level of individual, group or organisational performance (rather than hours worked on the job). Performance pay that is based on the level of expected job performance could be included in the base pay; however, when it is based on outputs (i.e. increased gross profit or increased sales volume) it is not consolidated into the base bay.

> **performance pay**
> Pay individuals receive based upon their individual, group and/or organisational performance.

In 1999, research indicated that organisations worldwide were increasingly replacing traditional rigid pay systems with flexible performance pay plans, such as discretionary bonuses, incentives and profit sharing schemes (Flynn, 1999). This shift occurred because the contemporary system links pay and performance more tightly and increases the variability of pay.

DISCRETIONARY BONUS

A **discretionary bonus** is a discretionary reward provided after the event, which makes no guarantee that future work and effort will be rewarded similarly (O'Neill, 1995). A bonus is *reactive* performance pay as the pay is dependent upon the organisation's discretion. Organisations could strategically use this scheme to help promote a good employer image and to increase employee loyalty.

> **discretionary bonus**
> A reward provided after goal achievement with the understanding that future success on a similar task may not be similarly rewarded.

INCENTIVES

An **incentive** focuses on a person's performance by establishing specific individual performance criteria or objectives and rewarding the achievement of these criteria. An incentive is *proactive* performance pay as the pay is dependent upon the performance. Based upon goal setting theory and expectancy theory, organisations should utilise incentives to motivate employees to achieve their performance criteria. For example, salespeople are typically offered incentives based upon meeting their performance criteria on sales output and revenue. Today, there are various contemporary incentives such as customer service incentives and key contributor incentives to support the strategic direction of the organisation. Incentives are categorised at the individual, group and organisational (profit sharing schemes) level.

> **incentive**
> Focuses on a person's performance by establishing specific individual performance criteria or objectives and rewarding the achievement of these criteria.

1. *Individual incentives* include piece rate, standard hour plans, merit pay and sales incentives and are based on individual performance. Piece-rate pay gives employees a payment for each item produced (e.g. a basket maker would receive a piece rate for every basket made). Standard hour plans set pay rates based on

the completion of a job in a predetermined time period (e.g. a consultant receives payment for eight hours of training preparation for a one-day training program regardless of whether the preparation took more or less time). Merit pay refers to an increase in base pay depending on how successfully employees met the performance objectives (e.g. achieving the objective of selling 20 mobile phones within a month). Sales incentive plans permit salespeople to be paid for conducting a number of duties that are not necessarily reflected in their sales volumes (e.g. building excellent customer relationships) and/or based upon percentage or volume of sales. For example, in the hotel industry, employees may receive a sales incentive plan when large group bookings are made.

2. *Group incentives* refer to payment over and above individual base pay when one's group exceeds the group's performance criteria (e.g. at the production level). Group incentives include team compensation, the Scanlon Plan, Rucker Plan, Improshare and earnings-at-risk plans. Scanlon Plan rewards are paid when employees participate in improving productivity and reducing costs. Rucker Plan rewards are paid when the sales value of production (SVOP) expected per wage dollar is exceeded. Improshare is gain sharing based on exceeding the expected productivity for a predetermined time period. Earnings-at-risk plans are used as an incentive to encourage employees to achieve higher output and quality standards by placing a portion of their base salary at risk of loss (e.g. 20 per cent performance loading which is lost if the predetermined performance level is not met).

3. *Organisation-wide incentives* usually include profit sharing incentives (where most employees receive a share of the organisation's profits, such as 10 per cent) and gain sharing incentives (where most employees share the achievement of organisational productivity objectives which led to incremental cost-saving gains). Rather than dictating control under the bonus scheme, profit sharing and gain sharing enhance participation, commitment and loyalty and benefit both the individual and the organisation's strategic goals.

The stock option is also an organisation-wide incentive which gives employees the right to buy a certain number of shares in the organisation for a stated period of time. Likewise, the employee share ownership plan (ESOP) offers employees free or discounted shares to develop a sense of ownership and long-term focus and commitment to the organisation. In Australia, executives are likely to have their incentives linked to financial objectives (e.g. net profit before tax) and the overall performance of a specific function (e.g. growth in sales revenue or production output) (PA Consulting Group, 1994).

ADVANTAGES AND DISADVANTAGES OF PERFORMANCE PAY

Every HR manager should be aware of the advantages and disadvantages of performance-based pay. Performance pay is most useful when:
- it focuses on the key performance objectives (quality and/or quantity) that produce employee and organisational gains;
- it is linked to the achievement of competitive important results;
- teamwork and unit cohesiveness are fostered by paying individuals on team work results;

- it is used to distribute the outcomes of success to those responsible for producing that success. For example, a department head will be ultimately responsible for the financial gain or loss for the department. Hence, the head will share the success when their department outperforms the performance expectation.

There is, however, a case against performance-based pay. Kohn (1993) argues that performance-based pay makes inadequate psychological assumptions about such pay and presents the following seven cases against performance-based pay.

1. Extrinsic motivators do not alter the fundamental attitudes behind behaviours. They only bring temporary reinforcement and not long-term change. They undermine intrinsic motivation as the work is no longer self-directed (Deci & Ryan, 1985). As highlighted earlier, some people value money less than others (Mitchell & Mickel, 1999) and thus attitude would stay the same despite pay increase.
2. It treats symptoms and not underlying causes. Performance-based pay cannot be used as a substitute for effective management behaviours such as better job content, giving feedback and opportunity for self-motivated behaviours. If you want people to be motivated to do a good job, give them a good job to do.
3. It may reduce risk-taking behaviours to face challenging tasks and reinforce rigid behaviour. Thus it may jeopardise employees' innovation, creativity and internally motivated behaviours. Therefore, organisations should take into account employee risk preference in performance pay (Deckop, Merriman & Blau, 2004).
4. The performance standard could be perceived as unfair. For example, factory workers are told to increase their factory productivity by 100 per cent in order to receive their incentive pay.
5. Competitive attitudes among employees could emerge, hence, reducing work morale.
6. It creates friction between employees and management.
7. There is no consistent empirical evidence for a causal link between performance pay and performance.

PERFORMANCE MANAGEMENT

As covered extensively in Chapter 10, performance pay is determined by the effectiveness of the performance management process as performance management is a strategic process designed to improve individual and organisational performance. Performance-based pay should be determined via an employee's annual performance review. However, in reality, very few organisations possess a robust performance management and appraisal system that provides a clear link between performance and pay (O'Neill, 1995). Therefore, HR managers should refer to motivation theory on reinforcing the *right* performance and creating a clear link between performance and reward expectancy when analysing performance pay strategies.

TRAINING AND DEVELOPMENT

In the performance review, managers should consider the link between pay and performance in determining employees' training and development needs (e.g. teamwork abilities, customer service skills, machine handling). As reward management views 'improved performance' as the final objective, training and development is an important precursor and consequence of improved performance as indicated in Figure 11.3.

BLOCK 3: EMPLOYEE BENEFITS

employee benefits
All financial rewards that are not paid directly in cash to the employee, such as subsidised meals and superannuation.

Employee benefits (or indirect financial rewards) are all financial rewards that are not paid directly in cash to the employee (e.g. concierge services, crèche facilities, flexi time, pension, medical coverage, company cars, subsidised meals and legislated benefits such as superannuation, annual leave and sick leave). Employee benefits refer to services that are purchased by the employer for the employee's use; however, they do not affect employees' perceptions of their remuneration unless they understand the monetary value it holds for them.

In summary, total remuneration may be calculated using the following equation:

$$\text{Total remuneration} = \text{Block 1} + \text{Block 2} + \text{Block 3}$$

HR managers can use this simple equation to determine reward strategies for employees, in line with organisational goals. The equation is also flexible and companies can strategically integrate these blocks to serve their core values and strategic plan best. For example, if a company's strategy was to expand the business based on excellent customer service, they could set the sales representatives' base pay higher than the market value, increase the performance pay based upon customer satisfaction feedback and sales output, and offer company cars to their top sales representatives. By doing so, they could develop a strategic competitive advantage.

WHAT FACTORS INFLUENCE PAY?

As individuals and organisations are unique, it is reasonable to expect that remuneration (and pay) would be affected by a myriad of factors both internal and external to the organisation. An HR manager needs to be aware of these when designing and developing such strategies.

The internal factors that may affect pay strategies include:

1. *Pay strategy.* Setting an organisation's pay policy to lead, lag or match competitors' pay.
2. *Worth of a job.* Managers need to establish the internal equity of pay within the organisation.
3. *Relative worth of an employee.* Managers need to decide the degree to which employees should be rewarded for their performance (i.e. performance pay).
4. *Ability to pay.* Organisations should consider the current and future financial resources (including profits) to pay employees.

The external factors that may affect pay strategies include:

1. *Labour market conditions.* Employees' pay is affected by socioeconomic conditions, government regulations, policies and practices and the presence of unions. For example, labour market conditions also affect substitutability (i.e. how easily staff can be replaced). In Australia, increasing skill migration

has increased the substitutability of employees, which reduces pay competitiveness. In addition, a limited supply of people at an executive level also affects companies, which may create pay strategies to prevent them from leaving. This is also known as the 'golden handcuffs', which is a pay strategy designed to entice the executive to remain with the company for a certain period of time.

2. *Area market rate.* An organisation's pay for a job is influenced by the pay for similar jobs in the marketplace, establishing external equity.

3. *Cost of living.* Managers need to consider employees' financial conditions, such as local housing, natural disasters and inflation, which require companies to adjust pay based on increases in some accepted measure of prices.

4. *Social values.* Family and cultural values should be taken into consideration when pay is determined. A recent study showed that Indians tend to possess strong collectivist values and family values are related to their pay satisfaction (Bordia & Blau, 2003).

BLOCK 4: NON-FINANCIAL REWARD

One of the most pressing concerns that HR managers experience when developing reward strategies is how to motivate employees continually to perform to the best of their ability. Although most people are motivated by financial rewards, non-financial rewards play an equally important role in reward management because they are generally the most powerful performance motivators in an organisation's reward management process. Non-financial rewards focus on the needs of people for recognition, self-determination, achievement, responsibility and personal growth, which contribute to motivation, commitment and improved performance. Further, non-financial rewards are expected to increase an employee's motivation. For example, research confirms that there is a positive relationship between individual autonomy, skill development, a learning environment and intrinsic motivation (Gilbert, 1994). Therefore, organisations should strategically leverage non-financial rewards to decrease financial reward costs. Notably, non-financial rewards pay more attention to 'soft HRM' issues and are expected to meet higher-order needs (refer to Maslow's hierarchy of needs theory discussed in Chapter 2).

In summary, improved performance may be calculated using the following equation (see Figure 11.3):

$$\text{Improved performance} = \text{Block 1} + \text{Block 2} + \text{Block 3} + \text{Block 4}$$

The preceding sections on essential building blocks of the reward management process covered the practical steps needed to build an effective reward strategy. It also illustrated that reward management takes a critical role in the SHRM implementation process by incorporating performance management and training development practices. Of course, reward management is also linked to other parts of SHRM implementation. For example, great employee benefits (such as those offered by Southwest Airlines) can dramatically affect the recruitment pool, widening the employee selection options and increasing the ability to gain a competitive advantage through effective HRM.

Contemporary reward strategy features

Pay has undergone a tremendous transformation from rigid and inflexible and tenure-based pay to flexible pay in response to the demands of a dynamic changing environment (Lewis, 2000). Under this new belief about pay, the key reward features that HR managers need to consider are discussed next (Lawler, 2000). These features help determine pay strategies designed to improve individual and organisational performance.

EMPLOYABILITY PAY

Employability pay is based upon the notion of an employability contract. An employability contract refers to 'employability security', that is, an adult to adult partnership between employers and employees. Employability pay based upon this contract is expected to achieve a win–win situation as employees contribute to business objectives and employers pay employees for their desired performance in return (Schuster & Zingheim, 1992). In other words, employees' performance is becoming an important indicator of job security in today's business environment. This notion fits with the expectancy theory approach to motivation as employees expect better pay as they contribute more toward business objectives.

PERSON-BASED PAY

Organisations should pay individuals according to what their human capital is worth in the context of the labour market and inside the organisation. Usually, person-based rewards are based on personality attributes (e.g. leadership and communication) and personal knowledge, skill and ability (e.g. computer knowledge). Person-based rewards reflect an organisation's developmental approach to cope with a competitive environment. A particular person attribute that serves business objectives (e.g. customer satisfaction through excellent customer service) should be rewarded more than other attributes (e.g. hotel management knowledge or administrative skills). By establishing a pay policy to offer more to those employees who acquired strategic skills and contributed more to the success of the organisation, the organisation can achieve a better 'return on human capital' (Beatson, 1995).

MARKET-DETERMINED PAY

Market-determined pay means rewarding high-performing individuals at or above the market rate, while colleagues are rewarded below the market rate. In today's continuously changing external environment there is a general shift toward performance pay in contemporary organisations. This is because a person's ability to contribute to high organisational performance reaps a competitive edge in the marketplace, thus is advantageous for the achievement of strategic organisational goals.

In contrast to the conventional job evaluation process, which merely emphasises internal relativity, this trend has led organisations to focus more on external equity, which is market-determined pay aimed at retaining high-performing and value-adding employees. For example, the advent of technology has certainly increased the market value of electronic engineers. Consequently, this is reflected in the increased pay that engineers are receiving today in the automobile industry.

TEAM-BASED REWARDS

The increasing popularity of self-managed work teams (SMWTs) has led organisations to value team-based rewards (e.g. gain sharing). SMWTs are commonly used in most organisations as a way to achieve organisational goals effectively through increased empowerment and responsibility. Team-based pay aims to reinforce behaviour that reaps effective teamwork through group coordination, developing a sense of loyalty to the team. Behaviours such as willingness to share and agreement regarding the team objectives allow employees the ability to express different viewpoints which would then be rewarded. For example, establishing points-based competition between teams can promote a cooperative and collegial spirit between team members and may contribute to the achievement of team objectives.

However, it is important to take note that teams do not guarantee positive performance. Term members may be willing to express different points of view although this may not necessarily lead to better solutions. Thus, team-based rewards should pay members based on the achievement of team goals; for example, if sales volume has increased by 20 per cent then all team members are rewarded equally. While team-based pay encourages group performance, managers need to strike a balance between individual performance and an individual's performance in the team to ensure that members who are not contributing equally are not unfairly rewarded, as this may create team resentment and cancel out the effect of team-based pay.

LOW DEGREE OF HIERARCHY

It is common in many organisations today to shift from hierarchical reward systems to 'boundaryless' reward management. This new reward management style aims to foster performance improvement through employees' multiskilling and flexibility to work with a wide range of employees. Hierarchical pay systems, in contrast, tend to reinforce the status-based pay that politically differentiates employees' interactions, thus inhibiting the speed of performance improvement. The hierarchical pay also encourages wrong behaviours that are associated with upward mobility at the expense of individuals improving performance. Therefore, low hierarchical, broadband pay is believed to serve the business objective in a much more speedy, flexible and strategic manner (refer to the discussion on broadbanding earlier in the chapter).

AIM OF REWARD MANAGEMENT

The preceding explanation of the essential building blocks of total reward management, coupled with contemporary reward features, summarises the aim of reward management in the contemporary business context. In order to cope with today's dynamic changing environment, reward management should aim to:

- support the achievement of the organisation's strategic objectives;
- help communicate the organisation's desired behaviours, values and performance expectations (e.g. more customer-friendly behaviours, increased production output per hour);
- support organisational cultural change such as changing performance criteria from role based on bureaucratic structure to functionality based on less hierarchical structure;
- indicate the behaviours that will link to performance pay through performance management;
- promote employee development through performance pay and broadbanding;
- compete in the labour market by paying market-competitive pay;
- motivate all workers through a strategic reward system (base pay, performance pay and employee benefits) and non-financial rewards;
- promote flexibility to cope with the dynamic changing environment;
- provide a cost-effective pay structure; and
- achieve fairness and equity by rewarding people based on internal equity as well as external equity (cf. Armstrong & Murlis, 2004).

Contemporary SHRM Application Tool

Imagine that you are an HR manager for the state police, which employs over 2000 staff across 300 police stations to serve a local community of three million people. The vision of your organisation is to make a difference by providing a safer local community. Today, the state police has a growing operation with strong government support. Recently, you became a recipient of the prestigious WorkSafe Awards from the state government.

Seeing the recent intensified and higher crime rate in the community, you are faced with a challenge of how to attract, motivate and retain the top-performing police officers. State government supports recruitment of an additional 400 police officers, and you have decided to take the opportunity to provide a better reward strategy to increase the pool of high-calibre policy officers. Simultaneously, however, you are faced with a challenge of meeting the drastically changed social demographics and values of your police workforce. For example, the average age of your police workforce has escalated from 21 years old to 30 years old, encompassing four generations of officers today. The workforce is also characterised by more officers who have received tertiary education and have a wider range of work and life experience. Furthermore, current officers' intrinsic reward preferences have shifted from a focus on job security to a focus on better career prospects. The SHRM Application Tool example demonstrates the reward strategies derived to meet your employees' current demands and also to meet your organisation's objective of serving the community better (refer to Figure 11.6).

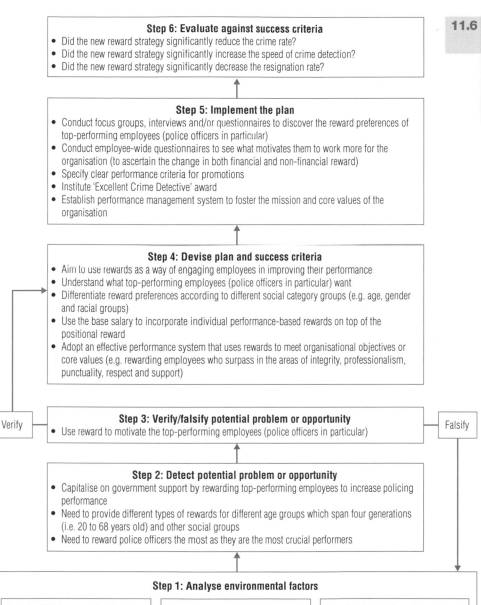

11.6 FIGURE
SHRM Application Tool:
problem — reward strategy

Step 6: Evaluate against success criteria
- Did the new reward strategy significantly reduce the crime rate?
- Did the new reward strategy significantly increase the speed of crime detection?
- Did the new reward strategy significantly decrease the resignation rate?

Step 5: Implement the plan
- Conduct focus groups, interviews and/or questionnaires to discover the reward preferences of top-performing employees (police officers in particular)
- Conduct employee-wide questionnaires to see what motivates them to work more for the organisation (to ascertain the change in both financial and non-financial reward)
- Specify clear performance criteria for promotions
- Institute 'Excellent Crime Detective' award
- Establish performance management system to foster the mission and core values of the organisation

Step 4: Devise plan and success criteria
- Aim to use rewards as a way of engaging employees in improving their performance
- Understand what top-performing employees (police officers in particular) want
- Differentiate reward preferences according to different social category groups (e.g. age, gender and racial groups)
- Use the base salary to incorporate individual performance-based rewards on top of the positional reward
- Adopt an effective performance system that uses rewards to meet organisational objectives or core values (e.g. rewarding employees who surpass in the areas of integrity, professionalism, punctuality, respect and support)

Verify

Step 3: Verify/falsify potential problem or opportunity
- Use reward to motivate the top-performing employees (police officers in particular)

Falsify

Step 2: Detect potential problem or opportunity
- Capitalise on government support by rewarding top-performing employees to increase policing performance
- Need to provide different types of rewards for different age groups which span four generations (i.e. 20 to 68 years old) and other social groups
- Need to reward police officers the most as they are the most crucial performers

Step 1: Analyse environmental factors

Step 1a: HR issues: Monitor/analyse data (past, present and future)
- Growing operations with strong government support
- Recipient of WorkSafe Awards – lowest attrition rate in history
- Huge recruitment campaign through newspaper, magazine and online employment site advertisements, as well as television advertising
- Employment pool aimed at reflecting the diversity of the community it serves – number of female police has increased from 10% to 20%

Step 1b: Internal/organisational environment
- Vision to make a difference to the community by providing a safer community
- Aim to be the best policing organisation in the world
- Organisation's core values are integrity, professionalism, punctuality, respect and support
- Employees' intrinsic reward preference shifted from job security to career prospects
- Employment of over 2000 people serving a population in excess of 3 million with 300 police stations

Step 1c: External environment
- Changing career patterns, different way of working (e.g. flexible work hours)
- Increasingly diverse police workforce
- Skill shortage in police workforce
- Average age of police workforce has escalated from 21 to 30 years and officers are more likely to be tertiary educated and have a range of work experiences
- Rise in the rate of crime in the local community
- Strong government commitment to increase number of top-performing police officers

A view from the field   **Reward management: is an incentive plan the answer?**

Incentive- or commission-based reward systems tend to be the norm in jobs where sales or billings targets are the basis for judgements about performance. This practice is common across a wide range of industries from retail to professional services. In most of these types of jobs, remuneration increases significantly as the employee sells more or wins more business.

There are a number of possible approaches to reward management within these fields. Some organisations use a simple approach of a base salary with commission paid as a percentage of any sales or business achieved. Variations on this theme include a stepped scale, which breaks income performance targets into stages. Such approaches are designed to provide greater incentives to perform and the rewards earned by performance are provided in incremental steps. For example, the first $50 000 generates 5 per cent commission, the next $50 000 generates 10 per cent commission and so on.

Reward systems, which are heavily weighted towards incentives and bonuses, can certainly drive effort and performance as some employees thrive in an environment where results are closely tied to financial benefits. The question remains, 'Is it all about money'? Certainly most employees want to be sure they are paid appropriately; however, the priority placed on additional financial benefits seems to vary from individual to individual.

Incentives can also have a negative effect, driving self-oriented behaviour among employees, which can be counterproductive to the long-term profitability of a business. Territorial behaviour is an example of self-oriented behaviour. Typically a consultant would guard their territory and the associated group of clients from others in their company as a means to ensure their targets are achieved. In one management consultancy firm a consultant was heard to claim a large Telecommunications firm as his client. The manager of that consultant was surprised by that claim of complete ownership given that the client had some 20 000 employees, and was far too large to be 'the client' of only one consultant. Further discussion revealed the consultant was fearful of losing his foothold and the potential earnings from that lucrative client. His behaviour was in fact restricting his company's ability to provide service to the client and improve the amount of business written with that client. The company's reward management system in that situation was encouraging driving behaviours that were undesirable.

The drive to achieve targets can cause the focus of an employee to be on quantity at the cost of quality. This type of focus is of great concern to clients as it is likely to have a detrimental effect on the overall quality of services provided. A director of a major Australian recruitment agency reports that many major corporations now require reward structures for recruitment consultants to be specified as part of the process to bid for work in their organisations. She explained that it is not unusual to be quizzed at length about the intricacies of the approach to reward management. 'Major clients want to be assured that our approach to reward management is balanced, that customer orientation and quality outcomes are valued and rewarded as well as filling vacancies (with associated income targets).'

So the challenge remains as to how to structure rewards best to maximise motivational factors and deliver valued rewards in functions where sales or billings targets are critical to short-term business success. The balance needs to be struck with an emphasis allowing for high-quality work and relationships with customers for long-term business sustainability.

One common response to this challenge has been to structure the rewards in a way which encourages and rewards team-oriented behaviour as well as individual performance. The bonus pool is split to reward individual performance and team performance. Some organisations go as far a three way split: individual, team and overall business performance. This split encourages and rewards individual performance, highlights the importance of the team and rewards the consolidated team effort. The change in emphasis is intended to encourage collaboration and collective responsibility for overall (team and/or organisation) outcomes for clients and the company.

With a view towards reinforcing longer-term business sustainability, some companies in the HR consultancy field have ventured into reward management structures that reflect those of their large corporate clients. In these approaches, part of the employee's bonus is paid in cash, and part is paid as shares in the company they work for. These shares are held in trust on behalf of the employee for a specified period (usually for at least one year, and sometimes two or three years) after which time ownership of the shares transfers to the employee. This approach has a number of advantages. It is a long-term investment for the employee and there are some taxation benefits as, depending on the design of the scheme, concessional Capital Gains Tax rates may apply when ownership of the shares transfers to the employee and the shares are sold. In addition, this approach gives the employee a share in the business and its future, and an income stream from any dividends that are paid. Therefore, if the business performs they continue to benefit as an employee and a shareholder. This strategy is also a retention strategy as employees may commit to stay and wait for their shares to become available to them.

Such incentive schemes can work well where it is less important for employees to have a short-term focus. Hence, in general, they are more likely to apply at management levels where the focus of the role is both to achieve short-term revenue targets and to grow the business over time. However, there are some flaws in this approach too. If large amounts of bonus are paid this way then employees may 'discount' the value of the bonus they get. The amount an employee eventually gets varies with the share price, so it can go down as well as up and employees have to wait a long time for part of their bonus, and, in some cases, may have to leave some of their previously earned bonuses behind if they resign. This may lead to a bonus scheme being less of a motivator than the company might like.

The human resource consultancy field is probably one of the most competitive and results-focused parts of the professional services industry. Put simply, consultants in HR consulting either make their numbers or they are out, there is little margin for failure. New consultants are likely to be accommodated for a training period (from three to six months) after which they are required to 'feed' themselves by developing contacts and writing business.

Peter George is the General Manager of Consulting and e-learning divisions at Talent 2, an A$90 million publicly listed consulting firm. He has extensive experience in the HR consultancy field in Australia and Europe and has valuable insights to offer in this area, having worked in a very large multinational consultancy firm as head of its European operation and in start-up 'boutique' consultancy organisations. Mr George agrees that it is critical to hit those numbers, but it is necessary to do so in a way which sustains your own performance and that of the business. 'Consultants who are driven towards financial goals at the cost of all others tend to churn and burn in this industry', says Mr George.

HR consultancy tends to be a relationship-based industry, which means the ability to establish and nurture relationships with clients and colleagues is critical. According to Mr George, 'Those who have longevity in this industry tend to have a generosity of spirit, which extends to customers and clients. They are facilitators and information sharers, creating networks and opportunities for themselves, colleagues and clients; it just happens that most are good sales people as well'.

Reward management in an HR consultancy is complex and important for the attraction and retention of talented staff. The industry is highly competitive (both within companies and between companies) as companies compete for business. Employees' skills are highly transferable between the players in the industry and, as a result, employees tend to be very mobile.

Mr George comments that the reward management system provides the framework; however, as in any area of management, the art is in the application of it and the active management of the employees. 'People who choose to work in this field are often ambitious, driven and entrepreneurial. The incentive-based models can work very effectively with these people. There is a clear line of sight between their efforts, their achievements and their rewards. Other issues more related to how they go about it or behavioural aspects of their performance need to be monitored and managed. It is equally important to make clear the way things are done around here, the values and norms and reinforce those.'

At first glance, it would appear that an incentive scheme would be an easy fit in these types of functions as it is based on a straightforward assessment of whether or not targets have been met. An examination of the application of these types of reward management systems reveals that it is more complex than simply achieving targets and reward management systems should be designed and applied to take account of the specific long- and short-term goals, and the desired culture, of the organisation.

Mr George comments that it might seem that an incentive scheme is a relatively blunt instrument for use in measuring performance. 'Many of the consultants I have managed are great at customer relationships, are very strategic in their approach in fact, they are skilled and capable people but at the end of the day if they don't win business, they don't perform. Winning business is a true measure of performance, one that takes away all the trimmings. A client will have met three or four consultants from different companies when considering who to engage to complete an assignment. The consultant who ultimately wins the business has understood the client requirements, responded appropriately and won the client's confidence. There is an unquestionable element of skill in getting a client to "open their wallet" to you. A sustained performance in this type of environment is a true indicator of performance proficiency and deserves reward.'

An incentive program is perhaps not such a blunt instrument, in fact according to Mr George it is a crude but sharp instrument for measuring value added to clients and overall performance of a consultant in their industry.

Discussion questions

1. What are the arguments presented in this case for and against an incentive-based reward management system?
2. How would you design a reward management system to support the desired organisation culture and achieve business sales targets?
3. Do you think it is possible to run a sales organisation successfully without an incentive program?

CEOs slammed | **A manager's challenge**

Imagine having a job worth a few million dollars. For most people, this is a dream that will never become reality. So, how can it be achieved? The answer is simple: become a CEO! Around the globe, exorbitant CEO payouts have become a recent trend, with shareholders and the public outraged at the excessive figures bestowed upon CEOs in recent years. Adding fuel to the fire is the fact that not only do CEOs receive significant remuneration while performing the job, but it is also common for multimillion dollar sums to be paid to executives who end their contracts early. In effect, they are awarded significant cash amounts and don't even have to work. What a life!

Australian banks are notorious for large salaries and payouts for CEOs, with ANZ CEO John McFarlane securing a $7.2 million remuneration package over the 2004/2005 financial year. ANZ tallied a record profit of more than $3 billion over the same period, with the combined salary of executives sitting at more than $16 million, a significant increase from the previous year. Westpac CEO David Morgan was also awarded a significant payment of $9.1 million in light of the company's $2.82 billion profit.

Opposition has been rife among shareholders and employees, with an increased reluctance to accept excessive payments to those holding executive positions. Shareholders' reaction reflected some dissent with the announcement of CBA's $12 million long-term remuneration package of incoming CEO Ralph Norris, with a 10 per cent vote against the package. CBA's Chairman, John Schubert, defended the payment, claiming that a competitive market necessitated increased salaries to attract suitable contenders for top positions. Shareholder backlash was similarly evident at the 2005 Fairfax AGM, where there were accusations connecting staff retrenchments and a $4.5 million payout to retiring CEO Fred Hilmer. Fairfax management claimed that the timing of 55 job cuts was entirely coincidental, praising Hilmer for his success in his position.

The situation appears to be out of hand in some companies, with Southcorp CEO Tom Park awarded $10 million after only *five* months with the wine company in 2001, then catapulted to another top-level executive position with another company. Anger over payments has been tempered by justifications of the demands of such high level jobs, but ultimately affects the viability of the company from the top down. Perhaps Fairfax will be the first of many to question these practices and provide the opportunity for a more efficient and sustainable business in the long term.

In the meantime, CEOs will continue to do it tough at the top!

Source: Adapted from Anonymous (2005), 'Fairfax defends staff cuts at AGM', *The Age*, 18 November; Anonymous (2005), 'ANZ CEO McFarlane pocketed $7.2m', *The Sydney Morning Herald*, 15 November; Anonymous (2005), 'Westpac CEO received $9.1m last year', *The Sydney Morning Herald*, 9 November; Kirby, J. (2005), 'Tom Park, a top gun with the golden handshake', *The Age*, 30 October; O'Sullivan, M. (2005), 'CBA boss's pay deal ticked, but tentatively', *The Sydney Morning Herald*, 29 October.

Summary

This chapter addressed the important issue of reward management. It began with a definition of reward management, which refers to the strategic formulation and implementation of equitable rewards in a way that aligns with the strategic direction and values of an organisation. Reward management plays a crucial part in the strategic management process as it helps organisations attract, motivate and retain employees who possess strategic attributes such as knowledge, skills and values that are aligned with the organisation's strategy. The way employees have been rewarded has changed dramatically over the years, from a rigid, inflexible and tenure-based pay to a flexible pay that bridges reward and business strategies, enabling companies to compete in the dynamic business environment. Therefore, HR managers today need to be more strategic in establishing flexible reward systems to align with the dynamic environment, including what is being offered by their competitors. This ensures that companies attract and retain the 'best' employees and the ability to achieve a competitive advantage is fostered. Rewards are designed and developed in a variety of ways; however, it is imperative that they align with organisational goals and aim to improve organisational, group and individual performance. Of course, the type of reward offered is unique to the company and will usually depend on the company size, culture and profitability, as well as the incumbent's position.

A reward is defined as an item (either tangible or intangible) which is received in recognition for behaviour or output, and may be classified as either intrinsic or extrinsic. Intrinsic rewards refer to rewards which are sourced from inside of, or internal to, the individual, for example the pleasure or value received from the content of the work or a plaque awarded for employee of the month (tangible). In contrast, extrinsic rewards refer to rewards which are sourced outside of, or external to, the individual and they are usually financially related. For example, direct financial rewards include profit-sharing and stock options, and indirect financial rewards include factors such as medical insurance or a car. As employees are motivated differently, the type of reward they prefer depends on the individual and HR managers need to be aware of this when developing reward strategies. Therefore, managers are advised to refer to motivational theories (i.e. content and process theories) to help them understand how and why employees are motivated and wish to be rewarded. It is also important, when undergoing this process, to be aware of individual and organisational needs to ensure they are congruent in the development of effective reward strategies.

There are four simple building blocks which are designed to assist an HR manager in the development of reward strategies. The first block, *base pay*, addresses how much employees should be paid just for turning up to work. This forms the foundation of reward management. Depending on the employees' contract and the organisational needs and capabilities (such as financial resources), employees may either be paid a salary or a wage and this forms the base of their pay. In the Australian context, there are several ways that base pay can be determined, such as an award, Australian Workplace Agreement (AWA), certified agreement, collective bargaining and award-free individual contracts, and the recent industrial relations reform has significantly impacted upon base pay, as well as employer and employee rights. Base pay can also be determined by establishing the internal and external equity of a job which influences pay-level satisfaction. Internal equity reflects the equity (or relative) value associated with jobs and people within the organisation's internal labour market, whereas external equity refers to the levels of pay for similar jobs in the external labour market.

The second block in the total reward management process is *performance pay*. Performance pay is a payment individuals receive based upon their individual, group and/or organisational performance and is also referred to as variable pay, contingency pay or pay at risk. There are various types of performance pay, such as a discretionary bonus, an incentive (i.e. individual, group and organisational), and profit-sharing schemes. Although performance pay can be advantageous for the company because it focuses on key performance objectives and is linked to the achievement of competitively important results, it can also be disadvantageous. For example, it may reduce risk-taking behaviours to face challenging tasks and reinforce rigid behaviour.

The third block addresses *employee benefits*, which refer to all financial rewards that are not paid directly in cash to the employee. For example, this might include crèche facilities, flexi time, pensions, subsidised meals and superannuation. Employee benefits refer to services that are purchased by the employer for the employee's use; however, they do not affect employees' perceptions of their remuneration unless they understand the monetary value it holds for them. After HR managers have determined blocks one, two and three, the total remuneration for employees may be calculated via the following equation: *Total remuneration = Block 1 + Block 2 + Block 3*. Managers can use this equation to determine reward strategies for employees that are congruent with organisational goals. However, managers should also be aware of factors which may influence pay strategies, such as internal factors (i.e. the worth of a job and the company's ability to pay) and external factors (i.e. labour market conditions and the relative cost of living).

Although total remuneration may be calculated using the remuneration equation, it is also important to consider non-financial rewards, which is the fourth block. This is important because not all employees are motivated by financial rewards, and this type of reward focuses on the needs of people for recognition, self-determination, achievement, responsibility and personal growth, which contribute to motivation, commitment and improved performance. Therefore, an adapted equation that HR managers may use to determine improved performance is: *Improved performance = Block 1 + Block 2 + Block 3 + Block 4*.

The chapter concluded with a discussion on contemporary reward strategy features. These include employability pay, person-based pay, market-determined pay, team-based rewards, low degree of hierarchy and the aim of reward management. By considering these features, HR managers can design reward strategies that foster continuous improvement and the ability to develop a strategic competitive advantage.

Key terms

award	external equity	reward
award-free individual contract	extrinsic rewards	reward management
broadbanding	incentive	reward strategy
certified agreements	internal equity	salary
collective bargaining	intrinsic rewards	the factor comparison system
discretionary bonus	job evaluation	the point system
employee benefits	performance pay	wage

Review questions

11.1 Before reward systems can be designed and implemented strategically with SHRM goals, what is it first necessary for an HR manager to do? Illustrate your answer with examples and define key terms.

11.2 People usually differ in how they prefer to be rewarded. What is the difference between intrinsic and extrinsic rewards? How do you think a junior sales assistant at a fast food restaurant would like to be rewarded? How would this compare to a senior accountant at a top accounting firm in London?

11.3 Reward management is closely associated with motivational theory. How do content and process theories differ and how does each relate to reward management? Which motivational theory would you prefer for your own reward management?

11.4 Referring to the essential building blocks of the total reward management process, briefly explain how reward strategies may be developed, taking into consideration recent Australian industrial relations reforms.

11.5 An HR manager can choose the type of reward (or pay) strategy that is employed within an organisation. Identify and briefly describe each of the three strategies. If you were the HR manager of a mid-sized company, which strategy would you adopt for: (a) a university lecturer, (b) a stock broker, and (c) a carpenter? Provide justifications for your answers.

Exercises

1.1 Visit Mercer Human Resource Consultant's website (www.mercerhr.com). Select the Knowledge Centre icon to reveal current articles in SHRM. Using the SHRM Application Tool, critically analyse one of the presented articles.

11.2 Visit the website of a company you are familiar with or have an interest in and develop reward strategies based on what they suggest about their vision, mission, core values or business strategies. For example, the Hilton Hotel's vision statement is: 'Our vision is to be first choice of the world's travellers. Hilton intends to build on the rich heritage and strength of our brands by: Consistently delighting our customers, investing in our team members, delivering innovative products and services through continuously improving performance'. What reward strategies would you develop for this company?

11.3 Establish a reward strategy using the four essential building blocks based upon the following business objectives: (a) excellent customer service, (b) excellent innovation and creativity, and (c) just-in-time delivery.

References

Adams, J. S. (1963), 'Toward an understanding of inequity', *Journal of Abnormal and Social Psychology*, vol. 67, pp. 422–36.

Alderfer, C. P. (1969), 'An empirical test of a new theory of human needs', *Organizational Behavior and Human Performance*, vol. 8, pp. 142–75.

Armstrong, M. & Murlis, H. (2004), *Reward Management*, Kogan Page, London.

Beatson, M. (1995) *Labour Market Flexibility, Employment Department*, Research Series, April, No. 48, Employment Department, Sheffield.

Bordia, P. & Blau, G. (2003), 'Moderating effect of allocentrism on the pay referent compassion-pay level satisfaction relationship', *Applied Psychology*, vol. 52, no. 4, pp. 499–514.

Deci, E. & Ryan, R. (1985), *Intrinsic Motivation and Self-Determination in Human Behaviour*, Plenum Press, New York.

Deckop, J. R., Merriman, K. K. & Blau, G. (2004), 'Impact of variable risk preferences on the effectiveness of control by pay', *Journal of Occupational and Organisational Psychology*, vol. 77, pp. 63–80.

Fisher, C. D., Schoenfeldt, L. F. & Shaw, J. B. (1999), *Human Resource Management*, Houghton Mifflin, Boston.

Flynn, J. (1999), 'Use of performance based pay spreads across continental Europe, survey says, *Wall Street Journal*, vol. 17, p. 1.

Gerhart, B., Minkoff, H. B. & Olsen, R. N. (1995), 'Employee compensation: Theory, practice, and evidence', in *Handbook of Human Resource Management*, eds G. R. Ferris, S. D. Rosen & D. T. Barnum, Blackwell, Cambridge.

Gilbert, D. (1994), 'Merit pay increases are a mistake: A response', *Compensation & Benefits Review*, March–April, pp. 23–5.

Guzzo, R. A. & Katzell R. A. (1987), 'Effects of economic incentives on productivity: A psychological view', in *Incentives, Cooperation, and Risk Sharing: Economic and Psychological Perspectives on Employment Contracts*, ed. H. R. Nalbantian, Rowman and Littlefield, Totowa, NJ.

Hay Group Method of Job Evaluation (2005), <http://www.haygroup.com/>, accessed 22 November 2005.

Kerr, S. (1995), 'On the folly of rewarding A, while hoping for B', *Academy of Management Executive*, vol. 9, no. 1, pp. 7–14.

Kessler, I. & Purcell, J. (1992), 'Performance related pay: Objective and application', *Human Resource Management Journal*, vol. 2, no. 3, pp. 16–33.

Kohn, A. (1993), 'Why incentive plans cannot work', *Harvard Business Review*, September–October, pp. 54–63.

Lawler, E. E. (1981), *Pay and Organizational Effectiveness,* McGraw-Hill, New York.

Lawler, E. E. (2000), *Rewarding Excellence: Pay Strategies for the New Economy*, Jossey-Bass, San Francisco.

Lewis, L. (2000), 'Exploring Lawler's new pay theory through the case of Finbank's reward strategy for managers', *Personnel Review*, vol. 29, no. 1, pp. 10–28.

Locke, E. A. (1968), 'Toward a theory of task motivation and incentives', *Organizational Behaviour Human Performance,* vol. 3, pp. 157–89.

Maslow, A. H. (1954), *Motivation and Personality*, Harper E. Row, New York.

Mitchell, T. R. & Mickel, A. E. (1999), 'The meaning of money: An individual-difference perspective' *Academy of Management Review*, vol. 24, no. 3, pp. 568–78.

O'Neill, G. L. (1995), 'Linking pay to performance: Conflicting views and conflicting evidence', *Asia Pacific Journal of Human Resources*, vol. 33, no. 2, pp. 20–35.

PA Consulting Group (1994), *Perspectives on Top Management Rewards*, PA Consulting Services, Sydney.

Schuster, J. & Zingheim, P. (1992), *The New Pay: Linking Employee and Organisational Performance*, Lexington, New York.

Skinner, B. F. (1953), *Science and Human Behavior*, Macmillan, New York.

Taylor, F. W. (1911), *The Principles of Scientific Management*, Harper, New York.

Tripp, T. (2004), 'Best Perks: Southwest Airlines', <http://www.vault.com/nr/newsmain.jsp?nr_page=3&ch_id=401&article_id=21007&cat_id=1089>, accessed 13 October 2004.

Vroom, V. (1964), Work and Motivation, John Wiley, New York.

12 Chapter

The defining features of an effective HR practitioner

INTRODUCTION

The core aim of this book has been to highlight the fact that effective HRM comes from an accurate understanding of the particular business context your organisation is operating in (i.e. internal and external), knowledge of the latest research and theory relating to the management of people in organisations, and the ability to transform that knowledge into practice as demonstrated through the SHRM Application Tool. The purpose of this chapter is to highlight the defining features of an effective HR practitioner. These features include an accurate understanding of what motivates human behaviour, thinking that reflects the processes depicted in the SHRM Application Tool, remembering that 'what gets measured gets done' and, thus, attention to HR metrics is critical, and considering the social as well as financial impacts of HRM.

Objectives

The primary objective of this chapter is to provide an understanding of what effective HR is and to enable you to utilise the SHRM Application Tool in practice.

After reading this chapter you should be able to:

- distinguish between 'best principles' and 'best practice';
- understand the significance of having a systems perspective when applying the SHRM Application Tool in a dynamic work environment;
- explain the strategic importance of having HR metrics in an organisation;
- differentiate between multiple levels of HR metrics and identify their utility at each level;
- understand the use of horizontal and vertical gap analysis when using a multilevel metrics model;
- discuss the importance of linking HRM to social and environmental outcomes, in addition to financial outcomes.

Effective SHRM is about 'best principles' not 'best practices'

There are numerous examples of organisations adopting so-called '**best practices**'. Best practices are thought of as an ideal or 'model' mode of practice, and they are identified from highly successful organisations. Other organisations wanting this same success are often tempted to simply adopt the best practice (i.e. a new software program), only to find that it isn't as successful in their own company. This is because it is not the best practice alone that yields success but rather the principles behind it (i.e. whether it aligns with the organisation's culture, structure and strategy). For example, consider the true case of a company which observed a competitor using Lotus Notes® (an email and communication software program) actively to collaborate on projects and share information. Had the SHRM Application Tool been used, the company would have realised that the reason this technology worked for their competitor was not a consequence of the software alone. Rather, it was because the software was supported by an organisational culture of collaboration and knowledge sharing. In the absence of such a culture, the company attempted to use Lotus Notes® but soon discovered that their investment proved only to be an expensive email system and, for it to be effective, an appropriate culture needed to be developed (not just the purchase of the software).

The error of focusing on best practices rather than best principles is commonly observed in HR decision making when companies move an HR policy or practice across national borders as there is a myriad of cultural factors that need to be taken into consideration (as discussed in Chapters 5 and 7). For example, an American-owned multinational found the 'Employee of the month' recognition an effective motivator in its US subsidiaries. Subsequently, it asked its Australian subsidiary to implement the same recognition scheme. After the Australian managers tried the scheme but with very different results (employees were

best practice
Practice thought of as an ideal or 'model' mode of practice.

demotivated by being singled out from their workmates), the Australian subsidiary decided to deal with the American directive by simply rostering employees for the award – in effect, carrying out a nonsensical activity in order to give the appearance to headquarters that its policies were being complied with and were effective. Therefore, this was an ineffective and wasteful activity that the Australian subsidiary adopted, which was also incongruent with the overall goals of the company and its organisational culture. Had the Australian subsidiary simply discussed this issue with the US subsidiary, a more appropriate, effective and meaningful initiative could have been implemented.

These examples underscore the importance of adopting not the practice of effective companies but rather the underlying principles about managing human behaviour which led to their development of the 'best practice'. In other words, it is important to keep in mind that the 'best practice' is 'best' for the specific circumstances of the company which developed it; it is the end result (i.e. Step 6) of the SHRM Application Tool.

Recognition of what effective SHRM is reveals the many exciting possibilities available to organisations in managing their people. Effective SHRM is not dependent on the culture one is operating in or the amount of resources one has; it is about innovative thinking. Take, for example, a case of a bus operator in outback Queensland whose business must run on very narrow profit margins. At first glance, the owner of this small business might think that providing a reward system beyond the standard wage is beyond reach. Certainly this would be a likely conclusion if the owner were to rely on looking at what other companies were offering or the types of reward systems described in many textbooks. However, if the owner considered the underlying principles of best practice reward systems, it would become clear that such systems are based on what employees value. With this as a starting point, the owner decided to develop an innovative reward system that was specific to his business. He asked his employees (i.e. the bus drivers) what non-financial factors they valued in their job. The bus drivers had no difficulty in coming up with a list, including factors such as driving the newest bus, preferred bus routes and shifts and first choice at picking timing of holiday leave. With this in mind, the owner then chose from both intrinsic and extrinsic rewards to motivate his employees (see Chapter 2 for a discussion on motivation). Now that the owner had identified the rewards, he then linked these to desired performance levels and ensured a method for assessing best performance was in place. Therefore, the effective SHRM is not purely for large corporations but rather for all types of organisations: big, small, national, international, private, pubic, not-for-profit, diverse, etc. Any type of organisation which employs people can benefit from effective SHRM.

The SHRM Application Tool presented as the foundation of this book ensures that HR decision makers draw on the best available research and theory on people management and develop practices based on these which accord with the unique features of the business and its operating environment. The technique is simple to learn, easy to use and provides a framework which can be used by anyone to transform theory and research into innovative practices that address specific business challenges and opportunities.

Effective SHRM is an evolutionary dynamic process not a static set of routines

The SHRM Application Tool highlights effective HRM as a dynamic process, involving ongoing and systematic environmental scanning and analysis of organisational objectives, strategies and policies. Accordingly, it promotes 'systems thinking' or the consideration of the elements of an HR activity and the processes that interconnect them (cf. Espejo, 1994). Systems thinking has been shown to be critical to dealing with the complexity, dynamism and uncertainty of contemporary management (Flood, 1999), and necessary for effective SHRM (Walker, 1999).

Effective SHRM has more to do with the HRM system than specific practices (Barney & Wright, 1998). The system must be continually fine-tuned and its components (i.e. policies and practices) must be monitored to ensure they are addressing the underlying causes of behaviour and that they align with one another. Effective SHRM therefore reflects continuous learning processes. It requires a flexible mindset, mechanisms which ensure the availability of the most accurate information at the time required, reflecting on what can be learned from the past while thinking about the needs and demands of the future. As what is measured gets attended to and done, HR metrics play an essential role in diagnosing issues in the organisation, monitoring the internal and external environment and identifying and tracking changes.

Human resource management metrics

At this point, it is clear that the HR function can play a fundamental role in an organisation's overall success. It is for this reason that an organisation should be able to measure clearly the impact of its HR investments and ensure that they are in line with the organisation's strategic goals. This is done by using **HR metrics**.

HR metrics can be used to monitor:

- what is going on within an organisation;
- what effects any changes implemented within the organisation are having; and
- the value being added to the organisation through its human resources.

HR metrics may be taken at a number of levels. These include assessing changes within persons, between persons, between groups, between departments, between sites and between organisations. It is essential that information is collected at each of these levels as collecting data at multiple levels provides the organisation with more information than if they were simply to collect metrics at one level. Further, as has been demonstrated throughout this text and with the SHRM Application Tool, effective HRM takes a dynamic and systems view of organisations, which mean specific activities need to be examined collectively, not just individually, and also over time. The focus of the remainder of this section is on demonstrating both why and how collecting information at multiple levels is important.

HR metrics
Measurements used by an organisation to evaluate the impact of its human resource investments and ensure that they are in line with the organisation's strategic goals.

LEVELS OF MEASUREMENT

WITHIN-PERSON METRICS

within-person metrics
Measurements used to analyse differences within an individual person.

within-person variability
Changes that occur in an individual from moment to moment.

Within-person metrics are used to measure differences within an individual person. People, unlike machines, are not static entities, rather they can change from moment to moment. This is known as **within-person variability**. When examining the implications of within-person variability in relation to performance at work (and specifically to emotions at work), Fisher and Noble (2004) found substantial variability within individual people as to their perceptions of their skill for undertaking the task, the difficulty of the task they were undertaking, the level of interest they had in the task, the effort that they put in to doing the task, their perception of their performance of the task and the emotions that they had related to the task. This indicates that it is important for organisations to take within-person metrics in order to gain an understanding of the task and situational variables that influence how much effort employees exert and, hence, what will lead them to performing at a higher level.

Examples of areas where metrics may be used to measure changes at the within-person level include:

- Motivation
- Effort
- Interest and boredom
- Performance
- Stress

Once these metrics have been collected, they can be useful in assisting in HR activities such as job design. By understanding what generates and maintains an individual's interest, stimulates motivation and leads them to put in a high degree of effort, the HR manager can adjust an individual's job design accordingly. For example, think of a book keeper working for a large wholesaler who every Friday generates invoices to send out to customers for orders placed in that week. Within-person metrics may reveal that the book keeper loses interest in the task when doing the invoices all at once, resulting in less time being spent on ensuring no mistakes have been made. By redesigning the job so that the employee spends two hours at the end of each day generating invoices for the orders placed that day, the book keeper does not lose interest in the task at hand and fewer mistakes will be made.

BETWEEN-PERSON METRICS

between-person metrics
Measurements used to analyse differences between people.

Between-person metrics are used to measure differences between people. While it is possible, for example, to measure differences within an individual's levels of motivation, it is also possible to measure differences between people. Examples of metrics which can be measured at the between-person level include:

- Personality traits
- Aptitude
- Organisational citizenship behaviours (OCBs)
- Emotion management skills (e.g. emotional intelligence)
- Honesty
- 'G' or general intelligence

These between-person measures are useful in assisting HR activities such as recruitment and selection. Let's take the example of a service provider who places a high value on customer service. First, metrics such as personality tests can assist in identifying the individual differences which are associated with success on the job. Once these are identified, they can be used in the recruitment and selection of new employees. For example, if interpersonal communication and conflict management skills were identified as being characteristics of successful service providers in making the decision on which applicant would be most suited to the position, the recruitment process would emphasise these skills in the job description and the selection process would involve taking measures of the applicants on these skill dimensions. This would help the company to determine which applicant would perform the best in interactions with customers under difficult circumstances.

GROUP-LEVEL METRICS

Group-level metrics can be used to measure variables at the group level. This level of measurement is particularly important considering that now, more than ever, organisations are using work teams to increase efficiency and effectiveness (Shaw & Barrett-Power, 1998). Examples of metrics which can be measured at the group level include:

group-level metrics
Measurements used to analyse differences between groups.

- Performance
- Cohesion
- Conflict
- Communication integration
- Morale
- Turnover
- Group satisfaction

Measurement at this level will help a group leader to determine what they need to do to ensure that the group's climate is such that it will bring about the highest possible level of performance. To illustrate this point, consider an organisation which has a large number of culturally diverse employees. Diversity research has revealed that while diverse work teams present the potential for increased innovation and creativity, they also tend to have lower levels of group cohesion (Fujimoto *et al.*, 2000). In order to ensure that the organisation is able to benefit from the benefits of having diverse employees they could take group-level metrics to determine the extent to which teams within the organisation have an inclusive team climate. This would help them in making decisions about what sort of training and development workshops would be of benefit to the employees. For example, if the metrics revealed that employees perceived the team climate to be exclusionary (i.e. as evidenced by the existence of subgroups and conflict), then this would indicate to HR managers that diversity-based training would be of benefit to employees and the organisation. On the other hand, if the metrics revealed employees perceived the team climate to be inclusive (i.e. no subgroups), this would reveal to HR managers that diversity-based training is not necessary and that employees and the organisation would benefit more from skill-based training.

This approach can also be applied to examining issues between departments or different sites of the organisation.

ORGANISATIONAL-LEVEL METRICS

organisational-level metrics
Measurements used to evaluate an organisation's overall position.

Organisational-level metrics can be used to provide an organisation with information about its overall position. Examples of organisational-level metrics include:

- Organisational culture
- Organisational climate
- Corporate social responsibility (CSR)
- Organisational performance

In many cases, making sense of these metrics will involve benchmarking or collecting data on the positioning of competitor organisations on these same metrics. For example, an oil company that obtained its ranking on a corporate social responsibility questionnaire would want to interpret its score in the context of scores of other companies in its industry. Similarly, changes in overall levels of job satisfaction are known to be affected by general attitudes toward the economy; being able to compare the job satisfaction level of one's organisation with other organisations can help managers identify whether the change is organisation specific or reflects a change in the labour force at large.

DETERMINING FIT AMONG HR METRICS

A mistake that is often made when using HR metrics is developing and using metrics for each individual function or activity without thinking about the 'bigger picture'. When using HR metrics, it is important to ensure that they are in line with (1) the other organisational functions, and (2) the organisation's strategic goals. It is for this reason that we advocate using a multilevel metrics model that will allow measurement of human resources at the within-person, between-person, group and organisational levels.

multilevel metrics model
A model that allows the measurement of human resources at the within-person, between-person, group and organisational levels.

When using a **multilevel metrics model** it is necessary to undertake a gap analysis both vertically and horizontally to ensure that HR functions at each level are consistent and that there are no gaps which may prevent the organisation from reaching its strategic goals. A gap analysis, which was discussed in Chapter 1, involves looking at what the organisation is currently doing and what it needs to be doing to reach its strategic goals.

Vertical gap analysis examines the alignment between HR activities happening at the organisation level, the group/department/site level, the individual level and the within-individual level. For example, if one of the key performance management criteria for an organisation is customer focus, yet the organisation fails to include customer interaction skills as part of its selection criteria, a gap analysis will reveal this gap and indicate that the organisation needs to adjust its selection criteria to ensure that all criteria are in line with each other.

Horizontal gap analysis examines the alignment between HR activities targeted at the within-individual level, between HR activities targeted at individuals within a group and between HR activities targeted at groups/departments/sites of the organisation. For example, if the performance management process is being implemented differently in different organisational departments, the gap analysis would identify this and assess whether those differences have any negative implications for the goals and legal obligations of the organisation.

Effective SHRM is underpinned by a value-driven culture

The values and philosophy of an organisation have been linked to organisational success (Kirn *et al.*, 1999). The values and beliefs driving people management are crucial to the type of HRM system adopted in an organisation and its ultimate impact on employee behaviour and attitudes (Monks & McMackin, 2001, p. 59).

The history of HRM (see Chapter 1) illustrates how the philosophical stance or paradigm about work and employees one adopts affects the direction and target of both research and practice. The paradigm adopted determines the values, objectives and methods one will develop and advocate. An effective HR practitioner will know what their paradigm is, clearly communicate that paradigm to others and work in an organisation that supports that paradigm.

There is evidence to suggest that the paradigm that is most relevant to the contemporary business context contains the following values and beliefs.

- Recognition of the whole person. That is, employee behaviour is affected not only by what is happening in the workplace but also by their personal lives. Effective HRM takes this fact into account as much as is feasible.
- The social environment within the organisation influences employee behaviour for better or for worse. Effective HRM promotes a positive social environment.
- The physical environment the employee works in influences behaviour, emotions, attitudes and motivation. Effective HRM ensures a healthy and secure physical environment.
- The emotions employees experience at work influence their behaviour. Effective HRM recognises the emotional aspects of work and working and ensures employees are supported in the management of these.
- The quality of relationships with one's supervisor and co-workers affects work behaviour and attitudes. Effective HRM promotes inclusion and constructive conflict and addresses destructive conflict.
- Employee behaviour is a product of personal and environmental characteristics. Effective HRM ensures high-quality interpersonal relationships, appropriate organisational systems, clear goals and performance criteria, a healthy work environment and consideration of person–job fit.
- Employee behaviour is better served by HRM policies and practices which focus on motivation through support rather than through fear.

The future of HRM and HRM in the future

Part of being an effective leader in business is to think about what the future is likely to hold in terms of both challenges and opportunities. In asking this question of HRM, it is useful to consider both how the theory and practice of HRM might be different in the future as well as how business might be different and the people management implications of these.

Let's begin by considering what business might be like in the future. Already we have witnessed shifts in how business is valued in society. The **triple bottom line** view has highlighted for business, society and governments the importance of what metrics are used to indicate successful business performance. In particular, the triple bottom line suggests that it is inappropriate to rely on financial performance indicators alone. Rather, this approach suggests that business success is measured by good performance on financial, social and environmental indicators. Although the current ability accurately to assess environmental and social impact in any meaningful way is questionable, the view that business should contribute to the wellbeing of the environment and society does foreshadow the possibility that current notions of economics and business performance may shift away from a material focus to a wellbeing focus. For HRM, a key implication would be the need to link the management of people to social and environmental outcomes in addition to financial ones. Examples of non-financial outcomes that HRM may need to show it affects include cognitive moral development, corruption, distributive justice, diversity openness, inclusion, crime, economic development, poverty alleviation, education, corporate citizenship, environmental impact, human rights, empowerment to exercise civil and employment freedoms and rights and power to negotiate work choices.

The increasing expectations of consumers, employees, communities and governments regarding the purpose of business in society and how it should operate will undoubtedly require greater integration of HRM with the other functions within an organisation as well as integration with the broader community. The SHRM Application Tool can be used to assist in identifying key issues as well as aligning the HRM system with other organisational functions and external demands. It can also assist in examining the assumptions and values of different stakeholder groups and a critical analysis of the organisation's own paradigms.

triple bottom line
A company reporting system that advocates the notion that the traditional company reporting framework should be extended to include not just financial outcomes but environmental and social outcomes also.

Contemporary SHRM Application Tool

The SHRM Application Tool in each chapter has demonstrated how HRM metrics are designed and used with respect to one aspect of the overall HRM system. The purpose of this last example of the application tool is to show you how the tool can be used at the 'big picture' level, in particular, how HR managers should examine the entire set of HR metrics. In other words, this example shows how the application tool can assist in assessing the fit among HR metrics at the within-person, between-person, group and organisational levels.

Imagine you are an HR manager of a large multinational finance company in Australasia. Since her appointment six years ago, the CEO of this company has been very enthusiastic about celebrating workforce diversity. Today, top management is committed to making full use of every individual's talent in the pursuit of organisational success. Under the auspices of celebrating diversity, the

HR director has been asked to create a range of specific initiatives and programs to fill in the gaps between HR activities as well as the gap between HR activities and the diversity-oriented strategy of this company. The example SHRM Application Tool presented in Figure 12.1 demonstrates how an HR manager should consider HR issues at every level by using HR metrics.

FIGURE 12.1
SHRM Application Tool: fit assessment

Step 6: Evaluate against success criteria
- After 3 years, by what percentage did the horizontal integration of diversity initiatives increase minority representation at the executive level?
- By what percentage did employee fairness increase (e.g. from assessment of relationship between ethnicity, status, performance and pay)?
- By what percentage did diversity-related complaints reduce?

Step 5: Implement the plan
- Conduct focus groups, interviews and/or surveys to discover the (a) struggles minority members are facing and (b) ambiguity line managers are facing about diversity management

Horizontal integration of diversity management
- Form a two-hour training workshop focused on diversity as an asset to senior managers and line managers. Develop a practical skill set on how to train employees to foster their diverse talents
- Form a career development and counselling plan for minority members
- Create a statistical dataset of ethnicity against pay, promotion and job status to ensure employment fairness
- Performance appraisal of senior managers to emphasise cross-cultural management skills
- Recruitment criteria should include diversity openness
- Establish diversity celebration days in the company calendar such as multicultural food day and indigenous celebration day

Step 4: Devise plan and success criteria

Individual metrics
- Senior managers need training on how to motivate their employees to appreciate diversity and to capitalise on diverse talents
- Counselling or career development plan is needed for minority members to reduce their stress in relation to perceived lack of career opportunity
- Educate line managers to increase the diversity-openness in their personality

Between-person metrics
- Recruitment needs to ensure that not only culturally diverse employees are recruited but those that value diversity
- Each job description should include diversity-open behaviours

Group metrics
- Group leaders need to be trained to create diversity-open climate in their groups

Verify

Step 3: Verify/falsify potential problem or opportunity
- Capitalise on workforce diversity better through various initiatives and programs (organisational-level metrics)

Falsify

Step 2: Detect potential problem or opportunity
- Lack of minority members at the executive level
- Significant increase in culturally diverse employees reflects the diversity in the community we serve
- Workers still struggle with the concept of diversity management and valuing diversity

Step 1: Analyse environmental factors

Step 1a: HR issues: Monitor/analyse data (past, present and future)
- Shifted to diversity management focus 6 years ago with the new CEO from offshore being very alarmed at lack of diversity management in Australia
- People still struggle with the concept of diversity management
- Compared to ethnicity statistics of 6 years ago, 20% increase in ethnic diversity; however, still lack minority representation at the executive level
- Began an education strategy to train new employees about valuing diversity

Step 1b: Internal/organisational environment
- Organisational culture to celebrate workforce diversity
- Aim to fully utilise individual and group talents to achieve high organisational performance
- Organisation's core values are openness, respect and fairness
- The core business consists of retirement savings, investment, insurance, banking and financial planning
- Very culturally diverse company achieved through diversity-oriented recruitment and induction strategy

Step 1c: External environment
- Approximately 45% of Australian population is born overseas or has at least one parent born overseas
- 200 languages spoken in Australia
- Ageing workforce
- Approximately 25% of workforce consists of people born overseas
- Commonwealth government-initiated multicultural policy
- Increasing cultural tension in communities and workplaces since September 11 incident

A view from the field

The basis for this case study lies in a series of corporate changes that were implemented at the Australian Taxation Office (ATO). The changes (which have been revolutionary in improving the work aspects of employees, as well as the tax compliance of the wider community) were introduced through identification of a new HR system which was appropriate for the future of the organisation. An overarching objective of the change initiative was to achieve a cultural change at the ATO that could complement its corporate strategy. In particular, the CEO delegated to the HR team the challenge of devising an implementation strategy to move the organisation from an 'entitlement culture' to a 'performance culture'. Further, it was found that the HR functions at the ATO had gradually evolved to taking a secondary role in the corporate agenda. This deterioration of the HR role was variously attributed to continuous downsizing, change initiatives, redundancy programs and the threat of outsourcing HR functions. Consequently, the situation had resulted in a complex network of HR activities operating independently within the business, often in competition and conflicting with other internal activities, resulting in poor people management.

The HR system that was developed in response to the issues identified above integrated a number of SHRM theories and ideas that have appeared over the last decade or so in the HRM literature. These theories included such concepts as the resource-based view of human capital, human resource architecture and its vertical and horizontal fit within the organisation, and HR systems and roles. In essence, the HR system model adopted by the ATO represented a holistic approach which was developed out of 'best principles' identified in the academic literature. The ATO made a purposeful shift of its philosophical stance about people and people management. Importantly, it clearly articulated this new paradigm in terms of assumptions. These are given below:

Assumption No. 1 – People are vital to an organisation's success
This first assumption is supported by human capital theory and the resource based view. The logic underpinning this assumption is that in order to obtain the required value human resources should be configured in a manner congruent with the business requirements of the organisation.

Assumption No. 2 – There are several ways organisations can enable their human capital to be used to improve organisational performance
The second assumption is that organisations can enhance human capital through effective HR systems, high-performing work practices, a flexible workforce and the development of human capital. However, it is acknowledged that not every HR function is capable of increasing human capital or improving organisational performance. To be able to do so, such HR functions need to achieve vertical and environmental fit (the fit between current and future business directions of the organisation and its environment in relation to the HR policy). Simultaneously, an organisation should ensure its HR functions achieve a horizontal fit, which is the internal congruence with its other processes. HR architecture is assumed to be the enabler of this horizontal, vertical and environmental fit.

Assumption No. 3 – When delivering complex strategic HRM design, the four major roles of HR need to be operating in a focused and proficient way
The ATO believes HR should carry out four major roles: strategic partner, change agent, administrative expert and employee champion. These activities are viewed as needing to function in a collaborative and focused manner.

Assumption No. 4 – Each of the four HR roles listed above could be located in various parts of the HR function
The ATO believes that the above-stated HR roles could be located in different divisions of the HR function. Therefore, careful consideration of the HR architecture and the business context of the organisation was needed in order to determine whether the roles should be a part of the core corporate function, technological services,

centralised services, decentralised services or external services. It was also assumed that consideration needed to be given to the four levels of architecture, business structure and the context of operation when assigning locations for HR functions.

Steps in the implementation process

The following steps show how the ATO implemented the new HR system. The thinking illustrated in this case is a good example of how the principles captured in the SHRM Application Tool enable effective HRM at the level of the entire HRM system. It is important to note that many of the steps outlined only provide guidance in the form of a checklist for the practitioners; in effect these steps often overlap and are better represented as phases of organisational change. It is also important to note that the steps are not necessarily consecutive in time.

Step 1: Decide on the organisation's current and future human capital requirements

Systems thinking and methodology was used by the ATO implementation team to identify the types of people currently available and those who would be required in the future given the organisation's goals and vision. Analysis included consideration of the business direction, labour force characteristics, business environment, organisational performance and business systems. HR's involvement in this process was expected to be provided by the senior HR manager acting in the role of strategic partner.

Step 2: Develop a human resource philosophy

It is of significance that an organisation has explicated a set of values or a philosophy articulating the role of HR within the organisation. At the ATO, the executive leadership developed a philosophy consisting of three distinct components: (1) a vision for a 'performance culture' supported by a mutual 'partnership' like the relationship between management and employees, (2) behavioural change directed at achieving corporate goals and better client relations, and (3) a statement of specific future HR and employment arrangements.

Step 3: Assess the HR configuration required

A framework was developed at the ATO to assess the HR configuration once the required human capital was agreed upon. This tool considered the various types of work in the organisation (e.g. management, law, field operations) with regard to their uniqueness and value to the organisation. Based on the analysis, suitable employment modes (e.g. internal development, contracting and acquisition) were adopted to attain the most suitable HR configuration. Once a configuration was established, the design of a suitable HR system that met the needs of the HR configuration was undertaken.

Step 4: Assess the implications of the HR configuration against the philosophy of the organisation

It is important that the HR configuration of an organisation is compatible with the organisational philosophy. In the case of the ATO, a typology was utilised to evaluate both the uniqueness and the value of human capital with respect to the nature of core business and the corporate philosophy (see Figure 12.2).

Step 5: Design an HR architecture to deliver the required human capital

Once the HR configuration was agreed upon, the next phase of the process was the design of an HR architecture that ensured vertical and horizontal alignment within the organisational system. At the ATO, several HR sub-systems were recognised to have been in operation. These included workforce design and planning; employment; learning; conditions and environment; and performance. Furthermore, it was acknowledged that supporting subsystems such as internal communications, alignment, organisational design and change management may need to be incorporated into a holistic HR system, especially if the organisation concerned is large. Additionally, common organisational aspects such as IT tools, systems and processes need to be incorporated within a common infrastructure of the architecture in order to enhance horizontal fit. Operations of each HR subsystem could be enacted separately as long as they were harmonious with the overall HR design, to ensure vertical

12.2 FIGURE
HR configuration framework

alignment. The HR architecture at the ATO was a product of a four-tier process of design, infrastructure, operations and assurance that established both vertical and horizontal alignment in the organisation.

Step 6: Determine the HR processes required to meet the human capital requirements
The project team at the ATO recognised that the HR architecture must be designed with optimal flexibility capabilities to meet the ongoing human capital needs. Furthermore, an evaluation was conducted to ensure the HR processes would be able cost effectively to match the human capital requirements in the organisation. The evaluation essentially involved the comparison of human capital against the required HR processes. The results of the analysis indicated that in some areas of the HR processes generic services would be able to provide the services, whereas in others areas specialised services were required on a work-type basis.

Step 7: Determine the location of HR functions in the business
The final step of the model involved determining desirable locations for various HR functions, depending on the specific structure and requirements of the organisation. At this stage, the ATO was provided with a number of specific recommendations. These were:

1. The core corporate function, incorporating design and management of the HR system, organisation design, policy, change management and assurance management should be centrally located.
2. The common infrastructure, including generic IT-based systems, such as payroll, establishment, capability management and performance, should be centrally managed, but not as part of the core function.
3. The management of conditions, including the negotiation of industrial agreements, should be centralised.
4. All operational activities, including employment, performance management, learning programs and specific delivery of certain conditions, should be decentralised and based close to the client.
5. The operations could be decentralised according to work type and/or location, depending on the nature of the activity and efficiency gains involved.

This extract highlights, through a real case example, how a theoretical model can be successfully operationalised using SHRM Application Tool principles. The resulting HRM system represents a holistic framework which has a very practical application even in a highly complex organisation such as the ATO.

Discussion questions

1. How does the HR architecture facilitate horizontal, vertical and environmental fit in organisations?
2. Explain the function of the four major roles of human resources in the SHRM model.
3. Discuss the importance of the corporate philosophy in implementing the HR configurations.

Source: Adapted from Molineux, J. & Härtel, C. E. J. (2005), 'A model for the implementation of strategic human resource management', paper presented at the 19th Annual ANZAM Conference, 8 December, Canberra, Australia.

A manager's challenge

Australia's greatest resource goes unnoticed

Human resources are vital to any business, and valuing this resource is the key to successful business. But what will the future hold for Australian businesses? Will human resources still be viewed as a company's most valuable resource? These are questions all HR managers should be asking in light of today's dynamic business environment. The answer, it appears, is no longer to take a back seat to our international competitors. The time is right to get moving! Action is required to ensure longevity in an everchanging world market. Smart management means the ability to identify up and coming trends. Also important is the willingness to adapt business, even if this means abandoning previous plans. Innovative business design is paramount, as the majority of businesses are susceptible to various contingencies such as bankruptcy and takeovers. Yet, the key to ongoing success in any business is people. Although unpredictability plagues businesses, employees are indispensable for business success. SHRM is becoming the vital ingredient that boosts a company's most valuable asset – its employees. Strategies must be changeable, and strategic businesses that have survived are few and far between, but have one thing in common – people with foresight.

But is this enough for Australian businesses to survive? As a nation, Australia has a few success stories including Macquarie Bank, Wesfarmers and Toll and Patrick. Macquarie Bank's expansion has included toll roads infrastructure, water treatment plants and the media. Wesfarmers is responsible for such diverse businesses as Bunnings and Kleenheat Gas, yet had humble beginnings as a farmer's co-operative. Toll and Patrick joined forces after expanding into rail from roads and ports respectively. These companies are singled out by their willingness to branch out, take a chance and reassess their strategy. Australian furniture retailer Fantastic Furniture is not afraid of change, or of pursuing expansion. The company is keen to diversify, with plans for increasing stores, and has a willingness to embrace opportunities for acquisition and business innovation. This attitude and strategy seems to be paying dividends, with a 2004/2005 net profit rise of 12 per cent to $17.66m. Market success appears to be driven by a perceptive vision. Managing Director Julian Tertini emphasised the need to anticipate the trend of more competition, and focus on long-term prospects rather than short-term gains.

Good management is vital but the role of employees in generating a successful business must not be underestimated, despite the apparent lack of recognition from managers and executives. More than half of respondents surveyed in a poll by HR firm Towers Perrin expressed negative feelings towards their employment experience. Key areas that contributed to these feelings included excessive workload, lack of communication from management, lack of recognition and boredom. The good news is that the study found a positive correlation between positive emotions of employees and financial gains, a fact that should not be ignored. Executives are keen to make funds available for updating technology to maintain a competitive advantage but often fail to value their employees in the same manner. Australian businesses must maintain their competitive advantage – and to do so they must focus on their employees as the best asset they will ever have.

Source: Adapted from Anonymous (2005), 'Fantastic Furniture confident of growth', *The Age* (Business), 31 October; Gettler, L. (2005), 'The flyers and the flops', *The Age* (Business), 15 October; MacInnis, P. (2003), 'The human factor', *Computing Canada*, vol. 29, no. 3, p. 10.

Summary

This chapter has highlighted the features required of an effective HR practitioner. The first feature identified as being important for an HR practitioner is having an accurate understanding of what motivates human behaviour. Having this understanding will enable the practitioner to implement HR practices that are appropriate to the specific circumstances of the organisation they are dealing with rather than simply implementing those practices recognised as 'best practice'. This ability ensures innovative HRM.

The second feature identified as being important for an HR practitioner is thinking that reflects the processes depicted in the SHRM Application Tool. Throughout this book, the SHRM Application Tool has shown effective HRM to be an evolutionary dynamic process, involving ongoing and systematic environmental scanning and analysis of organisational objectives, strategies and policies. This, in turn, indicates that systems thinking is critical for dealing with the complexity, dynamism and uncertainty of the environment in which HR practitioners find themselves working today. The thinking reflected in the SHRM Application Tool involves a flexible mindset, accessing the most up to date and accurate information and reflecting on what can be learned from the past while thinking about the needs and demands of the future.

The third feature identified as being important for an HR practitioner is being able to develop and use appropriately HR metrics because what gets measured gets done. As the HR function plays a fundamental role in an organisation's overall success, the HR practitioner should be able to measure clearly the impact of HR investments and ensure that they are in line with the organisation's strategic goals. Specifically, HR metrics can be used to monitor what is going on within the organisation, what effects any changes implemented within the organisation are having and the value being added to the organisation through its human resources. HR practitioners can use these metrics to assess changes within persons, between persons, between groups, between departments, between sites and between organisations. When taking measurements at these different levels it is important to perform both a vertical and horizontal gap analysis in order to ensure that the HR functions at each level are consistent and there are no gaps which may prevent the organisation from reaching its strategic goals.

The final feature identified as being important for an HR practitioner is thinking of the social as well as financial effects of HRM. This feature will be of particular importance in the future as governments, citizens, consumers and environmental groups put more pressure on business to be good corporate citizens. The triple bottom line view suggests that business success is measured not only by financial indicators but also by social and environmental indicators. A key implication of this for the HR practitioner is the need to link management of people to social and environmental outcomes in addition to financial ones.

Key terms

best practice	HR metrics	triple bottom line
between-person metrics	multilevel metrics model	within-person metrics
group-level metrics	organisational-level metrics	within-person variability

Review questions

12.1 Why can focusing on best practices rather than best principles be an error for HR decision makers?

12.2 Define HR metrics and describe the levels at which they can be taken?

12.3 What are horizontal and vertical gap analyses and why are they important when using a multilevel metrics model?

12.4 The values and philosophy of an organisation have been linked to organisational success. Identify the seven values and beliefs that are suggested to be most relevant to the contemporary business context.

12.5 Thinking about HRM in the future, describe some of the HR outcomes that HR practitioners may need to demonstrate.

Exercises

12.1 Identify three best practices. What assumptions about an organisation's people, culture and circumstances do they rest upon? What does your analysis reveal about best practices versus best principles?

12.2 Identify metrics you could use for performance at the within-person, between-person, group, department and organisational level. How would you perform a gap analysis?

12.3 Design appropriate HR metrics at the individual, departmental and organisational level based on the triple bottom line principle.

References

Barney, J. B. & Wright, P. M. (1998), 'On becoming a strategic partner: The role of human resources in gaining competitive advantage', *Human Resource Management*, vol. 37, no. 1, pp. 31–46.

Espejo, R. (1994), 'What is systemic thinking?', *System Dynamics Review*, vol. 10, no. 2/3, pp. 199–212.

Fisher, C. D. & Noble C. S. (2004), 'A within-person examination of correlates of performance and emotions while working', *Human Performance*, vol. 17, no. 2. pp. 145–68.

Flood, R. L. (1999), *Rethinking the Fifth Discipline*, Routledge, London.

Fujimoto, Y., Härtel, C. E. J., Härtel, G. F. & Baker, N. J. (2000), 'Openness to dissimilarity moderates the consequences of diversity in well-established groups', *Asia Pacific Journal of Human Resources*, vol. 38, no. 3, pp. 46–61.

Kirn, S. P., Rucci, A. J., Huselid, M. A. & Becker, B. E. (1999), 'Strategic human resource management at Sears', *Human Resource Management*, vol. 38, no. 4, pp. 329–35.

Monks, K. & McMackin, J. (2001), 'Designing and aligning an HR system', *Human Resource Management Journal*, vol. 11, no. 2, pp. 57–72.

Shaw, J. B. & Barrett-Power, E. (1998), 'The effects of diversity on small work group processes and performance', *Human Relations*, vol. 51, no. 10, pp. 1307–25.

Walker, J. W. (1999), 'Perspectives', *Human Resource Planning*, vol. 22, no. 1, pp. 11–13.

Glossary

adaptation approach to SIHRM The use of either a globalised HR strategy and localised practices or a localised HR strategy and globalised practices.

arbitration Involves an independent moderator who mediates a meeting between the two parties and has the authority to make decisions.

assessment Used to determine the success of trainees and can be categorised as diagnostic, formative and summative.

assessment centres A selection technique comprising problem-solving and team-based activities where people are assessed and graded on their performance by assessors.

Australian Industrial Relations Commission A third party whose role is to act as mediator to resolve conflicts between management and employees.

award A formal, legally binding document that provides legal protection for five minimum conditions of employment.

award-free individual contract An agreement, such as an AWA, between an employer and a single employee.

balanced scorecard Translates an organisation's vision, mission, values and strategy into a comprehensive set of performance measures, which serve as the framework for a strategic management system (Kaplan & Norton, 1996b).

behaviour observation scale An appraisal tool that measures the frequency of desirable job-related behaviours observed.

behavioural orientation to learning Emphasises changing behaviour through reinforcement and punishment and is advocated by a number of behavioural psychologists.

behavioural science approach Focused management attention on dynamic systems, total organisational culture and climate, employee participation and an emphasis on both economic and humanistic concerns.

behaviourally anchored rating scales Produce a numerical rating, anchored by specific narrative examples of behaviours, ranging from very negative to very positive attributes of employee performance.

best practice Practice thought of as an ideal or 'model' mode of practice.

between-person metrics Measurements used to analyse differences between people.

biographical information blanks Any type of information collected regarding an applicant's personal history, experience or education.

brainstorming The process of idea generation via face to face groups.

broadbanding Collapsing a large number of salary grades into a few wide bands where each grade includes a wide range of jobs and salary ranges.

bullying Undesirable, unfavourable and inappropriate treatment experienced by employees within the workplace.

business case for diversity The improvement of opportunities and experiences for previously excluded minority groups which aims to improve overall organisational capability.

business ethics The stance and standard of behaviour concerning morals and ethics that an organisation may adopt.

career A series of work-related experiences over one's life.

career development The series of work-related training activities, experiences, tasks and relationships an employee undertakes.

career management An organisation's management activities aimed at helping employees with preparing, implementing and monitoring their career planning process.

career planning An employee's deliberate process to understand and to plan their work.

career plateau When the likelihood of an employee receiving significant job responsibilities or advancement is low.

central tendency When busy and untrained appraisers are tempted to rate everyone in the range of 'satisfactory' or 'adequate' regardless of their actual performance.

certified agreements Arise out of collective bargaining (usually involving unions) at the enterprise level to establish terms and conditions of employment, including a base pay.

code of conduct A company policy outlining company expectations and formal rules surrounding ethics, including legal implications and disciplinary action.

cognitive orientation to learning Emphasises changing behaviour though giving people information and the opportunity to process it mentally so they understand what correct behaviour is and how to perform it.

collaborative philosophy Managers acknowledge the legitimacy of stakeholder views and are open to partnerships and involvement.

collective bargaining The process of negotiation between a union and employers to reach agreement on wages and employment conditions.

collectivists Seek to benefit the group or community first.

commitment philosophy The development of an employee–employer relationship which maximises employee contribution and the application of skills and knowledge for the benefit of the organisation.

competitive advantage A process, system or source (i.e. social, cultural or human capital) that one company does better than their competitors.

conciliation Involves an independent moderator who mediates a meeting between the two parties and together they determine a solution.

conditioning A permanent change in behaviour.

conflict Occurs when people with different goals and perspectives interact.

conflict management skills Involve an understanding of not only how to manage conflict but also how other people manage conflict.

content theories Suggest that human beings have certain wants and needs that direct their behaviour.

contextual performance Behaviours that are discretionary, yet capable of nurturing the supporting sociopsychological environment within which the core business operates.

creativity The generation of ideas, including diverse, abstract and novel ideas.

critical incident method The documentation of highly effective or highly ineffective instances of performance in a journal designated for each employee.

cultural capital The value that can be placed on the core values and beliefs of the organisation and its people.

cultural knowledge Knowledge about such things as cultural practices and beliefs of cultures other than one's own.

culture The shared values, assumptions, beliefs and perceptions which guide the behaviour of organisational members.

Delphi technique Extracts the forecast from a group of experts who exchange several rounds of HR estimates, normally without meeting face to face, to increase the breadth of the HR forecast.

demand forecasting Involves estimating the quantity and quality of employees required to meet organisational objectives.

development The holistic growth of individuals in work and non-work roles as well as learning, adapting and handling the organisation's culture, policies and procedures.

diagnostic assessment Audience analysis within the training needs analysis.

direct discrimination A policy or certain behaviour which purposely treats one group less favourably than another.

discretionary behaviours The behaviours that fall outside of the formal job requirements and are not recognised within the reward system, which can be performed at the discretion of the employee.

discretionary bonus A reward provided after goal achievement with the understanding that future success on a similar task may not be similarly rewarded.

discrimination Any difference or preference based on race, gender, colour, religion, political beliefs or nationality which results in disadvantageous or unfair treatment regarding employment, occupation or status.

dissimilarity openness The extent to which an individual is open to people they perceive to be dissimilar to themself.

diversity management The planning, organising and controlling of diversity-friendly policies and practices, which is reflected in a open-minded organisational culture and climate.

diversity-open performance evaluations Achieved by including diversity criteria in organisational objectives and the evaluations of individual managers.

diversity-open recruitment and selection Recruiting the person(s) most suitable for the job regardless of diversity attributes.

diversity-open training and development Training and development that will foster understanding between all employees as well as provide all employees with equal opportunities to enhance their skills.

diversity-oriented HRM HRM policies and practices that aim to attract, employ, develop and promote high-potential diverse employees.

double-loop learning Identifying why the problem might be occurring, as well as how to solve it.

effective SHRM Involves understanding both the internal and external operational requirements of the business and the social and behavioural requirements of the business.

emotion management Dealing with your own and others' emotions as well as using emotions in decision making and problem solving.

emotional intelligence The ability to perceive and experience emotions which then guide emotional responses and promote intellectual growth.

employee benefits All financial rewards that are not paid directly in cash to the employee, such as subsidised meals and superannuation.

employee self-service systems Allow employees to access their own personal details.

employment relationship The working relationship between employers and employees which is a fundamental relationship in workplaces.

employment tests Standardised tests in which applicants perform a selected set of actual tasks that are physically and/or psychologically similar to those performed on the job (Ployhart, Schneider & Schmitt, 2006).

e-recruitment The process of recruiting via the intranet (internal) and Internet (external).

essay description Managers expressing their views on each employee's performance, and suggestions for future development, in their own words.

ethnocentric management orientation When employees from company headquarters fill key managerial positions and power and decision making are centralised at the head office.

evaluation Determining the success of the training program.

expatriation The process of sending a home-country national to a foreign country to work.

experiential learning cycles View individuals as self-directed learners who learn by trial and error.

external analysis The evaluation of the environment in which the company operates.

external attraction activities An organisation looking externally for its human resource needs.

external equity The levels of pay for similar jobs in the external labour market.

external labour supply Any person not currently employed with the company.

external locus of control The belief that our destiny is controlled by external forces, such as fate or luck.

external scanning Involves the systematic identification and analysis of key trends in the external environment and the monitoring of their impact on HR strategies.

extrinsic rewards Rewards which are sourced outside, or are external to, the individual.

factor comparison system Calculates the relative worth of jobs on a range of job-related factors, such as skills, mental effort and location.

focal behaviours Those behaviours that the employee is bound to perform according to their job description and psychological contract.

formative assessment Occurs during the training delivery to give trainees regular feedback on the task (rather than the person).

gap analysis Involves looking at what the organisation is currently doing and what it needs to be doing.

geocentric management orientation When the best person for the job, regardless of whether they are a home-country, host-country or third-country national, is used to fill key managerial positions.

globalisation The removal of geographical borders when conducting business so that cultural and distance barriers become obsolete as national markets fuse into one global market.

globalised approach to SIHRM The use of the parent company's HR strategy and practices globally.

grading Rating an employee's overall performance at a specific performance level, such as Superior, Good, Acceptable, Marginal and Unsatisfactory.

graphic rating scale Enables each employee to be rated on a bipolar scale (ranging from Unsatisfactory to Outstanding) based on individual traits.

group A collective body of individuals striving towards a common objective guided by an overarching organisational framework.

group-level metrics Measurements used to analyse differences between groups.

groupthink When people publicly agree with the group, yet privately do not.

halo effect When the assessor believes that an employee is inherently good or bad based upon one job-related factor, regardless of the employee's actual level of performance.

hard HRM The management of people via calculative, control-based activities.

horizontal integration The integration of HRM functions.

HR metrics Measurements used by an organisation to evaluate the impact of its human resource investments and ensure that they are in line with the organisation's strategic goals.

HRIS An integrated technological system which accumulates, stores, maintains and analyses all data relating to a company's human resources.

human capital The value that can be placed on people's knowledge, skills, abilities and expertise.

human processual intervention strategy Focuses on changing behaviours by modifying individual attitudes and values.

human relations movement A joint focus on people and production based on a concern for people and with an emphasis on communication and the need to treat employees with dignity and respect.

human resource management The formal part of an organisation responsible for all aspects of the management of human resources.

human resource perspective Views people as an organisation's most valuable asset and states that all business operations should consider employee implications and consequences because without employees the business would not exist.

human resource planning A dynamic planning process which involves ongoing environmental scanning and an analysis of organisational objectives, strategies and policies in order to ascertain the right quantity and quality of employees when and where necessary.

hygiene factors Characteristics of the work environment which minimise discomfort and insecurity.

implementation theory Focuses on specific intervention strategies that are designed to induce changes.

incentive Focuses on a person's performance by establishing specific individual performance criteria or objectives and rewarding the achievement of these criteria.

incremental change A series of small changes.

indirect discrimination A policy which appears to be non-discriminatory at the outset, but in practice results in discrimination.

individual knowledge Knowledge formed in an individual's mind.

individual level of analysis An analysis of training needs from an individual's perspective, based on how well they perform their job.

individualists Focus primarily on satisfying individual goals.

industrial organisation approach Based on an economic ideal and is focused on issues such as resource allocation and profit maximisation.

industrial relations The formal relations between management, employees, unions and the government through work rules and agreements.

innovation The introduction of a new process or system which ultimately provides benefits at the individual, team or organisational level.

input Source materials of the output such as labour hours, raw materials, land and capital.

internal analysis An audit of a company's core competencies, strengths, weaknesses, opportunities and threats.

internal attraction activities An organisation looking internally for its human resource needs.

internal equity The equity value associated with jobs and people within the organisation's internal labour market.

internal labour supply Comprises all employees currently employed with the company.

internal locus of control Implies that people control their own destiny through their decisions and actions.

internal scanning Involves analysing the internal environment of an organisation.

interviews Formal or information-guided discussions between a candidate and an organisational representative.

intranets Internal networks which contain company information and can only be accessed by organisational members.

intrinsic rewards Rewards which are sourced from inside, or are internal to, the individual.

job analysis A systematic analysis of the tasks, duties and responsibilities of a job as well as the necessary knowledge, skills and abilities a person needs to perform the job adequately.

job burnout Exhaustion experienced by employees as a result of their work efforts.

job context The situational and supporting information regarding the job, such as work climate and unspoken rules.

job description Outlines the broad nature of a job.

job design The way that an entire job is organised and categorised; focuses on the needs of the incumbent.

job enlargement The horizontal expansion of a job by allocating to it a variety of similar-level skills and new responsibilities.

job enrichment Involves the vertical expansion of a job by increasing the amount of employee control or responsibility.

job evaluation An analytical tool which determines the relative worth of the job with the aim of providing fair and objective pay.

job rotation Involves increasing task variety by shifting employees from one task to another task.

job satisfaction The level of contentment that an employee associates with their job.

job specialisation Involves employees performing standardised, repetitive tasks so that analysts can record what the job involves and how long it takes to perform each task.

key performance indicators Criteria incumbents should achieve for a particular job to be performed effectively.

knowledge The holistic combination of experiences and information which provides insight to make decisions, develop opinions and direct future behaviour.

knowledge management The process of developing and controlling the intellectual capital of employees.

knowledge transfer The movement of information, skills and ideas from one entity to another.

knowledge work Behaviour which results in the end product of knowledge being delivered.

knowledge workers Employees who produce knowledge work.

learning A lifelong change in attitudes, behaviours and cognition as a result of one's interaction with the surrounding environment.

learning organisation A type of organisation which has the ability to change continuously and adapt to new environments and circumstances, though the acquisition of new knowledge.

legal case for diversity When companies are required by law to adopt diversity-friendly policies such as equal employment opportunity and affirmative action.

legal obligation The legal responsibility that an employer has towards employees and vice versa.

leniency/strictness bias When the assessor tends to rate at one end of the rating scale (i.e. high or low) in a consistent manner.

level of cognitive moral development An individual's perception of what is right and wrong cognitively (i.e. what they think).

localised approach to SIHRM The development of HR strategy and practices to suit the local environment.

locus of control The perceived control over individual behaviour.

macro internal HR information Includes the organisational philosophy, culture, climate and structure.

management A process involving planning, organising, leading and controlling the human, financial and material resources of the organisation.

management by objectives A results-oriented method of performance appraisal, where measurable goals or criteria are jointly established by the supervisor and the subordinate.

manager self-service systems Allow managers to view and update employee records.

masculinity versus femininity The degree of masculine characteristics (i.e. material success and assertiveness) as opposed to feminine characteristics (i.e. concern and feelings for others and for relationships).

mental models Representations of events, interpretations and behaviours.

micro internal HR information Includes the current number of employees, their job-related skills, demographic characteristics, performance level, management skills and work attitudes.

Mind Mapping A process of visually recording ideas with words, colours, codes and symbols.

moral case for diversity When diversity is embraced for the purpose of equity creation where diverse employees are integrated throughout the organisation and rewarded without regard to their dissimilarity.

motivation factors Characteristics of the work environment which promote employee growth and development.

multilevel metrics model A model that allows the measurement of human resources at the within-person, between-person, group and organisational levels.

multiple regression A mathematical technique used to relate HR demand to several independent variables, such as sales output, product mix or per capita productivity.

negative ethical climate Implies that unethical behaviour is tolerated by organisational members, including management.

negotiation The process of resolving disputes or conflicts between two or more parties.

nominal group technique A group process where a small number of experts meet face to face.

occupational health and safety The health, safety and welfare of employees in the workplace. It is the effort to improve workplace conditions to prevent accidents and injury occurring at work, and developing systems to deal with rehabilitation and compensation.

online learning Virtual training and development – the process of acquiring and developing new knowledge via computer-based systems (such as intranets).

operational level of analysis The analysis of training needs from a job or operational perspective.

organisation transformation change Views organisations as complex human systems that consistently face new challenges.

organisational behaviour The study of each individual's and group's behaviours, attitudes and actions within an organisation.

organisational change Any alteration (whether planned or unplanned) which causes a shift in the status quo, and which affects the structure and resources of an organisation.

organisational culture A system of shared beliefs, values and assumptions which guide individual behaviour within the organisation.

organisational justice Focuses on individual reactions to organisational processes and outcomes.

organisational knowledge Formed through the interaction between organisational visions, cultures, strategies, technologies, and people.

organisational learning A system-wide approach to learning.

organisational-level metrics Measurements used to evaluate an organisation's overall position.

organisational level of analysis The analysis of training needs from an organisational point of view.

organisational resources Tangible (e.g. finances, equipment, land, buildings, raw materials) or intangible commodities (e.g. knowledge, social networks, community relationships, trade secrets).

organisational strategy Design of organisational decision making which determines the goals, purpose, objectives and direction of the company.

organisational structure The formal arrangement of roles, processes and relationships within the organisation.

orientation program A type of specific training program which assists new entrants as they encounter new job, workgroup, cultural, organisational, departmental and miscellaneous information.

output The accomplishment of target levels of productivity.

paternalistic philosophy When managers look after employees while maintaining high levels of control and hierarchy.

performance To accomplish, execute or carry out an ordered task or assignment.

performance appraisal A formal and mutually agreed upon system of planning and reviewing employee performance.

performance management A collective range of activities conducted by an organisation aimed at enhancing individual, group or unit-level performance with the overarching purpose of improving organisational performance in the long term.

performance pay Pay individuals receive based upon their individual, group and/or organisational performance.

person specification The knowledge, skills and abilities a person requires to perform the job adequately.

planned change Any deliberate, structured execution of a shift in the status quo.

pluralist HRM The perceived inevitable conflict between employers and employees, favouring strong union involvement.

point system Calculates a job's worth by assigning points to specific job factors.

polycentric management orientation When local managers are used to fill key managerial positions.

Porter's five forces A tool to model the influences in an organisation's environment and identify preferred strategic direction.

positive ethical climate Implies that the organisational culture encourages members to behave ethically and morally.

power distance The degree to which people accept an equal or unequal distribution of power in organisations and society.

prejudices The errors generated as a result of the positive or negative attitude held by the appraiser towards the employee.

process theories Highlight thought patterns that underlie the decision of whether or not to engage in certain behaviours.

protestant work ethic 'The degree to which individuals place work at or near the center of their lives' (Mudrack, 1997, p. 217).

psychological contracts Intangible, informal contracts that the employee perceives about their employment relationship.

psychological test A test designed to provide insight into human behaviour.

radical change Large-scale and drastic change. It is usually organisation-wide, innovative and planned.

realistic job preview Provides new employees with complete and accurate information about the job and the organisation to avoid a mismatch between the employee's expected and actual work experience.

recency effect When the performance appraisal is based on the most recent behaviours rather than the performance over the full review period.

recruitment The process of generating a pool of qualified candidates for a particular job who can contribute best to the strategic objectives of the organisation; involves identifying what jobs need to be filled and how the most suitable candidates will be attracted.

recruitment agencies External companies who supply human resources.

regiocentric management orientation When organisations are broken into regions and host-country or third-country nationals are used to fill key managerial positions.

relationship effect When the performance appraisal is affected by the quality of the supervisor and subordinate's relationship as opposed to the actual work performance.

reliability The degree to which interviews, tests and other selection procedures yield comparable data over a period of time and the degree to which two or more methods yield similar results or are consistent.

repatriation The process of acclimatising an expatriate to their home country and organisation.

resistance to change Any barrier that impedes a change from occurring.

resource-based view Internal resources, which are rare, valuable, inimitable and non-substitutable, can provide sources of sustainable competitive advantage (Boxall, 1996).

restructuring The reorganisation of a company to increase efficiencies and adapt to, and enter, changing markets.

reward An item (either tangible or intangible) which is received in recognition for behaviour or output.

reward management Concerned with the strategic formulation and implementation of equitable rewards in a way that aligns with the strategic direction and values of an organisation.

reward strategy The development, implementation and use of reward systems which enable individuals to complete work tasks that are aligned with organisational goals, structures and strategies.

risk management The process of measuring and assessing risk and developing systems to manage the risk successfully.

salary Pay that is paid consistently from period to period.

scientific management A method for managing people and work based on a concern for production and with an emphasis on efficiency.

selection The identification of candidates who can best contribute to the strategic objectives of the organisation and help in the quest to obtain a competitive advantage.

selection criteria Key work-related factors in making the decision to hire or not to hire a person.

self-service system A virtual HR menu where organisational members can make changes or additions to their personal details or access company policies or documents.

session plan A blueprint of the training program, which typically includes a particular skill and how it will be taught.

similarity attraction paradigm States that humans are inclined to be attracted to others they perceive to be similar.

single-loop learning Improving the company by identifying solutions.

skill obsolescence Reduced employee competence resulting from a lack of knowledge and skills to perform new work responsibilities, techniques and technologies.

skills inventory form A system which keeps track of employee skill development.

social capital The value that can be placed on the networks and relationships between people such as that gained from helping behaviours and sharing knowledge resources.

social categorisation theory States that people tend to categorise themselves and others into various social categories, namely 'in group' and 'out group' membership.

social identity theory States that group members attempt to achieve or maintain a positive self-image as a result of a favourable comparison between their social category and other groups.

societal perspective States that an organisation should carefully consider societal impacts before decisions are made.

sociological approach Based on a human ideal and is focused on issues such as satisfying behaviour, and profit sub-optimality.

sociotechnical systems design Aims for innovative ways of increasing productivity and worker satisfaction through redesigning workflow structures, work methods and work content.

soft HRM The management of people via activities designed to gain commitment and motivation.

standard The expected criteria of performance (e.g. quality, quantity or timeline).

strategic human resource management The process of human resource management which is driven by planning, foresight and analytical decision making.

strategic international HRM The management of employees in more than one country.

strategic international management Global strategic formulation and global strategic implementation.

strategic knowledge management The long-term process that uses both tacit and explicit knowledge to cultivate organisational learning, which is then shared among organisational members to achieve the strategic goal.

strategic management The process of managing with a long-term focus, and which is largely composed of strategy formulation and strategy implementation.

strategy formulation Includes setting a mission, vision, strategy, goals and values, coupled with a consideration of the external and internal environments.

stress Tension people experience when they are under considerable physical and psychological demand.

summative assessment A holistic assessment of the trainees' competencies at the end of a training session.

SWOT analysis Involves a scan of the organisation's internal and external environments in order to match the organisation's internal strengths (S) and weaknesses (W) with its perceived opportunities (O) and threats (T).

task performance The technical know-how, organisational knowledge repositories and skill base needed to engage in the core business of goods and/or service production.

technostructural intervention theory Focuses on improving work content, work method and work flow with the aim of lowering costs by replacing inefficient work practices, designs, material, methods and equipment with technologies.

Theory X The management assumption that employees prefer not to do work and need close supervision and control.

Theory Y The management assumption that employees can be given greater responsibility as they are highly motivated and will be creative if given a chance.

360-degree feedback A type of appraisal which collects views from people both in the job and holding jobs hierarchically above and below the position being analysed, providing a multifaceted view.

time orientation The degree to which long- or short-term consequences are considered.

traditional (or transactional) philosophy Work tasks are tightly scripted and little accountability is given to individual workers.

traditional perspective The perspective that an organisation's primary obligation is to its shareholders.

training The deliberate activities planned by an organisation to increase employee knowledge, skills and attitudes; occurs at particular times and in particular locations.

training needs analysis A tool used to identify the gap between the actual performance and the desired performance in the organisation.

trend projection A time series analysis where past information about the number of people hired (or requested) by the organisation over time is plotted on a graph so that HR trends and requirements can be forecast into the future.

triple bottom line A company reporting system that advocates the notion that the traditional company reporting framework should be extended to include not just financial outcomes but environmental and social outcomes also.

Tsui's multiple constituency model A model that states an organisation has multiple constituencies whose objectives may conflict or differ.

uncertainty avoidance The degree to which society takes risks or tolerates uncertain or ambiguous situations.

unitarist HRM An employment relationship where employers and employees assume common goals.

validity The extent to which something measures what it claims to measure.

vertical integration The integration of individual, group, functional and organisational objectives.

virtual HRM Computer technology used to recruit, train, develop and monitor human resources.

wage Hourly, daily or weekly payment based on the time worked.

within-person metrics Measurements used to analyse differences within an individual person.

within-person variability Changes that occur in an individual from moment to moment.

work motivation The stimulation of effort required to achieve, and maintain, organisational goals.

workforce diversity Any visible or invisible difference between organisational members.

workplace injury An injury or illness sustained: (a) as part of work activities; (b) in transit to or from the place of employment; or (c) by aggravation of pre-existing conditions where employment contributed to the injury (ABS, 2001).

Index

Page numbers followed by *fig* indicate figures; those followed by *tab* indicate tables.